EMERSON THE ESSAYIST

AN OUTLINE OF HIS PHILOSOPHICAL DEVELOPMENT
THROUGH 1836
with
SPECIAL EMPHASIS ON THE SOURCES AND
INTERPRETATION OF *NATURE*

Also

Bibliographical Appendices of General and Special Interest
to Students of American Literature, Emphasizing Thoreau,
Emerson, the Boston Library Society and Selected Documents of New England Transcendentalism.

By

KENNETH WALTER CAMERON

VOLUME

II

TRANSCENDENTAL BOOKS

DRAWER 1080
HARTFORD, CONNECTICUT 06101

COPYRIGHT 1945 AND 1972
BY KENNETH WALTER CAMERON

Engraved by W. B. Closson from the crayon drawing by Samuel Rowse.

RALPH WALDO EMERSON.

TABLE OF CONTENTS

VOLUME TWO

Part Five: Selected Documents of New England Transcendentalism

Part Six: Bibliographies, Letters, and
Miscellaneous

Part Seven: Index-Concordance to
Emerson's Sermons

Indexes

INDEX OF ALL REFERENCES TO THE TEXT OF *NATURE*

INDEX OF INDEXES

MATTERS NOT INCLUDED IN THE FINAL INDEX

FINAL INDEX

PART FIVE

SELECTED DOCUMENTS
OF NEW ENGLAND
TRANSCENDENTALISM*

---

* Numerals in brackets throughout the body of each text are the page numbers of the original article, book or manuscript.

I

ORATION ON GENIUS*

By SAMPSON REED

The world was always busy; the human heart has always had love of some kind; there has always been fire on the earth.[1] There is something in the inmost principles of an individual, when he begins to exist, which urges him onward; there is something in the centre of the character of a nation, to which the people aspire; there is something which gives activity to the mind in all ages, countries, and worlds. This principle of activity is love: it may be the love of good or of evil; it may manifest itself in saving life or in killing; but it is love.

The difference in the strength and direction of the affections creates the distinctions in society. Every man has a form of mind peculiar to himself. The mind of the infant contains within[2] itself the first[3] rudiments of all that will be hereafter, [59] and needs nothing but expansion; as the leaves and[4] branches and fruit of a tree are said to exist in the seed from which it springs. He[5] is bent in a particular direction; and, as some objects are of more value than others, distinctions must exist. What it is that makes a man great depends upon the state of society: with the savage, it is physical strength; with the civilized, the arts and sciences; in heaven, the[6] perception that love and wisdom are from the Divine.

There prevails an idea in the world,[7] that its[8] great men are more like God than others. This sentiment carries in its bosom sufficient evil to bar the gates of heaven. So far as a person possesses it, either with respect to himself or others, he has no connection with his Maker, no love for his neighbor, no truth in his understanding. This was at the root of heathen idolatry: it was this that[9] made men worship saints and images. It contains within[10] itself the seeds of atheism, and will ultimately make every man insane by whom it is cherished. The life which circulates in the body is found to commence in the head; but, unless it be traced through the soul up to God, it is merely corporeal, like that of the brutes.[11]

Man has often ascribed to his own power the effects of the secret operations[12] of divine truth. When the world is immersed in darkness, this is a judgment of the Most High; but the light is the effect of the innate strength of the[13] human intellect.

When the powers[14] of man begin[15] to decay, and approach an apparent dissolution,[16] who cannot see the Divinity? But what foreign aid[17] wants the man who is full of his own strength? God sends the lightning that[18] blasts the tree; but what credulity would ascribe to him the sap that[19] feeds its branches? The sight of idiotism leads to a train of religious reflections; but the face that is marked with lines of intelligence is admired for its own inherent beauty.[20] The hand of the Almighty is visible to all[21] in the stroke of death; but few see his face in the smiles of the new-born babe.

The intellectual eye of man is[22] formed to see the light, not to make it; and it is time that,[23] when the causes that[24] cloud the spiritual world are removed, man should rejoice in the [60] truth itself, and not that *he* has found it. More than once, when nothing was required but for a person to stand on this[25] world with his eyes open, has the truth been seized upon as a thing of his own making. When the power of divine truth begins to dispel the darkness, the objects that[26] are first disclosed to our view—whether men of strong understanding, or[27] of exquisite taste, or of deep learning—are called geniuses. Luther, Shakspeare, Milton, Newton, stand with the bright side towards us.

There is something which is called genius, that[28] carries in itself the seeds of its own destruction. There is an ambition which hurries a[29] man after truth, and takes away the power of attaining it. There is a desire which is null,[30] a lust which is impotence.[31] There is no understanding so powerful, that ambition may not in time bereave it of its

---

* This oration was delivered at Harvard on August 21, 1821, when Reed was candidate for the degree of Master of Arts. The text reproduced here is that found in *Æsthetic Papers*, ed. Elizabeth P. Peabody, Boston and N. Y., 1849, pp. 58-64. Verbal variations listed in the notes (to be found at the end of the oration) are those in a manuscript owned by the Ralph Waldo Emerson Memorial Association and formerly in the possession of Emerson himself. It bears the inscription: "Chas. C. Emerson from his friend, Joseph Lyman. Oct. 1830." See *Letters*, I, 306; III, 74. (Variants in capitalization, spelling and punctuation are ignored.)

last truth, even that two and two are[32] four. Know, then, that genius is divine, not when the[33] man thinks that[34] he is God, but when he acknowledges that his powers are from God. Here is the link of the finite with the infinite, of the divine with the human:[35] this is the humility which[36] exalts.

The arts have been taken from nature by human invention; and, as the mind returns to its God, they are in a measure swallowed up in the source from which[37] they came. We see, as they vanish, the standard to which we should refer them. They are not arbitrary, having no foundation[38] except in taste: they are only modified by taste, which varies according to the state of the human mind. Had we a history of music, from the war-song of the savage to the song of[39] angels, it would be a history of the affections that[40] have held dominion over the human heart. Had we a history of architecture, from the first building erected by man to the house not made with hands, we might trace the variations of the beautiful and the grand, alloyed[41] by human contrivance, to where they are lost in[42] beauty and grandeur. Had we a history of poetry, from the first rude effusions[43] to where words make one with things, and language is lost in nature, we should see the state of man in the language of licentious passion, in the songs[44] of chivalry, in the descriptions[45] of heroic valor, in the mysterious wildness of Ossian; till the [61] beauties of nature fall on the heart, as softly as the clouds on the summer's water. The mind, as it wanders from heaven, moulds the arts into its own form, and covers its nakedness. Feelings of all kinds will discover themselves in music, in painting, in poetry; but it is only when the heart is purified from every selfish and worldly passion, that they are created in real beauty; for in their origin they are divine.

Science is more fixed. It consists of the laws according to which natural things exist; and these must be either true or false. It is the natural world in the abstract, not in the concrete. But the laws according to which things exist, are from the things themselves, not the opposite. Matter has solidity: solidity makes no part of matter. If, then, the natural world is from God, the abstract properties, as dissected and combined, are from him also. If, then, science be from Him who gave the ten commandments, must not a life according to the latter facilitate[46] the acquirement of the former?[47] Can *he* love the works of God who does not love his commandments?[48] It is only necessary that the heart be purified, to have science like poetry its spontaneous growth. Self-love has given rise to many false theories, because a selfish man is disposed to make things differently from what God has made them. Because[49] God is love, nature exists; because God is love, the Bible is poetry. If, then, the love of God creates the scenery of nature, must not he whose mind is most open to this love be most sensible of natural beauties? But in nature both the sciences and the arts[50] exist embodied.

Science may be learned from ambition; but it must be by[51] the sweat of the brow. The filthy and polluted mind *may* carve beauties from nature, with which it has no allegiance:[52] the rose is blasted in the gathering. The olive and the vine had rather live with God, than crown the head of him whose love for them is a lust for glory. The man is cursed who would rob nature of her graces, that he may use them to allure the innocent virgin to[53] destruction.

Men say there is an inspiration in genius. The genius of the ancients was the good or evil spirit that attended the man. The moderns speak of the magic touch of the pencil, [62] and of the inspiration of poetry. But this[54] inspiration has been esteemed so unlike religion, that the existence of the one almost[55] supposes the absence of the other. The spirit of God is thought to be a very different thing when poetry is written, from what it is when the heart is sanctified.[56] What has the inspiration of genius in common with that of the cloister? The one courts the[57] zephyrs; the other flies them. The one is cheerful; the other, sad. The one dies; the other writes the epitaph. Would the Muses take the veil? Would they exchange Parnassus for a nunnery? Yet there has been learning, and even poetry, under ground. The yew loves the graveyard; but other trees have grown there.

It needs no uncommon eye[58] to see, that the finger of death has rested on the church. Religion and death have in the human mind been[59] connected with the same train[60] of associations. The churchyard is the graveyard. The bell which calls men to worship is to toll at their funerals, and the garments of the priests are of the color of the hearse and the coffin. Whether we view her in the strange melancholy that sits on her face, in her mad reasonings[61] about truth, or in the occasional convulsions that agitate her limbs, there are symptoms, not of life, but of disease and death. It is not strange, then, that genius, such as could exist on the[62] earth, should take its flight to the mountains. It[63] may be said, that great men are good men. But what I mean is, that, in the human mind, greatness is one thing, and goodness another; that philosophy is divorced from religion; that truth is separated from its source; that that which is called goodness is sad, and that which is called genius is proud.

Since things are so, let men take care[64] that the life which[65] is received be[66] genuine. Let the glow on the cheek spring from the warmth of the heart, and the brightness of the eyes beam[67] from the light of heaven. Let ambition and the love of the world be plucked up by their[68] roots. How can he love his neighbor, who desires to be above him? He may love him for a slave; but that is all. Let not the shrouds[69] of death be removed, till the living principle has entered. It was not till Lazarus was raised from the dead, and had received the breath of life, that the Lord said, "Loose him, and let him go."

[63] When the heart is purified from all selfish and worldly affections, then may genius find its seat in the church. As the human mind is cleansed of its lusts, truth will permit and invoke[70] its approach, as the coyness of the virgin subsides into the tender love of the wife. The arts will spring in full-grown[71] beauty from Him who is the source of beauty. The harps which have hung on the willows[72] will sound as sweetly as the first breath of heaven that moved the leaves in the garden of Eden. Cannot a man paint better when he knows that the picture ought not to be worshipped?

Here is no sickly aspiring after fame,—no filthy lust after philosophy, whose very origin is an eternal barrier to the[73] truth. But sentiments will flow from the heart warm as its blood, and speak eloquently; for eloquence is the language of love. There is a unison[74] of spirit and nature. The genius of the mind will descend, and unite with the genius of the rivers, the lakes, and the woods. Thoughts[75] fall to the earth with power, and make a language out of nature.

Adam and Eve knew[76] no language but their garden. They had nothing to communicate by words; for they had not the power of concealment. The sun of the spiritual world shone bright on their hearts, and their senses were open with delight to natural objects. In the eye were the beauties of paradise; in the ear was the music of birds; in the nose was the fragrance of the freshness of nature; in the taste was the fruit of the garden; in the touch, the seal of their eternal union.[77] What had they to *say*?

The people of the golden age have left us no monuments of genius, no splendid columns, no paintings, no poetry. They possessed nothing which evil passions might not obliterate; and, when their[78] "heavens were rolled together as a scroll," the curtain dropped between the world and their existence.

Science will be full of life, as nature is full of God.[79] She will wring from her locks the dew[80] which was gathered in the wilderness. By science, I mean natural science. The science of the human mind must change with its subject. Locke's mind will not always be the standard of metaphysics. Had we a description of it in its present state, it would make [64] a very different book from "Locke on the Human Understanding."

The time is not far distant. The cock has crowed. I hear the distant lowing of the[81] cattle which are grazing on the mountains. "Watchman, what of the night? Watchman, what of the night? The watchman saith, The morning cometh."[82]

TABLE OF VARIANTS

[1]*on earth*
[2]*in*
[3]Omitted.
[4]Ms. omits *leaves and*
[5]*Every one*
[6]Omitted.
[7]*in the world an idea*
[8]Omitted.
[9]*wh[ich].*
[10]*in*
[11]*corporeal life like the brute's.*
[12]*operation*
[13]Omitted.
[14]*power*
[15]*begins*
[16]*decay in apparent dissolution*
[17]Ms. reads *foresight* instead of *foreign aid.*
[18]*which*
[19]*which*
[20]Ms. omits entire sentence.
[21]Ms. omits *to all*
[22]*was*
[23]Ms. omits *that* and inserts it before the following *man.*
[24]*which*
[25]*the*
[26]*which*
[27]Omitted.
[28]*which*
[29]Omitted.
[30]*small*
[31]*importance*
[32]*make*
[33]*a*
[34]Omitted.

[35]*There is a kind of divine with human —of finite with infinite.*
[36]*that*
[37]*whence*
[38]*formation*
[39]*of the*
[40]*which*
[41]*(alloyed)?*
[42]*in the source of*
[43]*effusion*
[44]*song*
[45]*description*
[46]*participate*
[47]*this power.*
[48]Ms. omits entire sentence at this point, but records it at the bottom of the page without indicating its proper position.
[49]*Oh! because*
[50]*both science and the arts*
[51]*from*
[52]*alliance.*
[53]*to her*
[54]*the*
[55]Omitted.
[56]Entire sentence omitted.
[57]Omitted.
[58]*light*

[59]*been ever*
[60]*strain*
[61]*reasoning*
[62]Omitted.
[63]*It . . . proud.* appears in a footnote in the Ms.
[64]*beware*
[65]*that .*
[66]*is*
[67]Omitted.
[68]*the*
[69]*shroud*
[70]*invite*
[71]*growth*
[72]*willow*
[73]Omitted.
[74]*union*
[75]*Thus it will*
[76]*had*
[77]Ms. omits *in the touch, the seal of their eternal union.*
[78]*the*
[79]*good*
[80]*the dew from her locks*
[81]Omitted.
[82]*the morning cometh and also the night.*

II

OBSERVATIONS ON THE GROWTH OF THE MIND*

By SAMPSON REED

Nothing is a more common subject of remark than the changed condition of the world. There is a more extensive intercourse of thought, and a more powerful action of mind upon mind than formerly. The good and the wise of all nations are brought nearer together, and begin to exert a power, which though yet feeble as infancy, is felt throughout the globe. Public opinion, that helm which directs the progress of events by which the world is guided to its ultimate destination, has received a new direction. The mind has attained an upward and onward look, and is shaking off the errours and prejudices of the past. The gothic structure of the feudal ages, the ornament of the desert, has been exposed to the light of heaven; and continues to be gazed at for its ugliness, as it ceases to be admired for its antiquity. The world is deriving vigour, not from that which is gone by, but from that which is coming; not from the unhealthy moisture of the evening, but from the nameless influences of the morning. The loud call on the past to instruct us, as it falls on the rock of ages, comes back in echo from the future. Both mankind, and the laws and principles by which they are governed, seem about to be redeemed from slavery. The moral and intellectual character of man has undergone, and is undergoing a change; and as this is effected it must change the aspect of all things, as when the position-point is altered from which a landscape is viewed. We appear [4] to be approaching an age which will be the silent pause of merely physical force before the powers of the mind; the timid, subdued, awed condition of the brute, gazing on the erect and godlike form of man.

---

* This is a reprint of the first edition, Boston, 1826, p. 3ff. (Copy in New York Public Library).

These remarks with respect to the present era are believed to be just, when it is viewed on the bright side. They are not made by one who is insensible to its evils. Least of all are they intended to countenance that feeling of self-admiration, which carries with it the seeds of premature disease and deformity; for to be proud of the truth is to cease to possess it. Since the fall of man, nothing has been more difficult for him than to know his real condition, since every departure from divine order is attended with a loss of the knowledge of what it is. When our first parents left the garden of Eden, they took with them no means by which they might measure the depths of degradation to which they fell; no chart by which they might determine their moral longitude. Most of our knowledge implies relation and comparison. It is not difficult for one age, or one individual, to be compared with another; but this determines only their relative condition. The actual condition of man, can be seen only from the relation in which he stands to his immutable creator; and this relation is discovered from the light of revelation, so far as by conforming to the precepts of revelation, it is permitted to exist according to the laws of divine order. It is not sufficient that the letter of the Bible is in the world. This may be, and still mankind continue in ignorance of themselves. It must be obeyed from the heart to the hand. The book must he eat, and constitute the living flesh. When only the relative condition of the world is regarded, we are apt to exult over other ages and other men, as if we ourselves were a different order of beings, till at length we are enveloped in the very mists from which we are proud of being cleared. But when the relative state of the world is justly viewed from the real state of the individual, the scene is lighted from the point of the beholder with the chaste light of humility which never deceives; it is not forgotten that the way lies forward; the cries of exultation cease to be heard in the march of progression, and the mind, in whatever it learns of the past and the present, finds food for improvement, and not for vain-glory.

[5] As all the changes which are taking place in the world originate in the mind, it might be naturally expected that nothing would change more than the mind itself, and whatever is connected with a description of it. While men have been speculating concerning their own powers, the sure but secret influence of revelation has been gradually changing the moral and intellectual character of the world, and the ground on which they were standing has passed from under them, almost while their words were in their mouths. The powers of the mind are most intimately connected with the subjects by which they are occupied. We cannot think of the will without feeling, of the understanding without thought, or of the imagination without something like poetry. The mind is visible when it is active; and as the subjects on which it is engaged are changed, the powers themselves present a different aspect. New classifications arise, and new names are given. What was considered simple is thought to consist of distinct parts, till at length the philosopher hardly knows whether the African be of the same or a different species; and though the soul is thought to continue after death, angels are universally considered a distinct class of intellectual beings. Thus it is that there is nothing fixed in the philosophy of the mind; it is said to be a science which is not demonstrative; and though now thought to be brought to a state of great perfection, another century under the providence of God, and nothing will be found in the structure which has cost so much labour, but the voice "he is not here, but is risen."

Is then every thing that relates to the immortal part of man fleeting and evanescent, while the laws of physical nature remain unaltered? Do things become changeable as we approach the immutable and the eternal? Far otherwise. The laws of the mind are in themselves as fixed and perfect as the laws of matter; but they are laws from which we have wandered. There is a philosophy of the mind, founded not on the aspect it presents in any part or in any period of the world, but on its immutable relations to its first cause; a philosophy equally applicable to man, before or after he has passed the valley of the shadow of death; not dependent on time or place, but immortal as its subject. The light of this philosophy has begun to beam faintly on the world, and mankind will yet see their own moral and in- [6] tellectual nature by the light of revelation, as it shines through the moral and intellectual character it shall have itself created. It may be remarked also that the changes in the sciences and the arts are entirely the effect of revelation. To revelation it is to be ascribed, that the genius which has taught the laws of the heavenly bodies and analyzed the material world, did not spend itself in drawing the bow or in throwing the lance, in the chase or in war; and that the vast powers of Handel did not burst forth in the wild notes of the war-song. It is the tendency of revelation to give a right direction to every power of every mind; and when this is effected, inventions and discoveries will follow of course, all things assume a different aspect, and the world itself again become a paradise.

It is the object of the following pages not to be influenced by views of a temporal or local nature, but to look at the mind as far as possible in its essential revealed character, and beginning with its powers of acquiring and retaining truth, to trace summarily that development which is required, in order to render it truly useful and happy. It is believed that they will not be found at variance with the state of the public mind on the subject of education, whether of the child or the man.

It was said, *the powers of acquiring and retaining truth*, because truth is not retained without some continued exertion of the same powers by which it is acquired. There is the most intimate connexion of the memory with the affections. This connexion is obvious from many familiar expressions; such as remember me to any one, by which is signified a desire to be borne in his or her affections—do not forget me, by which is meant do not cease to love me—get by heart, which means commit to memory. It is also obvious from observation of our own minds; from the constant recurrence of those subjects which we most love, and the extreme difficulty of detaching our own minds or the minds of others from a favourite pursuit. It is obvious from the power of attention on which the memory principally depends, which if the subject have a place in our affections requires no effort; if it have not, the effort consists principally in giving it a real or an artificial hold of our feelings, as it is possible if we do not love a subject, to attend to it because it may add to our fame or our wealth. It is obvious from the [7] never fading freshness retained by the scenes of childhood, when the feelings are strong and vivid, through the later periods of life. As the old man looks back on the road of his pilgrimage, many years of active life lie unseen in the valley, as his eye rests on the rising ground of his younger days; presenting a beautiful illustration of the manner in which the human mind when revelation shall have accomplished its work, shall no longer regard the scene of sin and misery behind, but having completed the circle, shall rest as next to the present moment on the golden age, the infancy of the world. The connexion of the memory with the affections is also obvious from the association of ideas; since the train of thoughts suggested by any scene or event in any individual, depends on his own peculiar and prevailing feelings; as whatever enters into the animal system whenever it may arise, seems first to be recognized as a part of the man, when it has found its way to the heart, and received from that its impulse. It is but a few years, (how strange to tell,) since man discovered that the blood circulated through the human body. We have perhaps, hardly learned the true nature of that intellectual circulation, which gives life and health to the human mind. The affections are to the soul, what the heart is to the body. They send forth their treasures with a vigour not less powerful, though not material, throughout the intellectual man, strengthening and nourishing; and again receive those treasures to themselves, enlarged by the effect of their own operation.

Memory is the *effect* of learning, through whatever avenue it may have entered the mind. It is said the *effect*; because the man who has read a volume and can perhaps tell you nothing of its contents, but simply express his own views on the same subject with more clearness and precision, may as truly be said to have remembered, as he that can repeat the very words. In the one case, the powers of the mind have received a new tone; in the other, they are encumbered with a useless burthen—in the one, they are made stronger; in the other they are more oppressed with weight—in the one, the food is absorbed and becomes a part of the man; in the other it lies on the stomach in a state of crude indigestion.

There is no power more various in different individuals, than the memory. This may be ascribed to two reasons. [8] First, this partakes of every power of the mind, since every mental exertion is a subject of memory, and may therefore be said to indicate all the difference that actually exists. Secondly, this power varies in its character as it has more or less to do with time. Simple divine truth has nothing to do with time. It is the same yesterday, to-day and tomorrow. The memory of this is simply the development of the mind. But we are so surrounded by facts of a local and temporal nature; the place where, and the time when, make so great a part of what is presented to our consideration; that the attribute is mistaken for the subject, and this power sometimes appears to have exclusive reference to time, though strictly speaking it has no relation to it. There is a power of growth in the spiritual man, and if in his progress we be able to mark as in the grain of the oak the number of the years, this is only a circumstance; and all that is gained would be as real if no such lines existed. The mind ought not to be limited by the short period of its own duration in the body, with a beginning and end comprising a few years; it should be poised on its own immortality, and what is learned, should be learned with a view to that real adaptation of knowledge to the mind which results from the harmony of creation, and whenever or wherever we exist, it will be useful to us. The memory has in reality, nothing to do with time, any more than the eye has with space. As the latter learns by experience to measure the distance of objects, so the consciousness of the present existence of states of mind, is referred to particular periods of the past. But when the soul has entered on its *eternal* state, there is reason to believe that the past and the future will be swallowed up in the present; that memory and anticipation will be lost in consciousness; that every thing of the past will be comprehended in the present, without any reference to time, and every thing of the future will exist in the divine effort of progression.

What is time? There is perhaps no question that would suggest such a variety of answers. It is represented to us from our infancy as producing such important changes, both in destroying some, and in healing the wounds it has inflicted on others, that people generally imagine, if not an actual person, it is at least a real existence. We begin with time in the primer, and end with reasoning about the [9] foreknowledge of God. What is time? The difficulty of answering the question, (and there are few questions more difficult,) arises principally from our having ascribed so many important effects to that which has no real existence. It is true that all things in the natural world are subject to change. But however these changes may be connected in our minds with time, it requires but a moment's reflection to see that time has no agency in them. They are the effects of chemical, or more properly perhaps, of natural decompositions and reorganizations. Time, or rather our idea of it, so far from having produced any thing, is itself the effect of changes. There are certain operations in nature, which depending on fixed laws, are in themselves perfectly regular; if all things were equally so, the question how long? might never be asked. We should never speak of a late season, or of premature old age; but every thing passing on in an invariable order, all the idea of time that would remain with respect to any object, would be a sort of instinctive sense of its condition, its progress or decay. But most of the phenomena in the natural world are exceedingly irregular; for though the same combination of causes would invariably produce the same effect, the same combination very rarely occurs. Hence in almost every change, and we are conversant with nothing but changes, we are assisted in ascertaining its nature and extent, by referring it to something in itself perfectly regular. We find this regularity in the apparent motions of the sun and moon. It is difficult to tell how much our idea of time is the effect of artificial means of keeping it, and what would be our feelings on the subject, if left to the simple operations of nature—but they would probably be little else than a reference of all natural phenomena to that on which they principally depend, the relative situation of the sun and earth; and the idea of an actual succession of moments, would be in a measure resolved into that of cause and effect.

Eternity is to the mind what time is to nature. We attain a perception of it, by regarding all the operations in the world within us, as they exist in relation to their first cause; for in doing this, they are seen to partake somewhat of the nature of that Being on whom they depend. We make no approaches to a conception of it, by heaping day upon day or year upon year. This is merely an accumu- [10] lation of time; and we might as well attempt to convey an idea of mental greatness by that of actual space, as to communicate a conception of eternity by years or thousands of years. Mind and matter are not more distinct from each other than their properties; and by an attempt to embrace all time we are actually farther from an approach to eternity than when we confine ourselves to a single instant—because we merely collect the largest possible amount of natural changes, whereas that which is eternal approaches that which is immutable. This resembles the attempt to ascend to heaven by means of the tower of Babel, in which they were removed by their pride from that which they would have approached, precisely in proportion to their apparent progress. It is impossible to conceive of either time or space without matter. The reason is, they are the effect of matter; and as it is by creating matter that they are produced, so it is by thinking of it that they are conceived of. It need not be said how exceedingly improper it is to apply the usual ideas of time and space to the Divine Being; making him subject to that which he creates.

Still our conceptions of time, of hours, days or years, are among the most vivid we possess, and we neither wish nor find it easy to call them in question. We are satisfied with the fact, that time is indicated on the face of the watch; without seeking for it among the wheels and machinery. But what is the idea of a year? Every natural change that comes under our observation, leaves a corresponding impression on the mind; and the sum of the changes which come under a single revolution of the earth around the sun, conveys the impression of a year. Accordingly, we find that our idea of a year is continually changing, as the mind becomes conversant with different objects, and is susceptible of different impressions; and the days of the old man as they draw near their close, seem to gather rapidity from their approach to the other world. We have all experienced the effect of pleasure and pain in accelerating and retarding the passing moments; and since our feelings are constantly changing, we have no reason to doubt, that they constantly produce a similar effect, though it may not be often noticed. The divisions of time then, however real they may seem to be, and however well they may serve the common purposes of conversation, cannot be supposed to convey the same im- [11] pression to any two minds, nor to any one mind in different periods of its existence. Indeed, unless this were the fact, all artificial modes of keeping it, would be unnecessary. Time then, is nothing real so far as it exists in our own minds.

Nor do we find a nearer approach to reality, by any analysis of nature. Every thing as was said, is subject to change, and one change prepares the way for another; by which there is growth and decay. There are also motions of bodies both in nature and art, which in their operation observe fixed laws; and here we end. The more we enter into an analysis of things, the farther are we from finding any thing that answers to the distinctness and reality which are usually attached to a conception of time; and there is reason to believe that when this distinctness and reality are most deeply rooted, (whatever may be the theory) they are uniformly attended with a practical belief of the actual motion of the sun, and are indeed the effect of it. Let us then continue to talk of time, as we talk of the rising and setting of the sun; but let us think rather of those changes in their origin and effect, from which a sense of time is produced. This will carry us one degree nearer the actual condition of things; it will admit us one step further into the temple of creation—no longer a temple created six thousand years ago, and deserted by him who formed it; but a temple with the hand of the builder resting upon it, perpetually renewing, perpetually creating—and as we bow ourselves to worship the "I am," "Him who liveth forever and ever, who created heaven and the things that are therein, and the earth and the things that are therein, and the sea and the things that are therein," we may hear in accents of divine love the voice that proclaims "that there shall be time no longer."

It is not the living productions of nature, by which the strongest impression of time is produced. The oak over which may have passed a hundred years, seems to drive from our minds the impression of time, by the same power by which it supports its own life, and resists every tendency to decay. It is that which is decayed, though it may have been the offspring of an hour—it is the ruined castle mouldering into dust, still more, if the contrast be strengthened by its being covered with the living productions of nature— it is [12] the half consumed remains of some animal, once strong and vigorous, the discoveries of the undertaker, or the filthy relics of the catacomb, by which the strongest impression of time is conveyed. So it is with the possessions of the mind. It is that which is not used, which seems farthest in the memory, and which is held by the most doubtful tenure; that which is suffered to waste and decay because it wants the life of our own affections; that which we are about to lose because it does not properly belong to us—whereas that truth, which is applied to the use and service of mankind, acquires a higher polish the more it is thus employed, like the angels of heaven, who forever approximate to a state of perfect youth, beauty and innocence. It is not a useless task then, to remove from our minds the usual ideas of time, and cultivate a memory of things. It is to leave the mind in the healthy, vigorous and active possession of all its attainments, and exercise of all its powers—it is to remove from it, that only which contains the seeds of decay and putrefaction; to separate the living from the dead; to take from it the veil by which it would avoid the direct presence of Jehovah, and preserve its own possessions without using them.

Truth, all truth is practical. It is impossible from its nature and origin, that it should be otherwise. Whether its effect be directly to change the conduct, or it simply leave an impression on the heart, it is in the strictest sense practical. It should rather be our desire to use what we learn, than to remember it. If we desire to use it, we shall remember it of course; if we wish merely to remember, it is possible we may never use it. It is the tendency of all truth to effect some object. If we look at this object, it will form a distinct and permanent image on the mind; if we look merely at the truth it will vanish away, like rays of light falling into vacancy.

Keeping in view what has been said on the subject of time then, the mind is presented to us, as not merely active in the acquirement of truth, but active in its possession. The memory is the fire of the vestal virgins, sending forth perpetual light; not the grave, which preserves simply because annihilation is impossible. The reservoir of knowledge should be seated in the affections, sending forth its influence throughout the mind and terminating in word and deed, if I [13] may be allowed the expression, merely because its channels and outlets are situated below the watermark. There prevails a most erroneous sentiment, that the mind is originally vacant, and requires only to be filled up; and there is reason to believe, that this opinion is most intimately connected with false conceptions of time. The mind is originally a most delicate germ, whose husk is the body; planted in this world, that the light and heat of heaven may fall upon it with a gentle radiance, and call forth its energies. The process of learning is not by synthesis, or analysis. It is the most perfect illustration of both. As subjects are presented to the operation of the mind, they are decomposed and reorganized in a manner peculiar to itself, and not easily explained.

Another object of the preceding remarks upon time, is that we may be impressed with the immediate presence and agency of God, without which a correct understanding of mind or matter can never be attained; that we may be able to read on every power of the mind, and on every particle of matter the language of our Lord, "My Father worketh hitherto, and I work." We usually put the Divine Being to an immense distance, by supposing that the world was created many years ago, and subjected to certain laws, by which it has since been governed. We find ourselves capable of constructing machines, which move on without our assistance, and imagine that the world was constructed in the same way. We forget that the motions of our machines depend on the uniform operation of what we call the laws of nature; and that there can be nothing beyond, on which these depend, unless it be the agency of that Being from whom they exist. The pendulum of the clock continues to move from the uniform operation of gravitation. It is no explanation, to say that it is a law of our machinery that the pendulum should move. We simply place things in a situation to be acted upon by an all-pervading power—but what all-pervading power is there by which gravitation is itself produced, unless it be the power of God?

The tendency of bodies to the earth, is something with which from our childhood we have been so familiar; something which we have regarded so much as a cause, since in a certain sense it is the cause of all the motions with which we are acquainted; that it is not agreeable to our habits of thinking, to look at it as an effect. Even the motions of [14] the heavenly bodies seem completely accounted for, by simply extending to these phenomena the feelings with which we have been accustomed to regard the tendency of bodies to the earth; whereas if the two things were communicated at the same period of life, they would appear equally wonderful. An event appears to be explained, when it is brought within the pale of those youthful feelings and associations, which in their simplicity do not ask the reason of things. There is formed in the mind of the child, from his most familiar observations, however imperfect they may be, as it were a little nucleus, which serves as the basis of his future progress. This usually comprises a large proportion of those natural appearances, which the philosopher in later periods of life, finds it most difficult to explain. The child grows up in his Father's house, and collects and arranges the most familiar operations and events. Into this collection, he afterwards receives whatever history or science may communicate, and still feels at home; a feeling with which wonder is never associated.

This is not altogether as it should be. It is natural for the mature mind to ask the cause of things. It is unsatisfied when it does not find one, and can hardly exclude the thought of that Being, from whom all things exist. When therefore we have gone beyond the circle of youthful knowledge, and found a phenomenon in nature, which in its insulated state fills us with the admiration of God; let us beware how we quench this feeling. Let us rather transfer something of this admiration to those phenomena of the same class, which have not hitherto directed our minds beyond the fact of their actual existence. As the mind extends the boundaries of its knowledge, let a holy reference to God descend into its youthful treasures. That light which in the distance seemed to be a miraculous blaze, as it falls on our own native hills may still seem divine, but will not surprise us; and a sense of the constant presence of God will be happily blended with the most perfect freedom.

Till the time of Newton, the motion of the heavenly bodies was in the strictest sense a miracle. It was an event which stood alone, and was probably regarded with peculiar reference to the Divine Being. The feeling of worship with which they had previously been regarded, had subsided into a feeling of wonder; till at length they were [15] received into the family of our most familiar associations. There is one step further. It is to regard gravitation wherever it may be found, as an effect of the constant agency of the Divine Being, and from a consciousness of his presence and co-operation in every step we take, literally "to walk humbly with our God." It is agreeable to the laws of moral and intellectual progression, that all phenomena, whether of matter or mind, should become gradually classified; till at length all things, wherever they are found; all events, whether of history or experience, of mind or matter; shall at once conspire to form one stupendous miracle, and cease to be such. They will form a miracle, in that they are seen to depend constantly and equally on the power of the Lord; and they will cease to be a miracle, in that the power which pervades them, is so constant, so uniform and so mild in its operation, that it produces nothing of fear, nothing of surprise. From whatever point we contemplate the scene, we feel that we are still in our Father's house; go where we will, the paternal roof, the broad canopy of heaven is extended over us.

It is agreeable to our nature, that the mind should be particularly determined to one object. The eye appears to be the point, at which the united rays of the sun within and the sun without, converge to an expression of unity; and accordingly the understanding can be conscious of but one idea or image at a time. Still there is another and a different kind of consciousness which pervades the mind, which is coextensive with every thing it actually possesses. There is but one object in nature on which the *eye* looks directly, but the whole body is pervaded with nerves which convey perpetual information of the existence and condition of every part. So it is with the possessions of the mind; and when an object ceases to be the subject of this kind of consciousness, it ceases to be remembered. The memory therefore, as was said, is not a dormant, but an active power. It is rather the possession than the retention of truth. It is a consciousness of the will; a consciousness of character; a consciousness which is produced by the mind's preserving in effort, whatever it actually possesses. It is the power which the mind has of preserving truth, without actually making it the subject of thought; bearing a relation to thought, anal[o]gous to what this bears to the actual [16] perception of the senses, or to language. Thus we remember a distant object without actually thinking of it, in the same way that we think of it, without actually seeing it.

The memory is not limited, because to the affections viewed simply as such, number is not applicable. They become distinct and are classified, when connected with truths, or from being developed are applied to their proper objects. Love may be increased, but not multiplied. A man may feel intensely, and the quantity and quality of his feeling may affect the character of his thought, but still it preserves its unity. The most ardent love is not attended with more than one idea, but on the contrary has a tendency to confine the mind to a single object. Every one must have remarked, that a peculiar state of feeling belongs to every exercise of the understanding; unless somewhat of this feeling remained after the thought had passed away, there would be nothing whereby the latter could be recalled. The impression thus left exists continually in the mind; though as different objects engage the attention, it may become less vivid. These impressions go to comprise the character of an individual; especially when they have acquired a reality and fixedness, in consequence of the feelings in which they originated, having resulted in the actions to which they tend. They enter into every subject about which we are thinking, and the particular modification they receive from that subject gives them the appearance of individuality; while they leave on the subject itself, the image of that character which they constitute. When a man has become acquainted with any science, that state of the affections which properly belongs to this science, (whatever direction his mind may take afterwards) still maintains a certain influence; and this influence is the creative power by which his knowledge on the subject is reproduced. Such impressions are to the mind, what logarithms are in numbers; preserving our knowledge in its fulness indeed, but before it has expanded into an infinite variety of thoughts. Brown remarks, "we will the existence of certain ideas, it is said, and they arise in consequence of our volition; though assuredly to will any idea is to know that we will, and therefore to be conscious of that very idea, which we surely need not desire to know, when we already know it so well as to will its actual existence." The author does not discriminate between look- [17] ing at an object and thence desiring it, and simply that condition of feeling between which and certain thoughts there is an established relation, so that the former cannot exist to any considerable degree without producing the latter. Of this exertion of the will, every one must have been conscious in his efforts of recollection. Of this exertion of the will the priest must be conscious, when (if he be sincere) by the simple prostration of his heart before his maker, his mind is crowded with the thoughts and language of prayer. Of this exertion of the will, the poet must be conscious, when he makes bare his bosom for the reception of nature, and presents her breathing with his own life and soul. But it is needless to illustrate that of which every one must be sensible.

It follows from these views of the subject, that the true way to store the memory is to develop the affections. The mind must grow, not from external accretion, but from an internal principle. Much may be done by others in aid of its development; but in all that is done, it should not be forgotten, that even from its earliest infancy, it possesses a character and a principle of freedom, which *should be* respected, and *cannot* be destroyed. Its peculiar propensities may be discerned, and proper nutriment and culture supplied—but the infant plant, not less than the aged tree, must be permitted, with its own organs of absorption, to separate that which is peculiarly adapted to itself; otherwise it will be cast off as a foreign substance, or produce nothing but rottenness and deformity.

The science of the mind itself will be the effect of its own development. This is merely an attendant consciousness, which the mind possesses of the growth of its own powers; and therefore it would seem, need not be made a distinct object of study. Thus the power of reason may be imperceptibly developed by the study of the demonstrative sciences. As it is developed, the pupil becomes conscious of its existence and its use. This is enough. He can in fact learn nothing more on the subject. If he learns to use his reason what more is desired? Surely it were useless, and worse than useless, to shut up the door of the senses, and live in indolent and laborious contemplation of one's own powers; when if any thing is learned truly, it must be what these powers are and therefore that they ought not to [18] be thus employed. The best affections we possess will find their home in the objects around us, and, as it were, enter into and animate the whole rational, animal and vegetable world. If the eye were turned inward to a direct contemplation of these affections, it would find them bereft of all their loveliness; for when they are active, it is not of them we are thinking, but of the objects on which they rest. The science of the mind then, will be the effect of all the other sciences. Can the child grow up in active usefulness, and not be conscious of the possession and use of his own limbs? The body and the mind should grow together, and form the sound and perfect man, whose understanding may be almost measured by his stature. The mind will see itself in what it loves and is able to accomplish. Its own works will be its mirror; and when it is present in the natural world, feeling the same spirit which gives life to every object by which it is surrounded, in its very union with nature it will catch a glimpse of itself, like that of pristine beauty united with innocence, at her own native fountain.

What then is that development which the nature of the human mind requires? What is that education which has heaven for its object, and such a heaven as will be the effect of the orderly growth of the spiritual man?

As all minds possess that in common which makes them human, they require to a certain extent the same general development, by which will be brought to view the same powers however distinct and varied they may be found in different individuals; and as every mind possesses something peculiar, to which it owes its character and its effect, it requires a particular development by which may be produced a full, sincere and humble expression of its natural features, and the most vigorous and efficient exertion of its natural powers. These make one, so far as regards the individual.

Those sciences which exist embodied in the natural world, appear to have been designed to occupy the first place in the development of all minds, or in that which might be called the general development of the mind. These comprise the laws of the animal, vegetable, and mineral kingdoms. The human mind, being as it were planted in nature by its heavenly Father, was designed to enter into matter, and detect knowledge for its own purposes of growth and nutrition. This gives us a true idea of memory, or rather of what memory [19] should be. We no longer think of a truth as being laid up in a mind for which it has no affinity, and by which it is perhaps never to be used; but the latent affections as they expand under proper culture, absolutely require the truth to receive them, and its first use is the very nutriment it affords. It is not more difficult for the tree to return to the seed from which it sprung, than for the man who has learned thus, to cease to remember. The natural sciences are the basis of all useful knowledge, alike important to man in whatever time, place or condition he is found. They are coeval with our race, and must continue so long as the sun, moon and stars endure. Before there were facts for the pen of history to record, or vices for the arm of law to restrain, or nations for the exhibition of institutions for the government of themselves, and intercourse with each other; at the very creation, these were pronounced good in the general benediction—and when history shall have finished her tale of sin and wo, and law shall have punished her millions of offenders, and civil society shall have assumed every possible form, they will remain the same as when presented in living characters to the first parents of the human race. Natural philosophy seems almost essential to an enlightened independence of thought and action. A man may lean upon others, and be so well supported by an equal pressure in all directions, as to be apparently dependent on no one; but his independence is apt to degenerate into obstinacy, or betray itself in weakness, unless his mind is fixed on this unchanging basis. A knowledge of the world may give currency to his sentiments and plausibility to his manners; but it is more frequently a knowledge of *the world* that gives light to the path and stability to the purposes. By the one he may learn what coin is current, by the other what possesses intrinsic value. The natural world was precisely and perfectly adapted to invigorate and strengthen the intellectual and moral man. Its first and highest use was not to support the vegetables which adorn, or the animals which cover its surface; nor yet to give sustenance to the human body—it has a higher and holier object, in the attainment of which these are only means. It was intended to draw forth and mature the latent energies of the soul; to impart to them its own verdure and freshness; to initiate them into its own mysteries; and by its silent and humble dependence on its creator, to leave on them [20] when it is withdrawn by death, the full impression of his likeness.

It was the design of Providence, that the infant mind should possess the germ of every science. If it were not so, they could hardly be learned. The care of God provides for the flower of the field, a place wherein it may grow, regale with its fragrance, and delight with its beauty. Is his providence less active over those, to whom this flower offers its incense? No. The soil which produces the vine in its most healthy luxuriance, is not better adapted to the end, than the world we inhabit to draw forth latent energies of the soul, and fill them with life and vigour. As well might the eye see without light, or the ear hear without sound; as the human mind be healthy and athletic, without descending into the natural world, and breathing the mountain air. Is there aught in eloquence, which warms the heart? She draws her fire from natural imagery. Is there aught in poetry to enliven the imagination? There is the secret of all her power. Is there aught in science to add strength and dignity to the human mind? The natural world is only the body, of which she is the soul. In books science is presented to the eye of the pupil, as it were in a dried and preserved state; the time may come when the instructer will take him by the hand, and lead him by the running streams, and teach him all the principles of science as she comes from her maker, as he would smell the fragrance of the rose without gathering it.

This love of nature, this adaptation of man to the place assigned him by his heavenly Father, this fulness of the mind as it descends into the works of God, is something which has been felt by every one, though to an imperfect degree; and therefore needs no explanation. It is the part of science, that this be no longer a blind affection, but that the mind be opened to a just perception of what it is, which it loves. The affection, which the lover first feels for his future wife, may be attended only by a general sense of her external beauty; but his mind gradually opens to a perception of the peculiar features of the soul, of which the external appearance is only an image. So it is with nature. Do we love to gaze on the sun, the moon, the stars and the planets? This affection contains in its bosom the whole science of astronomy, as the seed contains the future tree. It is the office of the instruct- [21] er, to give it an existence and a name, by making known the laws which govern the motions of the heavenly bodies, the relation of these bodies to each other, and their uses. Have we felt delight in beholding the animal creation, in watching their pastimes and their labours? It is the office of the instructer to give birth to this affection, by teaching the different classes of animals with their peculiar characteristics, which inhabit the earth, air, and sea. Have we known the inexpressible pleasure of beholding the beauties of the vegetable world? This affection can only expand in the science of botany. Thus it is that the love of nature in the mass, may become the love of all the sciences; and the mind will grow and bring forth fruit from its own inherent power of development. Thus it is that memory refers to the growth and expansion of the mind; and what is thus, as it were incorporated into its substance, can be forgotten only by a change in the direction of the affections, or the course of conduct of the individual analogous to that in his physical man, by which his very flesh and bones are exchanged for those of a different texture; nor does he then entirely cease to remember, inasmuch as he preserves a sense of his own identity.

It is in this way the continual endeavour of Providence, that the natural sciences should be the spontaneous production of the human mind. To these should certainly be added, poetry and music; for when we study the works of God as we should, we cannot disregard that inherent beauty and harmony in which these arts originate. These occasion in the mind its first glow of delight, like the taste of food as it is offered to the mouth; and the pleasure they afford, is a pledge of the strength and manhood after-wards imparted by the sciences.

By poetry is meant all those illustrations of truth by natural imagery, which spring from the fact that this world is the mirror of him who made it. Strictly speaking, nothing has less to do with fiction, than poetry. The day will come, and it may not be far distant, when this art will have another test of merit than mere versification, or the invention of strange stories; when the laws by which poetry is tested, will be as fixed and immutable as the laws of science; when a change will be introduced into taste corresponding to that which Bacon introduced into philosophy, by which both will [22] be confined within the limits of things as they actually exist. It would seem that genius would be cramped; that the powers of invention would be destroyed; by confining the human mind, as it were, at home, within the bounds which nature has assigned. But what wider scope need it have? It reaches the throne of God; it rests on his footstool. All things spiritual and natural are before it. There is as much that is true as false; and truth presented in natural imagery, is only dressed in the garments which God has given it.

The imagination was permitted for ages to involve the world in darkness, by putting theory in the place of fact; till at length the greatest man revealed the simplest truth, that our researches must be governed by actual observation. God is the source of all truth. Creation, (and what truth does not result from creation?) is the effect of the Divine Love and Wisdom. Simply to will and to think with the Divine Being, result in creating; in actually producing those realities, which form the ground-work of the thoughts and affections of man. But for the philosopher to desire a thing, and to think that it existed, produced nothing but his own theory. Hence it was necessary that he should bring his mind into coincidence with things as they exist, or in other words with the truth.

Fiction in poetry must fall with theory in science, for they depend equally on the works of creation. The word fiction however is not intended to be used in its most literal sense; but to embrace whatever is not in exact agreement with the creative spirit of God. It belongs to the true poet to feel this spirit, and to be governed by it; to be raised above the senses; to live and breathe in the inward efforts of things; to feel the power of creation, even before he sees the effect; to witness the innocence and smiles of nature's infancy, not by extending the imagination back to chaos, but by raising the soul to nature's origin. The true poetic spirit, so far from misleading any, is the strongest bulwark against deception. It is the soul of science. Without it, the latter is a cheerless, heartless study, distrusting even the presence and power of Him to whom it owes its existence. Of all the poetry which exists, that only possesses the seal of immortality, which presents the image of God which is stamped on nature. Could the poetry which now prevails, be viewed from the future, [23] when all partialities and antipathies shall have passed away, and things are left to rest on their own foundations; when good works shall have dwindled into insignificance from the mass of useless matter that may have fallen from them, and bad ones shall have ceased to allure with false beauty; we might catch a glimpse of the rudiments of this divine art, amid the weight of extraneous matter by which it is now protected, and which it is destined to throw off. The imagination will be refined into a chaste and sober view of unveiled nature. It will be confined within the bounds of reality. It will no longer lead the way to insanity and madness by transcending the works of creation, and as it were, wandering where God has no power to protect it; but finding a resting-place in every created object, it will enter into it and explore its hidden treasures, the relation in which it stands to mind, and reveal the love it bears to its Creator.

The state of poetry has always indicated the state of science and religion. The Gods are hardly missed more, when removed from the temples of the ancients, than they are when taken from their poetry; or than theory is when taken from their philosophy. Fiction ceases to be pleasing when it ceases to gain credence; and what they admired in itself, commands much of its admiration now, as a relic of antiquity. The painting which in a darkened room only impressed us with the reality, as the sun rises upon it discovers the marks of the pencil; and that shade of the mind can never again return, which gave to ancient poetry its vividness and its power. Of this we may be sensible, by only considering how entirely powerless it would be, if poetry in all respects similar were produced at the present day. A man's religious sentiments, and his knowledge of the sciences, are so entirely interwoven with all his associations; they shed such light throughout every region of the mind; that nothing can please which is directly opposed to them—and though the forms which poetry may offer, may sometimes be presented, where this light begins to sink into obscurity; they should serve, like the sky and the clouds, as a relief to the eye, and not like some unnatural body protruding on the horizon, disturb the quiet they are intended to produce. When there shall be a religion which shall see God in every thing, and at all times; and the natural [24] sciences not less than nature itself, shall be regarded in connexion with Him—the fire of poetry will begin to be kindled in its immortal part, and will burn without consuming. The inspiration so often feigned, will become real; and the mind of the poet will feel the spark which passes from God to nature. The veil will be withdrawn, and beauty and innocence displayed to the eye; for which the lasciviousness of the imagination and the wantonness of desire may seek in vain.

There is a language, not of words but of things. When this language shall have been made apparent, that which is human will have answered its end, and being as it were resolved into its original elements, will lose itself in nature. The use of language is the expression of our feelings and desires; the manifestation of the mind. But every thing which is, whether animal or vegetable, is full of the expression of that use for which it is designed, as of its own existence. If we did but understand its language, what could our words add to its meaning? It is because we are unwilling to hear, that we find it necessary to say so much; and we drown the voice of nature, with the discordant jargon of ten thousand dialects. Let a man's language be confined to the expression of that which actually belongs to his own mind; and let him respect the smallest blade which grows and permit it to speak for itself. Then may there be poetry which may not be written perhaps, but which may be felt as a part of our being. Every thing which surrounds us, is full of the utterance of one word, completely expressive of its nature. This word is its name; for God, even now could we but see it, is creating all things, and giving a name to every work of his love, in its perfect adaptation to that for which it is designed. But man has abused his power, and has become insensible to the real character of the brute creation, still more so, to that of inanimate nature, because in his selfishness, he is disposed to reduce them to slavery. Therefore he is deaf. We find the animal world, either in a state of savage wildness, or enslaved submission. It is possible that as the character of man is changed, they may attain a midway condition equally removed from both. As the mind of man acknowledges its dependance on the Divine Mind, brutes may add to their instinct submission to human reason; preserving an [25] unbroken chain from our Father in Heaven, to the most inanimate parts of creation. Such may be supposed to have been the condition of the animal, on which the King of Zion rode into Jerusalem; at once free and subject to the will of the rider. Every thing will seem to be conscious of its use; and man will become conscious of the use of every thing.

It may be peculiar, and is said with deference to the opinions of others, but to my ear, rhymes add nothing to poetry, but rather detract from its beauty. They possess too strongly the marks of art, and produce a sameness which tires, and sometimes disgusts. We seek for them in vain in nature, and may therefore reasonably presume that they spring out of the peculiar state of the public taste, without possessing any real foundation in the mind itself; that they are rather the fashion of the dress, than any essential part. In the natural world we find nothing which answers to them, or feels like them—but a happy assemblage of living objects springing up, not in straight lines and at a fixed distance, but in God's own order, which by its apparent want of design, conveys the impression of perfect innocence and humility. It is not for that which is human to be completely divested of the marks of art; but every approach towards this end, must be an approach towards perfection. The poet should be free and unshackled as the eagle; whose wings, as he soars in the air, seem merely to serve the office of a helm, while he moves on simply by the agency of the will.

By music is meant not merely that which exists in the rational world, whether in the song of angels or men; not merely the singing of birds and the lowing of cattle, by which the animal world express their affections and their wants—but that harmony which pervades also all orders of creation; the music of the harp of universal nature, which is touched by the rays of the sun, and whose song is the morning, the evening and the seasons. Music is the voice of God, and poetry his language, both in his word and works. The one is to the ear, what the other is to the eye. Every child of nature must feel their influence. There was a time, when the human mind was in more perfect harmony with the Divine Mind, than the lower orders of creation; and the tale of the harp of Orpheus, to which [26] the brutes, the vegetables and the rocks listened, is not altogether unfounded in reality—but when the selfish and worldly passions usurped the place of love to our God and our neighbour, the mind of man began to be mute in its praise. The original order was reversed. The very stones cry out, and we do well to listen to them.

There is a most intimate and almost inseparable connexion between poetry and music. This is indicated by the fact that they are always united. Nothing is sung which has not some pretensions to poetry; and nothing has any pretensions to poetry, in which there is not something of music. A good ear is essential to rhythm; and rhythm is essential to verse. It is the perfection of poetry, that it addresses two senses at once, the ear and the eye; that it prepares the affections for the object before it is presented; that it sends light through the understanding, by forming a communication between the heart of man, and the works of God. The character of music must have always harmonized with that of poetry. It is essential to the former that it should be in agreement with our feelings; for it is from this circumstance, that it derives its power. That music which is in unison with the Divine Mind, alone deserves the name. So various is it found in the different conditions of man, that it is hardly recognized as the same thing. There is music in the war-song of the savage, and in the sound for battle. Alas! how unlike that music which proclaimed peace on earth and good will towards men. Poetry and music like virtuous females in disguise, have followed our race into the darkest scenes to which the fall has brought them. We find them in the haunts of dissipation and vice; in the song of revelry and lewdness. We meet them again kindling the fire of devotion at the altar of God; and find them more and more perfect, as we approach their divine origin.

There prevail at present two kinds of music, as diverse as their origins; profane and religious. The one is the result of the free, unrestrained expression of natural feelings; the other, of a kind which indicates that these feelings are placed under restraint. In the one, there is often something of sensuality; in the other of sadness. There is a point in moral improvement, in which the sensual will be subdued, and the sorrowful disappear; which will combine the pleasure [27] of the one, with the sanctity of the other. When a sense of the presence of God shall be coextensive with the thoughts of the mind, and religion shall consecrate every word and action of our lives; the song of Zion will be no longer sung in a strange land. The Divine Love, the soul and essence of music, will descend, not in the thunders of Sinai, but will seem to acquire volume, as it tunes the heart in unison with itself, and the tongue in unison with the heart. The changes in the character of our music, which may be the effect of the gradual regeneration of the world, are hardly within the reach of conjecture.

Enough has been said to illustrate generally, the influence of the natural world in the development of the mind. The actual condition of society operates to produce the same effect, with hardly less power. In this, are comprised the religious and civil institutions of one's own country; that peculiar character in which they originate; and a knowledge of the past, as by disclosing the origin and progress of things, it throws light on the prospect actually before us. As the philosophy connected with the natural world, is that in which the mind may take root, by which it may possess an independence worthy a being whose eternal destiny is in his own hands—so the moral and civil institutions, the actual condition of society, is the atmosphere which surrounds and protects it; in which it sends forth its branches, and bears fruit. The spiritual part of man is as really a substance, as the material; and is as capable of acting upon spirit, as matter is upon matter. It is not from words of instruction and advice, that the mind of the infant derives its first impetus; it gathers strength from the warmth of those affections which overshadow it, and is nourished by a mother's love, even before it has attained the power of thought. It is the natural tendency of things, that an individual should be brought into a situation, in which the external condition of the place, and the circle of society in which he is, are particularly adapted to bring forth to view his hereditary character. The actual condition of the human mind, is as it were the solid substance, in which the laws of moral and intellectual philosophy and political economy, (whatever may be their quality) exist embodied, as the natural sciences do in the material world. A knowledge of those laws, such as they exist, is the natural consequence [28] of the development of the affections, by which a child is connected with those that surround him. The connexion of mind is not less powerful or universal than that of matter. All minds, whatever may be their condition, are not unconnected with God; and consequently not unconnected with each other. All nations, under whatever system of government, and in whatever state of civilization, are under the Divine Providence, surely but almost imperceptibly advancing to a moral and political order, such as the world has not yet seen. They are guided by the same hand, and with a view to the same destiny. Much remains to be done, and more to be suffered; but the end is certain. The humblest individual may, nay *must* aid in the accomplishment of this consummation. It is not for time or space to set limits to the effects of the life of a single man. Let then the child be so initiated into a knowledge of the condition of mankind, that the love at first indulged in the circle of his father's family, shall gradually subside into a chaste and sober love of his country; and of his country, not as opposed to other countries, but as aiding them in the same great object. Let the young mind be warmed and cherished by whatever is chaste and generous in the mind of the public; and be borne on to a knowledge of our institutions, by the rich current of the disposition to preserve them.

Thus it is that the child is no sooner brought into this world, than the actual condition both of the world itself, and of society, acts powerfully to draw forth the energies of his mind. If mankind had retained that order in which they were created, this influence in co-operation with the Divine, would have been sufficient, as it was designed to have been, for all the purposes of God. Nature, the very image of divine loveliness, and the purest affections of the heart, which approach still nearer the same origin, acting together on the infant mind; it would seem as if the effect would be almost as certain, as any process of growth which is witnessed among the productions of the natural world. But man is fallen—and the operation of this influence in different conditions of society, may produce different results; but in none is sufficient to capacitate him for that life of usefulness and happiness, for which he was designed. The influence of society cannot be sufficient, since this cannot raise a man above its own level; and the society of earth is no longer [29] the society of heaven. This influence may bring forward all the warlike energies of the young savage, and direct them in their utmost vigour to the destruction of his enemies and of the beasts of the forest; and he may look onward with rapture to the happy hunting grounds beyond the grave. What disappointment awaits him in the other world, all of us may easily imagine. This influence may bring forth and gratify the unchaste and beastly passions of the Turk; and he may look forward, with his Koran in his hand, to a heaven of sensuality and crime. It need not be said how widely different will be found the reality. Christians generally are standing in expectation of a happiness as boundless in extent, as it is undefined in its nature; and with an infinite variety of passions in whose gratification alone they have experienced delight, are expecting a heaven in which simple useless enjoyment will rise like a flood and immerse the mind. The result must of necessity be as various, as the condition of the individuals by whom it is anticipated. Still there is a society yet in its coming, unseen though not unseeing, shrouded from the rest of the world by the very brilliancy of its own light, which would resist the impulse of every evil affection, and look for heaven simply in the delight of that which is chaste, pure and holy; which by removing that which renders duty undelightful, would draw nigh to the only source of real enjoyment; which would find its happiness and its God, in the very commandments which have been the terrour of the world; to which the effect is no longer doubtful, since it is made acquainted with the cause, and which as it anticipates no reward, will meet with no disappointment. When this society shall be fully established on the earth, the voice of the Lord will be no longer obstructed as it descends from above the heavens;—"*Suffer little children to come unto me and forbid them not, for of such is the kingdom of God.*"

The influence of the natural world however beneficial it may prove, is not such as it was designed to have been. Man has ever sought a condition in nature, which should correspond with the state of his own mind. The savage would pine and droop, if too suddenly removed to scenes of civilization, like grass which had grown in rank luxuriance under the shade of the oak, if the branches were cleft and it was at once exposed to the power of the sun. The charac- [30] ter of all the lower orders of creation has suffered a change in consequence of that in the condition of man, the extent of which cannot be measured. That the sun was darkened at the crucifixion of our Lord, was no miracle. It was as much the natural consequence of that event, as its present lustre is of His glory. It is not then for these the objects of nature, to restore to us that moral order, the want of which has wrought such changes on themselves.

There is then another power which is necessary to the orderly development of the mind; the power of the Word of God. This indeed has been implied in all the preceding remarks. No possessions and no efforts of the mind are unconnected with it, whatever may be the appearance. Revelation so mingles with every thing which meets us, that it is not easy for us to measure the degree to which our condition is affected by it. Its effects appear miraculous at first, but after they have become established, the mind as in the ordinary operations of nature, is apt to become unconscious of the power by which they are produced. All growth or development is effected from within, outward. It is so with animals; it is so with vegetables; it is so with the body; it is so with the mind. Were it not for a power within the soul, as the soul is within the body, it could have no possibility of subsistence. That the growth of the material part depends on the presence of that which is spiritual, is obvious from the fact, that at death the former falls to decay. If it were possible for God to be detached from our spiritual part, this would decay likewise. The doctrine then of the immortality of the soul is simply, "I in my Father, and ye in me and I in you." It is the union of the Divine, with the human— of that from which all things are, and on which they depend the Divine Will, with man through the connecting medium of Divine Truth. It is the tendency of the Bible to effect this union, and of course to restore a consciousness of it. It is a union which God desires with all, therefore even the wicked who reject it, partake of his immortality, though not of his happiness. When in the process of regeneration, this union is accomplished, the fear of dissolution will be as impossible in this world as in the other; and before this is effected, the fear of dissolution may exist there, as well as here. It is not the place where a person is, but the condition of mind which is to be regarded; and [31] there is no antidote against the fear of death, but the consciousness of being united with the fountain of life. But it is asked, how can the fear of death exist after it has actually taken place? The separation of the spiritual and material part so far as the nature of their connexion is understood, can produce no fear. Were it not for evil in ourselves, it would rather wear the appearance of a state of uncommon quiet. There is upon no subject a more powerful tendency to instinctive knowledge, than upon that of death. The darkness with which it is veiled, presents but a lamentable picture of our present condition. It is its own dissolution of which the mind is afraid; and that want of conjunction with God which renders this fear possible here, may render it possible any where. It is the sole object of the Bible to conjoin the soul with God; and as this is effected it may be understood in what way the Holy Spirit operates interiously to produce its development. It is not a mere metaphor, it is a plain and simple fact, that the Spirit of God is as necessary to the development of the mind, as the power of the natural sun to the growth of vegetables and in the same way. But let us remember, that as in nature the heat and light may be converted into the most noxious poison; so the Spirit of God in itself perfectly pure and holy, may be converted into passions the most opposite to its nature. It is left to us to open our hearts to its influence, by obeying its commandments. "If ye love me, keep my commandments; and I will pray the Father, and he shall give you another comforter that he may abide with you forever." "He that believeth on the Son *hath* everlasting life;" and he will become conscious of living and growing from God.

It is not consistent with the nature of things, that the full practical effect of a subject should be at once revealed to the mind. The child is led on to a knowledge of his letters, by a thousand little enticements, and by the tender coercion of parental authority, while he is yet ignorant of the treasures mysteriously concealed in their combinations. The arts have been courted merely for the transient gratification they afford. Their connexion with religion and with the sciences is beginning to be discovered; and they are yet to yield a powerful influence in imparting to the mind, its moral harmony and proportions. The sciences themselves have been studied principally as subjects of speculation and [32] amusement. They have been sought for the gratification they afford, and for the artificial standing they give in society, by the line of distinction which is drawn between the learned and the vulgar. The discovery of their connexion with the actual condition of man, is of later origin; and though their application to use is yet in its infancy, they are beginning to throw a light on almost every department of labour, hitherto unexampled in the annals of the world. Religion too has been a subject of speculation, something evanescent, a theory, a prayer, a hope. It remains for this also to become practical, by the actual accomplishment of that which it promises. It remains for the promise of reward to be swallowed up in the work of salvation. It remains for the soul to be restored to its union with God—to heaven. Christianity is the tree of life again planted in the world; and by its own vital power it has been, year after year, casting off the opinions of men, like the external bark which partakes not of its life. It remains for the human mind to become conformed to its spirit, that its principles may possess the durability of their origin.

Such are the effects to be anticipated from the Bible in the development of the mind. It has begun the work, and will perfect it in each individual, so far as by a life according to the commandments he becomes willing that it should. There is within it a secret power, which exerts an influence on the moral and intellectual world, like that of the sun on the physical; and however long and successfully it may be resisted by some, not the less certain in its effect on the ultimate condition of society. I am aware that in these remarks, I am ascribing to the spirit of God, to the spirit of the Word, a power which some may be unwilling to allow to it. The Bible is thought to resemble other books, and to be subject to the same laws of criticism; and we may be sometimes in danger of becoming insensible to its internal power, from the very mass of human learning, with which it is encumbered. "Is not this the carpenter's son?"

There is one law of criticism, the most important to the thorough understanding of any work, which seems not to have been brought sufficiently into view in the study of the Bible. It is that by which we should be led by a continued exercise of those powers which are most clearly demonstrated in an authour; by continued habits of mind and action; to [33] approximate to that intellectual and moral condition, in which the work originated. If it were desired to make a child thoroughly acquainted with the work of a genuine poet, I would not put the poem and lexicon in his hand and bid him study and learn—I would rather make him familiar with whatever was calculated to call forth the power of poetry in himself, since it requires the exercise of the same powers to understand, that it does to produce. I would point him to that source from which the author himself had caught his inspiration, and as I led him to the baptismal fount of nature, I would consecrate his powers to that Being from whom nature exists. I would cultivate a sense of the constant presence and agency of God, and direct him inward to the presence chamber of the Most High, that his mind might become imbued with His spirit. I would endeavour by the whole course of his education to make him a living poem, that when he read the poetry of others, it might be effulgent with the light of his own mind. The poet stands on the mountain with the face of nature before him, calm and placid. If we would enter into his views, we must go where he is. We must catch the direction of his eye, and yield ourselves up to the instinctive guidance of his will, that we may have a secret foretaste of his meaning—that we may be conscious of the image in its first conception—that we may perceive its beginnings and gradual growth, till at length it becomes distinctly depicted on the retina of the mind. Without this, we may take the dictionary in our hands and settle the definition of every word, and still know as little of the lofty conceptions of the author, as the weary traveller who passes round in the farthest verge which is visible from the mountain, knows of the scenery which is seen from its summit. It has been truly said that Johnson was incapable of conceiving the beauties of Milton. Yet Johnson was himself a living dictionary of Milton's language. The true poet, when his mind is full, fills his language to overflowing; and it is left to the reader to preserve what the words cannot contain. It is that part which cannot be defined; that which is too delicate to endure the unrestrained gaze; that which shrinks instinctively from the approach of any thing less chaste than itself, and though present, like the inhabitants of the other world, is unperceived by flesh and blood, which is worth all the rest. This acknowledges no dwelling-place [34] but the mind. Stamp the living light on the extended face of nature, beyond the power of darkness at the setting of the sun, and you may preserve such light as this, when the mind rises not to meet it in its coming.

If it were desired to make an individual acquainted with a work in one of the abstract sciences, this might be best effected by leading him gradually to whatever conduced to the growth of those powers on which a knowledge of these sciences depend; by cultivating a principle of dependence on the Divine Being, a purity and chastity of the affections, which will produce a tranquil condition, of all things the most favourable to clear perceptions; by leading him to an habitual observation of the relations of things, and to such continued exertion of the understanding, as calling into use its full powers without inducing fatigue, may impart the strength of the labourer, without the degradation of the slave; in a word, by forming a penetrating, mathematical mind, rather than by communicating mathematical information. The whole character and complexion of the mind will be gradually changed; till at length it will become (chemically speaking) in its very nature an active solvent of these subjects. They fall to pieces as soon as they come in contact with it and assume an arrangement agreeable to that of the mind itself, with all the precision of crystallization. They are then understood—for the most perfect understanding of a subject is simply a perception of harmony existing between the subject and the mind itself. Indeed the understanding which any individual posseses of a subject might be mathematically defined $\frac{\text{the subject proposed,}}{\text{the actual character of his mind}}$; and there is a constant struggle for the numerator and denominator to become the same by a change in the one or the other, that the result may be unity, and the understanding perfect.

There is an analogy, (such as may exist between things human and things divine) between that discipline which is required in order to understand a production of taste or science, and that which is necessary to a clear perception of the truths of the Bible. As it is requisite to a full sense of the beauties of poetry, that the individual should be himself a poet, and to a thorough knowledge of a work of science that he should not merely have scientific information, but a scientific mind; so it is necessary to a knowledge of the Bible, [35] that the mind should be formed in the image and likeness of God. An understanding of the Word is the effect of a life according to its precepts. It requires, not the obedience of the rich man who went away sorrowful, but the obedience of him who holds every other possession, whether it consist in the acquirements of the mind or in earthly property, in subjection to the Holy Spirit within him. "If ye will do the will of God, ye shall know of the doctrines" is a law of exegesis, before which false sentiments will melt away like frost before the rising sun. There is within the mind the golden vein of duty, which if followed aright will lead to an increasing brightness, before which the proudest monuments of human criticism will present an appearance like that of the dark disk of this world, as the eye of the dying man opens on the scenes of the other.

The world is beginning to be changed from what it was. Physical power instead of boasting of its deeds of prowess, and pointing with the tomahawk or the lance to the bloody testimonies of its strength, is beginning to leave its image on the rugged face of nature, and to feel the living evidence of its achievements, in the happy circle of domestic life. It remains for intellectual strength to lose the consciousness of its existence in the passions subdued, and to reap the reward of its labours, not in the spoils of an enemy, but in the fruits of honest industry. It remains for us to become more thoroughly acquainted with the laws of moral mechanism. Instead of making unnecessary and ineffectual exertions in the direct attainment of truth, it remains for us to make equal efforts to cleanse our own minds and to do good to others; and what was before unattainable will become easy, as the rock which untutored strength cannot move, may be raised by a touch of the finger.

The Bible differs from other books as our Lord differed from men. He was born of a woman, but His Spirit was the everlasting Father. It is humble in its appearance, as nature is when compared to art; and some parts which Providence has permitted to remain within the same cover, have often attracted more attention than that which is really divine. From the very nature of perfect innocence its presence is unnoticed, save by him by whom it is loved. Divine Love, in its perfect thoughtlessness of itself, enters the atheistical [36] heart, unperceived. Such an one thinks meanly of those who think humbly of themselves, and with perfect humility the last vestige of reality disappears. To him, both nature and the Word are like a deserted building, through which as he passes, he is conscious of nothing but the sound of his own footsteps; but to him whose heart opens to the Divine Influence, this building appears to assume from the internal cause of its creation, the symmetry of perfect proportions, till at length as he becomes more and more conscious of the presence with which it is filled, he sees no temple, "for the Lord God Almighty, and the Lamb are the temple." The Word resembles the hebrew language in which much of it is written. To him who knows not its spirit, it is an empty form without sound or vowel; but to him who is alive to the Divine Influence it is filled with the living voice of God.

The Bible can never be fully understood, either by making it subservient to natural reason, or by blindly adopting what reason would reject; but by that illumination of the understanding and enlargement of the reason, which will result from a gradual conformity to its precepts. Reason now, is something very different from what it was a few centuries past. We are in the habit of thinking that the mode of reasoning has changed; but this appears to be merely an indication of a change which has taken place in the character of the mind itself. Syllogistic reasoning is passing away. It has left no permanent demonstration, but that of its own worthlessness. It amounts to nothing but the discernment and expression of the particulars which go to comprise something more general; and as the human mind permits things to assume a proper arrangement from their own inherent power of attraction, it is no longer necessary to bind them together with syllogisms. Few minds can now endure the tediousness of being led blindfold to a conclusion, and of being satisfied with the result merely from the recollection of having been satisfied on the way to it. The mind requires to view the parts of a subject, not only separately but together; and the understanding in the exercise of those powers of arrangement by which a subject is presented in its just relations to other things, takes the name of reason. We appear to be approaching that condition which requires the union of reason and eloquence, and will be satisfied with neither without the other. We neither wish to see an ana- [37] tomical plate of bare muscles, nor the gaudy daubings of finery; but a happy mixture of strength and beauty. We desire language neither extravagant nor cold; but bloodwarm. Reason is beginning to learn the necessity of simply tracing the relations which exist between created things, and of not even touching what it examines lest it disturb the arrangement in the cabinet of creation—and as in the progress of moral improvement, the imagination (which is called the creative power of man) shall coincide with the actively creative will of God, reason will be clothed with eloquence as nature is with verdure.

Reason is said to be a power given to man for his protection and safety. Let us not be deceived by words. If this were the particular design, it should be found in equal perfection in every condition of the mind; for all are in equal need of such a power. It is the office of the eye to discern the objects of nature, and it may protect the body from any impending injury; and the understanding may be useful in a similar way to the spiritual man. Reason is partly a natural and partly an acquired power. The understanding is the eye with simply the power of discerning the light; but reason in the eye whose powers have been enlarged by exercise and experience, which measures the distance of objects, compares their magnitudes, discerns their colours and selects and arranges them according to the relation they bear to each other. In the progress of moral improvement no power of the mind, or rather no mode of exercising the understanding, undergoes a more thorough and decisive change than this. It is like the change from chaos to creation; since it requires a similar exercise of the understanding in man to comprehend creation, to what it does in God to produce it; and every approach to Him by bringing us nearer the origin of things, enables us to discover analogies in what was before chaotic. This is a change which it is the grand design of revelation to accomplish; reason should therefore come to revelation in the spirit of prayer, and not in that of judgment. Nothing can be more intimately, and necessarily connected with the moral character of an individual, than his rational powers, since it is his moral character which is the grand cause of that peculiar classification and arrangement which characterizes his mind; hence revelation in changing the former, must change the latter also.

[38] The insufficiency of reason to judge of the Bible, is obvious on the very face of revelation from its miracles. The laws of Divine Operation are perfectly uniform and harmonious; and a miracle is a particular instance of Divine Power, which for a want of a more interiour and extended knowledge of the ways of God, appearing to stand alone, and to have been the result of an unusual exertion of the Divine Will, creates in the minds of men, what its name implies, a sensation of wonder. That there are miracles in the Bible, proves that there are laws of the Divine Operation and of the Divine Government, which are not embraced within the utmost limits of that classification and arrangement, which is the result of natural reason. While therefore human reason professes to be convinced of the reality of revelation from its miracles, let it humble

itself before them. Let it bow itself to the earth, that it may be exalted to a more intimate acquaintance with these heavenly strangers. Let it follow the Lord in the regeneration, till the wonderful disappear in the paternal. Miracles are like angels who have sometimes been visible to men—who would much more willingly have introduced them to an acquaintance with the laws and society of heaven, than have filled them with fear and consternation. They are insulated examples of laws as boundless as the universe, and by the manner in which we are affected by them, prove how much we have to learn, and how utterly incompetent we are to judge of the ways of God, from that reason, which is founded on our own limited and fallacious observation. The resurrection of our Lord must have been a very different miracle to the ang[el]s at the sepulchre, from what it was to Mary. They saw it from the other side of the grave, with a knowledge of the nature of that death which they had themselves experienced; she saw an insulated fact not at all coincident with her views on the subject of which it was an illustration. They saw the use and design of that which had been accomplished; she saw the sepulchre and the linen clothes lying. As they gazed intensely at the same subject, the veil of heaven was withdrawn, and they beheld each other, face to face. She was filled with fear; they with love and compassion. If Mary were to persist in judging of this subject from her own reason; from a knowledge of those laws with which she was previously acquainted; how could her views ever become an- [39] gelic? How could the dark cloud of admiration be ever filled with the rich light of the rising sun?

Man alone of all created things, appears on his own account to want the full measure of his happiness; because he alone has left the order of his creation. He stands even at the present period half-convinced of the reality of the future state. It is the design of revelation to restore to him that moral condition, in which he will possess as necessarily the consciousness of immortality, as the brute does that of existence—for a consciousness of existence united with that of union with God, is a consciousness of eternal life. Let us come to the Bible then, with no hopes of arbitrary reward, and no fears of arbitrary punishment; but let us come to it, as to that which if followed aright, will produce a condition of mind of which happiness will be the natural and necessary consequence.

It is often said that the Bible has nothing to do with metaphysics or the sciences. An individual, whatever be his condition, always retains to a certain extent, a consciousness of his moral and intellectual character, and the more this character is exalted, the more minute and discriminating will be this consciousness. Who is it that formed the human mind, and who is here endeavouring to restore it to its true order? The Bible has the mind for its subject, that condition of mind which is heaven for its object, and the Father of mind for its author. Has it nothing to do with metaphysics? It has indeed nothing to do with that metaphysics which we shall leave with our bodies in the graves; but of that, which will shine with more and more brilliancy, as the passage is opened, not through distant regions of space, but through the secret part of our own souls to the presence of God, it is the very life and being. Can omniscience contemplate the happiness of the mind, without regard to its nature? Were we disposed to improve the condition of the savage, what course should we pursue? Should we not endeavour to change his habits of mind and body, by teaching him the arts of civilization; instructing him in the sciences; and gradually introducing him to that portion of social order which is here attained? And are not all these most intimately connected with our own condition of mind? Are they not merely the expression of its countenance? In the same way is it the endeavour of the Divine Mind in the Bible, to restore all to his own image and likeness—and [40] to say that the Bible has nothing to do with metaphysics, is to say that the present condition of the mind has nothing to do with what it should be, and that present metaphysics have nothing to do with religion. It is said that the Bible has nothing to do with the sciences. It is true that it does not teach them directly, but it is gradually unfolding a condition of mind, out of which the sciences will spring as naturally, as the leaves and blossoms from the tree that bears them. It is the same power which acts simultaneously to develop the soul [it]self, and to develop nature—to form the mind and the mould which is destined to receive it. As we behold the external face of the world, our souls will hold communion with its spirit; and we shall seem to extend our consciousness beyond the narrow limits of our own bodies, to the living objects that surround us. The mind will enter into nature by the secret path of him who forms her; and can be no longer ignorant of her laws, when it is a witness of her creation.

I have endeavoured to illustrate generally, in what way the natural sciences, the actual condition of society, and the Word of God are necessary to the development of all minds, in a manner analogous to that in which the earth, the atmosphere and the sun combine to bring forth the productions of nature. I shall say but a few words with respect to that particular development, which is requisite to the full manifestation of the peculiar powers possessed by any individual.

It is well known that at a certain period of life, the character of a man begins to be more distinctly marked. He appears to become separated from that which surrounds him—to stand in a measure aloof from his associates—to raise his head above the shadow of any earthly object into the light of heaven, and to walk with a more determined step on the earth beneath. This is the manifestation of a character which has always existed, and which has, as it were been accumulating by little and little, till at length it has attained its full stature.

When a man has become his own master, it is left to himself to complete his own education. "He has one Father, God." For the formation of his character thus far, he is not in the strictest sense accountable; that is, his character is not as yet so fixed, but that it is yielding and pliable. It [41] is left to himself to decide, how far it shall remain in its present form. This is indeed a period of deep responsibility. He has taken the guidance of a human being, and is not the less accountable, that this being is himself. The ligament is now cut asunder by which his mind was bound to its earthly guardian, and he is placed on his own feet, exposed to the bleak winds and refreshing breezes, the clouds and the sunshine of this world, fully accountable to God and man for his conduct. Let him not be made dizzy from a sense of his own liberty, nor faint under his own weight; but let him remember that the eye of God is now fixed full, it might almost be said anxiously upon him.

It is with the human mind, as with the human body. All our race have those limbs and features, and that general aspect, from which they are denominated men. But on a nearer view we find them divided into nations possessed of peculiar appearance and habits, and these subdivided into families and individuals, in all of which there is something peculiarly their own. The human mind (speaking in the most general sense) requires to be instructed in the same sciences and needs the same general development, and is destined to make one common and universal effort for its own emancipation. But the several nations of the earth also, will at a future period, stand forth with a distinctness of character which cannot now be conceived of. The part which each is to perform in the regeneration of the world, will become more and more distinctly marked and universally acknowledged; and every nation will be found to possess resources in its own moral and intellectual character, and its own natural productions, which will render it essential to the well-being and happiness of the whole. Every government must find that the real good of its own people precisely harmonizes with that of others; and standing armies must be converted into willing labourers for the promotion of the same object. Then will the nations of the earth resemble the well organized parts of the same body, and no longer convert that light which is given them for the benefit of their brethren, into an instrument by which they are degraded and enslaved.

But we stop not here. Every individual also possesses peculiar powers, which should be brought to bear on society in the duties best fitted to receive them. The highest de-[42] gree of cultivation of which the mind of any one is capable, consists in the most perfect development of that peculiar organization, which as really exists in infancy, as in maturer years. The seed which is planted, is said to possess in miniature the trunk, branches, leaves and fruit of the future tree. So it is with the mind; and the most that can possibly be done, is to afford facilities by which its development may be effected with the same order. In the process of the formation of our minds, there exists the spirit of prophecy; and no advancement can create surprise, because we have always been conscious of that from which it is produced. We must not seek to make one hair white or black. It is in vain for us to attempt to add one cubit to our stature. All adventitious or assumed importance should be cast off, as a filthy garment. We should seek an employment for the mind, in which all its energies may be warmed into existence; which, (if I may be allowed the expression) may bring every muscle into action. There is something which every one can do better than any one else; and it is the tendency and must be the end of human events, to assign to each his true calling. Kings will be hurled from their thrones and peasants exalted to the highest stations, by this irresistible tendency of mind to its true level. These effects may not be fully disclosed in the short period of this life, but even the most incredulous must be ultimately convinced that the truth is no respecter of persons, by learning the simple fact that a man cannot be other than what he is. Not that endless progression in moral goodness and in wisdom are not within the reach of any one; but that the state will never arrive, when he may not look back to the first rudiments—the original stamina of his own mind; and be almost able to say, I possessed all at the time of my birth. The more a person lives in singleness of heart, in simplicity and sincerity, the more will this be apparent.

It becomes us then to seek and to cherish this *peculium* of our own minds, as the patrimony which is left us by our Father in heaven—as that by which the branch is united to the vine—as the forming power within us, which gives to our persons that by which they are distinguished from others—and by a life entirely governed by the commandments of God, to leave on the duties we are called to perform, the full impress of our real characters. Let a man's ambition to be great, [43] disappear in a willingness to be what he is; then may he fill a high place without pride, or a low one without dejection. As our desires become more and more concentrated to those objects which correspond to the peculiar organization of our minds, we shall have a foretaste of that which is coming, in those internal tendencies of which we are conscious. As we perform with alacrity whatever duty presents itself before us, we shall perceive in our own hearts, a kind of preparation for every external event or occurrence of our lives, even the most trivial, springing from the all-pervading tendency of the Providence of God to present the opportunity of being useful wherever there is the disposition.

Living in a country whose peculiar characteristick is said to be a love of equal liberty, let it be written on our hearts, that the end of all education is a life of active usefulness. We want no education which shall raise a man out of the reach of the understanding or the sympathies of any of his species. We are disgusted with that kind of dignity which the possessor is himself obliged to guard; but venerate that which, having its origin in the actual character of the man, can receive no increase from the countenance of power, and suffer no diminution from the approach of weakness—that dignity in which the individual appears to live rather in the consciousness of the light which shines from above, than in that of his own shadow beneath. There is a spiritual atmosphere about such an one, which is at once its own protection, and the protection of him with whom it is connected—which while it is free as air alike to the most powerful and the most humble, conveys a tacit warning that too near an approach is not permitted. We acknowledge the invisible chain which binds together all classes of society, and would apply to it the electric spark of knowledge with the hand of tenderness and caution. We acknowledge the healthy union of mental and bodily exercise, and would rather see all men industrious and enlightened, than to see one half of mankind slaves to the other, and these slaves to their passions. We acknowledge that the natural world is one vast mine of wisdom, and for this reason it is the scene of the labours of man; and that in seeing this wisdom, there is philosophy, and in loving it, there is religion. Most sensibly do we feel that, as the true end of instruction is to prepare a man for [44] some particular sphere of usefulness; that when he has found this sphere, his education has then truly commenced, and the finger of God is pointing to the very page of the book of his oracles, from which he may draw the profoundest wisdom. It was the design of Providence that there should be enough of science connected with the calling of each, for the highest and holiest purposes of heaven. It is the natural world from which the philosopher draws his knowledge; it is the natural world in which the slave toils for his bread. Alas! when will they be one? When we are willing to practise what we learn, and religion makes our duty our delight. The mass of mankind must always labour; hence it is supposed that they must be always ignorant. Thus has the pride of man converted that discipline into an occasion of darkness and misery, which was intended only to give reality to knowledge, and to make happiness eternal. Truth is the way in which we should act; and then only is a man truly wise, when the body performs what the mind perceives. In this way, flesh and blood are made to partake of the wisdom of the spiritual man; and the palms of our hands will become the book of our life, on which is inscribed all the love and all the wisdom we possess. It is the light which directs a man to his duty; it is by doing his duty that he is enlightened—thus does he become identified with his own acts of usefulness, and his own vocation is the silken chord which directs to his heart, the knowledge and the blessings of all mankind.

III

THE FREE AGENCY OF MAN*

By Sampson Reed

The end of the divine providence is a heaven out of the human race; and, in all its operations, it protects the freedom of man in a manner which could be only the effect of the divine love for this end. Nothing can be appropriated by man but in a state of liberty. Consequently, it is only in this state that man can be reformed, regenerated, and be receptive of heavenly love and happiness. Therefore, the divine love of the liberty and of the salvation of man are essentially the same. A person is truly free, in proportion as he suffers himself to be led by the Lord. The celestial angels are free in the highest sense, because they are receptive of the love of the Lord in a purer state than others. This love is perfect freedom; being essential good, and in the constant effort to do that which is good. The divine freedom being infinite, utterly precludes the possibility of acting otherwise than in conformity to the laws of Infinite Wisdom.

The operation of the divine love is immediately upon the involuntary principle of man —called involuntary, because it is entirely above his own controul. Of the existence of this principle, we have a kind of consciousness. We cannot, however, make it an object of thought, any more than we can see the spirit with the natural eye; for a higher principle of the mind may conceive of a lower, but not *vice versa*. This would be to invert the order of creation. The mediate effect of the operation of the divine influx is the voluntary principle. This, in true order, is an exact correspondence of the involuntary—that principle in which the individual, (acknowledging that the love, as it descends, is divine, and this love being such as to desire to be that of another,) acts as of himself, yet from the Lord. This is the mar- [50] riage of the Lord with the church. But the voluntary principle in man is, in consequence of the fall, entirely perverted. It is therefore provided by the Lord, in order to the preservation of human liberty, that the influx should be directly from the involuntary into the intellectual. Had not this been so ordered, it would have been impossible to do other than evil. But the intellectual, being capable of an elevation above the voluntary, may see the true light; and, by conformity to it, a new voluntary principle will be formed in the intellectual. There is then a new and a higher kind of liberty. The will was before determined by the free exercise of the understanding; the understanding now resumes its proper place, and becomes the servant of the will.

The distinction between the involuntary and the voluntary principle, is apparent in the different organs of the body. Those organs whose operation is not subject to our own controul, correspond to the involuntary principle. Such are the heart, and most of the viscera. In the lungs, corresponding to the intellectual, the involuntary and the voluntary meet. Our breathing is sometimes the effect of our own volitions, and sometimes not; and, as an individual is introduced into a society of heaven, though his respiration may be voluntary, he cannot but respire with that society, in the same way as he acts as of himself from the Lord.

The relation between the involuntary and voluntary is such that man cannot, by any immediate act of his own mind, destroy his natural life; for lower principles cannot ascend into higher; though natural disease and death can hardly fail to be ultimately produced, by a continued resistance to the divine order. If the lungs were altogether a voluntary organ, death might be produced at the pleasure of the individual; but involuntary respiration will press in, and thwart his efforts. His power to destroy his own life is not from within outward, but from without inward; and in thus counteracting the divine order and influx consists spiritual death also. Not that it is in the power of an individual in the other world to destroy his own existence; for life is constantly flowing in from the Lord above his reach. But the lower principles, which are under his controul, may be destroyed, and rendered utterly unreceptive of his heavenly life.

---

* "Thoughts on the Divine Providence, Considered in Relation to the Free Agency of Man," *N J M*, I (1827-1828), pp. 49-52.

It is supposed, that the voluntary principle of man exists only when it is called forth in what is usually termed an act of volition. That the voluntary powers of man are in constant operation, whether he be quiet or active, is obvious from the state of the voluntary muscles. For, immediately on sleep, when these powers are suspended, the head falls, and all these muscles become relaxed. Hence we see why, in the Word, the Jews are called a stiff-necked people. For the muscles about the neck are particularly [51] under the province of the voluntary principle; and this expression becomes the true ultimate by which self-will is expressed in the letter of the Word.

The very wonderful manner in which human liberty is protected by the divine providence, is very apparent in our progression from infancy to old age. Previous to birth, the involuntary principle only is operative; but, at this time, the lungs respire, and the voluntary principle begins to manifest itself, though in an exceedingly faint, and almost imperceptible degree. The principles are developed in the same order in which they are designed to exist after their development; from inmost to ultimates: and are developed in such a gradual and tender manner, that, if society was such as to fully cooperate with the divine endeavour from within, every obstacle to the descent of the true order of heaven, which occurs from infancy to manhood, would be freely met and overcome. Brutes are born directly into an instinctive knowledge of whatever their condition requires; but the Lord thus gently unfolds the power of man, in order that there may be nothing of coercion; but that the individual himself may fully cooperate in their development, and thus become a voluntary medium of divine influx. It was said, that, in infancy, the voluntary principle had hardly begun to operate. The infant is nearly passive, and his motions are mostly involuntary. He does not will or think, according to the usual understanding of volition and thought; but possesses that kind of consciousness which we should have, if we ascended, within ourselves, above those principles which appear to be at all the work of our own hands. Thus to ascend into the elements and beginning of our own creation, where the Lord *stretcheth forth the heavens;* and thence, by our cooperation, to permit the lower principles of the mind to be formed after the same pattern, is *to be born again, to become as little children,* to ascend to where the good and the true are perpetually born within us from the Lord, to return, as it were, to our own infancy, save that the innocence of infancy, as it now descends, becomes clothed with the wisdom and strength of manhood. The infant is associated with the celestial angels, of whom our Lord said, that they *do always behold the face of my Father, who is in the heavens;* and the term of infancy is of considerable duration, in order that the highest principles of the mind may acquire strength to overcome the resistance to divine order, which hereditary evil will perpetually offer beneath; or if, in later periods, he be borne away by his own will, he may yet not be entirely insensible to the presence of the Lord within him, by which his evils may still possibly be curbed and subdued; so that *the wolf also shall dwell with the lamb; and the leopard shall lie down with the kid; and the calf, and the young lion, and the fatling,* [52] *together; and a little child shall lead them.* Each succeeding period of life presents an image of what is seen in infancy. It is the perpetual endeavour of the Lord, as the interior principles are formed, thence to descend into those which are beneath, that all may be made in his image and likeness; and this is effected so far as it can be done consistently with the freedom of the individual. But the state of the world is now such, that, as hereditary evils begin to operate,—though the Lord is not the less present in his endeavours to check them,—if his presence continued to be perceived, it would act as a restraint. This, therefore, is not permitted; for the freedom of every one is preserved, as the only possible ground of his salvation. It is the same infinite love which evades the eye of the atheist, and warms the hearts of the celestial angels.

As the lower principles of the mind can be formed in true correspondence to those within, only in a state of the perfect freedom of the individual; so, after he has been borne away by his evils, the lower principles must be reformed freely, as of himself, in order that the internals may be restored by the Lord.

The sense in which the liberty of man peculiarly resides, is the taste; inasmuch as it is here that he decides whether that which is offered shall, or shall not be appropriated, and make a part of him; for, after it has entered the stomach, he has no further power. Hence Swedenborg says, "inasmuch as the taste corresponds to perception, and to the affection of knowing, of understanding, and of growing wise, and the life of man is in that affection, therefore it is not permitted to any spirit, or to any angel, to flow into man's taste; for this would be to flow into the life which is proper to him."

IV

ON ANIMALS*

By SAMPSON REED

There is perhaps no subject generally less understood, than that of creation. This may be owing to the fact that external creation corresponds to that which is internal, or to regeneration; and that the one cannot be understood without the other. All things material are produced from things spiritual; and when this is seen and acknowledged, the mind is borne outward into the external universe, by the very power which constantly creates this universe.

Man differs essentially from animals, in that he has a spiritual mind, a distinct spiritual formation within the natural, adapted to spiritual uses, as the latter is to uses in this world; and in that he is capable of changing the quality of his affections, from good to bad, or by the power which is constantly given him from the Lord, from bad to good. This change is effected by means of the elevation of his understanding above his will, in consequence of which he is able, from religious motives, to lead a life in opposition to his own propensities. Animals are incapable of separating the affection from the thought. They are adapted to certain fixed ends, and to nothing else; and though their tendencies may be in some degree affected by the circumstances in which they are placed by man; (as vegetables are affected by the cultivation they receive, or by the influences of heat and light to which they are exposed,) it is not in their own power independently, to change or control them. It is otherwise with man. By his power of elevating his understanding above his affections, he is capable of looking down and condemning his own dispositions, and by following the truth even in opposition to his own will, of conjunction with the Lord. All the thoughts of animals necessarily flow outwards into the things of this world, and hence at death, when this [24] is no longer possible, they are altogether dissipated. But man is capable of looking within himself; of receiving from the Lord the idea of the Lord, and by a life according to the commandments, of loving God, which love is necessarily as eternal as He is from whom it proceeds, and to whom it is directed.

It was said that all creation is from within outwards; from spiritual to natural. The body is produced from the soul. Man having in his own freewill alienated himself from God, evil dispositions are hereditarily transmitted from one generation to another. The divine influx of love and wisdom is forever the same; but it is changed according to the state of the recipients. The existing evils in the human race are thus satisfactorily accounted for, by the nature of free agency. But animals also are forms of certain existing affections, from which they are created; nor have they now, or ever had they power to change those affections. How then can we account for those evil beasts and reptiles, which are forms of affections which have no prototype in the Creator? It is impossible for the Lord to communicate an affection which does not exist in himself; and it is impossible that these animals should have changed their character like man, from good to evil. The spiritual sense of the Sacred Scriptures affords the only possible explanation. From this we learn that bad animals correspond to, and are produced by the affections of evil spirits and men; thus that they are created by the divine influx as it is perverted by the hells—and that good animals correspond to and are produced by the affections of good spirits and men; thus that they are created by the Lord through the heavens. The fact that some animals are symbolical, is we believe universally admitted. The lamb is another name for innocence; the fox for cunning. The manner in which animals are spoken of in the Word, can leave no doubt on the mind of any, that they are in some general way, representative of the different affections and characters of men. But though it were folly in any to deny the general fact, few are prepared to admit those particular correspondences, without which, this general fact could not exist. Mankind regard the Word, much as they regard nature. They suppose that God exercised some general supervision over both; but it belongs to the New Church to recognise his presence, as well in the smallest portion of matter, as in every jot and tittle of the Sacred Scriptures—to perceive that the general outlines of his image, are the effect of the innumerable rays of his glory.

---

* "On Animals," *N J M*, II (1828-1829), 23-29.

We believe that we state the fact, when we say that with a large proportion of scientific men, there exists a doubt in regard to the immortality of man, which arises from their view of him in his relation to the brute creation. Mere sensual reason can discover no arguments in favour of the immortality of the one, which go [25] not also to prove that of the other. Nor is it possible that it should; for it has no faith in Him who "is the way, the truth and the life." Some may assent to the fact, by saying that it is so revealed; but few have learned to admit at the same time that the perfection of right reason consists in its coincidence with that which is revealed; and though to silence our doubts by a forced submission to revelation may sometimes be well, to remove the moral ground of those doubts by obedience to revelation, is always better. It is said that there is a gradual chain—that between the lowest grade in the human species, and the highest in the brute creation, the difference is exceedingly small, and that animals and vegetables imperceptibly run into each other. Such reasoners would do well to bear in mind that the difference between men and brutes, is a difference not in the degree of affection and intelligence manifested, but in their kind; and that no possible increase of brute feeling and intelligence can bring them a whit nearer to a resemblance of man. It is as though we should trace a stream from where it is muddy and impure to where it is clear and transparent—still it is water, and can with no more propriety be called *light* in one place than in the other. Or it may be compared to two parallel lines, both ascending, which can never meet. Mere sensual reasoners, though they may do something towards making men brutes, can do nothing towards making brutes men; and if the distance appears to be diminished, it must be by the moral effect of their arguments on themselves, and not by any power they possess of producing conviction in others.

To this degraded state of natural science, and to these pernicious consequences which necessarily result from the separation of spiritual and natural things; the study of anatomy as it is usually pursued, appears to be particularly favourable. This as it is itself the noblest of the sciences; so in the general perversion of all things, it has become the most debased. Such is the state of things that it is generally expected that from this study, the faith of the student will at least be shaken, if not undermined. All of man that is cognizable by the natural senses, is in the process of dissection laid fairly before them; and those, whose minds are open to no other evidence, have an opportunity to see the extent and nature of their faith. The futility of merely natural, experimental science is fairly tested. The jewel is broken to pieces, in order to learn of what it is composed. The process of examination is the process of destruction. It is gravely stated, that during the agonies of a cruel dissection, an animal unmindful of herself was constantly licking her young; and thus is proved the existence and the strength of this love. Alas! there is another way of being convinced of the same fact, that of cultivating affections equal to those manifested by this poor brute. [26] There are two ways of studying the science of natural things; the one by co-operating with the Lord in their creation; the other with the hells in the effort to destroy them. The principle of vitality shuns the dissector's knife; the mere anatomist finds a house without an inhabitant, and remains as ignorant of that which is spiritual as he was when he begun; but he who seeks first the kingdom of God, may hereafter find all these things added unto him, and may even attain to a knowledge of the minutiæ of anatomy, from the light of distinct consciousness.

We would not be understood altogether to disparage the study of natural experimental science in the way in which it is usually pursued; for we think it probable that the existing state of evil in the world, may render this process in some measure necessary. But we wish to acknowledge ourselves, and to see others acknowledge that it is rendered necessary by our own evils. It will then no longer foster the natural pride and atheism of the human heart; but will be as it should be, a constant memento of human depravity. The author of new discoveries will no longer exult in the vast extent of his own intellect and acquirements; but will see distinctly, that there was something in his own evil heart, which till now withheld the rays of the sun of the spiritual world from this portion of natural science. Instead of thinking of what he has himself accomplished, he will be able to acknowledge that he is himself the only obstacle to further advancement. He will study the natural sciences as the clouds collect the rain with which they refresh and fertilize the earth; by receiving within himself the influences of the sun of the spiritual world, by which the thoughts and affections of the natural man are as it were caught up into heaven, that they may be made to return with renewed life, and make glad the kingdoms of this world.

Rightly to understand natural science, is to understand the true uses of natural things. But all things of this world have respect, either directly or indirectly, to the spiritual and immortal part of man; and are created for it and from it. How can those therefore understand natural science, whose minds rest on the ultimate effect, without any knowledge of this relation? Suppose a watch for the first time to be submitted to the inspection of a savage. He is pleased with the motion of the wheels—he gradually learns the connexion of the parts—he may even make some rude imitation. Yet is all this an idle curiosity, and he may cast it away as a useless toy, unless its true use be disclosed to him, in unfolding its relation to the sun. Yet such precisely is the extent of scientific knowledge among those in the world who are usually called learned; save that the savage could hardly fail to be deeply impressed with the feeling, that he was in the presence of superior intelligence. Natural objects are analyzed and classified, [27] and made, in a limited degree, to subserve the uses of the body. But here the chain is broken. The relation in which the body itself and all its appendages stand to the spiritual man, for which they are and were created, is not known or acknowledged. It is with peculiar satisfaction, in such a posture of affairs, that we sometimes meet with a work which appears to possess the *true spirit—the fountain and the stream—the living, active source* of natural philosophy.

The following extract is from a work which deservedly occupies the highest place in the estimation of scientific men. We may have occasion to notice it further hereafter:

"There are two tribes in the animal kingdom that seem placed in contrast with each other, both by their habits and by their structure. One of these is carniverous, living by rapine and bloodshed, and cannot be rendered subservient to our domestic purposes; while the other is herbiverous or graniverous, is quiet in its habits, and easily domesticated. Amongst insects we find the representatives of both: those of the first tribe are distinguished by their predaceous habits, by the open attacks, or by the various snares and artifices which they employ to entrap and destroy other insects. They may usually be known by their powerful jaws, or instruments of suction; by their prominent or ferocious eyes; by the swiftness of their motions, either on the earth, in the air, or in the water; by their fraud and artifice in lying wait for their prey.

"These analogies ascending from the insect, terminate in races of a corresponding character and aspect amongst the *mammalia*, and thus lead us towards *man* himself, or rather to men in whose minds those bad and malignant qualities prevail, which when accompanied by power, harass and lay waste mankind; and thus ascending from symbol to symbol, we arrive at an animal who in his own person unites both matter and spirit, and is thus the member both of a visible and invisible world: and we are further instructed by these symbols, perpetually recurring under different forms; in the existence of evil and malignant spirits, whose object and delight is the corporeal and spiritual ruin of the noble creature who is placed at the head of the visible works of God.

"The other tribe of animals that I mentioned of a milder character, may be looked upon as represented by many herbiverous, or not carniverous, insects: amongst others, the Lamellicorn beetles imitate them by their remarkable horns, so that they wear the aspect of miniature bulls, or deer, or antelopes, or rams, or goats,—whether these horns are processes of the head or of the upper jaws.

"From insects, the ascent upwards, with regard to *form*, is by some of the branchiostegous fishes which symbolize the horns of [28] cattle; with regard to *character*, by the various species of *Cyprinus* and other similar genera. Amongst the birds, the *Gallinæ* and *Anseres*—from which orders we derive our domestic poultry, whether terrestrial or aquatic—and our game, form the step next below the ruminants, or cattle: and we are thus again led towards man, and symbolically instructed in those domestic and social qualities which endear us to each other, best promote the general welfare, and render us most like good spirits and the Divinity himself; of whom the perpetual recurrence of animals exhibiting these amiable and useful qualities, is calculated to impress upon us some notion." Introduction to Entomology, by Kirby and Spence, vol. iv.

In the general abuse and perversion of all things, the true uses of animals cannot be supposed to be understood except to an exceedingly limited and imperfect degree. These uses cannot be justly appreciated without right affections; for animals are the forms of affections. In the heavens the affections of the angels are manifested externally by the presence of innocent and useful animals. With what feelings would these be regarded by those, with whom the wanton destruction of similar animals in this world, has been called emphatically *sport*?

The proportion of animals, the use of which is known, is probably exceedingly small in comparison with those whose use is not acknowledged. It might appear very strange to most people, should they be told that, independently of any obvious external advantages derived from animals, man could not exist without them. Yet such is probably the fact. The Lord still suffers the devils to enter into the swine, and unclean beasts, and reptiles. The burning fires of hell are permitted to take *a form*, to pass in a measure *out of* the hearts of evil spirits. And this is a permission of Infinite Love and Wisdom, by which the condition of the hells is rendered more tolerable than it otherwise would be; and by which men in this world are in some measure relieved from their influences. In like manner, the affections of the angels necessarily pass forth *out of* themselves; for this is their essential tendency. They then appear alive, as really they are, for love is life, and become manifest in forms to which they truly correspond. In the spiritual world, the animals that appear, possessing no real existence independent of those affections from which they are constantly produced, disappear on the change of these affections. They are not thought of in the way that they are in this world, but instead of them, those things to which they correspond. But in the natural world, they assume a fixedness which it is not possible should belong to them in the spiritual. In the spiritual world they are simply the *forms, the bodies* of affections; but in the natural world, it is possible that there should [29] exist bodies even exterior to, and dependent on these. This also is a provision of the Divine Love and Wisdom; since the things without us not being necessarily dependent on our internal state, a means of reformation is afforded, which could not otherwise exist. But when all disposition to reformation is eradicated, this order of things would be a source of pain, without a possibility of its being useful.

The manner in which the smallpox, one of the most loathsome and dangerous diseases, becomes modified in animals, by which man himself gains protection from danger, is probably a true illustration of their use to us in regard to those diseases which are spiritual.

V

PRELIMINARY ESSAY*

By JAMES MARSH

Whether the present state of religious feeling, and the prevailing topics of theological enquiry among us, are particularly favourable to the success of the work herewith offered to the public, can be determined only by the result. The question, however, has not been left unconsidered; and however that may be, it is not a work, whose value depends essentially upon its relation to the passing controversies of the day. Unless I distrust my own feelings and convictions altogether, I must suppose, that for some, I hope for many, minds, it will have a deep and enduring interest. Of those classes, for whose use it is more especially designated in the author's preface, I trust there are many also in this country, who will justly appreciate the objects at which it aims, and avail themselves of its instruction and assistance. I could wish it might be received, by all who concern themselves in religious inquiries and instruction especially, in the spirit, which seems to me to have animated its great and admirable author; and I hesitate not to say, that to all of every class, who shall so receive it, and peruse it with the attention and thoughtfulness, which it demands and deserves, it will be found by experience to furnish what its title imports, "AIDS TO REFLECTION" on subjects, upon which every man is bound to reflect deeply and in earnest.

What the specific objects of the work are, and for whom it is written, may be learned in few words from the preface of the author. From this too, it will be seen to be

---

* Pages vii—liii from S. T. Coleridge, *Aids to Reflection*, (1st American edition), Burlington, Vt., 1829. James Marsh, the editor, in his "Advertisement" committed the whole "to the candour of the Christian public with the hope and prayer, that it may promote among us the interests, which cannot be long separated from each other, of sound philosophy and of true religion." (Marsh's errata have been corrected. See his list on page 399 of the *Aids*).

professedly didactic. It is designed to aid those, who wish for instruction, or assistance in the instruction of others. The plan and com- [viii] position of the work will to most readers probably appear somewhat anomalous; but reflection upon the nature of the objects aimed at, and some little experience of its results, may convince them, that the method adopted is not without its advantages. It is important to observe, that it is designed, as its general characteristic, to aid REFLECTION, and for the most part upon subjects, which can be learned and understood only by the exercise of *reflection* in the strict and proper sense of that term. It was not so much to teach a speculative system of doctrines built upon established premises, for which a different method would have been obviously preferable, as to turn the mind continually back upon the premises themselves—upon the inherent grounds of truth and error in its own being. The only way, in which it is possible for any one to learn the science of words, which is one of the objects to be sought in the present work, and the true import of those words especially, which most concern us as rational and accountable beings, is by reflecting upon, and bringing forth into distinct consciousness, those mental acts, which the words are intended to designate. We must discover and distinctly apprehend different meanings, before we can appropriate to each a several word, or understand the words so appropriated by others. Now it is not too much to say, that most men, and even a large proportion of educated men, do not reflect sufficiently upon their own inward being, upon the constituent laws of their own understanding, upon the mysterious powers and agencies of reason, and conscience, and will, to apprehend with much distinctness the objects to be named, or of course to refer the names with correctness to their several objects. Hence the necessity of associating the study of words with the study of morals and religion; and that is the most effectual method of instruction, which enables the teacher most successfully to fix the attention upon a definite meaning, that is, in these studies, upon a particular act, or process, or law of the mind—to call it into distinct consciousness, and assign to it its proper name, so that the name shall thenceforth have for the learner a distinct, definite, and intelligible sense. To impress upon the reader [ix] the importance of this, and to exemplify it in the particular subjects taken up in the work, is a leading aim of the author throughout; and it is obviously the only possible way by which we can arrive at any satisfactory and conclusive results on subjects of philosophy, morals, and religion. The first principles, the ultimate grounds of these, so far as they are possible objects of knowledge for us, must be sought and found in the laws of our being, or they are not found at all. The knowledge of these terminates in the knowledge of ourselves, of our rational and personal being, of our proper and distinctive humanity, and of that Divine Being, in whose image we are created. "We must retire inward," says St. Bernard, "if we would ascend upward." It is by self-inspection, by reflecting upon the mysterious grounds of our own being, alone, that we can arrive at any rational knowledge of the central and absolute ground of all being. It is by this only, that we can discover that principle of unity and consistency, which reason instinctively seeks after, which shall reduce to a harmonious system all our views of truth and of being, and destitute of which all the knowledge, that comes to us from without, is fragmentary, and in its relation to our highest interests as rational beings, but the patch-work of vanity.

Now, of necessity, the only method, by which another can aid our efforts in the work of reflection, is by first reflecting himself, and so pointing out the process and marking the result by *words*, that we can repeat it, and try the conclusions by our own consciousness. If he have reflected aright, if he have excluded all causes of self-deception, and directed his thoughts by those principles of truth and reason, and by those laws of the understanding, which belong in common to all men, his conclusions must be true for all. We have only to repeat the process, impartially to reflect ourselves, unbiassed by received opinions, and undeceived by the idols of our own understandings, and we shall find the same truths in the depths of our own self-consciousness. I am persuaded that such for the most part, will be found to be the case with regard to the principles developed in the present work, and that those, who, [x] with serious reflection and an unbiassed love of truth, will refer them to the laws of thought in their own minds, to the requirements of their own reason, will find there a witness to their truth.

Viewing the work in this manner, therefore, as an instructive and safe guide to the knowledge of what it concerns all men to know, I cannot but consider it in itself, as a work of great and permanent value to any christian community. Whatever indeed tends to awaken and cherish the power, and to form the habit, of reflection upon the great constituent principles of our own permanent being and proper humanity, and upon the abiding laws of truth and duty, as revealed in our reason and conscience, cannot but promote our highest interests as moral and rational beings. Even if the particular conclusions, to which the author has arrived, should prove erroneous, the evil is comparatively of little importance, if he have at the same time communicated to our minds such powers of thought, as will enable us to detect his errors, and attain by our own efforts to a more perfect knowledge of the truth. That some of his views may not be erroneous, or that they are to be received on his authority, the author, I presume, would be the last to affirm; and although in the nature of the case it was impossible for him to aid reflection without anticipating and in some measure influencing the results, yet the primary tendency and design of the work is, not to establish this or that system, but to cultivate in every mind the power and the will to seek earnestly and steadfastly for the truth in the only direction, in which it can ever be found. The work is no farther controversial, than every work must be, "that is writ with freedom and reason" upon subjects of the same kind; and if it be found at variance with existing opinions and modes of philosophizing, it is not necessarily to be considered the fault of the writer.

In republishing the work in this country, I could wish that it might be received by all, for whose instruction it was designed, simply as a didactic work, on its own merits, and without controversy. I must not, however, be supposed ignorant [xi] of its bearing upon those questions, which have so often been, and still are, the prevailing topics of theological controversy among us. It was indeed incumbent on me, before inviting the attention of the religious community to the work, to consider its relation to existing opinions, and its probable influence on the progress of truth. This I have done with as severe thought as I am capable of bestowing upon any subject, and I trust too with no want of deference and conscientious regard to the feelings and opinions of others. I have not attempted to disguise from myself, nor do I wish to disguise from the readers of the work, the inconsistency of some of its leading principles with much that is taught and received in our theological circles. Should it gain much of the public attention in any way, it will become, as it ought to do, an object of special and deep interest to all, who would contend for the truth, and labour to establish it upon a permanent basis. I venture to assure such, even those of them who are most capable of comprehending the philosophical grounds of truth in our speculative systems of theology, that in its relation to this whole subject they will find it to be a work of great depth and power, and whether right or wrong, eminently deserving of their attention. It is not to be supposed, that all who read, or even all who comprehend it, will be convinced of the soundness of its views, or be prepared to abandon those, which they have long considered essential to the truth. To those, whose understandings by long habit have become limited in their powers of apprehension, and as it were identified with certain *schemes* of doctrine, certain *modes* of contemplating all that pertains to religious truth, it may appear novel, strange, and unintelligible, or even dangerous in its tendency, and be to them an occasion of offence. But I have no fear, that any earnest and single-hearted lover of the truth as it is in Jesus, who will free his mind from the idols of preconceived opinion, and give himself time and opportunity to understand the work by such reflection as the nature of the subject renders unavoidable, will find in it any cause of offence, or any source of alarm. If the work become the occasion of controversy at all, [xii] I should expect it from those, who, instead of *reflecting* deeply upon the first principles of truth in their own reason and conscience and in the word of God, are more accustomed to *speculate*—that is, from premises given or assumed, but considered unquestionable, as the constituted point of observation, to look abroad upon the whole field of their intellectual visions, and *thence* to decide upon the true form and dimensions of all which meets their view. To such I would say with deference, that the merits of this work cannot be determined by the merely relative aspect of its doctrines, as seen from the high ground of any prevailing metaphysical or theological system. Those on the contrary who will seek to comprehend it by reflection, to learn the true meaning of the whole and of all its parts, by retiring into their own minds and finding there the true point of observation for each, will not be in haste to question the truth or the tendency of its principles. I make these remarks, because I am anxious, as far as may be, to anticipate the causeless fears of all, who earnestly pray and labour for the promotion of the truth, and to preclude that unprofitable controversy, that might arise from hasty or prejudiced views of a work like this. At the same time I should be far from deprecating any discussion, which might tend to unfold more fully the principles, which it teaches, or to exhibit more distinctly its true bearing upon the interests of theological science and of spiritual religion. It is to promote this object, indeed, that I am induced in the remarks which follow to offer some of my own thoughts on these subjects, imperfect I am well aware, and such as, for that reason, as well as others, worldly prudence might require me to suppress. If, however, I may induce reflecting men, and those who are engaged in theological enquiries especially, to indulge a suspicion, that all truth, which it is important for them to know, is not contained in the systems of doctrine usually taught, and that this work *may be* worthy of their serious and reflecting perusal, my chief object will be accomplished. I shall of course not need to anticipate in detail the contents of the work itself, but shall aim simply to point out what I consider its distinguishing and es- [xiii] sential character and tendency, and then direct the attention of my readers to some of those general feelings and views on the subject of religious truth, and of those particulars in the prevailing philosophy of the age, which seem to me to be exerting an injurious influence on the cause of theological science and of spiritual religion, and not only to furnish a fit occasion, but to create an imperious demand, for a work like that which is here offered to the public.

In regard then to the distinguishing character and tendency of the work itself, it has already been stated to be didactic, and designed to aid reflection on the principles and grounds of truth in our own being; but, in another point of view, and with reference to my present object, it might rather be denominated A PHILOSOPHICAL STATEMENT AND VINDICATION OF THE DISTINCTIVELY SPIRITUAL AND PECULIAR DOCTRINES OF THE CHRISTIAN SYSTEM. In order to understand more clearly the import of this statement and the relation of the author's views to those exhibited in other systems, the reader is requested to examine in the first place, what he considers the *peculiar doctrines of christianity*, and what he means by the terms *spirit* and *spiritual*. A synoptical view of what he considers peculiar to christianity as a revelation is given on pp. 127—128, and, if I mistake not, will be found essentially to coincide, though not perhaps in the language employed, with what among us are termed the evangelical doctrines of religion. Those who are anxious to examine farther into the orthodoxy of the work in connexion with this statement, may consult the articles on ORIGINAL SIN and REDEMPTION beginning at pp. 159 and 187, though I must forewarn them, that it will require much study in connexion with the other parts of the work, before one unaccustomed to the author's language and unacquainted with his views, can fully appreciate the merit of what may be peculiar in his mode of treating those subjects. With regard to the term *spiritual*, it may be sufficient to remark here, that he regards it as having a specific import, and maintains that in the sense of the N. T. *spiritual* and *natural* are contra-distinguished, so that what is spiritual is different [xiv] *in kind* from that which is natural, and is in fact *super*-natural. So, too, while morality is something more than prudence, religion, the spiritual life, is something more than morality. For his views at large, the reader may recur to note 29, and the references there made.

In vindicating the peculiar doctrines of the christian system so stated, and a faith in the reality of agencies and modes of being essentially spiritual or supernatural, he aims to show their consistency with reason and with the true principles of philosophy, and that indeed, so far from being irrational, CHRISTIAN FAITH IS THE PERFECTION OF HUMAN REASON. By reflection upon the subjective grounds of knowledge and faith in the human mind itself, and by an analysis of its faculties, he develops the distinguishing characteristics and necessary relations of the natural and the spiritual in our modes of being and knowing, and the all-important fact, that although the former does not *comprehend* the latter, yet neither does it preclude its existence. He proves, that "the scheme of Christianity, though not discoverable by reason, is yet in accordance with it —that link follows link by necessary consequence—that religion passes out of the ken of reason only where the eye of reason has reached its own horizon—and that faith is then but its continuation." Instead of adopting, like the popular metaphysicians of the day, a system of philosophy at war with religion, and which tends inevitably to under-mine our belief in the reality of any thing spiritual in the only proper sense of that word, and then coldly and ambiguously referring us for the support of our faith to the *authority* of revelation, he boldly asserts the reality of something distinctively spiritual in man, and the futility of all those modes of philosophizing, in which this is not recognized, or which are incompatible with it. He considers it the highest and most rational purpose of any system of philosophy, at least of one professing to be christian, to investigate those higher and peculiar attributes, which distinguish us from the brutes that perish—which are the image of God in us, and constitute our proper humanity. It is in his view the proper business and the duty of the Chris- [xv] tian philosopher to remove all appearance of *contradiction* between the several manifestations of the one DIVINE WORD, to reconcile reason with revelation, and thus to justify the ways of God to man. The methods by which he accomplishes this, either in regard to the terms in which he enunciates the great doctrines of the gospel, or the peculiar views of philosophy, by which he reconciles them with the subjective grounds of faith in the universal reason of man, need not be stated here. I will merely observe, that the key to his system will be found in the distinctions, which he makes and illustrates between *nature* and *free-will*, and between the *understanding* and *reason*. For the first of these distinctions the reader may consult note 29, and for the other, pp. 135—154, and note 59. It may meet the prejudices of some to remark farther, that in philosophizing on the grounds of our faith he does not profess or aim to solve all *mysteries*, and to bring all truth within the comprehension of the understanding. A truth may be mysterious, and the primary ground of all truth and reality must be so. But though we may believe what "passeth all *understanding*," we *cannot* believe what is *absurd*, or contradictory to *reason*.

Whether the work be well executed, according to the idea of it, as now given, or whether the author have accomplished his purpose, must be determined by those who are capable of judging, when they shall have examined and reflected upon the whole as it deserves. The inquiry which I have now to propose to my readers is, whether the idea itself be a rational one, and whether the purpose of the author be one, which a wise man and a christian ought to aim at, or which in the present state of our religious interests, and of our theological science specially needs to be accomplished.

No one, who has had occasion to observe the general feelings and views of our religious community for a few years past, can be ignorant, that a strong prejudice exists against the introduction of philosophy, in any form, in the discussion of theological subjects. The terms *philosophy* and *metaphysics*, even *reason* and *rational* seem, in the minds of those most de- [xvi] voted to the support of religious truth, to have forfeited their original, and to have acquired a new, import, especially in their relation to matters of faith. By a philosophical view of religious truth would generally be understood, a view, not only varying from the religion of the bible in the form and manner of presenting it, but at war with it; and a *rational* religion is supposed to be of course something diverse from revealed religion. A philosophical and rational system of religious truth would by most readers among us, if I mistake not, be supposed a system deriving its doctrines not from revelation, but from the speculative reason of men, or at least relying on that only for their credibility. That these terms have been used to designate such systems, and that the prejudice against reason and philosophy so employed, is not, therefore, without cause, I need not deny; nor would any friend of revealed truth be less disposed to give credence to such systems, than the author of the work before us.

But, on the other hand, a moment's reflection only can be necessary to convince any man, attentive to the use of language, that we do at the same time employ these terms in relation to truth generally in a better and much higher sense. *Rational*, as contradistinguished from *irrational* and *absurd*, certainly denotes a quality, which every man would be disposed to claim, not only for himself, but for his religious opinions. Now, the adjective *reasonable*, having acquired a different use and signification, the word *rational* is the adjective corresponding in sense to the substantive *reason*, and signifies what is conformed to reason. In one sense, then, all men would appeal to reason, in behalf of their religious faith: they would deny that it was *irrational* or *absurd*. If we do not in this sense adhere to reason, we forfeit our prerogative as rational beings, and our faith is no better than the bewildered dream of a man who has *lost his reason*. Nay, I maintain that when we use the term in this higher sense, it is impossible for us to believe on any authority what is directly *contradictory* to reason and *seen to be so*. No evidence from another source, and no authority could convince us, that a proposition [xvii] in Geometry, for example, is false, which our reason intuitively discovers to be true. Now supposing, (and we may at least suppose this,) that reason has the same power of intuitive insight in relation to certain moral and spiritual truths, as in relation to the truths of Geometry, then it will be equally impossible to divest us of our belief of those truths.

Furthermore, we are not only unable to believe the same proposition to be false, which our reason sees to be true, but we cannot believe *another proposition*, which by the exercise of the same *rational faculty* we see to be incompatible with the former, or to contradict it. We may, and probably often do, receive with a certain kind and degree of credence opinions, which reflection would show to be incompatible. But when we have reflected, and *discovered* the inconsistency, we cannot retain *both*. We *cannot* believe two contradictory propositions *knowing* them to be such. It would be *irrational* to do so.

Again, we cannot conceive it possible, that what by the same power of intuition we see to be universally and necessarily true should appear otherwise to any other rational being. We cannot, for example, but consider the propositions of Geometry, as necessarily true, for all rational beings. So, too, a little reflection, I think, will convince any one, that we attribute the same necessity of reason to the principles of moral rectitude. What in the clear day-light of our reason, and after mature reflection, we see to be right, we *cannot* believe to be wrong in the view of other rational beings in the distinct *exercise* of their Reason. Nay, in regard to those truths, which are clearly submitted to the view of our reason, and which we behold with distinct and steadfast intuitions, we necessarily attribute to the *Supreme Reason*, to the Divine Mind, views the same, or coincident, with those of our own reason. We cannot, (I say it with reverence and I trust with some apprehension of the importance of the assertion) we *cannot* believe that to be *right* in the view of the supreme reason which is clearly and decidedly wrong in the view of our own. It would be contradictory to reason, it would be ir- [xviii] rational to believe it, and therefore we cannot do so, till we lose our reason, or cease to exercise it.

I would ask now, whether this be not an authorized use of the words reason and rational, and whether so used they do not mean something. If it be so—and I appeal to the mind of every man capable of reflection, and of understanding the use of language, if it be not—then there is meaning in the terms *universal reason*, and *unity of reason*, as used in this work. There is, and can be, in this highest sense of the word, but one reason, and whatever contradicts that reason, being seen to do so, cannot be received as matter either of knowledge or faith. To reconcile religion with reason used in this sense, therefore, and to justify the ways of God to man, or in the view of reason, is so far from being irrational, that reason imperatively demands it of us. We cannot, as rational beings, believe a proposition on the grounds of reason, and deny it on the authority of revelation. We cannot believe a proposition in philosophy, and deny the same proposition in theology; nor can we believe two incompatible propositions on the different grounds of reason and revelation. So fast, and so far, as we compare our thoughts, the objects of our knowledge and faith, and by reflection refer them to their common measure in the universal laws of reason, so far the instinct of reason impels us to reject whatever is contradictory and absurd, and to bring unity and consistency into all our views of truth. Thus, in the language of the author of this work, (p. 6,) though "the word *rational* has been strangely abused of late times, this must not disincline us to the weighty consideration, that thoughtfulness, and a desire to rest all our convictions on grounds of right reason, are inseparable from the character of a Christian."

But I beg the reader to observe, that in relation to the doctrines of spiritual religion —to all that he considers the peculiar doctrines of the Christian revelation, the author assigns to reason only a *negative* validity. It does not teach us, what those doctrines are, or what they are not, except that they are not, and cannot be, such as contradict the clear convictions of right [xix] reason. But his views on this point are fully stated in the work, and may be found by the references in note 43. The general office of reason in relation to all, that is proposed for our belief, is given with philosophical precision in the Appendix, pp. 390—391.

If then it be our prerogative, as rational beings, and our duty as Christians, to think, as well as to act, *rationally* to see that our convictions of truth rest on grounds of right reason; and if it be one of the clearest dictates of reason, that we should endeavor to shun, and on discovery should reject, whatever is contradictory to the universal laws of thought, or to doctrines already established, I know not by what means we are to avoid the application of philosophy, at least to some extent, in the study of theology. For to determine what *are* the grounds of right reason, what are those ultimate truths, and those universal laws of thought, which we cannot rationally contradict, and by reflection to compare with these whatever is proposed for our belief, is in fact to philosophize; and whoever does this to a greater or less extent, is so far a philosopher in the best and highest sense of the word. To this extent we are bound to philosophize in Theology, as well as in every other science. For what is not rational in theology, is, of course, irrational, and cannot be of the household of faith; and to determine whether it be rational in the sense already explained or not, is the province of philosophy. It is in this sense, that the work before us is to be considered a philosophical work, viz. that it proves the doctrines of the Christian faith to be rational, and exhibits philosophical grounds for the *possibility* of a truly spiritual religion. The *reality* of those experiences, or states of being, which constitute experimental or spiritual religion, rests on other grounds. It is incumbent on the philosopher to free them from the contradictions of reason, and nothing more; and who will deny, that to do this is a purpose worthy of the ablest philosopher and the most devoted christian! Is it not desirable to convince all men, that the doctrines, which we affirm to be revealed in the gospel, are not contradictory to the requirements of reason [xx] and conscience. Is it not, on the other hand, vastly important to the cause of religious truth, and even to the practical influence of religion on our own minds, and the minds of community at large, that we should attain and exhibit views of philosophy and doctrines in metaphysics, which are at least compatible with, if they do not specially favour those views of religion, which, on other grounds, we find it our duty to believe and maintain. For, I beg it may be observed, as a point of great moment, that it is not the method of the genuine philosopher to separate his philosophy and religion, and adopting his principles independently in each, leave them to be reconciled or not, as the case may be. He has and can have rationally but one system, in which his philosophy becomes religious, and his religion philosophical. Nor am I disposed in compliance with popular opinion to limit the application of this remark, as is usually done, to the mere external evidences of revelation. The philosophy which we adopt will and must influence not only our decision of the question, whether a book be of divine authority, but our views also of its meaning.

But this is a subject, on which, if possible, I would avoid being misunderstood, and must, therefore, exhibit it more fully, even at the risk of repeating what was said before, or is elsewhere found in the work. It has been already, I believe, distinctly enough stated, that reason and philosophy *ought* to prevent our reception of doctrines claiming the authority of revelation only so far as the very necessities of our rational being require. However *mysterious* the thing affirmed may be, though "it passeth *all understanding*," if it cannot be shown to contract the unchangeable principles of right reason, its being incomprehensible to our understandings is not an obstacle to our faith. If it contradict reason, we *cannot* believe it, but must conclude, either that the writing is not of divine authority, or that the language has been misinterpreted. So far it seems to me, that our philosophy ought to modify our views of theological doctrines, and our mode of interpreting the language of an inspired writer. But then we must be cautious, [xxi] that we philosophize rightly, and "do not call *that* reason, which is not so." (See p. 205.) Otherwise we may be led by the *supposed* requirements of reason to interpret metaphorically, what ought to be received literally, and evacuate the Scriptures of their most important doctrines. But what I mean to say here is, that we cannot avoid the application of our philosophy in the interpretation of the language of Scripture, and in the explanation of the doctrines of religion *generally*. We cannot avoid incurring the danger just alluded to of philosophizing erroneously, even to the extent of rejecting as irrational that, which tends to the perfection of reason itself. And hence I maintain, that instead of pretending to exclude philosophy from our religious enquiries, it is vastly important, that we philosophize in earnest—that we endeavor by profound reflection to learn the *real* requirements of reason, and attain a true knowledge of ourselves.

If any dispute the necessity of thus combining the study of philosophy with that of religion, I would beg them to point out the age since that of the Apostles, in which the prevailing metaphysical opinions have not distinctly manifested themselves in the prevailing views of religion; and if, as I fully believe will be the case, they fail to discover a single system of theology, a single volume on the subject of the christian religion, in which the author's views are not modified by the metaphysical opinions of the age or of the individual, it would be desirable to ascertain, whether this influence be accidental or necessary. The metaphysician analyzes the faculties and operations of the human mind, and teaches us to arrange, to classify, and to name them, according to his views of their various distinctions. The language of the Scriptures, at least to a great extent, speaks of subjects, that can be understood only by a reference to those same powers and processes of thought and feeling, which we have learned to think of, and to name, according to our particular system of metaphysics. How is it possible then to avoid interpreting the one by the other? Let us suppose, for example, that a man has studied and adopted the philosophy of Brown, is it possible for him to interpret the 8th chap- [xxii] ter of Romans, without having his views of its meaning influenced by his philosophy? Would he not unavoidably interpret the language and explain the doctrines, which it contains, differently from one, who should have adopted such views of the human mind, as are taught in this work? I know it is customary to disclaim the influence of philosophy in the business of interpretation, and every writer now-a-days on such subjects will assure us, that he has nothing to do with metaphysics, but is guided only by common sense and the laws of interpretation. But I would like to know how a man comes by any common sense in relation to the movements and laws of his intellectual and moral being without metaphysics. What is the common sense of a Hottentot on subjects of this sort? I have no hesitation in saying, that from the very nature of the case, it is nearly, if not quite, impossible for any man entirely to separate his philosophical views of the human mind from his reflections on religious subjects. Probably no man has endeavored more faithfully to do this, perhaps no one has succeeded better in giving the truth of Scripture free from the glosses of metaphysics, than Professor Stuart. Yet, I should risk little in saying, that a reader deeply versed in the language of metaphysics, extensively acquainted with the philosophy of different ages, and the peculiar phraseology of different schools, might ascertain his metaphysical system from many a passage of his commentary on the Epistle to the Hebrews. What then, let me ask, is the possible use to the cause of truth and of religion, from thus perpetually decrying philosophy in theological enquiries, when we cannot avoid it if we would? Every man, who has reflected at all, has his metaphysics; and if he reads on religious subjects, he interprets and understands the language, which he employs, by the help of his metaphysics. He cannot do otherwise.—And the proper enquiry is, not whether we admit our philosophy into our theological and religious investigations, but whether our philosophy be right and true. For myself, I am fully convinced, that we can have no right views of theology, till we have right views of the human mind; and that these are to be acquired [xxiii] only by laborious and persevering reflection. My belief is, that the distinctions unfolded in this work will place us in the way to truth, and relieve us from numerous perplexities, in which we are involved by the philosophy, which we have so long taken for our guide. For we are greatly deceived, if we suppose for a moment, that the systems of theology, which have been received among us, or even the theoretical views, which are now most popular, are free from the entanglements of wor[l]dly wisdom. The readers of this work will be able to see, I think, more clearly the import of this remark, and the true bearing of the received views of philosophy on our theological enquiries. Those, who study the work without prejudice and adopt its principles to any considerable extent, will understand too how deeply an age may be ensnared in the metaphysical webs of its own weaving, or entangled in the net, which the speculations of a former generation have thrown over it, and yet suppose itself blessed with a perfect immunity from the dreaded evils of metaphysics.

But before I proceed to remark on those particulars, in which our prevailing philosophy seems to me dangerous in its tendency, and unfriendly to the cause of spiritual religion, I must beg leave to guard myself and the work from misapprehension on another point, of great importance in its relation to the whole subject. While it is maintained that reason and philosophy, in their true character, *ought* to have a certain degree and extent of influence in the formation of our religious system, and that our metaphysical opinions, whatever they may be, *will*, almost unavoidably, modify more or less our theoretical views of religious truth *generally*, it is yet a special object of the author of the work to show, that the spiritual life, or what among us is termed experimental religion, is, in itself, and in its own proper growth and developement, essentially distinct from the forms and processes of the understanding; and that, although a true faith cannot contradict any universal principle of speculative reason, it is yet in a certain sense independent of the discursions of philosophy, and in its proper nature beyond the reach "of positive *science* [xxiv] and theoretical *insight.*" "Christianity is not a *Theory*, or a *Speculation;* but a *Life.* Not a *Philosophy* of Life, but a Life and a living process." It is not, therefore, so properly a species of knowledge, as a form of being. And although the theoretical views of the understanding, and the motives of prudence which it presents, may be, to a certain extent, connected with the developement of the spiritual principle of religious life in the Christian, yet a true and living faith is not incompatible with at least some degree of speculative error. As the acquisition of merely speculative knowledge cannot of itself communicate the principle of spiritual life, so neither does that principle, and the living process of its growth, depend wholly, at least, upon the degree of speculative knowledge with which it co-exists. That religion, of which our blessed Saviour is himself the essential Form and the living Word, and to which he imparts the actuating Spirit, has a principle of unity and consistency in itself, distinct from the unity and consistency of our theoretical views. This we have evidence of in every day's observation of Christian character; for how often do we see and acknowledge the power of religion, and the growth of a spiritual life, in minds but little gifted with speculative knowledge, and little versed in the forms of logic or philosophy. How obviously, too, does the living principle of religion manifest the same specific character, the same essential form, amidst all the diversities of condition, of talents, of education, and natural disposition, with which it is associated; everywhere rising above nature, and the powers of the natural man, and unlimited in its goings on by the forms in which the understanding seeks to comprehend and confine its spiritual energies. "There are diversities of gifts, but the same spirit;" and it is no less true now, than in the age of the Apostles, that in all lands, and in every variety of circumstances, the manifestations of spiritual life are essentially the same; and all who truly believe in heart, however diverse in natural condition, in the character of their understandings, and even in their theoretical views of truth, are *one* in *Christ Jesus.* The essential faith is not to be found in the understand- [xxv] ing or the speculative theory, but "the *Life,* the *Substance,* the *Hope,* the *Love*—in one word, the *Faith*—these are Derivatives from the practical, moral, and Spiritual Nature and Being of Man." Speculative systems of theology indeed have often had little connexion with the essential spirit of religion, and are usually little more than schemes resulting from the strivings of the finite understanding to comprehend and exhibit under its own forms and conditions a mode of being and spiritual truths essentially diverse from their proper objects, and with which they are incommensurate.

This I am aware is an imperfect, and I fear may be an unintelligible view, of a subject exceedingly difficult of apprehension at the best. If so, I must beg the reader's indulgence, and request him to suspend his judgment, as to the absolute intelligibility of it, till he becomes acquainted with the language and sentiments of the work itself. It will, however, I hope, be so far understood, at least, as to answer the purpose for which it was introduced—of precluding the supposition, that, in the remarks which preceded, or in those which follow, any suspicion is intended to be expressed, with regard to the religious principles or the essential faith of those who hold the opinions in question. According to this view of the inherent and essential nature of Spiritual Religion, as existing in the *practical reason* of man, we may not only admit, but can better understand, the possibility of what every charitable christian will acknowledge to be a fact, so far as human observation can determine facts of this sort—that a man may be truly religious, and essentially a believer at heart, while his understanding is sadly bewildered with the attempt to comprehend and express philosophically, what yet he feels and knows spiritually. It is indeed impossible for us to tell, how far the understanding may impose upon itself by partial views and false disguises, without perverting the will, or estranging it from the laws and the authority of reason and the Divine Word. We cannot say, to what extent a false system of philosophy and metaphysical opinions, which in their natural and uncounteracted tendency would go to destroy all religion, may [xxvi] be received in a christian community, and yet the power of spiritual religion retain its hold and its efficacy in the hearts of the people. We may perhaps believe that, in opposition to all the might of false philosophy, so long as the great body of the people have the Bible in their hands, and are taught to reverence and receive its heavenly instructions, though the church may suffer injury from unwise and unfruitful speculations, it will yet be preserved; and that the spiritual seed of the Divine Word, though mingled with many tares of worldly wisdom, and philosophy falsely so called, will yet spring up, and bear fruit unto everlasting life.

But though we may hope and believe this, we cannot avoid believing, at the same time, that injury must result from an unsuspecting confidence in metaphysical opinions, which are essentially at variance with the doctrines of revelation. Especially must the effect be injurious, where those opinions lead gradually to alter our views of religion itself, and of all that is peculiar in the Christian system. The great mass of community, who know little of metaphysics and whose faith in revelation is not so readily influenced by speculations not *immediately* connected with it, may, indeed, for a time, escape the evil, and continue to "receive with meekness the ingrafted word." But in the minds of the better educated, especially those who think, and follow out their conclusions with resolute independence of thought, the result must be either a loss of confidence in the opinions themselves, or a rejection of all those parts of the christian system which are at variance with them. Under particular circumstances, indeed, where both the metaphysical errors, and the great doctrines of the christian faith, have a strong hold upon the minds of a community, a protracted struggle may take place, and earnest and long continued efforts may be made to reconcile opinions, which we are resolved to maintain, with a faith which our consciences will not permit us to abandon. But so long as the effort continues, and such opinions retain their hold upon our confidence, it must be with some diminution of the fulness and simplicity of our faith. To a greater or less degree, accord- [xxvii] ing to the education and habits of thought in different individuals, the Word of God is received with doubt, or with such glozing modifications as enervate its power. Thus the light from heaven is intercepted, and we are left to a shadow-fight of metaphysical schemes and metaphorical interpretations. While one party, with conscientious and earnest endeavors, and at great expense of talent and ingenuity, contends for the faith, and among the possible shapings of the received metaphysical system, seeks that which will best comport with the simplicity of the gospel, another more boldly interprets the language of the gospel itself, in conformity with those views of religion to which their philosophy seems obviously to conduct them. The substantial being, and the living energy, of that WORD, which is not only the light but the life of men, is either misapprehended or denied by all parties; and even those who contend for what they conceive the literal import of the gospel, do it—as they must to avoid too glaring absurdity—with such explanations of its import, as make it to become, in no small degree, the "words of man's wisdom," rather than a simple "demonstration of the spirit, and of power." Hence, although such as have experienced the spiritual and life-giving power of the Divine Word, may be able, through the promised aids of the spirit, to overcome the natural tendency of speculative error, and, by "the law of the spirit of life" which is in them, may at length be made "free from the law of sin and death," yet who can tell how much they may lose of the blessings of the gospel, and be retarded in their spiritual growth when they are but too often fed with the lifeless and starveling products of the human understanding, instead of that "living bread which came down from heaven." Who can tell, moreover, how many, through the prevalence of such philosophical errors as lead to misconceptions of the truth, or create a prejudice against it, and thus tend to intercept the light from heaven, may continue in their ignorance, "alienated from the life of God," and groping in the darkness of their own understandings.

But however that may be, enlightened christians, and espe- [xxviii] cially christian instructers, know it to be their duty, as far as possible, to prepare the way for the full and unobstructed influence of the Gospel, to do all in their power to remove those natural prejudices, and those errors of the understanding, which are obstacles to the truth, that the word of God may find access to the heart, and conscience, and reason of every man, that it may have "free course, and run, and be glorified." My own belief, that such obstacles to the influence of truth exist in the speculative and metaphysical opinions generally adopted in this country, and that the present work is in some measure at least calculated to remove them, is pretty clearly indicated by the remarks which I have already made. But, to be perfectly explicit on the subject, I do not hesitate to express my conviction, that the natural tendency of some of the leading principles of our prevailing system of metaphysics, and those which must unavoidably have more or less influence on our theoretical views of religion, are of an injurious and dangerous tendency, and that so long as we retain them, however we may profess to exclude their influence from our theological enquiries, and from the interpretation of Scripture, we can maintain no consistent system of Scriptural theology, nor clearly and distinctly apprehend the spiritual import of Scripture language. The grounds of this conviction I shall proceed to exhibit, though only in a very partial manner, as I could not do more without anticipating the contents of the work itself, instead of merely preparing the reader to peruse them with attention. I am aware, too, that some of the language, which I have already employed, and shall be obliged to employ, will not convey its full import to the reader, till he becomes acquainted with some of the leading principles and distinctions unfolded in the work. But this, also, is an evil, which I saw no means of avoiding without incurring a greater, and writing a book instead of a brief essay.

Let it be understood, then, without farther preface, that by the prevailing system of metaphysics, I mean the system, of which in modern times Locke is the reputed author, and the leading principles of which, with various modifications, more [xxix] or less important, but not altering its essential character, have been almost universally received in this country. It should be observed, too, that the causes enumerated in the Appendix of this work, pp. 393—395, as having elevated it to its "pride of place" in Europe, have been aided by other favouring circumstances here. In the minds of our religious community especially some of its most important doctrines have become associated with names justly loved and revered among ourselves, and so connected with all our theoretical views of religion, that one can hardly hope to question their validity without hazarding his reputation, not only for orthodoxy, but even for common sense. To controvert, for example, the prevailing doctrines with regard to the freedom of the will, the sources of our knowledge, the nature of the understanding as containing the controlling principles of our whole being, and the universality of the law of cause and effect, even in connexion with the arguments and the authority of the most powerful intellect of the age, may even now be worse than in vain. Yet I have reasons for believing there are some among us, and that their number is fast increasing, who are willing to revise their opinions on these subjects, and who will contemplate the views presented in this work with a liberal, and something of a prepared feeling, of curiosity. The difficulties, in which men find themselves involved by the received doctrines on these subjects, in their most anxious efforts to explain and defend the peculiar doctrines of spiritual religion, have led many to suspect, that there must be some lurking error in the premises. It is not, that these principles lead us to *mysteries*, which we cannot comprehend—they are found, or believed at least by many, to involve us in *absurdities*, which we can comprehend. It is necessary, indeed, only to form some notion of the distinctive and appropriate import of the term spiritual, as opposed to natural in the N. T., and then to look at the writings, or hear the discussions, in which the doctrines of the spirit and of spiritual influences are taught and defended, to see the insurmountable nature of the obstacles, which these metaphysical dogmas throw in the way of the most powerful minds. To [xxx] those who shall read this work with any degree of reflection, it must, I think, be obvious, that something more is implied in the continual opposition of these terms in the N. T., than can be explained consistently with the prevailing opinions on the subjects above enumerated; and that, through their influence our highest notions of that distinction have been rendered confused, contradictory, and inadequate. I have already directed the attention of the reader to those parts of the work, where this distinction is unfolded; and had I no other grounds than the arguments and views there exhibited, I should be convinced, that so long as we hold the doctrines of Locke and the Scotch metaphysicians respecting power, cause and effect, motives, and the freedom of the will, we not only can make and defend no essential distinction between that which is *natural*, and that which is *spiritual*, but we cannot even find rational grounds for the feeling of *moral obligation*, and the distinction between *regret* and *remorse*.

According to the system of these authors, as nearly and distinctly as my limits will permit me to state it, the same *law of cause and effect* is the *law of the universe*. It extends to the *moral* and *spiritual*—if in courtesy these terms may still be used—no less than to the properly *natural* powers and agencies of our being. The acts of the *free-will* are pre-determined by a cause *out of the will*, according to the same law of cause and effect, which controls the changes in the physical world. We have no notion of *power* but uniformity of antecedent and consequent. The notion of a power in the will to act *freely*, is therefore nothing more than an inherent capacity of *being acted upon*, agreeably to its *nature*, and according to a *fixed law*, by the motives which are present in the *understanding*. I feel authorized to take this statement partly from Brown's philosophy, because that work has been decidedly approved by our highest theological authorities; and indeed it would not be essentially varied, if expressed in the precise terms used by any of the writers most usually quoted in reference to these subjects.

I am aware that variations may be found in the mode of [xxxi] stating these doctrines, but I think every candid reader, who is acquainted with the metaphysics and theology of this country, will admit the above to be a fair representation of the form in which they are generally received. I am aware, too, that much has been said and written to make out consistently with these *general* principles, a *distinction* between *natural* and *moral* causes, natural and moral ability, and inability, &c. But I beg all lovers of sound and rational philosophy to look carefully at the *general* principles, and see whether there be, in fact, ground left for any such distinctions of this kind as are worth contending for. My first step in arguing with a defender of these principles, and of the distinctions in question, as connected with them, would be to ask for his definition of *nature* and *natural*. And when he had arrived at a distinctive *general* notion of the import of these, it would appear, if I mistake not, that he had first subjected our whole being to the law of nature, and then contended for the existence of something which is *not* nature. For in their relation to the law of moral rectitude, and to the feeling of moral responsibility, what difference is there, and what difference can there be, between what are called *natural* and those which are called *moral* powers and affections, if they are all under the control of the *same universal law* of cause and effect. If it still be a mere nature, and the determinations of our will be controlled by causes out of the will, according to our nature, then I maintain that a moral nature has no more to do with the feeling of responsibility than any other nature.

Perhaps the difficulty may be made more obvious in this way. It will be admitted that brutes are possessed of various *natures*, some innocent or useful, others noxious, but all alike irresponsible in a moral point of view. But why? Simply because they act in accordance with their *natures*. They possess, each according to its proper nature, certain appetites and susceptibilities, which are stimulated and acted upon by their appropriate objects in the world of the senses, and the relation—the law of action and reaction— subsisting between these specific susceptibilities and their corresponding outward ob- [xxxii] jects, *constitutes* their nature. They have a power of selecting and choosing in the world of sense the objects appropriate to the wants of their nature; but that nature is the *sole law* of their being. Their power of choice is *but a part of it*, instrumental in accomplishing its ends, but not capable of rising *above* it, of controlling its impulses, and of determining itself with reference to a purely *ideal law*, distinct from their nature. They act in accordance with the law of cause and effect, which constitutes their several natures, and cannot do otherwise. They are, *therefore*, not *responsible*—not capable of *guilt*, or of *remorse*.

Now let us suppose another being, possessing, in addition to the susceptibilities of the brute, certain other specific susceptibilities with their correlative objects, either in the sensible world, or in a future world, but that these are subjected, like the other to the same binding and inalienable law of cause and effect. What, I ask, is the amount of the difference thus supposed between this being and the brute? The supposed addition, it is to be understood, is merely an addition to its nature; and the only power of will belonging to it is, as in the case of the brute, only a capacity of choosing and acting uniformly in accordance with its nature. These additional susceptibilities still act but as they are acted upon; and the will is determined accordingly. What advantage is gained in this case by calling these supposed additions *moral* affections, and their cor- relative stimulants *moral* causes? Do we thereby find any rational ground for the feeling of *moral* responsibility, for conscience, for remorse? The being acts *according to its nature*, and why is it *blameworthy* more than the brute? If the moral cause existing *out of the will* be a power or cause which, in its relation to the specific susceptibility of the moral being, produces under the same circumstances uniformly the same result, according to the law of cause and effect; if the acts of the will be subject to the same law, as mere links in the chain of antecedents and consequents, and thus a part of our nature, what is gained, I ask again, by the distinction of a moral and a physical nature. It is still *only* a nature under the law of [xxxiii] cause and effect, and the liberty of the moral being is *under the same condition* with the liberty of the brute. Both are free to follow and fulfil the law of their nature, and both are alike *bound by that law*, as by an adamantine chain. The very conditions of the law preclude the possibility of a power to act otherwise than according to their nature. They preclude the very idea of a free- will, and render the feeling of moral responsibility not an enigma merely, not a mystery, but a self-contradiction and an absurdity.

Turn the matter as we will—call these correlatives, viz. the inherent susceptibilities and the causes acting on them from without, *natural*, or *moral*, or *spiritual*—so long as their action and reaction, or the law of reciprocity, (see note 67), which constitutes their specific natures, is considered as the *controlling law* of our *whole being*, so long as we refuse to admit the existence in the will of a power capable of rising *above this law*, and controlling its operation by an act of absolute *self*-determination, so long we shall be involved in perplexities both in morals and religion. At all events, the only method of avoiding them will be to adopt the creed of the necessitarians entire, to give man over to an irresponsible nature as a better sort of animal, and resolve the will of the Supreme Reason into a blind and irrational fate.

I am well aware of the objections that will be made to this statement, and especially the demonstrated incomprehensibleness of a self-determining power. To this I may be permitted to answer, that, admitting the power to originate an act or state of mind to be beyond the capacity of our understandings to comprehend, it is still not contradictory to reason; and that I find it more easy to believe the existence of that, which is simply incomprehensible to my understanding, than of that, which involves an absurdity for **my** reason. I venture to affirm, moreover, that however we may bring our understandings into bondage to the more comprehensible doctrine, simply because it is comprehensible under the forms of the understanding, every man does, *in fact*, believe himself possessed of freedom in the higher sense of self-determination. Every [xxxiv] man's conscience *commands* him to believe it as the only rational ground of moral accountability. Every man's conscience too betrays the fact, that he does believe it, whenever for a moment he indulges the feeling either of moral self-approbation, or of remorse. Nor can we on any other grounds justify the ways of God to man upon the supposition, that he inflicts or will inflict any other punishment, than that which is simply remedial or disciplinary. But this subject will be found more fully explained in the course of the work. My present object is merely to show the necessity of some system in relation to these subjects different from the received one.

It may perhaps be thought, that the language used above is too strong and too positive. But I venture to ask every candid man, at least every one, who has not committed himself by writing and publishing on the subject, whether, in considering the great questions connected with moral accountability and the doctrine of rewards and punishments, he has not felt himself pressed with such difficulties as those above stated; and whether he has ever been able fully to satisfy his reason, and there was not a lurking contradiction in the idea of a being created and placed under the law of its nature, and possessing at the same time a feeling of moral obligation to fulfil a law above its nature. That many have been in this state of mind I know. I know, too, that some, whose moral and religious feelings had led them to a full belief in the doctrines of spiritual religion, but who at the same time had been taught to receive the prevailing opinions in metaphysics, have found these opinions carrying them unavoidably, if they would be consequent in their reasonings, and not do violence to their reason, to adopt a system of religion which does not profess to be spiritual, and have thus been compelled to choose between their philosophy and their religion. In most cases indeed, where men reflect at all, I am satisfied that it requires all the force of authority, and all the influence of education, to carry the mind over these difficulties; and that then it is only by a vague belief, that, though we cannot see how, yet there must be some method of reconciling what seems to be so contradictory.

If examples were wanting to prove that serious and trying difficulties are felt to exist here, enough may be found, as it [xxxv] has appeared to me, in the controversy respecting the nature and origin of sin, which is at this moment interesting the public mind. Let any impartial observer trace the progress of that discussion, and after examining the distinctions, which are made or attempted to be made, decide whether the subject, as there presented, be not involved in difficulties, which cannot be solved on the principles, to which, hitherto, both parties have adhered; whether, holding as they do the same premises in regard to the freedom of the will, they can avoid coming to the same conclusion in regard to the nature and origin of sin; whether, in fact, the distinctions aimed at must not prove merely verbal distinctions, and the controversy a fruitless one. But in the September number of the Christian Spectator, the reader will find remarks on this subject, to which I beg leave to refer him, and which I could wish him attentively to consider in connexion with the remarks which I have made. I allude to the correspondence with the editors near the end of the number. The letter there inserted is said to be, and obviously is, from the pen of a very learned and able writer; and I confess it has been no small gratification and encouragement to me, while labouring to bring this work and this subject before the public, to find such a state of feeling expressed, concerning the great question at issue, by such a writer. It will be seen by reference to p. 545 of the C. S., that he places the *"nucleus* of the dispute" just where it is placed in this work and in the above remarks. It will be seen, too, that by throwing authorities aside, and studying his own mind, he has "come seriously to doubt," whether the received opinions with regard to *motives*, the law of *cause and effect*, and the *freedom of the will*, may not be erroneous. They appear to him "to be bordering on fatalism, if not actually embracing it." He doubts, whether the mind may not have within itself the adequate cause of its own acts; whether indeed it have not a self-determining power, "for the power in question involves the idea of originating volition. Less than this it cannot be conceived to involve, and yet be *free* agency." Now this is just the view offered in the present work; and, as it seems to [xxxvi] me, these are just the doubts and conclusions, which every one will entertain, who lays aside authority, and reflects upon the goings-on of his own mind, and the dictates of his own reason and conscience.

But let us look for a moment at the remarks of the editors in reply to the letter above quoted. They maintain, in relation to original sin and the perversion of the will, that from either the *original* or the *acquired* strength of certain natural appetites, principles of self-love, &c., "left to themselves," the corruption of the heart will certainly follow. "In every instance the will does, in fact, yield to the demands of these. But whenever it thus yielded, *there was power to the contrary; otherwise there could be no freedom of moral action.*" Now I beg leave to place my finger on the phrase in italics, and ask the editors what they *mean* by it. If they hold the common doctrines with regard to the relation of cause and effect, and with regard to *power* as connected with that relation, and apply these to the acts of the will, I can see no more possibility of conceiving a *power to the contrary* in this case, than of conceiving such a power in the current of a river. But if they mean to assert the existence in the will of an *actual* power to rise above the demands of appetite, &c., above the law of nature, and to decide *arbitrarily,* whether to yield or not to yield, then they admit, that the will is not determined *absolutely* by the extraneous *cause,* but is in fact *self*-determined. They agree with the letter-writer; and the question for them is at rest. Thus, whatever distinctions may be attempted here, there can be no real distinction, but between an irresponsible nature and a will that is self-determined. The reader will find a few additional remarks on this topic in note 45, and for the general views of the work is again referred to note 29, and the references there made. To the subject of that note and to the great distinction between nature and the will, between the natural and the spiritual, as unfolded in the work, I must beg leave, also, again to request the special and candid attention of the reader. I must beg, too, the unprejudiced attention of every reader, friendly to the cause of practical and [xxxvii] spiritual religion, to the tendency of this part of the author's system, and of the remarks hazarded above.

I cannot but be aware, that the views of the will here exhibited will meet with strong prejudices in a large portion, at least, of our religious community. I could wish that all such would carefully distinguish between the author's views of the doctrines of religion, and the philosophical grounds, on which he supposes those doctrines are to be defended. If no one disputes, and I trust no one will dispute, the substantial orthodoxy of the work, without first carefully examining what has been the orthodoxy of the church in general, and of the great body of the reformers, then I could hope it may be wisely considered, whether, as a question of philosophy, the metaphysical principles of this work are not in themselves more in accordance with the doctrines of a spiritual religion, and better suited to their explanation and defence, than those above treated of. If on examination it cannot be disputed that they are, then, if not before, I trust the two systems may be compared without undue partiality, and the simple question of the truth of each may be determined by that calm and persevering reflection, which alone can determine questions of this sort.

If the system here taught be true, then it will follow, not, be it observed, that our religion is necessarily wrong, or our essential faith erroneous, but that the *philosophical grounds,* on which we are accustomed to defend our faith, are unsafe, and that their *natural tendency* is to error. If the spirit of the gospel still exert its influence; if a truly spiritual religion be maintained, it is in *opposition* to our philosophy, and not at all by its aid. I know it will be said, that the practical results of our peculiar forms of doctrine are at variance with these remarks. But this I am not prepared to admit. True, religion and religious institutions have flourished; the gospel, in many parts of our country, has been affectionately and faithfully preached by great and good men; the word and the spirit of God have been communicated to us in rich abundance; and I rejoice, with heartfelt joy and thanksgiving, in the belief, that thereby multitudes have been regenerated to a new and [xxxviii] spiritual life. But so were equal or greater effects produced under the preaching of Baxter, and Howe, and other good and faithful men of the same age, with none of the peculiarities of our theological systems. Neither reason nor experience indeed furnish any ground for believing, that the living and life-giving power of the Divine Word has ever derived any portion of its efficacy, in the conversion of the heart to God, from the forms of metaphysical theology, with which the human understanding has invested it. It requires, moreover, but little knowledge of the history of philosophy, and of the writings of the 16th and 17th centuries to know, that the opinions of the reformers and of all the great divines of that period, on subjects of this sort, were far different from those of Mr. Locke and his followers, and were in fact essentially the same with those taught in this work. This last remark applies not only to the views entertained by the eminent philosophers and divines of that period on the particular subject above discussed, but to the distinctions made, and the language employed, by them with reference to other points of no less importance in the constitution of our being.

It must have been observed by the reader of the foregoing pages, that I have used several words, especially *understanding* and *reason*, in a sense somewhat diverse from their present acceptation; and the occasion of this I suppose would be partly understood from my having already directed the attention of the reader to the distinction exhibited between these words in the work, and from the remarks made on the ambiguity of the word reason in its common use. I now proceed to remark, that the ambiguity spoken of, and the consequent perplexity in regard to the use and authority of reason, have arisen from the habit of using, since the time of Locke, the terms understanding and reason indiscriminately, and thus confounding a distinction clearly marked in the philosophy and in the language of the older writers. Alas! had the *terms* only been confounded, or had we suffered only an inconvenient ambiguity of language, there would be comparatively little cause for earnestness upon the subject; or had our views of the things [xxxix] signified by these terms been only partially confused, and had we still retained correct notions of our prerogative, as rational and spiritual beings, the consequences might have been less deplorable. But the misfortune is, that the powers of understanding and reason have not merely been blended and confounded in the view of our philosophy, the higher and far more characteristic, as an essential constituent of our proper humanity, has been as it were obscured and hidden from our observation in the inferior power, which belongs to us in common with the brutes that perish. According to the old, the more spiritual, and genuine philosophy, the distinguishing attributes of our humanity—that "image of God" in which man alone was created of all the dwellers upon earth, and in virtue of which he was placed at the head of this lower world, was said to be found in the *reason* and *free-will*. But understanding these in their strict and proper sense and according to the true *ideas* of them, as contemplated by the older metaphysicians, we have literally, if the system of Locke and the popular philosophy of the day be true, neither the one nor the other of these—neither reason nor free-will. What they esteemed the image of God in the soul, and considered as distinguishing us specifically, and so vastly too, above each and all of the irrational animals, is found, according to this system, to have in fact no real existence. The reality neither of the free-will, nor of any of those laws or ideas, which spring from, or rather constitute, reason, can be authenticated by the sort of proof which is demanded, and we must therefore relinquish our prerogative, and take our place with becoming humility among our more unpretending companions. In the ascending series of powers, enumerated by Milton, with so much philosophical truth, as well as beauty of language, in the fifth book of Paradise Lost, he mentions

> *Fancy* and *understanding*, whence the soul
> REASON receives. And reason is her *being*,
> Discursive or intuitive.

But the highest power here, that which is the BEING of the soul, considered as any thing differing in kind from the under- [xl] standing, has no place in our popular metaphysics. Thus we have only the *understanding*, "the faculty judging according to sense," a faculty of abstracting and generalizing, of contrivance and forecast, as the highest of our intellectual powers; and this we are expressly taught belongs to us in common with brutes. Nay, these views of our essential being, consequences and all, are adopted by men, whom one would suppose religion, if not philosophy, should have taught their utter inadequateness to the true and essential constituents of our humanity. Dr. Paley tells us in his Nat. Theology, that only "CONTRIVANCE," a power obviously and confessedly belonging to brutes, is necessary to constitute *personality*. His whole system both of theology and morals neither teaches, nor implies, the existence of any specific difference either between the understanding and reason, or between nature and the will. It does not imply the existence of any power in man, which does not obviously belong in a greater or less degree to irrational animals. Dr. Fleming, another reverend prelate in the English church, in his "Philosophy of Zoology," maintains in express terms, that we have no faculties differing in kind from those which belong to brutes. How many other learned, and reverend, and wise men adopt the same opinions, I know not; though these are obviously not the peculiar views of the individuals, but conclusions resulting from the essential principles of their system. If, then, there is no better *system*, if this be the genuine philosophy, and founded in the nature of things, there is no help for us, and we must believe it—*if we can*. But most certainly it will follow, that we ought, as fast as the prejudices of education will permit, to rid ourselves of certain notions of prerogative, and certain feelings of our own superiority, which somehow have been strangely prevalent among our race. For though we have indeed, according to this system, a little *more* understanding than other animals—can abstract and generalize and fore-cast events, and the consequences of our actions, and compare motives *more* skilfully than they; though we have thus *more* knowledge and can circumvent them; though we have *more* power and can subdue [xli] them; yet, as to any *distinctive* and *peculiar* characteristic—as to any inherent and essential *worth*, we are after all but little better—though we may be better off—than our dogs and horses. There is no essential difference, and we may rationally doubt—at least we might do so, if by the supposition we were rational beings—whether our fellow animals of the kennel and the stall are not unjustly deprived of certain *personal rights*, and whether a dog charged with trespass may not *rationally* claim to be tried by a jury of his *peers*. Now however trifling and ridiculous this may appear, I would ask in truth and soberness, if it be not a fair and legitimate inference from the premises, and whether the *absurdity* of the one does not *demonstrate* the utter falsity of the other. And where, I would beg to know, shall we look, according to the popular system of philosophy, for that "image of God" in which we are created? Is it a thing of *degrees?* and is it simply because we have something *more* of the same faculties which belong to brutes, that we become the objects of God's special and fatherly care, the *distinguished* objects of his Providence, and the *sole* objects of his Grace?—"Doth God take care for oxen?" But why not?

I assure my readers, that I have no desire to treat with disrespect and contumely the opinions of great or good men; but the distinction in question, and the assertion and exhibition of the higher prerogatives of reason, as an essential constituent of our being, are so vitally important, in my apprehension, to the formation and support of any rational system of philosophy, and—no less than the distinction before treated of—so pregnant of consequences to the interests of truth, in morals, and religion, and indeed of all truth, that mere opinion and the authority of names may well be disregarded. The discussion, moreover, relates to facts, and to such facts, too, as are not to be learned from the instruction, or received on the authority, of any man. They must be ascertained by every man for himself, by reflection upon the processes and laws of his own inward being, or they are not learned at all to any valuable purpose. We do indeed find in ourselves then, as no one [xlii] will deny, certain powers of intelligence, which we have abundant reason to believe the brutes possess in common with us in a greater or less degree. The functions of the understanding, as treated of in the popular systems of metaphysics, its faculties of attention, of abstraction, of generalization, the power of forethought and contrivance, of adapting means to ends, and the law of association, may be, so far as we can judge, severally represented more or less adequately in the instinctive intelligence of the higher orders of brutes. But, not to anticipate too far a topic treated of in the work, do these, or any and all the faculties which we discover in irrational animals, satisfactorily account to a reflecting mind for all the phænomena, which are presented to our observation in our own consciousness? Would any supposable addition to the *degree* merely of those powers which we ascribe to brutes render them *rational* beings, and remove the sacred distinction, which law and reason have sanctioned, between things and persons? Will any such addition account for our having—what the brute is not supposed to have—the pure *ideas* of the geometrician, the power of ideal construction, the intuition of geometrical or other necessary and universal truths? Would it give rise, in irrational animals, to a *law of moral rectitude* and *to conscience*—to the feelings of moral *responsibility* and *remorse?* Would it awaken them to a reflective self-consciousness, and lead them to form and contemplate the *ideas* of the *soul*, of *free-will*, of *immortality*, and of GOD. It seems to me, that we have only to reflect for a serious hour upon what we mean by these, and then to compare them with our notion of what belongs to a brute, its inherent powers and their correlative objects, to feel that they are utterly incompatible—that in the possession of these we enjoy a prerogative, which we cannot disclaim without a violation of reason, and a voluntary abasement of ourselves—and that we must therefore be possessed of some *peculiar* powers—of some source of ideas *distinct* from the understanding, differing *in kind* from any and all of those which belong to us in common with inferior and irrational animals.

[xliii] But what these powers are, or what is the precise nature of the distinction between the understanding and reason, it is not my province, nor have I undertaken, to show. My object is merely to illustrate its necessity, and the palpable obscurity, vagueness, and deficiency, in this respect, of the mode of philosophizing, which is held in so high honour among us. The distinction itself will be found illustrated with some of its

important bearings in the work, and in the notes and Appendix attached to it; and cannot be too carefully studied—in connexion with that between nature and the will—by the student who would acquire distinct and intelligible notions of what constitutes the truly spiritual in our being, or find rational grounds for the possibility of a truly spiritual religion. Indeed, could I succeed in fixing the attention of the reader upon this distinction, in such a way as to secure his candid and reflecting perusal of the work, I should consider any personal effort or sacrifice abundantly recompensed. Nor am I alone in this view of its importance. A literary friend, whose opinion on this subject would be valued by all who know the soundness of his scholarship, says, in a letter just now received, "if you can once get the attention of thinking men fixed on his distinction between the reason and the understanding, you will have done enough to reward the labour of a life. As prominent a place as it holds in the writings of Coleridge, he seems to me far enough from making too much of it." No person of serious and philosophical mind, I am confident, can reflect upon the subject, enough to understand it in its various aspects, without arriving at the same views of the importance of the distinction, whatever may be his conviction with regard to its truth.

But indeed the only ground, which I find, to apprehend that the reality of the distinction and the importance of the consequences resulting from it will be much longer denied and rejected among us, is in the overweening assurance, which prevails with regard to the adequateness and perfection of the system of philosophy which is already received. It is taken for granted, as a fact undisputed and indisputable, that this is the most enlightened age of the world, not only in regard to [xliv] the more general diffusion of certain points of practical knowledge, in which, probably, it may be so, but *in all respects;* that our whole system of the philosophy of mind as derived from Ld. Bacon, especially, is the only one, which has any claims to common sense; and that all distinctions not recognized in that are consequently unworthy of our regard. What those reformers, to whose transcendent powers of mind, and to whose characters as truly spiritual divines, we are accustomed to look with feelings of so much general regard, might find to say in favour of their philosophy, few take the pains to inquire. Neither they nor the great philosophers, with whom they held communion on subjects of this sort, can appear among us to speak in their own defence; and even the huge Folios and Quartos, in which, though dead, they yet speak—and ought to be heard—have seldom strayed to this side of the Atlantic. All our information respecting their philosophical opinions, and the grounds on which they defended them, has been received from writers, who were confessedly advocating a system of recent growth, at open war with every thing more ancient, and who, in the great abundance of their self-complacency, have represented their own discoveries as containing the sum and substance of all philosophy, and the accumulated treasures of ancient wisdom as unworthy the attention of "this enlightened age." Be it so.—Yet the "foolishness" of antiquity, if it be "of God," may prove "wiser than men." It may be found, that the philosophy of the reformers and their religion are essentially connected, and must stand or fall together. It may at length be discovered, that a system of religion essentially spiritual, and a system of philosophy that excludes the very idea of all spiritual power and agency, in their only distinctive and proper character, cannot be consistently associated together.

It is our peculiar misfortune in this country, that while the philosophy of Locke and the Scottish writers has been received in full faith, as the only rational system, and its leading principles especially passed off as unquestionable, the strong attachment to religion, and the fondness for speculation, by [xlv] both of which we are strongly characterized, have led us to combine and associate these principles, such as they are, with our religious interests and opinions, so variously and so intimately, that by most persons they are considered as necessary parts of the same system; and from being so long contemplated together, the rejection of one seems impossible without doing violence to the other. Yet how much evidence might not an impartial observer find in examining the theological discussions that have prevailed, the speculative systems, that have been formed and arrayed against each other, for the last seventy years, to convince him, that there must be some discordance in the elements, some principle of secret but irreconcilable hostility between a philosophy and a religion, which, under every ingenious variety of form and shaping, still stand aloof from each other, and refuse to cohere. For is it not a fact, that in regard to every speculative system, which has been formed on these philosophical principles,—to every new shaping of theory, which has been devised and gained its adherents among us,—is it not a fact, I ask, that, to all, except those adherents, the *system*—the philosophical *theory*—has seemed dangerous in its tendency, and at war with orthodox views of religion—perhaps even with the attributes of God. Nay, to bring the matter still nearer and more plainly to view, I ask, whether at this moment the organs and particular friends of our leading theological seminaries in New England, both devotedly attached to an orthodox and spiritual system of religion, and expressing mutual confidence as to the *essentials* of their mutual faith, do not each consider the other as holding a philosophical *theory* subversive of orthodoxy? If I am not misinformed, this is the simple fact.

Now, if these things be so, I would ask again with all earnestness, and out of regard to the interests of truth alone, whether serious and reflecting men may not be permitted, without the charge of heresy in RELIGION, to stand in doubt of this PHILOSOPHY *altogether;* whether these facts, which will not be disputed, do not furnish just ground for suspicion, that the principles of our philosophy may be erroneous, or at least in-[xlvi] duce us to look with candour and impartiality at the claims of another and a different system.

What are the claims of the system, to which the attention of the public is invited in this work, can be understood fully, only by a careful and reflecting examination of its principles in connexion with the conscious wants of our own inward being—the require-ments of our own reason and consciences. Its purpose and tendency, I have endeavoured in some measure to exhibit; and if the influence of authority, which the prevailing system furnishes against it can, and must be counteracted by any thing of a like kind— (and whatever professions we may make, the influence of authority produces at least a predisposing effect upon our minds)—the remark which I have made, will show, that the principles here taught are not wholly unauthorized by men, whom we have been taught to reverence among the great and good. I cannot but add, as a matter of simple justice to the question, that however our prevailing system of philosophizing may have appealed to the authority of Lord Bacon, it needs but a candid examination of his writings, especially the first part of his Novum Organum, to be convinced, that such an appeal is without grounds; and that in fact the fundamental principles of his philosophy are the same with those taught in this work. The great distinction, especially, between the understanding and the reason is clearly and fully recognized; and as a philosopher he would be far more properly associated with Plato or even Aristotle, than with the modern philosophers, who have miscalled their systems by his name. For farther remarks on this point, the reader is requested to refer to notes 50 and 59. In our own times, moreover, there is abundant evidence, whatever may be thought of the principles of this work here, that the same general views of philosophy are regaining their ascendancy elsewhere. In Great Britain there are not a few, who begin to believe, that the deep toned and sublime eloquence of Coleridge on these great subjects may have something to claim their attention besides a few peculiarities of language. At Paris, the doctrines of a rational and spiritual system of phi- [xlvii] losophy are taught to listening and admiring thousands by one of the most learned and eloquent philosophers of the age: and in Germany, if I mistake not, the same general views are adopted by the serious friends of religious truth among her great and learned men.

Such—as I have no doubt—must be the case, wherever thinking men can be brought distinctly and impartially to examine their claims; and indeed, to those who shall study and comprehend the general history of philosophy, it must always be matter of special wonder, that in a christian community, anxiously striving to explain and defend the doctrines of christianity in their spiritual sense, there should have been a long continued and tenacious adherence to philosophical principles, so subversive of their faith in every thing distinctively spiritual; while those of an opposite tendency, and claiming a near relationship and correspondence with the truly spiritual in the christian system, and the mysteries of its sublime faith, were looked upon with suspicion and jealousy, as unintelligible or dangerous metaphysics.

And here I must be allowed to add a few remarks with regard to the popular objec-tions against the system of philosophy, whose claims I am urging, especially against the writings of the author, under whose name it appears in the present work. These are various and often contradictory, but usually have reference either to his peculiarities of language, or to the depth—whether apparent or real,—and the unintelligibleness, of his thoughts.

To the first of these it seems to me a sufficient answer, for a mind that would deal honestly and frankly by itself, to suggest that in the very nature of things it is impos-sible for a writer to express by a single word any truth, or to mark any distinction, not recognized in the language of his day, unless he adopts a word entirely new, or gives to one already in use a new and more peculiar sense. Now in communicating truths, which the writer deems of great and fundamental importance, shall he thus appropriate a single word old or new, or trust to the vagueness of perpetual circumlocution? Admitting for [xlviii] example, the existence of the important distinction, for which this writer contends, between the understanding and reason, and that this distinction, when recognized at all, is confounded in the common use of language by employing the words indiscriminately, shall he still use these words indiscriminately, and either invent a new word, or mark the distinction by descriptive circumlocutions, or shall he assign a more distinctive and precise meaning to the words already used? It seems to me obviously more in accordance with the laws and genius of language to take the course, which he has adopted. But in this case and in many others, where his language seems peculiar, it cannot be denied that the words had already been employed in the same sense, and the same distinctions recognized, by the older and many of the most distinguished writers in the language. But the reader will find the author's own views of the subject in the Appendix, pp. 347—348, and pp. 355—357, and p. 397. See also note 22.

With regard to the more important objection, that the *thoughts* of Coleridge are *unintelligible*, if it be intended to imply, that his language is not in itself expressive of an intelligible meaning, or that he affects the appearance of depth and mystery, while his thoughts are common-place, it is an objection, which no one who has read his works attentively, and acquired a feeling of interest for them, will treat their author with so much disrespect as to answer at all. Every such reader *knows*, that he uses words uniformly with astonishing precision, and that language becomes, in his use of it—in a degree, of which few writers can give us a conception—a living power, "consubstantial" with the power of thought, that gave birth to it, and awakening and calling into action a corresponding energy in our own minds. There is little encouragement, moreover, to answer the objections of any man, who will permit himself to be incurably prejudiced against an author by a few peculiarities of language, or an apparent difficulty of being understood, and without enquiring into the cause of that difficulty, where at the same time he cannot but see and acknowledge the presence of great intellectual and moral power.

[xlix] But if it be intended by the objection to say simply, that the thoughts of the author are often difficult to be apprehended—that he makes large demands not only upon the attention, but upon the reflecting and thinking powers, of his readers, the fact is not, and need not be, denied; and it will only remain to be decided, whether the instruction offered, as the reward, will repay us for the expenditure of thought required, or can be obtained for less. I know it is customary in this country, as well as in Great Britain—and that too among men from whom different language might be expected—to affect either contempt or modesty, in regard to all that is more than common-place in philosophy, and especially "Coleridge's Metaphysics," as "too deep for them." Now it may not be every man's duty, or in every man's power, to devote to such studies the time and thought necessary to understand the deep things of philosophy. But for one, who professes to be a scholar, and to cherish a manly love of truth for the truth's sake, to object to a system of metaphysics because it is "too *deep* for him," must be either a disingenuous insinuation, that its depths are not worth exploring—which is more than the objector knows—or a confession, that—with all his professed love of truth and knowledge—he prefers to "sleep after dinner." The misfortune is, that men have been cheated into a belief, that all philosophy and metaphysics worth knowing are contained in a few volumes, which can be understood with little expense of thought; and that they may very well spare themselves the vexation of trying to comprehend the depths of "Coleridge's Metaphysics." According to the popular notions of the day, it is a very easy matter to understand the philosophy of mind. A new work on philosophy is as easy to read as the last new novel; and superficial, would-be scholars, who have a very sensible horror at the thought of studying Algebra, or the doctrine of fluxions, can yet go through a course of moral sciences, and know all about the philosophy of the mind.

Now why will not men of sense, and men who have any just pretensions to scholarship, see that there must of neces- [l] sity be gross sophistry somewhere in any system of metaphysics, which pretends to give us an adequate and scientific self-knowledge—to render comprehensible to us the mysterious laws of our own inward being, with less manly and persevering effort of thought on our part, than is confessedly required to comprehend the simplest of those sciences, all of which are but some of the phænomena, from which the laws in question are to be inferred? Why will they not see and acknowledge—what one would suppose a moment's reflection would teach them—that to attain true self-knowledge by reflection upon the objects of our inward consciousness—not merely to understand the motives of our conduct as conscientious christians, but to know ourselves scientifically as philosophers—must, of necessity, be the most deep and difficult of all our attainments in knowledge? I trust that what I have already said will be sufficient to expose the absurdity of objections against metaphysics in general, and do something towards showing, that we are in actual and urgent need of a system somewhat deeper than those, the contradictions of which have not without reason made the name of philosophy a terror to the friends of truth and of religion. "False metaphysics can be effectually counteracted by true metaphysics alone; and if the reasoning be clear, solid, and pertinent, the truth deduced can never be the less valuable on account of the depth from which it may have been drawn." It is a fact, too, of great importance to be kept in mind, in relation to this subject, that in the study of ourselves—in attaining a knowledge of our own being, there are truths of vast concernment, and lying at a great depth, which yet no man can draw for another. However the depth may have been fathomed, and the same truth brought up by others, for a light and a joy to their own minds, it must still remain, and be sought for by us, each for himself, at the bottom of the well.

The system of philosophy here taught does not profess to make men philosophers, or —which ought to mean the same [t]hing—to guide them to the knowledge of themselves, without the labour both of attention and of severe thinking. If it [li] did so, it would have, like the more popular works of philosophy, far less affinity, than it now has, with the mysteries of religion, and those profound truths concerning our spiritual being and destiny, which are revealed in the "things hard to be understood" of St. Paul and of the "beloved disciple." For I cannot but remind my readers again, that the author does not undertake to teach us the philosophy of the human mind, with the exclusion of the truths and influences of religion. He would not undertake to philosophize respecting the being and character of man, and at the same time exclude from his view the very principle which constitutes his proper humanity: he would not, in teaching the doctrine of the solar system, omit to mention the sun, and the law of gravitation. He professes to investigate and unfold the being of man *as man*, in his higher, his peculiar, and distinguishing attributes. These it is, which are "hard to be understood," and to apprehend which requires the exercise of deep reflection and exhausting thought. Nor in aiming at this object would he consider it very philosophical to reject the aid and instruction of eminent writers on the subject of religion, or even of the volume of revelation itself. He would consider St. Augustine as none the less a philosopher, because he became a christian. The Apostles John and Paul were, in the view of this system of philosophy, the most rational of all writers, and the New Testament the most philosophical of all books. They are so, because they unfold more fully, than any other, the true and essential principles of our being; because they give us a clearer and deeper insight into those constituent laws of our humanity, which as men, and therefore as philosophers, we are most concerned to know. Not only to those, who seek the practical self-knowledge of the humble, spiritually minded, christian, but to those also, who are impelled by the "heaven descended γνωθι σεαυτον" to study themselves as philosophers, and to make self-knowledge a science, the truths of Scripture are a light and a revelation. The more earnestly we reflect upon these and refer them, whether as christians or as philosophers, to the movements of our inward being—to the laws which reveal them- [lii] selves in our own consciousness, the more fully shall we understand, not only the language of Scripture, but all that most demands and excites the curiosity of the genuine philosopher in the mysterious character of man. It is by this guiding light, that we can best search into and apprehend the constitution of that "marvellous microcosm," which, the more it has been known, has awakened more deeply the wonder and admiration of the true philosopher in every age.

Nor would the author of this work, or those who have imbibed the spirit of his system, join with the philosophers of the day in throwing aside and treating with a contempt, as ignorant as it is arrogant, the treasures of ancient wisdom. "He," says the son of Sirach, "that giveth his mind to the law of the Most High, and is occupied in the meditation thereof, will seek out the wisdom of all the ancient." In the estimation of the true philosopher, the case should not be greatly altered in the present day; and now that two thousand years have added such rich and manifold abundance to those ancient "sayings of the wise," he will still approach them with reverence, and receive their instruction with gladness of heart. In seeking to explore and unfold those deeper and more solemn mysteries of our being, which inspire us with awe, while they baffle our comprehension, he will especially beware of trusting to his own understanding, or of contradicting, in compliance with the self-flattering inventions of a single age, the universal faith and consciousness of the human race. On such subjects, though he would call no man master, yet neither would he willingly forego the aids to be derived, in the search after truth, from those great oracles of human wisdom—those giants in intellectual power, who from generation to generation were admired and venerated by the great and good. Much less could he think it becoming, or consistent with his duty, to hazard the publication of his own thoughts on subjects of the deepest concernment, and on which minds of greatest depth and power had been occupied in former ages, while confessedly ignorant alike of their doctrines, and of the arguments by which they are sustained.

[liii] It is in this spirit, that the author of the work here offered to the public has prepared himself to deserve the candid and even confiding attention of his readers, with reference to the great subjects of which he treats.

And although the claims of the work upon our attention, as of every other work, must depend more upon its inherent and essential character, than upon the worth and authority of its author, it may yet be of service to the reader to know, that he is no hasty or unfurnished adventurer in the department of authorship, to which the work belongs. The discriminating reader of this work cannot fail to discover his profound knowledge of the philosophy of language, the principles of its construction, and the laws of its interpretation. In others of his works, perhaps more fully than in this, there is evidence of an unrivalled mastery over all that pertains both to logic and philology. It has been already intimated, that he is no contemner of the great writers of antiquity and of their wise sentences; and probably few English scholars, even in those days when there were giants of learning in Great Britain, had minds more richly furnished with the treasures of ancient lore. But especially will the reader of his works observe with admiration the profoundness of his philosophical attainments, and his thorough and intimate knowledge, not only of the works and systems of Plato and Aristotle, and of the celebrated philosophers of modern times, but of those too much neglected writings of the Greek and Roman Fathers, and of the great leaders of the reformation, which more particularly qualify him for discussing the subjects of the present work. If these qualifications, and—with all these, and above all—a disposition professed and made evident seriously to value them, chiefly as they enable him more fully and clearly to apprehend and illustrate the truths of the christian system,—if these, I say, can give an author a claim to a serious and thoughtful attention, then may the work here offered urge its claims upon the reader. My own regard for the cause of truth, for the interests of philosophy, of reason, and of religion, lead me to hope that they may not be urged in vain.

[liv] Of his general claims to our regard, whether from exalted personal and moral worth, or from the magnificence of his intellectual powers, and the vast extent and variety of his accumulated stores of knowledge, I shall not venture to speak. If it be true indeed, that a really great mind can be worthily commended, only by those, who adequately both appreciate and *comprehend* its greatness, there are few, who should undertake to estimate, and set forth in appropriate terms, the intellectual power and moral worth of Samuel Taylor Coleridge. Neither he, nor the public, would be benefited by such commendations as I could bestow. The few among us who have read his works with the attention which they deserve, are at no loss what rank to assign him among the writers of the present age; to those, who have not, any language, which I might use, would appear hyperbolical and extravagant. The character and influence of his principles as a philosopher, a moralist, and a christian, and of the writings by which he is enforcing them, do not ultimately depend upon the estimation in which they may now be held; and to posterity he may safely entrust those "productive ideas" and "living words"—those

"—truths that wake,"
"To perish never,"

the possession of which will be for their benefit, and connected with which, in the language of the son of Sirach,—"His own memorial shall not depart away, and his name shall live from generation to generation."

VI

THE INFINITE IN NATURE*

By THEOPHILUS PARSONS

Infinity and eternity, in the highest sense of these words, are predicable only of the Divine. From the Lord they exist in spiritual things; and the infinite and eternal of spiritual things, are again shadowed forth and represented in natural things.

No one natural thing is eternal; but there is in natural things a principle of continuous developement, of orderly and unbroken succession, and of unending reproduction, which represents [145] eternity, and is the form which eternal principles assume when they descend into this lowest sphere and are manifested in external things. Thus every individual tree must die and cease to be; because there is in its very nature a necessity of decay and termination. But every tree may ripen its seed, and its seed produce a tree, and this with an unceasing alternation, because to the continuance and activity of this principle of reproduction there is no necessary termination. If we go below things which vegetate, down to the mineral world, this principle of reproduction is less obvious, because we have come to an inferior class of things, where all the manifestations of life are less clear and science is more deficient. But it is not less real. Some minerals, those, for instance, which are crystalized, are almost like vegetables; but every stone and rock, whether it be a pebble or the core of a mountain, must in time disintegrate, and its component parts will thereafter gather together and form some new things for some new purposes. That is to say, whatever has been and whatever shall be is connected with what is, by a true and operative, though it may be an imperceptible, law. All external things exist because of internal things, and represent them; but the internal things which the things of external nature correspond to, are affections or thoughts, that is some states or conditions of the will or of the mind. Now no one state or condition of any man is eternal; it must pass away and be succeeded by another. Therefore no one thing which now exists will continue to exist forever, but there will always be an external or natural world as the basis or ultimate of the internal or spiritual world.

Infinity is also represented in nature. The Lord is the centre of all things; and man is the centre of all created things. Man is thus the definite and universal standard. Things depart from man into immeasurableness, both upwards and downwards, both into largeness and smallness, and this equally. This was always known to a certain extent, and it became better known as science advanced. As the time for the consummating manifestation of truth drew near, new means of science were provided for man, that natural forms of truth might be prepared, into which spiritual truths might descend. Thus the telescope was given that we might look upon the glittering sky with something better than vague admiration, with the knowledge that space is sown thick with innumerable worlds. The microscope is also given that we may advance in an opposite direction; that we may see every leaf to be a world to innumerable inhabitants, and know that the least fibres of our flesh are composed of fibrils, which [146] are again only a congeries of smaller but similarly compounded parts. There is no end to our progress on either side; the more perfect the instrument, and the farther discovery penetrates, the wider grows the field and the more certain is it that much remains to be discovered. Thus, the visible stars are commonly thought to be innumerable; yet they were all long ago counted and catalogued; their whole number, in both hemispheres, that is, in all parts of the sky, but little exceeds four thousand. The first rude telescope discovered many thousand more, and modern instruments, as they are more and more improved, disclose to us that every spot in the sky is covered with them more and more thickly, and science is every day strengthening the evidence that all these stars are suns and centres of inhabited systems. On the other hand the microscope discovers animals, active and full of life and manifestly provided with complex organs, and yet so small that multitudes may cluster around a point invisible to unaided human sight; and every improvement in this instrument discovers some new and more recondite fact of similar character.

There may never be a stop to the progress of science. Each generation may go forward from the farthest point which the preceding generation reached. But the limit of nature,

---

* "On the Infinite in Nature," *N J M*, IV (1830-1831), pp. 144-146 (Dec. 1830).

whether in its smallness or in its greatness, though it be perpetually approached, will never be reached. The oldest philosophy of which we have any distinct record, declares the Divine to be a circle whose centre is everywhere and whose circumference is nowhere.

The Lord alone can see all his creation, composing together one distinct unity, whose bounds are measured by his span; and he alone can discern the first principles and least forms of things, and look on nature when, in obedience to his word, it is beginning to exist.

VII

COLERIDGE'S LITERARY CHARACTER——GERMAN METAPHYSICS[1]

By FREDERIC HENRY HEDGE

There[2] is no writer of our times whose literary rank appears so ill-defined as that of Mr. Coleridge. Perhaps there is no one whose true standing in the literary world it is so difficult to determine. For ourselves we know not a more doubtful problem in criticism than this author and his works present. If it were lawful to judge men by what they are, rather than by what they have done, by the evidence they give of what they might accomplish, rather than by the value of that which they have accomplished, few would stand higher than Mr. Coleridge. His talents and acquirements, the original powers, and the exceeding rich cultivation of his mind, place him among the foremost of this generation. But this method of estimating a man's merit will hardly be thought righteous judgment in an age which is peculiarly prone to try every man by his works. Tried by his works, Mr. Coleridge, we fear, must ultimately fall, not only below the rank which nature and education had fitted him to maintain, but even below that which he now actually holds in the estimation of literary men.

As a prose-writer he has never been popular, though skilled beyond most men in the use of language, and writing on subjects of the deepest interest. As a poet, though gifted in no common degree with the essentials of the poetic character, he has not been successful. As a philosopher, though at once both subtile and profound, and deeply versed in all the mysteries of the inner man, he has gained little else than smiles of compassion and ominous shaking of heads by his metaphysical speculations. For a reconciliation of these several antitheses we must have recourse to the history of the man. In the "Biographia Literaria," by far the most entertaining, and in our opinion the most instructive of [110] his works, we have that history in part; the influences which operated most powerfully on our author's youth, and the elements both of thought and feeling which entered most largely into the formation of his literary character, are there set before us with great clearness and precision; and from the data which this book furnishes we are enabled to account for much that would otherwise be unintelligible in the doings and not-doings of this remarkable man. Nature, it would seem, had endowed Mr. Coleridge with a singularly fertile and creative mind,—a mind which, if left to itself with no other training than opportunity might supply, would have enriched the world with manifold and pleasing productions. The marks of this creative tendency are still visible in some of his poetical productions; we would mention in particular the "Ancient Mariner," and the tragedies.

But at an early period of his education, our author's mind acquired a bias which proved injurious to its productive faculty, and which, by changing the tendency of his intellect from the creative to the reflective, in process of time seduced him from the open

---

[1] Reprinted from *The Christian Examiner*, XIV (n.s. IX) [Boston, March, 1833], pp. 108-129. Hedge in this article was reviewing: (1) *Biographia Literaria*, N.Y., 1817; (2) *The Poetical Works of S. T. Coleridge*, (3 vols.), London, 1829; *Aids to Reflection*, ed. James Marsh, Burlington, Vt., 1829; and (4) *The Friend* (1st Am. ed.), Burlington, 1831.

[2] The text begins on page 109.

highway of literary fame, into more devious and darksome paths. We refer to the discipline which he received at the grammar school at Christ's-Hospital, as described in his life.[3] Such a discipline, though admirably adapted to invigorate the understanding, and to strengthen the judgment, was ill-suited to unfold a poet's talent, or to nourish creative genius of any kind. It was precisely the training to make a critic; and although we are unwilling to ascribe any irresistible influence to education alone, we cannot help believing that the strong tendency to criticism which has ever marked Mr[.] Coleridge's literary pursuits, is in part the effect of early discipline. We do not mean that Mr. Coleridge has at any period of his life been a writer of critiques, as that business is generally understood, but that he has ever inclined to comment upon the sayings and doings of others, rather than to say and do himself. This propensity, however, has not been exercised on literary subjects alone; it has found a wider scope and a freer field in deep and comprehensive speculations on topics of national and universal interest, particularly those which agitated Europe at the commencement of the present century. It has been [111] employed on knotty questions in politics, philosophy, and religion, it has canvassed the rights and duties of civil government, criticized the movements of nations, and passed judgment on the tendencies and characteristics of the age. The results of these speculations were first given to the world in "The Morning Post," and afterwards in "The Friend," a collection of original essays, which for depth of thought, clearness of judgment, sound reasoning, and forcible expression, have few rivals in the English language. For the American edition of this work, as also for the republication of the "Aids to Reflection," and "The Statesman's Manual," we take this opportunity of expressing our obligations to President Marsh. Next to the writer of a good book, he most deserves our gratitude, who in any way helps to increase its circulation. This praise is due, in an eminent degree, to Mr. Marsh; nor does this comprise the whole of his claims to our regard and good wishes; in the valuable dissertation which accompanies the "Aids to Reflection," he has done much to illustrate Mr. Coleridge's philosophical opinions, and has evinced a philosophical talent of his own, which we cannot but hope will some day be employed in more extensive undertakings.

To return to our author. After finding him engaged in the desultory and patch-work business of journal composition and essay writing, we are no longer surprised that he should have produced nothing of a more lofty and epic character. Whether the habit of small writing (under which name we include essays, reviews, and critiques of all kinds) be cause or effect, we shall not undertake to say; but certain we are, that this habit is always connected with an indisposition for more dignified and sustained efforts. From a skilful essayist we might expect excellence in small matters,—a spirited ode or a pointed epigram,—but never should we expect from such a one a well sustained epic poem, or perfect drama, a complete history, or system of philosophy. That species of talent which leads to fragmentary composition, will generally be found to be the offspring of a mind which loves rather to dwell on particulars than to contemplate universals, and is more accustomed to consider things in their special relations and minutest bearings, than to expatiate in large and comprehensive views. In such minds the centrifugal force is out of all proportion to the [112] centripetal; they are ever losing themselves in endless diffusion, without the ability to recover themselves in systematic results, or to concentrate their powers into regular and definite forms. Such a habit of mind is decidedly anti-creative, and therefore fatal to success in the higher departments of literary production. In proportion as the mind accustoms itself to dwell on particulars, it loses sight of unity and totality, and becomes incapable of contemplating or producing a whole. And herein, we conceive, lies the secret of Mr. Coleridge's failures. Here we have the answer to the oft repeated question, why a mind of such copious resources, so filled and overflowing with various and rich material, should have produced so little, and that little so loose and desultory.

Something more than abundance of material is wanted to constitute a perfect literary production. In every intellectual, as well as in every material creation, there are two essential elements, substance and form. Of substance Mr. Coleridge has enough, but in respect to form he is strikingly deficient, and being deficient in this, he wants that which constitutes the perfection of genius.

The characteristics of genius have been variously defined. To us it has always seemed, that, as there are two degrees of this mental quality, so there are also two characteristics, the one common to both degrees, the other peculiar to, and, indeed, constituting

---

[3] See *Biographia Literaria*, Chapter I.

the highest. The first characteristic is originality. By this we mean not merely a disposition to think and act differently from the rest of mankind, but the power of imparting novelty, and a sense of freshness to common thoughts and familiar objects. In poetry this faculty constitutes what is called the poetical feeling; it is that which distinguishes genuine poetry, whether metrical or unmetrical, from mere eloquence. In this quality Mr. Coleridge is by no means deficient. The following quotation may serve to illustrate our meaning; it is from the story of an orphan girl, contained in "The Friend."

"Maria followed Harlin, for that was the name of her guardian angel, to her home hard by. The moment she entered the door she sank down and lay at her full length, as if only to be motionless in a place of rest had been the fulness of delight. *As when a withered leaf that has long been whirled about by the gusts of autumn is blown into a cave or the hollow of a tree, it stops* [113] *suddenly, and all at once looks the very image of quiet.* Such might this poor orphan girl appear to the eye of a meditative imagination."

In the words which are here marked with Italics we have a plain but accurate description of an incident familiar to all of us. Nothing can be simpler, — perhaps some will think nothing could be less indicative of genius than the mention of such a circumstance. And yet it is this faculty of seizing upon a natural incident, of presenting it exactly as it is, without embellishment or emotion, yet at the same time making it impressive by gently emphasizing its most distinctive feature, and by diffusing over the whole a kind of ideality, — it is this faculty which gives life to poetry; it is this which gives to the poetry of the ancients in particular, its strange and peculiar charm. Who has not seen a leaf whirled about by the wind, and then lodged in the hollow of a tree? but who except a poet would have recalled the circumstance? who but a poet would have found in it an analogy to any thing in the moral world? This is to look upon nature with a poet's eye, and to interpret nature with a poet's sense. This is to clothe with new beauty, and as it were to sanctify, a common sight, so that it can never more seem common, nor pass unnoticed again. An incident thus selected from the daily spectacle of nature, and associated with a particular state of mortal being, becomes thenceforward and for ever a poetical image; by the poet's magic synthesis a natural object has become inseparably linked with a human feeling, so that the one must thenceforth always suggest the other. We feel assured that after reading this passage we shall never again behold the thing there described without a new sensation. We shall add a few extracts from Mr. Coleridge's poetry for the purpose of further illustrating what we mean by the *poetical feeling*.

The first is a description of nocturnal silence from the "Frost at Midnight."

> " 'T is calm indeed, so calm that it disturbs
> And vexes meditation with its strange
> And extreme silentness.
>   Sea, hill, and wood,
> With all the numberless goings-on of life
> Inaudible as dreams,
> Only that film which fluttered on the grate
> Still flutters there, the sole unquiet thing.
> Methinks its motion in this hush of nature
> Gives it dim sympathies with me, who live
> Making it a companionable form."

[114]

The following is from the same piece:

> " Therefore all seasons shall be sweet to thee,
> Whether the summer clothe the general earth
> With greenness, or the redbreast sit and sing
> Betwixt the tufts of snow on the bare branch
> Of mossy apple-tree, while the nigh-thatch
> Smokes in the sun-thaw. Whether the eave-drops fall
> Heard only in the trances of the blast,
> Or if the secret ministry of frost
> Shall hang them up in silent icicles,
> Quietly shining to the quiet moon."

How aptly is a well known state of mind described in the following passage from the ode, entitled "Dejection."

" A grief without a pang, void, dark, and drear,
  A stifled, drowsy, unimpassioned grief,
  Which finds no natural outlet, no relief
  In word or sigh or tear.

"The Ancient Mariner" is so full of beauties that we find it difficult to make a selection. The description of a vessel becalmed near the equator is probably familiar to many of our readers.

" All in a hot and copper sky
  The bloody sun at noon
  Right up above the mast did stand
  No bigger than the moon.
  Day after day, day after day
  We stuck, nor breath nor motion,
  As idle as a painted ship
  Upon a painted ocean."

The effects of a sudden breeze are set forth with the same nervous and graphic power.

" But in a minute she 'gan stir
  With a short uneasy motion,
  Backwards and forwards half her length
  With a short uneasy motion:
  Then, like a pawing horse let go,
  She made a sudden bound."

[115]

The influence of superstitious fears is portrayed with great truth.

" Like one who on a lonesome road
  Doth walk in fear and dread,
  And having once turned round, walks on
  And turns no more his head,
  Because he knows a frightful fiend
  Doth close behind him tread."

Sometimes the poetical merit consists solely in a happy choice of epithets.

" The moonlight *steeped* in *silentness*
  The *steady* weathercock."

In the following passage from "Christabel," the poetical feeling is equally diffused over the whole.

" There is not wind enough to twirl
  The one red leaf, the last of its clan
  That dances as often as dance it can,
  Hanging so light and hanging so high
  On the topmost twig that looks up at the sky."

The second characteristic of genius, that which distinguishes its highest degree, relates to form. It may be termed completeness, or the power of producing a well-proportioned whole. By a well-proportioned whole, we mean a work of art in which one central idea pervades, connects, and determines all the parts; where the greatest diversity of matter is nicely balanced by unity of purpose; where the same leading thought shines visibly through every variety of attitude and scene;—a work which, originating in a happy conception, and grounded upon a rational plan, has all its parts proportioned to that plan, pursues a consistent course, has beginning, middle, and end, moulds itself, as it were, by the self-determining power of its subject, into a compact and pleasing form, and produces, when finished, a simple and undivided impression. Thus a good literary composition may be known by the same test by which we judge of an architectural work, unity of design and totality of effect. Some of Shakspeare's plays, "Othello," for example, or "Romeo and Juliet," will illustrate our meaning, [116] Indeed, the greatest literary productions of ancient and modern times, whether dramatic, epic, or didactic, whether they be histories, orations, or systems of philosophy, all are marked with this characteristic. And not only literary productions, but all that is great in every department of intellectual exertion, a good painting, a masterpiece of sculpture, or in active life a masterpiece of policy, or in mechanics a useful invention, a well-contrived machine, any and every creation of the human mind, so far as it conforms to this standard, — unity and completeness, — is a work of genius. Genius then, in its most perfect state, is known by its *"perfect work."* A writer in whom this quality is wanting, betrays the defect in the loose and disjointed character of his composition. The difference between such a writer and one who possesses the quality we have described, is like the contrast we may suppose between the *coup d'œil* of an eagle who surveys whole landscapes from his perch amid the clouds, and the vision of an insect to whose microscopic eye the minutest object divides itself into numberless fragments. The difference in the productions of these men resembles that which distinguishes the growth of an organic from that of a mineral product; — the one developes itself into determinate forms by the evolution of a single germinal principle, the other irregularly swells its bulk by heterogeneous accretions. Mr. Coleridge is one of those in whom this quality of completeness, the power of producing a whole, is entirely wanting. We have never met with a writer whose works are so patched and ill made up. There does not occur to us at this moment a single production of his, which has the least pretensions to shape.

As to the charge of obscurity, so often and obstinately urged against Mr. Coleridge's prose writings, we cannot admit it in any thing like the extent in which it has been applied. So far as there is *any* ground for this complaint, it is owing to the author's excessive anxiety to make himself intelligible, an anxiety which leads him to present a subject in so many points of view, that we are sometimes in danger of losing the main topic amid the variety of collateral and illustrative matter which he gathers round it. We are inclined, however, to suspect that the greater part of this alleged obscurity exists in the mind of the reader, and not in the author. In an age when all classes read, and when a consequent demand [117] for popular works has rendered every thing superficial that could be made superficial, and excluded almost every thing that could not, when the best books in the language are the least read, when such works as Butler's Analogy and others of the same stamp are confined within the narrow circle of professional reading, — while at the same time complaints are heard that we have no good books to put into the hands of infidels, — when in religion and philosophy superficial treatises and books of amusement have almost supplanted scientific inquiry, — when, even in the department of taste, novels and tales supersede Shakspeare and Milton; — in such an age, we are not surprised to hear the charge of obscurity preferred against books whose only fault is that they deserve, and therefore require, a little more study than we are compelled to bestow upon a novel or a tract. It is to be feared that the men of this generation have been spoiled by the indulgence shown to their natural indolence, and made tender by the excessive pains which have been taken to render every thing easy and smooth. Our intellects are dwarfed and stunted by the constant stimulus of amusement which is mixed up with all our literary food. There is no taste for hardy application, no capacity for vigorous and manly efforts of the understanding. Whatever taxes the mind, instead of exciting it, is deemed a burthen. A hard word scares us; a proposition, which does not explain itself at first glance, troubles us; whatever is *supersensual* and cannot be made plain by images addressed to the senses, is denounced as obscure, or beckoned away as mystical and extravagant. Whatever lies beyond the limits of ordinary and outward experience, is regarded as the ancient geographers regarded the greater portion of the globe, — as a land of shadows and chimæras. In a treatise on mechanics or astronomy, many things would be unintelligible to one who is ignorant of mathematics; but would it be fair in such a one to charge the author with a difficulty which arises from his own ignorance? Some writers are clear because they are shallow. If it be complained that Mr. Coleridge is not one of these, we shall not deny a charge which is applicable also, and in a much greater degree to much wiser men. He is certainly not a shallow writer, but, as we think, a very profound one, and his style is for the most part as clear as the nature of his thoughts will admit. To those only is he [118] obscure who have no depths within themselves corresponding to his depths, and such will do well to consider, as Bishop Butler has said in reference to his own work, — "that the question is not whether a more intelligible book might have been written, but whether the subjects which he handles will admit of greater perspicuity in the treatment of them."

In a review of Mr. Coleridge's literary life, we must not omit to notice that marked fondness for metaphysics, and particularly for German metaphysics, which has exercised so decisive an influence over all his writings. Had it been given to him to interpret German metaphysics to his countrymen, as Mr. Cousin has interpreted them to the French nation, or had it been possible for him to have constructed a system of his own, we should not have regretted his indulgence of a passion which we must now condemn as a source of morbid dissatisfaction with received opinions, unjustified by any serious attempt to introduce others and better. From his vigorous understanding, his acute dialectic powers, his complete knowledge of the subject, his historical research, and power of expression, something more might have been expected than the meagre sketch contained in his autobiography.[4] That Mr. Coleridge has done so little in the way of original production in this department, we ascribe to the same mental defect which has already been remarked upon, namely, the preponderance of the reflective over the creative faculty, and the consequent inability to collect, and embody in systematic forms, the results of his inquiries. But though so ill-qualified for the work of production, one would think the translator of Wallenstein might have interpreted for us all that is most valuable in the speculations of Kant and his followers. It has been said that these works are untranslatable, but without sufficient grounds. That they are not translatable by one who has not an intimate acquaintance with the transcendental philosophy, is abundantly evident from the recent attempt which has been made in England to translate Tenneman. But in this respect, and indeed in every respect, Mr. Coleridge is eminently fitted for such a task; and it is the more to be regretted that he has not undertaken it, as the number of those who are thus fitted [119] is exceedingly small, while the demand for information on this subject is constantly increasing. We are well aware that a mere translation, however perfect, would be inadequate to convey a definite notion of transcendentalism to one who has not the metaphysical talent necessary to conceive and reproduce in himself a system whose only value to us must depend upon our power to construct it for ourselves from the materials of our own consciousness, and which in fact exists to us only on this condition.

[German Metaphysics]

While we are on this ground, we beg leave to offer a few explanatory remarks respecting German metaphysics,[5] which seem to us to be called for by the present state of feeling among literary men in relation to this subject. We believe it impossible to understand fully the design of Kant and his followers, without being endowed to a certain extent with the same powers of abstraction and synthetic generalization which they possess in so eminent a degree. In order to become fully master of their meaning, one must be able to find it in himself. Not all are born to be philosophers, or are capable of becoming philosophers, any more than all are capable of becoming poets or musicians. The works of the transcendental philosophers may be translated word for word, but still it will be impossible to get a clear idea of their philosophy, unless we raise ourselves at once to a transcendental point of view. Unless we take our station with the philosopher and proceed from his ground as our starting-point, the whole system will appear to us an inextricable puzzle. As in astronomy the motions of the heavenly bodies seem confused to the geocentric observer, and are intelligible only when referred to their heliocentric place, so there is only one point from which we can clearly understand and decide upon the speculations of Kant and his followers; that point is the interior consciousness, distinguished from the common consciousness, by its being an active and not a passive state. In the language of the school, it is a free intuition, and can only be attained by a vigorous effort of the will. It is from an ignorance of this primary condition, that the writings of these men have been denounced as vague and mystical. [120] Viewing them from the distance we do, their discussions seem to us like objects half enveloped in mist; the little we can distinguish seems most portentously magnified and distorted by the unnatural refraction through which we behold it, and the point where they touch the earth is altogether lost. The effect of such writing upon the uninitiated, is like being in the company of one who has inhaled an exhilarating gas. We witness the inspiration, and are astounded at the effects, but we can form no conception of the feeling until we ourselves have experienced it. To those who are

---

[4] See *Biographia Literaria*, Chapter 12.

[5] When we speak of *German* metaphysics we wish to be understood as referring to the systems of intellectual philosophy which have prevailed in Germany since Kant. Our remarks do not apply to Leibnitz, Wolf, or any of Kant's predecessors.

without the veil, then, any *exposé* of transcendental views must needs be unsatisfactory. Now if any one chooses to deny the point which these writers assume, if any one chooses to call in question the metaphysical existence of this interior consciousness, and to pronounce the whole system a mere fabrication, or a gross self-delusion, — to such a one the disciples of this school have nothing further to say; for him their system was not conceived. Let him content himself, if he can, with "that compendious philosophy which talking of mind, but thinking of brick and mortar, or other images equally abstracted from body, contrives a theory of spirit, by nicknaming matter, and in a few hours can qualify the dullest of its disciples to explain the *omne scibile* by reducing all things to impressions, ideas, and sensations." The disciples of Kant wrote for minds of quite another stamp, they wrote for minds that seek with faith and hope a solution of questions which that philosophy meddles not with, — questions which relate to spirit and form, substance and life, free will and fate, God and eternity. Let those who feel no interest in these questions, or who believe not in the possibility of our approaching any nearer to a solution of them, abstain for ever from a department of inquiry for which they have neither talent nor call. There are certain periods in the history of society, when, passing from a state of spontaneous production to a state of reflection, mankind are particularly disposed to inquire concerning themselves and their destination, the nature of their being, the evidence of their knowledge, and the grounds of their faith. Such a tendency is one of the characteristics of the present age, and the German philosophy is the strongest expression of that tendency; it is a striving after information on subjects which have been usually considered as beyond the reach of human intelligence, [121] an attempt to penetrate into the most hidden mysteries of our being. In every philosophy there are three things to be considered, the object, the method, and the result. In the transcendental system, the *object* is to discover in every form of finite existence, an infinite and unconditioned as the ground of its existence, or rather as the ground of our knowledge of its existence, to refer all phenomena to certain *noumena*,[6] or laws of cognition. It is not a *ratio essendi*, but a *ratio cognoscendi*; it seeks not to explain the existence of God and creation, objectively considered, but to explain our knowledge of their existence. It is not a skeptical philosophy;[7] it seeks not to overthrow, but to build up; it wars not with the common opinions and general experience of mankind, but aims to place these on a scientific basis, and to verify them by scientific demonstrations.

The method is synthetical, proceeding from a given point, the lowest that can be found in our consciousness, and deducing from that point "the whole world of intelligences, with the whole system of their representations." The correctness or philosophical propriety of the construction which is to be based upon this given point, this absolute thesis, must be assumed for a while, until proved by the successful completion of the system which it is designed to establish. The test by which we are to know that the system is complete, and the method correct, is the same as that by which we judge of the correct construction of the material arch, — continuity and self-dependence. The last step in the process, the keystone of the fabric, is the deduction of time, space, and variety, or, in other words, (as time, space, and variety include the elements of all empiric knowledge) the establishing of a coincidence between the facts of ordinary experience and those which we have discovered within ourselves, and scientifically derived from our first fundamental position. When this step is accomplished, the system is complete, the hypothetical frame-work may then fall, and the structure will support itself.[8]

[122] We have called the method synthetical; we should rather say that it is an alternation of synthesis and antithesis. Every synthesis, according to Fichte in the "Wissenschaftslehre,"[9] presupposes an antithesis; every antithesis, by limitation of the terms opposed, must be reconciled into a synthesis; in every new synthesis thus obtained, new antitheses are found; these again must be reconciled, and so on, till we come to a stand. The first proposition in the "Wissenschaftslehre" is stated thus, A = A. In this proposition the first term is a something, A unconditionally proposed; the second term

---

[6] Kant, *Kritik der re[i]nen Vernun[f]t*.

[7] Perhaps the writings of Fichte may be considered as an exception to this statement.

[8] We give the *ideal* of the method proposed; we are by no means prepared to say that this idea has been realized, or that it can be realized.

[9] Coleridge translates this word, "lore of ultimate science;" it means the science of knowing.

is the same A reflected upon. I propose A, and then, reflecting upon it, find that it is A. This identity arises not from any quality in the thing proposed; it exists solely in my own consciousness. A = A, because I, the being who proposed it, am the same with I, the being who reflects upon it. Consequently the proposition, A = A, is equivalent to the proposition, I = I. Again, I propose — A = — A, or A unconditionally denied not equal to A unconditionally proposed; consequently not equal to A, the object of reflection in the former proposition. Now the possibility of my denying A presupposes and depends upon my power of proposing or affirming A. — A is relative, and can exist only so far as A exists in my consciousness. Consequently, I, the being who now denies A, must be the same with I, the being who first proposed or affirmed A, otherwise — A might be equal to A. This is what is meant by identity of consciousness. I find then in consciousness, two opposites apparently incompatible with each other, absolute affirmation, and absolute negation. Here then is the first antithesis. Now how can these two things exist together? Why does not the one exclude the other? They can be reconciled only by the introduction of a new term.[10] This new term is the idea of divisibility or limitation. It is then no longer absolute, but partial affirmation and negation. What was first unconditionally affirmed to exist, and if allowed uncon- [123] ditional existence must of course exclude its opposite, is now allowed to exist only so far as its opposite does not exist, and the opposite exists only so far as this does not exist, i.e. they coexist by mutual limitation; they define and determine each other. The *I* proposes itself as divisible or limitable, and determined by the *not-I*, and it proposes the *not-I* as divisible and determined by the *I*, and here we have the first synthesis. In this synthesis we find new antitheses, which, by further qualification must be reconciled as the first was reconciled into new syntheses, and so on till we arrive at absolute unity, or absolute contradiction.

This mode of proceeding is peculiar to Fichte, but it is a form of the method used to a greater or less extent by all the philosophers of that school. Defining it by that which is common to all its forms, we may call it the method of synthetic conclusions from opposite terms. Kant first suggested this method in his treatise entitled "The use of Negative Quantities in Metaphysics." To *him*, the father of the critical philosophy, we are indebted for the successful cultivation of the preparatory, or, to use his own expression, the "propaideutic" branches of the science. He did not himself create a system, but he furnished the hints and materials from which all the systems of his followers have been framed. In his preface to the second edition of the "Critique of pure Reason," he makes us acquainted with the train of reasoning which led to the course he has adopted in his metaphysical inquiries. "He had been struck with the fact, that, while other departments of knowledge, availing themselves of scientific method, were constantly and regularly advancing, intellectual philosophy alone, although the most ancient of all sciences, and the one which would remain, though all the rest should be swallowed up in the vortex of an all-ingulphing barbarism, — intellectual philosophy alone, appears to be still groping in the dark, sometimes advancing and sometimes receding, but making on the whole little actual progress. How are we to account for this fact? Is a science of metaphysics impossible? Why then has nature implanted within us this ardent longing after certain and progressive knowledge on subjects of all others the most interesting to the human soul; or how can we place any confidence in our reason, when it fails us in the investigation of such topics as these? But perhaps the fault lies with us. [124] May not our want of success be owing to a wrong method? The science of geometry was probably for some time in the same condition that metaphysical inquiry is now; but ever since the demonstration of the equilateral triangle commonly ascribed to Thales, it has advanced in regular and rapid progression. Physical science has done the same since Bacon. It is evident that both these branches of knowledge are indebted for the success with which they have been cultivated, to the fortunate discovery of a right method. May not the want of such a method constitute the sole obstacle to the progress of metaphysical science? Hitherto philosophers have assumed that our cognitions are determined by the objects they represent. On this assumption it is evident that every attempt to establish any thing *a priori* concerning them (the objects) must be vain. Let us therefore try whether, in metaphysical problems, we may not succeed

---

[10] It was found necessary to abridge the process so much, that perhaps the conclusions may not appear strictly consequential. Let it be understood, then, that affirmation and negation stand for existence and non-existence,—the *I* and *not-I*,—which, of course, when absolute must eventually exclude each other.

better by assuming that the objects without us are determined by our cognitions. Copernicus, when he found that he could not explain the motions of the heavenly bodies on the supposition that the starry host revolves around the observer, changed his theory and made the observer revolve, and the stars stand still. Reversing this process, let us, since the supposition that our intuitions depend on the nature of the world without, will not answer, assume that the world without depends on the nature of our intuitions. Thus perhaps we shall be enabled to realize that great desideratum — *a priori* knowledge."

We have here the key to the whole critical philosophy, the very essence of which consists in proposing an absolute self as unconditionally existing, incapable of being determined by any thing higher than itself, but determining all things through itself. On this fundamental position, Fichte, in his "Wissenschaftslehre," endeavoured to found a system of consequential deductions, explanatory of the grounds of all human belief; a system which should serve as a foundation-science for all other sciences. With whatever success this attempt was attended in the author's own estimation, it has never been generally satisfactory to others. The system is altogether too subjective. The possibility of any knowledge of the absolute or self-existing, is denied; we can know only concerning our knowledge; man's personal freedom is the basis of all reality; with many other assertions of like character.

[125] Next to Fichte in the order of time, but differing widely from him as it respects the tendency of their respective systems, appears Schelling, the projector of the "natural philosophy" so called; a branch of transcendentalism which was afterwards more fully developed, and reduced to a system by Oken. If Fichte confined himself too exclusively to the subjective, Schelling on the other hand treats principally of the object, and endeavours to show that the outward world is of the same essence with the thinking mind, both being different manifestations of the same divine principle. He is the ontologist of the Kantian school. All knowledge, according to him,[11] consists in an agreement between an object and a subject. In all science, therefore, there are these two elements or poles, subject and object, or nature and intelligence; and corresponding to these two poles there are two fundamental sciences, the one beginning with nature and proceeding upward to intelligence, the other beginning with intelligence and ending in nature. The first is natural philosophy, the second transcendental philosophy. Of all the Germans who have trod the path of metaphysical inquiry under the guidance of Kant, Schelling is the most satisfactory. In him intellectual philosophy is more ripe, more substantial, more promising, and, if we may apply such a term to such speculations, more practical than in any of the others. Though in one sense a follower of Kant, he begins a new period, and may be considered as the founder of a new school. Of the other successors of Kant, Hegel, Oken, Fries, Reinhold, Krug, Plattner and others, our information would not enable us to say much, and our limits forbid us to say any thing. The three whom we have particularized are the only ones who appear to us to possess much individuality, or to have exercised much influence in the philosophical world. In designating these, we have done all that this brief sketch requires. We need only add, that the best histories of philosophy, and, with the exception of Cousin's, the only good ones we have, are productions of German philosophers.

If now it be asked, as probably it will be asked, whether any definite and substantial good has resulted from the labors of Kant and his followers, we answer, Much. More [126] than metaphysics ever before accomplished, these men have done for the advancement of the human intellect. It is true the immediate, and if we may so speak, the calculable results of their speculations are not so numerous nor so evident as might have been expected: these are chiefly comprised under the head of method. Yet even here we have enough to make us rejoice that such men have been, and that they have lived and spoken in our day. We need mention only the sharp and rightly dividing lines that have been drawn within and around the kingdom of human knowledge; the strongly marked distinctions of subject and object, reason and understanding, phenomena and noumena; — the categories established by Kant; the moral liberty proclaimed by him as it had never been proclaimed by any before; the authority and evidence of law and duty set forth by Fichte; the universal harmony illustrated by Schelling. But in mentioning these things, which are the direct results of the critical philosophy, we have by no means exhausted all that that philosophy has done for liberty and truth. The preeminence of Germany among the nations of our day in respect of intellectual culture, is universally

---

[11] Schelling, *Transcendentaler Idealismus.*

acknowledged; and we do fully believe that whatever excellence that nation has attained in science, in history, or poetry is mainly owing to the influence of her philosophy, to the faculty which that philosophy has imparted of seizing on the spirit of every question, and determining at once the point of view from which each subject should be regarded, — in one word, to the transcendental method. In theology this influence has been most conspicuous. We are indebted to it for that dauntless spirit of inquiry which has investigated, and for that amazing erudition which has illustrated, every corner of biblical lore. Twice it has saved the religion of Germany, — once from the extreme of fanatic extravagance, and again, from the verge of speculative infidelity. But, though most conspicuous in theology, this influence has been visible in every department of intellectual exertion to which the Germans have applied themselves for the last thirty years. It has characterized each science and each art, and all bear witness to its quickening power. A philosophy which has given such an impulse to mental culture and scientific research, which has done so much to establish and to extend the spiritual in man, and the ideal in nature, needs no [127] apology; it commends itself by its fruits, it lives in its fruits, and must ever live, though the name of its founder be forgotten, and not one of its doctrines survive.

We have wandered far from the subject of our critique. It is time we should return and take our final leave. It was not our intention in this brief review of Mr. Coleridge's literary merits to criticize in particular any one of the works whose titles stand at the head of this article. But the "Aids to Reflection," as containing an account of the author's religious views, demand a passing notice in a work like this. In his biography Mr. Coleridge describes the state of his mind, with respect to religion, previous to his leaving England, by saying that his head was with Spinoza, and his heart with Paul and John; which means, we presume, that he found it impossible to reconcile his religion with his philosophy. In another passage, he tells us that he was at this time a Unitarian, "or more accurately a *Psilanthropist*," which term he chooses to consider as synonymous with the former. We understand it very differently. Psilanthropism, according to our definition, means Humanitarianism, — a doctrine which has no more necessary connexion with the Unitarian faith than with the Roman Catholic. In the "Aids to Reflection," our author would have us believe that he has accomplished at last the wished for reconciliation between his head and his heart. To us the breach seems as wide as ever. In this work he appears as a zealous Trinitarian, and a warm defender of the doctrines of the English church. We have no doubt of his sincerity; but unless we err greatly, he has either misunderstood his own views, or grossly misinterpreted the doctrines of his church. His view of the Trinity, as far as we can understand it, is as consistent with Unitarianism, to say the least, as his former psilanthropic scheme. His opinion of the atonement is far from Orthodox; the idea of vicarious suffering he rejects with disdain. The strong expressions used by St. Paul in reference to this subject, he tells us are not intended to designate the *act* of redemption, but are only figurative expressions descriptive of its effects. The *act* of redemption he calls a "mystery," which term, as it may mean any thing, means, in reality, nothing. The other doctrines fare in the same way. Every thing is first mystified into a sort of imposing indistinctness, and then pronounced to be genuine Orthodoxy. [128] The truth is, Mr. Coleridge, though a great scholar, was not qualified in point of biblical learning for an undertaking like this. Many of his assertions, we are persuaded, would not have been hazarded, had he not taken his understanding of the New Testament for granted, but studied that book with the same diligence and perseverance which he appears to have bestowed upon other works. With these exceptions, however, we consider the "Aids to Reflection" as a very valuable work. The distinctions between prudence and morality, and between natural and spiritual religion, are sound and important.

On the whole, in summing up Mr. Coleridge's merits, we cannot but regard him as endowed with an intellect of the highest order, as a profound thinker, and a powerful writer, though not a successful poet or an amiable critic. As a translator, he has no equal in English literature. His prejudices are strong,[12] his tastes confined, his pedantry often oppressive, his egotism unbounded. Yet we can never read a chapter in any one of his prose works, without feeling ourselves intellectually exalted and refined. Never can we sufficiently admire the depth and richness of his thoughts, the beauty of his illus-

---

[12] Mr. Coleridge's prejudices against the French nation, and all that belongs to them, are unreasonable and absurd in the extreme. He is said, upon one occasion, during the delivery of a public lecture, in the presence of a numerous assembly, to have thanked God in the most serious manner for so ordering events, "that he was entirely ignorant of a single word of that frightful jargon, the French language."

trations, the exceeding fitness and force of all his words. If he is too minute in details to shine in the higher walks of literature, too anxious in the elaboration of single parts, to succeed in the total effect, it must be allowed that few compositions will bear so close an inspection, and still maintain their color and their gloss so well as his. If he divides nature and life and human art into too many particulars, it cannot be denied that his divisions, like those of the prism, give to each particular an individuality and a glory, which it did not possess while merged and lost in the whole to which it belonged. If he has produced far less than might have been expected from a mind so ready and and so rich, we will nevertheless cheerfully accord to him the credit which he claims in his own appeal against a similar charge. "Would [129] that the criterion of a scholar's utility were the number and moral value of the truths which he has been the means of throwing into the general circulation, or the number and value of the minds whom by his conversation or letters he has excited into activity, and supplied with the germs of their after-growth. A distinguished rank might not even then be awarded to my exertions, but I should dare look forward with confidence to an honorable acquittal."[13]

VIII

ON THE HUMAN FORM*

ANONYMOUS

Man is distinguished from the brute creation by his spiritual, moral and intellectual capacity; and by this superadded capacity he is a subject of Divine control and influence, which is distinct in kind and degree from that to which they are subject. [336] His moral and spiritual nature must be the subject of moral and spiritual laws. That which constitutes him man, therefore, makes him a subject of the Divine government and capable of acknowledging it and conforming to it. But only as he is conformed to the Divine law and influence, exercised in and upon him as a man, does it truly govern him as such; for in such conformity, only, is that government accomplished in him and its end attained. In rebelling against this government, he comes under another which was not intended to influence and form him as a man. Hence, on his proper reception of the Divine influence and obedience to Divine laws, depends his real humanity. He is truly human no otherwise and in no greater degree than as he receives and is influenced by laws which are truly Divine. His dereliction from that influence and government, is a dereliction from that state and nature in which his proper humanity consists.

It is man's reception of Divine law and influence, then, which makes him a human being, and his progressive reception of the same virtue from the same source which exalts and perfects his humanity. The Divine Being, unlike other masters, not only gives laws, but by his presence and influence within the recipient, gives also the ability to obey them. For this reason His truths and His laws, are not to be thought of separate from Himself operating in and by them. Divine truth given for the government of beings whose life and power of action is momentarily from the Supreme Source, supposes the presence and operation of the giver within it. The law and the power of obedience to it proceed from their source in conjunction. It can be only by man that they are separated in appearance. Divine laws are the Divine wisdom and are one with the Divine Being Himself. They are that, in and by which he operates and performs his will, and by and in which his will is manifested and known. His laws, then, are ever received and obeyed, if received and obeyed at all, in conjunction with the influence and power of the giver. As they become laws of life in the obedient recipient, they are conjoined in him with the influence of the Divine Spirit, and are the Comforter Himself, operating in the recipient to fulfill them and reap the fruits of obedience. It follows that in proportion as man is what the Divine Word—the Divine law and influence would make him, he partakes of qualities which are truly human, because he receives those which are in their origin truly Divine. It is thus he can be assimilated to Him in [337] whom they are Divinely human, and be restored to that image and likeness from which he has fallen.

---

[13] *Biographia Literaria,* Chapter 10.

* "On the Human Form and the Correspondence of Natural Things to Spiritual," *N J M,* VII (1833-1834), pp. 335-342; 374-380. (May-June, 1834).

Such being the relation of man to his Maker designed by creation and providence, he should know and acknowledge it, that he may fill it. We must look for a knowledge of God to His Word. In that only can He be known, because in and by that only He operates and manifests Himself. It is Himself in form and proceeding operation. It has been written, that is, divinely represented in types and letters. Thus is made permanently accessible to man, that means of knowing the Spiritual Word of God, of which that written language is only a corresponding natural, but divinely inspired, manifestation. The Divine Word assumed and revealed Himself in natural language for the same reason that He assumed and revealed Himself in a natural body. It was to approach the understanding of man and be received there, that His spirit might operate in his heart;—that thus the good and true might become one in him and he one with Heaven and with the Lord who fills Heaven. We can have no knowledge of God and a spiritual world except through natural mediums; so true it is with respect to man's natural formation and his intellectual and spiritual developement, that "that is first which is natural and afterwards that which is spiritual."

As in the written Word, God is clothed in natural language as a medium of manifesting Himself, so in the Word made flesh he was clothed with a natural body. Each is but the natural investiture of Him who creates and fills nature, and arranges it in His own Divine order. Each is but the proceeding of Him to the earth, His footstool, that He might reach man there and raise him to His throne. When the written Word, preparatory to his personal advent, no longer served as a medium of Divine operation to govern and save man—when inspired natural language could not join him with heaven by producing the order of heaven within him—when he had so receded from that order, that Divine influence through it could not effect his salvation, and the prince of this world and the powers of darkness usurping in him heaven's dominion, man in heart and soul and mind and strength, was estranged from the Lord his Maker—then was the fulness of time. There was but one means of saving man. The Lord bowed the heavens and came down. He assumed and invested Himself in that very nature which had so fallen from Him in all its properties, spiritual and thence natural. And, in the [338] order of Himself, in His works, imaged in the creation, growth, regeneration and salvation of man, He filled it and glorified it, till wholly one with Himself, the Word once flesh became His own heavenly manifestation and glory. Then it was that the darkness was under His feet. Only so could fallen humanity with all its attributes be brought into proper connexion with Humanity Divine. Only so could those attributes be lifted up and brought again to their original fountain, that it might be known whence they spring. Only so could the powers of darkness which had taken possession of them, be overcome and subdued, that man might follow and worship the Lord his God.

By presenting Himself on earth, either in natural language or a natural body, the Lord does not vacate his throne in the heavens. He does not circumscribe his presence by making nature sensible of it, or limit his influence by causing the imperfections of humanity and the powers of darkness to submit to it. He does not weaken His power by extending his dominion, or obscure His glory by assuming the instrument which is to display it. He took upon Himself a natural humanity that He might fill with Himself the laws of nature, and make them represent the laws of God. He glorified it from His own Divine Esse, the Father within, that the power of the Father might be known and acknowledged in the form and essence so rendered Divine in Him.

The natural humanity was glorified by communion with, and reception from the Father Divinely in the Son,—in a successive overcoming by Divine Good and Truth, or Divine Life flowing thence, of the evil and the false and all the powers of darkness which permissively assailed Him. All things of the Father were thus delivered to the Son, that the Son might have all power in heaven and earth. The process of glorification, of which the regeneration and salvation of man is a faint image, was the operation of "the Father who doeth the works," by His Divine Word, in and upon the nature assumed and in which He was, and the powers of darkness which permissively had access to it. It is expressed in natural language and manifested in a natural manner, because it was the Father in and by His own Word, operating in and upon nature to "fulfill all righteousness." He who was in the beginning with God, and was God, who *said* let there be light and there was light, shows us that the mode of His Divine existence and operation is His *Word*, the Divine Mind *speaking*, oper- [339] ating, creating and regenerating. Hence "by the Word of God were the heavens made and all the host of them by the breath of His mouth."

The effects of that glorification were progressively exhibited in Divine miracles,

Divine words, and Divine glory, a "doing of the works of the Father." Hence the power of the Father was received and exhibited in and by the Son, till all not of the Father in the Son was put off, and the Son manifesting and making manifest, became the express image of the Father's substance, which is unseen and unknowable but in Him.

The Divine Word thus embodied in natural humanity visibly before man, connects Himself with his works, to exalt his laws represented in them and fill them with His influence. Hence as the process of glorification proceeded and was perfected, the kingdom of the evil and the false, actually and prospectively, tottered to its foundation, and satan like lightning fell from heaven. Thus Humanity divinely glorified, the Father's own person, of an from Himself, reaches and fills all, orders and governs all, from Himself to nature. The Divine Humanity, then, in which the Lord is, is the medium of his power and glory to subdue the world to himself.

In formation, government and influence, like can only act in and upon its like; otherwise that which acts, destroys. All things are thus connected and subsist from God to inert nature. Had not man all inferior natures, some way in him, he never could have been lord of the creation beneath him. They receive from and through him in the way of control and influence; which do not destroy, because their essences are in him. Did not the Lord unite, divinely in Himself, that from which are the essential rudiments of all, man could never have been in His image and likeness. It is upon this principle that what is spiritual can act in and upon nature subsisting from it, by producing in it an image of itself as a recipient form of action and influence. Natural things are thus sustained and governed by spiritual influences within them; and these produce forms fitted for the reception and exhibition of their power, without which there would be no subsistence or connexion, but dissolution. Any other action of spirit in and upon nature, unlike to itself in essence, would destroy it, and not produce subsistence and connexion of one from the other.

The order of subsistence and that of existence are one. The Lord of and from His Divine Love, in and by His Divine Wisdom, gives existence and subsistence to a Spiritual Sun in [340] which He is; and to a spiritual world, whence our souls and minds have being and subsistence, and from the operation of all these, through and by a material sun and a material world, our natural bodies in which we are, have existence and subsistence in this natural degree of life. We are thus connected in and by a natural body through external senses with the world of nature, and through our spiritual form and essence, with a spiritual world. In and by a natural body we have actual perception of natural things only, but in and by that, is the formation for spiritual things. We have no actual perception, through material organs, of spiritual forms interior to natural ones, because like can only act in and upon its like, and our spiritual body is so harmoniously conjoined with its material covering, that all its outward actions flow through it, whilst that connexion subsists. Hence nothing can be presented to our exterior and actual perception, but things of like quality with the organs through which we perceive. It is by interior influx from a spiritual world, that we learn any thing of a spiritual nature and quality. This influx becomes identified in the recipient with himself, because it is ever in perfect harmony with his free-will and ruling love. It flows into natural forms of thought, because it is in and by nature that man has his spiritual formation and growth. Hence, although it be spiritual influx into the recipient according to his state of life, which induces and presents in harmony with his will and state, all his thoughts and feelings, the appearance is necessarily otherwise, because it is in and by his free-will, and in and by nature, the plane on which it acts through his understanding, that it is effected. Nature, therefore, is in apparent priority, both as to action and reality of being.

The chain of causes and effects, of production and subsistence, by which all things were and are formed and kept in their order, is under the control of a wise Providence extending to all. Its links can be broken and disappear only in him who must be, by derivation and dependently, man from the Lord who is independently and Divinely so. A departure in man from the order and influence of the Lord through heaven, gives existence in him to opposing qualities. His love becoming evil his thoughts cannot be true. He still carries with him, however, in his interior form, as well as exterior conformation, while he remains man, an image, of that order, in and by which the heavens and the earth, and angels and men were created. There is still in him a progression, of [341] and from the end aimed at, or his love, in and by its means, real or apparent truth, to an accomplishment in the effect, its form. There is in him an image of humanity within and without, though there be not a likeness of Him from whom it has receded. Did he not possess *that* he could never be restored to *this*. He is, therefore, capable of perceiving the form of good, that by embracing it he may feel its power. He can elevate his understanding to apprehend truth, and by willing obedience to it, may know it more fully in the good it contains.

Every effort is the expression and image of its cause, else it would not proceed from one cause rather than another. They are thus connected in the order of Divine creation, or it would be casual, or of man, and not of God. All our conceptions being originally formed in and by natural senses in communication with natural objects and events, from influx or action from within and above the senses themselves, they are mediums to us of that knowledge only which is on the same plane with them. This is the knowledge of natural forms and relations; for these senses cannot look above themselves or act of themselves, but only of and from that within them. All knowledge of any thing above them, therefore, originates in spiritual influx, or qualities of life made known by internal experience and flowing into natural forms and relations, thus taking their shape, though unlike in essence. It is thus the natural world and the spiritual are connected; and that connexion is founded in the order and nature of things, or all knowledge would be fallacy. We cannot conceive of a spiritual cause except in its relation to an effect out of itself in which it is imagined, or it would not be known to be such cause rather than another. We do not know the effect in its relation to such cause, till we experience interiorly to it, qualities of the cause which produce it. And we can conceive of these only as imaged in that. The knowledge of natural things and spiritual, of nature and the God of nature, thus depends on experimental knowledge, through different sources, one interior to the other, but acting in conjunction and not separated. Their separation abolishes the true knowledge of either. By these two witnesses every thing good and true must be established.

Every cause produces its image in its effect, that the effect may be known to proceed from it. The cause is known experimentally through another source, though conjointly in the [342] visible or conceivable effect, else it would be perfectly identified with the effect and not known as any thing distinct and in relation with it. Both the interior cause and its exterior form exhibited in the effect become one in our knowledge and conception of the cause. This illustrates the nature of spiritual influx, whether it be into a mere natural, moral, intellectual, or spiritual state of life. It is so perfectly in harmony with the free-will of the recipient, that flowing through it and taking its quality *in him*, it becomes in man, the man himself. Whatever love he is in, is to him the cause of things, and his perception of truth from that love, is the corresponding effect and image of it. He knows what this is only as it springs from that, and he conceives of that only as it is manifested and imaged in this. The love in which he is, therefore, is of necessity the God which he worships, and the truth real or apparent which flows thence, is merely the work of his hands, in and by which he is known to the worshipper.

All that is embraced as religious truth, thus takes, in the recipient, the character.of his will or love. By obedience to spiritual truth as given of the Lord, a natural state of life gradually gives place to a spiritual one, and man thence becomes receptive of a love whose quality bespeaks the Giver. And of and from that love, in and by the truth so made one in him, he can see and acknowledge that truth is not of man's discovery, or good of his attainment; that they have but one Source which needs only to be truly acknowledged for us to drink of its streams.

[374] The state of life in each individual is that in which the true or the false in his understanding are one with his love and life. In infancy, when our "angels do behold the face of the Father in heaven," and also more or less in subsequent childhood, there are implanted in all by influx from the Lord through heaven, rudiments of celestial love and innocence, with which truth is congenial. These states, are by Divine Providence stored up interiorly in the mind, to serve as means for man's regeneration. It is from these states that he can elevate his understanding above his ruling love in after life, to perceive spiritual truth, which by obedience, becomes in him a state of acquired life. Accordingly in proportion as truth so seen and obeyed has reference to the Lord, a new heart is formed in him. But affection is of no determinate character, till embodied and manifested by truth. Mere affection gives no distinctive knowledge; it must flow into its form, which is thought. It must reach the understanding, or it cannot be known whence it is, nor can it tend to any one object rationally.

For this reason, an abstract idea of power has no place in the understanding. We form no conception of it except as we conceive of the subject in which it is. In subjects void of life, it is called physical power; in the natural, animated creation, animal power. Taking its character from the subject in [375] which it is, we conceive of it by conceiving of that subject in form. We know by experience in ourselves, that is, by spiritual influx, of nothing which can produce motion but life. We have no conception of power, then, but the power of life made known in ourselves, which is the power of affection, good or evil, in and by thought. That kind of life which is moral, rational, intellectual and spiritual, we can conceive of in a human form only. Yet we may, by imagination and fancy, associate the peculiar qualities of that life with things having no real existence, or by negation of all conceivable form, with vacuity. Hence we can imagine airy nothings, and give them in poetical fancy, local habitations and names.

All our conceptions are originally formed by influx from within outward to perception of natural objects in the plane of nature. By memory the world without becomes a world in our minds, but it teaches us nothing spiritual till our love is so. Still all knowledge which we can have of spiritual things, by whatever means, while acting in and by a material body in this world, must be embodied and represented to our understanding, in and by, natural ideas thus acquired.

Spiritual things, therefore, can only be expressed and imaged in nature by something of determinate character which is not exclusively in either world, but common to both. This is *form*. In this world it has the fixedness of matter; in the other, the changeableness of state, which belongs to affection and thought. It is in both worlds from the same origin, being the corresponding effect and image of the spiritual cause and essence which it flows from, and which fills it. It is in both worlds, because it flows by influx from the spiritual world into the natural, which subsists from it. It necessarily presents to us the exterior of matter, by means of the bodily senses, whilst we inhabit a material body. But it can present to our conception spiritual things, in their true nature and character, only according to our reception of spiritual life from the Lord. And this, because it is only in receiving Him by love and obedience, that we become recipients of that life from Him, by influx through heaven, to which all good things in nature and the truth with which they are one, correspond.

We have actual perception only of natural forms and their relations by the bodily senses. But man is forbidden to *make unto himself* any graven image or likeness of any thing in heaven above, in the earth beneath, or in the waters under the earth. He is forbidden to have any love and any thoughts, but such [376] as he receives in loving the Lord above all things, and his neighbor as himself. By that only can his natural, selfish, and worldly love be subdued and removed, that he may truly know the Lord, of and from the good and truth which He gives, and worship Him only.

We have no actual perception of spiritual things, exteriorly or through the bodily senses in this world. This renders it necessary that we should be told of the distinct existence of a spiritual world, that our conceptions may cease to be identified with nature, and our life remain merely natural. Therefore the ten commandments, the truths of which already existed more or less among men, were ratified on Mount Sinai by Divine inspiration, that they might be the vehicle of heavenly influence and order, by conjoining man's thoughts with heaven. For this reason there is a Written Word. And to remove the evils which had accrued to man from that love which is opposite to heaven, the Lord assumed and glorified a natural humanity, and subdued thereby the powers of the evil and the false, which had overwhelmed the world. For a similar reason the internal sense of the Word, disclosing the spiritual laws and principles from which natural laws flow, is now made known.

The expression of the cause in the effect, the correspondence of natural effects to spiritual causes, is not arbitrary, but founded in true order. It is from this correspondence of the natural world to the spiritual, that a spiritual cause and qualities may be represented in the natural world. It is from this, that God, who is a Spirit, can reveal Himself through natural mediums, and in his own order of creation. It is from this, that words of natural language originating in the subsistence of natural from spiritual things, may be through heaven and man, so assumed, arranged, and filled by Divine inspiration from the Lord, as to be the natural expression, the corresponding image and sign, in the natural world and mind, of what in itself, is not natural, or of man, but spiritual and Divine. It is from this correspondence, that the natural world is to man a preliminary state of existence to the spiritual.

Were there not common to both worlds an exterior mode and form of being, or manifestation of being and qualities, inherent in the order of Divine creation, and thus flowing from the Lord himself, nothing of God and spiritual things could be manifested to man's understanding. All impression thence would be the blind affection of animal nature. But there being this harmony of exterior with interior knowledge, by [377] the influx of spirit into nature, as into an analogous self, in a lower and distinct sphere of being; we can conceive of spiritual things from their resemblances in nature, according as spiritual life flows into the understanding. The correspondence of this world to the spiritual is substantially imaged in our spiritual form and natural conformation. Without this we could have no spiritual knowledge whatever.

It is as this order of things is more or less perfectly admitted and acted upon in all our thoughts of God and a spiritual world, that we conceive of any thing distinct from materiality or physical power. As it is lost sight of, or really denied, all conception of spirit must be as vague and inane, as of the substratum of matter, which may be fancied and talked about.

Between the two limits of conceiving of things, as they actually exist in nature on the one hand, and as they are in heaven on the other, lies the domain of wild imagination, and false poetry, as also of false doctrine. Truth is congenial with good. There is a tendency in the latter to clothe itself with the other. The poet, in whose heart the fire of heavenly love has been kindled by a spiritual life, inhales a purer atmosphere than that of nature. And in proportion as its purity elevates him from the pride and confirmations of evil love and false doctrine, his conceptions approach the truth as it is in the world above. To the actual correspondence of this world with that within and above it, poetry owes its power. It is from this, that the true poet with his feet standing on the earth, his affections and thoughts in heaven, can draw thence the fire and the light which warms and illuminates the world below. But if his visions do not spring from the influx of heavenly love into its appropriate form, a pure and orderly life, he cannot conduct the influence of a spiritual world to this, in an orderly and salutary way.

The influx of life from the Lord is perfectly one in itself with its exterior manifestation of truth, but becomes separated in the human understanding. And this separation takes place in man, in proportion as he recedes from one degree of spiritual life to a lower, and to a merely moral, intellectual or natural state of mind. The knowledge of what truth is, and what life is, is respectively thus destroyed in him; life, becoming identified in his mind with his mere animal existence, the nature of which he knows not, and is therefore perhaps willing to ascribe to the Lord; truth, with his own achievement and discovery which he claims to himself. His truth in [378] both respects bears witness of itself, and its witness cannot be true. It is not conjoined in him with the Source of truth. His mind is divided, and from that state he cannot know and acknowledge the true God and eternal life. He naturally imagines, in this state, two or more Persons in Divine Revelation; one an unknown Fountain of life, the Father of his animal being, and a delegated Lord over his understanding merely, who by some meritorious achievement, such as that understanding suggests, does something, or gives him some light by which he may *seek his own way* to his Maker.

In such a state, therefore, who the Father and the Son are, cannot be known. The latter becomes involved in all the uncertainty of speculative theory, in which such an understanding finds itself; and the former in the darkness of absolute vacuity, where the understanding reaches not, though it imagine it.

It is in the Word of God alone, when permitted to disclose its treasures, that we can learn what life is, and what truth is, and know the Father in the Son, and the Son in the Father, the one Lord of all life and truth. His Word stands in the relation to Him of a divine effect from a Divine Cause. The cause is Himself in his Divine Love and Wisdom. But the Divine Influx of good and truth proceeding from the Lord, in passing through heaven puts on the quality and form of all, till it becomes clothed with that form and quality of the good and the true, which the natural mind is receptive of. This is a natural and literal description of spiritual operations in and by natural ones.

The Word was spoken and written of Divine Love in and by Divine Wisdom, thus from the Spirit of the Lord. Hence Divine Good and Truth are together, interiorly in the Word, in marriage union. And there are two expressions, one bearing reference to good and the other to truth, thence flowing in union throughout the Word in its natural sense. It is a joint expression of these two principles, which in some way constitute all life and mind, according to the subject in and by which they are imaged. When imaged in and by a celestial or spiritual mind and state, celestial and spiritual good and truth, respectively, are expressed, as it were nakedly in the letter. When in and by the natural mind and state unperverted, higher degrees of good and truth, are expressed by moral good and truth, as existing in the moral man merely. When imaged in and by the natural mind perverted, the good and the true are expressed by what appears so to that mind and state. In this case, good and truth of the celestial and [379] spiritual state are expressed by their opposites, as existing in the mind and state of man so perverted.

All states of humanity, in this way, are imaged and expressed in the Word, one interior to another; and the Lord in his Divine Human, with whom it is one, flows into all and exists together with all in its natural sense. And that in like manner as He was, Immanuel, God with us, in a natural body, and as He is in the midst of, and together with, every individual in all his natural operations and thoughts, though he knows Him not. The Lord, in assuming and glorifying a natural humanity by birth in nature, and thence by influx of life, was in all these states, and bore them all in his own form. Thus in the natural and literal Word of God, dwells all the fulness of the Godhead bodily, operating of and from, and in and by His own Divine Love and Wisdom, from His throne to His footstool. He was in all by actual accomplishment, and filled and does fill all, as his own Form of Being and power.

The whole Word, in all its senses, is that in and by which the Lord Himself is imaged and expressed to us, as received and known in all states, celestial, spiritual and natural, in their different grades. Man cannot receive the spiritual sense of the Word in his life, but as he receives and acknowledges the Lord within him as his only Spiritual Sun, the Sole Giver of all his spiritual good and truth. The mere natural sense of the Word is descriptive of the manner in which the Lord is received and known in the natural mind, respectively, according to its states. The Lord's outward raiment is thus divided amongst men, but Divine Providence guards the vesture which has no seam.

The Lord is the spiritual cause, and his written Word the effect in which only He can be truly known. We have seen that an effect cannot be known as proceeding from this or that cause, till the qualities of the cause are experienced; and that both must be jointly and harmoniously one in the conception, or neither is truly known. The cause is interior to the effect, and must be known within it by interior experience, and not by outward investigation only. It is a Word of Life, and by sincere reception of it, in truly obeying it, man becomes a living image and effect of the Spiritual Cause, operating upon and in him; and can conceive of Humanity Divine by its faint resemblance in himself. And this, in the same degree that the Word and the Spirit which fills it are one in him. Thus only can he enter into the heavenly marriage of the good and the true, of spiritual truth in his understanding, with its good in [380] his life, the preliminaries of which union must be settled and its bonds tied on earth, that its fruits may be reaped in heaven, where they neither marry nor are given in marriage, being already as the angels.

IX

STUDY OF THE WORKS OF NATURE*
By Fordyce Mitchell Hubbard

The material world in which we live is full of meaning. It is written all over, within and without, with characters of wisdom and mystery and beauty. Every fragment is of itself a true and appropriate symbol, nor is there a nook so secluded, that it does not contain, or a material form so scanty that it does not express, as really as the more stupendous, yet ever unobtrusive manifestation of nature, its peculiar import. The sun while it discharges its appointed function in giving light and heat to man, bears a witness that cannot be mistaken, to a wisdom and majesty, that are not in it; nor less by its obedience to the same laws, does the most worthless pebble. To the practised eye, every flower, every crested surge, every existence animate and inanimate through the whole range of nature, is a sentence traced by the finger of God; to the tuned ear, every voice of melody, and of discord too, is an utterance which the fitting sentiment within interprets.

I said to a practised eye—and doubtless Nature does not disclose her secrets, but to him who seeks patiently, and with much earnestness! Yet some of her larger exhibitions, as they can not escape the notice, so they must press in upon the mind even of the most

* Reprinted from *The Biblical Repository and Quarterly Observer* (of Andover and Boston), VI (1835), pp. 173-187 (July).

heedless, something of what he who made them, designed them to represent. The change of seasons with their imposing array of boundless and profuse magnificence, and the beautiful and wonderful developements of Nature's working economy, with their lesson of wisdom and kindness and love, every body sees and feels. And there are few men, to whom the melancholy wind of Autumn, as it whirls from its stalk the yellow leaf, is not a remembrancer of that kindred decay which awaits the glory of humanity; or of that dissolution still further onward, when shall perish, of Nature herself, all that can die. Or when her slumbering powers awake in the freshness of Spring, few who do not find in the springing shrub and the unfolding flower, a something which sustains the hope, that that which decays may revive, and that which dies, may not die for- [174] ever. Few minds are there so engrossed and besotted, that they do not sometimes stumble on thoughts like these; and fewer still who have felt their power and know their worth, who will not always welcome their return.

Suppose a human mind, awakened in the ripened manhood of his powers—his first sensation would present a twofold problem—to account to himself for the mystery of his own being, and next of that other outward existence which, while it reveals him to himself, his first consciousness assures him is not himself. The inquiry would, no doubt, force itself upon him as of primary and commanding interest, which Milton has ascribed to our first parent:

> "Thou Sun," said I, "fair light,
> And thou enlightened earth, so fresh and gay,
> Ye hills, and dales, ye rivers, woods, and plains,
> And ye that live and move, fair creatures, tell,
> Tell, if ye can, how came I thus, how here?"
> *Par. Lost, Book 8th.*

And long ere the intense eagerness of that question should be satisfied, would arise another of hardly less interest, whence this material world? Why those manifold and varied forms of beauty? this magnificent overarching sky? These lifted and heaven sustaining hills? These flower gemmed and quiet vales? These fountains sparkling and rejoicing in the light of day? And thus while every sense would become an inlet of exquisite and ever increasing delight, this same questioning would endlessly recur, furnishing new queries and new satisfactions. But alas! man is not so. His spirit is given him in weakness, and the first faint notices of sense come to a feebler intellect within, and in their earliest entrance are mingled with pain—the earthly inheritance of man—and when the child is fairly conscious of himself, and begins to find a curious pleasure in watching and meditating on the works of God around him; he is taken away from Nature, who was ordained his playfellow at once and his Teacher, and delivered over to human tutors, who fashion him after the prudence of this world, and make him believe that the learning of books is better than the doctrine of Nature, and teach him cunning instead of wisdom, and that to think nobly, and feel generously, and act bravely, is but folly, and that is the only true discretion, to be rich, and win favor, and live princely.

My readers have all doubtless seen a fragment by a popular [175] poet among us, (I forget the exact words) in which, he imagines a child, having laid aside his sports, as twilight is coming on, and leaning out of the parlor window, and watching the receding light and fading splendors of the western sky; as his eye catches a star dimly glimmering through the flush of evening, he turns to his father and exclaims in childish simplicity and wonder, "Father, God has made a star!" It was indeed a childlike thought, yet created intellect cannot compass a vaster.

But how few men can bring themselves back to the fresh purity of childhood and indulge such thoughts and feelings! A long familiarity with these scenes has deadened their impression, and that which should have been the occasion of strengthening and keeping forever alive the sentiment of beauty within us, has worn out and banished it! In how many does the sun coming "forth from his chambers" and fulfilling his glorious circuit, excite no sense but that of warmth, no feeling but that of convenience? And the moon walking in her brightness "and the stars which faint not in their watches neither are weary," serve only to guide the benighted traveller, or at most to soften a landscape.

A glance at the history of the human mind will show, however, that men in every stage of civilization, and in every variety of circumstances, have understood in the appearances around them a meaning deeper than meets the eye; and therefore that the Author of Nature designed them to be so understood. And here it is obvious to remark that this tendency would naturally be most conspicuous in nations, which stand midway between extreme barbarism, and high refinement, and perhaps most in the earlier stages of the transition, when free scope and abundant action is given to the natural tendencies of the mind, not yet embarrassed by the forms and restrictions which cultivated society necessarily implies, nor strangled by unnatural excitement in partial and absorbing pursuits. As the youth in whom the hurrying cares of business, and the all controlling power of custom have not dried up the greenness of his spirit, will find a wonder in the commonest occurrence at which his elder and more mature companion may smile, but from which he may learn a lesson of profound wisdom.

This tendency manifests itself in what is common to all, at least to all uncivilized nations, the notion of a prophetic power, supposed to reside in certain phenomena and events both ordinary and extraordinary. Hence the popular superstition of [176] omens —the belief in which is founded to some extent, though not entirely on this principle, and which retains its hold with more or less tenacity in the best informed and strongest minds. Thus the sudden decaying of a flourishing tree, the spilling of salt, the hooting of an owl, have been and still are reckoned ominous of evil. An unconsuming flame curling around the head of the youthful Servius betokened a future crown, and a bee settling on the lip of a cradled infant intimated the eloquence of Plato. Thus too the wise man in his lonely turret, high among the palaces of Babylon, and the shepherd as he watched his flocks at midnight on the plains of Chaldea, saw in the aspects and movements of the planetary world, an inner sense,—a mysterious relation to the alike strange vicissitudes of human life, and the otherwise undisclosed determinations of human destiny. It is shown more clearly in the religious notions of those nations, which have no other revelation than that of Nature; because in the frame of man the foundations of taste and of religion are intimately allied, and to some extent the same; or at least the religious instinct is more or less regulated in the forms it assumes, by the sentiment of taste. The untutored negro, when he prostrates himself on the reedy bank of his native stream, and adores the Deity of the stream in the shape of the crocodile, or bows before the poison tree, in reverence to the God of poisons, obeys this native impulse of humanity; no less than the disciple of Zoroaster, who climbs the highest mountain tops, unsoiled by the profane footsteps of trade or of curiosity, where the air is ever pure, and the sun greets the earth with its earliest light, to pay his vows and offer his incense to the visible symbols of Divinity, to his mind themselves Divinities; or the outcast Guebre, who with forbidden and untold of rites, worships an ever burning flame—to him the elemental principle of nature. But no where do we find it more conspicuous, than in the popular theology of "pagan Greece"—a sketch of which may be best given in the language of one, who has wonderfully combined in his description, historical accuracy with poetic beauty, and philosophical spirit.

> In that fair clime, the lonely herdsman, stretched
> On the soft grass through half a summer's day,
> With music lulled his indolent repose:
> And, in some fit of weariness, if he,
> When his own breath was silent, chanced to hear
> A distant strain, far sweeter than the sounds
> Which his poor skill could make, his fancy fetched, [177]
> Even from the blazing chariot of the Sun,
> A beardless youth, who touched a golden lute,
> And filled the illumined groves with ravishment.
> The nightly hunter, lifting up his eyes
> Towards the crescent moon, with grateful heart
> Called on the lonely wanderer who bestowed
> That timely light, to share his joyous sport:
> And hence, a beaming goddess with her nymphs,
> Across the lawn, and through the darksome grove,
> Swept in the storm of chase.
>   The traveller slaked
> His thirst from rill or gushing fount, and thanked
> The Naiad. Sunbeams, upon distant hills
> Gliding apace, with shadows in their train,
> Might, with small help from fancy, be transformed
> Into fleet Oreads, sporting visibly.
> The zephyrs, fanning as they passed, their wings,
> Lacked not, for love, fair objects, whom they moved

With gentle whisper. Withered boughs grotesque,
Stripped of their leaves and twigs by hoary age,
From depth of shaggy covert perching forth,
In the low vale, or on steep mountain side;
And, sometimes, intermixed with stirring horns
Of the live deer, or goat's depending beard;
These were the lurking Satyrs, a wild brood
Of gamesome deities; or Pan himself
The simple shepherd's awe inspiring God!
                                    Wordsworth's Excursion.

The same tendency is shown in the different values which men set on the various orders of being in nature, when the rule of estimation will be found to be some power, or active principle within, invisible, and inferred, not palpable to sense, but to thinking. Hence, a shapeless stone is passed unnoticed; a crystal more valued, because it is constructed on some principle or power working within it,—the vegetable creation has a higher worth, as involving an infinity of higher and to the seeming, living powers co-operating and controlling each other to the production of an infinity of semi-animate results essentially alike, yet partially diverse—in animals still higher powers and a greater worth, the uncombined fragments of an understanding, and the dawning of a moral nature—in man the yet higher powers of will and reason and fellowship.

The various meanings of Nature may be mainly reduced to [178] two classes—the logical, addressing itself to the understanding, and comprehended by the reason,—and the tasteful or moral, addressed to the sentiments, and apprehended and perhaps shaped by the imagination—the first, that which she presents to the eye of a philosopher; the second, that which she conveys to the mind of a poet. The logical includes those laws and forms of matter and motion, which can be precisely measured, and enunciated by the formulae of mathematics; comprising also those principles of moving force, and the great living energy, of which these laws and forms themselves are but the formulae and manifestations. The distinction between these two orders of meaning, may be compared to that between a finely chiselled statue in the perfect form and exact dimensions of a man, and the form and dimensions only, and the same marble wrought into the Laocoon, writhing and crushed in the serpent's folds, expressing his sacred horror, and parental anguish. Or it may perhaps be better illustrated by the different feelings which would arise in the mind of an anatomist and of a child, in looking on the pleasant countenance of a mother. The anatomist sees a combination of bones and processes, and articulations, the circulation of the blood, the insertion and movements of muscles. The child rests his head upon his mother's bosom, and with his eye upturned in quiet confidence to the face which has been wont to repay his every look with a smile; sees, and thus first learns, the calmness of contentment, or the joy of a satisfied affection, the intenseness of a mother's love, the chastened pensiveness of resignation, or the subdued glow of a fervent devotion.

Diverse as are the ideas imparted to these two minds, so unlike are the impressions produced in the two classes of those who, each in his own way study Nature; and in the elements of character generated by them; or rather by one of them, since the mechanical philosophy has no direct moral *sense* and of course has no *direct* effect on moral character.

"Homo naturae minister et interpres," said Lord Bacon; and expressed the office and commission of man. Yet even he seems not fully to have understood, at least he has nowhere in his works fully unfolded, more than half this sentiment. While he has given to the world a method for the physical, or as it is called scientific, interpretation of nature, incomparably better than any one who had gone before him, and demonstrably true, he has nowhere left us a clue, to the still profounder and more [179] subtile, the moral and spiritual meaning of the universe. The physical investigation of nature, the study of its material laws, its stated modes of motion and operation, has occupied the acutest intellects, ever since the foundation of the world; and though in some respects its progress has not been rapid enough to satisfy a reasonable expectation; yet in others it has reached the limits of desire, as it has reached the bounds of human possibility. In the ascertaining of ultimate facts, I do not conceive it possible for man to go beyond the Newtonian theory of the universe, at least in the same direction. Yet the whole system of physical truth is enclosed and sustained by a circle of superior and transcendant truth, the bounding line of which, the wisdom of man has not yet attained. The master mind of Newton has intimated its perception of this fact, in the hypothesis he felt himself constrained to make to account for the principle of gravitation. The physical study of nature, as it ministers most directly and most powerfully to the necessity and convenience of man, has received his first and almost exclusive attention; while that knowledge of it, which is intimately allied to his moral and more important being, crowded out by seemingly more pressing need, has been neglected and almost forgotten. Another reason for this neglect may lie in the nature of the pursuit itself; for while its first lessons are obvious, its method is deep-hidden and obscure; and I fully believe that the man, if any such there be, who shall give to the world the true principles of determining this meaning, will receive in the applause of a discerning and well disciplined future, a fame higher than that of Bacon and worthier than that of Plato. If indeed—and the doubt is far from an impertinent one,—language can now convey such a method; and if it be not left in the decrees of nature, to each individual to begin his researches where his fathers begun, and as they did, leave to his children no relic, or trace of his labors.

With these views of the difficulty inhering in the subject, I can make no pretensions to modesty in declining to enter upon the discussion of it. A volume could only furnish hints upon it; and after the labor of a life, I might find myself master of only its alphabet. And were I competent even, to give an ample exposition, I should choose to offer only detached and fragmentary thoughts; for a theory in the mind is a stationary thing, or enlarges only like a crystal, by accretion, while hints have a germinating and productive power.

[180] I purpose simply and briefly to state some differing views, which have been entertained of nature; and some of the conditions under which one may become a true lover of Nature, and attain some measure of success in the right apprehension of her meaning.

The *first class*, if it be not a misnomer, to call them lovers of Nature, who find in her a value indeed, but no worth, may be represented by the man, who, being asked, "what is the use of rivers," replied, "to feed canals." It includes all those who find in Nature, no higher use than to serve the convenience of man, and whose rule of appreciation is bodily pleasure and advantage. Such a man would see more beauty in a snug brick dwelling-house, than in all the glories of the Parthenon. I once heard of a lad, not remarkable for intelligence, who gravely propounded the query, "what becomes of the fire, when it goes out." Were I to choose between the two, I could not but prefer the dawning sense of mystery implied in that question, to the unthinking complacency of him, who can perceive in fire, one of the most wonderful of nature's powers and combinations, nothing but the heat it produces. These are your so called practical men!

The character of the *second class* is one step higher and may be defined an *indolent* recipience of forms and colors. They prefer a circle to a square, a smooth surface to a rough one, the graceful curve of a spreading elm to the ragged and straggling branches of an apple-tree—because Nature has, in the very frame of man, made it necessary that he should be better pleased with one of these forms than the other; he likes to see the rainbow, and a gorgeous sunset, and prefers a green meadow to a brown and barren heath, because no one who has a notion of colors, can help being pleased with such sights. He bends to the coercing impulses of his nature thus far, but falls back and deserts her here, simply for want of thought. To a mind working differently, or working at all, a sunset is more than form and color. Its own fancy invests every object of vision, with new light and beauty. The clouds far off in the sky are transformed into the snow-clad and everlasting Alps and snowy vallies stretching interminably between—again they become golden palaces of rare and surpassing splendor, or frowning and battle-mented castles—again, a single cloud floating along in the sun's track, becomes an island of calmness and repose resting on the bosom of the deep, richer than the gardens of the [181] Hesperides, and more peaceful than the fabled Atlantis. Why does the same object strike two persons so differently? Simply because the mind of one is dormant, in relation to this subject; and of the other active, and the constant and sole creator of its own enjoyment. Indeed it is an universal truth applying to the study of Nature of every kind—that the discoveries which we suppose we make in her works, are the sole products of our minds. The feelings, principles, ideas, have their first if not their only being there, and are disclosed to our consciousness, by an outward and natural correspondence. The scientific laws, for instance, seem to have been constituted on the principles of geometry, the elements of which are not in nature though its materials are, but are generated in the reason, and exist for it alone. So the sentiments of beauty, grandeur, order, harmony, the feelings of interest and attachment, are in and for the soul alone, existing there anterior to the circumstances which occasion their developement, and independent of them. This is very manifest in the *Third Class*—those in whom the feelings and sentiments which certain objects excite, are local, arbitrary, and personal—arising in all men, yet from no common principle—taking different forms, attaching to different objects, and dependent on associations peculiar to each individual or tribe. The peculiarity of this class seems to be, that each imparts to the object of his regard, and thus finds in it, some human interest, associating it in some way, with the worth and joy, or with the sorrow and feebleness of humanity. The branching elm or the silvered sycamore, which shaded the sports of our childhood, will not be easily forgotten. The brook which witnessed our first exploits in trout-fishing, the well, with its rickety sweep and mossy curb-stone, which slaked our thirst, and the sloping green sward, where we refreshed ourselves after the labors of the day were over, will recur to us with a feeling, which we cannot impart to another, and which another cannot feel. The Swiss pedlar, as he returns from his wearisome pilgrimage, and catches a glimpse of the iced top of the highest Alps, enjoys in that sight what the curious tourist knows nothing of—he sees in some deep valley far beneath that summit, the cottage where his boyish days were spent, the form of his sister, or perchance one dearer, fading in the distance as he parted from her, and receives again his mother's last kiss, his father's blessing. In the same class is the superstitious man, who finds a peculiar value in a fragment of the cord, which has [182] ended the life of a felon, and the Enthusiast who finds it in a wilted leaf from the tomb of Virgil.

In the *Fourth Class*, the predominant idea, is that of active powers, and principles enveloped by material forms. To such an eye a single plant or tree presents a mystery for almost endless meditation—not merely a curious collection of matter, juices and solids, bark and fibres, a pleasant greenness and a beautiful shape—there is something beneath all this—a system of living agencies, each working out its own purpose, and all tending by mutual inter and counter action, to a single and grand ultimate result. The skeleton of this view is the science of physiology—the Spirit, an inner and peculiar life.

The *fifth* and last view of Nature which I shall mention, is the Christian, the crown and glory of which is that in every form and work it sees plainly the hand of God. A human Spirit, walking in the twilight of reason, must, it would seem, almost unavoidably take refuge in pantheism and polytheism, to satisfy its religious wants. And the likelihood of his choosing one or the other, would depend mainly on his greater or less cultivation. One who perceives the many various powers which the world every where presents to his observation, each in appearance working separately, and accomplishing its own end, would naturally deify each—if he had not by long discipline risen to apprehend the unity, which pervades and animates all things. And *with* this idea, if not spiritually instructed, he would consider the whole system as itself *the* unity, a vast animated principle, and worship this *one*, as the all in all. But we, whose reason has been illuminated and informed, by a personal revelation of him, who is the ground of all being, and for the knowledge and manifestation of whom, we are taught that the material no less than the moral universe was created—we cannot fail to discern him, in all things. To us the precept of the Son of Sirach might be a rule in all our contemplations of nature. "Look upon the rainbow, and praise Him who made it; very beautiful is it in the brightness thereof; it compasseth the heaven about with a glorious circle, and the hands of the Most High have bended it."

But not only does the world persuade us of power and wisdom in the Framer of it. Every where around us, we find single products, which, taken singly, distinctly express to us the idea of beauty—manifold in the appearances, which reveal it, yet in each and all the same magnificent idea. Thus as the [183] firmament of heaven is reflected no less distinctly in a fountain, or in a dew drop, than in the ocean, so every order of created things in its proportion, and the vast whole according to its measure, is a true type of the Infinite, Eternal, Uncreated Beauty.

And further still—Nature does not merely shadow forth to us the ideal beauty and the perfections of the Deity. As man, though a spirit, is akin to earth, and was fashioned of it, and made to reach knowledge, through his organized connection with it; so in the constitution of things *it* was made a counterpart and to us a symbol of the moral world, of which we also form a part, and which is wonderfully within the material world, and yet above it, and for the sustaining and exhibition of which the material world was framed. Not that every moral truth has its adequate representation in nature; but the resemblances are numberless, our poetry and common language are full of them, and the mind that searches cannot fail to find them. Light is a symbol of knowledge, the water lily of hope and faith. The relation of a child to its parent is an earthly similitude of the high and cheering truth that God is "the Father of our spirits."

A profoundly meditative mind, recently gone from among us, speaking of Nature as a revelation, furnishes a proof and an example:

"It has been the music of gentle and pious minds in all ages, it is the poetry of all human nature, to read it in a figurative sense, and to find their correspondencies and symbols of the spiritual world. I have at this moment before me, in the flowery meadow, on which my eye is now reposing, one of its most soothing chapters, in which there is no lamenting word, no one character of guilt or anguish. For never can I look and meditate on the vegetable creation without a feeling similar to that with which we gaze at a beautiful infant that has fed itself asleep at its mother's bosom, and smile in its strange dream of obscure, yet happy sensations. The same tender and genial pleasure takes possession of me, and this pleasure is checked and drawn inward, by the same whispered remonstrance, and made restless by a similar impulse of aspiration. It seems as if the soul said to herself; from this state hast thou fallen! Such shouldest thou still become! But what the plant *is* by an act, not its own and unconsciously, *that* must thou *make* thyself to *become!* must by prayer and by unresisting spirit *join* at least, with the preventive and assisting grace, to *make* thyself, in that light of con- [184] science which inflameth not, and with that knowledge which puffeth not up." *

And though the resemblances are often fanciful, if controlled by a sound discretion, and a pure mind, they may not mislead or be profitless. I will give one more example from a sketch of great beauty by Mrs. Hemans—the Woodwalk. A father is telling his son, the significancy popularly ascribed to certain plants—among others the arum leaf, "the folding leaf with dark brown stains:"

> "These deep inwrought marks
> The villager will tell thee
> Are the flower's portion from the atoning blood
> On Calvary shed. Beneath the cross it grew,
> And in the vase-like hollow of its leaf,
> Catching from that dread shower of agony,
> A few mysterious drops; transmitted thus
> Unto the groves and hills their sealing stains."

Of the conditions under which one may attain some true insight into the meaning of Nature I shall mention only two. It will be doubtless understood however, that a certain degree of mental culture is a necessary pre-requisite, and that this degree must be enlarged as the mind makes progress in this knowledge. But more intimately connected with this study of Nature, as that on which success essentially depends, is the right cultivation of the tastes and sentiments, and these are the constitutive elements of what is commonly intended by the love of Nature. Not less essential, at least to its richest enjoyment and highest kind, are a clear moral discernment, and daily and familiar meditation on objects of moral interest, the chastening of the affections and the purifying of the heart. Among pagan nations even the most refined, the love of Nature has never so far as we know, been a prominent feature of character national or individual. The barrenness of the Greek and Roman classics in this respect is remarkable. Taste is not religion. The contemplation of nature is not the contemplation of God. But communion with God is the best preparation for the followship with nature, and that spirit only which has come awed, and humbled, and blissful from His presence is fully fitted for it.

One condition is an active sense of mystery. This is of a complex nature, resulting from restless ignorance and unsatis- [185] fied curiosity. It is the surest and most permanent ground of continued intellectual and moral advancement, superior to the vulgar stimulants of avarice and ambition, in the degree of its effects, as it is more lasting in its operation, and more excellent in its kind. In this most of all are men deficient. Childhood is full of it—but as the boyish questioner is too often unable to find an answer in himself, and is seldom aided by his elders, and is thus compelled to postpone his satisfaction till experience shall have made him wiser, he grows up to a forgetfulness of his own queries, in a familiarity with all wonders, which impairs his perceptions, and he becomes blind indeed. Still Nature is full of mystery, overshadowing and alluring to him who contemplates her aright; and he who has not sometime felt that the humblest flower asked him questions, he could not answer, and that the origin,

---

* Coleridge's Aids, p. 376, Am. Ed.

and growth and decay of an affection was an enigma he could not unravel, may be deemed almost hopeless for growth and for good.

I have already intimated that while nature contains ideas and principles which she discloses to the soul that is fitted to receive them; the sentiments which she expresses to us are often the original creations of our own feelings, and are found in nature because they are first found in us. The second condition then must obviously be a harmony of our Spirit with the Spirit of the Universe. I do not speak of a coincidence of our will with the Supreme will, or a correspondence of our affections with His Laws, or an obedience to the laws of matter—though the latter would be a valuable auxiliary to this attainment, and the former its highest and completing form—but of a harmony of our temper with the general aspects and, as I may say, feelings of Nature. Doubtless she speaks a various language—she has a voice of sympathy for the saddened and the mourning, gently rebukes and recalls the erring, and with fine and delicate influences heals the broken hearted. But the conflicts of the passions are alien and uncongenial— she withdraws from such, like Astraea to an upper sky of peace and rest. The proud and the vain find no response, for to them she is a stranger. In the heart which is the dwelling of sensuality and earthliness, her wings are clogged and her bright plumage tarnished, by its foul and pestilent mists. But she resides alway with the pure, the meek, and the holy. She loves best a gladsome spirit, and he who has issuing from his own breast a stream of deep, gentle, joyful feeling, who is full of the tender impulses of humanity and quietly fulfilling [186] all the offices of love, shall find her dwelling within him, as light and music in a gushing fountain.

It may not be amiss to hint at a few of the reasons, which seem to attach something of peculiar worth to this Love and Study of Nature, though he who possesses the love, and has made any attainment in the study, can hardly need them, and he who has not, may not readily apprehend their pertinence or feel their force.

Man has not too many sources of enjoyment, and he may not in honesty of heart, turn away from any indication of one, till he has fairly tried it; though the discipline which leads to it may be peculiar, and require even that the thoughts and feelings be remodelled, old principles displaced and new ones awakened in the soul. A greener vegetation may shoot up from the decayed and moulded trunk. The gratifying of this love of nature furnishes a real enjoyment, as he who feels it well knows, and which he who has it not, cannot deny. It is pure too, for it is communion with the pure. Nature stands in her main forms and energies, as God made her—perfect. The elements work freely and harmoniously. The taint of sin is not there, "the trail of the serpent" has not passed over them, the images of nature cannot defile. And being thus pure and perfect, they aid to cherish the sense of beauty, and establish the principles of taste in the mind which contemplates them. Nay, the cultivation of taste is but a developement of the idea of the perfect, which idea, when man meditates on himself, he finds not at all, or only by contrast; while he finds it in nature direct and manifest.

In the character of every individual man, from the various principles running through it, all of which modify and influence one another, almost any one may be selected, and under certain limitations, fairly considered as the type of the man; and this because there is an essential affinity among the principles of human thought and feeling, by which those of the same kind are allied and made to coalesce. A true relish for simple beauty is seldom joined with habits of sensuality, for they are of diverse natures and will not blend. The feeling of compassion usually associates with itself, mildness, patience, forbearance. Thus a Love of Nature, by the peculiar sympathy which exists between them, attracts to itself, and sustains, and strengthens all the "finer issues" of our being—pure and steadfast affection, a preferring attachment to the true, the generous, the noble, a [187] reverence for order, and a sense of dependency, a delicate sentiment of beauty and propriety diffusing itself over all objects of human regard, a fondness for the social, the domestic, the homebred. The Lover of Nature can hardly be an undutiful son, he can hardly fail to be a better father, a more obedient subject, and a holier Christian. Indeed all these gradations of character are but stages, high yet subordinate, in the education of man for the higher and spiritual duties of religion. The character thus formed is fitted to apprehend and embrace religious truth— there is a correspondence, and a tallying of one with the other. A man thus trained is more likely, other things being equal, to become a Christian, and having become one, he is more likely to be true and faithful, because he has auxiliars to his spiritual life, which none other has, and which make his sight the stay and upholding of his faith.

"The Angel of the Lord encampeth round about them that fear him," is verified to him in another sense than that of protection. Nature, a sealed book to the sealed mind, becomes as "the mountain full of chariots and horses of fire" to the opened eyes of the servant of the prophet—her rebukes, and warnings, and encouragements and consolations are every where around him—in the stable mountain, and the fleeting cloud, the falling dew and the unheeded and down trodden weed.

X

THE TRUE MESSIAH*
By G. OEGGER

Introduction

There is but one way to form to ourselves a just and exact idea of the person of Jesus Christ. This is, to bring ourselves into a state in which we shall not profane the holy truth. If we succeed, (a condition without which God is forced to blind us,) we must then look attentively and impartially at the Old and New Testaments. The first of these conditions depends principally on individuals and on Him who holds in his hand the heart of man; but history is within the domain of criticism, and reasoning may be submitted to analysis. It is then under this last interesting point of view that we intend to perform a useful task. We hope to infuse into the spirits of our readers, some portion of the salutary convictions which, for some years, have been our sweetest consolation. We draw some hope of success from the career we have run; which has brought us to those points of view, from which we could perceive the strong and the weak sides of most of the philosophical and religious opinions in vogue in the nineteenth century. An idea of the language of nature, must necessarily arouse the curiosity of even those who are most indifferent on the subject of religion; and that idea is the predominent one in our work. Yet, to shorten a work which may still be too serious for the frivolous tendency of the age, we shall confine ourselves principally to Saint John, the most sublime of the evangelists, only tracing back, occasionally, to these two principal sources, the most striking passages of the other extatic writers. Anticipating, on the other hand, the impatience of those readers who, before engaging in our dissertations, inquire what will be the result of the examination which we propose to make, we will here declare directly, that this examination may result for him as it has resulted for us—in the belief of the absolute divinity of Jesus Christ, and the thorough conviction that he who believes this, believes the whole truth. Such a promise is well worth the trouble of reading some pages with attention, even though it be previously known that the subject is to be Christianity. The distinction of truth into Christian truth and philosophical truth, is an absurdity which should never have entered any well organized mind. We will inform the reader, then, that, when we began [4] our work, we were, what he perhaps is, a deist, or something very near it, and that, when we finished it, we found ourself a Christian, and a Christian more deeply convinced than any theologian, because our conviction was the result of the free and lawful use of our individual reason. Indeed, the evidence accumulated by this new method of studying the holy books, which consists in reading them as written, from beginning to end, in the language of nature, are more than sufficient to convince any man of good faith, or rather any man of good will, that Jesus Christ was not merely an extraordinary man, or a Prophet, greater than the others; that he was not merely an image of divinity, a spark of divinity, or an eternal Son of God, distinct from him as to personality; but that he was Jehovah himself, Jehovah in person; that, by making himself Jesus Christ, the hidden God, the metaphysical and incomprehensible God manifested himself; that it was by making himself Jesus Christ, that the infinite Being entered into communication with finite beings engrossed in matter; in a word, that, by appearing on the confines of his creation, to show his erring children as much love as he had shown them power, the God became also Redeemer.

---

* The True Messiah; or The Old and New Testaments, examined according to the Principles of the Language of Nature, Boston (Pub. by E. P. Peabody), 1842, p. 3ff. (Copy in Boston Public Library.) This work is a translation of the introductory portions of Oegger's Le Vrai Messie, Paris, 1829, apparently made by Miss Peabody herself. It was probably her uncorrected manuscript that Emerson used in July and August, 1835. See Journals, III, 505, 506, 512, 525, 527.

Our ideas will, without doubt, appear extraordinary to more than one class of readers; but who will dare to reproach us for them? When, in the nineteenth century, Christianity still appears in so precarious a state that philosophy dares to doubt its ultimate triumph, what danger can there be in trying some great means? Does not an impartial view of Christian society, for eighteen hundred years past, with its hateful and inconceivable divisions, authorize us in suspecting that, from the first, some great error has been committed which has obstructed the work of the regeneration of the universe? and that, in consequence, there is some great obstacle which must be removed before truth can make its way? Is it not more than probable that the Infidels, and all those Christians, who are Christians only in name, would long ago have embraced the true faith, if the true faith had been rightly presented to them? Is it not more than probable that the miserable descendants of Israel, as well as those of our philosophers, who seek truth sincerely, would long ago have acknowledged the God who has manifested himself upon our globe, if his majesty had not been degraded, as it were, before their eyes? If, in consequence, our deep conviction should be charged with temerity, if our courage should occasion scandal, we shall not retract, convinced as we are, with Saint Chrysostom, that, even if truth should cause scandal, it were better even to suffer this scandal than to let truth perish.

What has most emboldened us in this great enterprise, is the entire certainty that we have acquired, of being definitely on the road to that language of Nature, which, as every one will easily conceive, must have preceded all languages of convention; in which, indeed, we have found the greater part of our holy books to be written, and which sheds over them collectively a light too strong and unexpected for deism to resist.

Nothing is more comfortable to sound philosophy than the belief in the primitive existence of a language of nature. The greatest names in the learned world stand at the head of those philosophers who have occupied themselves with what they called a universal language, of which, accordingly, they experienced the advantages, and which they [5] did not believe it impossible to realize upon our globe among educated men. The only difference between the language of nature and that of which our philosophers had conceived the idea is, that the former would be of less service in our terrestrial relations than in those in which we are one day to stand, with the universality of beings, in that world in which all other worlds flow together, and in which we shall need means of communication much more extensive than those required by our material existence.

The philosophical moralist, who is fully convinced of the immortality of man, ought therefore to be convinced also of the actual existence of a language, quite distinct from that which consists in sounds which are articulated by means of the elasticity of the air, and which have merely a conventional meaning. The thinking moralist will easily believe that, even on our terrestrial globe, however material it may now be with its degraded inhabitants, there must have existed, in times of greater perfection, means of communication different from those which are of mere convention; for, to establish conventions, it is absolutely necessary to be able previously to explain one's self. Rousseau advanced the greatest of paradoxes, when he said that the savage state was the primitive state of man: on the contrary, the savage state is nothing but the state of our greatest degradation, when, as we have become incapable of raising ourselves, God is obliged to come to our relief. All knowledge, says Plato, is remembrance, and all ignorance is forgetting. Primitively man must have been perfect, at least, in his kind; and consequently he must have had a perfect language, a language which cannot have been lost but in the lapse of ages, and of which the traces may be found, when Philosophy will direct her researches to that point.

A general idea of the language of nature may be formed, from the application that we have made of its principles to a new explanation of several passages from the Holy Scriptures. We will here offer only a few preliminary reflections which may enable the reader to enter into our whole idea.

People generally have an idea, before they have reflected more profoundly, that when God produced our visible universe, the choice that he made of forms and colors for animals, plants, and minerals, was entirely arbitrary on his part. But this idea is entirely false. Man may sometimes act from whim; God never can. The visible creation, then, can not, must not (if we may use such expressions) be anything but the exterior circumference of the invisible and metaphysical world; and material objects are necessarily *scoriæ* of the substantial thoughts of the Creator; *scoriæ* which must always preserve an exact relation to their first origin; in other words, visible nature must have a spiritual and moral side. For God every thing is, every thing exists: "create" conveys not the same idea to him as to us. For God, to create is only to manifest. The universe, even in its minutest details, existed for God as really before the creation as after it, because it existed in him substantially, as the statue exists in the block of marble from which the sculptor extracts it. By the creation, we only have been enabled to perceive externally a portion of the infinite riches existing in the divine essence. The perfect, especially, must have always thus existed in God. The imperfect alone can have received a kind [6] of creation by means of man, a free agent, though under the influence of a Providence which never loses sight of him. Neither the form nor the color, then, of any object in nature, can have been chosen without a reason. Every thing we see, touch, smell; every thing, from the sun to a grain of sand, from our own body with its admirable organs, to that of the worm; every thing has flowed forth, by a supreme reason, from that world where all is spirit and life. No fibre in the animal, no blade of grass in the vegetable kingdom, no form of crystalization in inanimate matter, is without its clear and well-determined correspondence in the moral and metaphysical world. And if this is true of colors and forms, it must, by a still stronger reason, be said of the instincts of animals, and the far more astonishing faculties of man. Consequently the most imperceptible thoughts and affections which we imagine we have conceived by our own power; the compositions which we consider our own in the regions of philosophy and literature; the inventions which we believe we have made in the arts and sciences; the monuments that we think we are erecting; the customs that we fancy we establish in the things which men consider great, as in the most insignificant transactions of civil and animal life; all this existed before us; all this is simply given to us, and given with a supreme reason, according to our different immediate wants. An infinitely little degree of consent to receive, which forms our moral liberty, is the only thing that we have for our own. And merely by an inspection of the objects by which a man is surrounded, or of some of the customs which he has adopted, a superior intelligence can undoubtedly determine the moral worth of his being; for according as moral beings (for whom alone inferior nature exists) modify themselves, that nature must admit emblems analogous to the new perfections or degradations.

And, indeed, but for all these emblems of life which creation offers, there would be no appreciable moral idea or moral sentiment, no possible means, we fear not to say it, for God to communicate a thought, an affection, to his creature, any more than for one feeling creature to communicate it to another. Above all, there would be no possible communication between the present state of man and his state of transformation; all is annihilated, all is broken up in feeling or thinking nature; the most interior life of the intelligent being is effaced and returns to nothing.

This truth may be rendered palpable by examples. If there had never been a father according to nature, could you form any idea of that portion of the goodness of God which corresponds to the tenderness of a father for his children? Could you ever know anything of what paternal tenderness is? If there had never in nature existed a generous man, could you form any conception of what generosity is? If you had never loved anything upon earth, would it be possible for you to have the least idea of what love can be? Or, (to choose our own examples in the descending order,) could you, without the defects, the maladies, and the defilements of the human body, represent to yourself the shameful vices which are analogous to them in the moral man? If you had never seen animals tormented, killed, devoured, could the idea of cruelty and barbarity be communicated to your mind? In fine, if you had never heard anything of the persecutions, the treacheries [7] which sometimes reign upon earth, could your soul receive even the first germ of the ideas of hatred, perfidy, atrocity? The thing really appears impossible.

Besides, the consideration of the necessity of indicating, by visible and tangible emblems, moral distinctions which would be otherwise imperceptible, alone explains those terrible phenomena, those monstrosities and those disgusting images, evidently unworthy of the Creator, which nature offers to the eyes of degraded man. The abyss of our being cannot be revealed, but by the appreciable phenomena of life. It is with us, in this respect, as with the Creator himself, in whose image we were created, and to the knowledge of whom we cannot rise but by means of his visible wonders. Nature is like a book in which we may read the perfections of God, or as a mirror in which we may see them reflected. The same must be said of man, and of the different phenomena

of his manner of living, of feeding and clothing himself. Matter furnishes us with
steps by which to rise to pure substances; and we must have also emblematic substances and images, that we may dart into the moral and metaphysical world; for
which reason the Creator has been obliged to come himself to meet us, crossing the
abyss which separates us from his first essence. As Cre[a]tor, God must have means of
communication analogous to those which he has imparted to us, that we might observe
him. We are created men, and God is uncreated man. It was at the immediate point
between the infinite which is all, and the finite which is nothing, that God and man met.
And this point is life, life manifested, life revealed by emblems. Before all languages of
convention and of articulated sounds, when the Creator wished to manifest or reveal
himself for the first time to man, how could he have done it but by showing himself to
that man under the substantial form of a father, the natural emblem of God Creator?
In truth, the human mind could never find a different emblem, nor imagine any different
means of communicating the first idea of the Creator to any secondary intelligence
whatever. We shall learn, in another place, that, when men would not acknowledge for
their Creator that ineffable Being who appeared to them as Father, that Being must
employ, to defend his rights, the means which we call the Redemption of the human
race, the divine means which he chose to show men that he was wiser, more powerful,
and, above all, better than them all, that immense system, which, led down from the
remotest times, to its entire execution, with an infinite knowledge, wisdom and goodness,
at least overwhelms the mortal whose heart it cannot touch.

The indispensable necessity of what we call emblems of life, shows that our future
existence itself cannot be so metaphysical as is sometimes imagined. There must still
be, in our state of transformation, substantial images, appreciable forms, objects seen,
felt, perceived, as in the material world. If not, any existence whatever, happy or unhappy, is but a real chimera. The future life is, evidently, Berkeley's world. That
philosopher was wrong only in not making a clear distinction between the substance
world and the matter world, or in not perceiving the shade which separates them; for
if it is true that matter exists, it is also true that it has extension and impenetrability
only as far as the Creator wills, and only for the beings whom he designs particularly
for that purpose. If there were really the infinite [8] between matter and spirit, the
impossibility of the creation might be reasonably maintained.*

---

* If we should here be asked, by a very natural curiosity, what we shall see in the
other world, and what we shall do there, we would answer without hesitation, resting on
the indispensable necessity of natural emblems, that we shall there see around us, as in
the material world, a more or less extensive horizon, filled with a greater or less number
of substantial images taken from known nature, and that we shall there be occupied
nearly as we are occupied upon earth when we seek shelter, food and clothing: only
these images will then be in exact correspondence with our moral being: the firmament
representing our celestial relations; the different objects of nature, our social affections;
and the soil which bears us, the nature of our confidence in Him who alone can make it
firm under our feet. As to our different occupations, they will be those which Heaven
shall judge most proper to characterize constantly the interior of our moral being, and
the different ways in which we seek to appropriate to ourselves the spiritual nourishment of love and truth, in other words, to satisfy all our moral wants. All these ideas,
though new, will not surprise those philosophers who know that nature is always
conformable to herself, or, as Leibnitz expresses it, she never does anything by leaps
and bounds. According to this philosophic apothegm, our future existence will, in reality,
differ from the present only by a slight variation; and this variation is that from a
material to a substantial world. We shall pass to the future existence, as we enter into
an agreeable dream; all nature will accompany us there. This truth receives an increase
of probability, or rather of proof, from the fact that, examined without those prejudices
that rise from the vague idea of an infinite power, never checked by the bounds of the
impossible, by simplicity or propriety, I might even say, geometrically examined, the
chain of beings is nearly complete here below in the three kingdoms, and consequently
that the nature which we know, itself contains all the elements necessary to the eternal
happiness of sensitive creatures; which renders alike impossible and useless the destruction of the images of visible nature, for the future existence. It is sentiment which
makes happiness, and not knowledge; and therefore the circle of possible things must be
much more restricted than is commonly thought. Try to suppress the horizon of celes-
t[i]al and terrest[r]ial images by which you are surrounded, the real Eden in which you
are placed; what will remain to form the pretended heaven of a blessed spirit? There
will remain nothing. And if those same images, clothed in an entirely spiritual and moral
character, are sufficient for your happiness, why suppress them, or why even substitute
others for them?

Then, in short, the moral and metaphysical universe, as rising successively to secondary degrees, (that is to say, to all which are not Jehovah,) cannot be conceived possible but by analogous emblems in the universe of phenomena; material phenomena for the physical world, substantial phenomena for that which is not physical. The moral and metaphysical world is, for us, as if anchored, as if rooted in the visible world, upon which it rests as upon an indispensable basis.

Any one may learn these truths from daily experience, without any great reasoning. Do but take a dictionary of morals, and examine the terms in it. You will see that all of them, from the first to the last, are derived from corporeal and animal life. The birth, growth, decay and death of the body, its state of health or of sickness, of strength or of weakness, have alone furnished correspondent ideas in the moral man. Each member of that body, considered in relation to its terrestrial use and employment, offers the same results. All the emblems that can be supplied by agriculture, the arts and trades, the different manners among men of feeding and clothing themselves, have been laid under contribution to furnish the means for characterizing the different varieties of moral and intellectual life, in individuals as in societies; and, but for all those emblems furnished by nature herself, the [9] moral and metaphysical world would have remained entirely buried in the eternal abyss.

Thence, then, the reality of a language of nature, which reality Philosophy should still admit, even if none of the letters of the immense alphabet which was made use of in speaking it, could be found; for that language is, after all, nothing but the perception of the emblems of life and intelligence, which nature contains in her bosom, and the faculty of transmitting that perception to other beings.

Still, we are very far from admitting that the dictionary of the language of nature is entirely lost; the traces of it might be found even in the languages of convention, necessarily derived from it, if the Bible were not alone sufficient to put us in possession of so precio[u]s a science. That book, so little known and so little appreciated by the self-styled enlightened universe, has not served to preserve for us the Hebrew language only, it has also furnished us with all the necessary materials for the understanding of the language of nature.

A certain number of our first ecclesiastical writers, such as the apostle Paul, Lactantius, Origen, Jerome and others, were evidently on the road to that language, as their particular manner of writing demonstrates; but by a secret judgment of Heaven, the precious traces were almost immediately abandoned by their successors. Men have treated these writers as mystics, as they now do all those who profess to see in the word of God something more than in an ordinary book. From the times of Theophilus, says Horsley, the great art of interpreting the Old Testament consisted in finding in everything types and emblems. If, instead of ridiculing this art, men had endeavored to learn how far it was well-founded, they would have better understood the mysteries of the love and wisdom of the Father, and they would not have wandered for eighteen centuries in the labyrinth of human thoughts. The word of God must necessarily be more rich and more fruitful in sense, than all the vain writings of the learned; its meaning must indeed be infinite.

Therefore, by abandoning the false method of the school, which consists in taking each text as if isolated, (by which the most contradictory things may be proved,) and studying the holy books as a whole, we may acquire an absolute certainty that all extatic men, from Abraham to the last of the prophets, and, after them all, the Redeemer himself, though expressing themselves by words of the conventional language in use at that time, yet always spoke the language of nature, and that the sense conveyed by it was the principal, if not the only one which they really meant to transmit to posterity. To speak only of Jesus Christ, it was to that language that he endeavored to accustom his apostles during the three years that he lived with them; it was that language that frequently perplexed them so much, which forced them to solicit explanations of their Master apart, and even to entreat him not [to] speak thus in parables. When a similitude, a comparison, is followed through all its branches, and sustained as long as those of Jesus Christ were, a real language results from it, which is inwoven with the ordinary discourse, and conveys a consistent sense, higher than the natural sense though parallel with it. Only recollect how far Jesus Christ carried the moral signification of the words eat and drink, and you will see that a new dictionary, a dictionary still to be made, is necessary to understand the Holy Scriptures; a book which not only is obscure, but which has been till now [10] closed and sealed in a thousand ways; and that, only by the aid of that dictionary, it will be possible to find the immense riches which the hand of the Eternal has concealed in it. He who has the least idea of the emblems of nature and their signification, reads the Bible as if with a microscope; he sees in it what he had never seen in it before; it seems to him like another book. It is like Egyptian hieroglyphics read by means of Champollion's system. Jesus Christ says, "Man lives by the word of God, as he lives by bread." The grain of which bread is made is that divine word. Bread is the substance of God, which man ought to appropriate to himself, because God is goodness and truth, and the moral man should be nothing else. Therefore the body and flesh of Jesus Christ are also that bread; because Jesus Christ is nothing but the Word or Divine Truth, incarnated through love for man. The daily bread recalls a daily appropriation of goodness and truth, which are God. The miraculous multiplications of bread, wrought by Jesus Christ, signify the abundance of the examples of virtue provided for men by infinite mercy. I have bread to eat that you know not of, said the Lord to the apostles; my food is to do the will of my Father. He who eats of the bread that I give him, shall not die, but he shall live forever. And this bread is my own flesh; you must eat me, or you can have no life in you. Inconceivable and repulsive expressions in the sense of the conventional language, but, in the language of nature, equally rich and true! I am, says Jesus Christ again, the bread of life come down from Heaven, grossly figured by the manna which your fathers ate in the desert: my flesh is consequently a true nourishment, as my blood is a true drink. And that, adds he, ought not to offend you; for these words are spirit and life; the flesh, inasmuch as it is flesh, profiteth nothing. Take and eat this bread in remembrance of me, says he, the evening before his death; it is the body which will be delivered for you to-morrow; and that means—Appropriate to yourself constantly more and more truth and love, which are God, by remembering unceasingly my examples. See, I stand at the door and knock; if any man will open to me, I will enter, and eat with him, and he with me.

Who does not see that the eating here spoken of, is entirely spiritual? and that these last words especially must be translated thus: If any man will open to me his heart, I will love him and he will love me. God cannot eat with us in any other way than by love, nor, consequently, we with him. That other passage of Saint John, where Jesus Christ says, Even as I live by the Father, so shall he who will eat with me live by me, makes this truth so clear, that the most marked folly alone could doubt it.

But this is not all. The comparison of material manducation, with the appropriation of love and truth which constitute the happiness of immortal man, is carried still farther in the Gospel. The sower, it is there said, is God; the field in which he sows, is the heart of man, in which that seed is to germinate; it is a whole church which is to bear fruit in the time of harvest. The wheat represents men loving God; the light straws, chaff,—souls without moral worth. The granary contains the riches of heaven; the fire of hell consumes the tares. The fan is the judgment upon the good and the bad. Three measures of flour or dough represents the kingdom of the heavens; the leaven of the Pharisees, false doctrines, hateful disputes. Even the mill pre- [11] serves an analogous signification; at the renewal of the Church two women shall be turning the mill-stone in a mill; the one shall be taken, the other left. Because of their different manner of announcing the word of God, such a particular church will be approved, such another disapproved, at the time of the arrival of the Son of Man. A mill-stone, hung to the neck of a scandalous man, and thrown with him into the sea, will be a blessing to him; for that mill-stone represents the means of appropriating to himself the word of God, and the sea is merely a collection of natural truths, by which man may be prepared for the reception of divine truths, as we shall soon see; water being everywhere in the discourses of Jesus Christ, the emblem of truth.

As to eat, is to appropriate to ourselves the love of God, or moral goodness, so to drink, is to appropriate to ourselves his truth. Truth dilutes goodness, which, otherwise, could not incorporate with our soul, as goodness without truth is not appreciable to creatures; or, in other words, as goodness manifested thereby becomes truth. If you had asked water of me, said Jesus Christ to the Samaritan woman, I would have given you water which springs up into everlasting life. He who will drink the water that I shall give him, shall never thirst again. He who receives my doctrine, rivers of water shall spring up from his heart. These words need no commentary; nor do these, which Jesus Christ pronounced aloud while teaching in the temple: Let him who thirsts, come and drink. Follow me, I will make you fishers of men, said he to the apostles when he associated them in the preaching of the Gospel; for, from natural truths, they were to raise men to spiritual knowledges. Thence the custom of baptism, which is evidently only the emblem of the acquisition of the true doctrine, leading man to repentance and reformation; for, we repeat it, water, as making the mirror and reflecting the images of objects, is the hieroglyphic of truth, even more than of purification. Wine and blood, in the mouth of Jesus Christ, considered as drinks, have analogous significations. Only, these emblems will be of a higher degree; blood being nearer life, and moistening the very flesh of men and animals, while water generally moistens only the objects on which they feed; and wine, on the other hand, having more affinity with the spirit of man whose heart it rejoices, according to the emblematic expression of David; the only reason why they play so great a part in the Holy Scriptures, in which mention is constantly made of the blood of victims and of the vine of the Lord; of the ancient law, and of the blood of the Lamb, of the wine that makes the virgins of the new law to germinate. The first miracle of Jesus Christ was changing of water into wine, because the principal object of his Advent was to change natural truths into divine truths, and to substitute his doctrine for that of human wisdom. New wine is put into new bottles, he says, speaking of that doctrine. Take and drink, cried he, at the Last Supper, after having long prepared the apostles for such a language, take and drink; this wine is the blood of the new covenant; this is my blood which is shed for the remission of sins; this is the New Testament in my blood. And the apostles so well understood the signification of all these discourses of their Master, that they afterwards generally gave the name of New Testament to the volume which contains his doctrine. The blood of Jesus Christ, then, wherever it is spoken of in the Gospel, recalls and represents the collection of the truths of salvation announced by him to the world; truths which the [12] world refused to receive, as it proved by the fact, and by a material emblem, by shedding, upon Calvary, the blood of the Redeemer. And the same is to be said of wine; for wine itself is only an emblem of blood. I will drink no more of this juice of the vine until I drink it new in my Father's kingdom, must signify, as will be fully proved in the body of our work, the complete union of divine truth and divine love in the person of Jesus Christ; in other words, the glorification of the Word in the heavens. When we know thus the real signification of the words eat and drink (inasmuch as these actions are moral emblems,) we can easily find the reason for the choice of those words, cup and platter, which Jesus Christ uses in this reproach to the Pharisees: Blind Pharisee, cleanse first the inside of the cup and platter, that the outside may be clean also. Man, as the receptacle of God's goodness, is represented by the platter; and, as the receptacle of His truth, by the cup. In a material vessel, the purity of the exterior, as is well known, does not necessarily follow from the purity of the interior. We perceive also that these words, happy are they who hunger and thirst after righteousness, are not chosen without reason, but that they are entirely in the genius of the language of nature. And, finally, we clearly understand that obscure text of Saint John: There are three in heaven who bear witness, the Father, the Word, and the Spirit; and these three are but one same thing: there are also three who bear witness upon earth; spirit, water, and blood, and these three relate to the same thing; in which water signifies the natural truths which announce God; blood, the evangelical truths which reveal him; and spirit, the invisible action of Him who alone can make us perceive any truth whatever, even if announced to us by a prophet. These three relate to the same thing, because reason and the Gospel, and extatic persons, speaking by the spirit, agree in declaring that the true God is no other than the Christ manifested in the flesh. We shall see, elsewhere, that Father is God in his essence, or as to his love and his power: Word, God in his form, or truth, divine wisdom, which has been called Speech or Son; and Spirit, God in his immediate action upon the soul, or the interior of all spiritual beings.

The knowledge of natural emblems, or of the universal language, has thrown, upon the whole word of God such a light, that even the mystery of the holy supper is fully revealed. Is it possible, indeed, after observing all the correspondences, which we have here pointed out to our readers, and after recollecting that Jesus Christ had said that his body was bread, before he said that bread was his body; and that before saying that wine was his blood, he had said that blood was truth—is it possible for any one to misunderstand it? Is it not clear as daylight that, in all this, he spoke only of the appropriation of the divine love and divine truth. And is not that dogma of the transubstantiation, which has had the effect of keeping men away from the holiest and most touching practice upon earth or in the heavens; is it not as absurd as it would be to attempt to maintain that the word of God is really corn, that Jesus Christ is a real vine, or that evangelical truths are indeed water and blood?*

[13] It would be easy for us to make the same remarks upon a number of other natural emblems, which were familiar to Jesus Christ in his instructions; such as stone, sand, house, door, shepherd, sheep, tree, sun, moon, stars; by which it may be seen, beyond a doubt, that, even in his apparently most simple discourses, he always spoke the language of nature. Stone, to select that example, is God, the eternal rock, and the eternal truth, general principles, mother truths, are particular stones detached from this rock; a house, a temple, built with these stones, is a religious system perfectly consistent in all its parts; built upon the rock, your house is eternal as God; built upon the incoherent sand of human thoughts, the torrent of tribulations overturns it; a whole city, founded upon the rock, is a collection of regular and unshakeable systems; built upon a mountain, such a city enlightens a whole country; finally, built entirely of precious stones, that same city is the general union of all the divine truths which can work the salvation of the human race; in other words, it is the New Jerusalem coming down out of heaven from God.

We must, in consequence, know something of the language of nature; we must have studied the genius of it a little, before we can understand what the extatic men intended to say; and, for want of this science, Rome, as well as the other Christian societies, successively detached from her, by the increase of light, have very naturally misinterpreted the Gospel upon different points. Indeed, it would be miraculous if this were not the case. For, how could men but be misled, when they took, grossly and literally, the words Father, Son, eat, drink, go up, come down, send, in discourses in which the divine essence only is spoken of? The truths of salvation were unavoidably enveloped in a human language by Him who came out from eternal splendors to visit our obscure retreat; and, to have the pure gold and silver of doctrine and truth, we must know how to separate his language from the dross and the scoriæ. The emblematic language is, as we have shown, founded upon the very nature of things; any other language would have been absurd in the mouth of God Redeemer. Discourses addressed to only a fraction of the creation of beings, would have been unworthy of Jesus Christ. The language of nature, or the universal language, has advantages which no conventional one can unite. That alone can be rendered as rich and concise as the Creator judges necessary on occasion; that alone can be understood in the eternal society of the univer- [14] sality of beings, in which the simple idea of a language, by articulate sounds, would appear an absurdity. Even while he made use of a conventional language as an instrument, the Being of beings still addressed himself to his whole creation, by weaving into that another language which was universal. In effect, the creation is to him but a unity; and it must always be comprehensible to all beings, from the highest angel to the most perverse of the demons; with only this difference, that the more intelligence a being has, the better he unravels the sense of these oracles; while he who is unworthy to receive them, seeing, seeth not, and hearing, understandeth not. This object, we repeat, is indispensable in the relations of the Creator with a society of degraded beings, and it can be attained only by natural emblems.

And if the contemporaries of Jesus Christ did not comprehend all the riches of his doctrine, it is because it could not and ought not to be: I should still have many things to say to you, but you are not now in a state to understand them, said the Lord to the

---

* I conjure those of my Roman Catholic brethren who still believe in a literal transmutation of substances, not to regard the word absurd as an insulting attack: nothing but the force of truth could wrest it from me. It will soon be seen that I also oppose, frequently and forcibly, not the Most Holy and Most Adorable Trinity, before which every created intelligence ought to be as nothing, but a Trinity of really distinct persons —and this without any hostile intention. I know that these two important points were so difficult to understand, without the knowledge of the language of nature, that all the errors into which they have led mankind, are excusable. As God was triple, it was easy to believe him three, and not to love him the less for it. Jesus Christ, in the idea of transcendental philosophy, might be supposed to be placed entirely out of time and space, even considered as man; and, therefore, some might easily persuade themselves of the possibility of eating, more or less really, the flesh of the Son of Man, and yet be very faithful and very loving Christians. In the eyes of the Lord, the zeal of the heart easily effaces the mistakes of the mind. And one proof that the errors we have mentioned, though serious in themselves, could be tolerated till now, is, that Eternal Wisdom has not seen fit to correct them sooner.

apostles. What would now be thought of Jesus Christ, if, to make his divine nature understood at his time, he had said, for example, suppressing the emblems of Father and Son: The first cause is the universal I; I who speak to you, I am that same universal I, particularly manifested! The world was really not then sufficiently advanced. It was necessary for the human race to be cultivated by degrees, under the influence of spirit and virtue from on high; it was requisite for it to learn to reflect profoundly; for it to rise, with Philosophy, entirely above the notions of time and space, that it might appreciate all the discourses and all the steps of its Eternal Benefactor. But that blessed epoch has arrived in its turn. Not only isolated individuals, but the whole mass of the human race is now ready to enter truly into the views of divine love. Eighteen hundred years have but just passed, and the eternal plan of God Redeemer may be developed! A third explosion of infinite mercy, to use the expression of a philosophical journal, may take place; and, at the moment when the universe believes itself nearest to deism, it may be on the point of becoming more truly Christian than it has ever been before.

Finding ourselves thus placed on the road to the language of nature, by the inspired books, we may now, without fear of being misled, cite some of the emblems of nature, which men themselves have preserved in their speech without knowing that they really belonged to a distinct language. Thus the general instinct of mankind has long since determined the moral signification of the sun, as well as that of his heat and light. The sun has always been the principal emblem of the Divinity upon earth; his heat that of love, and his light that of truth: thence, in times of superstition and barbarity, the adoration of the sun, and the worship of fire, was found with almost all people. Gold also signifies, generally among all nations, what is precious; stone, what is solid; fat, what is rich; and a hundred other emblems, which it would be tedious to repeat. In general, the fewer conventional words people had, the more they needed natural emblems; and when they had no conventional terms at all, which is quite conceivable, at least of moral terms, then they had absolutely nothing but emblems in their language.

There is one of these emblems at which we must stop, for a moment, because of its importance; it is that of man, which has not always [15] been remarked as much as those that are without us; because exterior objects generally strike us much more than our own being. In all times, some profound minds have perceived that man was the most perfect possible emblem; consequently, the natural and true emblem of all that can be called intelligence and life. The name microcosm, or world in little, given to man by the ancient sages, would be enough to prove it. The human form is, in truth, a real form of love and wisdom; capable, in itself alone, of characterizing all the possible varieties of the moral being, taken in its complex state. Living, intelligent existence could not have any other form than the human. The angel is nothing but the man spirit, or the substantial man. And God himself, when we would reflect on him, is really conceived by the human mind in no other way than as a divine man. The divine man is the only perceptible side of God; his infinite essence remaining eternally concealed in that man or in that form, which we conceive not as void and metaphysical, in the sense ordinarily attached to that word; but full and substantial; since God, to appear as man, need not create that man; he needs only show him. Another thing that renders man so interesting an emblem, is the relation in which he stands to all the other living beings that we perceive upon the earth. After this king of nature, all other animals, always less perfect forms of life, always inclining the head more and more towards the ground, are emblems of the different varieties of degraded life or intelligence. When man is what he ought to be, he differs from the angel only by the weight of matter; when man degrades himself, he runs through all the degrees of inferior life, figured by animals; each animal, by its forms and instincts, offering a particular variation of that life. The whole quadrant, from the zenith to the horizon, or from the perpendicular to the horizontal line, is thus filled up. Man and the serpent form the right angle; other animals fill the whole quadrant; and any other kind of beings is geometrically impossible.

We will not here cite a greater number of natural emblems to prove our theory; the body of our work will supply them in abundance; for, in looking, under this same point of view, upon all the objects of nature, both dead and living, and on the innumerable phenomena that they present in a whole globe as in every atom of that globe, it must be seen clearly that, always preserving a real, though distant relation with some variety of life or intelligence, they not only may serve to characterize them, but that they really do characterize them. Even the dust and the dirt have also their fixed significations. They represent all that is low and vile; for the low, the vile, the abject, and the disgusting, are found, in the moral world, by the side of the great, the noble, and the elevated. It is evidently from a dim remembrance of all those necessary relations between the moral and phenomenal worlds, that man derives his decided taste for comparisons, of which all the other figures of rhetoric are, in fact, only varieties. Thence comes man's irresistible taste for fables and parables; those sure means of making the multitude receive ideas of the just and the unjust, but by which people have been too often led to compose absurd mythologies. The passage from the language of nature to languages of convention, was made by such insensible degrees that they who made it never thought of tracing the latter back to their source. They knew [16] not the road they had traveled; but the distance appeared striking when they became attentive to it. Primitively, men could not name objects, they must show them; not corporeally, it is true, but substantially and by the force of thought; as those objects exist in God, and as we still perceive them in dreams, in which there is evidently something more than imagination.*

An immediate communication of thoughts and sentiments is quite as conceivable, and even more simple than all those which are made by means more or less distant; and such a communication is so rich that it suffers no comparison with the poverty of all the others. When that primitive faculty of seeing and showing the immediate object of thought, and the natural emblem of sentiment was weakened, then, only, exterior signs came to join it. Thence the language of gestures, spoken at first more particularly by the eyes, the mouth, and the particular composition of the face, which at length introduced conventional sounds, and all exterior signs, such as are still found among the deaf and dumb; and, finally, those offered by hieroglyphics and writing the Scripture. At the epoch when the two manners of speaking (that by natural emblems and that by articulate sounds) were mixed, then resulted the language which is now called prophetic or extatic, in which conventional words are used only to recall the more significant emblems of nature.

It is in this last language, evidently double, we repeat, that we have found to be written the greater number of the books which antiquity has transmitted to us as inspired. To understand the Bible, therefore, it is not enough to understand the Hebrew, the Greek, the Latin, or any other idiom into which it is translated; but it is necessary also to understand the language of nature; for the sacred writers, primitively, borrowed from the language used in their times, only the words necessary to retrace the natural images which speak of themselves. Hence those strange things found in the prophets, which have so much shocked superficial philosophers; those monstrous images, uniting the discordant members of many different animals; for, in speaking of collective societies, or of different traits of moral character in the same individual, the prophets were forced to amalgamate primitive emblems, and to form of them compounds, such as are remarked, principally, in Ezekiel, Daniel, and Saint John. All that was entirely in the genius of the language of nature, and, consequently in the essence of things; and to ridicule the animals, the horns, the wheels covered with eyes, of the prophets, the white horse of the Apocalypse, is like those ignorant beings who laugh when they see Chinese writing or Egyptian hieroglyphics.†

[17] Such are the considerations that have induced us to publish this essay. Studying the Holy Scriptures ourselves, with this new key, we have seen so clearly the real intentions of the Creator and Redeemer of the human race, that we should deem ourselves guilty, if we did not impart our ideas to a world, so bewildered in all its religious conceptions, that scarce anything is to be found in it but atheism or superstition.

Besides, the present is not an unfavorable moment to call on the world to examine anew, to examine seriously and reflectingly, those great events which have substituted Christianity for idolatry, upon our globe. The philosophy of the nineteenth century is really not that of the eighteenth. Since the last European revolutions, which were moral

---

* Unless it be admitted that by that imagination we can form Berkeley's whole world, and consequently all possible worlds.

† In speaking of religious matters, Voltaire most frequently joked; he did not reason. As to Dupuis, he had not made himself master of the subject he treated. An attentive perusal of Kreutzer's symbolics, (a very useful work to the philosopher who wishes to undertake the study of the language of Nature,) furnishes evidence excluding all doubt, that the ancient pagan religions, with their different mythologies and cosmogonies, generally arose from the language of Nature misunderstood; and that, consequently, the completion of the Christian religion, the only true one, will consist in that same language being regained and carried to a certain degree of perfection.

as well as physical, Philosophy, from being a materialist, as she was, has become, in a great measure, a spiritualist. Many of our modern thinkers have at length perceived the truth of that prediction of Plato, that "they who will deliver themselves to profound researches, (in all that belongs to morals and religion,) with a humble mind, and fly that irreligious and unphilosophic mania of deciding, of cutting short everything at the first sight of difficulties, will find that what seemed to them most incredible is often what was most certain and most evident. Some great names are already linked with those new and radiant doctrines, of a world of light, a world of substance, everywhere enclosed in a world of matter; the only true, the only life-giving doctrines; doctrines which must, sooner or later, triumph.*

We will not here speak of those phenomena which seem as if they must familiarize even the medical science with those ideas which extend our world through illimitable space. It is well known that some distinguished physicians in France, as well as in Germany, rising above the two opposite kinds of prejudice, have examined, with some attention, that particular state of organization produced by magnetic manipulations, or the laying on of hands, since called *provoked extasy;* and they have admitted the reality of surprising phenomena, evidently known to the ancients, which show that man, even while in the bonds of corporeal existence, may sometimes rise above organization, and thus be more or less free from time and space. The words seer, prophet, and inspired, thus begin to seem less strange to these philosophers; as the traces of the emblematic, or prophetic language, often reappear in the state of exaltation produced by magnetism. Some modern philosophers are even convinced by them, of the reality of certain communications between men, who, laying off their material envelope, have passed into that world of light, which plays in the midst of all the globes, as the rays of the sun play in a globe of crystal, and in which the emblematic language is spoken, and men still living upon earth who do not yet know any languages of convention and articulate sounds.†

---

* At the head of these names stands that of M. Royer Collard, and the school which he has formed.

† The proofs, by reasoning that we have offered, of the primitive existence of a natural language, among intelligent beings, appeared to us so clear and convincing, that we thought it unnecessary to crowd this introduction with citations from ancient authors who had the same opinion with ourselves, or related facts capable of supporting them. Yet the following remarks may find a place here, where we have touched on the delicate question of animal magnetism.

The Pythagorean Epicharmus already spoke as follows, of what I call substantial forms. "The art of playing on the flute, is undoubtedly separate from the man who plays on it. It is the same of what is well, or what is good; goodness is necessarily a thing separate from the man who possesses it." And Alcimus adds: "The soul learns certain things by means of the senses, and others without their aid, because it considers these things in themselves;" which very clearly proves that the ancients frequently attached the idea of reality to what, for the moderns, has been but an abstract quality. (See Diogenes Laertius, iii. 14, 12.) Philopones asserts that he has seen in one of the best books of Aristotle upon good, or philosophy, these expressions: "The ideas, or forms of things, contain their matter, as numbers contain the things numbered; for matter being in itself a thing undetermined, that is to say, without real attributes; it is only forms that make objects." (De An. page 17, Venice, 15, 35.) According to Pythagoras and his disciples, things alone were objects in themselves, that is to say, real and eternal, though immaterial objects: while material objects, as far as they were material, were in themselves nothing. Their ideas approached very near those brought forward among us by Berkeley, upon the non-existence of matter, as something in itself; and, consequently, when they spoke of the eternal world, they frequently meant only the substantial forms of this world; such as we see them, and feel them, in the state of dreaming. In this connection, the recent somnambulic phenomena, observed in Germany, seem to have enabled some of her philosophers to understand the ancients better than they have ever been understood before. "Timeus," says Tiedmann, in his Life of Pythagoras, page 545, "promises those who observe the prescribed rules, the sight of the gods, (that is, of their transformed ancestors); we cannot but conclude from this, that the Pythagoreans had found the means of being in a real state of extasy;" (that is, a state in which the interior and immortal man, being awake during a transient sleep of the body, can very naturally converse with those whose material organs sleep, definitely, the sleep of death.)

Stillingfleet, who is known to have studied antiquity most profoundly, was convinced, like ourselves, that, originally, the name of a thing signified its essence. Whoever will consult the "Origines Sacræ," will find there the confirmation of almost all our ideas.

[18] But, besides modern medicine being very far from consistent with itself, upon these various points; besides it being dangerous to seek to establish communications, of this kind, between the natural world and the universe of human spirits, on account of the degradation of our being, which necessarily prevents our entering into communication with any but the degraded beings who are found in unison with us; and as we are not in a state to understand them aright, even if they were disposed to be useful to us; we regard magnetic phenomena as of very little use to morals and religion, though we should be very far from discouraging any who wish to confirm their belief in immortality, by experiments in artificial somnambulism, by becoming eye-witnesses of the physical, or moral, penetration of certain extatic individuals, in whom the future state of man, disengaged from the dullness of matter, is seen as palpably as any other phenomenon in nature.

The enlightened Christian never needed those tardy experiments by which human sciences think, from time to time, to add to his faith. It was always enough, to make him perceive the finger of God, to observe with an impartial eye the admirable harmony of the old and new [19] Testaments, and the immense system evidently above the power of all created intelligences. But it is not thus with those merely nominal Christians, who, in reality, know not what they believe, and who, as they cannot disentangle the truth from the absurd pretensions, with which it has been mixed, envelope, in equal scorn, religious abuses and the most indispensable principles of morals and religion. It is not thus, above all, with those numerous miscreants of the day, who often have such terrible prejudices to surmount, who often have not the first idea, the first notion of an immortal life, disengaged from the clogs of matter. To all such, the most simple bridge becomes the most precious thing; and the idea of the language of Nature, found in the holy books, has appeared to us most proper to represent this bridge; and the eagerness with which we have seized on it, is proportioned to the number of those who are to pass over it.

We have divided our work into two parts; the first treats of the true nature of Jesus Christ; the second on the true sense of his doctrine.

Father Kircher was convinced that the first language could not be conventional. Clement, of Alexandria, said, in direct terms, that the ancients sometimes recounted their actions by a course of symbols. It was from Egypt that Greece received the use of symbols, her mythology, her temples for the cure of the sick, and the giving of oracles; and Egypt had found all those things only by means of her extatic men, her priests and priestesses. It is impossible to resist the evidence furnished by history, on this subject, and confirmed by new experience in these last times. Aristeus Proconensis, who lived at the time of Cyrus, is represented, by his contemporaries, as a man who could make his soul leave his body, and return to it, at will; he was, evidently, nothing else than a somnambulist. Socrates himself, as all know, entered, from time to time, into magnetic exaltation; this must be the origin of the demon, or familiar spirit, attributed to him. "These demons of the Pythagoreans, said Diogenes Laertius, (demons, who, as we have already said, were no other than the substantial men of their ancestors,) influence mortals by the presentiments and dreams which they give them; they send them health and sickness, and reveal to them hidden things and future events." Every one knows the cabalistic science of the Rabbins, which has been defended by more than one strong head, in past times, and which the progress of science has forced some modern philosophers to view with a little less disdain. Finally, all the passages of Saint Paul's epistles, in which he traces rules touching the order to be preserved among those who speak unknown tongues, those who have visions, revelations, and those who interpret dreams, prove that the laying on of hands, observed by him, resembled, entirely, our modern experiments on provoked extasy. It was necessary then, as now, to try the spirits if they be of God, and to set apart imaginary or simulated exaltation, imposture, and folly. And what the apostles themselves have taught us, on this subject, enables us to enter into details on what the Holy Fathers, and the first ecclesiastical writers, who, without a single exception, all admitted extasies, cures, and possessions, and spoke of them as phenomena known to all the world, the pagan as well as the Christian. Tertullian alone wrote seven books upon extasy; and he became a montanist only because he suffered himself to be deceived by the extatic Montan and his two companions, prophetesses or somnambulists, as they may be called. Really, he must be very ignorant of ancient authors, who can believe that the peculiar state of organization, which Dr. Bertrand calls the extatic crisis, has not been known to all ages; that it has not frequently constituted the principal object of the researches of nations, in relation to worship, as well as to the healing science, and that most of the religions in the world did not have those astonishing phenomena for a first principle.

Hieroglyphic Keys

[21] Before beginning our explanation of the principal pas[s]ages of the Holy Scriptures, according to the principles of the astonishing language, the existence of which we have just pointed at, we should most heartily wish to present, to our reader, the dictionary which has guided us. But, as the words of Rousseau will apply to this case, that our book would be as large as the world, and then we should not have exhausted our subject, we will limit ourselves to a few very general data; simple keys, by means of which the reader can, by himself, penetrate farther into the immense domains of nature. Meanwhile, our whole dictionary will be reduced to the following words:

    I.   GOD; LOVE, TRUTH.
   II.   SUN; HEAT, LIGHT.
  III.   MAN; GOODNESS, KNOWLEDGE.
  IV.   LIVE; EAT, DRINK.
   V.   ANIMAL KINGDOM; VEGETABLE KINGDOM, MINERAL KINGDOM.
  VI.   CREATION; PRODUCTION, DESTRUCTION.
 VII.   SUBSTANCE; FORM, COLOR.
VIII.   TO WALK; TO ASCEND, TO DESCEND.
  XI.   MIDST; RIGHT, LEFT.
   X.   POINTS; NUMBERS, ELEMENTS.

I. GOD; LOVE, TRUTH. Because God, in his first essence, is the Great-Whole, the Infinite Being, he is nothing for us, unless he concentrate the rays of his eternal glory upon a determined point; in other words, unless he present himself to man, under man's image and likeness. Indeed, we cannot perceive, or grasp the idea of God, even when we consider him in the first great division of his being, as love, goodness, or power; and as truth, order, or wisdom. Not only does his being already escape us, when we turn our attention to those two great attributes, but those attributes themselves are not known to us, save by the natural emblems of which they are the abstractions. How, indeed, can we know love, if not by the heart? And how can we know truth, if not by the objects that reveal it to us? Thus arises an absolute im- [22] possibility for any created intelligence to reach God, except by means of the emblem of a man-God, or a God-man. Therefore, man is the true hieroglyphic of the Divinity; a hieroglyphic, infinite in its details, even when man is considered only as a material form, since his material form itself, is but the emblem of his moral being.

II. SUN; HEAT, LIGHT. The truth which we have just declared must be perceived by every impartial mind, which will give it the slightest attention; but men have not, generally, sought God in that most natural type, the perfection of human nature. Guided, probably, by the secret consciousness of the degradation of their own being, they have, almost invariably, begun by seeking God in an emblem of the second order, an inanimate emblem, and, on that account, less susceptible of degradation, but, also, less susceptible of a mere physical perfection; we speak of the star of day. Indeed, all the inconceivable qualities, remarked in the Divine Being, are found typified almost as inconceivably in the sun. The sun in the firmament, that star always the same, that star always new, appears as one only, dazzling the eyes of mortals, infinite by its light, present to the whole earth, and the principle of life to all nature. Its two essential qualities, heat and light, also correspond, the former to love, the latter to truth. Mysterious fire! in thy progress, as in the nature of thy rays, men know thee clearly, only by thy benefits. Everything in the world is nourished, formed, by thy substance, from the tenderest grass-blade to the hardest diamond. Hence the millions of hieroglyphics which any one may easily find. All the phenomena of reflected light, all the colors, preserve some distant relation with the moral world; from white, which represents complex truths, to black, which recalls the darkness of absolute ignorance; from scarlet, which casts the brilliancy of fire and flame, to the faintest violet, scarcely able to indicate the forms of objects. And this amazing comparison of dead light with spiritual light, may be carried into the mysteries of refraction and transmission. Light, in whatever way we view it, under whatever point of view we consider it, always answers to some variety of truth; and man's eye, the emblem of his soul, is really nourished by light, in the contemplation of the whole creation.

III. MAN; GOODNESS, SCIENCE. We have already, in our Introduction, said a word of man; and, in the body of our work, will be found quite a detailed sketch of the numerous hieroglyphics of his different organs. We will say, then, simply, that all that can be remarked in the vegetable, instinctive, and animal parts of his being, is likewise found in his moral being, and the former is but a detailed hieroglyphic of the latter. As the external man is constantly occupied in acquiring personal qualities, and in amassing possessions which will make him respected in the world, so the immortal man is every moment acquiring the celestial knowledges, and virtues, which render him worthy of the eternal society; and those different metaphysical qualities are made perceptible, even in their least varieties, by the infinite hieroglyphics of earthly acquisitions; hieroglyphics of which the substantial images will, necessarily, accompany man in his state of transformation; what do I say? which probably accompany him in his present state, though unknown to him. Man, like all animals, may be viewed [23] as a hollow cylinder, through which pass emblematic matters. Around this are ranged the different organs of the senses, more or less numerous, more or less developed, according to the subjects, and which, reviewed in the same way, give a mass of moral hieroglyphics, which it is not in human power to number. And here, also, may be remarked this characteristic difference, that goodness perfects, rather than science, because goodness relates to love, science to truth. Considered as a collection of levers, or of any powers whatever, man still offers an admirable subject of contemplation. The hand is, in itself, a whole apparatus; indeed, every finger is one. These apparatuses are always divided into three distinct levers, for reasons which we shall give when we speak of the hieroglyphic of numbers. The thumb, situated at the root of the hand, is the most considerable force of the same apparatus; and therein it corresponds to the shoulder and the hip, which are similarly situated. By an act of the will, of three levers man makes one. When a force is overcome, it is as if in three successive efforts; first, the hand is exerted, then the elbow, then the shoulder; and man is vanquished. Thus are distributed upon the human form, as upon a scale of proportion, the hieroglyphic points of all the possible varieties of moral powers. From the data that we already have on this subject, we may, one day, perhaps, give the particular correspondence of each finger and each joint.

IV. LIVE; EAT, DRINK. God is life; man lives: in other words, with man, life is progressive; with God, not. Everything in man is done by insensible degrees; the Creator himself cannot invert this order. For this reason, the human body increases, and decreases, equally, by accessions and losses, which are remarked only with time. Even love and truth, which are possessed exclusively by God, can be applied to man, only by imperceptible degrees. Hence that admirable economy of the restoration of the degraded human race, accomplished in a proportionate lapse of time; an essential truth, which we must never lose sight of, for an instant, when we wish to judge correctly of the course of God Redeemer. Eating, in the physical man, relates, also, to love, and drinking, to wisdom; and that, even in their minutest details. This is true of nourishment, in general, as of clothing, which also recalls love, or charity, by its warmth, and truth, by its colors and forms.

V. ANIMAL KINGDOM; VEGETABLE KINGDOM, MINERAL KINGDOM. All animals, by their corporeal forms, as well as by their instincts, are hieroglyphics of the different degradations of human nature, or of detached parts of the collection of organs of life, called man. Examine animal forms geometrically, from man, who represents the perpendicular, to the reptile which forms the horizontal line, and then applying to those forms the rules of the exact sciences, which God himself cannot change, we shall see that visible nature contains them all; that the combinations of the seven primitive forms, are entirely exhausted, and that, therefore, they can represent all possible varieties of morality. Hence the immense chain of moral types, offered by all animals, in their more and more imperfect manners of providing for their frail existence; types which appear, sometimes, arbitrary, and [24] even strange, to the eyes of the superficial philosopher, who is yet no more superficial than the philosophic naturalist, who has studied the delicate relation of forms, and instincts, in their endless details, and who knows that every fibre is placed, by a supreme reason, in the worm as in the elephant. As to the two other kingdoms, the vegetable kingdom is a degradation of the animal kingdom, by the suppression of all voluntary motion; and the mineral kingdom, a degradation of the vegetable kingdom by the suppression of all perceptible motion whatever. But the distant relation of the good and the true, is found to be always preserved. The young grass, for instance, is the symbol of a productive power in its germ; the tree, that of a faculty provided with all the means necessary for the production of fruits of all kinds. The same is true of minerals. The different manners of crystalization were certainly not abandoned to chance, nor chosen without some moral reason, by supreme Goodness and Wisdom. Only warmth, in the mineral kingdom, is generally less than in the preceding, as in that, it is less than in the first.

VI. CREATION; PRODUCTION, DESTRUCTION. If for God to create is not an act, properly speaking, that is to say, an effort, for man to do good is to create with God and by God. And to do evil is to create in a still more real sense; for, in evil, man acts alone; God does not create with him. The perfect emblems needed no Creation. They were all found in the Infinite Being, in the absolute Being, who can give everything because he has everything. But, as to the imperfect emblems, they were all necessarily created; from the emblem of fraternal hatred, pictured on the face of the first sinner, to that of a crucified, which is an outraged God. In the simultaneous order, the infinite is said to create, or produce the finite; the whole is said to create, or produce the part. All that produces, is Creator, or Father; all that is produced, is Son, or Truth. Substance produces form; form produces color, &c. Production refers to good, to affirmation, to reality, to order, to harmony; destruction, to evil, to negation, to falsity, to disorder, to discord. Nature, in her beauty, is the emblem of the first; terrible phenomena, elements in convulsion, the emblem of the second. The admirable economy of men and animals, reproducing themselves, offers the hieroglyphic of all moral bodies, which, also, have their birth, their time of growth, and of decay. When the moral body is considered as having life, it is represented by living being, more or less developed; when that body is without life, but regular, it is figured by a dead body, or a statue more or less perfect, more or less finished. All divine harmony is typified by different degrees of legitimate loves and unions; all discord, all sin, all error, by different degrees of illegitimate loves and unions. And this correspondence is sustained even in inorganic unions, the attractions or repulsions of matter. Otherwise, it would be metaphysically impossible that all those moral varieties should become appreciable to created intelligence.

VII. SUBSTANCE; FORM, COLOR. Substance is all that is real. The Creator is substance in the supreme degree. All that we see and touch, in nature, is emblematic of that substance. In this sense, the objects that we perceive in the state of dreaming, are as much sub- [25] tances as any others. In man, it is the flesh that represents the substance, or the foundation of his being; the various forms of this flesh represent his qualities. And, again, flesh, as substance, relates to love; forms and colors, to truth. Moreover, all possible geometrical forms are moral types; and, considered in their primitive developments, they cannot be more numerous than the primitive variety of colors. The three dimensions, length, breadth, and thickness, consequently, have their fixed significations; but thickness should be named first, as it relates to substance. These dimensions must make exactly the parallel of the centre, of the right and left, which will be spoken of soon. Just now, we considered men, and animals, as crooked cylinders, or as vases, containing such emblematic matters as may characterize their being. Let the reader now extend this idea to everything that is crooked; he will have, first, the horizon and the cope of the heavens surrounding him, like immense curves, figuring eternity; he will then have the edifices, made by the hand of man, of all forms and sizes, from the hieroglyphic temple, the abode of the divinity, or, rather, of Divine Truth, to the smallest vase, to the smallest box. And all the details, considered in their relation to the primitive form, with the universal form, which is man, supply the type of some moral variety, more or less distant from the first source.

VIII. WALK; GO UP, COME DOWN. The action of walking is the general emblem of life and social relations. In its origin, locomotion, with man, is of a very simple nature; but, afterwards, he varies it at will; the horse, the elephant, the carriage, the vessel, receive him by turns. He even makes to himself wings, and rises towards the heaven. Hence the innumerable hieroglyphics of life and social relations, all the different varieties of which may be found and appreciated. Human intelligence itself, as an abstract part, putting in motion all that apparatus, is figured by it in its different developments. And, in that, the degree of elevation of the soil has, also, its particular signification. To go up, is taken in a good sense, and recalls an approach to uncreated goodness; thence the custom of the ancients to worship upon mountains. To go down, is taken in the opposite sense. These two emblems are always the complete reverse of each other, when applied to the vice of pride and the virtue of humility, as, in general, all emblems may be. On the other side, to sit down is to cease to act, to be fixed, it is to rest, and even to rest upon ourselves. To be down, is to rest upon God, upon the eternal rock. The pagans called the earth the mother of all nature; the Christian knows that that mother is no other than He who would not forsake his children, even if a nursing mother could forget the child that she had borne beneath her bosom. Hence, then, the innumerable hieroglyphics of the sleep of night, of awakening, of the succession of days, and of labors, and even that of bed, which represents faith, and covering, which represents charity.

IX. MIDST; RIGHT, LEFT. The midst, in general, represents perfection, the centre of a whole; and thus, in the first place, the Being of beings, placed entirely out of time and space. The right recalls goodness, power; the left, truth, wisdom. The same may be said of that hieroglyphic, as of that of substance, form, and color. That of [26] points and directions, which follows, also relates to it, and will explain it entirely, so that we need say no more of it here.

X. POINTS; NUMBERS, ELEMENTS. Placing man at the zenith, he has behind him the east, before him the west, at his right the north, at his left the south. In this state of things, the east represents to him the invisible Creator, the hidden God, whom faith alone can reach. The east, characterized by the march of the sun, the material emblem of the Divinity, also designates an increase in goodness and truth; and, therefore, the west designates an analogous decrease; as the north recalls a loss in charity, and the south a progress in truth. Here, the order which we are about to remark, in relation to the good and the true, is found reversed,* since man has goodness, or love, at his left, and truth, or wisdom, at his right. But these things should always be judged, above all, with relation to that God in whose presence man stands. And, moreover, man himself, naturally placed by the Creator, at first, in a state of possible increase, consequently in a state of full and entire moral liberty, ought to make the first use of this noble faculty in seeking his Creator, in turning freely towards Him. Thence a moral signification of all the directions towards the different points of immensity, to which as many points in the human body correspond to characterize them. These points are still more real in the interior nature of our being, than they are in the physical universe. As we have already said, the human soul cannot be considered without that collection of organs called man; and, therefore, it cannot be conceived of without right, left, and all the other consequent directions. The points of height are already known to us, as recalling nobility, elevation of soul; those of depth, as recalling baseness and abjection. Considered in motion, the upward direction represents, also, celestial life; the opposite direction, infernal life. Beings of a superior perfection, when they appear, are seen descending from above; degraded beings arrive from below, though places, in themselves, are nothing determined, as forms offer only relative sizes. The whole front of man corresponds, also, to kindness, and the whole back, to aversion. The same instinct causes friendship to advance, and horror and disgust to recoil. Even the different forms of the body, among mankind, designate, as they create, the different affections.

The numbers which relate to points, have, also, their fixed significations. But they could not be understood without very extensive and metaphysical considerations. The analogy, which necessarily exists between this matter and all the rest, must supply the place of proof. Unity relates to God; duality to love and truth. Thus, duality relates to man, who, for this reason, was created male and female; the husband representing, rather, wisdom, the wife, rather, goodness. Trinity, or the number three, always designates the perfection of a being, or an object, probably, because of the three distinct relations that the human mind may discover therein. The astonishing properties of the number seven, and of the sabbath of human nature, will be amply discussed in [27] the body of our work. We will here add only a word, on the numbers ten and twelve, just to indicate to our readers that certain numbers cannot, in any case, be entirely arbitrary. The decimal which is taken from the number of our fingers, is, therefore, founded in the nature of things, since the Creator could not choose that number without reason. The same is true of the dozen. The different parts of the day and night, for example, could never have been divided in a different proportion. The four radical points, which serve as their base, two of which are in the horizon, the other two in the zenith and nadir, necessarily cause twelve or twenty-four numbers, which, likewise, have a proportionate importance in the Holy Scriptures, as we will show.

Finally, the four elements, in all their immense details, offer, to the reflecting mind, moral emblems so numerous, that no philosopher can count them. The earth, as a solid foundation, as a basis sustaining the king of nature, man with the upright brow, refers to God, the eternal support of his creatures. As productive of all sorts of fruits, agreeable to the taste and the sight, the earth may incessantly remind us of the human society, the church of God. The air, with its winged inhabitants, the atmosphere, with

---

* If the author here had turned man towards the east, as the angels always place themselves, in the heavens, he would not have found the order of right and left, with regard to good and truth, reversed.—TRANSLATOR.

its innumerable phenomena, everywhere announce the invisible action of a hidden God, his immensity, his inexhaustible goodness towards all that breathe, united to a majesty equally imposing and terrible. Water, as transparent element, reflecting with the exactness of a mirror, the images of objects, (when it is calm,) represents, with all the myriads that find life in it, the different kinds and degrees of truths; and that, in opposition to the habitable earth, which relates rather to goodness and substance. And as to fire, it refers us to the sun, from which it emanates; and, therefore, it represents charity, and knowledges among beings, weak images of their Author, who is uncreated Love and Truth.

We believe that this sketch, short and imperfect as it is, will be enough to awaken the attention of all classes of readers, and to prove to them that our explanations of the Holy Books will not be arbitrary, like those which have been hitherto given.

XI

THE PHYSICAL CONDITION OF THE WORLD*

By Thomas H. Perry

The natural world is the nursery of man. Throughout every department of nature, utility and design are characteristic of the laws both of animate and of inanimate existence. It matters not how seemingly unimportant be the subjects of our consideration —whether our views be general or particular; restricted now to individual phenomena, or opening upon the whole comprehensive range of mutual adaptedness and relation; we witness every where, the same invariable principles.

But as we rise in the scale of being; as we ascend from effects to their causes; from matter to mind; from things material to things immaterial; and approximate towards the universal centre; the laws of creative Wisdom become more and more distinctly marked;—the parts which lie beneath us, are irradiated by a light shed upon them from above, until the works of creation apparently the most insignificant, are rendered replete with interest and instruction—oracles vocal with the responses of benevolence and wisdom. But no where is the law of moral utility more distinctly visible, than in the connexion between man and the world which he inhabits.

The relation of the satellites of the solar system to their primaries is but a miniature image of that which those primaries themselves sustain to their common centre. So, in a manner analogous, as mankind depend upon the sun of the moral world, does the system of which they form the centre, depend upon them.

Man is the being, for the development of whose intellectual [59] and moral faculties the physical world, with all its appurtenances of continuous and successive life, has been called into existence. While all things else are ephemeral, man only is immortal. The various modifications of vegetable and animal life but minister to his wants, perpetuate their species, and are again resolved into their original elements.

And it is, as we believe, in order to subserve in a more perfect manner, than could otherwise have been possible, the purposes of its formation,—to adapt itself to the altered state of the human mind, that the condition of the physical world has been successively changed. The ultimate objects of creation could not have been otherwise secured. That man should descend into the world of nature, and there become conversant with the ultimate forms which existence assumes, is essential to the *free* and orderly development of his rational and moral powers.

It is a law which obtains not more in the vegetable and animal kingdoms, than with reference to man, that, whatsoever is destined to continue, is as it were, by an effort of principles from within, slow and constant in its increase, whilst that which springs up with sudden, instantaneous luxuriance, is of ephemeral duration. If, then, the moral nature of man is alone destined to survive, as the sole and exclusive product of all this complicated machinery, his embryo susceptibilities must be suffered to be gradually and successively developed.

But while man is deriving so much from the world of nature, while he here finds that in which has faculties and affections may take root, and from which they rise expanded, matured, and invigorated,—he is also exerting both an obvious and secret influence upon

* "The Physical Condition of the World Dependent upon the Moral Character of Man," N J M, IX (1835-1836), pp. 58-62. (October, 1835).

its condition. The human mind does not require, nor will it admit, the same process of development now as formerly; and the soil in which it is implanted, and the moral atmosphere by which it is surrounded, have therefore been modified to meet its exigencies. When man departed from the state of pristine innocence and simplicity, in which he was originally created, inferior natures felt a corresponding change. Nor do we believe it to be a wild and chimerical idea, a mere fancy of the poet, or whim of speculative philosophy, that when the moral nature of man shall have become renovated, when he shall have returned to the laws of order from which he has wandered; when the chords of human society shall again vibrate in harmonious unison, and mutual benevolence shall characterize the intercourse of man with man,— [60] inferior natures, also, yielding to the resistless impulse of an influence from within, will again find their place in the scale of being, and the same universal harmony be restored which reigned on the morning of creation.

For pain and suffering are as repulsive to the yearnings of benevolence now as they ever were. The bestowment of happiness is not less the continual effort of the Author of our existence now than when the human race was first called into being. And were it not for the existence of evil, the consequent misery, which it produces, would be as impossible now as then.

This change is now in the very act of being effected. We behold it, in the altered aspect of external nature, wherever the influence of civilization has been felt. We behold it in the wonderful achievements of human intelligence—in the successive submission of the energies of the physical world to the powers of the mind—and in the timid, awed, subdued condition of the brute, as he gazes on the image of his Creator—cowers beneath the glance of a superior nature,—or bows his submissive neck obedient to his authority.

The laws, which immutable Omniscience establishes, are as much of universal application in one department of his works as in another—in the world of mind as in the world of matter.

Nor are we disposed to regard the apparent deviations from the usual course of nature, which the pen of inspiration has recorded, evincing as they do in the clearest manner possible, the subserviency of things material to things spiritual, as other than the effects of the legitimate operation of principles which, because they lie in a region elevated above our present state of attainment, and are visible only in a light too dazzling for our natural vision, are at present concealed from our view.

A single muscle which, in its lifeless state, a few ounces only would be sufficient to sunder, when acting under the influence of the mind, is often known to exert a force which, estimated by the exact principles of mathematical science, is truly astonishing. In the economy of the human body the ordinary laws, even of chemical affinity, seem to be, in a wonderful manner, transcended. And the medical faculty assure us, that diseases of the body are both produced, modified and removed, by the influence of the mind.

If, then, the object of human existence is the formation of moral character; if matter exists but to subserve the wants of mind; and if the laws which govern the former are known to [61] be in subjection to those which govern the latter; if every inferior principle must yield to the operation of a superior, and if the laws of matter have thus yielded; and if such is the influence of individual minds upon those particular portions of matter with which they are more immediately associated,—how, in view of the facts recorded in history, sacred or profane, or elicited by daily experience, shall we repudiate, as unphilosophical, the necessary conclusion, that the physical condition of the world is dependent upon the moral character of man. Or who will venture to assert, that when in the progress of moral advancement, the disorders of human society shall cease to exist; when we shall have learned to act from purer and more exalted motives; when sordid selfishness and demoniac ambition shall no longer be suffered to belittle and pollute humanity; to array mankind in envious and jealous animosity; nor be appealed to and fostered as motives of action;—the time may not yet arrive, when the pernicious, the ferocious, and the terrible, shall disappear in the useful, and inferior natures learn to regard man as a friend and a protector, rather than to fear him and to detest him, as a common enemy, a tyrant, and a scourge.

But it is reserved for the men of other ages, to witness the consummation of those changes in the aspect of things, which the gradual renovation of the moral nature of man is yet in the very act of commencing; but which, as the wheels of reform move on, it will certainly effect.

This relation between him and the world which he inhabits, is not, however, useful to man, merely as the means of developing his faculties, irrespective of the manner of such development. While, by compelling subjection to the laws which govern his physical **constitution**, it imperceptibly infuses into the expanding embryo, the first principles of obedience, and thus induces a state more consonant with the laws of moral order, and better adapted to receive them, it also furnishes him with a mirror, in which may be seen, evidently reflected in appropriate colors, his own rational and moral condition. Though, as the lord of this sublunary creation, he is ever prone to pride himself upon his fancied superiority, he finds, even in the disorder and confusion which his follies and his crimes have introduced, the record of the steps of his deviations. He beholds it in the apparent external distraction which Providence permits to exist as the proper ultimates of human evil, alike in the diseases which prey upon his physical con- [62] stitution, in the ferocity of the tiger, the venom of the serpent, and in the fatal poison of the deadly night-shade. On what side soever he turns himself, he witnesses every where the consequences of his aberrations, and under circumstances in which, because, perhaps, he does not consider them as exclusively his own, he is comparatively free from the temptation to palliate or excuse them, he beholds faithfully and forcibly depicted, his own passions, feelings and propensities.

XII

PSYCHE*

By Amos Bronson Alcott

[iii]   **Psyche's Influence on Man's Soul**
   She taketh man's *spirit* by the hand, and, now, flying through the empyrean, she vivifieth his *imagination;* clears the vision of his faith by her radiant glories; then she descendeth midway and with him surveyeth the domain of earth, quickening his *reason* with the Forms of Being; and, anon, she falleth down to the ground; descendeth below its surface; filleth his *sense* with facts and things for his *fancy* till all his being teemeth with her life, so that he riseth, as if by his own might, on the wings of a hallowed *faith* into the realms of Beatific Being, taking Nature into his [iv] heart. He mastereth the *outward* by the inspiring influence of her divine agency. He *findeth* his *genius* in her and *representeth* it in Nature.

[iv]   **Nature and Man**
   And thus it is that Nature and Man are *one*. Infinite sympathies wed them together. Man is alone and naked without the presence and renewal of Nature. Nature both feedeth and clothe[th] his body, and this becometh the alert instrument of the Spirit by virtue of Nature's bounty. The soul liveth on Nature—is renewed by it day by day in all its external functions—and, while giving it laws, finds its own well-being in submitting to their enactments. Childhood feeleth this, and woe to him that striveth to break the divine bonds that unite him with it!

---

   * The title page of the manuscript from which the following excerpts have been taken reads thus: PSYCHE / or / The Breath of Childhood. / In Four Books / Boston / 1835-'36 /. It is a philosophical journal of Alcott's observations of his three little daughters, begun Wednesday, June 24, 1835, the day Elizabeth was born, and ended exactly one year later, Friday, June 24, 1836. It is the earlier of two manuscripts bearing the same heading, the second of which has for its title page the following: PSYCHE / AN / EVANGELE; / in / Four Books. / Boston: / 1838 /. Both are owned by Mr. F. Wolsey Pratt of the Middlesex School, Concord, Massachusetts. The first contains iv + 503 + about 20 pages called "interleaves"; the second assigns 346 to the last page of writing. Emerson read the first through page 284 in early February, 1836, and the remainder after August 2 of that year. The second and later manuscript Emerson read and criticized in June, 1838. (For evidence, see Emerson, *Letters*, II, 4-6, 138-141, and *The Journals of Bronson Alcott*, ed. Odell Shepard, Boston, 1938, p. 78). Portions of the first are reprinted here, chiefly those passages which Emerson said were worthy of being saved out of what was otherwise a rather bulky and unpublishable manuscript. Pages that interested Emerson were: 46, 57-58, 67, 76, 87-96, 105-112, 118-119, 133-136, 149, 161, 167, 182-183, 223, 227-234, 241-242, 251-260, 267-268, 275-277, 279-284. In the following excerpts, I have been obliged to improve punctuation, correct misspellings, and systematize capitalization. The page numbers in brackets at the left of the headings are references to the original manuscript. The plus sign after a numeral indicates an interleaf.

[12 + 1] **Psyche Prefers Summertime**

Psyche maketh her advent in the season of verdure. She cometh forth upon the outward scene in early summertime. Nature hath prepared, for her, beautiful objects of sense to greet her first outlook on her serene visage. She welcomes her by all her rich garniture and smileth in complacency from all her vine-clad arbours—from her quivering leaves, her bland airs, and gentle harmonies of birds, and murmur of waters. Nature is enrobed in her rich vestments. Her attire is worthy the first look of a god, when [12 + 2] descending to explore the confines of its domain and take upon itself the features of its tenants.

[12 + 2] **Appropriate Season for Childbirth**

Nor is there wanting a fit dwelling nor a sympathetic friend for the reception of the celestial visitant. Nature hath a kindly look. Her apartments are all in fit order, and within them hath she placed a matron, whose maternal instincts have prepared vestments—comforts for the naked, helpless divinity while on its self-sacrificing mission in the flesh. The arms of Providence are spread wide-open to receive the newcomer; maternal arms second the providential behest. The young divinity is ushered into terrestrial life. His body is enrobed in the garment of Time; and Nature, Providence, man, unite to cherish him.

[12 + 4] **The Advent of a Spirit**

The advent of a spirit is a phenomenon that no words can body forth. We can find no types in external nature adequate to the purpose. Even to the spiritually minded and loving receiver of the sacred trust of a child, there cometh no expressive image wherein to set his Idea or represent his feeling. The paternal instinct recognizeth no form fit for its embodiment. It findeth all save the reality but mock phantasy. To see the Godhead made flesh and sent as a living image of the Father—this is the Idea that lieth at the base of the human reason. Faith alone [12 + 5] apprehendeth it. Sense cannot embody it in aught save the living organ itself. The Supernatural is quickened into life and asketh for its own forms of significance. These are the child itself—the "very Incarnate Word," which neither the reason nor the external sense comprehendeth. The Absolute dawneth upon the being of man for a moment and then retreateth into the Universal, which for this brief moment it seemeth to leave in condescension to the feeble optics of humanity.

[12 + 6] **Advent of a Child—A Parental Invocation**

She comes! From Heaven she dawns upon my sight,
On Earth's dark scenes to pour her holy light!
In sense and flesh, the Infinite to see,
And feel that heavenly mystery—TO BE!

She comes in Nature's tenderest, fondest name—
Daughter of God! 'Tis she—the same—the same!
Mine is she too—my own, my latest child—
Myself wrapt in Divinity, yet unbeguiled!

Blest infant—God's and mine—yet to me given
That I might feel anew my being's heaven!
In love and faith to urge my human way,
Till transient time be lost in immortality!

Love thee I will, for thou didst first love me.
My faith shall quicken as I gaze on thee!
My spirit lift me from this vale of things
And point me heavenward to the King of Kings!

[13] **God in Flesh**

And this "round thing" is God—is man—is a spirit, subsisting *in* and *by* the godlike and the human! Incarnate One! Rudiment of Divinity! Seed of God in husk of flesh! Form moulded on the Divine Spirit! Humanity foretelling Divinity, related to the past and the future by the tie of the flesh! Immortal in spirit—dateless in being—yet fresh and new, frail and mortal, in form visible! I seek in vain to apprehend thee: to ascertain thy [14] being, thy faculties, thine endowment, thy Self! I look into my own being, but there do I find nought that thou dost not reimage in fuller radiance and grandeur. I seek for that Idea that floats ever and anon around the depths of my apprehension, and yet I find no emblem so fit as thou seemest to be to typify my thought of the Infinite! In thee I see the All that filleth my being. In the fullness of thy nature I embody my conception of the Whole. I am. Thou art. God is. And in this sublime synthesis thou art the middle term; nor can any resolve this into its trinal members without *beginning* and *ending* in thee. Time antedates and dates and stretches backwards and forwards into the period whence it came and whence it runneth; and thou art, in thy youth and age, but the horologe of its transit! Thou art [15] not Time, but maketh it apprehendable in the emblems of space through the instruments of the senses. Thou art and wast before time, and by virtue of that time-transcending memory, of which thou art the emblem, thou revivest in this as yet unexperienced scene the life of the Eternal. The clock that striketh—the sun that riseth or setteth at thy birth-time— are but sense-marks and sounds to the ears and eyes of Creation's outdwellers. Other keepers of thy ongoing there are in the Spirit's reckoning! Nay, Time's horologe is set by thee, and the orb of day performeth its circling courses to tell the story of thy date! Thou art not Nature. Thou art that of which Nature is but the show. Matter is thy shadow as thou passest in thy haste on the errand of good. Nature but shows *where* thou *now* art, but telleth naught of thy birthplace or coming!

Mysterious Existence

[16]
Thou breakest forth from the labouring womb of Nature and cometh upon our sight, the prophet at once of the past and the future. Our experience runneth back and loseth itself in thee; it goeth forward and carrieth thee along with us as the diviner of our destiny. Thou art, and there can be no start nor stop, or in these there cometh prophecies that announce undated permanence and being. Thou outrunnest all start and stop; thou art the emblem of everlasting, never-beginning being!

Quietude of Spirit

[25]
The babe was very quiet, sunk in the life of the Spirit, but seldom looking out into the scene of things. Being, in its new-found senses, lives mainly in the organic functions. Yet soon will the Spirit find access to the outward world and begin its mysterious kennings on things. Doth the Spirit sleep? Doth it ever lose itself in the dim and dark negative of unconsciousness? No, it cannot! It *is* consciousness; *this* is its life and being, and the apprehensions of sense are but the findings of its own absolute life in the shapes and shows of things. These are but the Spirit's indices. They all point inward and [26] guide the soul back to its life and source in the Spirit's Ideal, where alone are the quickening activities and powers of shape and being. The Spirit never sleepeth. Its life is a wakeful life—and not the less when the material eye is closed and the moment-measuring eyelids tell no more the Spirit's acts to the senses. There is stir within, though the countenance giveth no sign of its flitting life. The inner drama goeth on, though nought appears to the spectators of sense. Slumber is not unconsciousness, and the quiet repose of the newborn infant is but spiritual self-retirement, as if the celestial stranger feared to enter unbidden rudely upon the senses that tempt it from its inner courts to throw off the scents of its [27] being to the gaze of mortals! Reluctantly doth it look back upon the scenes it hath been called to leave and with longing, lingering look—the eye backturned—assume the garments of sense as it hath those of clay!

Nature Imageth Spirit

[38]
Now clearly doth it appear to the thoughtful that childhood regards all outward things as the emblems and exponents of its own inner being! Nature is a vast glass in which the child ever delighteth to behold his own image, and everything that he seeth hath connexions with him—reimageth some form of his being—is wedded by some mystic tie to his spirit. How important then is it that this hidden meaning, of which his heart hath the dim sense, should be unfolded to him; and his relations to the Invisible, of which his spirit is the glowing symbol, be made a fact of his consciousness! Sad is the lot of those who are divorced from Nature and then left to wander in the darkness of materialism. Yet this materialism is the inevitable result of starving the sense of the beautiful in childhood.

The Nursery Is Often Bare

[38 + 1]
How devoid of life, greenness, beauty, all that renews and quickens the soul, are the nurseries and the homes of innumerable spirits that come into this lower world and tenant the clay! Doth aught that can lift the Spirit from the presence of the environing clay address the light? Bare and full of deformity is the dwelling. Oft bare and naked (save that soul-interesting visage that Nature ever weareth) is the scene without. Yet here liveth a spirit, claiming representation of all below the sun (types of the spiritual and physical universe) to satisfy its wants and unfold its powers in full

luxuriance, strength and unity. One or two of its heavenly functions are put in play, yet many sleep or sluggishly perform their unconscious task without the glow and [38 + 2] quickening life that maketh existence a joy and a good. The eyes are put out. The ears are stopped. Physical sensations absorb the soul's notice. The animal being sucks away the forces that were intended to feed and sustain the spiritual. Fancy is subjected to the bestial instincts. Sense is submerged in sensuality, or, stolid and arid in its function, lives on a life of indifference or apathy. This is too often the process through which humanity passes, by the negligence, indifference or false valuations of parents. The nursery and the dwelling—the early scene of life's beholding—are all bare, and what wonder if the Spirit, finding nought on which to feed and renew itself, folds itself in torpor or jumps into the excesses of sense and instinct!

[45]   Want of Nursery Maids

Herein do I fail, that I cannot have supervision and control, cooperation and sympathy. The spirit that I would invoke for the nursery cometh not. Other and strange spirits, [46] wizards from the cauldron and broomstick, are admitted; and what baleful influence do they shed over the being of childhood! Girls in foreign costume and outlandish dialect are made the substitutes of maternal tendance. And how can the listening ear, the curious eye and imitating hands of childhood escape the foul-sighted example? As well might we ask purity and propriety of thought and manner from the tenant of the sty as to expect from our children, while we surround them by impurity and unsightliness, the immaculate virtue and grace that we profess as our end. Purity imparts purity; grace inspires grace; docility and love are the reflex acts of themselves. And not in the low and vulgar spirit is the act of *tending* the pure and exalted. Jesus was in the manger, but the pure Mary was there to nurture, and how [47] much came from the mother that the child adopted into Christianity in riper years is left to conjecture. That much of the mind of Jesus owed its form to her cherishing love we cannot question. A mother so full of faith, so trustful of the supernatural impulses within her, so ideal in her temperament, so devout, as was Mary, must have transfused into her child not a little of her faith and devotion. And such a son must have imbibed it as the genial aliment of his being. The Lord God required a pure and heavenly-minded mother to cherish the spiritual within him, and to such a mother was he committed by Providence. The divine germ was thus unfolded into life. The Beautiful, the True and the Good were manifested in transcendent proportion. *Genius* was incarnated and dwelt in the person of the Son of Man.

[48]   Genius A Common Gift

And thus doth Genius enter the dwelling of every parent and plead for the cherishing favour that shall disclose its light. Genius is the prime endowment of humanity. It is the life of every spirit. It belongeth to every spirit. Yet how seldom doth it show forth its glory amidst the things of time and sense! And why? Because it findeth nought to warm, quicken and renew; but everything to chill, to blunt, and destroy. Life is without the sacred flame. The nursery is bare. Imagination configureth nought for the fancy of childhood. Nature remaineth without explanation. The heart apprehendeth not the lessons of Providence, and where is the tuition—systematic and loving—that the Spirit needeth to quicken and strengthen its powers? Genius fades out at last. The surmise of life's morning goeth out in the doubts of age!

[53]   The Smile of Conscious Joy

And this same Elizabeth I took in my arms today that I might perchance tempt forth the indwelling vision and fix it for a moment on my own face. She was lively and essaying her will on surrounding things. As she lay before me, drinking in the influences of things, I sought communion by fixing my eye intently upon hers and seeking to catch the flitting spirit as it passed by its socket and rolled around the orb of vision. Radiating the spiritual as I could, I succeeded in presenting an emblem of the Spirit's joy, which she did, for a moment, apprehend and gave the answering smile. She fixed her eye on me with a deep intensity of vision. Yet a moment of endeavour, and the free will was disenthralled from the instinctive, and the vision was given her of living, individual [54] being. Then came the smile—the sense—the upfilling joy— from the Spirit's life, from the fount whence cometh all love, all bliss, all peace, and repose that bloweth into the ample heart of man.

[57]   Idea of Immortality

The adult may doubt; the child never. The adult may seek, and seeking illusions may find them to reimage his own disbelief in the human heart's affections. He may see and sympathize with the transits of Nature through the emblems of decay, but these the child deemeth proofs of his own immortality. He peopleth the solitudes and the tombs with life. He maketh all things tell the story of continuance. There is no stop in his thought; and where the sense droppeth him, the heart taketh him up and lifteth him above things into the blessed and pure realities of faith. There is no sepulchre that bindeth its tenant. "He is not here; he is risen!" is the language of his spirit, and he saith, "Come see the place where the spirit lay!" but addeth, "It is gone!" in the glad spirit of prophecy.

[58] **Spirit Cannot Apprehend Death**

The child feedeth on the sense and ever hath the dim vision of the Immortal in his spirit. And it is because this is the absolute life of his being that he cannot apprehend death. The sense of life is within him, and the void of death is no more than a phantom —a mere fancy picture—an incarnated fear—doubt—despair—all deriving their seeming existence to the thinking spirit from itself. Yet devoid of meaning are they. They are life minus life plus death—misimaging phantasies, bewildering enigmas, which seem and yet are not. Death presupposes a faith in life, and this faith redeems the idea from a negative value. It takes out of it the notion of stop, cessation, which have no type in the Spirit. Mortality pertains to nought save the forms and organs—the embodying of life. It is but the generalization and exponent of change. It is a [59] negation of the Spirit—a cypher over the faith of being. It seemeth to be by illusion of sense. The shadow is, because there is substance.

[59] **Spirit Endoweth Nature With Life**

The child lives. Therefore, all that he thinketh and feeleth and expecteth receiveth life in his configuring ideal, since the life that stirreth within him endoweth all with its own essence. The blessed gift he bestoweth on all. Nature is made alive. Sense is substantiated in his vision. His inner life eddieth around itself, and he perceiveth the successive circlings that image themselves on the surface of his consciousness. A spirit moveth over the face of the waters. The Infinite and Immortal is pictured in his thought. Its calm is the emblem of death.

[60]
> Doth not the farmer's hope—the scattered grain—
> Lie in the darksome earth 'mid winter's reign?
> Yet did he fail to sow it? No, not he—
> When spring should come, he knew 'twould harvest be.
> Hope is the sower; faith the quickening beam.
> The child believes, and reapeth every dream.
> Even as the corn-seed lifteth up its head,
> Doth childhood's spirit vivify the dead.   *1 Cor.* 15:17.
> And, in the perilous hour that fancy sees,
> The death-pang blesses, and at once relieves.

[61] **Harmony of Development**

The babe comes forth in quiet harmony. She wakes up the slumbering senses and puts them on their watches as the sentinels of the Spirit. She looks out more than she did, defines voices more readily, discovers their direction, and detects movements. She sympathises in expressions of countenance with a nicer intelligence, apprehending in these phenomena some of the mysterious functions of the life that enacteth itself within. She is free from organic obstruction. Pain forms no item of her experience. The cravings of the organic functions are fed and satisfied. She [62] cries but seldom; often smiles. The prevailing temper of her spirit seems that of repose—deep, still, sustained peace. She is quiet, self-satisfied, self-subsistent. On the ocean of the Infinite doth her spirit calmly lie as a simple wavelet, unagitated by distant storms.

[62] **Repose of Spirit**

Yet how difficult it is to sustain a young and susceptible creature in this kingdom of quietude—of self-repose—in which every function of the spirit performs its appropriate office, and each works for the other, and all for each! How easy to break in upon this harmony and cause the agitated waves of evil from without to mingle their turbid streams with the clear and lucid elements of the original fount of spiritual life! To fulfil this complex work is thy work, O Parent, and woe be to thee if thou be faithless to [63] thy sacred trust. Better were it for thee that thou hadst remained in the universal consciousness without the sense of thy individual will, than to have come into this scene of being, to cherish the angels of the Divinity, for thou pollutest them and makest them the children of the earth.

[66] **Cities Starve the Spirit**

And waiving these, there are causes at work on them, as on all young natures at this season confined in cities, that tend to prostrate the spiritual in our nature. Much of the petulance—most that annoys both parent and child—has its origin in the artificial arrangements of society and things in cities. Parents transmit the influence as they imbibe it from the bare and lifeless aspects of things around them. They have little true and genial sympathy with the beauty and serenity of Nature. Brick walls, paved streets, rattling chariots, and all the bustle and stir, the false glitter and show of a city, are not the best supporters [67] of the senses; nor are the men and women who move amid these shows always the simplest and purest. Their influence is not like that of Nature. It is not on such fare that a young spirit can satisfy itself. Nought is there to supply the cravings of the sense of the beautiful; nought to beautify and refresh the imagery of the imagination; nought for the heart's purest longings; nought for the poetry of life. The temple of the Spirit is Nature—beautiful, simple, ever-renewing Nature, undimmed by the awkward essays of man's art—of that for which the city prides itself, but which, with all her pretense, is but the mockery of Nature—a mockery to which man, long survilized,* approximates, his mind growing prim, stiff, wanting the air and gracefulness of essential humanity. Sickly sensibilities [68] ape the healthful life of the soul, and the whole being becomes barren and puny.

[68]   The Country Quickens and Renovates
Man, indeed, can never flourish and put forth all his powers in their full luxuriance and strength by relying solely on the imagery and influence of a city. He does not get the benefit of creation's ample provisions. He starves his spirit in some sort. He seeks to feed it with unsubstantial fare. Doth he drink of the pure spring? Doth he tread the mountain heights, parley with the elements, commune with the quietude and repose of Nature? Doth he behold the Divinity ever first and uppermost in his senses, view the things and creatures that have followed the simple path of their being, unbeguiled by art's deceptive wiles? No! These he liveth not upon, and he is dead!

[72]   The Face is the Spirit's Visor
Behind this mask are we, and by a curiosity which time never quenches nor satiates do we still obey the instinct—heaven-given—to pry behind that we may find ourselves. How soon the child beginneth the work. Hardly is he a tenant of this outer world, ere he begins this same mystic kenning of things, and how truly doth he ken! He findeth himself behind the scene, and he painteth this Self-Image from the Type that we set before him from ourselves! Perchance we give him a Demon-Image. Yet he taketh it and calleth it an angel of light. He investeth the unsightly born with his own ideal beauty, and none knoweth the deformity save the deformed themselves, in whose image they apprehend the self-shape as it is. Strange that we never saw our veritable face—the flesh-and-blood that tells all our spirit's history!

[76]   Culture of the Imagination
There are few works suited to the minds of the young, whose spiritual sense finds little on which to feed. Even our variety of works of pure fancy is small. Besides Grimm's *Tales* from the German, "The Story Without An End," and a few of the early English fictions, now almost gone out of use, we have nothing for the young. Works of fiction are, indeed, sedulously shut out of the nursery and schoolroom in many instances, and it is beginning to be a sin to have that very unprofitable faculty of imagination. The Beautiful in form, sentiment, idea, and art, is excluded.

[87]   The Gospel of Childhood
The gospel of childhood—who hath written it? The Infant Christ—who hath delineated it? Who even hath found the meaning of the facts given in the records of the Evangelists? The Ideal Child—who hath represented it by setting it forth in fit words —incarnated it for the vision of the little ones that dwell among us? We have neither the spiritual nor the flesh-and-blood picture that is wanted. The Child-Saviour hath not yet been fully revealed to us in the simple ways of holiness. Childhood hath not as yet a gospel. There is no intelligible saviour for it—no example—no [88] full revelation of its own divine humanity. The Incarnation hath not taken place for it, and if it be lost, it is for the want of this flesh-and-blood Type of Itself.

[88]   Saviour of Childhood
Yet shall not one arise of simple heart and clear apprehension to image forth this being? One who shall apprehend the facts of everyday life in their sublime simplicity, and record in fit phrase and living theory the great life of the Spirit in childhood? Truly, I sometimes feel as if inspired to the work. Nought is there wanting but the divine vision, and this shall come if I live true and faithful to the Ideal. Even these

---

* Either a coined word or a badly written "formalized."

simple pages may become part of the great record, for now and then do I seem to rise to the pure and perfect, and find the words glittering with life!

[89] Who Apprehendeth the Spirit of Childhood?

Yet amid the innumerable wants of childhood, not as yet even apprehended by the wiser minds of the time, how shall I unfold the grounds of these wants and* hint even at the means of supply? Everything seems to be wanting—the apprehending mind, in the first place. Can I but get the clear vision, then shall the rest follow. Apprehending principles, defining elements, I shall be led to methods—processes of setting these forth. But who is sufficient for these things? For they are, indeed, the great things of the Spirit—and the Spirit in its first essayings on the works of space, in time, by the instrumentality of body. Who apprehendeth his own spirit or remembereth the life of infancy and childhood with that vividness of affection to conceive even of what goeth [90] on in the pure and loving spirit of an infant? Verily, none knoweth these things. In their own mysterious life are they hidden. Only a transient vision of them is vouchsafed to man in his incarnate state. Can the Son of Man fully apprehend the Son of God, not being as yet lifted up to the seraphic life of the Spirit, and yet without the reassurance of the Absolute? To the pure and docile-minded, however, some revelations shall be made. I may come in for mine in so far as I am pure and faithful. Let me then search out the Indwelling Life as it passeth by in fitful vision, making its transit across the beings of my little ones. Shall not the mystery of life open before me as I advance? Day by day do the deeds and things find some interpretation and shed their light around me as [91] a glory. Am I in the transfiguring cloud, communing with the Invisible, building my tabernacle therein, and feeling that "it is good to be there?"

[91] Oracle of the Spirit

Not until I am there shall I find the solution of the spiritual problem that my spirit laboureth to solve as the mission upon which it hath come. I would settle some disputed points in the theology of the time. I would shadow forth truth not only to the head, but inspire it into the heart and make principle visible in the concrete. Too long hath humanity been perplexed by the complex scheme of being that hath been current. Its simple sublimity hath not been set forth as it may. Life has been a mysterious thing; childhood, a [92] perplexity, over which the light of certainty hath not dawned. We have had no axioms of spiritual science growing out of our being. We have had no settled notions of our humanity.

[92] Philosophy of Spirit

Yet there is, I will believe, a philosophy of our being. It is a philosophy that includes in its broad sweep all elements, all combinations, and embodiments of elements, taking in the child and running on to the adult, antedating our terrestrial life and outdating its continuance—a vision, bifaced, bisighted, running backward to beginning and forward to ending, and without absolute stop, stay, or setting out! Its outline is Christianity, and Christ is its filling up. The synthesis and the analysis are united and are *one* in Him! Apprehend, O Spirit, and reveal!

[93] Subtlety of Spirit

And in the prosecution of this endeavour, I come to the close of a day. And now as the shades of evening devolve upon the past—the shadowy things of this same day— shall I know what hath been brought forth for record and representation on these pages, whereon I purpose to delineate, as I may, the subtle life of the Spirit that energizeth in the bodies of these little ones, and without weariness or stop essayeth all its unimagined, unuttered things. I know not what the day hath tempted forth from their Ideal. Joys and sorrows, hopes and fears, images and ideas, sentiments and thoughts, instincts and senses, have all been busy—all conspiring to open out into the life of the visible, the inner being, and to vehicle aright its powers and susceptibilities for the great mission of self-insight and self-mastery.

[94] Omnipotence of Spirit

Verily, this is an ever-going agency. It stoppeth not; it faltereth not. On it passeth, and is there any terrestrial incumbrance that overmastereth it? Doth death? O no! Death removeth the incumbrance. Death setteth it free—lifteth it out of the body— taketh all shackle from its functions. Life it is. This is its vision—its consciousness. And out of this cometh the objective being that giveth substance to the day that it honoreth.

[95] Entrance of Evil into Spirit

How early doth this demon from without enter the young heart! Nursery menials

---

* The Ms. reads "and to."

bring it in. The imaged passion becomes a type for the little imitator. Boisterous words, violent [96] gestures, threats, reproofs, punishments, passions, "all envy, malice, wrath, and uncharitableness," become the atmosphere of the young spirit; and how can it escape evil, while tempted by everything of sense? Wonderful is the strength of the young celestial. He liveth in the midst of evil, and how strong is he for a while in withstanding it! If beguiled at last, it was almost against his will. With appetites, instincts, senses, passions, all alive to the outward, how can he scarce escape? He will fall; but who is there to raise him up and make his mischance a lesson? Who shall lead him through the gate of repentance into the fold through which he hath broken, more in ignorance than in guilt? Alas! There are none, too often, to lead the wanderer back—none to teach him the error of his way, and so he goeth down the dark paths of error till he forgetteth the sweet repose once his own!

[97] Revelation of Spirit to Spirit

There are absolute elements—simple, few, definite—the productive powers of humanity. The growth of our being, as a whole, is indicated by the integrity of each of these members. Spirit is the trunk of which these are the branches; and these determine its productivity. These may be represented in a diagram. Thus,

REVELATION (i.e., the influence of the Divine Spirit on the human spirit) is, in order,	1. The Sense of the Beautiful.
	2. The Sentiment of the Good.
	3. The Idea of the True.

[97] The Sense of the Beautiful

It is in this order and through these faculties [98] that the Divine Spirit reveals his own perfection to the spirit of man. All revelation begins in sense. It is typified in the Beautiful, whether of spiritual or physical being. There can be no true apprehension of beauty without a spiritual act. This is the *first revelation*, and it is coeval with human consciousness, being its element and ground. With it the infant begins his kennings on things. Simple beauty is the charm that liveth in his Ideal, and every type delighteth him. He loseth himself in it, and by the apprehension of it is led onward to the second burst of spiritual glory that cometh upon him.

[98] The Sentiment of the Good

This is the sentiment of the Good. As the dawn betokeneth and is the herald of the day, even so is the sense of the Beautiful the antepast of the Good. Yet is the morning not the full and meridian light. This cometh at noon in the round-orbed sun. As the [99] morning announceth the promise of the noon, doth the Good prophesy the True; and in these three is the Revelation complete. |Sense|Sentiment|Idea|—these are the Spirit's functions, and human nature is but the complex activity of these agencies. They are the members of that sublime synthesis, under which incarnate man is to be studied, and by the analysis and apprehension of which, the theory of our being is revealed.

$$God \quad : \quad Sense \quad : \quad : \quad Beauty$$
$$God \quad : \quad Sentiment \quad : \quad : \quad Good$$
$$God \quad : \quad Idea \quad : \quad : \quad Truth$$

Thus standeth the problem for the human spirit's action thereon. He that worketh out the first member is *feeling* after God. He that espouseth the second is *enacting* God. He only that extendeth his endeavour to the third *apprehendeth* Him in his thought and completeth [100] the Revelation by applying all his faculties to the great Intuition. On him hath the Divinity fully wrought. He alone hath wrought, being a co-worker with the Original.

[100] Childhood—A Revelation of Spirit

And the infant enters into this first work at once. There is no delay. The Revelation is upon him. It radiateth from him. He is it. His senses are the functions that cannot rest. Toward the Beautiful they stray out of themselves and will not return till they have found it. Early may it be found! Elizabeth hath already found it. Her notice was arrested today by the sight of flowers on the mantel of the nursery, and so deep-felt was her delight that she smiled at the vision. The sense of the Beautiful found representation in the flower-emblem expressive of beauty.

[102] Childhood—An Emblem of the Spiritual

The infant is to all the emblem of goodness. To childhood it is emphatically. Beauty of form, countenance, motion—its very freedom from all resentment, its simple trust, its serene and placid spirit, its joyous and ever-gleeful temper, its sympathy with all things around it, its very weaknesses and imperfections—all tend to make the impression of good on the heart of a child—and this, to become an embodiment of the sentiment that is enkindled in his heart—not the less a type of goodness to him, though the sense of evil hath not by contrast found apprehension in the mind of the little one. Wherever there is Beauty, the element of the Good hath been at work, and, though hidden in its workings, the visual or spiritual sense feeleth the divine agency and takes it as one of the revelations of the Holy and True. Beauty is, indeed, but the countenance of Goodness [103] and Truth. It is the herald of the two. As the face of man lighteth and announceth the forthcoming sentiment and the mouth prepareth to utter it in fit passage, even so doth Beauty image forth the sentiment of the Good and announce the living words of Truth in the vivid and spirit-beholding Idea.

[103]   Nature—The Face of the Spiritual
Nature, in the simple grandeur of her countenance, revealeth to the eye of man the dim image of her own Idea, and the living heart findeth the meaning which the head announceth. Creation is the face of the Divine Spirit. Whoso looketh on this face with a simple and trusting heart shall interpret her mysterious meanings and not want words fit to image the Living Idea, which that same face shadows forth to the eyes of sense.

[103]   Genius Representeth the Spiritual
The child hath this good and trusting heart, [104] and he ever looketh out upon the face of his Father, as this same Father ever revealeth himself to his truth-loving spirit within. And wherever he looketh forth, he seeth the same divine expression and knoweth that it is his Father's. Ever thus doth the poet, the artist, the philosopher, apprehend; and this simple apprehension cometh from the same living trust in Nature and the quickening influence that it lendeth to the Spirit's vision. Beauty is revealed, whether of Truth or of Good, and the charm and the tint and the form are ever its accompaniment. Beauty spreadeth itself out before them, and they are its revealers to the senses and reason of man. And in contemplating it, all men return for a moment to the simple apprehension of childhood, and both child and adult accept the delineation as a type of their sentiment and Idea.

[105]   Spirit Endoweth Nature
The Spirit endoweth every sensible thing with its own individual life. As this is, so are the things upon which it rests its vision, for it is this same vision that formeth every separate image around the heart and quickeneth it in the mind. A child makes all things like himself. They are imaged after his own Ideal. As he thinks, feels, sees, acts, so is he; and to this he conformeth the external. And thus is it pictured in him.

[105]   Self-Finding
This morning I saw Elizabeth while her mother was preparing her for the day. The form and motions of an infant—how beautiful! How expressive is every motion—every articulation [106] of its members! Beautifully did she lie in her mother's lap, exposing the vestment of the Spirit to the view, while from her countenance radiated the indwelling life of which this same body was the visible shaping and sign. How open were her arms! How confidingly did she stretch them forth toward that nature on whom she now relies for that sustaining influence which shall supply the waste and exhaustion of the animal functions of the flesh, into which she hath just entered! How ardently doth she seek, by an instinctive sense, among the shapes and shows of things visible, for types of her own Ideal, asking body to her thoughts and endowing all that she beholds with the life of her own being. Doth there aught of doubt image itself in her countenance or gesture? Doth she look downward for light and life? O, no! She looketh *upward* and *beyond* the visible as she [107] looketh *from above* and *beyond* it. She looketh on the visible because her vision hath been disciplined on the invisible. The dim, flesh-imaged shapes are but transcripts of her spiritual apprehension; and hardly doth she know them, so imperfect are they—so inaccurate is the counterfeit. Her position is, in itself, a prayer of aspiration; her breathing life, an ascription. She hath faith; she hath love; she is bent heavenward. She turneth toward the source of Spirit by the sense that worketh deep within her, even as the sunflower towards the radiant light on which it feeds! And her smiles (drawn from everything she beholds), the delicate ear, the exquisite touch, the sense of perfume—over all parts of this body doth the spiritual influence circulate, coming to the surface of every member and testing every outward thing. All is alive, because the quickening agency flows into all. And [108] how fresh and new! Spring morning is a fit emblem of this newness. The vivifying breath of morning is a type of its freshness.

[108] Mirror of Sense

Verily, in every motion, in every look, in every sense and instinct and function of the child, doth the Infinite Spirit labour. And with these frail instruments doth it seek to apprehend and repossess the Idea of the Infinite (which is the life of the mind) and to represent it in finite imagery. The imagery of sense is a mirror in which the Spirit surveys its own features, beholding itself in the magnificent glass of Nature! And how readily doth the child go upon this mission! How quickly he begins his survey of the mysterious Outward! How strong his faith in it! How doth it charm him from day to day! How joyfully doth he [109] renew his task on each successive morning and continue it with short sessions of rest throughout the livelong day! From hour to hour, from moment to moment, ever as constant as his own flitting pulse, is the charmed work. And all his wakeful life is a glad sense of vision—of sentiment—and thought. His whole soul cometh forth in all its might to realize that which his heart conceiveth or his spirit willeth. Of the kingdom of sense, he seeketh an early conquest, for he comes armed with celestial weapons, and why should he not triumph? Yea, he shall triumph, if assisted in these hours of his weak pupilage. He shall "overcome the world," for he hath more than the world already in his possession. He cometh to prove the reality of his faith and the depth of his love in order to apprehend it himself.

[110] Nature and Man Nurse the Spirit

And the other two little ones are now in happier mood. Under the administration of a nursery maid of more lively, joyous, sustained spirit they seem to thrive. Could I add the beautiful vision of Nature at this season, they* would dilate in happiness. They pine for the country. They need the repose of Nature. Not the human face alone, though the type of joy and serenity is adequate to quicken all the powers of the spirit. Nature's myriad-imaged countenance—the sign of all that lives in their spirits—is wanted; or all that remains within untempted will there lie dormant. Nature—human and physical—this is the quickening agency. It bringeth forth the faculties of the Spirit. It is the stimulus of humanity. Let no parent starve the child of its humanizing influences. In early spring let him take his young progeny to commune with her in her manifold variety, and fill them with her life.

[111] Nature Quickens the Spirit

I am desirous of taking Anna and Louisa into the country to pass a month with them. Could I do this, not a little of their life would be seized for this record, which now wholly escapes me. This excursion they need. It would do more to diversify and renovate their associations, to quicken the true being of their hearts, modify their dispositions and meliorate their habits, than anything else within my means. They would be brought more under my immediate supervision. The accidents of their being, now lost in the monotony of a city, would be noted. Of their favorite amusements, choice phrases and common images—of the true history of their spirits, in short, I should put myself in possession. Their range of thought, their vocabulary, their prevailing tendencies, whether to good or evil, would be revealed to me.

[112] Journey with the Children

It is my intention to take them to my own native village—to my mother's. There, amidst the wildness of Nature and the scenes of my own mind's formation, can I be to them, for a while, the father that I image in my Ideal. Childhood's young life would revisit me. Surrounded by the emblems of my germinating sentiments and fancies, I should bring forth that which, when distant, lieth latent in my being. I should return to the being as well as to the scenes of my childhood, and with theirs write off, in living words, types of the things and thoughts that quickened my being—the history of my own life—with theirs. The father shall be seen in the son's forming being; the language of his thoughts and sentiments, in the imagery that surrounds his paternal home.

[116] Invocation to the Spirit

O thou unapproachable, unapprehensible Spirit—the Inspirer of the infant and of the adult, of our sleeping or of our waking life, yet of whose life and being we can form no visible image! There is no likeness of thee in the heaven above or in the earth beneath or in the waters under the earth. Thou canst not be apprehended by the senses nor worshipped aright by the fleshly reason of man. Thou art known by the [117] communication of thyself alone, and whoso hath not been inspired by thee and is possessed by this afflux of thyself knoweth not himself, nor can he be conscious of thy being. Even faith and reason are but the reflex shadows of thyself. They bind their

---

* Ms. reads "and they."

being in thee, and without thee are not at all. How can dwellers in clay apprehend thee as thou art in thy absolute life? Thanks to the Perfected, thou hast in him incarnated thyself; and man through him hath fellowship with thee by attaining the assurance and the sense of his humanity. In him thou mirrorest forth thyself and becomest a God of flesh.

[117] Jesus—The Emblem of the Perfect

And in the being of childhood—"the angel that ever retains a vision of thine Image" —thou art revealed to us. In the dream thou visitest them, and in waking life. And yet how doth man pass heedlessly by thy comings, knowing thee not, having [118] no sense of thy presence. He hath lost the sense and the apprehension. In dim and fitful glimpses the Infinite cometh up in his spirit, but it soon departs. He hath no faculty to detain it in his thought. The outward hath overshadowed him, and he liveth and is lost in the shadow!

[118] The Imaging of the Perfect

Yet all the time doth thy influence work in the hearts of thy children. It stirreth them to the charities of love. It leadeth them to the holy engagements of wedlock. It quickeneth their very bodies, and they reimage their love in the forms of the flesh! But not always do they feel thy holy influence, nor do they see aught in these forms save the material. They trace not thy outline—the heavenly features that thou hast assumed. They linger around organs. They are curious of functions. They image hidden and [119] ignoble delights; dwell among instruments when they should apprehend uses and ends. Verily, these [propagate] impurity in the world. Lust taketh the sacred functions of love and peopleth the earth with its own progeny. Man maketh himself a brute, and he begetteth his like. What else can he perpetuate if he do not love and be simple?

[119] Lust Perpetuateth Itself

Let none think of hiding his impurities from even the world's eye. He cannot escape the penalty of disobedience. The violated law scatters and compensates itself in the beings of his offspring.* In them will his own sins be reimaged to his senses. As living reproofs will they meet his eyes in his daily ways. His own life flows in them. If it be physical, he must perceive in humiliation and feel the injustice and wickedness of his crime. He is in them, and they are a part of him. They suffer [120] in and for his sins, and he knoweth it. And nought, perhaps, can scarce redeem them from the penalty.

[124] Central Force of Spirit

Spirit—this is the centre around which every faculty rangeth itself to do the bidding of this Central Force. As a fountain it floweth forth and runneth through the whole being. It penetrateth the whole. It is the Force of which all these functions are the exponent and sign. *In* it, all are substantiated; *by* it, all are nurtured. It is the energy of this that moveth and sendeth them on their separate errands. They are the servants of the Spirit and await its bidding.

[133] Consciousness Is the Sense of the Infinite

The sense of the Infinite is universal. It is an original element of every human being, and the influence of one mind over another is determined by the degree in which he inspires this sense and manifests its grounds to another. The philosopher gains credence in proportion as he represents this sense in the reason of man; the artist, in the heart; the hero, in life. It must be embodied to the senses—made flesh and blood—take the semblance of fact. A reliance on this sense alone is the true principle and cause of success. No man ever accomplished a mission without it. Jesus [134] appealed to it constantly. It was the universal consciousness to which he addressed all his sublime teachings, and it was this that apprehended his miracles. Every word, every act, every apprehension of his, was a miracle; and all humanity acknowledged the presence of the supernatural in him.

[134] Humanity Liveth on the Infinite

Man, indeed, liveth and feedeth on this same supernatural sense. Through this doth all his spiritual life flow. Give the supernatural, and all else taketh its place. All else outrageth the same divine life. Immortality is the light that shineth forth from the spiritual sense and maketh the heart of man to throb with the sublime hope that, as he hath ever lived, so will he never die. Believest thou not this, proud skeptic? Then thou dost not believe thou livest; for unless thou acknowledgest this thou art not a living being, and thy doubt is [135] thy grave! To live is to acknowledge a god, and to know God is to know of neither beginning nor end. Thou hast the Idea. Where didst thou get

---

* Coleridge, *Table Talk*, Vol. II, p. 52. [Alcott's note].

it, and who gave it to thee. And, moreover, who made thee capable of drinking it in and apprehending it?

[135]   Nature Illustrates Spirit

Nothing is complete until it is enacted. A fact is Spirit having consummated its particular mission, attained its end, fully revealed itself. In it is the Infinite signified by the finite. And in the apprehension of a fact, all man's being hath wrought, even the will, since he can apprehend nothing that hath no type in his consciousness and hath not been enacted in some humble measure. The apprehension partakes of the character of more or less the same in kind, differing only in degree. Hence facts are the evidences of spiritual operations, and prove that Spirit hath been at work [136] in the instances to which they refer. They are the phenomena of spirit. The miracles of a religion—the facts of a religion—are the illustrations of the spiritual power of that religion. The more of the supernatural the religion embodies, the stronger the evidence in its favor, provided there be no infraction of spiritual laws—no surrender of the supernatural to the natural—no treachery of matter or spirit.

[136]   Organization Illustrates Spirit

Breathing is a spiritual fact. Its proof is in itself. The instruments and organs *illustrate* the miracle; they do not *prove* it. Birth is a miracle. There are many analogies in Nature, but no proofs of this spiritual fact. The proof is itself. It is the completion of a spiritual process and is full. A new series begins in it. Life is a miracle. Its evidence is in itself. We cannot apprehend any other.

[149]   Punishment

Doth a kind and pious parent ever punish his child? Yea, in proportion to his love and piety he punisheth him, and he showeth these mainly in the spirit with which he inflicts it: not in anger, not in severe and rebuking words, not in the amount of suffering that he giveth, but in the penitence that he exciteth, the hope that he bringeth forth, the faith in conscience, and the virtuous resolve that he inspireth with the success and beauty of his discipline. Unless he touch the heart of his child—unless he open before him the sacred nature that the child hath belied—and awaken in him a deep and humble penitence and a self-sacrificing purpose, he hath done no [150] good. He may have done an injury to the spiritual being of his child, although the punishment may have been administered by the most fit methods and, as a form, be perfect in its kind. Not so is Spirit administered unto. He who deals with a young being in anger or in the exercise of a wanton authority shall pay the forfeit of his rashness and impiety. Spirit will not then be subdued. Only to its own force will it submit. Violence only setteth it against the assaulting power. It causeth reaction, and the wounded spirit putteth itself on the defensive, calleth all instruments to its aid, and biddeth defiance to arbitrary power. It entrencheth itself in its own citadel and plyeth its forces against violence. Not so is the parent to excite his child. One voice and one word he hath, and this the child ever apprehendeth. [151] It is the voice of love, sympathising in his spiritual state and proffering aids and encouragement to lift the violated spirit from the evils into which, more in ignorance or weakness than in guilt, it hath fallen.

[159]   Childhood—A Revelation

Verily, a child is a revelation from the Infinite One. And this revelation is made to every parent. To him the Living Word is made flesh and dwelleth in his very presence, even before his very eyes. And, as if to give a more touching and affecting view of the relation between him and the Revealing One, the child taketh the fleshly image of the parent, and he cannot look upon him without the sense of his own identity coming over him with an overmastering force. And his affinity [160] with the Godhead through this living type—this incarnation of the Idea of himself and of God—is revealed to him as from the mouth of the Holy One! God is supernaturally before him and displayeth his hidden mysterious nature through the body and manners of his little one!

[160]   God in Childhood

And the inner functions of this being—the spiritual life that gusheth out and sparkleth around his child! A glory shineth around his head. In him the Divine Radiance dawneth upon the parent; and if he have the lingering sense of the godlike within him, this emblem must quicken it into life and activity. That spirit is of God. It is heavenly. It is the supernatural. It is a revelation in the flesh. It is the son of the Divine Parent. It is the offspring of the earthly also.

[161]   Sense of God's Presence

There are periods in the life of everyone when a sense of loneliness comes over the spirit, and the idea of isolation from the Universal overpowers, for a passing moment, the associations of the mind. Such moods are not, perhaps, common. To a spiritually minded person they cannot be. He is accustomed to regard himself, as it were, in the presence and under the care of the Presiding Spirit. He is surrounded by the signatures of his care—by the tokens of his love. All his wonted associations include the idea of a friend and protector. Spirit is enstamped on all his ideas. From his heart there comes a sentiment of community. Desertion enters not into his [162] thought. In the all-pervading Life and Love he enters for his humble share, and surrounding beings participate in the same beneficence.

[167] Confusion of Waking and Sleeping Life

She† often wakes and calls for her father—for mother—and is not easily appeased sometimes even when they assure her of their wakefulness. And her dreams are so vivid and impressive that they are taken for realities of sense, and she refers to them afterward as facts in her experience. So strong is her faith in them that no reasoning, not even the faith she places in the assurance of her parents, makes her relinquish the conviction. Thus unconsciously, even to us, perchance, doth our waking and sleeping life coalesce and lose their separate forms in one predominating [168] sentiment or idea, and take a common unity in the Spirit, from whence they sprang into life and shaping.

[168] Life is Bifold

And why spend all the time of sleep in a mere negative life? Why waste one third of our terrestrial existence sunk in the forgetfulness of sleep? It cannot be. It is not in harmony with the Creator's wise purposes. We do sleep. We dream. Sometimes the dream is revived by the facts of our waking life. Sometimes it floweth so imperceptibly and simply into our thought, spreading over the aggregate of our spirits, that we lose sight of it as a dream; and it cometh up in our consciousness as an original thing. But whence and where come all our ideas? Where but from that inexhaustible fountain of the Spirit. And when they come is but a question of time, in order to give us a history—outward, sensible—of our thought. Dreams are spiritual; and, for aught we know, all thoughts are dreams in the process of coming to us.

[171] Vivacity of Imagination

Anna was much interested this morning in a picture representing the contrasted effects of good and evil. She spent some time over it. Her love of the Beautiful leads her to take much satisfaction in pictures. When very young, the accuracy of her eye was obvious, and her volumes of picture books served to feed and develope this sense. She associates with every scene the spiritual and intellectual as well as moral and physical relations which it is suited to awaken and embody. Her memory is already teeming with tales thus connected with these graphic scenes. Indeed, her ideas and feelings (all that represents her inmost life) is embodied in this picturesque way, [which is] the first communicating medium between the Spirit and Nature—the primal language of Spirit. For Nature to the child is a [172] mysterious hieroglyphic—an emblem of the subtle life that flows through the child's spirit and seeks manifestation, shaping, body, in the objects of the material creation. Of him we may say, adopting the beautiful lines of the poet* (himself an unspoiled child of Nature—one of her fancy-filled offspring—ever delighting and ever bringing her mystic meanings to light):

> Symbolical is all that meets the sense,
> One mighty alphabet for infant minds,
> And man, in this low world, placed with his back
> To bright Reality, that he may view
> With young unwounded ken, the substance
> From the shadow.

[181] Sundry Counsels To Those Training a Child

Beguile not its heart by thy carnal policy. Divest it not of its simplicity by the

---

† Anna Alcott.

* The poet is S. T. Coleridge. Alcott is apparently quoting him from memory and hence the inaccuracy. Lines 17-22 of "The Destiny of Nations" read as follows:

> For all that meets the bodily sense I deem
> Symbolical, one mighty alphabet
> For infant minds; and we in this low world
> Placed with our backs to bright Reality,
> That we may learn with young unwounded ken
> The substance from its shadow.

pretences and affectations of cunning. Be not an example of evil and thus give it the authority of thine own way. Perplex it not by maxims drawn from the world. Shape not its heart by [182] false pretences of the flesh. Dim not its mind by animal indulgence. Keep not the bodily appetites before it nor debauch its fancy by images of impurity. Talk not of the outward as the end of any pursuit. Disappoint not its trifling affections by fixing them on unworthy or unfaithful objects. Make neither the reason nor the understanding the ultimates of action. Speak not of bodily pain as the dreaded evil of life nor of death as the close of all that confess joy and delight. Teach it not to distrust its own conscience nor to doubt the divinity of its being. Delineate life as no low existence—as the sole source of good. Disturb him not nor confound his moral senses and spiritual revelation by the perplexing exhibitions of vice and evil in the world. Give no existence to these save what our [183] imperfect apprehension assigns them. Leave not to mere acts the great truth that there is in thine heart a sense of Providence. Conceal not thy faith in the Invisible. Leave nothing out of God by disjointing and breaking up his works. Speak not slightingly of these works nor check his spiritual vision when the child sees more in these works than thou dost. Do not hesitate to follow him, if thou canst, in his flights toward the Invisible. Is he poetic? Laugh not at his image. Is he romantic? Stifle not the sentiment. Is he imaginative? Bring him not down to terrene. Doth he say and feel much that thou canst not apprehend? Reverence the prophecy and seek to find out its mysterious meaning. Think not that he cannot teach thee nor that he is taught only of the world, and thou of God. He will soon teach thee more of God than thou hast [184] learned from all other sources. He will be a Revealed Word to thee, and thou shalt find wisdom to discharge thy mission.

[193] Childhood—A Prophet

Sure as the morning comes, the little one arouses herself from the inner consciousness of dreams and all the phantom imagery of sleep to look out upon the outward scene whereon man enacteth the drama of his inmost purposes and desires. Out she looketh to resume her own mysterious communion with the things and persons whom God hath placed before and around her, and to find, if she may, some new meaning to her heart's ideal—some fuller revelation of the spirit that liveth within her, whose quickening influences are ever endowing all that she beholds with their own divine and conscious light! The prophet within is ever telling her some new tale of the outer life and leading [194] her vision to apprehend the fulfilment of the prophecy.

[194] Spirit Issues Through the Heart

Ever doth the *heart* precede the *head*, and the first is the herald and prophet of the other. As in infancy and childhood the heart is the foreteller and seer of life's purposes and prospects, and the head becometh the co-worker to bring up the labour and carry out its completion; even so should it be in the days of adolescence, for then is the heart the same divine prophet. And woe to him who hath distrusted the prophecy and taken counsel of the blind and shortsighted head—which is but the humble interpreter and representative of the heart's purposes, but never the rival or predecessor! Whoso listeneth to the teachings of the heart shall become wise. He shall know of the doctrine, whether it be of God or of man, while he that seeketh to apprehend all by his head shall stumble and fall over the truths that his heart loveth and shall become a fool in very deed.

[195] Revelation Cometh Through the Heart

In the pure and loving heart are there truths and principles which it shall take the head long to apprehend and explain, and in this is its special mission to the individual. Study thy heart, O Man! In this is thy humanity. In this is the history of thy nature. In this is the fact and surety of thy immortality. And insofar as thou apprehendest this sacred emblem of thy being, art thou inspired by the revelations of God and made capable of understanding thy inheritance in the truths of the Gospel of his Son. In this is thy faith, thy hope, thy love, thy life, and not till thou hast penetrated the mysteries of thy heart canst thou discharge thy duties to thyself or thy friend.

Childhood liveth upon its own simple, loving, trusting heart, and hence its serene peace, its joy, and holy faith. Childhood is the mirror [196] of the serene, the confiding, the blessed. Look thou often upon it, O Parent, and find that peace without which thou canst neither be thyself nor be a parent to thy child!

[223] Charm of Spirit

Parent, what thinkest thou that thy little one is doing from early morn to evening late as he sitteth or essayeth his senses in silence, asking little of thee save his needful sustenance and thy sympathetic glances to renew from time to time his sense of the human by sympathy with thee? What chasm is there in this outward sense which to thee, perchance, is devoid of all interest? He sitteth, perhaps, in the confinement of the nursery. He hath but a small space of his Father's infinite mansion to look out upon and essay his exhaustless life thereon, yet how doth he busy himself all the livelong day and find ever-renewing interest in the objects of his confinement! Affluent is Spirit. He investeth his poverty with its richness. He peopleth the little space around him from his ever-teeming Ideal, [224] and, though mid finite things, hath an infinitude of images within his spirit. And with this he essayeth the nakedness of his domicile! While thou art, perhaps, barren, he is rich and fruitful, and by sympathizing with him, thou mayest, perhaps, revive thine own Ideal and be reborn into the same blessed Kingdom that he hath not as yet died out of.

[227] ### Growth of the Spiritual

As the flower openeth out its beauties and cometh out to our vision by slow and imperceptible advances, unfolding its secret properties unseen by the eye of man, even so doth childhood disclose its latent powers, stealing gradually upon the mind and eye with the sense of its inner being and endeavourings. It shapeth forth its destiny by subtle handiwork, which no man apprehendeth. It worketh noiselessly. It displayeth no scaffolding—no framework—around its purpose, for it is its own scaffolding—its own framework, and all is lost in the central principle, even as the rose is the stalk, the blossom and the [228] leaves. Nature is ever a unity. She pusheth forth her hidden forces in harmonious developement. She conformeth the organ to the power and so bringeth all forth in every complex process as to present the idea of wholeness to the eye of sense. Each part grows in the subtle favour of the whole, for all are as one in purpose. All tend as one to the common centre of completion, and all are unfolded in due proportion and appropriate fullness and grace. Nature in every member uniteth perfection, for to each she hath awarded its completion, coordinating all to her own spiritual Ideal.

[228] ### Wholeness of Spirit

It is thus that Elizabeth dawneth upon my sight, displaying grace in grace, yet all lost and blended in each so that the effect is that of a complete whole. The part is lost [229] in the whole; the whole, in the parts; and each is the emblem of the other. The soul shapeth itself in the organs. The organs reimage the soul. God is in every function. Every function becometh such by favour of his indwelling force.

[229] ### God in Every Member

She openeth her *eyes*. This is of God, whose eye radiateth in her spirit and seeketh the image of himself in his terrestrial works. She turneth her *ear*. This, too, is of God, for a heavenly sound cometh forth from the depths of his immensity, borne on the wings of the air that surrounds her, and she catcheth the noise. She extendeth her hands. Of God she doeth it, since in her frame are the divine instincts through which the heavenly forces circulate on their earthly [230] errands and call in the organic functions to fulfil their behest. She *smileth*. In that smile beameth the joy of the Divinity from the delighted harmony of her heart. She *crieth*. That harmony hath been disturbed by some infraction of the divine laws, and the voice of suffering breaketh upon the ear. The grieved countenance betokeneth the inner disharmony to the eye, for the Divinity bewaileth in these sensible forms the evil that besetteth its course and tampereth with its rights. She *thinketh*. God energizeth in the holy temple of her spirit, and she hath the sense of his presence and worshippeth him in fit spirit. In her *faculties* and *endowment*—in Nature as presented to her senses—in herself as she findeth images of consciousness—doth the Divinity reveal his being and perfections, and she is charmed by the untold story. And [231] time is the hour that she chooseth to unfold the hidden meaning of this unending tale, for the full disclosure of which not time, but Eternity, shall avail. On the Dial of Eternity the hand of her being hath its brief hour. It pointeth to the time of her birth. This it hath passed. Over the remaining seconds and minutes it is moving onward, and each day and night is the vibration (each throb of the animal pulse) the indication of its approaching, yet time-fulfilling, exit into the hours of Eternity!

> Yea—the soul is Heaven's own time-piece,
> And the selfsame bell rings out our exit
> That rings in our birth. Life is *one* hour
> On Immortality's vast dial-plate
> Sense-imaged. 'Tis a hand divine
> Th'escapement setteth of a human soul!

[232] **False Time**

Yet easy is it for man to derange this heavenly instrument. Easy is it for those who are the appointed observers and upwinders, if need be, of childhood's horologe to disturb the serene harmony, the accurate movement of the Spirit's purpose. How often is it set to the time of sense. How soon is it graduated to the hours of earth and the true time lost for the Spirit's livings. The clock of Heaven striketh the hour, but no bell from the earth regardeth it. No eye spanneth the wide dial-plate and beholdeth the pointing index that prophesies the destinies of the terrestrial!

[232] **Adoration of Childhood**

Parent, thou art, or thou shouldest be, a faithful observer of the celestial phenomena. Thou shouldest apprehend the signs of the human firmament and be [233] wise as were the Eastern Magi to find the true stars of immortality and to offer the gifts of thy love and the worship of thy faith to infant Divinity, whom God hath sent to thee and which thou callest thine own! Worship God. How? As did the Wise Men. Worship the spiritual in thy child—the "God with thee." Believe him IMMANENCE, and he shall be all—even more than thou believest, since he hath a faith in his Father which, perchance, thou hast in part lost, and goeth about his Father's business while thou art inquiring of him the cause of his dealing so with thee.

[233] **Childhood—A Sign of the Spiritual**

The spiritual phenomena are thine to study. Ask not for a material sign, as did the sensual and sense-darkened cavillers [234] at the sayings of the Heavenly Seer, who apprehended the spiritual laws and subordinated the outward to their force, never mistaking the sign for the substance, but asserting the omnipotence of spirit over matter and ruling it at his will. Thou seek[est] a sign? Well, thou hast them. Thy child is a sign. Nature is a sign. Time and space are all emblematic of thy duty. What sayest thou to smiles, to tears, to hopes, to fears, to joys and sorrows, to wants and satisfactions, to doubts and assurances, to all the shifting phenomena of a day's life of thy little one? Are these insignificant to thee, and canst thou neither see nor divine aught from them of the spiritual life that is thus made to utter itself to thee? These are the true signs. Study them and be wise.

[240] **Prevalence of Spiritual Agency**

Frailty—what is it but the emblem of the flitting, flowing, fluid element of matter! Well is it that the Divinity hath incorporated the spirit which he delegateth to his children and made all its changes to tell at once the story of his continuance and growth by the evanescent passings to and fro of the visible natures that he beholdeth. Emblems are they all of the Spirit's universal prevalence, which is the subtle agent of every change and signifieth its recondite life by the agitations to which it subjecteth all terrestrial things. Man is a [241] *body*, as he seemeth to his bodily senses. He holdeth familiar companionship with the flesh that he carrieth about himself and whose instruments he employs—whose sufferings and joys seem to be his own. He is also a *spirit*, and he knoweth not that he *is* save by the signs that he putteth forth through these bodily organs to satisfy the longing senses of his spirit with something that shall remind him of his inner life. In every function of his animal constitution is he striving with all the force of delegated power to reassure himself of his very being and prove to himself that he is himself and not another. In the nervous, muscular movements—in the rushings of the blood through his system—in the throbbing, ever-going pulse not less than in the instincts and senses of his being—is he essaying to find the absolute life of [242] which this delegated existence is but the emblem and the sign. Man's present being is the prophet of his future existence, and all his toils here are but the unskilful efforts of a novice in the high vocation to which he is called. The frail and brittle elements that he endeavoureth to shape forth, as well as the instruments that he employs like tools of glass or forms of clay, oft break in the using or crumble in the shaping. And himself, built up from the dust, findeth the perpetuity that he longeth for only in dropping his tools, relinquishing his work, casting off the frail garments of his mortality, and reassuming the spiritual nature that hath haunted him like a shadow and never left him while living this visible life! Childhood runneth after the shadow, and in smiles and tears—in all the experiences of this terrestrial existence—pursueth the heaven-descended phantom. Nor shall it find the blessed reality till death introduce it into its august presence! Nature is ever making, never made.

[251] **God Quickeneth All His Works**

Is not Nature—is not the spirit of man—*quick* with Divinity? How else doth the one undergo its manifold changes and the other put on so many varying phases? Do not these come from the ever-shifting evanescent life that acteth within and cometh now to the surface to unveil [252] its mysterious forces and then withdraweth itself into the centre of Nature, where it hath its nexus, and openeth out toward the spiritual relations to receive the divine affluence that ever floweth into its functions, as the light and air meet its sense from the material scene? The spiritual senses drink in the life of the spiritual, as the material sense doth the material influence. Doth not an *inholding* as well as *upholding* and *outholding* afflux sustain the functions—fleshly and spiritual— by which the Spirit is continued in its individual life, and standeth out against the universal forces—the rush and stir of beings and things in the universe? God floweth in. God floweth out. God encompasseth around, and in this eddy of spiritual forces, man holdeth his being and *is*, because all within, without, around him, *is*. He suffers the Divine Breath to enter. He inhaleth it by virtue of the [253] spiritual suction that is within. In the confluence of those agencies he attaineth a force that he calleth his own free will, and acteth with the laws that he cannot master and by which he becometh a separate will—an individual. Upborne as on these flowing waters he becometh, as it were, a part of the tide, and ebbeth and floweth with it as he willeth to follow its celestial courses. On the ocean of the Infinite—in the air of the Immeasurable—he becometh a wave, a breeze, and is carried, or wafted, by the strong currents that circulate through these unfathomable depths, across this infinite expanse.

[253] **Man's Free Will**

Man's force, his individual will, his free-agency, cometh by submission to the superiour Force that ever presseth against him, penetrateth into his very centre, cometh forth from [254] this centre and rusheth both out and into his very being. He findeth his own strength as he yieldeth it and is upborne by these superiour forces. He findeth his own faculties as he submitteth to the inflowing of these forces through every function of his being. By this docility—this suffering of the Divinity—doth he lade his spirit with Divinity, and all his powers are renewed. His *senses* are quickened; his *sentiments*, vivified; his *ideas*, vividly imaged; and he flourishes as a tree planted by the waterside, and putteth forth leaves, blossoms, fruit, in his season.

[254] **God Flows Through Man**

Accepting the conditions of his being, he barreth against nothing. He obeys the Divine Laws, and obedience bringeth life and light to his spirit. He is filled with the inspiration of the Divinity. God floweth into him. He floweth [255] and commingleth with God and is so laden with the fullness that he thirsteth after. By his resumption in God he findeth his own divine force and is lost to find himself. Infinitude filleth his apprehension, and by apprehending *more* than himself in the Divinity, he apprehendeth himself in his own littleness. The eye of his spiritual sense is cleared of its films, and he turneth it upon these celestial phenomena as he was wont when in the narrow sphere of the material senses to turn them upon the things of time. [Once] he had apprehended these as the emblems of the selfsame objects that he now apprehends with the glad sense of faith. He hath learned his alphabet and is now perusing the celestial page and findeth the meaning of the hieroglyphics that were wont to puzzle his understanding and bind his fancy. Then, by descending into Nature, [256] (assuming its frail instruments, suffering its conditions with meek, yet patient, endeavour) doth the Spirit rise again from its mission of self-sacrifice, as did Jesus, to the glorious liberty of a son of God.

[256] **Mission of Parents**

In this blessed work, O Parent, childhood pleadeth for thy aid. The Divinity taketh it along upon its ever-flowing tides. It filleth all its instinctive senses—spiritual, fleshly— with its forces. It is thy work to urge its submission to the currents that drive it along, to yield a willing obedience to the laws which glide through its functions, and to teach it to reverence these as prophetic guides to the haven of Blessedness. Easy is it for the unpracticed spirit to stand up against these agencies, to brave the omnipotence that it knoweth not—that it only feeleth and taketh [257] to be itself, and thus to wed itself to the disturbing reaction that engendereth passion, enervateth the flesh, and becometh appetite with all the family of lust that springeth up from the flesh, if once the spiritual law be invaded.

[257] **Counsels to Parents**

Strive then to keep this law inviolate. Guard well this freedom. Interpret (as fast as growing experience openeth forth the sense of the inner life and its adaptations to the outer relations) the mysterious oracle of conscience; and inspire, by dwelling on the consequences of its violation, a reverence for its sacred voice. Bring forth early the sense of God's presence in the consciousness of the child. Let him apprehend the Divine

Being in the functions of his very constitution. Let not God only be *in* his thought, *in* his heart, but let God BE his thought—his force. [258] So shall God be a perpetual presence—one with his consciousness—and not an abstract Being remote and invisible to his faith. He shall live and move and have his being in God. Yea, God shall be *him*, and he shall be God so far as he apprehendeth him in his conscience and willeth to obey the law that he there announceth to him. He shall have a sense of his Father. He shall know in whom he believeth. He shall be alive to the spiritual, nor shall sense hold dominion over him. The flesh shall obey the will of the Spirit, and this Spirit shall take counsel of conscience and of those whose work it is to interpret its sacred promptings to his dawning *senses*, his quickening *affections*, his forming *ideas*. Then shall God reveal himself without mist or obscurity to his docile child!

[265]   **Mystery of Spirit**

Mysterious Essence! All-pervading, all-configuring, all-apprehending, all-meaning Principle! Life! Spirit! Or by what name soever or under what form thou art conceived or presented! Who shall apprehend thee as thou art in thyself, or find thee as thou art found of these little ones who have not lost thee? I *know* thee only, save by *remembrance*—save now and then when thou seemest to come to me, yet with short stay and urgent haste doth leave me to feel my bereavement and to cherish with fond recollection the words that thou [266] didst* faintly whisper in mine ears while thou wert in my presence. Childhood is thus *meaning* to me, because it reminds me of thee. In it I behold the memorials of a past life. I see the relics of an age of innocence—of holiness—of purity—that neither time nor revolution have defaced nor destroyed. Thou comest up to me in the forms of these little ones as an inhabitant of a country once mine own, and thy familiar tones and gentle ways seem the manners of my native home—the language of my mother-tongue—and I seem beside thee but a stranger and sojourner here below. Yet thou seemest scarce to know of thy change. Thou lookest about upon the things around thee and seemest to know that these are thy Father's, deeming thyself still in one of his apartments—that the furniture is his and that this new wardrobe of Nature and [267] these vestments of flesh in which he hath decked thee are all his own. A familiar art thou in thy Father's dwelling. Thou hast been acquainted with all its many mansions, and in the one which he hath now prepared for thee thou dost not feel thyself alone! God, angels—these forms and beings shaped like thyself and obvious to thine outward senses—are thy companions. Thou art at home!

[267]   **Bivision**

Thou art at home because thou holdest thy court in Heaven, and this earth and the things thereof and the flesh in which thou art arrayed are but the emblems and mementos of thy Father's residence. So long as thou keepest vivid the remembrance of thy former mansion, will the shapes and shows and beings around thee fill thee with that home-delight and with all those associations that constitute happiness [268] and peace—the domestic charm of thy heart's young life. Thou wilt not feel this seeming absence—this short errand into the flesh—this communing with matter, with signs and shadows—this mock-being, where the *seeming* is but the *evidence* of the Light that IS—where *apprehension* findeth not the whole of its object, and *desire* still yearneth after what it hath lost—where the illusion of the *once known* giveth the hope of attaining—where *remembrance* and *expectation*, seeming to look from each other upon different scenes, are but the Janus-faces of the present moment and survey unknowingly the same tracts of the Celestial Heritage and Home!

[275]   **Holidays Too Infrequent**

As a people we are much too sparing of amusements. We are austere. We are devoid of that pliancy of heart and freshness of fancy which minister so much to the charm and, under prudent management, to the true good of life. Joy, mirth, sportiveness, the festival, the anniversary—are not less softening, mellowing, and improving than grief, sadness, sobriety, the fast, or the funeral. On many occasions, joy is the most efficient [276] minister to good. Marriage, birth, baptism, the New Year, the anniversary of these—are fit occasions for merriment, tempered, of course, with reverential regard for one's nature and its sacred functions. Were these occasions adopted into a national religion and associated with all that is sacred and loved in our nature, the influence over a people would be of the holiest character. Indeed, what else beside these are fitter themes for rejoicing or gratitude? The changes of Nature, the vicissitudes of life, as well as political events, are fit topics, but subordinate surely to these inherent claims of

---

* Ms. reads "dost."

our beings. Humanity hath a few sacred rights, simple but full of significance. These should be associated with all that is permanent and holy.

[277]   **Childhood Reneweth Nations**

The life and perpetuity of a people, as of the individual, depend mainly upon their faithfulness to the simple and joyous associations of childhood as these are adopted into their domestic, civil and religious institutions. The charms of early life must be thrown over all those means and influences by which the heart and mind is nurtured and formed, or the principle of vitality is wanting. It is this that invests humanity with its confiding hopes, its trusts, its assurances of permanence, and traces all its parts together.

[277]   **Perpetuity of Childhood**

Childhood must be prolonged and carried into age. The spiritual must not be suffered to die out of the associations of a people. It must embody itself in all the common interests, [278] wants, pursuits, enactments, festivals, fasts—in all that spring directly from the central and universal life of man. Institutions should but represent and enforce the spiritual. They should perpetual[ly] reveal to the mind of man his true means of enjoyment and provide at fit seasons—as wants or privations, gifts or losses befall him —the appropriate means of signifying his inner life and of finding sympathy either of joy or of grief, of gratitude or of [   ]* with his kind. The individual should not be lost amid his kindred, but found, and each and every man's life flow through all. All by being kept thus in a state of action would be renewed, strengthened, refreshed and preserved. A nation would be like a vigorous and flourishing youth, full of life-giving energy and the promise of manhood—without decay!

[279]   **Forms of Revelation**

A Revelation includes not only the announcement of absolute truths in their abstract forms, but an embodiment of these in concrete shaping and individuality. It must embrace the elements of the *ideal*, yet clothed in the raiment of the *real*. It must dispose of its varied phenomena—its events, its facts, its visible, tangible effects—and indicate the connexion, dependence, growth of these, from independent, original causes and principles. It must unite the spiritual and the material—bring within its sweeping synthesis every fraction, member, function, faculty, organ and thing which makes up the subject of the perfect whole.

[280]   **Universality of Revelation**

Revelation thus derives its authority over the mind and being of man from its universality. It claims to be an interpretation of the universe, and each and every product of the corporeal or spiritual world attests—because it is *itself* an expression— the authenticity of its claims. Each power, capacity, product, fact, of Nature yields its evidence to the divinity of its truths. Thus all things, all beings, become the exponents of its principles and grounds in the absolute, divine life, whence they derive their subsistence and growth. Each lives and moves and hath its individual being in the great whole and attests by its very life the existence of this Divine Original.

[280]   **Certainty of Revelation**

As the artist commends his work to the common mind by his faithfulness to the Ideal (embodying his thought in forms common to all—[281] to the child and to the adult— to the learned and to the unlearned—addressing the sense, which ever telleth the same story)—is ever true to external Nature; as the Divinity shapeth everywhere the things and beings that he incarnateth from one common image, even Himself—spreading over the face of external Nature and representing in the being of man his own celestial attributes, his unity—even so must a Revelation include the materials for man's inner and outer senses and be the object of universal assent; to doubt which would be as impossible as to deny existence or the forms that the sense ever bringeth to the soul from the visible and invisible worlds—[it] being its own truth, ground and object. Thus is Man, Nature, Providence, each a revelation and the record of these (if it include the whole)—the individual members in the [282] universal statement—the parts subordinated *to* and substantiated *in*, the whole.

[282]   **Terms of Revelation**

Thus doth a Revelation stand on itself and give ground and substance to all its parts. It contains origin, growth, completion—these being represented in *history*, of which *philosophy* is the object, *poetry* the form, *Nature* the subject—these embracing every interest of humanity, being the Exponents of Creation and the terms under which Revelation disposes its elements. Thus

---

* The manuscript is blank at this point.

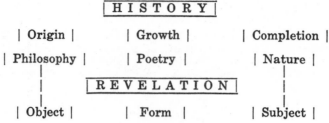

[283]　　　　　　　　　**Spirit in Act**

Every Revelation that hath gained the credence of man and hath been adopted as the rule of life, shaping the institutions and moulding the human being, hath embodied these elements. Life hath found within it every possible illustration: Poetry hath sung its divine aspirations; Philosophy unfolded the innate grounds and recondite mysteries of being; Nature hath proffered herself and all her manifold analogies as the subject and the expression of the Spirit's principles and truths. An energy above Nature (of which Nature is but the show, the sign, the emblem) is assumed, and the world of facts (phenomena, the visible scene) is deemed but the counterpart of the *Invisible Power* that moveth through them and impresseth its own individuality upon their docile elements. It is this Power that giveth *law* to matter. It is Spirit. And a *Revelation is the history of this Spirit in act.*

[284]　　　　　　　　**Gospel of Childhood**

Of the various media of Revelation, the child is, perhaps, the most significant of all. The *history of a child,* including its inner as well as outer movements, with its relations both spiritual and material and the varying phenomena of the sensual and the supersensual—this would be a Revelation indeed—an Incarnate Word to humanity. We have the history of an adult in the life of Jesus. In the Gospels both his inner and outer experience is given. The supremacy of the spiritual comes forth to our senses. The Word is incarnated, and man looketh on the face of his brother in the flesh, seeing in it the image of the Divine Life that he inheriteth. Yet the revelation of childhood hath not yet been promulgated. The "eyes have not seen nor the hands yet handled the Word of God" as presented in infancy. To the penning of this gospel, let me apply myself.

[368]　　　　　**Spirit Repairs the Waste of Body**

Yea, Spirit is the sublime architect of Nature—the builder of its temples, its bodies, the worship-place and the worshipper. It buildeth all things. It wasteth all things. Renovation is its working, and time is its workday. Decay hath no power save when it sleeps, and then it worketh with its master's tools. Matter is the element which it works —with which, by its own undetected skill, it moulds forth its inner objects to the outer senses and showeth their heavenly beauty and use. Yet this same wastes. The idol mouldereth. The arch giveth way. Man cannot cross the Stream of Time. Yet Spirit rebuildeth the bridge, and the terrestrial traveller findeth footway over the stream to the country of Immortality. Then renovation repaireth the waste of decay!

[369]　　　　　　　　　　**Birth**

Birth! It is a life-quickening word. It turneth the thought of man inward and backward to that dim sense of origin—to that stirring, instinctive Idea that lieth at the porch of time and looketh forth with its biformed visage upon a parent and on Eternity:
> "Not in entire forgetfulness,
> Nor yet in utter nakedness;
> But trailing clouds of glory do we come
> From God, who is our home."

[371]　　　　　　　**On Anna's Fifth Birthday**

She hath lost some of her heart's holiness—its tranquillity—its peace—its serene beatitude—by dalliance with things. She hath not been sustained at all times in her heart's integrity. The prophetic conscience hath not always been grounded in the understanding, nor the essaying will freed from the errors of ignorance, that mislead and beguile. She hath fallen, and hath not fully risen. Appetite hath sunk and clogged. Desire hath perplexed; passion, dimmed; fancy and sense, beguiled. She hath not staid all this time in her "Father's [372] Kingdom," wherein she was wont to disport herself in her young and celestial days ere a tenant of flesh, but hath forgotten some of the lore that was once her own. Earth hath despoiled her of these spiritual treasures, in part. Yet doth the same instinct urge her onward and upward, as if to revive the lost inheritance and reassure her of her divinity.

[372] ### Idolatry of Sense

"The sleep and the forgetting"—that cometh from the bifold nature that she now possesseth—the flesh and the objects of the senses. This causeth her to *dream;* and she scarce separateth the terrestrial from the celestial life, so inwrought and blended are they in her consciousness. Dreaming of Heaven, she thinketh its objects are on earth. Seeking embodiment for her heart, as she was wont in the morning of her being, she mistaketh [373] the objects of her senses for the things and beings of heaven, and awaketh not to the true perceptions save by the ministry of pain and disappointment, retribution flashing upon her spirit the living truth of her residence here below. She maketh idols of her ideas and incarnateth these in the crumbling objects of sense—nor findeth her mistake till her heart's faith is corrected—the *semblance* being the minister and herald of *substance!* Then disappointment leadeth her to the true sources of faith. The mutable elements around her fail so that she may be led to the immutable and the unfailing. Her trusts clasp at last the Spirit, whence alone they derive their support, resuming the blessed person whose image had seemed looking forth from every desire and object of the visible and loved. [374] Thus hath she run the human race, being brought to the selfsame goal whereunto all incarnate spirits must come to find the rewards that they seek.

[374] ### Shadow Skirmishes

Plying this celestial function on things—grasping divine images amid their shows—caught by the illusive shadows of reality—facing both the spiritual and material kingdoms, yet scarce knowing their domain from each other—the spiritual senses oft obscured by the physical—man alike with the child oft graspeth at the shadow while he deemeth it the substance, and intent on possessing it, he followeth after it, nor knoweth that it is his own shadow thrown before him by the celestial orb that shineth over his shoulders and casteth his image before. Truly, man with the child hath daily shadow-trials, and he deceiveth himself still.

[375] ### Spiritual Orphanage

He mistaketh his means and oft (as the child doth not) loseth his end and forgetteth his purpose. He wandereth away from the spiritual fold and herdeth with the wolves, belying his innocence and defacing his image. His birthday cometh around, and he is scarce reminded of his lineage and his Home! His heritage is forgotten. He striveth to associate himself with the earth and the beasts thereof, and dateth his origin from the building up of his body from the dust, thus cutting off his celestial connexions and putting out the idea of immortality from his *remembrance* and his *hope!*

[375] ### Loss of Eden

And having thus isolated himself from the Divine, denied his spiritual affinities, and set up his own claims to existence on this little island of Time, he carrieth on his brief [376] work, essayeth his divine instincts unknowingly on material things—an exile and an outcast on the earth! He hath shut out, as far as he may, the light of the past from his remembrance, and having done this there cometh into it no light for the future. The double gate that openeth into Time is closed. Neither memory nor hope (the folding doors thereof) reveal to him the country of his origin and home. Doubt hath bolted the doors, nor hath he the key that shall reopen either—neither the key of repentance nor of faith!

[376] ### Childhood—the Emblem of Eternity

Yet to childhood doth these folding doors stand wide open, and it seeth both before and behind. The vision of the past hath not departed nor the reflected phase of the future, and he hath the keys that give him passway whenever he desireth. Who art thou that vanishest them away and maketh him the prisoner of time and sense? [377] Parent, why doth God give thee children? Why doth he send thee at fit intervals these celestial messengers, but to remind thee of thy once-known, thine expected (though, perhaps, scarce remembered) home? Do these little ones come from the past out of which, a few years agone, thou wast born, and yet bring thee no tidings of thy celestial brotherhood—remind thee of none of the enjoyments of thy celestial life? Have the doors of the past (opening into immeasurable infinitude, which holdeth both thine own and the past of all derived beings and sweeps on and embraceth the future wherein thy yet unextinguished hope delighteth to range)—have these doors (as thy little one openeth and cometh in and goeth out before thee) given thee not one glimpse of thine heritage—thy home—nor afforded thee one hint of thy being's date and destiny?

[378] ### Childhood Bringeth a Message

Thy Father hath sent thee a message by the hand of this little one, and he giveth it to thee. Wilt thou receive it? Wilt thou apprehend it? Wilt thou be reminded of thy celestial as well as terrestrial relations and receive the heavenly visitor into thy family and be to him what he expecteth of thee? Fresh and new, let him quicken and renew thy nature. Born into the kingdom of flesh and sense, let him be to thee the emblem of innocence. Unclogged in his functions, take example and purify thyself from all the defilements of the flesh. Full of instinctive trust in thee and dependent as a physical creature upon thy care and kindness, let his helplessness remind thee of thine own spiritual weakness and quicken within thee the faith that reviveth the sluggish functions of thy spiritual life. Let his birth become the occasion of thine. Come [379] thou from the womb of the senses and of the flesh, in which thou art environed, even as thy child breaketh forth from his hiding place and, being inspired with the Almighty's breath, is a living and conscious thing. Regenerated in his functions, so be thou. Lifted into the light of this life, be thou lifted by the consideration of him into the light of another—even into the Supernatural. Before thee is the sacred emblem of the Supernatural—the birth of the body. Apprehend it, and be thou born again. Say not with the sense-beguiled Nicodemus, "How can these things be?" and disbelieve the Divine Teacher, asking an explanation that shall satisfy thy senses and shape itself in thine understanding. Thou canst as readily define the spiritual as the physical birth, for like the rushing wind they come upon us and ere the [380] ear hath sought its passage, it hath flitted by us, nor can we define either its coming or its going. It hath no signs for the senses. Its agency is too subtle for our coarse organs to apprehend, for these know only the flesh and the objects thereof. They penetrate not even to the origin and birthplace of these. The spiritual is apprehended only by its own senses. Open thine and be wise. Feel that a great process hath been wrought out within thy doors. The Spirit hath travailed and brought forth a soul. It hath enrobed it in flesh like unto thine. The spiritual offspring is put into thine arms. Nurse it—cherish it—love it—study it—for the Kingdom of Heaven is within it, and it cometh from "beholding its Father's face." How shall that smile soon depart from its countenance, though it hath put on a visor of flesh and feeleth all unused to the visage, if thou callest it forth and feedeth it with the smiles of thine own love!

[386]   The Infant Inheriteth a Spirit to Subordinate Nature

The infant enters into this corporeal life, bringing with him the patrimony that falleth to him of right as a descendant of a Heavenly One. He bringeth his inheritance of an everliving Spirit, and he cometh into the body to try the force of these immortal faculties on the [387] functions thereof. He cometh out of the pure realm of Spirit (wherein liveth his Father) upon an expedition against matter, some elements of which he hath incorporated around his very divine self, that by the feeling of the infirmities and weaknesses thereof, he may learn to subordinate it to the higher life which he bringeth with him. He liveth in Nature. He dwelleth in the flesh. The Incarnate One is he, and he feeleth his twofold life and entereth upon the mission of his own redemption from the tempting body and the things of his external senses, which enwrap him as in a confining womb. Yet he findeth an everliving instinct within him, which even in the earliest periods of his incarnate life seems to be living in his new assumed functions and to lift him from his low environment. [388] He laboreth in every little function of his body to regain the seeming good which he once possessed and to throw off the incumbrance that checketh his ascension. He hath assumed the flesh to conquer the flesh. He hath taken an individual body to test all its varied attributes and thus commune with the outer elements of his Father's universe. He hath come to find what there is in this realm of his Father's kingdom—in the domain of matter—that he can conquer and subordinate to his own being. He hath come to explore and to interpret by the prophetic and sagacious faculty that he feeleth within him.

[388]   Childhood Alert in its Mission

This is his advent. And how soon doth he begin the mission. The great problem which he came to solve he attacketh at once. [389] He delayeth not a moment. He lingereth not on his work. With an admiration lost in the vague wonder and surprise that cometh over him on finding himself in this new scene of being in which he half apprehendeth the shows and shapes of things and lives which he hath just left—with a sense, perplexing even as a lost thought when we hunt about in our past memories, and now the sought notion cometh into our consciousness, and then we lose it again—with a surmise, a gleam, a doubt, a shade, he looketh about him and seemeth to feel that he is still in his father's mansion, but all is strange and new. Yet he deemeth these objects and senses as having once been presented and experienced in some former state of being.

Nature is a familiar, though in a new visor. Flesh is a friend, [390] though she hath arranged herself in new habiliments. The life that now *is* seemeth to be both the remembrance and the hope of another—superior and certain. The twin factors of Eternity—past and future—stand in his thought, flow in his sense, as messages of Being. Time puzzleth him. Sense bewildereth. Place fractures. His original consciousness seems taken in pieces, and here he findeth a relic of its former framework, and there another. The Divine Synthesis is broken. Unity is spread out into diversity, and yet the central analogy, which is the Idea of his being, reappears in both sides of his consciousness. He seemeth to stand on the Arch of Time, and whether looking forward or backward, upward into the illimitable azure or downward into the immeasurable deep, he findeth emblems of his inner [391] thought. The Divine Idea gleameth up in his being, and he feeleth his kindred origin and destiny. The tide of time rolls onward under him and carrieth his thought to its original fount, even to the Eternal. The pervading air presseth and penetrateth and tosseth itself around him, but he inhaleth it and is reassured of his connexion with the Immortal. The pulse of things beateth within him. The quickening life is at the chambers of his heart, and he worshippeth—mutely, perhaps, yet assuredly worshippeth—and acknowledgeth his celestial lineage and expectation. There is a grandeur in Being!

[419] The True Church

Hath childhood a sabbath? Yea, all time is a sabbath to its celestial will. Worship is its perpetual labour, and the nursery is its temple; maternity, the image that receiveth its homage! Throughout the wide realm of space and in the period of time hath the Divinity created his altars and given the instinct of worship. The true and living God is that of the household. The divinely dedicated church is the nursery. The consecrated priest is the mother, for so hath the Supreme Object decreed. All organized Nature confirmeth the decree.

[420] Worship Beginneth in the Nursery

All worship beginneth in the nursery. All religion manifesteth itself at first at the maternal bosom. All revelation announceth itself, proclaiming its wide foundation whereon life is to build, on the paternal knee. Doth not the young worshipper turn his eye upward upon the maternal face, even while he satisfieth his instinctive sense, thus worshipping both in soul and in body? His first hour is the blessed Sabbath morn, and his last thought of the outward glideth from his spirit while he feedeth at the fountain. Sense worshippeth, and spirit accepteth the worship, for the heart lingereth around the maternal form, which is the image of the Divinity in the flesh, and claimeth its homage. Every hour is a holy time; each moment is a sabbath throughout the livelong day.

[425] Grandeur of Childhood

Grandeur, indeed, is the beating heart of childhood—a grandeur which none, not even the divine poet* in his divinest "Ode on Childhood," hath yet fully apprehended. Childhood is greater than Nature. It teemeth with Ideas for which Nature proffereth no image. It is above Nature—yea, above man—for yet unfallen, unbeguiled, it is an angel and [426] enjoyeth the beatific countenance of the Celestial Father in Heaven—even the selfsame face that Nature doth but dimly shadow forth to the external sense! The tide that floweth through that heart setteth back into the Infinite, and its perpetual ebb and flow—its systole and diastole—what are these but the circulations of the Divine Life through its very being?

[435] Threefold Being of the Spirit

The elements of the Spirit are threefold, and the faculties which are put in motion by these primal elements are threefold also. *Beauty, Truth* and *Good* are the *Absolute Being of the Spirit*. These are opened out and revealed to the spirit's consciousness through a series of influences which are instituted at the moment of incarnation, and ply their incessant agencies from this moment, taking Nature as their instrument on through every movement, till the structure wherein [436] they hold their central and primal force is taken down and returned again to the common elements from whence it was built up by virtue of the Absolute Agency. Spirit tempteth all outward things and beings, and, by reason of this tempting agency, is itself tempted forth and revealed to its own consciousness, taking matter as its plaything, its servant, its visible image. It writeth off the story of its *purposes* and delineateth its *works* upon the facile element

---

* Alcott probably refers to Wordsworth and to the "Ode on Intimations of Immortality."

of matter, doing all things by its own divine art. The pencil and the pen, the hand and the graver, are its own. Its *art* is above its *works*. It preserveth no fit representation of its being, for it findeth no elements out of itself, having the perpetuity of its own divine being, or subtle enough to be moulded into the form of its *celestial ideal*. [437] *Matter* floweth away; it stayeth not. Time crumbleth its forms and wasteth the proportions of *Beauty*, of *Truth*, and of *Good*, which it loveth to incarnate and perpetuate from its own prolific being.

[437] Industry of Spirit

Yet doth Spirit accept these conditions of waste and decay—of perpetual disappointment in its works—and still labour, still reveal, as far as finite and visible elements afford the instruments, its own celestial *love*. It bringeth forth *Beauty* and spreadeth it over the face of external Nature. It revealeth it to the *eye* and the *moral sense* of man. *Truth* it embodieth in *word* and in *act*, till the form thereof hath stamped itself on the *mind* of man, and he hath an *Idea* as well as an *Image*—till he hath seen through the *Idol* [438] to the *Idol-Maker* and found in his own spirit the *Creative Force* and *Shaper* of all outward images. And *Good* cometh to him through varied experiences of his manifold being—till he apprehendeth his relations both to himself and to the outward scenes that encompasseth him. His *sense* or *instinct* of the *Beautiful* revealeth the Absolute Beauty that dwelleth in his spirit as its essential life and being. His *apprehension* of the *True* unfoldeth to him the idea of Truth, that is the *ground* of his being. And his *sentiment* of the *Good* layeth hold on good as the object and end of his being—incorporateth* [it] with its own destiny. In this process doth every faculty and function, member and organ of his being find quickening stir and motion. Each [439] and every part beginneth its appointed work, and all prophesy their specific and general mission by their coordinating labours.

[474] Spirit Buildeth Itself a Temple Within

The Spirit is the master-builder. *Flesh* is but the instrument, and *matter* the material *by* which and *in* which the divine design is elaborated and shaped to the senses—whether sensual or intellectual—of man. [475] In things and ideas—the twofold objects of his senses—in these doth he set forth whatever actuateth his own spirit, and in the one or the other doth he fashion the indwelling, absolute, essential life of his being. He maketh of things and of ideas the revealings of himself. In these he fitteth the Infinite, the Godlike—configuring Nature according to the fancy of his own spiritual ideal. *Instinct* blends with *fancy*. *Fancy* associates with *light*. *Light* yields to *imagination;* and this, lifting itself above all into the Ideal, draws in the *understanding* and the *reason*, subordinating the realm of Nature and of Spirit to her own supervision as the envoy and oracle of the revealing, coordinating conscience, the judge and arbiter of the soul. The Godhead labours!

[491] Inbred Sin?

Yet thou art perhaps an unbeliever in the innocence—the holiness of infancy. Thou scoffest at the phenomena of childhood, seeing in these naught but confirmations of thine own theories of its innate, unmitigated depravity. Thou interpretest every sign that seemeth to thy sense as an indication of inbred holiness but as an illusion of the fancy—a mock semblance of goodness without the reality. Thou believest in EVIL, and findest it in thine own pure and holy one. Thou sayest that it is born with its very nature. Thou callest its weaknesses sins—its exasperation of the functions of the flesh, inbred guilt. Within its young bosom is eviled the hissing serpent, and thou approachest thy child as in fearing of the sting.

[492] Blasphemy of Childhood

Blasphemer! Belier of thy nature! Fallen spirit, dragging down the holiest ones of Heaven to thine own Pandemonium! Thou art an outcast and art planning the revolt of those whom God hath entrusted to thee. Thy child is no fallen, but a pure angel. Tempt it not from the worship and service of its Father in Heaven. Drag it not down to the vassalage of the flesh. Let it remain in Heaven. Let it possess the kingdom meant for it—even the kingdom of its own pure spirit. Invade not this celestial realm by thy blasphemous theories and the practice to which they lead. Believe as thy child believeth. Let him lead thee back to thy home—to the face of thy Father!

[496] Heaven-Tongue, or the Child's Language

And soon will the divine organ of the soul be loosed, discoursing to human ears the Spirit's celestial broodings while in the long hours of silence in the mute relations of

---

* Ms. reads "incorporates."

sense. Who shall tell the sense that cometh over the young spirit at its first *articulated* idea? Who, announce the rapture that filleth it when it heareth its own thought borne backward from the outward on the breathing pennons of the air, which it hath by its force set in motion? Speech! This is the birth of the spiritual force—the fruit of one revolution of the soul along with this temporal ball around the Infinite! Time-clad, the spirit beginneth to unfold the divine wardrobe and to bring forth treasures new and old for the dwellers on this naked and defenceless orb. Go, Parent, and be clad. Hold not the mockery of thy mother-tongue. Thou hast forgotten it. Thy child speaketh *heaven-tongue!*

[497]   **Celestial Life**

Listen to its accents. Perchance thou mayest revive thine own forgotten love—the sounds that were wont to greet thee in the glad morn of thy being while disporting thyself in the celestial nursery with thy fellow angels under the joyous supervision of thy Lord. Familiar words may come up in thy remembrance. Thou mayest regain thy mother-tongue—come again, as it were, a pure and holy child upon this scene of the terrestrial; and, fresh and new with the glittering array of celestial armour of holy associations, begin anew the career of thy spirit, made wise by the memory and the tuition of thy wandering, dubious, devious experience. Life may be revealed to thee even as it was at thy first birth-time, when from the confining womb (where thou didst fashion forth thy fleshly members) [498] thou didst burst forth into the joyous light of terrestrial day. Thou shalt be born again. Thy nature shall be regenerated. Thou shalt be purified from the grossness of appetite—from the excitements of passion —from the defilements of the flesh. Thy physical being shall be freed from the burden of thy lusts; thy spiritual functions assume their dominion over the whole of thy nature.

[498]   **Regeneration**

Thus renovated and restored to the primal unity of thy being, thou shalt be as a young and joyous child, radiant with the glories of celestial things. Earth shall be a temple in which thou shalt worship the Divinity that thou beholdest in all visible things. Thine imagination shall be quickened to the Beautiful. Thy reason shall apprehend the True. [499] Thy faith [shall] reveal the Good. Fancy shall spread over the *outward* and find new attestations of thy destiny. Love shall quicken the revelation of human immortality within thee. Thou shalt behold all things new. There shall be to thee a *new heaven and a new earth,* for the first shall have passed away in the glorious resurrection that hath happened to thee. Thou shalt be truly a child of God.

[499]   **The Child Typifies Renovation**

Can ye believe this, O ye Parents who have strayed away from the nursery of the Spirit, and, like wandering truants, disobeyed the command of your Divine Parent? Prodigal of your celestial heritage, ye have wasted its treasures on your lusts. Will ye have lost all filial regard and set at defiance the goodness of your Benefactor? [500] Self-estranged, ye have forgotten your lineage. Ye date your pedigree from earthly parents and speak of human bequests—of human tongues—having lost the *apprehension* and *language* of Heaven.

Go to your child. Peruse his face. Scan its lineaments. Apprehend its expression. Interpret its meanings. Go, then, and look in the mirror wherein thou deckest thy body forth so daintily, and see if the same lineaments are traced there—if the same expression lurks there—the same meanings bear truth to thy vision. Why? Thou art changed, and what a change! The angel is now a demon. The heavenly features are dimmed. Thou needest *regeneration.* Thy child is its emblem. Study it!

XIII

THE DOCTRINE AND DISCIPLINE OF HUMAN CULTURE*

By Amos Bronson Alcott

Idea of Man

Man is the noblest of the Creator's works. He is the most richly gifted of all his creatures. His sphere of action is the broadest; his influence the widest; and to him is given Nature and Life for his heritage and his possession. He holds dominion over the

---

* Boston (James Munroe and Company), 1836. It is apparently a resetting of pp.

Outward. He is the rightful Sovereign of the Earth, fitted to subdue all things to himself, and to know of no superior, save God. And yet he enters upon the scene of his labors, a feeble and wailing Babe, at first unconscious of the place assigned him, and needs years of tutelage and discipline to fit him for the high and austere duties that await him.

Idea of Education

The Art, which fits such a being to fulfil his high destiny, is the first and noblest of arts. Human Culture is the art of revealing to a man the true Idea of his Being—his endowments—[4] his possessions—and of fitting him to use these for the growth, renewal, and perfection of his Spirit. It is the art of completing a man. It includes all those influences, and disciplines, by which his faculties are unfolded and perfected. It is that agency which takes the helpless and pleading Infant from the hands of its Creator; and, apprehending its entire nature, tempts it forth—now by austere, and now by kindly influences and disciplines—and thus moulds it at last into the Image of a Perfect Man; armed at all points, to use the Body, Nature, and Life, for its growth and renewal, and to hold dominion over the fluctuating things of the Outward. It seeks to realize in the Soul the Image of the Creator.—Its end is a perfect man. Its aim, through every stage of influence and discipline, is self-renewal. The body, nature, and life are its instruments and materials. Jesus is its worthiest Ideal. Christianity its purest Organ. The Gospels its fullest Text-Book. Genius its Inspiration. Holiness its Law. Temperance its Discipline. Immortality its Reward.

History and Type of This Idea

This divine Art, including all others, or subordinating them to its Idea, was never apprehended, in all its breadth and depth of significance, till the era of Jesus of Nazareth. He it was that first revealed it. Over his Divine Intellect first [5] flitted the Idea of man's endowments and destiny. He set no limits to the growth of our nature. "Be Ye Perfect even as my Father in Heaven is Perfect," was the high aim which he placed before his disciples; and in this he was true to our nature, for the sentiment lives in every faculty and function of our being. It is the ever-sounding Trump of Duty, urging us to the perpetual work of self-renewal. It is the deep instinct of the spirit. And his Life gives us the promise of its realization. In his attributes and endowments he is a Type of our common nature. His achievements are a glimpse of the Apotheosis of Humanity. They are a glorious unfolding of the Godlike in man. They disclose the Idea of Spirit. And if he was not, in himself, the complete fulfilment of Spirit, he apprehended its law, and set forth its conditions. He bequeathed to us the phenomena of its manifestation; for in the Gospels we have the history of Spirit accomplishing its mission on the earth. We behold the Incarnate One, dealing with flesh and blood—tempted, and suffering—yet baffling and overcoming the ministries of Evil and of Pain.

Idea and Type Misapprehended

Still this Idea, so clearly announced, and so fully demonstrated in the being and life of Jesus, has made but little advance in the minds of men. Men have not subdued it to [6] themselves. It has not become the ground and law of human consciousness. They have not married their nature to it by a living Faith. Nearly two millenniums have elapsed since its announcement, and yet, so slow of apprehension have been the successors of this Divine Genius, that even at this day, the deep and universal significance of his Idea has not been fully taken in. It has been restricted to himself alone. He stands in the minds of this generation, as a Phenomenon, which God, in the inscrutable designs of his Providence, saw fit to present, to the gaze and wonder of mankind, yet as a being of unsettled rank in the universe, whom men may venture to imitate, but dare not approach. In him, the Human Nature is feebly apprehended, while the Divine is lifted out of sight, and lost in the ineffable light of the Godhead. Men do not deem him as the harmonious unfolding of Spirit into the Image of a Perfect Man—as a worthy Symbol of the Divinity, wherein Human Nature is revealed in its Fulness. Yet, as if by an inward and irresistible Instinct, all men have been drawn to him; and, while diverse in their opinions; explaining his Idea in different types, they have given him the full and unreserved homage of their hearts. They have gathered around the altars, inscribed with his perfections, and, through his name, delighted to address the God and [7] Father of Spirits. Disowning him in their minds, unable to grasp his Idea, they have

---

[xix]-liii of *Conversations with Children on the Gospels,* vol. I, published in December. The title page of the reprint bears a quotation from John 3:8, together with the tag: "Jesus in Conversation with Nicodemus."

deified him in their hearts. They have worshipped the Holiness which they could not define.

Era of Its Revival

It is the mission of this Age, to revive his Idea, give it currency, and reinstate it in the faith of men. By its quickening agency, it is to fructify our common nature, and reproduce its like. It is to unfold our being into the same divine likeness. It is to reproduce Perfect Men. The faded Image of Humanity is to be restored, and man reappear in his original brightness. It is to mould anew our Institutions, our Manners, our Men. It is to restore Nature to its rightful use; purify Life; hallow the functions of the Human Body, and regenerate Philosophy, Literature, Art, Society. The Divine Idea of a Man is to be formed in the common consciousness of this age, and genius mould all its products in accordance with it.

Means of Its Revival

The means for reinstating this Idea in the common mind, in order to conduce to these results, are many. Yet all are simple. And the most direct and effectual are by apprehending the Genius of this Divine Man, from the study of those Records wherein his career is delineated with so much [8] fidelity, simplicity, and truth. Therein have we a manifestation of Spirit, while undergoing the temptations of this corporeal life; yet faithful to the laws of its renovation and its end. The Divine Idea of Humanity gleams forth through every circumstance of his terrestrial career. The fearful agencies of the Spirit assert their power. In him Nature and Life are subordinated to the spiritual force. The Son of God appears on Earth, enrobed in Flesh, and looks forth serenely upon Man. We feel the significance of the Incarnation; the grandeur of our nature. We associate Jesus with our holiest aspirations, our deepest affections; and thus does he become a fit Mediator between the last age and the new era, of which he was the herald and the pledge. He is to us the Prophet of two millenniums. He is the brightest Symbol of a Man that history affords, and points us to yet fuller manifestations of the Godhead.

Ideal of A Teacher

And the Gospels are not only a fit Text-Book for the study of Spirit, in its corporeal relations, but they are a specimen also of the true method of imparting instruction. They give us the practice of Jesus himself. They unfold the means of addressing human nature. Jesus was a Teacher; he sought to renovate Humanity. His method commends itself to us. It is a beautiful [9] exhibition of his Genius, bearing the stamp of naturalness, force, and directness. It is popular. Instead of seeking formal and austere means, he rested his influence chiefly on the living word, rising spontaneously in the soul, and clothing itself at once, in the simplest, yet most commanding forms. He was a finished extemporaneous speaker. His manner and style are models. In these, his Ideas became like the beautiful, yet majestic Nature, whose images he wove so skilfully into his diction. He was an Artist of the highest order. More perfect specimens of address do not elsewhere exist. View him in his conversation with his disciples. Hear him in his simple colloquies with the people. Listen to him when seated at the well-side discoursing with the Samaritan woman, on the IDEA OF WORSHIP; and at night with Nicodemus, on SPIRITUAL RENEWAL. From facts and objects the most familiar, he slid easily and simply into the highest and holiest themes, and, in this unimposing guise, disclosed the great Doctrines, and stated the Divine Ideas, that it was his mission to bequeath to his race. Conversation was the form of utterance that he sought. Of formal discourse but one specimen is given, in his Sermon on the Mount; yet in this the inspiration bursts all forms, and he rises to the highest efforts of genius, at its close.

Organ of Instruction

[10] This preference of Jesus for Conversation, as the fittest organ of utterance, is a striking proof of his comprehensive Idea of Education. He knew what was in man, and the means of perfecting his being. He saw the superiority of this exercise over others for quickening the Spirit. For, in this all the instincts and faculties of our being are touched. They find full and fair scope. It tempts forth all the powers. Man faces his fellow man. He holds a living intercourse. He feels the quickening life and light. The social affections are addressed; and these bring all the faculties in train. Speech comes unbidden. Nature lends her images. Imagination sends abroad her winged words. We see thought as it springs from the soul, and in the very process of growth and utterance. Reason plays under the mellow light of fancy. The Genius of the Soul is waked, and eloquence sits on her tuneful lip. Wisdom finds an organ worthy her serene, yet imposing products. Ideas stand in beauty and majesty before the Soul.

Organ of Genius

And Genius has ever sought this organ of utterance. It has given us full testimony in its favor. Socrates—a name that Christians can see coupled with that of their Divine Sage—descanted thus on the profound themes in which he delighted. The market-place; the workshop; the public streets were [11] his favorite haunts of instruction. And the divine Plato has added his testimony, also, in those enduring works, wherein he sought to embalm for posterity, both the wisdom of his master and the genius that was his own. Rich text-books these for the study of philosophic genius. They rank next in finish and beauty, to the specimens of Jesus as recorded by his own beloved John.

Genius Alone Renews

It is by such organs that Human Nature is to be unfolded into the Idea of its fulness. Yet to do this, teachers must be men in possession of their Idea. They must be men of their kind; men inspired with great and living Ideas, as was Jesus. Such alone are worthy. They alone can pierce the customs and conventions that hide the Soul from itself. They alone can release it from the slavery of the corporeal life, and give it back to itself. And such are ever sent at the call of Humanity. Some God, instinct with the Idea that is to regenerate his era, is ever vouchsafed. As a flaming Herald he appears in his time, and sends abroad the Idea which it is the mission of the age to organize in institutions, and quicken into manners. Such mould the Genius of the time. They revive in Humanity the lost idea of its destiny, and reveal its fearful endowments. They vindicate the divinity of [12] man's nature, and foreshadow on the coming Time the conquests that await it. An Age preëxists in them; and History is but the manifestation and issue of their Wisdom and Will. They are the Prophets of the Future.

Genius Misapprehended

At this day, men need some revelation of Genius, to arouse them to a sense of their nature; for the Divine Idea of a Man seems to have died out of our consciousness. Encumbered by the gluts of the appetites, sunk in the corporeal senses, men know not the divine life that stirs within them, yet hidden and enchained. They revere not their own nature. And when the phenomenon of Genius appears, they marvel at its advent. They cannot own it. Laden with the gifts of the Divinity it touches their orb. At intervals of a century it appears. Some Nature, struggling with vicissitude, tempts forth the Idea of Spirit from within, and unlooses the Promethean God to roam free over the earth. He possesses his Idea and brings it as a blessed gift to his race. With awe-struck visage, the tribes of semi-unfolded beings survey it from below, deeming it a partial or preternatural gift of the Divinity, into whose life and being they are forbidden, by a decree of the Eternal, from entering; whose law they must obey, yet cannot apprehend. [13] They dream not, that this phenomenon is but the complement of their common nature; and that in this admiration and obedience, which they proffer, is both the promise and the pledge of the same powers in themselves; that this is but their fellow-creature in the flesh. And thus the mystery remains sealed, till at last it is revealed, that this is but the unfolding of human nature in its fulness; working free of every incumbrance, by possessing itself.

Idea of Genius

For Genius is but the free and harmonious play of all the faculties of a human being. It is a Man possessing his Idea and working with it. It is the Whole Man—the central Will—working worthily, subordinating all else to itself; and reaching its end by the simplest and readiest means. It is human nature rising superior to things and events, and transfiguring these into the image of its own Spiritual Ideal. It is the Spirit working in its own way, through its own organs and instruments, and on its own materials. It is the Inspiration of all the faculties of a Man by a life conformed to his Idea. It is not indebted to others for its manifestation. It draws its life from within. It is self-subsistent. It feeds on Holiness; lives in the open vision of Truth; enrobes itself in the light of Beauty; and bathes its powers in the fount of Temperance. It aspires after the [14] Perfect. It loves Freedom. It dwells in Unity. All men have it, yet it does not appear in all men. It is obscured by ignorance; quenched by evil; discipline does not reach it; nor opportunity cherish it. Yet there it is—an original, indestructible element of every spirit; and sooner or later, in this corporeal, or in the spiritual era—at some period of the Soul's developement—it shall be tempted forth, and assert its claims in the life of the Spirit. It is the province of education to wake it, and discipline it into the perfection which is its end, and for which it ever thirsts. Yet Genius alone can wake it. Genius alone inspire it. It comes not at the incantation of mere talent. It respects itself. It is strange to all save its kind. It shrinks from vulgar gaze, and lives in its own world. None but the eye of Genius can discern it, and it obeys the call of none else.

Wane of Genius

Yet among us Genius is at its wane. Human Nature appears shorn of her beams. We estimate man too low to hope for bright manifestations. And our views create the imperfection that mocks us. We have neither great men, nor good institutions. Genius visits us but seldom. The results of our culture are slender. Thirsting for life and light, Genius is blessed with neither. It cannot free itself from the in- [15] cumbrance that it inherits. The Idea of a Man does not shine upon it from any external Image. Such Corporeal Types it seeks in vain. It cries for instruction, and none satisfies its wants. There is little genius in our schoolrooms. Those who enter yearly upon the stage of life, bearing the impress of our choicest culture, and most watchful discipline, are often unworthy specimens of our nature. Holiness attends not their steps. Genius adorns not their brow. Many a parent among us—having lavished upon his child his best affections, and spared no pains which money and solicitude could supply, to command the best influences within his reach—sees him return, destitute of that high principle, and those simple aims, that alone ennoble human nature, and satisfy the parental heart. Or, should the child return with his young simplicity and truth, yet how unarmed is his intellect with the quiver of genius, to achieve a worthy name, and bless his race. The Soul is spilt out in lust; buried in appetite; or wasted in vulgar toils; and retreats, at last, ignobly from the scene of life's temptations; despoiled of its innocence; bereft of its hopes, and sets in the dark night of disquietude, lost to the race.

Cause of Declension

Yet not all depravity nor ignorance is to be laid at the door of our Institutions. [16] The evil has two faces. It is deeper in its origin. It springs from our low estimate of human nature, and consequent want of reverence and regard for it. It is to be divided between parents and institutions. The young but too often enter our institutions of learning, despoiled of their virtue, and are of course disabled from running an honorable intellectual career. Our systems of nursery discipline are built on shallow or false principles; the young repeat the vices and reproduce the opinions of parents; and parents have little cause to complain. They cannot expect fruits of institutions, for which they have taken so little pains to sow the seeds. They reap as they sow. Aiming at little they attain but little. They cast their own horoscope, and determine by their aim the fate of the coming generation. They are the organized Opportunity of their era.

Faith of Genius

To work worthily, man must aspire worthily. His theory of human attainment must be lofty. It must ever be lifting him above the low plain of custom and convention, in which the senses confine him, into the high mount of vision, and of renovating ideas. To a divine nature, the sun ever rises over the mountains of hope, and brings promises on its wings; nor does he linger around the dark and depressing valley of distrust and [17] of fear. The magnificent bow of promise ever gilds his purpose, and he pursues his way steadily, and in faith to the end. For Faith is the soul of all improvement. It is the Will of an Idea. It is an Idea seeking to embody and reproduce itself. It is the All-Proceeding Word going forth, as in the beginning of things, to incarnate itself, and become flesh and blood to the senses. Without this faith an Idea works no good. It is this which animates and quickens it into life. And this must come from living men.

Genius Alone Inspires

And such Faith is the possession of all who apprehend Ideas. Such faith had Jesus, and this it was that empowered him to do the mighty works of which we read. It was this which inspired his genius. And Genius alone can inspire others. To nurse the young spirit as it puts forth its pinions in the fair and hopeful morning of life, it must be placed under the kindly and sympathising agency of Genius—heaven-inspired and hallowed—or there is no certainty that its aspirations will not die away in the routine of formal tuition, or spend themselves in the animal propensities that coexist with it. Teachers must be men of genius. They must be men inspired. The Divine Idea of a Man must have been unfolded from their being, and be a living presence. Philosophers, and Sages, and Seers, [18]—the only real men—must come as of old, to the holy vocation of unfolding human nature. Socrates, and Plato, and the Diviner Jesus, must be raised up to us, to breathe their wisdom and will into the genius of our era, to recast our institutions, remould our manners, and regenerate our men. Philosophy and Religion, descending from the regions of cloudy speculation, must thus become denizens of our common earth, known among us as friends, and uttering their saving truths through the mouths of our little ones. Thus shall our being be unfolded. Thus the Idea of a man be reinstated in our consciousness. Thus Jesus be honored among us. And thus shall Man grow up, as the tree of the primeval woods, luxuriant, vigorous—armed at all points, to brave the winds and the storms of the finite and the mutable—bearing his Fruit in due season.

Idea of Inspiration

To fulfil its end, Instruction must be an Inspiration. The true Teacher, like Jesus, must inspire in order to unfold. He must know that instruction is something more than mere impression on the understanding. He must feel it to be a kindling influence; that, in himself alone, is the quickening, informing energy; that the life and growth of his charge preëxist in him. He is to hallow and refine as he tempts forth the soul. He is [19] to inform the understanding, by chastening the appetites, allaying the passions, softening the affections, vivifying the imagination, illuminating the reason, giving pliancy and force to the will; for a true understanding is the issue of these powers, working freely and in harmony with the Genius of the soul, conformed to the law of Duty. He is to put all the springs of Being in motion. And to do this, he must be the personation and exampler of what he would unfold in his charge. Wisdom, Truth, Holiness, must have preëxistence in him, or they will not appear in his pupils. These influence alone in the concrete. They must be made flesh and blood in him, to reappear to the senses, and reproduce their like.—And thus shall his Genius subordinate all to its own force. Thus shall all be constrained to yield to its influence; and this too, without violating any Law, spiritual, intellectual, corporeal—but in obedience to the highest Agency, co-working with God. Under the melting force of his Genius, thus employed, Mind shall become fluid, and he shall mould it into Types of Heavenly Beauty. His agency is that of mind leaping to meet mind; not of force acting on opposing force. The Soul is touched by the live coal of his lips. A kindling influence goes forth to inspire; making the mind think; the heart feel; the pulse throb with his own. He arouses every faculty. He awakens the Godlike. He images the fair and full features of a Man. And thus doth he drive at will the drowsy Brute, that the Eternal hath yoked to the chariot of Life, to urge man across the Finite!

Hallowed Geniuses

To work worthily in the ministry of Instruction, requires not only the highest Gifts, but that these should be refined by Holiness. This is the condition of spiritual and intellectual clearness. This alone unfolds Genius, and puts Nature and Life to their fit uses. "If any man will know of the Doctrine, let him do the will of my Father," said Jesus; and he, who does not yield this obedience, shall never shine forth in the true and full glory of his nature.

Quenching of Genius

Yet this truth seems to have been lost sight of in our measures of Human Culture. We incumber the body by the gluts of the appetites; dim the senses by self-indulgence; abuse nature and life in all manner of ways, and yet dream of unfolding Genius amidst all these diverse agencies and influences. We train Children amidst all these evils. We surround them by temptations, which stagger their feeble virtue, and they fall too easily into the snare which we have spread. Concupiscence defiles their functions; blunts the edge [21] of their faculties; obstructs the passages of the soul to the outward, and blocks it up. The human body, the soul's implement for acting on Nature, in the ministry of life, is thus depraved; and the soul falls an easy prey to the Tempter. Self-Indulgence too soon rings the knell of the spiritual life, as the omen of its interment in the flesh. It wastes the corporeal functions; mars the Divine Image in the human form; estranges the affections; paralyzes the will; clouds the intellect; dims the fire of genius; seals conscience, and corrupts the whole being. Lusts entrench themselves in the Soul; unclean spirits and demons nestle therein. Self-subjection, self-sacrifice, self-renewal are not made its habitual exercises, and it becomes the vassal of the Body. The Idea of Spirit dies out of the Consciousness; and Man is shorn of his glories. Nature grows over him. He mistakes Images for Ideas, and thus becomes an Idolater. He deserts the Sanctuary of the Indwelling Spirit, and worships at the throne of the Outward.

Means of Reform

Our plans of influence, to be successful, must become more practical. We must be more faithful. We must deal less in abstractions; depend less on precepts and rules. We must fit the soul for duty by the practice of duty. We must watch and enforce. Like unsleeping Providence, we [22] must accompany the young into the scenes of temptation and trial, and aid them in the needful hour. Duty must sally forth an attending

Presence into the work-day world, and organize to itself a living body. It must learn the art of uses. It must incorporate itself with Nature. To its sentiments we must give a Heart. Its Ideas we must arm with Hands. For it ever longs to become flesh and blood. The Son of God delights to take the Son of Man as a co-mate, and to bring flesh and blood even to the very gates of the Spiritual Kingdom. It would make the word Flesh, that it shall be seen and handled and felt.

Spiritual Culture

The Culture, that is alone worthy of Man, and which unfolds his Being into the Image of its fulness, casts its agencies over all things. It uses Nature and Life as means for the Soul's growth and renewal. It never deserts its charge, but follows it into all the relations of Duty; at the table it seats itself, and fills the cup for the Soul; caters for it; decides when it has enough; and heeds not the clamor of appetite and desire. It lifts the body from the drowsy couch; opens the eyes upon the rising sun; tempts it forth to breathe the invigorating air; plunges it into the purifying bath; and thus whets all its functions for the duties of the coming day. And when toil and amusement have [23] brought weariness over it, and the drowsed senses claim rest and renewal, it remands it to the restoring couch again, to feed it on dreams. Nor does it desert the Soul in seasons of labor, of amusement, of study. To the place of occupation it attends it, guides the corporeal members with skill and faithfulness; prompts the mind to diligence; the heart to gentleness and love; directs to the virtuous associate; the pure place of recreation; the innocent pastime. It protects the eye from the foul image; the vicious act; the ear from the vulgar or profane word; the hand from theft; the tongue from guile;—urges to cheerfulness and purity; to forbearance and meekness; to self-subjection and self-sacrifice; order and decorum; and points, amid all the relations of duty, to the Law of Temperance, of Genius, of Holiness, which God hath established in the depths of the Spirit, and guarded by the unsleeping sentinel of Conscience, from violation and defilement. It renews the Soul day by day.

Self-Apprehension

Man's mission is to subdue Nature; to hold dominion over his own Body; and use both these, and the ministries of Life, for the growth, renewal, and perfection of his Being. As did Jesus, he must overcome the World, by passing through its temptations, and vanquishing the Tempter. [24] But before he shall attain this mastery he must apprehend himself. In his Nature is wrapt up the problem of all Power reduced to a simple unity. The knowledge of his own being includes, in its endless circuit, the Alphabet of all else. It is a universe, wherein all else is imaged. God—Nature—are the extremes, of which he is the middle term, and through his Being flow these mighty Forces, if, perchance, he shall stay them as they pass over his Consciousness, apprehend their significance—their use—and then conforming his being to the one; he shall again conform the other to himself.

Childhood a Type of the Godhead

Yet, dimmed as is the Divine Image in Man, it reflects not the full and fair Image of the Godhead. We seek it alone in Jesus in its fulness; yet sigh to behold it with our corporeal senses. And this privilege God ever vouchsafes to the pure and undefiled in heart; for he ever sends it upon the earth in the form of the Child. Herein have we a Type of the Divinity. Herein is our Nature yet despoiled of none of its glory. In flesh and blood he reveals his Presence to our senses, and pleads with us to worship and revere.

Misapprehension of Childhood

Yet few there are who apprehend the significance of the Divine Type. Child- [25] hood is yet a problem that we have scarce studied. It has been and still is a mystery to us. Its pure and simple nature; its faith and its hope, are all unknown to us. It stands friendless and alone, pleading in vain for sympathy and aid. And, though wronged and slighted, it still retains its trustingness; still does it cling to the Adult for renovation and light.—But thus shall it not be always. It shall be apprehended. It shall not be a mystery and made to offend. "Light is springing up, and the dayspring from on high is again visiting us." And, as in times sacred to our associations, the Star led the Wise Men to the Infant Jesus, to present their reverent gifts, and was, at once, both the herald and the pledge of the advent of the Son of God on the earth; even so is the hour approaching, and it lingers not on its errand, when the Wise and the Gifted, shall again surround the cradles of the New Born Babe, and there proffer, as did the Magi, their gifts of reverence and of love to the Holiness that hath visited the earth, and shines forth with a celestial glory around their heads;—and these, pondering well, as did Mary, the Divine Significance, shall steal from it the Art—so long lost in our Consciousness—of unfolding its powers into the fulness of the God.

Renovation of Nature

[26] And thus Man, repossessing his Idea, shall conform Nature to himself. Institutions shall bear the fruits of his regenerate being. They shall flourish in vigor and beauty. They shall circulate his Genius through Nature and Life, and repeat the story of his renewal.

Human Renewal

Say not that this Era is distant. Verily, it is near. Even at this moment, the heralds of the time are announcing its approach. Omens of Good hover over us. A deeper and holier Faith is quickening the Genius of our Time. Humanity awaits the hour of its renewal. The renovating Fiat has gone forth, to revive our Institutions, and remould our Men. Faith is lifting her voice, and, like Jesus near the Tomb of Lazarus, is uttering the living words, "I am the Resurrection and the Life, and he that Believeth, though dead in doubts and sins, shall be reassured of his Immortality, and shall flourish in unfading Youth! I will mould Nature and Man according to my Will. I will transfigure all things into the Image of my Ideal."—And by such Faith, and such Vision, shall Education work its mission on the Earth. Apprehending the Divine Significance of Jesus—yet filled with the assurance of coming Messiahs to meet the growing nature of Man—shall inspired Genius go forth to [27] renovate his Era; casting out the unclean spirits and the demons that yet afflict the Soul. And then shall Humanity, leaving her infirmities, her wrongs, her sufferings, and her sins, in the corrupting grave, reappear in the consciousness of Physical Purity; Inspired Genius; and Spotless Holiness. Men shall be one with God, as was the Man of Nazareth.

PART SIX

———

BIBLIOGRAPHIES, LETTERS, AND
MISCELLANEOUS

CATALOGUE OF BOOKS,*

Composing the Library of the late Rev. *William Emerson,* to be sold at PUBLIC AUCTION, on TUESDAY, 27th of August instant, at the Theological Library in Chauncey-Place. Sale to commence at 10 o'clock, A.M.

1 AMES's Works, 8vo.
2 Appendix to New Testament, by James Winthrop.
3 American Biographical and Historical Dictionary.
4 Adam's View of Religions, 8vo.
5 American Review, 2 vols. 8vo.
6 Adam's History of New-England abridged.
7 Aikin's Letters.
8 Novum Testamentum, Baskerville, 8vo.
9 Alexander's Introduction.
10 Adam's Essay on Electricity, by Wm. Jones, 8vo.
11 B e n e v o l e n c e of the Deity, 8vo. (Chauncy.)
12 Christian Monitor, 8 vols, 12mo. bound.
13 Adams's Lectures on Rhetoric and Oratory, 2 vols.
14 Bibla Sacra, 2 vols.
15 Campbell's Rhetoric, in 4 vols. bound in 2, 8vo. (Castellis) Lond. 1726.
16 Joseph Bingham's Antiquities of the Christian Church. 2 vols. folio, scarce.
17 Brooke's Gazetteer, 8vo.
18 Biblia Heberica, 8vo. (fine copy.)
19 Clarke's Introduction.
20 Caustic's Petition.
21 Burkitt's New Testament, 1 vol. folio Lon. Edition (fine copy.)
22 Belsham's Elements of the Philosophy of the Mind.
23 Brown's Dictionary, 2 vols. 8vo.
24 Blair's Lectures, 2 vols. 8vo.
25 Belknap's American Biography, 2 vols. 8vo.
26 Parkhurst's Hebrew Lexicon, quarto.
27 Bancroft's Life of Washington, 8vo.
28 Boston Collection of Hymns.
29 Bysche's Art of Poetry, 2 vols.
30 Brattle Street Church Hymns.
31 Belknap's Dissertations.
32 Cruden's Concordance, quarto.
33 Clark on the Evangelists, 2 vols. 8vo.
34 Century and Dedication Sermons, 8vo.
35 Confessions of Faith, 8vo.
36 Catalogus Bibliothecæ Harvardianæ, interleaved, 8vo.

37 Chauncy's View of Episcopacy, 8vo.
38 Watson's Theological Tracts, 6 vols. 8vo.
39 Claude on the Composition of a Sermon, 2 vols. 8vo. Rob. Robertson's edition.
40 Clarke's Ovid, 8vo.
41 Funeral Orations of Thucydides, Plato, and Lysias, 8vo. Oxon. 1746.
42 English Dictionary, Walker and Johnson's, 8vo.
43 Chambaud's Grammar, (French) 8vo.
44 Bibliographical Dictionary, including Dr. Harwood's View of the Classicks, 6 vols. 12mo.
45 Conquest of Canaan, 8vo.
46 Cicero's Orations, translated by Guthrie, 3 vols. 8vo.
47 Church History.
48 Clarke's Discourses.
49 Collier's Reflections, 2 vols.
50 Doddridge's Lectures, quarto.
51 Church Hymns and Psalms.
52 Clarke's Funeral Discourses.
53 Durham's Astro Theology, 8vo.
54 Dialogues on Education, by Harris, 2 vols. 8vo.
55 Dufief's Nature Displayed, 2 vols. 8vo.
56 Priestley's System of Biography.
57 Damberger's Travels.
58 Elements of Elocution, by Walker, 8vo.
59 Dr. Emmons's Sermons, 8vo.
60 Enfield's History of Philosophy, 2 vols. 8vo.
61 General View of the Doctrines of Christianity, 8vo.
62 Evans's Sketch of Religious Denominations.
63 Enfield's Prayers, 8vo.
64 Election Sermons, 3 vols. bound, 8vo.
65 Edwards on the Will, 8vo.
66 Everlasting Gospel by Siegvolck).
67 Eulogies on Washington, bound in 1 vol. 8vo.
68 Francklin's Sermons on the Relative Duties, 8vo.
69 Ferguson's Astronomy, quarto.
70 Epistola Facciolati, 8vo.

---

* William Emerson died on May 12, 1811. The sale of his books probably took place on August 27 of the same year.

71 Cyclopædia of Arts and Sciences, (by Rees) Amer. Edition, 27 Nos. quarto.
72 Foster's (Dr. James) Sermons, 4 vols. 8vo.
73 Fast and Thanksgiving Sermons, 8vo.
74 Gentleman's Magazine for the year 1739.
75 Doddridge's Family Expositor, with Critical notes, 6 vols. 8vo.
76 Fawcett's Sermons, 2 vols. 8vo.
77 French Exercises.
78 Funeral Sermons, 3 vols. 8vo. (bound)
79 Friendly Dialogue on the nature of Duty.
80 Gli Animali Parlenti, 3 vols. 8vo.
81 Grove on the Lord's Supper.
82 Greek Rudiments, 8vo.
83 Geddes' Biblical Criticism, quarto.
84 Gravesande's Philosophy, 8vo.
85 Gregory's Economy of Nature, 3 vols. 8vo.
86 Gray's Key to the Old Testament, 8vo.
87 Hoole's Tasso, 2 vols. 8vo.
88 Hutchinson's Xenophon (translated into Latin) 8vo.
89 Geddes's Bible, 2 vols. quarto.
90 Harris's Tour, 8vo.
91 Holmes' Rhetoric.
92 Hierocles, (Greek and Latin)
93 Griesbach's Novum Testamentum, 2 vols. 8vo.
94 Humane Society Discourses.
95 Græcum Lexicon a Hederico, quarto.
96 Holmes's American Annals. 2 vols. 8vo.
97 Hutchinson's History of Massachusetts, 2 vols. 8vo.
98 Index to the Bible, (Dr. Priestley.)
99 Jones's Essay on the Church.
100 Jervis's Hymns.
101 Hutchinson's Philosophy, 2 vols. quarto.
102 Heathen Philosophy, (by Priestley) 8vo.
103 Heynei Apollodori, Tom. I and II. 11 vols.
104 Hindoo Rajah, 2 vols.
105 Henry on Prayer.
106 Hooper's Medical Dictionary.
107 Soame Jenyns's Works, 4 vols.
108 Hutchinson's Inquiry on Beauty, 8vo.
109 Hervey's Meditations, 2 vols. large 8vo.
110 History of New England, (Adams) 8vo.
111 Jones's Hymns.
112 Psalms and Hymns.
113 Institutio Græcæ.

114 Institutions of Moses, 8vo. (Dr. Priestley's Comparison.)
115 Junius's Letters, 2 vols.
116 Kippis's Hymns and Psalms.
117 Titus Livius, 10 vols.
118 Lavater's Physiognomy.
119 Letters to a Student.
120 Political Cabinet, 8vo.
121 Libanii Epistolæ.
122 Life of Sir William Jones, 8vo.
123 Lempriere's Classical Dictionary, 8vo.
124 Latin Rudiments, (British Edition) 8vo.
125 Literary Magazine, or American Register, 2 vols.
126 Mathematics, (Webber's) 2 vols. 8vo.
127 Morse's Geography.
128 Morehead's Discourses, 8vo.
129 Literary Miscellany, 2 vols. 8vo.
130 McKnight on the Epistles, 6 vols. 8vo.
131 Macneill's Poems, 2 vols.
132 Miscellany.
133 British Classicks, containing the Rambler, Idler, Tatler, Citizen of the World, Mirror, Goldsmith's Essays, Shenstone's Essays, Adventurer, Connoissuer, The World, and the Guardian, all the sets complete, 32 vols.
134 Missionary Magazine, 2 vols. 8vo. for 1803.
135 Opera Lactantii, 8vo.—á Bünemanæ Lips. 1739, an excellent edition.
136 Locke on the Human Understanding, 2 vols. 8vo.
137 Lawson's Lectures, 8vo.
138 Madoc, a Poem, 2 vols. 8vo.
139 Life of Johnson, by Chandler, President of King's College, N. Y.
140 Kett's Elements, 2 vols. 8vo.
141 Monthly Anthology, 9 vols. 8vo.
142 Neumanni (Casparis) De Punctio Hebrorum, 8vo.
143 Miller's Retrospect, 2 vols. 8vo.
144 Minot's History, 2 vols. 8vo.
145 Memoirs of Cumberland, 8vo.
146 Morse's Gazetteer, 2 vols. 8vo.
147 Memoirs of the American Academy, 2 vols. 4to.
148 New-England Biographical Dictionary, by Dr. Eliot, 8vo.
149 Percy's Key to the New Testament.
150 Tate and Brady's Psalms and Hymns.
151 Pyle on the Acts and Epistles, 3 vols. 8vo.
152 Pilgrim.
153 Political Tracts, 4 vols. 8vo.
154 Pope's Works, 6 vols. 8vo.
155 Proud's Hymns.

156 Philosophie de Descarte.
157 Paley's Philosophy, quarto.
158 Orton's Discourses, 8vo.
159 Ossian's Poems.
160 Orton's Letters to a young Clergyman.
161 Pearce's Longinus, 8vo.
162 Neal's Puritans, 2 vols. 8vo. 2d edition, 1732.
163 New London Magazine, 2 vols. 8vo.
164 Satyricon T. Petroni Arbitri, quarto.
165 Preacher's Directory, quarto.
166 Orations, 2 vols. 8vo.
167 Nomina Hebræa, Chaldæa, Græca et Latina.
168 Calamy's Nonconformist's Memorial, 3 vols. 8vo. (Palmer's edition, 1802.)
169 Psalms and Hymns, 8vo.
170 Monthly Magazine, vols. 15, 16 and 17, for the years 1803 and 4.
171 Massachusetts Agricultural Society Papers, 2 vols. 8vo. from the year 1793 to 1809.
172 Massachusetts Magazine for the year 1796, 8vo.
173 Orton's Exposition, 6 vols. 8vo.
174 Priestley on the Corruptions of Christianity, 2 vols.
175 Ordination Sermons, 4 vols. 8vo.
176 System of Notation, (by Pelham).
177 Stuart's White on Colds.
178 Rumford's Essays, 2 vols. 8vo.
179 Reply to Wilberforce.
180 Rollin's Antient History, 8 vols. 8vo.
181 Medical and Agricultural Register, 8vo.
182 Prideaux's Connections, 4 vols. 8vo.

183 Robertson's Charles the Fifth, 4 vols. 8vo.
184 Treatise on Influx.
185 Miscellany, 14 vols. 8vo.
186 Trinity Hymns.
187 Sermons, 2 vols. 8vo.
188 Spectator, 8 vols.
189 Reflections by Zimmerman, 8vo.
190 Sermons by Wadsworth.
191 Priestley's Church History, 6 vols. 8vo.
192 Shakespeare, 8 vols.
193 Wakefield's New Testament, 2 vols. 8vo.
194 Reformed Pastor, abridged, by S. Palmer.
195 Swift's Works, 24 vols.
196 Swinton's Travels, 8vo.
197 Universal Salvation, 8vo.
198 J. Tillotson's Works, 10 vols. 8vo.
199 Theological Tracts, 22 vols. 8vo.
200 Watson's Apology.
201 The Wife.
202 Bos's Septuagint, with maps, 2 vols. 4to. 1709.
203 Watts's Works, 7 vols. 8vo.
204 Pursuits of Literature, 8vo.
205 Trumbull's History of Connecticut, 2 vols. 8vo.
206 Travels of Anacharsis the Younger, in Greece. 5 vols. 8vo.
207 View of Heresies, (by M'Farland.)
208 Whiston's Lectures, 8vo.
209 Walker's Key, 8vo.
210 Winthrop's Journal, 8vo.
211 Warren's History, 3 vols. 8vo.
212 Washington's Political Legacies, 8vo.

WHITWELL & BOND, *Auctioneers.*

BOOK BORROWERS OF THE BOSTON LIBRARY SOCIETY
(1793——1850)

The Boston Athenæum, a proprietary library founded in 1807, is well known to scholars, but the Boston Library Society, a like organization, founded in 1792,[1] is almost a stranger to competent researchers in the fields of history and literature. Commonly called by the abbreviated name of "The Boston Library," it has been occasionally confused with the younger institution, and no attempt, I believe, has been made in recent years to investigate its interesting history. That the subject deserves attention will be immediately apparent after a consideration of the following facts: The Rev. William Emerson, father of R. W. E., was a trustee from 1805 to 1810,[2] and a shareholder from 1800. His widow, Mrs. Ruth Emerson, inherited all his privileges at the time of her husband's death in 1811, withdrawing books until May 7 (or May 12), 1846. A large number of the scholarly people of Boston, moreover, held shares during the nineteenth century, and many were friends and associates of Ralph Waldo Emerson.

In October, 1939, because of diminishing income, after one hundred and forty-seven years of service to New Englanders, the Boston Library was moved into the Athenæum under terms congenial to both corporations, but the books were disposed of as follows. Out of approximately 50,000 volumes possessed at that time, the Athenæum took 5,686. The Boston Public Library and other local organizations were then given the opportunity to take several hundred others. Finally, Harvard University purchased about 10,000 volumes of fiction and 20,000 volumes of non-fiction, of which it retained respectively 6,500 and 12,000.[3] The remainders were sold to the Wesleyan University Library in Middletown, Connecticut. The official records of the Boston Society, however, were deposited in the Athenæum together with the incomplete card catalogue. There they still remain.

Of special importance to researchers in New England history and literature are the extant charging lists, resembling those of the Boston Athenæum and the Harvard College Library, to which I called attention in 1941.[4] They contain the records of book borrowers and the titles (or numbers) of the volumes withdrawn, together with dates. For the convenience of scholars distant from Boston, four years ago I published the names of patrons of the Athenæum up through the year 1850,[5] and intend in the following pages to set forth a similar directory of those who used the Boston Library during the same period. Of what appear originally to have been twenty-two manuscript charging books, all but two have survived and

---

[1] See *Athenaeum Items*, No. 17 [Boston, Mass., November, 1939], for a brief account of both institutions and of the merger.

[2] See Samuel S. Shaw, *The Boston Library Society: Historical Sketch*, Boston, 1895.

[3] The books kept by Harvard are now being catalogued. Most of them are being shelved in the Deposit Library.

[4] See Cameron, *Emerson's Reading*, pp. 11-16.

[5] *Ibid.*, pp. 131-139.

will be referred to by key letters. Scholars should note that dates of the
volumes overlap, and the use of them is occasionally confusing:

I	(1793-1797)	A	XII	(1829-1833)	L
II	(1800-1805)	B	XIII	(1833-1838)	M
III	(Missing)		XIV	(Missing)	
IV	(1808-1809)	D	XV	(1838-1841)	R
V	(1809-1811)	E	XVI	(1841-1844)	S
VI	(1811-1814)	F	XVII	(1844-1847)	U
VII	(1813-1818)	G	XVIII	(1847-1850)	V
VIII	(1818-1820)	H	XIX	(1851-1853)	..
IX	(1818-1822)	I	XX	(1853-1855)	..
X	(1821-1825)	J	XXI	(1855-1864)	..
XI	(1825-1833)	K	XXII	(1863-1867)	..

Students should not overlook two other important library collections of
the same era: The Boston Mercantile Library Association,[6] which still
maintains an office in Boston, published the names of its subscribers at
regular intervals in the printed catalogues of its holdings.[7] The Boston
Society of Natural History still preserves its charging lists and other early
records, but most of its manuscripts are now in permanent war storage
and not available.

THE DIRECTORY[8]

A

Abbot, James L.	UV		Amory, John	AB
Abbot, Joseph H.	V		Amory, Jonathan	ADEFGHIJKLMRSUV
Abbot, Robina	U		Amory, Rufus G.	B
Abbot, Samuel L.	FGHIJLMRSU		Amory, Mrs. Sarah	FGHIJKLMR
Adams, Asher	RU		Amory, Thomas C.	ABDEFGHIMRU
Adams, Benjamin	HIJKLM		Amory, Mrs. Thos. C.	LRSV
Adams, Joseph H., Jr.	UV		Andrews, Caleb	K
Adams, Phineas	HIJKL		Andrews, Ebenezer T.	AB
Adams, Thomas	B		Andrews, James	BGHIJKLMR
Adams, W. H.	V		Andrews, William	AB
Albree, John	MR		Andrews, William T.	HIJKLMRSUV
Alden, Rev. Timothy	E		Appleton, Benjamin B.	RSUV
Alexander, Giles	BDEF		Appleton, Nathan	ABG
Allen, Charles J. F.	SUV		Appleton, Nathaniel J.	B
Allen, James M.	U		Appleton, Nathaniel W.	ABL
Alley, Nathaniel	GHIJKLMRSUV		Apthorp, George H.	JK
Allen, James M.	KLMRS		Apthorp, John T.	B
Alley, Nathaniel, Jr.	EF		Armstrong, Samuel	DEM
Alleyne, F. S. B.	M		Armstrong, Samuel T.	KLMR
Alwyn, Will C.	M		Atkinson, George	RSUV
Ames, Fisher	ABE		Austin, James T.	DEFGHIJ
			Austin, Nathaniel	FGHIJKLM
			Austin, Nathaniel, Jr.	ABD

---

[6] It was incorporated in 1845 and merged with the Boston Public Library in 1877. It
was famous for its public lectures and had a reputation for paying a liberal honorarium
to its lyceum speakers. During its early years, George Barrell Emerson, second cousin
of R. W. E., was a leading spirit. Two other Emersons were patrons: William Emerson
and Frederick Emerson.

[7] See *A Catalogue of Books of the Boston Mercantile Library Association*, Boston,
1844. Other editions appeared in 1850, 1858 and 1869.

[8] The professions and street addresses of those listed can in most cases be found in
the appropriate volumes of the series of Boston Directories. The spelling of names
cannot be guaranteed here or elsewhere.

Austin, Samuel, Jr.	GHI
Austin, William	RSUV
Ayer, Joseph C.	S
Aylwin, William C.	HIJKRSUV

B

Babcock, Martha	ABE
Babcock, Samuel H.	LMR
Bacon, Francis	SUV
Badger, Willard	HIJK
Bailey, Ebenezer	LMR
Baker, Henry F.	RS
Baker, John	BEHIJKLM
Baker, Luke	ABD
Baker, Luther	KL
Balch, Joseph	HIJKLMRSUV
Baldwin, Aaron	HIJKLMRSUV
Baldwin, Enoch	KLMRSUV
Baldwin, J. F.	UV
Balfour, Walter	M
Ballard, Joseph	JK
Ballard, Lewis	V
Ballister, Joseph	MRSU
Bancroft, John	R
Bancroft, Thomas	KMR
Bangs, Benjamin	HIJKLMRSUV
Barnard, Josiah	GH
Barrell, Hannah	A
Barrett, Hannah	B
Barrett, Samuel	AB
Barry, Henry	LM
Barry, M. O.	UV
Barry, William	ABDEFGHIJK
Bartlett, Julia	GHI
Bartlett, Percival W.	V
Bartlett, Thomas	ABEFGH
Bartlett, William P. G.	V
Bass, Henry	HIJKLMR
Bates, Dr. George	MRSUV
Bates, J.	R
Batterman, Elizabeth	KLMRSUV
Baxter, John	AB
Bazin, Abraham	EFGH
Bazin, John	ABDEFG
Beals, Samuel	GHRSUV
Beals, Samuel J.	LM
Belknap, Andrew E.	ABD
Belknap, Jeremiah	ABDEFGHI
Bell, Joseph	SUV
Bell, Shubael	ABEG
Bellows, John	HI
Benjamin, Park	R
Bigelow, Jacob	FHI
Bingham, Caleb	ABDEFGH
Binney, Charles	U
Binney, Matthew	SU
Bishop, Jane Gore	V
Blake, George	ABEF
Blake, James H.	R
Blake, Mrs. Sarah	KM
Blake, William	AB
Blake, William P.	AB
Blanchard, Edward	EFGHIJKLMR
Blanchard, Hezekiah	HI
Blanchard, J. H. T.	RSUV
Blanchard, Joshua P.	ABDEFGHIJKLMRSU
Blanchard, William G.	D
Bliss, Alexander	KL
Boardman, B. G.	R

Boardman, B. G., Jr.	M
Boies, Jeremiah Smith	ABKLMRS
Bolles, John A.	R
Bolles, Matthew	UV
Bond, C. V.	B
Bond, George	HIJRS
Bond, Nathan	AB
Bowditch, Nathaniel	JK
Bowdlear, Samuel G.	UV
Bowdoin, James	ABGLM
Bowen, James	UV
Bowers, Isaac	ABDEFG
Bowers, Phineas	AB
Bowman, Edmund	B
Boyden, Dwight	R
Boyden, Uriah A.	V
Boyes, William	A
Brackett, Abigail	AB
Bradbury, Charles	JKLMRSUV
Bradford, Gamaliel	KM
Bradford, John	LMRSUV
Bradford, William B.	V
Bradlee, James P.	D
Bradlee, Joseph P.	KLMRSUV
Bradlee, Samuel	ABRSUV
Bradley, James II	D
Bradley, Samuel	BE
Bray, John	DEFGHIJKLMRSUV
Breed, John	ABD
Brewer, Gardner	LMRS
Brewer, Thomas	ABDEFGHIJKLMRSUV
Bridge, Charles	GHI
Bridge, Samuel	DEFR
Bridge, Samuel H.	HIJK
Bridge, Samuel James	LM
Brigham, Elisha	HIJ
Bright, John	ABDEFGHIJ
Brimmer, J. A.	B
Brimmer, Martin	HIJKMR
Brinley, George	GHIJKLM
Brodhead, Daniel D.	UV
Brooks, B. F.	U
Brooks, Charles	RSUV
Brooks, Francis A.	V
Brooks, Peter Chardon	AB
Brown, Augustus	V
Brown, Charles	KLMRSUV
Brown, George M.	RSUV
Brown, James	G
Brown, Dr. John B.	HIJKLMRSUV
Brown, Stephen	LMRS
Brownless, Samuel	AB
Bryant, Dr. John	GHIJKLMRSUV
Bulfinch, Charles	ABDEFGH
Bulfinch, G. S.	R
Bulfinch, Thomas	AB
Bull, Epaphras	E
Bullard, William S.	R
Burley, Susan	UV
Burroughs, George	ABD
Burton, Hazen J.	S
Bussey, Benjamin	ABDEFGHIJKLMRS

C

Cabot, Henry	R
Cabot, Richard C.	UV
Cabot, Samuel	KRS
Caldwell, Josiah F.	AB
Calef, Josiah	DE

Callender, Sally Brown	DB	Crane, Dr. Phineas M.	V
Callender, Sarah B.	EFGHIJ	Crehore, Thomas	KLM
Callender, T. B.	K	Crocker, Robert	H
Capen, Lemuel	SUV	Crofts, William	B
Carey, Samuel	F	Crombie, Benjamin	GHIJKLM
Carnes, Francis	DEFGHIJ	Culter, G. H.	V
Carnes, John	JKM	Culter, R. C.	V
Carter, David	R	Cummings, Jacob A.	GH
Carter, Oliver	SUV	Cunningham, Eli M.	L
Cary, Charles S.	RSUV	Cunningham, Ephraim	R
Cary, George B.	RSUV	Cunningham, Ephraim M.	M
Cary, Isaac H.	U	Cunningham, George	HIJK
Cary, Samuel	E	Cunningham, James	AB
Cary, Thomas G.	RSU	Cunningham, Joseph L.	BDEFHIJK
Caskins, Thomas F.	F	Curtis, Betsey	AB
Caughey, Sarah B.	V	Curtis, Charles P.	HIJKMRSU
Chace, Caleb	UV	Curtis, John (of Roxbury)	AB
Chacon, Don Raymondo	K	Curtis, Nathaniel, Jr.	V
Chadwick, Ebenezer	JK	Curtis, Thomas	AB
Chandler, Gardiner	BD	Curtiss, John	A
Chandler, Gardiner L.	ABEFGHIJ	Cushing, Lucy L.	SUV
Chandler, Mary Ann	JKLMRSU	Cushing, Thomas	HIJR
Channing, Susan C.	HIJK	Cushing, Thomas P.	JKMRSUV
Channing, Susan E.	MRS	Cutler, James	AB
Channing, Walter	HIJK	Cutter, George H.	SU
Channing, Rev. William E.	RSUV	Cutter, James	A
Chapman, Henry	HIJKLMR	Cutter, Ralph C.	SUV
Chapman, Mary G.	RSUV		
Chase, Thomas G.	FGHIJ		
Chickering, Horatio	MSUV	**D**	
Chickering, Horatio C.	R		
Chickering, John W.	KLM	Dagget, Henry L.	R
Child, George H.	U	Damon, Albert H.	R
Choate, Rufus	R	Dana, George	RS
Clapp, David, Jr.	RSUV	Danforth, Caroline	K
Clarke, James W.	RSUV	Danforth, Catharine	L
Clarke, John	AB	Danforth, Isaac	RSU
Clarke, June	K	Danforth, J.	V
Clarke, Dr. Samuel	ABGHIJKLM	Danforth, Dr. Samuel	HIJK
Cleland, Charles	G	Darby, Elias H.	B
Clement, Job S.	V	Darling, Francis D.	R
Cleveland, Charles	HI	Darnforth, Isaac	R
Cochran, William	GHIJKL	Darracott, George	HIJKMRSUV
Cochrayne, Mary	M	Davenport, George	L
Codman, [?]	M	Davies, Joshua Gee	AB
Codman, Mrs. Catharine	HIJKLR	Davies, Nathan	AB
Codman, John	AB	Davis, Edward G.	JK
Coffin, Francis	LM	Davis, Mrs. Eleanor	EFGHIJK
Coffin, George W.	LMRSU	Davis, James	HIJKMRSUV
Coffin, Dr. John G.	DEFGHIJK	Davis, John	ABDEF
Cole, Charles	LS	Davis, John D.	DE
Cole, Charles, Jr.	LMRSU	Davis, John W.	GHIJKLMRSUV
Coles, Mrs. Margaret C.	JK	Davis, Joshua G.	DEF
Collins, Deborah B.	S	Davis, William S.	AB
Collins, John H.	SU	Davison, Thomas	RSUV
Colman, Rev. Henry	HIJ	Dawes, Thomas, Jr.	ABD
Coolidge, Joseph	ABD	Day, James	EFG
Cordis, Thomas	HIJ	Deane, William R.	RSUV
Cordwell, Robert H.	K	Deblois, George	ABDEFGH
Cordwell, William	DEFGHIJ	Delany, Lizzie	V
Cordwell, William, Jr.	AB	Dennie, Thomas	ABDEFGHIJKLMRS
Cormerais, Henry	SUV	Dennison, William	J
Cotting, Uriah	ABDEFGHI	Derby, Elias H.	LMSUV
Cotton, John	ABDEFGHIJKLMRSUV	Derby, Elias H., Jr.	AR
Cotton, Mrs. Mary	HI	Derby, Richard C.	HIJKLM
Cotton, Nathan D.	UV	Devens, Charles	V
Cotton, Solomon	BDEFGJK	Dewhurst, William	RSUV
Coverly, Samuel	ABDEFGHIJ	Dexter, Dr. Aaron	ABDEFGHIJKMRSUV
Coverley, Samuel, Jr.	LM	Dexter, Franklin	JKMRS
Crackbon, Lemuel	LM	Dexter, Thomas A.	HI
Crane, Joshua	RSUV	Dimmock, John L.	SUV
		Dixon, Thomas	R

Doane, George B.	KLMRSUV
Doane, Samuel B.	HIJKLMRS
Domett, Henry W.	V
Donnison, William	ABDEFGHIJKLM
Dorr, Ebenezer	B
Dorr, Elizabeth Flinn	B
Doubleday, John G.	AB
Downer, Samuel	ABDEFGHIJKLMRSUV
Downes, John Tilestone	AB
Dowse, Edward	AB
Driscoll, Cornelius	RSUV
Dunbar, John D.	V
Dunn, James C.	JK
Dunn, Samuel	ABEFGHI
Dupee, Horace	RSU
Dupee, James A.	V
Dutton, George	V
Dwight, Edmund	H
Dwight, Rev. Sereno E.	HI
Dwight, William H.	HIJK
Dyer, Joseph C.	D

E

Eastburn, John H.	UV
Eaton, Allen	G
Eaton, Rev. Asa	DEFG
Eaton, Samuel A.	S
Eaton, William G.	KLMRSV
Eckley, David	D
Eckley, Rev. Joseph	A
Edes, Edward, Jr.	AB
Eldridge, Edward	MR
Eliot, Dr. Ephraim	FGHIJK
Eliot, Rev. John	ABDEFGHIJKLMRSUV
Elliott, John, Jr.	S
Ellis, Calvin	AB
Ellis, Luther	DEFGHIJKLMRSUV
Emerson, Benjamin D.	L
Emerson, George B.	JK
Emerson, Mrs. Ruth	GHIJKRSU
Emerson, Rev. William	BDEFG
English, James L.	SUV
Esty, Alexander R.	V
Etheridge, Edward	L
Eustis, Jacob	ABEFGH
Everett, Otis	HIJKLMR

F

Fairbanks, Charles B.	RS
Fales, Samuel	BDEFGHIJKLMRSUV
Fales, William A.	HIJ
Fales, Mrs. William A.	J
Farley, Frederick A.	HIJK
Farrington, Dr. Thomas	BDEFGHIJKLMRSUV
Faulkner, Luther	RSU
Fenno, James W.	UV
Field, Joseph	EFGKMRSUV
Field, Joseph, Jr.	BD
Fisher, F.	U
Fisher, Samuel	HIJ
Fisk, Abijah	HIJ
Fisk, John J.	MR
Fitch, Caroline M.	SUV
Fitch, Jeremiah	HIJKLMRS
Fitch, Jonas	?
Fitz, Albert	MR

Flaherty, Thomas J. O.	L
Fleming, J. W. C.	KLMR
Fletcher, Richard	RSUV
Fling, George W.	JK
Flinn, Elisabeth	AB
Flint, Waldo	SUV
Folsom, Charles	SU
Foster, Archibald	KLMRSUV
Foster, George	U
Foster, James H.	HIJKLMRSUV
Foster, Henry G.	DEFGHIJKMRSV
Foster, James H.	U
Foster, John S., Jr.	EFG
Foster, Joseph	ABDEFGH
Fowle, George W.	SU
Fowle, William B.	HIJ
Fox, John	ABDEFG
Francis, Ebenezer	LMRS
Frazier, Nathan	B
Frazier, Nathan, Jr.	A
Freeman, James	ABHI
French, Charles E.	V
French, Hannah E.	R
French, John	HIJKLMRV
French, John A.	KLSUV
Frothingham, Rev. Nathaniel L.	GHIJ
Fuller, Abraham W.	GHIJKLMRSUV
Fuller, Henry H.	LMRSUV
Fuller, Timothy	EF
Furness, Nathaniel H.	EFGHI
Furness, Rebecca Thwing	B
Furness, William	DEFG

G

Gage, John	MR
Gallison, John	GHI
Gannett, Agnes J.	SUV
Gardiner, Elizabeth	RSUV
Gardiner, John	L
Gardiner, Samuel J.	HI
Gardiner, William H.	LR
Gardner, Francis	RSUV
Gardner, John	AB
Gardner, J. S. J.	D
Gardner, John S.	AB
Gardner, Lemuel	ABDE
Gardner, Robert	AB
Gardner, Samuel	AB
Gardner, Samuel J.	GH
Gassett, Henry	HIJKLMRSUV
Gassett, Henry, Jr.	UV
Gassett, Oscar	R
Gates, Jacob	EF
Gates, William	G
Gerry, Mrs. Ann	HIJKL
Gerry, Elbridge	JKLRS
Geyer, Frederic William	AB
Geyer, Frederic William, Jr.	B
Gibbons, Louise A.	V
Glover, John B.	M
Goddard, George A.	S
Goddard, William	KLMRSU
Goodridge, James L.	R
Goodwin, Timothy	AB
Gordon, William	H
Gore, Christopher	AB
Gore, Jeremiah	ABEHIJK
Gore, Jeremiah, Jr.	ABDEFG

Gore, John	AB
Gore, Samuel	ABDEFGHIJKLMR
Gorham, Benjamin	KLMRSUV
Gorham, Frederick	BDE
Gorham, Dr. John	HIJKL
Gorham, Stephen	EFGHIJK
Gould, Benjamin A.	LMRSUV
Gould, Frederick	SUV
Gray, Edward	BDE
Gray, Francis C.	FGHIJKMRSUV
Gray, Francis H.	SUV
Gray, Frederick T.	KLR
Gray, Horace	HIJKRSUV
Gray, John C.	RSUV
Gray, Samuel C.	UV
Gray, Thomas, Jr.	L
Greele, Samuel	HI
Greely, Samuel	HIJ
Green, Mary	EFGJ
Green, Matthew	G
Green, Samuel S.	DE
Greene, Miss Anne R.	KLM
Greene, David	ABDEF
Greene, Hannah	DEFGHIJKLMRSUV
Greene, John Singleton C.	LR
Greene, Miss Mary	EHIJKMRSUV
Greene, Nancy	AB
Greene, Thomas	AB
Greenleaf, Daniel	AB
Greenleaf, John	AB
Greenleaf, Thomas	AB
Greenough, David	BDEFGHI
Greenwood, William P.	DEFG
Guardenier, John	MRS
Guild, Benjamin	HIJK
Gurney, Nathan	V

H

Hale, Moses L.	K
Hale, Nathan	G
Hall, Adin	SUV
Hall, Ebenezer	A
Hall, Ebenezer III	AB
Hall, Edward	V
Hall, Isaac	DE
Hall, Jacob	MR
Hall, James	ABDEFGHIJ
Hall, Jonathan P., Sr.	ABDEFGHIJKLMRSUV
Hall, Jonathan P., Jr.	HIJKLMRSUV
Hall, Joseph	ABDEFGHIJKLM
Hall, Joseph, Jr.	H
Hall, Nathaniel, Sr.	ABD
Hall, Nathaniel, Jr.	AB
Hall, Samuel	AB
Hallet, George	RSU
Hallet, Henry S.	UV
Hallowell, Robert	AB
Hammatt, Charles	BDEFGHIJKLMRSUV
Hammatt, Mary	JK
Hancock, John	DEFGHIJKLMRSUV
Harris, John	GJK
Harris, Jonathan	ABDE
Harris, Mary D.	SUV
Harris, Samuel	FG
Harris, Samuel D.	KLMRSUV
Harris, Rev. T.	D
Harris, Rev. Thaddeus M.	EFGHIJKLMRS
Harris, William	FGHIKLMRSUV

Harris, William, Jr.	HIJK
Hartshorn, John	RSUV
Haskell, Andrew W.	L
Haskell, John	B
Haskins, John, Jr.	AB
Haskins, Thomas	ABDEFGHIJKLMR
Haven, Franklin	SUV
Havens, Thomas	MRS
Hayden, Caroline	M
Hayden, Catherine	RSU
Hayes, Francis B.	SU
Hayt, George Gracie	A
Hayward, Caleb	DEF
Hayward, Charles	GHI
Hayward, John	AB
Hayward, John S.	LM
Hayward, Dr. Lemuel	HIJKLMRSUV
Haywood (See "Hayward")	
Head, Joseph	ABDEFGHIJKLM
Healy, Mark	RSUV
Heard, John	MR
Heard, John, Jr.	HIJK
Heath, Charles	LMRSUV
Henshaw, Joseph B.	GHI
Hewes, Robert	B
Hewes, Robert, Jr.	D
Hichborn, Thomas	A
Hicks, James H.	R
Higginson, George	B
Higginson, Henry	DFGHIJKLMR
Higginson, James P.	HIJKLM
Higginson, Martha S.	HI
Higginson, Stephen	UV
Higginson, Stephen, Jr., 1st	ABDE
Higginson, Stephen, Jr., 2nd	AB
Higginson, Stephen III	K
Hildreth, Richard	LMR
Hill, Henry	ABDE
Hill, Samuel	AB
Hills, Joseph S.	LMR
Hinckley, Nabby	ABDEFGH
Hitchborn, Thomas	B
Hodgdon, Alexander	AB
Homans, John	LMSUV
Homer, David	LM
Homer, Eliza	RS
Homer, Jonathan (of Newtown)	AB
Homer, Samuel J. M.	SUV
Hooper, William R.	U
Horton, Samuel, Jr.	G
Hosmer, Zelotes	K
Hovey, Abijah W.	UV
How, John	B
Howard, Abigail	AB
Howard, Mrs. Catherine Hayden	S
Howard, Samuel	AB
Howard, William	?
Howe, George	RSUV
Howe, Hall J.	RSUV
Howe, John	ABEFHIJKLMRSUV
Howe, Jonathan	DUV
Howe, Joseph N.	RSUV
Hubbard, Charles T.	UV
Hubbard, Sally	B
Hubbard, Samuel	GHLMRSUV
Hudson, William H.	K
Hunt, George	G
Hunt, Samuel	ABDEFGRS
Hurd, Charles	B
Hurd, John Russell	ABE
Hurd, Jon. R.	D

I

Inches, Henderson	ABDEF
Inches, Susan	R
Institution for the Blind	
(See "New England")	
Ivy, Hannah	E

J

Jackson, Edward	GH
Jackson, Francis	LMRSUV
Jackson, John	ABD
Jackson, Salisbury	B
Jacobs, Benjamin	RS
James, Sally	HIJKL
Janes, Samuel	AB
Jarvis, Deming	KLMUV
Jarvis, Elizabeth Sarah	K
Jarvis, Leonard	AB
Jarvis, Mrs. Mary	RSUV
Jarvis, Sarah	M
Jarvis, William	AB
Jeffrey, John	AB
Jeffrey, Patrick	AB
Jeffries, Deborah	AB
Jeffries, Patrick	DEF
Jenks, William	K
Jewett, John Harris	M
Johnson, Benjamin	UV
Johnson, Samuel	KMRSUV
Johnson, Timothy	HIJKLMRS
Jones, John Coffin	HIJ
Jones, Thomas K.	ABEHIKL
Joy, Hannah Barret	ADEFGHIJKLM

K

Kane, D. H.	R
Kast, Frederick	AB
Kast, Sally Inman	BDEHI
Kelly, William H.	UV
Kettell, George P.	V
Kirkland, Rev. John T.	ABDEF
Knapp, George	DE
Knapp, John	HIJRS
Knowles, Sarah P.	M

L

Labree, John D.	SUV
Ladd, William G.	SUV
Lamb, Mary	E
Lamb, Robert	B
Lamb, Robert, Jr.	AB
Lamb, Thomas	B
Lamson, Rev. Alvan	JK
Lamson, Edwin	R
Lane, John W.	AHI
Langdon, John W.	K
Langdon, Mary (of Greenwood)	AB
Larkin, Benjamin	AB
Larkin, Ebenezer	B
Larkin, Ebenezer, Jr.	A
Larkin, Thomas Oliver	AB
Lash, Robert	DFGHIJKMRSUV
Lash, Robert, Jr.	E
Lathrop, John Lawson	R
Leach, James	B
Leach, Samuel	B
Leach, Thomas	DEFGHIJKLMR
Leach, William	B

Leaver, Benjamin	S
Lee, George G.	G
Lee, Hannah F.	HRSUV
Lee, Henry	LM
Lee, James, Jr.	SUV
Lee, Thomas	MRSUV
Leeds, Samuel, Jr.	AB
Lenzee, John T.	K
Leverett, William	ABDEFG
Lincoln, Benjamin, Jr.	R
Lincoln, Bradford	KLMRS
Lincoln, F. W.	UV
Lincoln, Jairus B.	RSUV
Linzee, John J.	KMRSUV
Littlehale, J. S.	RSUV
Littlehale, S. S.	LM
Lloyd, James	B
Lloyd, James, Jr.	AB
Locke, Ephraim	GHIJKL
Lodge, Giles	HIJKLMR
Loring, Caleb	ABDEFGHIJ
Loring, Charles G.	MR
Loring, Elizabeth J.	R
Loring, Henry	K
Loring, John F.	SU
Loring, John J.	K
Loring, Henry	JK
Loring, Relief	BDEFGHIJKLMRSUV
Lovell, R. S.	EF
Low, Peter	UV
Lowder, Samuel	DE
Lowell, Rev. Charles	HIJKLMRSU
Lowell, Charles R.	M
Lowell, Francis C.	ABDEGHIJK
Lowell, John, Sr.	HIJK
Lowell, John, Jr.	HI
Lowell, John S.	AB
Lucas, John	AB
Lyon, Gardner P.	JKLMRSUV
Lyon, Lawson	DEFGHI

M

McCarty, John	V
McCleary, Samuel F.	HI
McCleary, Samuel T.	HI
McClure, Thomas	DEFGHIJK
McIntire, Charles	R
Mack, David	V
Magee, James	AB
Mackay, T. B.	V
Mackay, William	GHMRSU
Mackay, William, Jr.	HIJK
McKean, Amy	HIJ
McKean, Rev. Joseph	ADEFG
McKeene, Joseph	BE
McLane, John	B
McLean, John	A
McLellan, George W.	V
McLellan, Isaac	HIJKM
Maloney, Bridget	V
Mandell, Moses J.	SUV
Mansfield, Isaac	JKMR
Marrett, Phillip	LMRSUV
Marshall, Josiah	RS
Marvin, Theophilus R.	SUV
Mason, Jonathan	UV
Mason, Jonathan, Jr.	B
May, George	UV
May, Henry Knox	ABEFGHIJKMRS
May, Col. Joseph	HIJKLMR

May, Perrin	BDEFGHIJKLMRS
May, Samuel	SUV
May, Thomas	DE
Mead, Samuel O.	U
Mellon, William	S
Melville, Thomas	DEFGHIJK
Meriam, Charles	RS
Meriam, Levi	JKLM
Meriam, Silence	UV
Metander, Giles	B
Miller, Capt. John	DEFGHJKLM
Miller, Samuel R.	BEGHIJK
Mills, James K.	KL
Minns, T. C.	B
Minns, Thomas	ABDEFGHIJKLMRSUV
Minns, William	KL
Minot, Christopher	ABDE
Minot, George	A
Minot, George R.	AB
Minot, John	AB
Minot, Timothy M.	AB
Minot, William	EFGHIJKLMRSUV
Montague, William H.	KLMRSV
Moody, William H.	RS
Moreton, Sarah	A
Morrill, Charles J.	UV
Morrill, James	HIJKLM
Morrill, Samuel	MRSUV
Morse, Elijah	H
Morse, Jedidiah	AB
Morton, Joseph	EF
Morton, Sarah	ABDEFGHIJ
Moulton, E. C.	B
Moulton, Ebenezer	BDEFGHI
Munroe, Edmund	DEFGHI
Murphy, James	B

N

Nancrede, Joseph	AB
Nazro, John	HIJKLMRSUV
Nazro, John G.	SU
New England Institution for the Blind	MRSUV
New, R. C.	B
New, Robert	AB
Newell, William	G
Newhall, Ezra F.	R
Newman, Henry	S
Newton, F. W.	V
Nichols, George	G
Nicholls, Isaac P.	RS
Niles, William J.	SU
Nye, J. W. P.	RSUV

O

Odin, George	E
Odin, John	DEFGHIJKLMRSUV
Odiorne, William H.	RS
Ogden, Jacob	D
Oliver, Abby K.	RS
Oliver, Benjamin L.	S
Oliver, Francis J.	ABEGHIJKLMRSU
Oliver, F. T.	D
Oliver, Henry J.	KLMR
Oliver, Nathaniel K. G.	FGJKL
Oliver, Nathaniel K.	E
Otis, Edmund B.	UV
Otis, Eliza H.	MRSUV
Otis, F.	E
Otis, Mrs. Fanny	FGHIJK

Otis, Fanny Russell	B
Otis, Harrison G., Jr.	HIJK
Otis, T.	B

P

Page, John C.	JKLM
Page, Thomas	R
Paine, Robert	A
Palmer, Miss Jerusha	JKL
Park, A. C.	RSUV
Park, Benjamin	M
Park, John	HIJKL
Park, Thomas B.	LM
Parker, Benjamin C. C.	GHI
Parker, Benjamin M.	UV
Parker, Charles A.	LM
Parker, Daniel	R
Parker, David	RSU
Parker, Mrs. Frances	JKLMR
Parker, Isaac	KLMRSUV
Parker, James	R
Parker, James Lloyd	FGHI
Parker, John	DRS
Parker, John, Jr.	EFGHIJKLM
Parker, Miss Maria	JKLMRSUV
Parker, Samuel	AB
Parker, Samuel D.	DEFRSUV
Parker, Thomas B.	K
Parker, William	MRUV
Parker, William T. M.	S
Parkes, James Lloyd	F
Parkman, Rev. Francis	SUV
Parkman, P. M.	V
Parkman, Samuel	ABDEFGHI
Parkman, William	RU
Parsons, Theophilus	K
Parsons, Thomas W.	M
Payne, William E.	KM
Payson, Mrs. Ruth	RSU
Payson, Samuel R.	RSU
Peabody, Asa	G
Peabody, Augustus	HIJKLMRSUV
Peck, W. H.	R
Peck, W. W.	SU
Peckman, Benjamin T.	L
Peirce, John	B
Peirce, Joseph	B
Peirce, Levi	AB
Pemberton, William W.	M
Penniman, Elisha	DEFGHIJKL
Penniman, Henry	UV
Percival, James	B
Perkins, Francis A.	UV
Perkins, James	ABEFGHIJ
Perkins, Samuel G.	ABDEFGHIJKMR
Perkins, Thomas H.	ABDEFGH
Perry, John	FGHIJKLM
Pettees, Henry	M
Petties, Henry	RSUV
Phelps, Charles A.	V
Phillips, John	ABDEFGHIJ
Phillips, Jonathan	GHIJKLM
Phillips, Willard	HIJK
Phillips, William	B
Phillips, William, Jr.	AB
Phipps, William	JKLM
Pickens, John	GHIJKLSUV
Pickering, John	R
Pickman, Benjamin T.	M
Pico, Richard L.	B
Pierce, John	A

Pierce, L.	B
Pierpont, Rev. John	JKLM
Pike, Charles A.	V
Pike, James	DEFGHIJKLMRSUV
Plimpson, Daniel	R
Poignand, David	ABDEFG
Pollock, Allan	ABDFGHIJKM
Pomeroy, George	B
Pomeroy, Samuel W.	AB
Pomroy, George	A
Pope, Paschal P.	MRSUV
Pope, Thomas B.	UV
Powers, Thomas	DEFGHIRSUV
Powers, Thomas J.	D
Pratt, William	HIJK
Preble, Caroline	HI
Preble, Ebenezer	ABDEFG
Prentice, Theodore	SUV
Prescott, William	HIJKMRSU
Prescott, William H.	JKMRSUV
Putnam, Catharine	GHIJKLM
Putnam, Samuel R.	MR

Q

Quincy, Edmund	KM
Quincy, Josiah	ABHIJK
Quincy, Samuel	RSUV

R

Rand, Robert	AB
Ranney, David G.	M
Redman, John	RSU
Reed, Ralph I.	BD
Renouf, Edward	S
Revere, Paul	ABEFGHIJKLMRSUV
Revere, Paul, Sr.	DE
Reynolds, William B.	RSUV
Rice, Henry G.	HIJK
Rich, Hannah	SU
Richards, Alice W.	K
Richards, Joseph	ABDEFGHIJ
Richards, Reuben	LMRSUV
Richards, Reuben, Jr.	L
Ritchie, Andrew	EFGHIJKLRSUV
Ritchie, Andrew, Jr.	F
Ritchie, William	HIJKLMRS
Robbins, Francis C.	UV
Robbins, Samuel D.	UV
Roberts, John G., and Co.	R
Robertson, Andrew	KM
Robertson, Thomas	HIJ
Robinson, James	D
Robinson, Jane	EFGHIJK
Roby, Joseph	AB
Rockwood, Ebenezer	EFG
Rogers, Abner	F
Rogers, John Gray	HIJKLMRSUV
Rogers, William S.	LMRSUV
Rollins, William	KLMRSUV
Ropes, John C.	V
Rose, Philip	AB
Russell, Benjamin	AB
Russell, Benjamin F.	V
Russell, Fanny	AB
Russell, Joseph	BE
Russell, Nathaniel P.	HIJKLMRSUV
Russell, Thomas	AB

S

Salisbury, Josiah	HIJ
Salisbury, Nancy	V

Salisbury, Samuel	ABEFGHKLMRSUV
Sanderson, Jacob	KLM
Sargent, Daniel	DE
Sargent, Daniel, Jr.	AB
Sargent, Henry	FGH
Sargent, John O.	LM
Saunderson, Jacob	FGHIJ
Savage, George	SUV
Savage, James	KLMRSUV
Savage, William	M
Saville, William O.	KL
Sawyer, Edward	HIJK
Sawyer, Frederick W.	SUV
Sawyer, James H.	UV
Sayles, Francis W.	V
Sayles, Willard	RSUV
Scholfield, Arthur	HIJKLMRSUV
Scollay, Mrs. Catharine	ABDEFGHRSUV
Scollay, Mercy	AB
Scollay, William	ABDEFGHIJKLM
Scudder, Charles	HIJK
Scudder, David	KM
Searle, George	G
Sears, Joshua	RS
Seaver, Amasa	G
Seaver, Benjamin	SU
Seaver, George	RS
Seaver, Zachariah	AB
Sewall, Joseph	HIJKLMRSU
Sewall, Thomas R.	LM
Shattuck, George	MR
Shattuck, Lemuel	RSUV
Shattuck, William	A
Shattuck, William, Jr.	B
Shaw, Barnabas	AB
Shaw, Lemuel	DEFGHIJKMRSUV
Shaw, Robert G.	K
Sheafe, Charles C.	R
Shear, P.	G
Shelton, Thomas J.	KMRSUV
Shelton, Thomas L.	S
Sherburne, William	ABDEF
Shimmin, William	K
Shirley, Irving, Jr.	DE
Shurtleff, Dr. N. B.	V
Sigourney, Elizabeth	KLMRS
Sigourney, John C.	HIJ
Sigourney, Nathaniel	AB
Sigourney, Sarah B.	HIJ
Simpson, Daniel P.	RSUV
Skelton, Samuel D.	V
Smallidge, Jeremiah	EFGH
Smith, Abiel	ABDEFG
Smith, Azor Orne	B
Smith, Barney	H
Smith, George	HI
Smith, Mrs. Hannah	HIJK
Smith, Henry	LMRSUV
Smith, Rev. Isaac	EFGHIJKL
Smith, Joseph	ABDE
Smith, Joseph M.	MR
Smith, Nathaniel	EFG
Smith, Rebecca Rose	KLM
Smith, William	ABDEFG
Snelling, Samuel, Sr.	ABDEFGHIJKM
Snelling, Samuel, Jr.	JKL
Snow, Gideon T.	HIJ
Sohier, Edward D.	SUV
Sohier, William D.	SUV
Somes, John	AB
Southard, Zibeon	UV

Southgate, Lyman	SUV	Ticknor, Elisha	DE
Southwick, Joseph	SUV	Ticknor, George	KR
Spear, Paul, Jr.	FGH	Ticknor, William B.	KLMR
Spooner, Andrew	EFG	Tidd, Jacob	E
Spooner, Andrew O.	A	Tidd, William	AB
Spooner, Andrew P.	B	Tilden, Bryant P.	HIJK
Spooner, William	ABDEFGHIJKLMR	Tilden, Calvin	L
Sprague, Charles	BGH	Tilden, Mary P.	LMRS
Sprague, Hosea	B	Tilden, Sarah	ABDEFGHIJK
Sprague, John	AB	Tisdale, Mace	M
Sprague, Peleg	RSUV	Todd, George	HIJ
Sprague, Seth	UV	Torrey, Henry William	R
Sprague, Seth, Jr.	SU	Torrey, John	M
Stackpole, Joseph Lewis	K	Torrey, John G.	RSUV
Staniford, Daniel	ABDEFGHIJ	Torrey, Samuel	LMR
Staniford, Daniel, Jr.	A	Torrey, Samuel, Sr.	ABDEFGHIJ
Stanwood, David	H	Townsend, Alexander	H
Stearns, David	A	Townsend, Charles	H
Stearns, G. L.	U	Townsend, David	BD
Stearns, George S.	KRS	Townsend, H.	V
Stearns, J. A.	V	Townsend, Isaac P.	KLMRSUV
Stevens, Edward L.	M	Tracy, Nathaniel	V
Stevens, Isaac	FGHIJKLMRSUV	Train, Enoch	RS
Stevens, L. M.	V	Trott, George	HIJ
Stevenson, William	LMRSUV	Tucker, James	E
Stillman, Samuel	UV	Tucker, John	J
Stimson, Caleb	BDEF	Tucker, Joseph C.	B
Stoddard, Edward	AB	Tucker, R. D.	G
Stodder, Charles	RS	Tucker, William	LM
Stone, Stephen S.	V	Tuckerman, Edward	KMR
Storer, Ebenezer	AB	Tuckerman, Gustavus	K
Storer, George	AB	Tudor, William	ABEG
Storers, E.	B	Tuttle, Daniel	AB
Storrs, Nathaniel	DEF	Tyler, John E.	R
Story, Joanna	LM		
Streeter, Sebastian	L		
Strong, Dr. Woodbridge	JK	**U**	
Sturgis, Charles	AB		
Sturgis, James P.	DEFGHIJKLMRS	Underwood, William	LMRSUV
Sturgis, William	GHIJKMRS	Upham, Charles	V
Stutson, Thomas	AB	Upham, Walter W.	V
Sullivan, George	GHIJ	Urquhart, Alexander	RS
Sullivan, John L.	B	Urquhart, William	R
Swett, S. W.	L		
Swett, Samuel	EFGHIJKLMRSUV	**V**	
Swift, John J.	RSU		
		Vaughan, Charles	ABDFHIJKLMRSUV
T		Vila, James	ABDEFGHIJKLMR
		Vinton, Alexander H.	UV
Talbot, William H.	UV		
Tappan, Charles	HIM	**W**	
Tappan, John	UV		
Teschemacher, H. F.	RSU	Wainright, Henry	RSUV
Thacher, Peter O.	KLMRSU	Wainright, Peter	SU
Thacher, Samuel C.	FG	Waldron, Samuel W.	R
Thatcher, Peter, Sr.	AB	Wales, Ephraim	AB
Thayer, Andrew E.	DE	Wales, S., Jr.	SV
Thayer, Charlotte	HI	Wales, Samuel	U
Thayer, John	B	Wales, Thomas B.	EFGHIJKLMRSUV
Thayer, Nathaniel F.	HIJK	Walker, Dudley	B
Thomas, Joshua	ABDEFG	Walker, Samuel	JK
Thomas, Nathaniel Gardner	ABDEFGH	Walker, Wildes P.	S
Thomas, Sarah E.	UV	Walley, Thomas	AB
Thompson, Abraham R.	EF	Walter, Arthur Maynard	B
Thompson, John H.	MR	Walter, Harriot	B
Thompson, Josiah	AB	Walter, Lynde	DEFGHIJKLMRU
Thorndike, Israel, Jr.	H	Walter, W. C., Jr.	B
Thurston, William	ABEFGHIJKM	Walter, William	ABDEFG
Thurston, Mrs. William	J	Walter, William Jr.	AB
Thwing, Rebecca	AB	Ward, Artemas	FGHIJKMRSUV
Ticknor, Benjamin	JK	Ward, Benjamin C.	EFGHIJKLM
		Ward, Charles T.	V
		Ware, Henry	A

Ware, Henry (of Hingham)	BD	Whitwell, Mrs. Lucy C.	KLM
Ware, Rev. Henry	HIJK	Whitwell, Samuel	LM
Ware, Paschal	V	Whitwell, Samuel, Jr.	JK
Warner, William A.	KLMR	Whitwell, William	BDEFG
Warren, Mrs. Abigail	HIJKL	Wigglesworth, Thomas	GHIJKMRSU
Warren, John	BEFG	Wight, Ebenezer	KLMRSU
Watson, Benjamin M.	SUV	Wight, Lothrop	RSU
Watson, Marston	B	Wilby, Francis	JK
Weare, Dow	B	Wilby, Frances	GHI
Webb, Elisha	D	Wild, Abraham	JK
Webb, Nathan	ABDEFGHIJKMSUV	Wild, Dr. Charles	KLMRSUV
Webb, Rufus	B	Wild, George C.	UV
Webb, William H.	AB	Wild, James C.	HIJKLMRSUV
Webster, Daniel	HIJKMRSUV	Wilde, George C.	SU
Webster, John W.	HIJK	Wilde, James C.	MSU
Webster, Redford	ABDEFGHIJKLM	Wiley, Thomas	R
Welch, William	AB	Wilkinson, Arthur	S
Weld, Daniel	HIJKLMRSUV	Willard, Joseph	SUV
Weld, William E.	GHI	Williams, Edward A.	V
Weld, William F.	SUV	Williams, Eliphalet	SU
Welles, Arnold, Jr.	AB	Williams, F. Thomas	B
Welles, Samuel	B	Williams, John	JKLMRSUV
Welles, Samuel, Jr.	AB	Williams, John D. W.	R
Wellington, David, Jr.	RSU	Williams, Nathaniel L.	JKLMRSUV
Wells, Mrs. Hannah	KLMRSUV	Williams, S. K.	RSUV
Wells, John	AB	Williams, Sally	AB
Wells, Samuel, Jr.	A	Williams, Samuel G.	R
Wells, Seth	ABDEFGHIJ	Williams, Thomas	ABDEFGHIJK
Wells, Thomas	EHI	Williams, Timothy	HIJK
Welsh, Thomas, Jr.	HJK	Williams, William	ABD
Welsh, William	AB	Winslow, Benjamin	V
Wentworth, Philip H.	S	Winsor, Henry	SUV
Werner, Charles	GHIJ	Winthrop, Thomas L.	BDEFGHIJKM
West, Benjamin	ABDEF	Witherbee, J. B.	RS
West, David	AB	Withington, Ebenezer	DEFG
Wheeler, Abner B.	RS	Withington, Elijah	E
Wheeler, Moses	FGHIJK	Withington, Newell	LM
Wheelwright, Caroline	RSUV	Wood, David G.	SU
White, Benjamin F.	RSUV	Wood, T. N.	G
White, William	AB	Woods, Samuel	MR
White, William B.	GHIJK	Woodward, Joseph	AB
Whiting, Ella	UV	Woodward, Stanley G.	V
Whiting, Ruggles	BD	Wright, John S.	RSUV
Whiting, William P.	GHIJKLMRS	Wyman, Charles	UV
Whitney, James	G	Wyman, Oliver C.	HIJ
Whitney, Joseph	KLMRSUV	Wyman, William	EFGHIJKLMRSUV
Whitney, William	KLMRSUV		
Whitwell, Benjamin	GHIJK	**Y**	
Whitwell, F. P.	B		
Whitwell, John P.	BDE	Yeaton, Benjamin	RSU

BOOKS BORROWED FROM THE BOSTON LIBRARY SOCIETY
BY RALPH WALDO EMERSON AND HIS MOTHER
(1815———1845)[1]

The rules of the Boston Library, to be found prefixed to the various editions of its printed catalogue,[2] permitted the members of a shareholder's immediate family to withdraw books in his name, and it is probably safe to assume that the Rev. William Emerson did not monopolize the many volumes which appear charged to him between 1800 and 1811, the year of his death. From 1811 until the share was formally transferred to his widow, Mrs. Ruth Emerson, in October, 1815, books continued to be charged on his account.[3] Their titles suggest that they were used for fireside reading and for helping the widow find spiritual comfort and strength to meet her heavy responsibilities. I have not attempted to edit the reading lists of this early period, but have preferred to begin transcription at October 19, 1815, when William Jr. was beginning his second year at Harvard and when Ralph Waldo, though but twelve, was writing letters filled with references to his extensive reading.[4]

Until my discovery of the Boston Library Society's manuscripts, one question had frequently disturbed me: Since R. W. E's book borrowings at the Athenæum began late[5] and since the restrictions at the Harvard College Library apparently limited the number of books which he was permitted to withdraw during college days and afterwards,[6] where did he obtain the many volumes which he mentions during his early years in the letters and in the published *Journals*?[7] All or most of his father's library had been sold at auction shortly after the funeral,[8] and one cannot suppose that Waldo's personal book collection could have been very large before he settled down in Concord in 1836. I believe, therefore, that the reading list which follows this brief introduction is a partial answer to that question, for there is evidence that the literature listed under Mrs. Ruth Emerson's name was not all intended for her. R. W. E. mentioned, for example, on July 3, 1819,[9] that he had lost "the list of French Books at Boston Lib."[10] On March 17,

---

[1] This list is intended to supplement Cameron's *Emerson's Reading*, by augmenting the scanty records of Emerson's earlier years.

[2] To be listed *infra*.

[3] See Charging Lists: "B" pp. 226 and 394; "D" p. 73; "E" pp. 60, 129 and [185]; "F" pp. 40, 212 and 327; "G" pp. 36 and 144.

[4] See *Letters*, I, pp. 1-31.

[5] He began reading at the Athenæum in 1830. See Cameron, *Emerson's Reading*, p. 17.

[6] *Ibid.*, pp. 44-49.

[7] The scholar should be cautioned against relying too much on the printed lists. A careful search throughout the accompanying text can double the number of references listed at the ends of the chapters. The index of the *Journals* is also inadequate for purposes of detailed bibliography.

[8] See the list of books sold at auction on pages 135-137 of the present volume.

[9] *Letters*, I, 87.

[10] Apparently Catalogue No. 2, a very useful supplement to the earlier catalogue. It appeared without title page in 1819. See *infra*.

1828,[11] he told a friend: "I had some years ago out of the Boston Library a Plato which was Englished from Mme. Dacier's French." The best evidence, however, for his heavy reliance on that institution is to be found by comparing the reading record with the footnotes and index of Professor Rusk's edition of the *Letters* and with the bibliographies in the printed *Journals*.

How far one may go in determining which books were read by R. W. E., which by his mother, and which by both or by others——is problematic. It becomes apparent at once that this appendix should be used in conjunction with all lists of his contemporary library borrowings, the *Complete Works*, the *Journals*, the *Letters*, the published sermons and, when ultimately edited, the early lectures. To assume, for example, that Emerson read the non-fiction and his mother all the novels and romances would be to ignore certain important facts. He *did* read novels throughout his life——especially historical novels——and there is much evidence for his acquaintance with good fiction in his works, especially in his addresses delivered abroad. It is, indeed, highly probable that while at Harvard and during the succeeding decade he read a great deal of it. At all events, the fact that such works as *Rob Roy* were taken from the Boston Library again and again suggests that Mrs. Emerson was not the only reader of the lighter books that entered her home.[12] We need, of course, to know more about the early family life of the Emersons and of the part the mother played in R. W. E's household from 1836 until her death in 1853. Even before the share was sold to Francis A. Perkins on May 12, 1846,[13] Emerson's contact with the Boston Library seems to have ended. The Athenæum, which then held first place among the proprietary libraries, seemed adequate to supplement his own growing collection of books.

---

[11] *Letters*, I, 228.

[12] In his letter to William Withington, dated July 27, 1822, Emerson wrote: "I have this moment finished the first vol of 'Fortunes of Nigel' which I fear is excluded from your reading Catalogue, because it is so unfortunate as to bear the name of a novel; but if masterly unrivalled genius add any weight to the invitation for a scholar to step out of his Greek & Hebrew circle of sad enchantments, that he may pluck such flowers of taste & fancy as never bloomed before to deck his strength withal,—why, then, he may read Scott, and particularly the latter novels. In this book there is nothing akin to any novels of another man; there is no unskilful crowding of incident,—indeed there is very little incident at all; the interest is maintained by the very elevated and animating, and yet perfectly natural tone of the conversation which is kept up. The youngest observer of human society recognizes circumstances corresponding entirely with the record of his own mind; and in all the strangeness and remoteness of the scenes and persons. I have twenty times borne witness to the sagacity of observations which I had many times felt to be true, without ever having expressed them. Our sternest scholars must admire the genius of this unrivalled seer, whose fruitful invention already surpasses the One thousand and One Tales of Arabian Entertainment. Next to Shakspeare he will stand highest with posterity. . . . Perhaps it is wasting your time to trouble you with my lucubra[tions] about novels and poetical idolatry. But, at the moment, I have it more at heart than aug[ht] else. . . . In American *books*,—we feel quite proud of 'Europe' (Alex Everett's) 'The Spy' and 'N England Tale.' " *(Transcribed from a photostat of the MS.)* Many novels, especially Scott's, are still to be found in the small bookcase in Emerson's study at Concord.

[13] See the MS. entitled, "List of Proprietors—Boston Library," now in the Athenæum. The date in the Charging List is May 7. The records to be edited are drawn from MS. volumes: "G" pp. 144, 316; "H" p. 168; "I" pp. 43, 308, 407; "J" pp. 154, 337; "K" pp. 51, 114, 213; "R" pp. 159, 160, 161; "S" p. 180; "U" p. 146.

Beside the novels and Dacier's *Plato,* Emerson had his eye on the tempting array of French works to be found in the Library Society's alcoves. In 1818, moreover, he apparently read Broughton's *Selection from the Popular Poetry of the Hindoos* (London, 1814), a work which seems not to be mentioned in most discussions of his orientalism. Another popular work on the present inventory was the *Arabian Nights' Entertainments.* I shall say no more in introducing this new material. The scholar will, doubtless, find uses enough for the facts which the records reveal in abundance. As for the condition of the manuscripts, one will find them about the same as other library records of the period.[14] In deciphering them the editor needs to look for the *original* date of borrowing a book rather than for the date of renewal, which so often is scratched over the former. I have not reproduced the numbers "7," "17" and their multiples, which appear so often in the final column of the accounts because they were merely the sums imposed as fines for each week a book was kept out beyond the usual five-week loan period. The Emersons, it seems, did not object to spending money for overdue books! As for the tools used in identifying the listings and in checking them, I submit the following important works of reference:

(A) *Shelf Catalogue of the Boston Library.* It is a folio manuscript, begun *ca.* 1793 and continued until about 1845. It is valuable because it classifies books by shelf and position and indicates frequent changes of arrangement.

(B) The surviving card catalogue, now incomplete and, since the sale of the volumes to many institutions, broken up into a variety of bundles. If it is ever reconstituted, it should prove valuable to those working on early reading lists.

(C) *List of Proprietors———Boston Library.* This is a manuscript that provides a careful record of the names of the original founders and all shareholders. It records all transfers of shares until the late nineteenth century.

(D) Printed catalogues, especially those listed below.[15] Those starred were most useful because they contain more complete information about bibliographical matters:

    *1) *Catalogue No. 1 of Books in the Boston Library, October 1, 1815,* Boston, 1815.

    *2) *Catalogue No. 2 of Books in the Boston Library, Franklin Place,* [Boston, 1819]. (It is a supplement to the first.)

    3) *Catalogue of Books in the Boston Library, June, 1824,* Boston, 1824.

    4) *Catalogue of Books in the Boston Library, June, 1830,* Boston, 1830.

    *5) *A Catalogue of the Books of the Boston Library Society in Franklin Place, January, 1844,* Boston, 1844.

Mrs. Ruth Emerson moved to 24 Franklin Place, very near the Boston Library, sometime in 1820.[16] One may surmise that her primary purpose was to give her growing sons ready access to a large collection of books.

---

[14] See Cameron, *Emerson's Reading,* p. 12.

[15] I did not use all the printed catalogues. There are pamphlet inventories of 1797, 1805 and 1807. There were also supplemental catalogues issued in 1835, 1849 and 1855.

[16] See *Letters,* I, 94.

1 8 1 5 *

Oct. 19	(1)	Hayley, *Philosophical . . . Essay on Old Maids* (1)	Oct. 21
Oct. 19	(2)	Pearsall, *Contemplations on the Ocean etc.*	Oct. 21
Oct. 19	(3)	Tacitus, *Works of Cornelius Tacitus* (1)	Nov. 11
Oct. 21	(4)	Staël-Holstein, *Influence of the Passions*	Nov. 11
Oct. 21	(5)	Tucker, *Abridgment of the Light of Nature*	Nov. 11
Nov. 11	(6)	Inchbald, *The British Theatre* (3)	Nov. 16
Nov. 16	(7)	Tacitus, *Works of Cornelius Tacitus* (2)	Dec. 9
Nov. 16	(8)	Wakefield, *Mental Improvement*	Dec. 9
Nov. 16	(9)	Goldsmith, *History of the Earth* (3)	Dec. 21
Dec. 9	(10)	Sturm, *Reflections on the Works of God* (1)	Dec. 23
Dec. 23	(11)	Sturm, *Reflections on the Works of God* (1)	Jan. 11
Dec. 23	(12)	Fennell, *Apology for the Life of James Fennell*	Jan. 25
Dec. 23	(13)	*Edinburgh Review* (22)	Jan. 11

1 8 1 6

Jan. 11	(14)	Sévigné, *Letters from the Marchioness* (1)	Jan. 27
Jan. 13	(15)	Hamilton, *A Series of Popular Essays* (1)	Feb. 8
Jan. 27	(16)	Edgeworth, *Moral Tales for Young People* (2)	Feb. 24
Feb. 8	(17)	Hamilton, *A Series of Popular Essays* (2)	Feb. 24
Mar. 16	(18)	*Arabian Nights' Entertainments* (2)	Mar. 30
Mar. 16	(19)	Trimmer, *Sacred History* (1)	Apr. 6
Mar. 16	(20)	Edgeworth, *Popular Tales* (2)	Apr. 30
Mar. 30	(21)	Cicero, *The Tusculan Disputations*	Apr. 20
Mar. 30	(22)	Edgeworth, *Moral Tales for Young People* (1,3)	Apr. 20
Apr. 6	(23)	Franklin, *Works*[?] *Complete Works*[?] (1)	Apr. 11
Apr. 11	(24)	*Arabian Nights' Entertainments* (1)	Apr. 20
Apr. 20	(25)	Edgeworth, *Popular Tales* (2)	Apr. 27
Apr. 20	(26)	Cicero, *The Tusculan Disputations*	May 18
Apr. 20	(27)	Edgeworth, *Moral Tales for Young People* (2)	Apr. 27
Apr. 27	(28)	Hamilton, *A Series of Popular Essays* (1)	May 2
Apr. 27	(29)	Porter, *The Two Princes of Persia*	May 2
May 2	(30)	Cordiner, *Remarkable Ruins . . . North Britain* (2)	May 16
May 2	(31)	*New Moral Tales* [Not identified.] (1)	May 16
May 16	(32)	Goldsmith, *The Roman History* (1)	June 20
May 16	(33)	Goldsmith, *History of the Earth* (1,2)	June 8
May 18	(34)	*Bell's British Theatre* (3)	June 25
May 25	(35)	Hamilton, *A Series of Popular Essays* (2)	June 20
June 8	(36)	*The Two Pilgrims; a romance* (1)	June 20
June 20	(37)	Marmontel, *Memoirs*[?] *Incas* [?] *Moral Tales* [?] (1)	June 25

---

* The first column lists the date of withdrawal. The second is the editor's item-numbering system, to be used in the bibliography at the end of the yearly lists. The final column indicates the dates of return of books. Parentheses after the titles contain references to series and volume: Roman numerals always refer to series; Arabic always refer to the number of the volume.

June 25	(38)	Smith, *Essays on Philosophical Subjects*	Sept. 5
July 27	(39)	Goldsmith, *The Roman History* (2)	Aug. 17
Aug. 1	(40)	Cordiner, *Remarkable Ruins . . . North Britain* (2)	Aug. 24
Aug. 17	(41)	Logan, *Sermons*	Sept. 5
Aug. 24	(42)	Inchbald, *The British Theatre* (5)	Sept. 5
Sept. 5	(43)	Shakespeare, *The Poems of Shakespeare*	Sept. 19
Sept. 5	(44)	Southey, *Letters . . . by Don Espriella*	Sept. 19
Sept. 19	(45)	Tucker, *Abridgment of the Light of Nature*	[Oct.] 31
Sept. 19	(46)	Campbell, *The Pleasures of Hope*	[Oct.] 31
Sept. 19	(47)	Alison, *Sermons on Particular Occasions*	[Oct.] 31
Nov. 16	(48)	Burney, *Traits of Nature* (1)	Dec. 14
Nov. 23	(49)	Chateaubriand, *The Martyrs* (1,2)	Dec. 19
Dec. 14	(50)	Opie, *Simple Tales* (1)	Jan. 23
Dec. 19	(51)	Ligne, *Letters and Reflections*	Jan. 23
Dec. 19	(52)	Godwin, *Life of Geoffrey Chaucer* (1)	Jan. 23

1 8 1 7

Jan. 23	(53)	Hazlitt, *Eloquence of the British Senate* (1)	Jan. 30
Jan. 23	(54)	[Burke? or Pratt?] *Sublime and Beautiful*	Jan. 31
Jan. 23	(55)	Terentius, *Comedies* (tr. George Colman)	Jan. 31
Jan. 30	(56)	Aitchison, *Encyclopædia Perthensis* (1)	Jan. 31
Feb. 13	(57)	Klopstock, *The Messiah* (tr. Collyer)	Feb. 31
Feb. 13	(58)	[Clarke? or Fleury?] *Ancient Israelites*	Feb. 31
Feb. 13	(59)	Kames, *Essays on Principles of Morality*	Feb. 20
Feb. 15	(60)	*The Christian Observer* (10)	Feb. 20
Feb. 15	(61)	Brunton, *Self-control, a Novel* (1)	Feb. 20
Mar. 20	(62)	Bruce, *Travels to . . . Source of the Nile* (1)	Apr. 12
Mar. 20	(63)	Clarke, *Travels in Various Countries: Pt. II*	Mar. 29
[? ?]	(64)	Robertson, *History of . . . Charles V* (2,3,4)	[Apr. ?] 29
[? ?]	(65)	Cappe, *Discourses on Devotional Subjects*	Apr. 29
Apr. 12	(66)	Edgeworth, *The Absentee: a tale* (2)	Apr. 29
Apr. 19	(67)	Staël-Holstein, *Letters on Writings of Rousseau*	May 10
Apr. 26	(68)	Knox, *Elegant Extracts . . . of Poetry* (1)	May 3
May 3	(69)	Adams, *Lectures on . . . Philosophy* (1,5)	June 7
May 10	(70)	Robertson, *The History of Scotland*	July 10
June 7	(71)	*American Journal of Science* (I.1)	July 10
June 7	(72)	Adams, *Lectures on . . . Philosophy* (1,2,5)	Aug. 30
July [10]	(73)	Cuthbertson, *Forest of Montalbano* (1,2)	July 20
July [10]	(74)	*American Journal of Science* (I.2)	July 20
July 26	(75)	Scott, *Tales of My Landlord* ([I?].1)	Aug. 7
Aug. 7	(76)	*Encyclopædia* [*Britannica?*] or [*Rees' Cyclo.?*] (10)	Aug. 28
Aug. 28	(77)	Johnson, *Journey to Western Islands of Scotland*	Sept. 11
Sept. 11	(78)	Johnson, *The Rambler* (2)	Sept. 30
Sept. 11	(79)	Sherlock, [Wm.? or Thomas?], [See bibliography.] (1)	Sept. 13
Sept. 11	(80)	Coote, *History of Modern Europe*	Sept. 18
Sept. 13	(81)	*The Christian Observer* (13)	Oct. 18
Sept. 18	(82)	Wilcocks, *Roman Conversations* (1)	Oct. 20

Sept. 20	(83)	Ségur, *Women: their Condition and Influence* (1)	Oct. 25
Sept. 25	(84)	Barbauld, *Poems* (1)	Oct. 2
Oct. 2	(85)	Elsley, *Annotations on the Four Gospels* (1)	Oct. 4
Oct. 2	(86)	Goldsmith, *Abridgment of History of England*	Oct. 18
Oct. 4	(87)	*The Christian Observer* (14)	Oct. 18
Oct. 23	(88)	*The Christian Observer* (15)	Nov. 22
Nov. 6	(89)	Clarkson, *A Portraiture of Quakerism* (1)	Nov. 22
Nov. 22	(90)	Wardlaw, *Discourses on Socinian Controversy*	Nov. 27
Dec. 6	(91)	Knox, *Elegant Extracts* [? *in Prose*] (1)	Dec. 31
Dec. 6	(92)	Depping, *Evening Entertainments*	Jan. 15

1 8 1 8

Jan. 1	(93)	White, *Letters on England* (1)	Jan. 10
Jan. 1	(94)	Genlis, *Sacred Dramas* (tr. Holcroft)	Jan. 10
Jan. 10	(95)	Mass. Hist. Soc., *Collections* (II.3,4)	Jan. 29
Jan. 15	(96)	*Arabian Nights' Entertainments* (1,4)	Jan. 31
Jan. 15	(97)	Depping, *Evening Entertainments*	Jan. 29.
Jan. 29	(98)	*The Christian Observer* (10,15)	Feb. 19
Jan. 29	(99)	Milton, *The Poetical Works* (Todd) (1,2)	Feb. 19
Feb. 12	(100)	*Arabian Nights' Entertainments* (3)	Feb. 19
Mar. 19	(101)	Stewart, *Travels over the Globe etc.* (1)	Mar. 26
Mar. 21	(102)	Goldsmith, *The Grecian History* (1)	Mar. 26
Mar. 21	(103)	Milton, *Paradise Lost* (1)	May 2
Mar. 26	(104)	Chalmers, *Evidence and Authority of Revelation*	Apr. 9
Apr. 4	(105)	*Arabian Nights' Entertainments* (1)	Apr. 9
Apr. 9	(106)	Cappe, *Critical Remarks on Scripture* (1,2)	Apr. 23
Apr. 11	(107)	Chalmers, *Series of Discourses on Revelation*	May 21
Apr. 23	(108)	Buckminster, *Sermons*	May 23
May 2	(109)	Milton, *Paradise Lost* (1)	May 23
May 21	(110)	Goldsmith, *History of England* (1,2)	May 23
May 23	(111)	Richardson, *History of Sir Charles Grandison* (1,2)	May 23
June 4	(112)	More, *Strictures on System of Female Education* (1)	June 18
June 13	(113)	Cappe, *Critical Remarks on Scripture* (1)	June 13
June 13	(114)	Tooke, *The Pantheon . . . of the Heathen Gods*	July 23
June 18	(115)	Buckminster, *Sermons*	July 23
June 27	(116)	Goldsmith, *The Roman History* (2)	July 23
July 9	(117)	Florian, *Œuvres Complètes* (4)	July 30
July 23	(118)	Tooke, *The Pantheon . . . of the Heathen Gods*	Oct. 17
July 25	(119)	Tacitus, *Life of Cnæus Julius Agricola*	Aug. 15
July 30	(120)	Florian, *Œuvres Complètes* (3)	Aug. 13
Aug. 15	(121)	Trimmer, *Sacred History* (1)	Aug. 29
Aug. 20	(122)	Gillies, *History of Ancient Greece* (1)	Aug. 29
Aug. 29	(123)	Broughton, *Selections from Poetry of the Hindoos*	Sept. 5
Sept. 5	(124)	*The Spectator* (1,2,3)	Oct. 24
Sept. 24	(125)	Jay, *Short Discourses to be read in Families* (1)	Oct. 3
Oct. 3	(126)	*Aristotle's Ethics and Politics* (Gillies) (1)	Oct. 10
Oct. 10	(127)	*Quintilian's Institutes of the Orator* (1)	Oct. 17
Oct. 17	(128)	Cappe, *Discourses on Devotional Subjects*	Oct. 24

Oct. 24	(129)	*The Spectator* (4,5)	Nov. 21
Nov. 12	(130)	*Arabian Nights' Entertainments* (1)	Dec. 12
Nov. 21	(131)	Apollonius Rhodius, *Argonautics* (Preston) (1)	Dec. 26
Dec. 12	(132)	Horsley, *Sermons*	Jan. 2
Dec.[?12]	(133)	Pearson, *Memoirs of the Rev. Claudius Buchanan*	Jan. 30
Dec. 26	(134)	*Arabian Nights' Entertainments* (2,3)	Jan. 7

1 8 1 9

Jan. 7	(135)	*The Spectator* (1)	Jan. 21
Jan. 9	(136)	Boswell, *Life of Samuel Johnson* (1,2,4)	Jan. 28
Jan. 21	(137)	Yates, *A Vindication of Unitarianism*	Feb. 4
Jan. 28	(138)	Beattie, *The Minstrel . . . with Other Poems*	Jan. 30
Jan. 30	(139)	Wardlaw, *Unitarianism Incapable of Vindication*	Feb. 6
Jan. 30	(140)	Allston, *The Sylphs of the Seasons etc.*	Feb. 4
Feb. 4	(141)	Johnson, *Journey to Western Islands of Scotland*	Feb. 18
Feb. 4	(142)	Wakefield, *Mental Improvement*	Feb. 18
Feb. 6	(143)	Edgeworth, *Tales of Fashionable Life* (2,3)	Feb. 13
Feb. 13	(144)	Watts, *The Improvement of the Mind*	Feb. 18
Mar. 6	(145)	*Ferguson's Astronomy* (1 + plates)	Mar. 11
Mar. 6	(146)	Edgeworth, *Tales of Fashionable Life* (2)	Mar. 11
Mar. 6	(147)	Edgeworth, *Popular Tales* (1,2)	Mar. 25
Mar. 11	(148)	Taylor, *Discourses on Various Subjects* (1)	Mar. 25
Mar. 25	(149)	Staël-Holstein, *Letters on Writings of Rousseau*	Apr. 3
Mar. 25	(150)	Coleridge, *Biographia Literaria*	Mar. 27
Mar. 25	(151)	Chalmers, *Series of Discourses on Revelation*	Apr. 3
Mar. 27	(152)	Godwin, *Mandeville: tale of the 17th Century* (1)	[Apr. 3]
Apr. 3	(153)	Kirwan, *Sermons, with Sketch of his Life*	Apr. 15
Apr. 3	(154)	Robertson, *History of . . . Charles V* (1,2)	Apr. 15
Apr. 3	(155)	Porter, *Don Sebastian: An historical novel* (2)	Apr. 15
Apr. 15	(156)	Jebb, *Works: Theological, Medical etc.* (1,2)	May 2
Apr. 22	(157)	*The Spectator* (1)	May 13
May 10	(158)	Moore, *Lalla Rookh, an Oriental Romance*	May 29
May 13	(159)	Scott, *Rob Roy* (1,2)	May 22
May 20	(160)	Chateaubriand, *The Martyrs* (1)	May 22
May 22	(161)	Hazlitt, *Lectures on the English Poets*	June 10
May 22	(162)	La Fontaine, *Œuvres Complettes* (5)	July 3
May 29	(163)	Taylor, *The Identity of Junius Established*	June 10
June 10	(164)	Southey, *Letters . . . by Don Espriella*	July 1
June 19	(165)	Tacitus, *Works of Cornelius Tacitus* (1)	July 31
July 3	(166)	Montolieu, *La Ferme aux Abeilles*	Aug. 5
July 8	(167)	Ramsay, *History of the United States* (1)	Sept. 18
July 31	(168)	Tacitus, *Works of Cornelius Tacitus* (1)	Aug. 14
Aug. 7	(169)	Marmontel, *Nouveau Contes Moraux* (1)	Sept. 16
Aug. 14	(170)	Beresford, *Miseries of Human Life*	Sept. 2
Sept. 2	(171)	Tytler, *Considerations on State of India* (1)	Sept. 4
Sept. 4	(172)	*The Christian Observer* (15)	Oct. 9
Sept. 16	(173)	Tibullus, *Elégies de Tibulle* (Mirabeau) (1,3)	Oct. 14
Sept. 16	(174)	Southey, *Letters . . . by Don Espriella*	Oct. 30

Oct. 9	(175)	Congreve, *Poems*	Oct. 14
Oct. 14	(176)	Tibullus, *Elégies de Tibulle* (Mirabeau) (2)	Nov. 20
Oct. 14	(177)	*The Christian Observer* (13)	Nov. 20
Oct. 30	(178)	*American Journal of Science* (I.1)	Dec. 4
Nov. 20	(179)	Staël-Holstein, *Considérations sur la Révolution* (1)	Dec. 30
Nov. 20	(180)	Jouy, *The Paris Spectator, or l'hermite* (1)	Dec. 4
Dec. 4	(181)	Hunt, *The Feast of the Poets etc.*	Dec. 23
Dec. 4	(182)	*The Monthly Anthology and Boston Review* (2)	Dec. 23
Dec. 23	(183)	Tressan, *Œuvres choisies de Comte de Tressan* (7,8)	Jan. 29
Dec. 23	(184)	Carey, *Vindiciæ Hibernicæ, or Ireland Vindicated*	Dec. 23
Dec. 23	(185)	Mathias, *Pursuits of Literature*	Dec. 30
Dec. 30	(186)	Plato, *Works of Plato Abridg'd* (M. Dacier) (1,2)	Jan. 20

1 8 2 0

Jan. 13	(187)	Hazlitt, *The Round Table* (1)	Jan. 22
Jan. 20	(188)	Campbell, *An Essay on English Poetry*	Jan. 27
Jan. 22	(189)	Enfield, *Institutes of Natural Philosophy*	Jan. 27
Jan. 27	(190)	Edgeworth, *Moral Tales for Young People* (1)	Jan. 29
Jan. 29	(191)	Staël-Holstein, *Influence of the Passions*	Feb. 19
Jan. 29	(192)	Bacon, *The Essays, or Councils Civil and Moral*	Feb. 19
Jan. 29	(193)	Baillie, [*?Miscellaneous*] *Plays*	Feb. 19
Mar. 18	(194)	Sargent, *The Life of Alexander Smith*	Apr. 8
Mar. 18	(195)	Staël-Holstein, *Corinne ou l'Italie* (1)	Apr. 15
Apr. 8	(196)	Hazlitt, *The Round Table* (1)	May 13
Apr. 15	(197)	Plato, *Works of Plato Abridg'd* (M. Dacier) (1)	May 13
Apr. 15	(198)	Staël-Holstein, *Delphine*, Paris, 1809. (1)	May 13
Apr. 27	(199)	Wordsworth, *Poems by William Wordsworth* (1,2)	May 6
May 6	(200)	Adams, [J. Q.? or George?] *Lectures* (1)	May 18
May 13	(201)	Boccaccio, *The Decameron* (1)	May 20
May 13	(202)	Dryden, [*?Critical and Miscellaneous Prose Wks.*] (3)	May 13
May 13	(203)	Dryden, *Works* (Scott) (11,12,13)	May 27
May 18	(204)	Burns, *The Works of Robert Burns* (3)	May 20
May 20	(205)	*The Quarterly Review* (21)	June 15
May 20	(206)	Butler, *Hudibras, in Three Parts* (1)	June 15
May 27	(207)	Plato, *Works of Plato Abridg'd* (M. Dacier) (1)	June 15
June 3	(208)	Morgan, *O'Donnel; a National Tale* (2)	June 8
June 8	(209)	Taylor, *Discourses on Various Subjects* (1)	July 20
June 8	(210)	Percy, *Reliques of Ancient English Poetry* (1)	June 10
June 10	(211)	[Le Sage:]* *The Devil upon Two Sticks* (1,2)	June 29
June 15	(212)	Campbell, *Poetical Works of Thomas Campbell* (2)	June 13
June 17	(213)	Wirt, *The Old Bachelor* (2)	July 8
June 29	(214)	Byron, *The Siege of Corinth . . . Parisina*	July 1
July 1	(215)	Moore, *Lalla Rookh, an Oriental Romance*	July 13
July 8	(216)	Lavater, *Physiognomy*	Sept. 2

---

* Since the author's name is not given in the charging list, Emerson might have used *The Devil upon Two Sticks in England*, (3 vols.) London, 1811.

July 13	(217)	Porter, *The Scottish Chiefs: a Romance* (1,2)	Sept. 29
July 20	(218)	Taylor, *Discourses on Various Subjects* (2)	Sept. 2
July 29	(219)	Ossianic Poems: *The Poems of Ossian* (1)	Aug. 12
Aug. 12	(220)	Ramsay, *History of the United States* (1)	Aug. 17
Aug. 17	(221)	Scott, *Rob Roy* (1,2)	Sept. 7
Sept. 2	(222)	Massinger, *Plays of Philip Massinger* (1,2)	Sept. 14
Sept. 2	(223)	Porter, *Fast of St. Magdalen, a Romance* (1)	Sept. 7
Sept. 7	(224)	Edgeworth, *Moral Tales for Young People* (2)	Sept. 7
Sept. 7	(225)	Taylor, *Sermons on Different Subjects*	Sept. 7
Sept. 7	(226)	Montaigne, *Essais*, Paris, 1802. (1)	Sept. 9
Sept. 7	(227)	Dryden, *Works* (Scott) (17)	Sept. 9
Sept. 9	(228)	Taylor, *Discourses on Various Subjects* (3)	Sept. 16
Sept. 9	(229)	Edgeworth, *Moral Tales for Young People* (2)	Sept. 14
Sept. 14	(230)	Scott, *Rob Roy* (1)	Sept. 14
Sept. 14	(231)	Edgeworth, *Tales of Fashionable Life* (1)	Sept. 14
Sept. 14	(232)	Massinger, *Plays of Philip Massinger* (3,4)	Sept. 28
Sept. 14	(233)	Edgeworth, *Popular Tales* (2)	Sept. 21
Sept. 16	(234)	Edgeworth, *Essays on Professional Education*	Sept. 28
Sept. 21	(235)	Froissart, *Sir John Froissart's Chronicles* (1 + plates)	Oct. 7
Sept. 28	(236)	Taylor, *Discourses on Various Subjects* (3)	Sept. 30
Sept. 28	(237)	Nares, *Thinks-I-to-Myself: a Tale*	Oct. 7
Sept. 30	(238)	Livius, *Roman History* (1)	Dec. 16
Oct. 7	(239)	Taylor, *Discourses on Various Subjects* (3)	Dec. 2
Oct. 7	(240)	Scott, *Roy Rob* (1,2)	Oct. 14
Oct. 14	(241)	*Arabian Nights' Entertainments* (4)	Oct. 28
Oct. 28	(242)	Roland, *Works of J. M. Phlipon Roland* (1,2)	Nov. 11
Nov. 11	(243)	Bacon, *Works* (1)	Dec. 21
Dec. 2	(244)	Beloe, *The History of Herodotus* (1)	Dec. 21
Dec. 16	(245)	Livius, *Roman History* (1)	Mar. 31
Dec. 21	(246)	*Edinburgh Review* (5)	Dec. 23
Dec. 21	(247)	Bacon, *Works* (1)	Feb. 3
Dec. 23	(248)	Scott, *Waverley; or 'Tis Sixty Years Since* (1)	Feb. 3

1 8 2 1

Jan. 4	(249)	Dearborn, *Memoir on . . . the Black Sea* (1 + Atlas)	Feb. 1
Jan. 27	(250)	Thucydides, *History of the Peloponnesian War* (1)	Feb. 1
Feb. 1	(251)	Burton, *The Anatomy of Melancholy*	Feb. 17
Feb. 3	(252)	Buckminster, *Sermons*	Feb. 8
Feb. 8	(253)	Byron, *The Siege of Corinth . . . Parisina*	Feb. 10
Feb. 10	(254)	Watts, *Sermons on Various Subjects*	Mar. 17
Feb. 22	(255)	Lyman, *The Political State of Italy*	Mar. 24
Feb. 24	(256)	*The Monthly Anthology and Boston Review* (4)	Mar. 3
Mar. 3	(257)	Godwin, *History of the Life of Wm. Pitt*	Mar. 8
Mar. 8	(258)	Aikin, *General Biography* (7)	Mar. 29
Mar. 17	(259)	Stewart, *Gen'l View of Progress of Philosophy* (1)	Apr. 26
Mar. 29	(260)	Scott, *Ivanhoe: A Romance* (1)	Apr. 29
Mar. 31	(261)	Livius, *Roman History* (1)	Apr. 26
Apr. 19	(262)	Hazlitt, *Lectures on the English Poets*	May 12

Apr. 26	(263)	Schlegel, [August ? or Friedrich ?][1] (1)	June 2
May 12	(264)	Scott, *The Lay of the Last Minstrel*	May 19
May 17	(265)	*Aristotle's Ethics and Politics* (Gillies) (1)	June 2
May 19	(266)	Burnett, *Specimens of English Prose Writers* (1)	June 2
June 16	(267)	Gibbon, *Decline and Fall of the Roman Empire* (1789) (1)	June 23
June 28	(268)	Priestley, *Lectures on History and Gen'l Policy* (1,2)	July 19
July 21	(269)	Schlegel, [August ? or Friedrich ?][2] (2)	July 28
July 23	(270)	Sturm, *Reflections on the Works of God* (2)	Aug. 25
July 19	(271)	McCrie, *The Life of John Knox*	July 28
July 28	(272)	Scott, *The Monastery: A Romance* (1,2)	Aug. 2
July 28	(273)	Robertson, *History of . . . Charles V* (2)	Sept. 1
Aug. 2	(274)	Montesquieu, *Œuvres Complettes* (5)	Aug. 9
Aug. 9	(275)	Grimm, *Correspondance Littéraire etc.* (1)	Aug. 16
Aug. 16	(276)	Montesquieu, *Œuvres Complettes* (4)	Aug. 25
Aug. 25	(277)	Hume, *The History of England* (4)	Sept. 13
Aug. 25	(278)	Simonde, *De la Littérature du Midi de l'Europe* (3)	Sept. 8
Sept. 1	(279)	Hume, *The History of England* (1)	Sept. 8
Sept. 8	(280)	Robertson, *History of . . . Charles V* (3)	Sept. 27
Sept. 8	(281)	Pascal, *Pensées* (1)	Sept. 15
Sept. 13	(282)	Rabelais, *Œuvres de Maitre François Rabelais* (1)	Sept. 15
Sept. 15	(283)	Simonde, *De la Littérature du Midi de l'Europe* (1)	Oct. 6
Sept. 15	(284)	*Edinburgh Review* (16)	Sept. 22
Sept. 22	(285)	Dunlop, *The History of Fiction* (1)	Oct. 4
Sept. 27	(286)	Irving, *A History of New York* (Knickerbocker) (1)	Oct. 4
Oct. 4	(287)	Burney, *The Country Neighbors, or The Secret* (1)	Oct. 4
Oct. 4	(288)	Smith, *The Theory of Moral Sentiments*	Nov. 3
Oct. 6	(289)	La Harpe, *Lycée, ou Cours de Littérature* (1,2)	Nov. 22
Oct. 20	(290)	Hallam, *View of Europe during Middle Ages* (1,2,3,4)	[ ][3]
Oct. 27	(291)	Froissart, *Sir John Froissart's Chronicles* (4 + plates)	Nov. 3
Nov. 3	(292)	Burr, *Reports of the Trials of Col. Aaron Burr* (1)	Nov. 8
Nov. 3	(293)	Adams, *Lectures on . . . Philosophy* (2)	Dec. 15
Nov. 8	(294)	Chalmers, *A History of . . . the Univ. of Oxford* (2)	Nov. 15
Nov. 17	(295)	*Ferguson's Astronomy* (1)	Nov. 29
Nov. 29	(296)	Cervantes, *History and Adventures of Don Quixote* (?1)	Jan. 3
Dec. 15	(297)	Adams, *Lectures on . . . Philosophy* (?2)	Jan. 3
Dec. 15	(298)	Adams, *Lectures on . . . Philosophy* (5)	Jan. 24

1 8 2 2

| Jan. 3 | (299) | Adams, *Lectures on . . . Philosophy* (1) | Jan. 24 |
| Jan. 3 | (300) | Chalmers, *A Sermon in the Tron Church, Glasgow* | Jan. 26 |

---

[1] The MS. reads: "Schlegels Drama 29.35." The word "Drama" suggests August Schlegel's *A Course of Lectures on Dramatic Art and Literature*, but that work has the call number "48.6." The number "29.35" is assigned to Friedrich Schlegel's *Lectures on the History of Literature*.

[2] The MS. reads: "Schlegel on Literature." No call number is given. Again the reference may apply equally well to either of the works cited in the preceding footnote.

[3] Renewed November 24 and again on December 15 for an additional five weeks' period.

Jan. 24	(301)	*Edinburgh Review* (18)	Feb. 14
Jan. 24	(302)	Enfield, [? *Hist. of Philos.* or ? *Institutes*]	Feb. 14
Jan. 26	(303)	Warburton, *Works* (Hurd) (9)	Feb. 28
Feb. 16	(304)	Mitford, *History of Greece* (1,2,3)	Apr. 6
Feb. 28	(305)	More, *Utopia* (Dibdin) (1,2)	Mar. 14
Feb. 28	(306)	Simonde, *Histoire des Républiques Italiennes* (4)	Mar. 14
Mar. 2	(307)	Paley, *Natural Theology*	Mar. 9
Mar. 9	(308)	Robertson, *The History of Scotland*	Mar. 21
Mar. 14	(309)	Simonde, *Histoire des Républiques Italiennes* (5,6,7)	May 16
Mar. 14	(310)	Staël-Holstein, *Corinne ou l'Italie* (1)	May 16
Mar. 21	(311)	Staël-Holstein, *De l'Allemagne* (1,2)	May 23
Apr. 6	(312)	Byron, *Childe Harold's Pilgrimage*	Apr. 13
Apr. 13	(313)	Scott, *Waverley; or 'Tis Sixty Years Since* (2)	Apr. 18
Apr. 18	(314)	Dallas, *Percival, or Nature Vindicated* (1)	Apr. 18
Apr. 20	(315)	*Edinburgh Review* (25)	May 16
May 16	(316)	Simonde, *Histoire des Républiques Italiennes* (9)	June 8
May 16	(317)	Petrarca, *Petrarch's View of Human Life*	May 25
May 23	(318)	Priestley, *Lectures on History and Gen'l Policy* (2)	June 8
June 20	(319)	Simonde, *Histoire des Républiques Italiennes* (10,11)	July 20
June 20	(320)	Priestley, *Lectures on History and Gen'l Policy* (2)	June 27
June 20	(321)	Mitford, *History of Greece* (4,5,6,7)	Aug. 8
June 27	(322)	Simonde, *De la Littérature du Midi de l'Europe* (3,4)	[?]
July 6	(323)	Priestley, *Lectures on History and Gen'l Policy* (2)	July 18
July 18	(324)	Bossuet, *Histoire Universelle* (1)	Aug. 8
July 20	(325)	Simonde, *Histoire des Républiques Italiennes* (12,13)	Aug. 8
Aug. 8	(326)	Simonde, *Histoire des Républiques Italiennes* (14)	Aug. 31
Aug. 8	(327)	Bossuet, *Oraisons Funèbres*	Aug. 8
Aug. 8	(328)	*Arabian Nights' Entertainments* (2,4)	Aug. 22
Aug. 8	(329)	Bossuet, *Histoire Universelle* (2)	Aug. 15
Aug. 15	(330)	Campbell, *The Philosophy of Rhetoric* (1)	Aug. 31
Aug. 22	(331)	[*Poets of Great Britain*] (1)	Oct. 5
Aug. 31	(332)	Percy, *Reliques of Ancient English Poetry* (1)	Sept. 19
Aug. 31	(333)	*Arabian Nights' Entertainments* (2,3)	Sept. 19
Sept. 19	(334)	[*Poets of Great Britain*] (3)	Sept. 26
Sept. 26	(335)	Brown, *Lectures . . . Philosophy of Human Mind* (1)	Oct. 10
Sept. 26	(336)	Alfieri, *Tragedies* (tr. Charles Lloyd) (1)	Oct. 10
Sept. 28	(337)	Stewart, *Gen'l View of Progress of Philosophy* (2)	Nov. 21
Oct. 5	(338)	Mitford, *History of Greece* (8)	Oct. 24
Oct. 19	(339)	Staël-Holstein, *Corinne ou l'Italie* (1)	Nov. 7
Oct. 24	(340)	Richardson, *Clarissa* (7)	Oct. 26
Oct. 26	(341)	Hope, *Anastasius, or Memoirs of a Greek* (2)	Nov. 2
Nov. 2	(342)	Gillies, *History of Ancient Greece* (4)	Nov. 7
Nov. 7	(343)	Gibbon, *Miscellaneous Works* (Sheffield) (2,3,4,5)	Nov. 23
Nov. 21	(344)	Richardson, *History of Sir Charles Grandison* (3)	Nov. 23
Nov. 23	(345)	Gibbon, *Miscellaneous Works* (Sheffield) (1)	Nov. 23
Nov. 23	(346)	Staël-Holstein, *Corinne ou l'Italie* (2,3)	Dec. 12
Nov. 30	(347)	Turner, *History of the Anglo-Saxons* (1,2,3,4)	Dec. 12

| Dec. 12 | (348) | *Edinburgh Review* (23,24) | Dec. 26 |
| Dec. 26 | (349) | Brown, *Lectures . . . Philosophy of Human Mind* (3) | Jan. 16 |

1 8 2 3

Jan. 4	(350)	Mitford, *History of Greece* (8,9)	Jan. 16
Jan. 9	(351)	Simond, *Switzerland; or A Journal of a Tour* (2)	Jan. 16
Jan. 16	(352)	Staël-Holstein, *Considérations sur la Révolution* (1,2)	Mar. 22
Jan. 16	(353)	Rousseau, *Œuvres* (13,14)	Mar. 22
Jan. 30	(354)	Grimm, *Correspondance Littéraire etc.* (5,8)	Mar. 22
Feb. 1	(355)	Campbell, *The Philosophy of Rhetoric* (1)	Feb. 13
Feb. 13	(356)	Staal, *Mémoires de Madame de Staal* (1,2)	Feb. 22
Feb. 22	(357)	Campbell, *The Philosophy of Rhetoric* (1)	Mar. 13
Feb. 27	(358)	Stewart, *Gen'l View of Progress of Philosophy* (1)	Mar. 13
Mar. 13	(359)	Campbell, *The Philosophy of Rhetoric* (2)	Apr. 2
Mar. 13	(360)	Mitford, *History of Greece* (10)	May 1
Mar. 22	(361)	O'Meara, *Napoleon in Exile* (2)	Mar. 29
Mar. 29	(362)	Erskine, *Speeches when at the Bar* (1)	Apr. 12
May ?1	(363)	Mitford, *History of Greece* (10)	June 7
May ?1	(364)	Staël-Holstein, *De l'Allemagne* (1,2)	June 7
May 3	(365)	*Edinburgh Review* (18)	June 7
July 12	(366)	Alison, *The Nature and Principles of Taste*	Aug. 2
July 12	(367)	Scott, *Tales of My Landlord* (III.1)	Aug. 2
July 26	(368)	Edgeworth, *The Modern Griselda*	July 31
July 31	(369)	Voltaire, *Théâtre* (1 or 6)	July 31
July 31	(370)	Hogg, *The Brownie of Bodsbeck etc.*	Aug. 2
Aug. 2	(371)	Gisborne, *Enquiry into Duties of Female Sex*	Aug. 9
Aug. 2	(372)	Mass. Hist. Soc., *Collections* (II.5)	Aug. 23
Aug. 2	(373)	Gibbon, *Miscellaneous Works* (Sheffield) (5)	Aug. 14
Aug. 9	(374)	Hume, *The History of England* (1,2,5,?8)	Nov. 29
Aug. 14	(375)	Milton, *The Prose Works* (Symmons) (1)	Nov. 29
Sept. 6	(376)	Staël-Holstein, *Lettres sur les Ouvrages de Rousseau*	Sept. 20
Nov. 1	(377)	*Edinburgh Review* (7)	Dec. 20
Nov. 27	(378)	Hume, *The History of England* (2)	Jan. 10
Dec. 20	(379)	Ellis, *Journal of the Late Embassy to China*	Feb. 26
Dec. 20	(380)	*Edinburgh Review* (24,29,30)	Feb. 21

1 8 2 4

Jan. ?10	(381)	Hume, *The History of England* (5,6,8)	[?]
Feb. 21	(382)	Franklin, *Complete Works in Philosophy etc.* (1,3)	May 22
Feb. 21	(383)	*Edinburgh Review* (22)	Apr. 10
Feb. 28	(384)	"Schlegel on Literature" (Cf. #263 and #269)	Apr. 10
Apr. 10	(385)	Burns, *The Works of Robert Burns* (1)	Apr. 10
Apr. 10	(386)	Montesquieu, *Œuvres Complettes* (1)	May 8
May 8	(387)	Brown, *Lectures . . . Philosophy of Human Mind* (3)	May 29
May 15	(388)	Hutchinson, *Hist. of Colony of Massachuset's Bay*	May 29
May 22	(389)	Franklin, *Complete Works in Philosophy etc.* (1,3)	May 29
June 26	(390)	Smith, *The Works of Adam Smith* (Stewart) (1,5)	Aug. 7
June 26	(391)	Bacon, *Works* (1)	Aug. 7

July 24	(392)	Dwight, *Travels in New England and New York* (2)	Aug. 7
July 31	(393)	Bradford, *History of Massachusetts* (1764-1775)	Aug. 14
Aug. 2	(394)	Milton, *The Prose Works* (Symmons) (1)	Oct. 2
Aug. 7	(395)	Smith, *The Works of Adam Smith* (Stewart) (1,5)	Oct. 2
Aug. 11	(396)	Hallam, *View of Europe during Middle Ages* (2)	Oct. 16
Sept. 11	(397)	Hume, *Philosophical Essays* (2)	Dec. 30
Oct. 2	(398)	Knox, [*Elegant Epistles?*]*	Oct. 23
Oct. 2	(399)	Plato, *The Republic* (Spens)	Oct. 23
Oct. 16	(400)	Fontenelle, *Conversations on Plurality of Worlds*	Nov. 20
Oct. 23	(401)	Hume, *The History of England* (2,3)	Nov. 20
Oct. 23	(402)	Drake, *Literary Hours, or Sketches etc.* (3)	Nov. 6
Nov. 6	(403)	Wilson, *The City of the Plague*	Nov. 20
Nov. 20	(404)	*The Quarterly Review* (21)	Nov. 20
Nov. 20	(405)	Bonnycastle, *Spanish America*	Jan. 15
Dec. 30	(406)	Hume, *Philosophical Essays* (2)	Feb. 3

1 8 2 5

Jan. 15	(407)	Mitford, *History of Greece* (1,2)	Feb. 3
Jan. 15	(408)	Mitford, *History of Greece* (3,4)	Jan. 29
Jan. 29	(409)	Galt, *Life and Administration of Card. Wolsey* (1)	Feb. 3
Feb. 3	(410)	Guicciardini, *History of Italy (1490-1532)* (1)	Feb. 24
Feb. 3	(411)	Fontenelle, *Conversations on Plurality of Worlds*	Feb. 5
Feb. 5	(412)	Ferguson, *Hist. of Progress &c. of Roman Republic* (1)	Feb. 24
Feb. 24	(413)	Hume, *The History of England* (4,5,6,7)	May 21
Mar. 19	(414)	Guicciardini, *History of Italy (1490-1532)* (3)	May 21
Apr. 16	(415)	Sully, *Mémoires de Sully* (2)	May 21
June 16	(416)	Hume, *The History of England* (7,8)	July 23
June 16	(417)	Sully, *Mémoires de Sully* (2)	July 23
July 14	(418)	Bacon, *Works* (4)	Aug. 1
July 23	(419)	Hume, *The History of England* (7,8)	Sept. 3
July 23	(420)	Sully, *Mémoires de Sully* (2)	Oct. 22
Aug. 18	(421)	Landor, *Imaginary Conversations* (I.1)	Oct. 22
Oct. 22	(422)	Euripides, *Tragedies* (tr. Potter) (1)	Dec. 10
Nov. 12	(423)	Warton, *The History of English Poetry* (1)	Dec. 10
Nov. 26	(424)	*Quarterly Review* (21)	Dec. 22
Nov. 26	(425)	Plato, *Works of Plato Abridg'd* (M. Dacier) (2)	Mar. 4
Dec. 10	(426)	Tacitus, *Works of Cornelius Tacitus* (2)	June 3
Dec. 22	(427)	Mitford, *History of Greece* (1)	[?]
Dec. 22	(428)	Simond, *Switzerland; or A Journal of a Tour* (1)	[?]
Dec. 29	(429)	Plutarchus, *Plutarch's Morals* (3)	Mar. 4

1 8 2 6

Jan. 12	(430)	Sedgwick, *Redwood, a Tale* (1,2)	Jan. 19
Jan. 19	(431)	Johnson, *Rasselas, Prince of Abyssinia*	Jan. 21
Jan. 21	(432)	Hume, *The History of England* (3,4,5)	[?]

---

* The MS. reads: "Elegant Extracts 7.23." The call number is that of *Elegant Epistles. Elegant Extracts* (Prose) and *Elegant Extracts* (Poetry) bear respectively the numbers 7.21 and 7.22.

Mar. 4	(433)	Fox, *Speeches in the House of Commons* (1)	June 1
Apr. 1	(434)	Staël-Holstein, *Considerations on Fr. Revolution* (1)	June 1
Nov. 24	(435)	Piron, *Œuvres Choisies d'Alexis Piron* (2)	[?]
Nov. 24	(436)	Disraeli, *Curiosities of Literature* (? ser.,1)	Apr. 3

1 8 2 8

Jan. 24	(437)	Marsh, *Politicks of Gt. Brit. and France* (1,2)	Feb. 2
Feb. 2	(438)	Woolrych, *Life of Sir Edward Coke*	May 1
Feb. 2	(439)	Eugène, *Mémoires du Prince Eugène de Savoie*	[?]
Feb. 2	(440)	Euler, *Lettres . . . sur Divers Sujets* (1)	[?]
Feb. 2	(441)	Genlis, *Jeanne de France* (1)	[?]
Feb. 2	(442)	Meissner, *Charles et Hélène de Moldorf*	[?]
Feb. 2	(443)	Staal, *Mémoires de Madame de Staal* (1,2)	[?]
Apr. 3	(444)	Goethe, *Memoirs of Goëthe*	May 15
May 15	(445)	Rousseau, *Œuvres* (13,14)	June 14
May 15	(446)	"Napoleon" [Not identified.] (1)	June 14
May 15	(447)	Cervantes, *Don Quichotte de la Manche* (Florian) (1,2)	June 14
Sept. 13	(448)	Edgeworth, *Leonora*	[?]
Sept. 13	(449)	Malthus, [*Political Economy?* or *Population?*]	Dec. 4
Sept. 13	(450)	Plutarchus, *Plutarch's Morals* (2,3)	Dec. 4
Dec. 4	(451)	Plutarchus, *Plutarch's Morals* (4)	Dec. 27
Dec. 4	(452)	Edgeworth, *The Modern Griselda*	Dec. 27
Dec. 27	(453)	Plutarchus, *Plutarch's Morals* (?3,4)	Jan. 22
Dec. 27	(454)	Winthrop, [*On Comets?* or *Settlement of Mass.?*]	Jan. 22

1 8 2 9

Jan. 22	(455)	Plutarchus, *Plutarch's Morals* (4,5)	Feb. 12
Jan. 22	(456)	Rush, [*Essays?* or *Medical Inquiries?*]	Feb. 12
Feb. 12	(457)	Plutarchus, *Plutarch's Morals* (4)	Feb. 26
Feb. 12	(458)	Richardson, *Clarissa* (7)	Feb. 26
Feb. 26	(459)	Cox, *Narratives of Lives of the Fathers*	Mar. 12
Feb. 26	(460)	Temple, *Works* (1)	Mar. 12
Feb. 26	(461)	Tooke, Επεα πτεροεντα, *or, The Diversions* (1)	Mar. 7
Mar. 7	(462)	Swift, *Gulliver's Travels*	Mar. 26
Mar. 12	(463)	Lamb, *Elia: Essays from London Magazine*	Mar. 26
Mar. 12	(464)	Porter, *The Scottish Chiefs: a Romance*	Apr. 14
Mar. 26	(465)	Lucretius, *Nature of Things* (ed. Good? Creech?)	Apr. 14
Apr. 14	(466)	Beaumont and Fletcher, *Dramatick Works* (1)	Apr. 16
Apr. 14	(467)	Porter, *The Scottish Chiefs: a Romance*	Apr. 18
Apr. 16	(468)	Richardson, *History of Sir Charles Grandison* (3)	Apr. 25
Apr. 16	(469)	*Xenophon's Memoirs of Socrates* (tr. Fielding)	May 14
Apr. 18	(470)	Massinger, *Plays of Philip Massinger* (1)	Apr. 21
Apr. 21	(471)	Richardson, *History of Sir Charles Grandison* (4)	Apr. 25
Apr. 25	(472)	Richardson, *History of Sir Charles Grandison* (5)	Apr. 30
Apr. 25	(473)	Richardson, *History of Sir Charles Grandison* (6)	May 16
Apr. 30	(474)	Epictetus, *All the Works now Extant* (Carter)	May 21
May 14	(475)	*Xenophon's Memoirs of Socrates* (tr. Fielding)	May 21
May 16	(476)	Richardson, *History of Sir Charles Grandison* (7)	May 23

May 23	(477)	Darwin, *Zoonomia, or Laws of Organic Life* (1,2)	May 30
July 23	(478)	*Aristotle's Ethics and Politics* (Gillies) (1)	Oct. 24
Aug. 22	(479)	*Aristotle's Ethics and Politics* (Gillies) (2)	Oct. 24
Oct. 10	(480)	Berkeley, [*Of Human Knowledge?* or *Querist?*]	Oct. 24
Oct. 24	(481)	Collinson, *Life of Thuanus, with Acc't of Writings*	Nov. 28
Oct. 24	(482)	Plutarchus, *Plutarch's Morals* (4)	Jan. 21
Oct. 24	(483)	Plutarchus, *Plutarch's Morals* (5)	Dec. 19
Dec. 5	(484)	Schiller, *History of Thirty Years' War* (1)	Dec. 12
Dec. 12	(485)	Schiller, *History of Thirty Years' War* (2)	Dec. 19
Dec. 19	(486)	Goethe, *Memoirs of Goëthe*	Jan. 26
Dec. 19	(487)	Southey, *Thalaba the Destroyer* (1?)	Jan. 2
Dec. 28	(488)	Plutarchus, *Plutarch's Morals* (4)	Feb. 16

1 8 3 0

Jan. 2	(489)	Southey, *Thalaba the Destroyer* [2?]	Jan. 2
Jan. 26	(490)	Dante Alighieri, *A Translation of the Inferno* (1)	Feb. 27
Feb. 18	(491)	Simonde, [? *Historical View of Lit. of Europe*] (2)	Apr. 15
Feb. 18	(492)	Plato, *Works of Plato Abridg'd* (M. Dacier) (1)	[Mar.] 2
Feb. 27	(493)	Simonde, [? *Historical View of Lit. of Europe*] (1)	Apr. 15
Feb. 27	(494)	Dante Alighieri, *A Translation of the Inferno* (1)	Apr. 1
Dec. 21	(495)	Marshall, *The Life of George Washington* (1,5)	Jan. 4
Dec. 21	(496)	Humboldt, *Personal Narrative of Travels* (3)	Jan. 4

1 8 3 1

Jan. 4	(497)	Humboldt, *Personal Narrative of Travels* (1)	Jan. 29
Jan. 29	(498)	Humboldt, *Personal Narrative of Travels* (2)	Feb. 26
Jan. 29	(499)	[? Humboldt, *Political Essay on Kingdom of*] *New Spain*	Feb. 5
Feb. 5	(500)	Cuvier, *Essay on the Theory of the Earth*	Mar. 5
Feb. 5	(501)	Bunyan, *The Pilgrim's Progress*	Feb. 22
Feb. 26	(502)	Erskine, *Speeches when at the Bar* (1)	Mar. 15
Mar. 15	(503)	Plato, *Works of Plato Abridg'd* (M. Dacier) (1)	Mar. 15
Mar. 15	(504)	Hutchinson, *Memoirs of Life of Col. Hutchinson* (2)	Mar. 15
Mar. 15	(505)	Gibbon, *Decline and Fall of Roman Empire* (1807) (1)	Mar. 17
Mar. 15	(506)	Gibbon, *Decline and Fall of Roman Empire* (1807) (2)	Mar. 26
Mar. 15	(507)	Plato, *Works of Plato Abridg'd* (M. Dacier) (2)	Mar. 31
Mar. 15	(508)	Irving, *Life and Voyages of Christopher Columbus* (2)	Apr. 16
Mar. 26	(509)	*Aristotle's Ethics and Politics* (Gillies) (1,2)	Apr. 16
Mar. 31	(510)	Mitford, *History of Greece* (1)	Apr. 16
Apr. 16	(511)	Irving, *Life and Voyages of Christopher Columbus* (2)	May 5
Apr. 16	(512)	Mitford, *History of Greece* (1)	Apr. 19
Apr. 16	(513)	Pascal, *Les Provinciales, ou Lettres* (1?)	May 5
Apr. 16	(514)	Poynder, *A History of the Jesuits* (1)	May 5
May 7	(515)	Grahame, *The Sabbath: a Poem . . . Sabbath Walks*	May 17
May 17	(516)	Barthélemy, *Travels of Anacharsis the Younger* (1)	May 28
May 28	(517)	Barthélemy, *Travels of Anacharsis the Younger* (2)	May 28

1 8 3 2

Mar. 29	(518)	"Life 14.2" (1)[1]	Apr. 28

---

[1] The call number "14.2" is that of *Aristotle's Ethics and Politics* (ed. Gillies). It is highly probable that "14.4" was intended: Teignmouth's *Life of Sir William Jones.*

May 26	(519)	Sheridan, *Lectures on the Art of Reading*	May 31
May 26	(520)	Haüy, *Elementary Treatise on Natural Philosophy* (1)	May 31
May 26	(521)	Klopstock, *The Messiah* (tr. Collyer)	May 31
Aug. 7	(522)	*Aristotle's Ethics and Politics* (Gillies) (1,2)	Aug. 11
Aug. 7	(523)	Scott, *Tales of My Landlord* (? ser.,2)	Aug. 11
Aug. 11	(524)	Butler, *Reminiscences*	Aug. 21
Aug. 11	(525)	*Family Library* (21)	Aug. 21
Aug. 21	(526)	Goethe, *Wilhelm Meister's Apprenticeship* (3)	Aug. 23
Aug. 23[2]	(527)	Walpole, *Private Correspondence* (3,4)	Aug. 25
Aug. 25	(528)	Sparks, *The Life of Gouverneur Morris* (1)	Aug. 28
Aug. 25	(529)	Grimm, *Mémoires Historiques, Littéraires etc.* (1)	Aug. 28
Aug. 28	(530)	Regnard, *Œuvres Complettes de Regnard* (5)	Sept. 4
Aug. 28	(531)	Williams, *Life &c. of Sir Thomas Lawrence, kt.* (1)	Sept. 4
Sept. 4	(532)	Walpole, *Reminiscences Written in 1788*	Sept. 6
Sept. 4	(533)	Richardson, *History of Sir Charles Grandison* (1,2)	Sept. 6
Sept. 6	(534)	Richardson, *History of Sir Charles Grandison* (3,4,5)	Sept. 8
Sept. 8	(535)	Richardson, *History of Sir Charles Grandison* (6,7)	Sept. 13
Sept. 8	(536)	Smollett, *Miscellaneous Works, with Memoirs* (1)	Sept. 13
Sept. 13	(537)	Petronius Arbiter, *Works in Prose and Verse*	Sept. 15
Sept. 13	(538)	Clarendon, *History of the Rebellion etc.* (1)	Sept. 15
Sept. 13	(539)	Roscoe, *The Italian Novelists* (1)	Sept. 13
Sept. 15	(540)	Clarendon, *History of the Rebellion etc.* (2)	Sept. 27
Sept. 15	(541)	Clarendon, *History of the Rebellion etc.* (3)	Sept. 18
Sept. 18	(542)	Clarendon, *History of the Rebellion etc.* (4,?5)	Sept. 27
Sept. 27	(543)	Dryden, *Works* (Scott) (2,3)	Sept. 29
Sept. 27	(544)	Clarendon, *History of the Rebellion etc.* (6)	Sept. 29
Sept. 29	(545)	Dryden, *Works* (Scott) (6)	Oct. 2
Sept. 29	(546)	*Library of Old English Prose Writers* (vol.?)*	Oct. 2
Sept. 29	(547)	Audubon, *Ornithological Biography* (vol.?)	Oct. 2
Oct. 2	(548)	Beaumont and Fletcher, *Dramatick Works* (3)	Oct. 23
Oct. 2	(549)	Clarkson, *A Portraiture of Quakerism* (1,2)	Oct. 23
Oct. 23	(550)	Spurzheim, *Outlines of Phrenology*	Oct. 25
Oct. 23	(551)	Martineau, *Five Years of Youth*	Oct. 25
Oct. 23	(552)	Warren, *Affecting Scenes from Diary of Physician*	Oct. 25

1 8 3 8

June 9	(553)	Gardiner, *The Music of Nature*	June 23
June 16	(554)	Hall, *Uncle Horace, A Novel* (1,2)	June 23
June 26	(555)	Boyle, *The State Prisoner: Tale of French Regency*	July 3
June 30	(556)	James, *One in a Thousand: Days of Henri Quatre* (1,2)	July 10
July 10	(557)	Humphrey, *Great Britain, France and Belgium* (1)	July 21

---

[2] "G. Bradford" is added to Mrs. Emerson's name at the head of the section covering August 23 through October, 1832. I assume that he was an accommodation bearer of books during R. W. E's or his mother's illness. He may have had full use of the share between 1833 and 1838, when Ruth Emerson's records reappear, but one cannot be certain. One charging list appears to be missing.

* See bibliography. The book withdrawn from this series could not have borne an imprint later than 1832.

July 10	(558)	Adams, *Dermot MacMorrogh . . . Historical Tale*	July 21
July 10	(559)	*Museum of Foreign Literature, Science & Art* (28)	Aug. 11
July 21	(560)	Brunton, *Self-Control: a Novel* (1,2)	Aug. 11
Sept. 6	(561)	Stephens, *Incidents of Travel in Egypt etc.* (1)	Sept. 22
Sept. 8	(562)	Beaconsfield, *Vivian Gray, a Novel* (1,2)	Sept. 22
Sept. 22	(563)	Abrantès, *Memoirs of Celebrated Women* (1)	Sept. 27
Sept. 22	(564)	Burney, *Geraldine Fauconberg, a Novel* (1)	Sept. 27
Sept. 22	(565)	Burney, *Geraldine Fauconberg, a Novel* (2)	Oct. 4
Sept. 27	(566)	Neal, *Keep Cool, a Novel* (1,2)	Oct. 4
Oct. 4	(567)	*Aunt Pontipool, a Novel* (1)	Oct. 9
Oct. 4	(568)	*Aunt Pontipool, a Novel* (2)	Nov. 10
Oct. 4	(569)	*Museum of Foreign Lit., Science & Art* (May,[1838])	Oct. 9
Oct. 9	(570)	Bury, *Love* (1,2)	Oct. 13
Oct. 13	(571)	Blessington, *Confessions of an Elderly Lady &c.* (1,2)	Oct. 16
Oct. 27	(572)	Rowson, *Trials of the Human Heart: a Novel* (1,2)	Nov. 10
Nov. 10	(573)	Caulaincourt, *Napoleon and His Times* (1)	Nov. 13
Nov. 10	(574)	Brooks, *Zóphiël, or The Bride of Seven*	Nov. 24
Nov. 10	(575)	*Museum of Foreign Lit., Science & Art* (Aug.,[1838])	Nov. 13
Nov. 13	(576)	Lytton, *Alice, or The Mysteries* (1)	Nov. 24
Nov. 13	(577)	Lytton, *Alice, or The Mysteries* (2)	Nov. 27
Nov. 27	(578)	Herbert, *The Brothers: A Tale of the Fronde* (1,2)	Dec. 4
Dec. 6	(579)	Hutton, *The Miser Married: A Novel* (1,2)	Dec. 13
Dec. 6	(580)	Byron, *Works* (1)	Jan. 5
Dec. 13	(581)	Lytton, *Ernest Maltravers* (1,2)	Jan. 5

1 8 3 9

Jan. 12	(582)	Staël-Holstein, *Considerations on Fr. Revolution* (1)	Feb. 23
Jan. 19	(583)	Lockhart, *Memoirs of Life of Sir Walter Scott* (2)	Feb. 7
Feb. 7	(584)	Porter, *Fast of St. Magdalen, a Romance* (1,2)	Feb. 12
Feb. 12	(585)	Dickens, *Oliver Twist* (1?)	Feb. 19
Feb. 12	(586)	*Blackwood's Edinburgh Magazine* (? May)	Feb. 19
Feb. 19	(587)	Dickens, *Oliver Twist* (1)	Feb. 21
Feb. 19	(588)	*Blackwood's Edinburgh Magazine* (Nov.)	Feb. 23
Feb. 21	(589)	Percy, *Reliques of Ancient English Poetry* (1)	Feb. 23
Feb. 23	(590)	Coleridge, *Poetical Works* (1)	Mar. 2
Feb. 23	(591)	Coleridge, *Poetical Works* (2)	Mar. 26
Feb. 23	(592)	Dickens, *Oliver Twist* (2)	[?]
Mar. 2	(593)	Coleridge, *Poetical Works* (3)	Mar. 21
Mar. 2	(594)	Southey, *Thalaba the Destroyer* (1)	Mar. 26
Mar. 26	(595)	Carlyle, *Sartor Resartus*	Apr. 6
Mar. 26	(596)	Southey, *Thalaba the Destroyer* (2)	May 11
Apr. 6	(597)	Carlyle, *Critical and Miscellaneous Essays* (1)	May 20
Apr. 9	(598)	*Tasso's Jerusalem Delivered* (tr. Hunt) (1)	May 23
Apr. 20	(599)	Lamb, *The Works of Charles Lamb* (1)	May 23
Apr. 23	(600)	Coleridge, *The Friend* (1st Am. ed.)	May 4
Apr. 23	(601)	James, *The Huguenot: Tale of French Protestants* (1)	Apr. 30
Apr. 30	(602)	James, *The Huguenot: Tale of French Protestants* (2)	May 4
May 4	(603)	Howard, *Outward Bound: A Merchant's Adventures* (1)	May 11

May 4	(604)	Sherer, *The Story of a Life*	May 11
May 11	(605)	Gardiner, *The Music of Nature*	June 4
May 11	(606)	Edgeworth, *Helen, a Tale* (1)	May 23
May 25	(607)	Edgeworth, *Helen, a Tale* (2)	June 4
May 25	(608)	Smith, *The Three Eras of Woman's Life*	June 4
Oct. 8	(609)	Percy, *Reliques of Ancient English Poetry* (1)	Nov. 5
Oct. 8	(610)	Ward, *De Vere, or The Man of Independence* (1,2)	Nov. 5

1 8 4 0

Jan. 16	(611)	Lardner, *The Cabinet Cyclopædia* (29)	[Jan.] 25
Jan. 16	(612)	Fay, *Norman Leslie. A Tale of Present Times* (1,2)	Jan. 18
Jan. 18	(613)	Longfellow, *Outre-mer; A Pilgrimage* (1)	Jan. 21
Jan. 18	(614)	Longfellow, *Outre-mer; A Pilgrimage* (2)	Jan. 25
Jan. 21	(615)	Coleridge, *Poetical Works* (3)	Feb. 1
Jan. 25	(616)	Sherwood, *The Works of Mrs. Sherwood* (7,8)	Feb. 1
Feb. 1	(617)	Carlyle, *German Romance: Specimens* (1,3)	Feb. 8
Feb. 1	(618)	Carlyle, *German Romance: Specimens* (4)	Feb. 15
Feb. 8	(619)	Sherwood, *The Works of Mrs. Sherwood* (9)	Feb. 11
Feb. 8	(620)	Coleridge, *Poetical Works* (2)	Feb. 11
Feb. 11	(621)	Smith, *Rejected Addresses*	Feb. 15
Feb. 11	(622)	*Constable's Miscellany of Orig. Publs.* (18)	Feb. 27
Feb. 15	(623)	*[Poets of Great Britain]* (1)	Feb. 27
Feb. 15	(624)	*Herbert's Poems and the Country Parson*	Apr. 28
Feb. 27	(625)	Lardner, *The Cabinet Cyclopædia* (93)	Mar. 21
Mar. 21	(626)	Austin, *Characteristics of Goethe* (1)	Apr. 4
Mar. 26	(627)	Jamieson, *Popular Ballads and Songs* (2)	Apr. 16
Apr. 4	(628)	Landor, *Pericles and Aspasia* (1)	Apr. 21
Apr. 16	(629)	Williams, *Mephistophiles in England* (1)	Apr. 21
Apr. 21	(630)	*Blackwood's Edinburgh Magazine* (44)	Apr. 28
Apr. 21	(631)	Carlyle, *Critical and Miscellaneous Essays* (2)	May 2
Apr. 28	(632)	Jamieson, *Popular Ballads and Songs* (1)	May 5
Apr. 28	(633)	Hall, *Marian, or A Young Maid's Fortunes* (1)	May 5
May 2	(634)	James, *The Gipsy: A Tale* (1)	June 6
May 5	(635)	Hall, *Marian, or A Young Maid's Fortunes* (2)	June 12
May 5	(636)	Marmontel, *Moral Tales*	June 30
May 19	(637)	*Edinburgh Review* (Jan.)	June 28
May 30	(638)	Longfellow, *Hyperion, A Romance* (1,2)	June 6
June 30	(639)	Gardiner, *The Music of Nature*	July 18
June 30	(640)	James, *The Gipsy: A Tale* (2)	July 18
June 30	(641)	Smith, *Tales of the Early Ages* (1)	July 18
July 18	(642)	Normanby, *Matilda: A Tale of the Day*	Sept. 12
July 18	(643)	Simms, *The Damsel of Darien* (1,2)	Aug. 8
Sept. 12	(644)	Bojardo, *The Orlando Innamorato*	Sept. 19
Sept. 12	(645)	Chaucer, *The Riches of Chaucer*	Sept. 19
Sept. 19	(646)	Martineau, *Deerbrook: A Novel* (1,2)	Sept. 22
Sept. 22	(647)	Staël-Holstein, *Delphine* (tr. from French) (1,2)	Oct. 13
Oct. 13	(648)	Austin, *Characteristics of Goethe* (2)	Oct. 22

Oct. 13	(649)	Beaconsfield, *Vivian Gray, a Novel* (1)	Oct. 22
Oct. 13	(650)	Beaconsfield, *Vivian Gray, a Novel* (2)	Oct. 24
Oct. 22	(651)	Beaconsfield, *Vivian Gray, a Novel* (3)	Oct. 24
Oct. 22	(652)	Carlyle, *Critical and Miscellaneous Essays* (1)	Nov. 24
Oct. 24	(653)	Jamieson, *Popular Ballads and Songs* (1)	[Oct.] 31
Oct. 24	(654)	Lytton, *Godolphin, or The Oath* (1)	[Oct.] 31
Oct. 31	(655)	Lytton, *Godolphin, or The Oath* (2)	Nov. 10
Nov. 10	(656)	Goethe, *Memoirs of Goëthe*	Nov. 24
Nov. 10	(657)	Roscoe, *The German Novelists* (2)	Dec. 8
Nov. 24	(658)	Velde, *Tales from the German* (Greene) (1)	Dec. 8
Nov. 24	(659)	Coleridge, *Poetical Works* (2)	Dec. 29
Dec. 8	(660)	Percy, *Reliques of Ancient English Poetry* (1,2)	Dec. 12
Dec. 12	(661)	Macaulay, *Critical and Miscellaneous Essays* (2)	Dec. 29
Dec. 12	(662)	Beyle, *The Life of Haydn . . . Life of Mozart*	Dec. 19
Dec. 19	(663)	Beyle, *The Life of Haydn . . . Life of Mozart*	Dec. 29
Dec. 29	(664)	Coleridge, *Poetical Works* (2)	Jan. 26

1 8 4 1

Jan. 7	(665)	Bulgarin, *Ivan Vejeeghen, or Life in Russia* (1)	Jan. 26
Jan. 7	(666)	Ferrier, *Marriage, A Novel*	Feb. 2
Jan. 26	(667)	Lee, *Life and Times of Thomas Cranmer*	Feb. 2
Feb. 11	(668)	Jesse, *Memoirs of the Court of England* (1,3)	Feb. 18
Feb. 18	(669)	Jesse, *Memoirs of the Court of England* (1)	Feb. 23
Feb. 23	(670)	Jesse, *Memoirs of the Court of England* (2,?3,4)	Mar. 2
Mar. 6	(671)	Maintenon, *Lettres, Précédées de sa Vie* (1)	Mar. 18
Mar. 6	(672)	Gardiner, *The Music of Nature*	Apr. 6
Mar. 18	(673)	Dover, *True History of the State Prisoner*	Apr. 20
Mar. 20	(674)	Bury, *Diary . . . of the Times of George IV* (1,2)	Apr. 27
Mar. 27	(675)	Hogg, *Winter Evening Tales* (2)	Apr. 3
Mar. 27	(676)	Dickens, *Posthumous Papers of Pickwick Club* (4)	Apr. 3
Apr. 3	(677)	James, *Henry of Guise, or The States of Blois* (1)	Apr. 6
Apr. 3	(678)	James, *Henry of Guise, or The States of Blois* (2)	Apr. 10
Apr. 6	(679)	Arnim, *Goethe's Correspondence with a Child* (1)	Apr. 13
Apr. 6	(680)	Fay, *The Countess Ida. A Tale of Berlin* (1)	Apr. 10
Apr. 10	(681)	Lytton, *Night and Morning. A Novel* (2)	Apr. 17
Apr. 10	(682)	Tuckerman, *Isabel, or Sicily. A Pilgrimage*	Apr. 24
Apr. 13	(683)	Fay, *The Countess Ida. A Tale of Berlin* (2)	Apr. 22
Apr. 17	(684)	Wilhelmine, *Mémoires de Frédérique Wilhelmine* (1)	May 13
Apr. 24	(685)	Austen, *Sense and Sensibility* (1)	May 13
May 13	(686)	Le Sage, *Histoire de Gil Blas de Santillane* (1)	June 1
May 13	(687)	Staël-Holstein, *Corinna, or Italy* (1,2)	June 1
July 10	(688)	Ward, *Fielding, or Society; Atticus; etc.* (1,2)	Aug. 7
July 10	(689)	Le Sage, *Histoire de Gil Blas de Santillane* (2)	Aug. 7
Aug. 7	(690)	Cottin, *Mathilde* (1,4)	Sept. 28
Aug. 7	(691)	Le Sage, *Histoire de Gil Blas de Santillane* (3)	Sept. 28
Sept. 30	(692)	Beyle, *The Life of Haydn . . . Life of Mozart*	Oct. 30
Sept. 30	(693)	Scott, *A Visit to Paris in 1814*	Oct. 9
Oct. 9	(694)	Simms, *Pelayo: A Story of the Goth* (1,2)	Oct. 16

Oct. 30	(695)	Norton, *The Wife, and Woman's Reward* (1)	[Nov.] 27
Oct. 30	(696)	Norton, *The Wife, and Woman's Reward* (2)	[Dec.] 4
Nov. 27	(697)	MacCarthy, *The Siege of Florence* (1)	Dec. 4
Nov. 27	(698)	Lever, *The Confessions of Harry Lorrequer*	Dec. 11
Dec. 4	(699)	Longfellow, *Hyperion, A Romance* (1)	Dec. 11
Dec. 4	(700)	Longfellow, *Hyperion, A Romance* (2)	Dec. 14
Dec. 11	(701)	Smith, *The Moneyed Man, or Lesson of a Life* (1)	Dec. 14
Dec. 11	(702)	Austin, *Fragments from German Prose Writers*	Dec. 14
Dec. 22	(703)	Richardson, *Clarissa* (1)	Dec. 25
Dec. 22	(704)	Richardson, *Clarissa* (2)	Dec. 27
Dec. 22	(705)	Jamieson, *Popular Ballads and Songs* (1)	Dec. 27
Dec. 25	(706)	Richardson, *Clarissa* (3)	Feb. 3
Dec. 27	(707)	Richardson, *Clarissa* (4)	Feb. 8
Dec. 27	(708)	Richardson, *Clarissa* (5)	Feb. 3

1 8 4 2

Feb. 3	(709)	Richardson, *Clarissa* (6)	Feb. 8
Feb. 3	(710)	Richardson, *Clarissa* (7)	Feb. 12
Feb. 8	(711)	Shelley, *Frankenstein, or The Modern Prometheus* (1)	Feb. 12
Feb. 8	(712)	Shelley, *Frankenstein, or The Modern Prometheus* (2)	Feb. 22
Feb. 12	(713)	Taylor, *Historic Survey of German Poetry* (1)	Feb. 22
Feb. 12	(714)	Austin, *Fragments from German Prose Writers*	Mar. 3
Feb. 22	(715)	Gore, *Greville, or A Season in Paris* (1,2)	Mar. 1
Mar. 3	(716)	Lester, *The Glory and the Shame of England* (1)	Mar. 10
Mar. 3	(717)	Pichler, *The Siege of Vienna*	Mar. 5
Mar. 5	(718)	La Rochejaquelein, *Mémoires. Ecrits par Elle-même*	Apr. 5
Mar. 17	(719)	Dickens *et al.*, *The Pic Nic Papers* (1,2)	Mar. 24
Mar. 24	(720)	Trollope, *Life . . . of Michael Armstrong* (1,2)	Mar. 29
Mar. 29	(721)	Hawthorne, *Twice-told Tales* (1)	Apr. 2
Mar. 29	(722)	Staël-Holstein, *Delphine* (tr. from French) (1)	Apr. 2
Apr. 2	(723)	Hazlitt, *Lectures on the English Comic Writers*	Apr. 19
Apr. 2	(724)	Hugo, *The Hunchback of Notre-Dame* (1)	Apr. 5
Apr. 5	(725)	Molière, *Œuvres* (4)	Apr. 16
Apr. 5	(726)	James, *Corse de Leon, or The Brigand* (1)	Apr. 12
Apr. 16	(727)	Cuthbertson, *Santo Sebastiano. A Novel* (1)	Apr. 19
Apr. 16	(728)	Cuthbertson, *Santo Sebastiano. A Novel* (2)	May 24
Apr. 19	(729)	Cuthbertson, *Santo Sebastiano. A Novel* (3)	May 24
May 7	(730)	Martineau, *Essential Faith of the Universal Church*	June 4
Sept. 20	(731)	Gallenga, *Italy: General Views* (1)	Oct. 13
Sept. 20	(732)	Gallenga, *Italy: General Views* (2)	Nov. 12
Oct. 13	(733)	Arblay, *Diary and Letters* (1)	Oct. 18
Oct. 18	(734)	Arblay, *The Wanderer, or Female Difficulties* (1,2)	Oct. 22
Oct. 22	(735)	Arblay, *The Wanderer, or Female Difficulties* (3)	Nov. 12
Nov. 12	(736)	Gallenga, *Italy: General Views* (2)	Dec. 7
Dec. 20	(737)	Lee, *Life of Jean Paul Frederic Richter* (1)	Dec. 27
Dec. 20	(738)	Lee, *Life of Jean Paul Frederic Richter* (2)	Dec. 20

1 8 4 3

Jan. 3	(739)	Gore, *Preferment, or My Uncle the Earl* (1,2)	Jan. 7

Jan. 3	(740)	Pickering, *The Prince and the Pedler* (1)	Jan. 10
Jan. 9	(741)	Hugo, *The Hunchback of Notre-Dame* (1,2)	Jan. 10
Jan. 10	(742)	Smith, *The Forsaken, A Novel* (1,2)	Jan. 17
Jan. 10	(743)	Pickering, *The Prince and the Pedler* (2)	Jan. 17
Jan. 17	(744)	Burney, *Clarentine, A Novel* (1,2)	Jan. 19
Jan. 17	(745)	Banim, *The Denounced. A Novel*	Jan. 28
Jan. 19	(746)	Burney, *The Country Neighbors, or The Secret* (1,2)	Jan. 28
Jan. 28	(747)	*Specimens of Foreign Standard Literature* (14)	Feb. 14
Jan. 28	(748)	Bury, *The Exclusives* (1,2)	Feb. 2
Feb. 2	(749)	*Aunt Pontipool, a Novel* (1,2)	Feb. 14
Feb. 14	(750)	Taylor, *Historic Survey of German Poetry* (2)	Feb. 28
Feb. 14	(751)	Voltaire, *Théâtre* (2)	Mar. 11
Feb. 14	(752)	Southey, *Chapters on Churchyards*	Feb. 28
Feb. 28	(753)	Taylor, *Historic Survey of German Poetry* (3)	Mar. 11
Mar. 11	(754)	Gardiner, *The Music of Nature*	Apr. 20
Mar. 11	(755)	*Madame de Sévigné and her Contemporaries* (1)	Mar. 21
Mar. 21	(756)	*Constable's Miscellany of Orig. Publs.* (52)	Mar. 25
Mar. 25	(757)	Lytton, *Eugene Aram. A Tale* (1,2)	Apr. 1
Apr. 1	(758)	Edgeworth, *Belinda* (1,2)	May 16
Apr. 22	(759)	Cervantes, *History and Adventures of Don Quixote* (1)	May 16

1 8 4 5

Mar. 11	(760)	Kendall, *Narrative of an Expedition from Texas* (1)	Mar. 18
Mar. 11	(761)	Jamieson, *Popular Ballads and Songs* (1)	Mar. 27
Mar. 18	(762)	Kendall, *Narrative of an Expedition from Texas* (2)	Mar. 25
Mar. 25	(763)	Kendall, *Narrative of an Expedition from Texas* (2)	Mar. 27
Mar. 27	(764)	Arblay, *Diary and Letters* (1)	Apr. 24
Mar. 27	(765)	Townshend, *Facts in Mesmerism*	Apr. 5
Apr. 5	(766)	Austen, *Pride and Prejudice* (1,2)	Apr. 24
Apr. 5	(767)	Moore, *Travels of an Irish Gentleman etc.*	May 3
May 10	(768)	Hazlitt, *Lectures on the English Poets*	June 14
May 10	(769)	*Family Dramatist* (3)	June 14

BIBLIOGRAPHY OF THE BORROWINGS OF
EMERSON AND HIS MOTHER*

A

ABRANTES, Laura Saint-Martin (Permon) Junot, *duchesse* d': *Memoirs of celebrated women of all countries*, (2v.) Philadelphia, 1835. [563]

---

* The numbers in brackets, following the date of publication, refer to the items in the foregoing annual lists. An asterisk (*) before one or two different editions of a work indicates the copy probably withdrawn. "B.L.S." after a work in this bibliography means that the information here given comes only from the printed catalogues of the Boston Library Society and that I have been unable to confirm the title or the place and date of publication elsewhere. A dash after an author's name indicates a shortening of the fuller form in the work immediately preceding.

ADAMS, George: *Lectures on natural and experimental philosophy . . . describing . . . the principal phenomena of nature*, (5v.) London, 1794.   [69, 72, 200? 293, 297, 298, 299]

ADAMS, John Quincy (1767-1848): *Dermot MacMorrogh, or, The conquest of Ireland. An historical tale of the 12th century*, (2d ed.) Boston, 1832.   [558]

ADAMS, John Quincy———: *Lectures on rhetoric and oratory*, (2v.) Cambridge (Mass.), 1810.   [200?]

AIKIN, John: *General biography, or Lives critical and historical of the most eminent persons of all ages*, (10v.) London, 1799-1815.   [258]

AITCHISON, Alexander: *Encyclopædia Perthensis, or Universal dictionary of knowledge*, (23v.) Perth, [1807].   [56]

ALFIERI, Vittorio, *count: Tragedies*. Tr. from Italian by Charles Lloyd, (3v.) London, 1815.   [336]

ALISON, Archibald (1757-1839): *Essays on the nature and principles of taste*, Dublin, 1790.   [366]

ALISON, Archibald———: *Sermons, chiefly on particular occasions*, Boston, 1815.   [47]

ALLSTON, Washington: *The sylphs of the seasons, with other poems*, Boston, 1813.   [140]

AMERICAN JOURNAL OF SCIENCE, The, (1st ser., v. 1-50) [N.Y. and] New Haven, 1819-1845.   [71, 74, 178]

APOLLONIUS *Rhodius: The Argonautics of Apollonius Rhodius*, tr. William Preston, (3v.) Dublin, 1803.   [131]

ARABIAN NIGHTS' ENTERTAINMENTS, The, (4v.) Philadelphia, 1812.   [18, 24, 96, 100, 105, 130, 134, 241, 328, 333]

ARBLAY, *Mme.* Frances (Burney) d': *Diary and letters of Madame d'Arblay*, ed. by her niece, (2v.) Philadelphia, 1842.   [733, 764]

ARBLAY, *Mme.*———: *The Wanderer, or Female difficulties*, (3v.) N.Y., 1818.   [734, 735]

ARISTOTELES: *Aristotle's Ethics and Politics, comprising his practical philosophy*, tr. with notes by John Gilles, (2v.) London, 1804.   [126, 265, 478, 479, 509, 518? 522]

ARNIM, Bettina (Brentano) von: *Goethe's correspondence with a child*, (1st Am. ed., 2v.) Lowell, 1841.   [679]

AUDUBON, John James: *Ornithological biography, or An account of the habits of the birds of the United States*, (5v.) Philadelphia etc., 1831-1839.   [547]

AUNT PONTIPOOL, A Novel, (2v.) Philadelphia, 1836.   [567, 568, 749]

AUSTEN, Jane: *Pride and Prejudice: a novel*, (2v.) Phila., 1832.   [766]

AUSTEN, Jane: *Sense and Sensibility: a novel*, (3v.) London, 1811.   [685]

AUSTIN, Sarah (Taylor): *Characteristics of Goethe: from the German of Falk, von Müller, etc.*, (3v.) London, 1833.   [626, 648]

AUSTIN, Sarah (Taylor), *translator: Fragments from German prose writers . . . with biographical sketches*, N.Y., 1841.   [702, 714]

B

BACON, Francis: *The Essays, or Councils civil and moral. With a table of the colours of good and evil and a discourse of the wisdom of the ancients*, London, 1701.   [192]

BACON, Francis: *Works*, (10v.) London, 1803.   [243, 247, 391, 418]

BAILLIE, Joanna: *Miscellaneous Plays*, London, 1804.   [193]

BANIM, John: *The Denounced*, [a novel], (2v. in 1) New York, 1830.   [745]

BARBAULD, Anna Letitia (Aikin): *Poems*, [edition unknown].   [84]

BARTHELEMY, Jean Jacques, *abbé: Travels of Anacharsis the younger in Greece during the middle of the fourth century [B.C.]*, (7v.) London, 1790-1791.   [516, 517]

BEACONSFIELD, Benjamin Disraeli, *1st earl of: Vivian Gray, a Novel*, (3rd Am. ed., 3v.) Philadelphia, 1827.   [562, 649, 650, 651]

BEATTIE, James: *The Minstrel, in two books: with some other poems*, London, 1784.   [138]

BEAUMONT, Francis *and* John FLETCHER: *Dramatick Works with Notes*, (10v.) London, 1778.   [466, 548]

BELL, John (1745-1831): *Bell's British Theatre*, (24v.) London, [n.d.] (B.L.S.). [34]

BELOE, William, *translator: The History of Herodotus*, (4v.) London, 1791. [244]

BERESFORD, James: *The Miseries of human life, or The last groans of Timothy Testy and Samuel Sensitive, with a few supplementary sighs from Mrs. Testy*, (1st Am. ed.) Boston, 1807. [170]

BERKELEY, George, *bp. of Cloyne: The Principles of Human Knowledge*, (2d ed.) London, 1734. [480?]

BERKELEY, George——: *The Querist; or Several queries proposed*, Glasgow, 1751. [480?]

BEYLE, Henri: *The Life of Haydn in a series of letters written in Vienna [by Giuseppe Carpani] Followed by the Life of Mozart [from the German of Schlichtegroll]. With observations on Metastasio and on the present state of music in France and Italy. Tr.* [by Robert Brewin]. Notes by William Gardiner. London, 1817; *Boston 1839. [662, 663, 692]

BLACKWOOD'S EDINBURGH MAGAZINE, (112v.) Edinburgh, 1817-1861. [586, 588, 630]

BLESSINGTON, Marguerite (Power) Farmer Gardiner, *countess of: The Confessions of an elderly lady and gentleman*, (2v.) Philadelphia, 1838. [571]

BOCCACCIO, Giovanni: *The Decameron, or Ten days entertainment* (with remarks on the life and writings of Boccaccio by [Edward Dubois]), (2v.) London, 1804. [201]

BOJARDO, Matteo Maria, *conte di Scandiano: The Orlando Innamorato*, tr. into prose from the Italian of Francesco Berni by Wm. Stewart Rose, Edinb. and London, 1823. [644]

BONNYCASTLE, *Sir* Richard Henry: *Spanish America, or A descriptive, historical, and geographical acc't of the dominions of Spain in the Western Hemisphere*, Phila., 1819. [405]

BOSSUET, Jacques Bénigne, *bp. of Meaux: Histoire universelle à Monseigneur le Dauphin. Pour expliquer la suite de la religion & des changements des empires*, (2v.) Paris, 1814. [324, 329]

BOSSUET, Jacques——: *Oraisons funèbres*, Paris (P. Didot l'aîné), 1814. [327]

BOSWELL, James: *The Life of Samuel Johnson*, (5th ed., 4v.) London, 1807. [136]

BOYLE, Mary Louisa: *The State Prisoner: a tale of the French Regency*, (2v. in 1) Philadelphia, 1838. [555]

BRADFORD, Alden: *History of Massachusetts from 1764 to July, 1775*, Boston, 1822. [393]

BROOKS, *Mrs.* Maria (Gowen): *Zóphiël, or The bride of seven. By Maria del Occidente* [*pseud.*], Boston, 1833. [574]

BROUGHTON, Thomas Duer, *translator: Selections from the popular poetry of the Hindoos*, London, 1814. [123]

BROWN, Thomas (1778-1820): *Lectures on the philosophy of the human mind*, (3v.) Andover, 1822. [335, 349, 387]

BRUCE, James: *Travels to discover the source of the Nile in the years 1768-1773*, (6v.) Dublin, 1790. [62]

BRUNTON, *Mrs.* Mary (Balfour): *Self-control, a novel*, (2v.) Phila., 1811. [61, 560]

BUCKMINSTER, Joseph Stevens: *Sermons, with a memoir of his life and character*, Boston, 1814. [108, 115, 252]

BULGARIN, Faddei Venediktovich: *Ivan Vejeeghen, or Life in Russia. By Thaddeus Bulgarin.* [Tr. George Ross], (2v.) Philadelphia, 1832. [665]

BUNYAN, John: *The Pilgrim's Progress*, Worcester, 1791; *Charlestown, 1821. [501]

BURKE, Edmund: *A philosophical enquiry into the origin of our ideas of the sublime and beautiful*, (6th ed. with add'ns) London, 1770. [54?]

BURNETT, George, *editor: Specimens of English prose writers*, (3v.) London, 1807. [266]

BURNEY, Sarah Harriet: *Clarentine, a novel*, (2v.) Phila., 1818. [744]

BURNEY, Sarah Harriet: *The Country neighbors, or The secret*, (2v.) N.Y., 1820. [287, 746] (This work comprises vols. 2-3 of *Tales of Fancy*).

BURNEY, Sarah Harriet: *Geraldine Fauconberg, a novel*, (2v.) Phila., 1817. [564, 565]

BURNEY, Sarah Harriet: *Traits of nature*, (2v.) Philadelphia, 1812. [48]

BURNS, Robert: *The works of Robert Burns, with an acc't of his life and a criticism*, (7th ed., 5v.) London, 1813. [204, 385]

BURR, Aaron, *defendant: Reports of the trials of Colonel Aaron Burr, for treason and for a misdemeanor in preparing the means of a military expedition against Mexico etc. Taken in shorthand by David Robertson,* (2v.) Philadelphia, 1808. [292]

BURTON, Robert: *The Anatomy of melancholy,* by Democritus Junior [*pseud.*], London, 1660. [251]

BURY, *Lady* Charlotte (Campbell): *Diary illustrative of the times of George IV* [with continuations. Ed. John Galt], (4v.) Philadelphia, 1838-1839. [674]

BURY, *Lady*———: *The Exclusives,* (2v.) New York, 1830. [748]

BURY, *Lady*———: *Love,* (2v.) Philadelphia, 1838. [570]

BUTLER, Charles: *Reminiscences,* N.Y., 1824. [524]

BUTLER, Samuel: *Hudibras, in three parts,* (2v.) Edinburgh, 1779. [206]

BYRON, George Gordon Byron, *6th baron: Childe Harold's pilgrimage, a romaunt: and other poems,* (1st Am. ed.) Phila., 1812. [312]

BYRON, George———: *The Siege of Corinth, a poem; Parisina, a poem,* (2d Am. ed.) New York, 1816. [214, 253]

BYRON, George———: *Works,* (11v.) Paris, 1823. [580]

C

CAMPBELL, George: *The Philosophy of rhetoric,* (2d. ed., 2v.) London & Edinburgh, 1801. [330, 355, 357, 359]

CAMPBELL, Thomas: *An essay on English poetry,* Boston, 1819. [188]

CAMPBELL, Thomas: *The pleasures of hope, with other poems,* N.Y., 1800. [46]

CAMPBELL, Thomas: *The poetical works of Thomas Campbell,* (2v.) Baltimore, 1810. [212]

CAPPE, Newcome: *Critical remarks on many important passages of scripture, together with dissertations upon . . . the New Testament. Memoirs of his life.* (2v.) York, 1802. [106, 113]

CAPPE, Newcome: *Discourses chiefly on devotional subjects. Memoirs of his life by Catharine Cappe, a sermon by Cappe, and a sermon by William Wood,* York, 1805. [65, 128]

CAREY, Mathew: *Vindiciæ Hibernicæ, or Ireland vindicated:* (An attempt to expose errors in the English historians), Philadelphia, 1819. [184]

CARLYLE, Thomas: *Critical and miscellaneous essays,* (2v.) Boston, 1838. [597, 631, 652]

CARLYLE, Thomas, *translator: German romance: Specimens of its chief authors,* (4v.) Edinburgh, 1827. [617, 618]

CARLYLE, Thomas: *Sartor Resartus. In three books.* [ed. R. W. Emerson], Boston, 1836. [595]

CAULAINCOURT, Armand Augustin Louis, *marquis* de: *Napoleon and his times,* (2v.) Philadelphia, 1838. [573]

CERVANTES SAAVEDRA, Miguel de: *Don Quichotte de la Manche, traduit de l'espagnol* par [Jean Pierre Claris de] Florian, (3v.) Paris, 1803. [447]

CERVANTES SAAVEDRA, Miguel de: *The history and adventures of the renowned Don Quixote.* Tr. Tobias Smollett, (4v.) Phila., 1803; (4v.) Phila., 1811 (B.L.S.). [296, 759]

CHALMERS, Alexander: *A history of the colleges, halls, and public buildings attached to the University of Oxford, including the lives of the founders,* (2v.) Oxford, 1810. [294]

CHALMERS, Thomas: *The evidence and authority of the Christian revelation,* Phila., 1817. [104]

CHALMERS, Thomas: *A series of discourses on the Christian revelation, viewed in connection with modern astronomy,* (2d Am. ed.) N.Y., 1817. [107, 151]

CHALMERS, Thomas: *A sermon delivered in the Tron church, Glasgow* (Nov. 19, 1817; *temp.* funeral of Princess Charlotte of Wales), New York, 1819. [300]

CHATEAUBRIAND, François Auguste René, *vicomte* de: *The martyrs, or The triumph of the Christian religion,* (3v.) New York, 1812. [49, 160]

CHAUCER, Geoffrey: *The riches of Chaucer: in which his impurities have been expunged, his spelling modernized etc.* by Charles Cowden Clarke, (2v. in 1) London, 1835. [645]

CHRISTIAN OBSERVER, The, conducted by members of the established church, (20v.) Boston, 1802-1822. [60, 81, 87, 88, 98, 172, 177]

CICERO, Marcus Tullius: *The Tusculan Disputations of Marcus Tullius Cicero. A new translation by a gentleman*, London, 1758. [21, 26] (Listed in the Charging Records as "Cicero's Questions.")

CLARENDON, Edward Hyde, *1st earl of: The history of the rebellion and civil wars in England, begun in the year 1641*, (7v.) Oxford, 1708 (B.L.S.). [538, 540, 541, 542, 544]

CLARKE, Adam: *History of the Ancient Israelites*, Baltimore, 1811 (B.L.S.). [58?]

CLARKE, Edward Daniel: *Travels in various countries of Europe, Asia and Africa: Pt. II: Greece, Egypt and the Holy Land*, New York, 1813. [63]

CLARKSON, Thomas: *A portraiture of Quakerism*, (3v.) N.Y., 1806. [89, 549]

COLERIDGE, Samuel Taylor: *Biographia literaria, or Biographical sketches of my literary life and opinions*, Philadelphia, 1818. [150]

COLERIDGE, Samuel Taylor: *The friend: a series of essays to aid in the formation of fixed principles*, (1st Am. ed.) Burlington, Vt., 1831. [600]

COLERIDGE, Samuel Taylor: *Poetical works*, (3v.) London (W. Pickering) and Boston, 1835. [590, 591, 593, 615, 620, 659, 664]

COLLINSON, John: *The life of Thuanus, with some account of his writings and a translation of the preface to his history*, London, 1807. [481]

COMBE, William: *The devil upon two sticks in England, being a continuation of Le Diable Boiteux of Le Sage*, (3v.) London, 1811. [211?]

CONGREVE, William: *Poems*, London, 1778 (B.L.S.). [175]

CONSTABLE'S MISCELLANY of original publications in the various departments of literature, the sciences, and the arts, (B.L.S. had 80v.) Edinburgh, 1826-1833. [622, 756] Vol. 18: Robert Chambers, *History of the Rebellion in Scotland in 1745 and 1746*. Vol. 52: Wm. C. Stafford, *History of Music*.

COOTE, Charles: *The history of modern Europe and a view of the progress of society (1763-1802). Being a continuation of Dr. [William] Russell's History*, (2v. in 1?) Philadelphia, 1811. [80]

CORDINER, Charles: *Remarkable ruins and romantic prospects of North Britain. With ancient monuments and singular subjects of natural history*, (2v.) London, 1788-1795. [30, 40]

COTTIN, *Mme.* Marie (Risteau): *Mathilde*, (4v.) Paris, 1810. [690]

COX, *Rev.* Robert: *Narratives of the lives of the more eminent fathers of the first three centuries*, London, 1817. [459]

CUTHBERTSON, Catherine: *Forest of Montalbano. A novel*, (4v.) Phila., 1810. [73]

CUTHBERTSON, Catherine: *Santo Sebastiano, or The young protector. A novel*, (3v.) Boston, 1832. [727, 728, 729]

CUVIER, Georges: *Essay on the theory of the earth*. Tr. from the French by R. Kerr, with notes by Robert Jamieson. (2d ed. enl.) Edinburgh, 1815. [500]

D

DACIER: See "Plato."

DALLAS, Robert Charles: *Percival, or Nature vindicated. A novel*, (2d ed., 4v.) London, 1802. [314]

DANTE ALIGHIERI: *A translation of the Inferno in English verse, with historical notes and the life of Dante*. [Added: Specimen of new tr. of Ariosto's *Orlando Furioso*]. By Henry Boyd. (2v.) Dublin, 1785. [490, 494]

DARWIN, Erasmus: *Zoonomia, or The laws of organic life*, (3v.) N.Y. & Phila., 1796-1797. [477]

DEARBORN, Henry Alexander Scammell: *A memoir on the commerce and navigation of the Black Sea, and the trade and maritime geography of Turkey and Egypt*, (2v. + Atlas) Boston, 1819. [249]

DEPPING, Georg Bernhard: *Evening entertainments, or Delineations of the manners and customs of various nations . . . and descriptions in natural history*, Phila., 1812. [92, 97]

DICKENS, Charles: *Oliver Twist*, (2v.) Phila. (Lea and Blanchard), 1839. [585, 587, 592]

DICKENS, Charles: *Posthumous papers of the Pickwick Club*, (5v.) Phila., 1836-1837. [676]

DICKENS, Charles, *editor: The Pic Nic Papers*, by Charles Dickens, W. H. Maxwell, Thomas Moore, Miss Strickland, Horace Smith, Leitch Ritchie and others, (2v.) [edition uncertain]. [719]

DISRAELI, Isaac: *Curiosities of literature,* (1st ser., 3v.) London, 1795 (B.L.S.) ; (2d ser., 3v.) London, 1824 (B.L.S.). [436]

DOVER, George Agar-Ellis, *1st baron: The true history of the state prisoner, commonly called the Iron Mask, extracted from documents in the French archives,* [edition uncertain]. [673]

DRAKE, Nathan, *M.D.: Literary hours, or Sketches critical and narrative,* (3v.) Sudbury, 1800. [402]

DRYDEN, John: *The critical and miscellaneous prose works, now first collected* [with a collection of his letters], ed. Edmond Malone, (3v. in 4) London, 1800. [202?]

DRYDEN, John: *Works. Illustrated with notes and a life by Walter Scott,* (18v.) London, 1808. [203, 227, 543, 545]

DUNLOP, John Colin: *The history of fiction, being a critical account of the most celebrated prose works of fiction, from the earliest Greek romances to the novels of the present age.* (3v.) Edinburgh, 1814. [285]

DWIGHT, Timothy: *Travels in New England and New York,* (4v.) New Haven, 1821. [392]

E

EDGEWORTH, Maria: *The absentee: a tale,* (2v.) New York, 1812. [66]

EDGEWORTH, Maria: *Belinda,* (2v.) Boston, 1814. [758]

EDGEWORTH, Maria: *Helen, a Tale,* (2v.) Philadelphia, 1834. [606, 607]

EDGEWORTH, Maria: *Leonora,* (2v.) London, 1806. [448]

EDGEWORTH, Maria: *The modern Griselda,* George Town, 1810. [368, 452]

EDGEWORTH, Maria: *Moral tales for young people,* (3v.) Phila., 1810. [16, 22, 27, 190, 224, 229]

EDGEWORTH, Maria: *Popular tales,* (2v.) Phila., 1804. [20, 25, 147, 233]

EDGEWORTH, Maria: *Tales of fashionable life,* (3v.) Boston, 1810. [143, 146, 231]

EDGEWORTH, Richard Lovell: *Essays on professional education,* (2d ed.) London, 1812. [234]

EDINBURGH REVIEW, (137v.) Edinburgh, 1802-1873. [13, 246, 284, 301, 315, 348, 365, 377, 380, 383, 637]

ELLIS, *Sir* Henry (1777-1855): *Journal of the proceedings of the late embassy to China* [Lord Amherst's], Philadelphia, 1818. [379]

ELSLEY, Heneage, *vicar of Burenston: Annotations on the four gospels and the Acts of the Apostles,* (2d ed., 3v.) London, 1812. [85]

ENCYCLOPÆDIA BRITANNICA (Dobson's edn. with supplement), (21v.) Phila., 1798-1803. [76?]

ENFIELD, William: *Institutes of natural philosophy, theoretical and experimental,* ed. Samuel Webber, (1st Am. ed.), Boston, 1802. [189, 302?]

ENFIELD, William: *The history of philosophy,* (2v.) Dublin, 1792. [302?]

EPICTETUS: *All the works of Epictetus which are now extant.* Tr. Elizabeth Carter, (2v.) London, 1768. [474]

ERSKINE, Thomas Erskine, *baron: Speeches, when at the bar, on subjects connected with the liberty of the press, and against constructive treasons.* Collected by James Ridgway, (2v.) New York, 1810. [362, 502]

EUGENE, *Prince of Savoy: Mémoires du Prince Eugène de Savoie, écrits par lui-même* [or rather by Charles Joseph, Prince of Ligne], Paris, 1810. [439]

EULER, Leonhard: *Lettres à une princesse d'Allemagne* [the *Princess of Anhalt-Dessau*] *sur divers sujets de physique et de philosophie,* (2v.) Paris, 1812. [440]

EURIPIDES: *Tragedies translated* [by Robert Potter], (2v.) London, 1781. [422]

F

FAMILY DRAMATIST, (6v. London, 1830. [769] (These six volumes were also published in America as the "Dramatic Series" of Harper's Family Library, N.Y., 1831———.) Vol. 1-3: *Massinger's plays.* Vol. 4: *Æschylus* Vols. 5-6: *Ford's plays.*

FAMILY LIBRARY, The, (80v.) London (Murray), 1829-1842. [525] Vol. 21: G. R. Gleig, *Hist. of the Brit. Empire in India* (1830)

FAY, Theodore Sedgwick: *The Countess Ida. A tale of Berlin,* (2v.) N.Y., 1840. [680, 683]

FAY, Theodore Sedgwick: *Norman Leslie. A tale of the present times*, (2v.) N.Y., 1835. [612]

FENNELL, James: *An apology for the life of James Fennell. Written by himself.* Philadelphia, 1814. [12]

FERGUSON, Adam: *The history of the progress and termination of the Roman republic*, (3v.) Dublin, 1783. [412]

FERGUSON, James: *Ferguson's astronomy explained upon Sir Isaac Newton's principles*, Philadelphia, 1809. (Also a vol. of *Plates illustrative of Ferguson's Astronomy*, Phila., 1809). [145, 295]

FERRIER, Susan Edmonstone: *Marriage, A novel*, [edition uncertain]. [666]

FLEURY, Claude: *The manners of the ancient Israelites, containing an account of their peculiar customs, ceremonies, laws, polity etc.*, [tr. E. Farneworth, i.e., Thos. Bedford]; much enlarged by Adam Clarke, (2d ed. enlarged) Manchester & London, 1805. [58?]

FLORIAN, Jean Pierre Claris de: *Œuvres complettes*, (nouv. éd. aug., 11v.) Paris, 1803. [117, 120]

FONTENELLE, Bernard Le Bovier de: *Conversations on the Plurality of Worlds* (with memoir of Fontenelle by Voltaire), London, 1809. [400, 411]

FOX, Charles James: *The speeches of . . . in the House of Commons*, (6v.) London, 1815. [433]

FRANKLIN, Benjamin: *The complete works in philosophy, politics, and morals, now first collected and arranged*, (3v.) London (J. Johnson), 1806. [23? 382, 389]

FRANKLIN, Benjamin: *Works of the late Dr. Benjamin Franklin, consisting of his life written by himself etc.*, (2v.) London (Longman etc.), 1806. [23?]

FROISSART, Jean: *Sir John Froissart's chronicles of England, France, Spain, and the adjoining countries* (tr. Thomas Johnes), (3d ed., 12v. in 6 + Plates) London, 1808. [235, 291]

G

GALLENGA, Antonio: *Italy, general views of its history and literature in reference to its present state. By L. Mariotti [pseud.]*, (2v.) London, 1841. [731, 732, 736]

GALT, John: *The life and administration of Cardinal Wolsey*, (2d ed.) London, 1817. [409]

GARDINER, William: *The music of nature, or An attempt to prove that what is passionate and pleasing in the art of singing, speaking, and performing upon musical instruments, is derived from the sounds of the animated world*, Boston, 1837. [553, 605, 639, 672, 754]

GENLIS, Stéphanie Félicité Ducrest de St. Aubin, *comtesse* de: *Jeanne de France*, (2v.) Paris, 1816. [441]

GENLIS, Stéphanie———: *Sacred dramas, written in French* (tr. Thomas Holcroft), London, 1786. [94]

GIBBON, Edward: *History of the decline and fall of the Roman empire*, (12v.) London, 1807. [505, 506]

GIBBON, Edward: *The history of the decline and fall of the Roman empire*, (14v.) Basil, 1789. [267]

GIBBON, Edward: *The miscellaneous works of . . ., with memoirs of his life and writings*, composed by himself, (ed. with notes by John Baker Holroyd, 1st Earl of Sheffield), (5v.) London, 1814. [343, 345, 373]

GILLIES, John: *The history of ancient Greece, its colonies and conquests*, (4v.) London, 1787. [122, 342]

GISBORNE, Thomas: *An enquiry into the duties of the female sex*, (2d ed.) London, 1797. [371]

GODWIN, William: *The history of the life of William Pitt, earl of Chatham*, (2d ed.) London, 1783. [257]

GODWIN, William: *Life of Geoffrey Chaucer, the early English poet* (incl. memoirs of John of Gaunt, etc.), (2d ed., 4v.) London, 1804. [52]

GODWIN, William: *Mandeville; a tale of the seventeenth century in England*, (3v.) Philadelphia, 1818. [152]

GOETHE, Johann Wolfgang von: *Memoirs of Goëthe*, New York, 1824. [444, 486, 656]

GOETHE, Johann Wolfgang von: *Wilhelm Meister's Apprenticeship* (tr. Thomas Carlyle), (3v.) Boston, 1828. [526]

GOLDSMITH, Oliver: *Abridgment of the history of England from the invasion of Julius Caesar to the death of George II,* London, 1787; London, 1800. [86]

GOLDSMITH, Oliver: *The Grecian history, from the earliest state to the death of Alexander the Great,* (2v.) London, 1790. [102]

GOLDSMITH, Oliver: *History of the earth and animated nature,* (8v.) Dublin, 1782. [9, 33]

GOLDSMITH, Oliver: *History of England,* (3v.) London, 1790. [110]

GOLDSMITH, Oliver: *The Roman history, from the founding of the city of Rome to the destruction of the Western Empire,* (2v.) London, 1789. [32, 39, 116]

GORE, *Mrs.* Catherine Grace Frances (Moody): *Greville, or A season in Paris,* (2v.) Philadelphia, 1841. [715]

GORE, *Mrs.*————: *Preferment, or My uncle the earl,* (2v.) N.Y., 1840. [739]

GRAHAME, James: *The Sabbath: a poem. To which are now added, Sabbath walks,* (1st Am. ed.) N.Y., 1805. [515]

GRIMM, Friedrich Melchior, *freiherr* von: *Correspondance littéraire, philosophique et critique,* (17v.) Paris, 1813. (B.L.S.) [275, 354]

GRIMM, Friedrich————: *Mémoires historiques, littéraires et anecdotiques tirés de la correspondance philosophique et critique,* (4v.) Londres, 1815. [529]

GUICCIARDINI, Francesco: *History of Italy from the year 1490 to 1532.* [Tr. by Austin Parke Goddard, with life of Guicciardini chiefly from Domenico Manni], (10v.) London, 1753. [410, 414]

H

HALL, *Mrs.* Anna Maria (Fielding): *Marian, or A young maid's fortunes. By Mrs. S. C. Hall,* (2v.) New York, 1840. [633, 635]

HALL, *Mrs.*————: *Uncle Horace, a novel,* (2v.) Philadelphia, 1828. [554]

HALLAM, Henry: *View of the state of Europe during the middle ages,* (4v.) Philadelphia, 1821. [290, 396]

HAMILTON, Elizabeth: *A series of popular essays illustrative of principles essentially connected with the improvement of the understanding, the imagination, and the heart,* (2v.) London, 1813. [15, 17, 28, 35]

HAUY, René Just: *An elementary treatise on natural philosophy by . . . Haüy* (tr. with notes by Olinthus Gregory), (2v.) London, 1807. [520]

HAWTHORNE, Nathaniel: *Twice-told tales,* (2v.) Boston, 1842. [721]

HAYLEY, William: *A philosophical, historical, and moral essay on old maids. By a friend to the sisterhood,* (3v.) Dublin, 1786. [1]

HAZLITT, William: *Eloquence of the British senate; a selection of speeches of parliamentary Speakers from the beginning of the reign of Charles I to the present time,* (2v.) New York, 1810. [53]

HAZLITT, William: *Lectures on the English comic writers,* (3d ed.) London, 1841. [723]

HAZLITT, William: *Lectures on the English poets. Delivered at the Surrey Institution,* (1st Am. ed.) Philadelphia, 1818. [161, 262, 768]

HAZLITT, William: *The round table,* (2v.) Edinburgh, 1817. [187, 196]

HERBERT, George: *Herbert's poems and the Country parson, with the life of the author from Izaak Walton,* London, 1809. [624]

HERBERT, Henry William: *The brothers. A tale of the Fronde,* (2v.) N.Y., 1835. [578]

HERODOTUS. See "William Beloe."

HOGG, James: *The brownie of Bodsbeck, and other tales,* Phila., 1818. [370]

HOGG, James: *Winter evening tales, collected among the cottagers in the south of Scotland,* (2v.) Edinburgh, 1820. [675]

HOPE, Thomas: *Anastasius, or Memoirs of a Greek written at the close of the eighteenth century,* (3v. in 2) New York, 1820. [341]

HORSLEY, Samuel, *bishop* (1733-1806): *Sermons,* New York, 1814. [132]

HOWARD, Edward: *Outward bound, or A merchant's adventures,* (2v.) Philadelphia, 1838. [603] (This work is wrongly attributed to Frederick Marryat.)

HUGO, Victor: *The hunchback of Notre-Dame* [with sketch of Hugo by Frederick Shoberl], (2v.) Philadelphia, 1834. [724, 741]

HUMBOLDT, Alexander, *freiherr* von: *Personal narrative of travels to the equinoctial regions of the new continent (1799-1804),* tr. Helen Maria Williams), (3v.) London, 1814 (B.L.S.). [496, 497, 498]

HUMBOLDT, Alexander———: *Political essay on the kingdom of New Spain* (tr. John Black), (4v.) London, 1814 (B.L.S.). [499?]

HUME, David: *The history of England, from the invasion of Julius Cæsar to the revolution in 1688* [with life written by himself], (8v.) London, 1790; (8v.) Edinburgh, 1810. [277, 279, 374, 378, 401, 413, 416, 419, 432]

HUME, David: *Philosophical essays. With the answer to his objections to Christianity by Dr. Campbell, and his life by Thomas Ewell*, (2v.) Phila., 1817. [397, 406]

HUMPHREY, Heman: *Great Britain, France and Belgium. A short tour in 1835*, (2v.) New York, 1838. [557]

HUNT, Leigh: *The feast of the poets, with notes, and other pieces in verse*, N.Y., 1814. [181]

HUTCHINSON, *Mrs.* Lucy (Apsley): *Memoirs of the life of Colonel Hutchinson, with original anecdotes*, (2v.) London, 1810. [504]

HUTCHINSON, Thomas: *The history of the colony of Massachuset's Bay, from the first settlement thereof in 1628* [until 1691], (2d ed.) London, 1765. [388]

HUTTON, Catherine: *The miser married. A novel*, (2v.) [Philadelphia, 1814]. [579]

I

INCHBALD, *Mrs.* Elizabeth (Simpson): *The British theatre, or A collection of plays which are acted at the Theatres Royal, Drury Lane, Covent Garden, and Haymarket, with biographical and critical remarks*, (25v.) London, 1808. [6, 42]

IRVING, Washington: *A history of the life and voyages of Christopher Columbus*, (1st ed., 3v.) New York, 1828. [508, 511]

IRVING, Washington: *A history of New York from the beginning of the world to the end of the Dutch dynasty*, by Diedrich Knickerbocker, (1st ed., 2v.) New York & Philadelphia, 1809. [286]

J

JAMES, George Payne Rainsford: *Corse de Leon, or The brigand: a romance*, (2v.) New York, 1841. [726]

JAMES, George———: *The gipsy: a tale*, (2v.) [? New York, 1835]. [634, 640]

JAMES, George———: *Henry of Guise, or The states of Blois*, (2v.) N.Y., 1839. [677, 678]

JAMES, George———: *The Huguenot. A tale of the French Protestants*, (2v.) N.Y., 1839. [601, 602]

JAMES, George———: *One in a thousand, or The days of Henri Quatre*, (2v.) Phila., 1836. [556]

JAMIESON, Robert, *editor: Popular ballads and songs from tradition, manuscripts, and scarce editions*, (2v.) Edinburgh, 1806. [627, 632, 653, 705, 761]

JAY, William: *Short discourses to be read in families*, (2v.) Hartford, 1807. [125]

JEBB, John (1736-1786): *Works: theological, medical, political and miscellaneous.* [With a memoir of Jebb by John Disney], (3v.) London, 1787. [156]

JESSE, John Heneage: *Memoirs of the court of England during the reign of the Stuarts, including the Protectorate*, (4v.) Philadelphia, 1840. [668, 669, 670]

JOHNSON, Samuel: *A journey to the western islands of Scotland*, (2v. in 1) Dublin, 1775. [77, 141]

JOHNSON, Samuel: *The Rambler*, (4v.) London, 1789. [78]

JOHNSON, Samuel: *Rasselas, prince of Abyssinia*, Dublin, 1788. [431]

JOUY, Étienne, *i.e.* Victor Joseph Étienne, *called* de: *The Paris spectator, or L'hermite de la Chaussée d'Antin, containing observations upon Parisian manners and customs* [ca. 1800], tr. W. Jerdan, (3v.) Philadelphia & Boston, 1816. [180]

K

KAMES, Henry Home, *lord: Essays on the principles of morality and natural religion* [with essays added concerning the proof of a deity], (2d ed.) London, 1758. [59]

KENDALL, George Wilkins: *Narrative of an expedition across the great southwestern prairies, from Texas to Santa Fé*, (2v.) New York, 1844. [760, 762, 763]

KIRWAN, Walter Blake: *Sermons, with a sketch of his life* [by Wilhelmina Kirwan?], Philadelphia, 1817. [153]

KLOPSTOCK, Friedrich Gottlieb: *The Messiah* (attempted from the German of Klopstock by Joseph and Mary Collyer), N.Y., 1795. [57, 521]

KNOX, Vicesimus, *compiler: Elegant Epistles, or A copious collection of familiar and amusing letters*, London, 1790. [398?]

KNOX, Vicesimus, *compiler: Elegant Extracts: or useful and entertaining passages in prose, selected for the improvement . . . in the art of speaking etc.*, (2v.) London, 1791. [91? 398?]

KNOX, Vicesimus, *compiler: Elegant Extracts, or useful and entertaining pieces of poetry*, (2v.) London, 1791. [68, 398?]

L

LA FONTAINE, Jean de (1621-1695) : *Œuvres complettes, précédées d'une nouvelle notice sur sa vie*, (6v.) Paris, 1814. [162]

LA HARPE, Jean François de: *Lycée, ou Cours de littérature ancienne et moderne*, (nouv. éd. augm., 15v.) Paris, 1816. [289]

LAMB, Charles: *Elia: essays which have appeared under that signature in the London Magazine*, London, 1823. [463]

LAMB, Charles: *The works of Charles Lamb* (prefixed by his letters and a sketch of his life by Thomas Noon Talfourd, (2v.) N.Y., 1838. [599]

LANDOR, Walter Savage: *Imaginary conversations of literary men and statesmen*, (1st ser., 2v.) London, 1824. [421]

LANDOR, Walter Savage: *Pericles and Aspasia*, (2v.) Philadelphia, 1839. [628]

LARDNER, Dionysius, *editor: The Cabinet Cyclopædia*, (133v.) London, 1830-1846. [611, 625]

> Vol. 29: Dunham, Samuel Astley: *History of Spain and Portugal*, (5 vols.) London, 1832-1833, vol. I.

> Vol. 93: Dunham, S. A. et al.: *Lives of the Most Eminent Literary and Scientific Men of Great Britain* (v. 1: Early British Writers. v. 2-3: British Dramatists), (3 vols.) London, 1836-1838, vol. II.

LA ROCHEJAQUELEIN, Marie Louise Victoire (de Donnissan), *marquise* de: *Mémoires. Ecrits par elle-même*, Paris, 1815. [718]

LAVATER, Johann Caspar: *Physiognomy, or The corresponding analogy between the conformation of the features and the ruling passions of the mind*, London, 1789. [216]

LEE, *Mrs.* Eliza (Buckminster): *Life of Jean Paul Frederic Richter*. Compiled from various sources. Together with his autobiography, (2v.) Boston, 1842. [737, 738]

LEE, *Mrs.* Hannah Farnham (Sawyer): *The life and times of Thomas Cranmer*, Boston, 1841. [667]

LE SAGE, Alain René: *The devil upon two sticks* [Added: Dialogues between some chimneys of Madrid], (2v.) London, 1793. [211]

LE SAGE, Alain René: *Histoire de Gil Blas de Santillane*, (4v.) Paris, 1802. [686, 689, 691]

LESTER, Charles Edwards: *The glory and the shame of England*, (2v.) N.Y., 1841. [716]

LEVER, Charles: *The confessions of Harry Lorrequer* [pseud.], Phila., 1841 (B.L.S.). [698]

LIBRARY OF THE OLD ENGLISH PROSE WRITERS, [ed. Alexander Young], (9v.) Cambridge, Mass., 1831-1834. [546]

> Vol. 1: Thos. Fuller, *Holy and Profane States* (1831)

> Vol. 2: Sir Philip Sidney, *Defense of Poesy* and John Selden, *Table Talk* (1831)

> Vol. 3: Sir Thomas Browne, *Works* (1831)

> Vol. 4: Owen Feltham, *Resolves* (1832)

> Vols. 5-6: Izaak Walton, *Lives of Donne, Wotton, Hooker, Herbert and Sanderson* (1832)

> Vol. 7: Hugh Latimer, *Select Sermons* (1832)

> Vol. 8: Jeremy Taylor, *Selections* (with life) (1833)

> Vol. 9: Sir Thomas More, *Utopia* and *History of King Richard III.* (1834)

LIGNE, Charles Joseph, *prince* de: *Letters and reflections of the Austrian field-marshal Prince de Ligne*, ed. by Baroness de Staël-Holstein. (Tr. D. Boileau), (2v. in 1) Philadelphia, 1809. [51]

LIVIUS, Titus: *Roman history*, (2v.) London, 1814. [238, 245, 261]

LOCKHART, John Gibson: *Memoirs of the life of Sir Walter Scott, bart.*, (2v.) Philadelphia, 1837. [583]

LOGAN, John (1748-1788): *Sermons*, (1st Am. ed.) Boston, 1804. [41]

LONGFELLOW, Henry Wadsworth: *Hyperion, a romance*, (2v.) New York, 1839. [638, 699, 700]

LONGFELLOW, Henry———: *Outre-mer; a pilgrimage beyond the sea*, (2v.) N.Y., 1835. [613, 614]

LUCRETIUS: *T. Lucretius Carus, Of the nature of things*, tr. Thomas Creech [System of Epicurean philosophy explained in the notes], (2v.) London, 1715. [465?]

LUCRETIUS: *The nature of things; a didactic poem.* (The original text with a tr. by John Mason Good), (2v.) London, 1805. [465?]

LYMAN, Theodore: *The political state of Italy*, Boston, 1820. [255]

LYTTON, Edward George Earle Lytton Bulwer, *1st baron: Alice, or the mysteries: a sequel to Ernest Maltravers*, (2v.) New York, 1838. [576, 577]

LYTTON, Edward———: *Ernest Maltravers*, (2v.) New York, 1837. [581]

LYTTON, Edward———: *Eugene Aram. A tale*, (2v.) New York, 1832. [757]

LYTTON, Edward———: *Godolphin, or The oath*, (2v.) [edition uncertain]. [654, 655]

LYTTON, Edward———: *Night and morning. A novel*, (2v.) New York, 1841. [681]

M

MACAULAY, Thomas Babington: *Critical and miscellaneous essays*, (4v.) Boston, 1840 etc. (B.L.S.) [661]

MacCARTHY, Daniel: *The siege of Florence; an historical romance*, (2v.) Phila., 1841. [697]

McCRIE, Thomas: *The life of John Knox, containing illustrations of the history of the reformation in Scotland, with biographical notices of the principal reformers*, New York, 1813. [271]

MADAME DE SÉVIGNÉ AND HER CONTEMPORARIES, (2v.) Phila., 1842. [755]

MAINTENON, Françoise d'Aubigné, *marquise* de: *Lettres, précédées de sa vie par L. S. Auger*, (2ᵉ éd., 4v.) Paris, 1815. [671]

MALTHUS, Thomas Robert: *An essay on the principle of population*, London, 1798. [449?]

MALTHUS, Thomas Robert: *Principles of political economy considered with a view to their practical application*, Boston, 1821. [449?]

MARMONTEL, Jean François: *The Incas, or The destruction of the empire of Peru*, (2v.) London, 1777. [37?]

MARMONTEL, Jean François: *Memoirs of Marmontel, written by himself*, (4v.) London, 1805; (4v.) London, 1806. [37?]

MARMONTEL, Jean François: *Moral tales*, (2v.) Edinburgh, 1775; (3v.) [edition uncertain]. [37? 636]

MARMONTEL, Jean François: *Nouveau contes moraux*, (4v.) Paris, 1801. [169]

MARSH, Herbert, *bp. of Peterborough: The history of the politicks of Great Britain and France, from the Conference at Pillnitz to the declaration of war against Great Britain*, (2v.) London, 1800. [437]

MARSHALL, John: *The life of George Washington* (with a view of the colonies planted by the English in North America), (5v.) Philadelphia, 1804-1807. [495]

MARTINEAU, Harriet: *Deerbrook, a novel*, (2v.) New York, 1839. [646]

MARTINEAU, Harriet: *The essential faith of the universal church, deduced from the sacred records*, Boston, 1833. [730]

MARTINEAU, Harriet: *Five years of youth, o[r] Sense and sentiment*, (1st Am. ed.) Boston, 1832. [551]

MASSACHUSETTS HISTORICAL SOCIETY: *Collections of . . .*, (1st ser., 10v.) Boston, 1795-1816; (2d ser., 10v.) Boston, 1814-1823. [95, 372]

MASSINGER, Philip: *The plays of Philip Massinger*, with notes by William Gifford, (2d ed., 4v.) London, 1813. [222, 232, 470]

MATHIAS, Thomas James: *Pursuits of literature. A satirical poem in four dialogues*, London, 1799. [185]

MEISSNER, August Gottlieb: *Charles et Hélène de Moldorf, ou Huit ans de trop, traduit de l'allemand* par Mme. Isabelle de Montolieu, Paris, 1814. [442]

MILTON, John: *Paradise lost; a poem in twelve books*, (2v.) Dublin, 1772; (2v.) Glasgow, 1776. [103, 109]

MILTON, John: *The poetical works of John Milton, with notes of various authors* [With acc't of Milton's life and writings by Henry J. Todd], (2d ed., 7v.) London, 1809. [99]

MILTON, John: *The prose works, with life etc.* by Charles Symmons, (7v.) London, 1806. [375, 394]

MITFORD, William: *History of Greece*, (10v.) London, 1795 (B.L.S.). [304, 321, 338, 350, 360, 363, 407, 408, 427, 510, 512]

MOLIERE, Jean Baptiste Poquelin: *Œuvres*, (6v.) Paris, 1804. [725]

MONTAIGNE, Michel de: *Essais*, (éd. stéréotype, 4v.) Paris, 1802. [226]

MONTESQUIEU, Charles Louis de Secondat, *baron: Œuvres complettes de Montesquieu* (avec vie de cet auteur), (6v.) Paris, 1816. [274, 276, 386]

MONTHLY ANTHOLOGY AND BOSTON REVIEW, The. Containing sketches and reports of philosophy, religion, history, arts, and manners [Nov., 1803———June, 1811], (10v.) Boston, 1804-1811. [182, 256]

MONTOLIEU, Isabelle (Polier), *baronne* de: *Le Ferme aux abeilles, ou les fleurs de lis, imité d'Auguste Lafontaine*, (2v. in 1) Paris, 1814. [166]

MOORE, Thomas: *Lalla Rookh, an oriental romance*, Philadelphia, 1817. [158, 215]

MOORE, Thomas: *Travels of an Irish gentleman in search of a religion*, Phila., 1833. [767]

MORE, Hannah: *Strictures on the modern system of female education. With a view of the principles and conduct prevalent among women of rank and fortune*, (2v.) Philadelphia, 1800. [112]

MORE, *Sir* Thomas: *A most pleasant, fruitful, and witty work of the best state of a public weale, and of the new isle called Utopia* (tr. Raphe Robinson, 1551) ed. T. F. Dibdin, (2v.) London, 1808. [305]

MORGAN, Sydney (Owenson), *lady: O'Donnel; a national tale*, (2v.) N.Y., 1814. [208]

MUSEUM OF FOREIGN LITERATURE, SCIENCE, AND ART, The: (45v.) Phila., 1822-1842. [559, 569, 575] (Vols. 29-45 are called "new series, 1-17.")

N

NARES, Edward: *Thinks-I-to-myself; a serio-ludicro, tragico-comico tale*, (1st Am. ed., 2v. in 1) Boston, 1812. [237]

NEAL, John: *Keep cool, a novel. Written in hot weather*, (2v.) Baltimore, 1817. [566]

NORMANBY, Constantine Henry Phipps, *1st marquis: Matilda, a tale of the day*, Philadelphia, 1825. [642]

NORTON, *Hon. Mrs.* Caroline (Sheridan): *The wife, and Woman's reward*, (2v.) New York, 1836. [695, 696]

O

O'MEARA, Barry Edward: *Napoleon in exile, or A voice from St. Helena. The opinions and reflections of Napoleon on the most important events of his life and government, in his own words.* (2d ed., 2v.) Philadelphia, 1822. [361]

OPIE, *Mrs.* Amelia (Alderson): *Simple tales*, (2v.) George Town, 1807. [50]

OSSIANIC POEMS: *The poems of Ossian.* Tr. James Macpherson (new ed., 2v.) London, 1790. [219]

P

PALEY, William: *Natural theology; or Evidences of the existence and attributes of the Deity. Collected from the appearances of nature*, Philadelphia, 1802. [307]

PASCAL, Blaise: *Pensées*, (nouv. éd., 2v.) Paris, 1812. [281]

PASCAL, Blaise: *Les provinciales, ou Lettres de Louis de Montalte*, (2v.) Paris, 1816. [513]

PEARSALL, Richard (1698-1762): *Contemplations on the ocean, harvest, sickness, and the last Judgement*, London, 1753. [2]

PEARSON, Hugh (1777-1856): *Memoirs of the life and writings of the Rev. Claudius Buchanan*, Philadelphia, 1817. [133]

PERCY, Thomas: *Reliques of ancient English poetry*, (3v.) London, 1812. [210, 332, 589, 609, 660]

PETRARCA, Francesco: *Petrarch's View of human life*, tr. Mrs. Susanah Dobson, London, 1797. [317]   (A translation of *De Remediis Utriusque Fortunæ*).

PETRONIUS ARBITER: *The works of Petronius Arbiter in prose and verse.* Tr. from the Latin by Mr Addison. (Life and character of his writings by St. Evremont), London, 1736. [537]

PICHLER, *Frau* Karoline (von Greiner): *The siege of Vienna*, Philadelphia, 1835. [717]

PICKERING, Ellen: *The prince and the pedler, or The siege of Bristol*, (2v.) N.Y., 1839. [740, 743]

PIRON, Alexis: *Œuvres choisies d'Alexis Piron*, (3v.) Paris, 1806. [435]

PLATO: *The Republic of Plato.* (Tr. H. Spens with a discourse on the philosophy of the ancients), Glasgow, 1763. [399]

PLATO: *The works of Plato abridg'd, with an account of his life, philosophy, morals and politicks, together with a translation of his choicest dialogues . . . Illustrated by notes.* By M. [André] Dacier. Translated from the French. (2v.) London, 1772. [186, 197, 207, 425, 492, 503, 507]

PLUTARCHUS: *Plutarch's Morals: translated from the Greek by several hands* [M. Morgan, S. Ford, W. Dillingham, T. Hoy and others], (3d ed., 5v.) London, 1694. [429, 450, 451, 453, 455, 457, 482, 483, 488]

[POETS OF GREAT BRITAIN], (3v.) Edinburgh, 1793. [331, 334, 623]   (Each author has a separate title page in each volume:)

　　Vol. 1: Chaucer, Surrey, Wyatt, Sackville;
　　Vol. 2: Spencer, Shakspeare, Davies, Hall;
　　Vol. 3: Drayton, Carew, Suckling.

PORTER, Anna Maria: *Don Sebastian, or The house of Braganza.* An historical novel, (2v.) Philadelphia, 1810. [155]

PORTER, Anna Maria: *The fast of St. Magdalen, a romance*, (2v.) N.Y., 1819. [223, 584]

PORTER, Jane: *The Scottish chiefs: a romance*, (2v.) N.Y., 1819. [217, 464, 467]

PORTER, Jand: *The two princes of Persia. Addressed to youth*, London, 1801. [29]

POYNDER, John: *A history of the Jesuits, to which is prefixed A reply to Mr. [Robert Charles] Dallas's defense of that order*, (2v.) London, 1816. [514]

PRATT, Samuel Jackson: *The sublime and beautiful of Scripture: being essays on select passages of sacred composition*, London, 1782. [54?]

PRIESTLEY, Joseph: *Lectures on history and general policy*, (2v.) London, 1793. [268, 318, 320, 323]

Q

QUARTERLY REVIEW, The: (148v.) London, 1809-1879. [205, 404, 424]

QUINTILIANUS: *Quintilian's Institutes of the orator, in twelve books* (Tr. from Latin acc. to the Paris edition of Rollin, with notes by J. Patsall), (2v.) London, 1744. [127]

R

RABELAIS, François: *Œuvres de Maitre François Rabelais, suivies des Remarques publiées en anglois par M. Le Motteux et traduites en françois* [par César de Missy], (nouv. éd., 3v.) Paris, 1798. [282]

RAMBLER, The: See "Samuel Johnson."

RAMSAY, David: *History of the United States from their first settlement as English colonies in 1607, to the year 1808.* (Continued to the treaty of Ghent by Samuel Stanhope Smith et al.), (3v.) Philadelphia, 1816-1817. [167, 220]

REES, Abraham: *Cyclopædia*, (41v. + 6v.) Philadelphia, [1810-1824]. [76?]

REGNARD, Jean François: *Œuvres complettes de Regnard*, (6v.) Paris, 1810. [530]

RICHARDSON, Samuel: *Clarissa, or The history of a young lady*, (4th ed., 7v.) London, 1751. [340, 458, 703, 704, 706, 707, 708, 709, 710]

RICHARDSON, Samuel: *The history of Sir Charles Grandison*, (7v.) London, 1754; (7v.) London, 1781. [111, 344, 468, 471, 472, 473, 476, 533, 534, 535]

ROBERTSON, William: *The history of the reign of the Emperor Charles V*, (new ed., 4v.) London, 1777. [64, 154, 273, 280]

ROBERTSON, William: *The history of Scotland during the reigns of Queen Mary and King James VI. till his accession to the crown of England*, (12th ed., 2v. in 1) London, 1791. [70, 308]

ROLAND DE LA PLATIERE, Marie Jeanne: *The works of J. M. Phlipon Roland, containing her philosophical and literary essays, written previous to her marriage; her correspondence and her travels etc.* (With preliminary discourse by L. A. Champagneux. Tr. from the French), (3v.) London, 1803 (B.L.S.). [242]

ROSCOE, Thomas, *translator: The German novelists: tales selected from ancient and modern authors in that language* (from earliest period to close of 18th century, with critical and biographical notices), (4v.) London, 1826. [657]

ROSCOE, Thomas, *translator: The Italian novelists, from the earliest period down to the close of the 18th century.* Tr. from the original Italian. (4v.) London, 1825. [539]

ROUSSEAU, Jean Jacques: *Œuvres,* (nouv. éd., 18v.) Paris, 1817. [353, 445]
　　　　Vols. 13-14: "Les Confessions."

ROWSON, *Mrs.* Susanna (Haswell): *Trials of the human heart, a novel,* (2v.) Phila., 1795. [572]

RUSH, Benjamin: *Essays, literary, moral and philosophical,* Phila., 1798. [456?]

RUSH, Benjamin: *Medical inquiries and observations upon the diseases of the mind,* Philadelphia, 1812. [456?]

S

SARGENT, Charles Lenox: *The life of Alexander Smith, captain of the island of Pitcairn; one of the mutineers on board H.M.S. Bounty.* Written by Smith himself etc., Boston, 1819. [194]

SCHILLER, Johann Christoph Friedrich von: *The history of the Thirty Years' War in Germany.* Tr. by Captain Blaquiere, (2v.) London, 1799. [484, 485]

SCHLEGEL, August Wilhelm von: *A course of lectures on dramatic art and literature.* Tr. John Black, (2v.) London, 1815. [263? 269? 384?]

SCHLEGEL, Friedrich von: *Lectures on the history of literature, ancient and modern* (tr. J. G. Lockhart), (2v.) Philadelphia, 1818. [263? 269? 384?]

SCOTT, John (1783-1821): *A visit to Paris in 1814, being a review of the moral, political, intellectual, and social condition of the French capital,* Phila., 1815. [693]

SCOTT, *Sir* Walter, bart.: *Ivanhoe; a romance,* (2v.) [edition uncertain]. [260]

SCOTT, *Sir* Walter: *The lay of the last minstrel, a poem,* Boston, 1807. [264]

SCOTT, *Sir* Walter: *The monastery: a romance,* (2v.) [edition uncertain]. [272]

SCOTT, *Sir* Walter: *Rob Roy,* (2v.) New York (Eastburn & Co.), 1818. [159, 221, 230, 240]

SCOTT, *Sir* Walter: *Tales of my landlord;* collected and arranged by Jedediah Cleishbotham [*pseud.*], (1st ser., 2v.) Philadelphia, 1817; (2d ser., 2v.) Philadelphia, 1818; (3d ser., 2v.) [edition uncertain]; (4th ser., 3v.) [edition uncertain]. [75, 367, 523]

SCOTT, *Sir* Walter: *Waverley; or, 'Tis sixty years since,* (2v.) Boston, 1815. [248, 313]

SEDGWICK, Catharine Maria: *Redwood, a tale,* (2v.) New York, 1824. [430]

SEGUR, Alexandre Joseph Pierre, *vicomte* de: *Women: their condition and influence in society.* Tr. from the French, (3v.) London, 1803. [83]

SEVIGNE, Marie (de Rabutin Chantal) *marquise* de: *Letters from the Marchioness de Sévigné to her daughter, the Countess de Grignan,* (7v.) London, 1801. [14]

SHAKESPEARE, William: *The poems of Shakespeare, to which is added an account of his life,* (1st Am. ed.) Boston, 1807. [43]

SHELLEY, *Mrs.* Mary Wollstonecraft (Godwin): *Frankenstein, or The modern Prometheus,* (2v.) [edition uncertain]. [711, 712]

SHERER, Moyle: *The story of a life,* New York, 1825. [604]

SHERIDAN, Thomas: *Lectures on the art of reading.* (Pt. I: Art of reading prose; pt. II: Art of reading verse), (2d ed.) London, 1781. [519]

SHERLOCK, Thomas, *bp. of London: Sermons,* (4v.) London, 1769 (B.L.S.). [79?] (This listing is taken from the ptd. catalogues of the Boston Library Society. I cannot identify this work in any other library. The shelf-list of the B.L.S. seems to imply———what I, indeed, suspect———that this work is really the *Discourses,* (4v.) etc.)

SHERLOCK, Thomas: *Several discourses preached at the Temple Church,* London, 1756. [79?]

SHERLOCK, William, *dean of St. Pauls: A practical discourse concerning death,* (26th ed.) London, 1751. [79?]

SHERLOCK, William: *A practical discourse concerning a future judgment*, London, 1731. [79?]

SHERWOOD, *Mrs.* Mary Martha (Butt): *The works of Mrs. Sherwood*, (16v.) New York (Harper), 1834-1858. [616, 619]

SIMMS, William Gilmore: *The damsel of Darien*, (2v.) Philadelphia, 1839. [643]

SIMMS, William Gilmore: *Pelayo: a story of the Goth*, (1st ed., 2v.) N.Y., 1838. [694]

SIMOND, Louis: *Switzerland; or A journal of a tour and residence in that country (1817-1819)* [With sketch of customs of ancient and modern Helvetia], (2v.) Boston, 1822. [351, 428]

SIMONDE DE SISMONDI, Jean Charles Léonard: *De la littérature du midi de l'Europe*, (4v.) Paris, 1813. [278, 283, 322]

SIMONDE DE SISMONDI, Jean——: *Histoire des républiques italiennes du moyen âge*, (2° éd., 16v.) Paris, 1818. [306, 309, 316, 319, 325, 326]

SIMONDE DE SISMONDI, Jean——: *Historical view of the literature of the south of Europe*, (tr. Thomas Roscoe), (4v.) London, 1823. [491? 493?]

SMITH, Adam: *Essays on philosophical subjects* (with an account of his life and writings by Dugald Stewart), Dublin, 1795. [38]

SMITH, Adam: *The theory of moral sentiments. To which is added a dissertation on the origin of languages*, (3d ed.) London, 1767; (7th ed., 2v.) London & Edinburgh, 1792. [288]

SMITH, Adam: *The works of Adam Smith* (with acc't of his life etc. by Dugald Stewart), (5v.) London, 1812. [390, 395]

SMITH, *Mrs.* Elizabeth Elton: *The three eras of woman's life*, (2v.) N.Y., 1836. [608]

SMITH, Horatio: *The moneyed man, or The lesson of a life*, (2v.) Phila., 1841. [701]

SMITH, Horatio: *Tales of the early ages. By Horace Smith*, (2v.) N.Y. (Harper), 1832. [641]

SMITH, Horatio *and* James SMITH: *Rejected addresses, or The new theatrum poetarum*. Revised by the authors, Boston, 1840. [621]

SMITH, Richard Penn: *The forsaken, a novel by the author of Caius Marius*, (2v.) Philadelphia, 1831. [742]

SMOLLETT, Tobias: *Miscellaneous works. With memoirs of his life and writings by Robert Anderson*, (6v.) Philadelphia, 1812. [536]

SOUTHEY, *Mrs.* Caroline Anne (Bowles): *Chapters on churchyards*, N.Y., 1842. [752]

SOUTHEY, Robert: *Letters from England: by Don M. A. Espriella [pseud.]*, (1st Am. ed.) Boston, 1807. [44, 164, 174]

SOUTHEY, Robert: *Thalaba the destroyer. A rhythmical romance.* (2v.) London, 1801; (2v.) Boston, 1812. [487, 489, 594, 596]

SPARKS, Jared: *The life of Gouverneur Morris, with selections from his correspondence and miscellaneous papers*, (3v.) Boston, 1832. [528]

SPECIMENS OF FOREIGN STANDARD LITERATURE, ed. George Ripley, (14v.) Boston, 1838-1842. [747]

    Vol. 14: *Songs and ballads*, tr. from Uhland, Körner, Bürger, and other German lyric poets. With notes. By Charles Timothy Brooks, Boston, 1842.

SPECTATOR, The, [by Addison, Steele and others], (8v.) Edinburgh, 1766. [124, 129, 135, 157]

SPURZHEIM, Johann Gaspar: *Outlines of phrenology. Being also a manual of reference for the marked bust*, Boston, 1832. [550]

STAAL, Marguerite Jeanne de, *baroness*: *Mémoires de Madame de Staal. Ecrits par elle-même*, (3v.) Londres, 1767. [356, 443]

STAEL-HOLSTEIN, Anne Louise Germaine (Necker) *baronne* de: *Considerations on the principal events of the French revolution. Posthumous work.* Ed. by the Duke de Broglie and Baron de Stael, (2v.) New York, 1818. [434, 582]

STAEL-HOLSTEIN, Anne——: *Considérations sur les principaux événemens de la révolution françoise. Ouvrage posthume etc.* (2° éd., 3v.) Paris, 1818. [179, 352]

STAEL-HOLSTEIN, Anne——: *Corinna; or Italy*, (2v.) Boston, 1808. [687]

STAEL-HOLSTEIN, Anne——: *Corinne ou l'Italie*, (3v.) Paris, 1812. [195, 310, 339, 346]

STAEL-HOLSTEIN, Anne——: *De l'Allemagne*, (2° éd., 3v.) Paris, 1814. [311, 364]

STAEL-HOLSTEIN, Anne——: *Delphine*, (6v.) Paris, 1809. [198]

STAEL-HOLSTEIN, Anne————: *Delphine,* (tr. from the French), (3v.) Phila., 1836. [647, 722]

STAEL-HOLSTEIN, Anne————: *Letters on the writings and character of Jean Jacques Rousseau,* London, 1814. [67, 149]

STAEL-HOLSTEIN, Anne————: *Lettres sur les ouvrages et le caractère de J. J. Rousseau,* (2° éd.) Paris, 1798. [376]

STAEL-HOLSTEIN, Anne————: *Treatise on the influence of the passions.* (With sketch of her life by the translator), London, 1798. [4, 191]

STEPHENS, John Lloyd: *Incidents of travel in Egypt, Arabia, Petræa and the Holy Land.* By an American, (2v.) New York, 1837. [561]

STEWART, Dugald: *A general view of the progress of metaphysical, ethical, and political philosophy since the revival of letters in Europe. In two dissertations.* (2v.) Boston, [1817?]-1822.* [259, 337, 358]

STEWART, John: *Travels over the most interesting parts of the globe, to discover the source of moral motion; communicated to lead mankind through the conviction of the senses to intellectual existence. In the year of man's retrospective knowledge by astronomical calculation 5000.* (2v.) London (J. Ridgway), [1790?]. [101] Vol. 2 has the title: *The Apocalypse of Nature wherein the Source of Moral Motion is discovered, etc.*)

STURM, Christoph Christian: *Reflections on the works of God and of his providence, throughout all nature, for every day in the year.* (Tr. from German into French and from French into English), (3v.) Dublin, 1791. [10, 11, 270]

SULLY, Maximilien de Béthune, *duc de: Mémoires de Sully, principal ministre de Henri-le-Grand,* (nouv. éd., 6v.) Paris, 1814. [415, 417, 420]

SWIFT, Jonathan: *Gulliver's travels,* [edition uncertain]. [462]

T

TACITUS: *The life of Cnæus Julius Agricola,* Glasgow, 1763 (B.L.S.). [119]

TACITUS: *The works of Cornelius Tacitus, with an essay on his life and genius.* Tr. Arthur Murphy, (4v.) Dublin, 1794; (2v.) London, 1813. [3, 7, 165, 168, 426] (Listed in the B.L.S. ptd. catalogues as "The History of Rome.")

TASSO, Torquato: *Tasso's Jerusalem delivered, an heroic poem.* (Tr. John Higgs Hunt), (2v.) London, 1818. [598]

TAYLOR, Jeremy (1613-1667): *Discourses on various subjects,* (3v.) Boston, 1816. [148, 209, 218, 228, 236, 239]

TAYLOR, John (1781-1864): *The identity of Junius with a distinguished living character established.* Including the supplement, consisting of fac-similes, N.Y., 1818. [163]

TAYLOR, John————: *Sermons on different subjects, left for publication,* Walpole, N.H., 1806. [225]

TAYLOR, William: *Historic survey of German poetry, interspersed with various translations,* (3v.) London, 1830. [713, 750, 753]

TEIGNMOUTH, *Sir* John Shore, *Lord: Life of Sir William Jones,* Phila., 1805. [518?]

TEMPLE, *Sir* William: *Works* (with life of the author), (4v.) London, 1757. [460]

TERENTIUS: *Comedies, translated into familiar blank verse.* By George Colman, London, 1802. [55]

---

* The "Advertisement" before "Dissertation First" is dated 1817; that before "Dissertation First, Pt. II," is dated 1821. Only the *first* dissertation (in TWO parts) seems to have ever been published. References to the "second" dissertation, during the Nineteenth Century, apparently mean the second part of the *first*. Boston copies of this edition show a variety of combinations. The two-volume set at the Boston Athenæum, for example, is put together as follows: Vol. I: Stewart's *First Dissertation (Part I)* bound with Wm. Thos. Brande, *Dissertation Third, exhibiting a general view of Chemical Philosophy* etc. Vol. II: Stewart's *First Dissertation* (Part II). The shelf-list of the B.L.S. reveals, under the shelf numbers on the left, the following:

91.31	Metaphysical Ethical & Political Philosophy		Vol 1st by Dugald Stewart
	2nd by Playfair	8vo	2 [vols.]
34.26	Dugald Stewart's 2 Dissertation	8vo	2 [vols.]	Brande (Wm
	Thomas) 3 do.	8vo	1 [vol.]

The volume by Playfair was, doubtless, John Playfair's *Dissertation on the Progress of Mathematical and Physical Science,* published in Boston.

THUCYDIDES: *History of the Peloponnesian war* (tr. by William Smith, with additions of three preliminary discourses), (2v.) London, 1781. [250]

TIBULLUS, Albius: *Elégies de Tibulle* (tr. into French prose by Honoré, comte de Mirabeau, avec contes et nouvelles), (3v.) Paris, 1798. [173, 176]

TOOKE, Andrew: *The Pantheon, representing the fabulous histories of the heathen gods and illustrious heroes in a short, plain, and familiar method*, London, 1787. [114, 118]

TOOKE, John Horne: Επεα πτεροεντα. *Or, The diversions of Purley*, (1st Am. ed., 2v.) Philadelphia, 1806-1807. [461]

TOWNSHEND, Chauncy Hare: *Facts in mesmerism, with reasons for a dispassionate inquiry into it*, New York, 1843. [765]

TRESSAN, Louis Elisabeth de la Vergne, *comte* de: *Œuvres choisies de comte de Tressan*, (12v.) [Paris, 1787-1791]. [183]

TRIMMER, *Mrs.* Sarah (Kirby): *Sacred history, selected from the scriptures with annotations etc., calculated to facilitate study of Holy Scripture in schools and families*, (6v.) Gloucester, 1788. [19, 121]

TROLLOPE, *Mrs.* Frances (Milton): *The life and adventures of Michael Armstrong, the factory boy*, (2v.) New York, 1840. [720]

TUCKER, Abraham: *An abridgment of the Light of nature pursued*, London, 1807. [5, 45]

TUCKERMAN, Henry Theodore: *Isabel, or Sicily. A pilgrimage*, Phila., 1839. [682]

TURNER, Sharon: *The history of the Anglo-Saxons from their first appearance above the Elbe to the Norman conquest*, (4v.) London, 1802-1805. [347]

TWO PILGRIMS, The: a romance. [Anonymous], (2v.) London, 1805. [36]

TYTLER, Alexander Fraser: *Considerations on the present political state of India*, (2v.) London, 1816. [171]

V

VELDE, Karl Franz van der: *Tales from the German by Nathaniel Greene*, (2v.) Boston, 1837. [658]

VOLTAIRE, François Marie Arouet de: *Théâtre*, (9v.) Paris, 1809. [369, 751]

W

WAKEFIELD, *Mrs.* Priscilla (Bell): *Mental improvement: or The beauties and wonders of nature and art in a series of instructive conversations*, (1st Am. ed.) New-Bedford, 1799. [8, 142]

WALPOLE, Horace, *earl of Orford*: *Private correspondence of Horace Walpole. Now first collected*. (4v.) London, 1820. [527]

WALPOLE, Horace————: *Reminiscences, written in 1788, for the amusement of Miss Mary and Miss Agnes B***y* [with letters and Walpoliana], Boston, 1820. [532]

WARBURTON, William, *bp. of Gloucester*: *Works, with life etc.* by Richard Hurd, (12v.) London, 1811. [303]

WARD, Robert Plumer: *De Vere, or The man of independence*, (2v.) N.Y., 1831. [610]

WARD, Robert Plumer: *Fielding, or Society; Atticus, or The retired statesman; St. Lawrence*, (3v.) Philadelphia, 1837. [688]

WARDLAW, Ralph: *Discourses on the principal points of the Socinian controversy*, Boston, 1816 (B.L.S.). [90]

WARDLAW, Ralph: *Unitarianism incapable of vindication: a reply to James Yates's "Vindication of Unitarianism,"* Boston, 1816 (B.L.S.). [139]

WARREN, Samuel: *Affecting scenes; being passages from the diary of a physician*, (2v.) New York, 1831. [552]

WARTON, Thomas: *The history of English poetry*, ed. Richard Price, (4v.) London, 1824. [423]

WATTS, Isaac: *The improvement of the mind, or A supplement to the act of logic*, London, 1792. [144]

WATTS, Isaac: *Sermons on various subjects, divine and moral*, London, 1740. [254]

WHITE, Joshua E.: *Letters on England: comprising descriptive scenes, with remarks on the state of society, domestic economy, habits of the people etc.*, (2v.) Phila., 1816. [93]

WILCOCKS, Joseph (1723-1791): *Roman conversations; or A short description of the antiquities of Rome; interspersed with characters of eminent Romans, and reflections religious and moral*, (1st ed., 2v.) London, 1792. [82]

WILHELMINE, *consort of Frederick William, margrave of Beyreuth: Mémoires de Frédérique Sophie Wilhelmine de Prusse, margrave de Bareith*, (2v.) Paris, 1813 (B.L.S.) [684]

WILLIAMS, D. E.: *Life and correspondence of Sir Thomas Lawrence, kt.*, (2v.) London, 1831. [531]

WILLIAMS, Robert Folkestone: *Mephistephiles in England; or the confessions of a prime minister*, (2v.) New York, 1835. [629]

WILSON, John (1785-1854): *The city of the plague, and other poems*, Edinburgh, 1816. [403]

WINTHROP, John (1588-1649): *A journal of the transactions and occurrences in the settlement of Massachusetts and the other New-England colonies from 1630-1644*, Hartford, 1790. [454?]

WINTHROP, John (1714-1779): *Two lectures on comets. Also an essay on comets by A. Oliver Jr.*, Boston, 1811. [454?]

WIRT, William *et al.: The old bachelor* [Thirty-nine essays reprinted from the *Richmond Enquirer*, written by Wm. Wirt, Dabney Carr, St. George Tucker and others, modelled after those of the *Spectator*. Some signed with fictitious names], (2v.) Baltimore, [1818]. [213]

WOOLRYCH, Humphry William: *The life of Sir Edward Coke*, London, 1826. [438]

WORDSWORTH, William: *Poems by William Wordsworth, including Lyrical Ballads and the miscellaneous pieces of the author, with add'l poems, a new preface, and a supplementary essay*, (2v.) London, 1815. [199]

X

XENOPHON: *Xenophon's Memoirs of Socrates; with the Defence of Socrates before his judges*, tr. Sarah Fielding, (3d ed.) London, 1788. [469, 475]

Y

YATES, James: *A vindication of Unitarianism, in reply to Mr. Wardlaw's discourses of the Socinian controversy*, Boston, 1816. [137]

ADDITIONS TO THE CENSUS*

(A Census of Extant Copies of the First Edition of Emerson's *Nature*, Boston, 1836.)

FIRST ISSUE   (Page 94 misnumbered 92)

No.	Binding	Color	Page Length	Marginalia	Inscriptions or Original Owners
F28	CR	Chocolate brown	7⅝	(p)	"Geo: Forbes"
F29	CR	Medium brown	7⅝	(p)	"Rev. N. L. Frothingham with the respects of R. W. Emerson"
F30	DR	Brown	7⅝		"Rev. Dr. Walker with Respects of the Author"
F31	A	Green	7⅝	(p) (e?) (m)	
F32	B	Light brown	7⅝	(m) (n)	Bookplate: Library of W. H. Robinson "Wm. H. Robinson" "From Prof. C. F. Hudson's Library"
F33	A	Greenish blue	7 7/16		"D. MacGregor"
F34	AQ	Dull brown	7⅝	(m) (p)	"Miss M. M. Emerson from her affectionate nephew, R. W. E."
F35	?	Green			Inscribed to "W. Burton."

* For a complete description of twenty-seven copies of the "first issue" and thirty copies of the "second issue," see *Nature (1836)* by R. W. Emerson, ed. with introd., index-concordance and bibliographical appendices by Kenneth Walter Cameron, N. Y., 1940, pp. xvii—xxvi. Abbreviations used in the tables include:

(var.) Variation in spine of the binding.

(rbd) Copy has been rebound.

(m) Marginal notes, corrections, comments, or scoring of passages by previous owners.

(let.) Contains an Emerson letter.

(p) Page 32, line 9, is corrected by a caret before "facts"; "Spiritual" is written usually in the margin. In line 10, the "s" of "Spirits" is crossed out.

(e) Emerson's handwriting.

(n) Not in Emerson's hand.

Corrections and additions to this census should be sent to Kenneth W. Cameron, c/o State College of the University of North Carolina, Raleigh, N. C.

SECOND ISSUE (All pages correctly numbered)

No.	Binding	Color	Page Length	Marginalia	Inscriptions or Original Owners
S31	DR	Light blue	7½	(p) (e?) (m)	"H. B. Townsend / Oct. 22, 1836." Bookplate of Francis Wilson.
S32	GQ	Brown	7⅜	?	"A. C. Spooner, May 11th, 1837." Bookplate of Arlo Bates
S33	DR	Brick	7½	?	"H. W. W / Henry W. Wellington." "H. W. Wellington, 1836"
S34	(rbd)			(m)	[No fly-leaf; many notes.]
S35	KT	Light brown	7		
S36	IQ	Chocolate brown	7⅜		"W. Hinman" "M. Morris"
S37	JS	Dark brown or black	7¼		
S38	DR	Blue-green	7½	(p)	
S39	(rbd)		7½		[Rebound by Zaehnsdorf.] "234" at foot of page [3].
S40	I	Light brown	7⅜	(p) (e?) (m)	"Mary Russell from her friend R. W. E. Concord / Nov. 1841." "To Ellen [?Waters?]"
S41	DR	Dark brown	7½	(p) (e?)	"Presented by Jas. B. Congdon Esq."
S42	?	Black	?	?	"C. M. Fitch"
S43	?	?	?	?	[Signature of Nathaniel Hawthorne on title page]

UNIDENTIFIED (Issue unknown. Location of copy uncertain. Data wanted.)

U 1	Reddish brown	Presentation inscription of Wendell Phillips followed by the signature of B. Green.
U 2	?	Inscribed by R. W. Emerson to J. F. Clarke
U 3	Maroon cloth	"To William Allen from his friend and classmate D. H. Thoreau . . . June 25th '37."

NAMES MENTIONED IN INSCRIPTIONS AND BOOKPLATES

ADAMS, Sarah H.	F1	HINMAN, W.	S36
ALLEN, William	U3	HUDSON, Prof. C. F.	F32
ARNIM, Bettina von	F1	LOWELL, John Jr.	F7
BARRETT, James	S24	MacGREGOR, D.	F33
BARTLETT, Robert	S2	MORRIS, M.	S36
BATES, Arlo	S32	MUNROE, William	S3
BEARD, J. R.	F23	NEWTON, W. T.	S4
BETTINA VON ARNIM	F1	PALMER, George Herbert	S7, S11
BOWEN, Francis	F22	PERKINS, L. H.	S25
BROS[MAN?], Emma T.	F16	PHILLIPS, Wendell	U1
BURTON, W[arren]	F35	ROBINSON, William H.	F32
CARLYLE, Thomas	F10	RODMAN, Thomas P.	F4
CARR, William	S25	RUSSELL, Mary	S40
CLARKE, James Freeman	U2	S., C.	F21
COFFIN, Miss Ann E.	F12	SALISBURY, Mrs. Stephen	S6
CONGDON, James B.	S41	SAMPSON, Ira	S10
DANA, Dr. Charles L.	S24	SHEPARD, Mary	F13
DANA, Henry Swan	S24	SILSBEE, M. C.	S5
DURFEE, Samuel Slater	S17	SPOONER, A. C.	S32
EGAN, James	F6	STARRETT, Vincent	F15
EMERSON, Mary Moody	F34	STEDMAN, ?	S28
EMERTON, R. W.	S19	T., J. F.	F21
FITCH, C. M.	S42	THAYER, The Misses	S8
FORBES, George	F28	THOREAU, Henry David	S12, U3
FROTHINGHAM, Rev. Nathaniel L.	F29	TOTMAN, Stark	S28
FULLER, Margaret	F1	TOWNSEND, H. B.	S31
GREEN, B[eriah]	U1	VERY, Jones	F19
GRIMM, Herman	F1	WALKER, Rev. Dr. [James]	F30
HASKINS, Miss Elizabeth	F13	WARE, Henry Jr.	F23
HASTY PUDDING CLUB	F8	[WATERS?], Ellen	S40
HAWTHORNE, Nathaniel	S43	WELLINGTON, Henry W.	S33
HAYES, E. W.	F15	WILLIAMS, J. M.	F2
HIGGINSON, Thos. Wentworth	S2	WILSON, Francis	S31

OWNERS OF THE COPIES LISTED IN THE TABLES[1]

Andover-Harvard Theological Library	Harvard Divinity School, Cambridge, Mass.	F30, F31, S37
Barrow, Mrs. James S.[2]	2050 Third Avenue North, Napa, California.	F34
Bennett, Whitman	41 West 57th Street, New York City, N. Y.	F33
Conger, George P.	University of Minnesota, Minneapolis, Minn.	S33
Goodspeed's Book Shop	18 Beacon Street, Boston, Mass.	S32
Lehigh University Library	Bethlehem, Pa.	S31
Massachusetts Historical Society	1154 Boylston Street, Boston, Mass.	F29
Mayers, Arthur	c/o The Mayers Company, 1240 South Main Street, Los Angeles, Cal.	F32
New Bedford Free Public Library	New Bedford, Mass.	S41
New York Public Library (H. W. and A. A. Berg Coll'n)	Fifth Avenue at 42nd Street, New York City, N. Y.	S40
New York State Library	University of the State of N. Y., Albany, N. Y.	S38, S39
Scribner Bookstore	597 Fifth Avenue, New York City, N. Y.	S35, S36
University of Illinois Library	Urbana, Illinois.	S34
Wallace, Mrs. J. B.	Canaan Street, Canaan, N. H.	F28

---

[1] All owners are not known, many of the listings having been taken from *Book Prices Current* and other auction catalogues.

[2] Among Mrs. Barrow's other holdings are:

(a) Emerson's *Poems*, Boston, 1847.
"Hannah U. Parsons with the affectionate regards of her Cousin R. W. E."
(b) Stael-Holstein's *Influence of Literature upon Society* (1813), vol. II.
(c) Stael-Holstein's *Germany* (1814).
"Mary Moody Emerson, 1830. Will Rev. R. Waldo Emerson accept this old book in token of the gratitude and affection of one whose oddities are past, whose affections yet live and may be conscious of their earthly objects."
(d) Letter of William Emerson, Oct. 7, 1793. (Printed *supra*.)
(e) Letter of Ralph Waldo Emerson, Feb. 24, 1834. (Printed *supra*.)
(f) Letter of Ellen T. Emerson to "Cousin Hannah" Parsons, Concord, 6 Feb. 1888.

BOOKS THOREAU BORROWED FROM HARVARD COLLEGE LIBRARY

The energy of American scholarship has not yet been turned fully upon Thoreau largely, perhaps, because so much yet remains to be done with Emerson, but a decade or two hence one may expect to find the works of the hermit of Walden investigated by careful editors, and his reading scrutinized for its many influences upon his writing and character. Signs of an awakening are evident in Professor Adams' monograph on Thoreau's choice of books through 1841,[1] and in Professor Utley's portrayal of Thoreau's study methods as demonstrated in the use of Columella.[2] As far as I have been able to determine, however, apart from the evidence in Utley's paper scholars have either neglected the bibliographical help which the Harvard College charging lists provide or considered the records too difficult to be quickly or easily analyzed in an investigation of limited scope. That such an aid cannot be long ignored will become increasingly apparent as the field attracts more students, and in publishing it now I hope to help those now distant from Boston and those who later may work intensively in the Concord group. To include such records in a volume on Emerson is not undesirable. Lines of research in the works of both Americans tend to converge at so many points that it is wise, especially in matters of bibliography, to recognize the interrelations.

Besides examining the published writings for clues to literary and philosophical influences, the future editor will quickly turn to the inventory which Thoreau made of his library in 1840, the original manuscript of which is now preserved in the Henry E. Huntington Library.[3] It was transcribed and printed, but not thoroughly edited, by F. B. Sanborn in 1917,[4] and must later be rehandled before it can be made permanently useful as a work of reference. Next in importance should be the Harvard charging lists, which appear in the following pages. I have discussed elsewhere the condition of the manuscripts in the university archives and mentioned the tools with which one must work in unraveling the tangled and abbreviated entries.[5] With one's equipment must go a measure of Job's patience, for the difficulties often appear insuperable. The fact that the set of Harvard Library shelf lists is incomplete (especially as regards a shelving system employing such designations as "A.4.3" and "B.3.1") has been especially troublesome in the present research and accounts for a few gaps, fortunately not serious. The record here is rich and interesting, and will speak for itself. It is, perhaps, superfluous to say that the books which Harvard

---

[1] See Raymond Adams, "Thoreau's Literary Apprenticeship," *S P*, XXIX (1932), 617-629.

[2] See Francis L. Utley, "Thoreau and Columella: A Study in Reading Habits," *N E Q*, XI (1938), 171-180. See also Arthur Christy, "A Thoreau Fact-Book," *Colophon*, part XVI (March, 1934).

[3] Listed under "HM 945" as *Index Rerum*, a signed holograph manuscript of thirty-eight leaves.

[4] See Franklin B. Sanborn, *The Life of Henry David Thoreau*, Boston & N.Y., 1917, pp. 505 *et seq.*

[5] See Cameron, *Emerson's Reading*, pp. 12-13.

furnished Thoreau between 1849 and 1860 helped him to keep his heart "in the Highlands"——of Canada, England, Wales and Switzerland——to name only a few countries in which his mind chose to wander, and that as he roamed thither as on by-paths, he always arrived in the end at a satisfying rediscovery of his own beloved Concord.

1 8 3 3[1]

Sept. 3	(1)	Butler, *The life of Erasmus, with historical remarks*	....
Sept. 11	(2)	Hall, *Travels in Canada and the U. S. in 1816 and 1817*	....
Sept. 18	(3)	Banks, *History of the life and reign of Peter the Great*	....
Sept. 18	(4)	Marmontel, *Moral tales, translated from the French* (1)	....
Sept. 25	(5)	Cox, *Adventures on the Columbia River ... among Indians*	....
Sept. 25	(6)	McKenney, *Sketches of a tour to the Lakes*	....
Oct. 2	(7)	"France" "2.4.7" [unidentified] (1,2)[2]	....

1 8 3 4

Jan. 8	(8)	Irving, *Life and voyages of Christopher Columbus* (1,2,3,4)	....
Jan. 22	(9)	Irving, *Companions of Columbus*[3]	....
Jan. 29	(10)	Harwood, *Grecian antiquities: An account of the Greeks*[4]	....
Feb. 5	(11)	Fisk, *Greek exercises, containing substance of syntax*	....
Feb. 12	(12)	Irving, *Chronicle of Conquest of Grenada* (1,2)	....
Feb. 12	(13)	Cleveland, *An epitome of Grecian antiquities*	....
Feb. 19	(14)	Child, *Hobomok, a tale* [and] *The Rebels*	....
Mar. 5	(15)	Barney, *Biographical memoir of Com. Joshua Barney*	....
Mar. 5	(16)	Cochrane, *Journal of residence and travels in Columbia* (1)	....
Mar. 12	(17)	al-Asma'i, *Antar, a Bedoueen romance* (Part I) (1,2,3)	....
Mar. 19	(18)	Bullock, *Six months' residence and travels in Mexico* (2)	....
Mar. 26	(19)	Gray, *The vestal, or A tale of Pompeii*	....
Apr. 23	(20)	Knox, *Elegant extracts, or useful ... pieces of poetry* (1)	....
Apr. 23	(21)	"Lewis & Clapperton" "10.1.4"[5] [unidentified] (1)	....
Apr. 30	(22)	Wilson, *Memoirs of life and times of Daniel De Foe* (1)	....
Apr. 30	(23)	Goldsmith, *History of England (with continuation)* (1,2)	....
May 7	(24)	Sigourney, [? *Traits of the aborigines of America*]	....
May 28	(25)	Mills, *History of the crusades for the ... Holy Land* (1)	....
June 10	(26)	Marshall, *History of the colonies ... of North America*	....
Sept. 16	(27)	Bailey, *Essays on formation and publication of opinions*	....
Sept. 16	(28)	Grimani, *New and improved grammar of Italian language*	....
Sept. 30	(29)	Barrow, *A voyage to Cochinchina in 1792 and 1793*	....

----

[1] See first footnote to the list of Emerson's reading for an introduction to editorial method.

[2] The margin reads: "C. S. Wheeler for Thoreau."

[3] In the margin: "A. G. Peabody for Thoreau."

[4] In the margin: "A. G. Peabody."

[5] I surmise that the volume referred to consisted of a work by Meriwether Lewis and another by Hugh Clapperton, though I have no positive evidence. Clapperton published his *Journal of a second expedition into the interior of Africa* in London, 1829.

Sept. 30   (30)   Waddington, *Journal of visit to parts of Ethiopia*   ....
Oct.   7   (31)   *Treasury of knowledge and library of reference* (1,2)   ....
Oct. 14   (32)   Metastasio, *Dramas and other poems* (tr. Hoole) (1)   ....
Oct. 14   (33)   Southey, "A.13.6" or "A.15.6"[6] (15)   ....
Oct. 21   (34)   Rollin, *Ancient history of the Egyptians* (1)   ....
Oct. 28   (35)   Hederich, *Lexicon manuale Graecum*   ....
Nov. 11   (36)   Morrell (Mrs. Abby *or* Benjamin ?), *Narrative*   ....
Nov. 11   (37)   Wines, *Two years and a half in the navy* (1)   ....

1 8 3 5

Jan. 13   (38)   Dumont, *Recollections of Mirabeau*   ....
Jan. 13   (39)   Ranking, *Historical researches on . . . Peru, Mexico etc.*   ....
Jan. 20   (40)   Racine, *Œuvres* (1,2)   ....
Feb. 10   (41)   Euripides, *Alcestis* (Wagner); *Ion* (Hülsemann)   ....
Feb. 17   (42)   Burgh, *The dignity of human nature etc.* (2)   ....
Feb. 24   (43)   Langtoft, *Chronicle . . . improv'd by Robert of Brunne* (1)   ....
Mar.   3   (44)   Goldsmith, *Miscellaneous works* (3)   ....
Mar. 17   (45)   *Edinburgh review* (35,48)   ....
Apr. 21   (46)   Shakespeare, *The Plays of William Shakespeare* (1,3,4)   ....
May   5   (47)   Godwin, *Life of Geoffrey Chaucer* (1,2)   ....
June   9   (48)   Scapula, *Lexicon Græco-Latinum*   ....
June 16   (49)   Peirce, *A history of Harvard University*   ....
Sept.   3   (50)   Rollin, *Ancient history of the Egyptians* (1 + Atlas)   ....
Sept.   3   (51)   Homerus, *Ilias cum brevi annotatione* (Heyne) (1)   ....
Sept.   3   (52)   Chaucer, *The Canterbury tales of Chaucer* (1,2,5)   ....
Sept. 17   (53)   Tucker, *The light of nature pursued* (2)   ....
Sept. 28   (54)   Wilson, *American ornithology* (5)[7]   ....
Oct.   5   (55)   Grimani, *New and improved grammar of Italian language*   ....
Oct. 29   (56)   Rollin, *Ancient history of the Egyptians* (3)   ....
Nov.   5   (57)   Rollin, *Ancient history of the Egyptians* (4,5,6,7,8)   ....

1 8 3 6

Apr. 28   (58)   Metastasio, *Dramas and other poems* (tr. Hoole) (1)   ....
Apr. 28   (59)   Chateaubriand, *Œuvres complètes* (6)   ....
Apr. 28   (60)   Homerus, *The Iliads and Odysses* (tr. Tho. Hobbes)   ....
May   5   (61)   Chateaubriand, *Œuvres complètes* (7)   ....
Sept.   5   (62)   Anville, [*Complete body of ancient geography*][8]   ....
Sept.   5   (63)   Schlegel, *Lectures on the history of literature* (1)   ....
Sept.   5   (64)   Peirce, *A history of Harvard University*   ....
Sept. 15   (65)   Coleridge, *Introductions to Greek classic poets* (Pt.I)   ....
Oct.   3   (66)   Schlegel, *Lectures on the history of literature* (2)   ....
Oct. 13   (67)   *North American Review* (9)   ....

---

[6] Apparently the Harvard Library had its own arrangement for the miscellaneous volumes of Robert Southey's poetry and prose. I have been unable to discover it.

[7] Margin reads: "Stearns."

[8] The shelf-list calls it: "Atlas of Ancient Geography." See "Rollin" in the Bibliography for another possibility.

Oct. 27 (68) Milton, *Poetical works of John Milton* (ed. Todd) (1,5,6)   ....
Oct. 27 (69) "Notes on Milton" "B.11.5" [unidentified]   ....
Nov. 10 (70) Cowper, *Works* (3)   ....
Dec. 5 (71) Milton, *The prose works of John Milton* (Symmons) (7)   ....

1 8 3 7

Jan. 9 (72) [Chalmers, *The works of the*] *English poets* (3)   ....
Jan. 9 (73) Bailey, *Essays on formation and publication of opinions*   ....
Jan. 12 (74) Cox, *Adventures on the Columbia River . . . among Indians*   ....
Jan. 16 (75) Brackenridge, *Journal of voyage up the river Missouri*   ....
Jan. 19 (76) Brosses, *Terra australis cognita: or Voyages* (1)   ....
Jan. 25 (77) Goldsmith, *The Roman history* (2)   ....
Jan. 30 (78) *The Gentleman's magazine* (n.s.,5)   ....
Feb. 6 (79) Milton, *Poetical works of John Milton* (ed. Todd) (5)   ....
Feb. 9 (80) Milton, *The prose works of John Milton* (Symmons) (7)   ....
Feb. 20 (81) Audubon, *Ornithological biography* (1,2,3)   ....
Mar. 9 (82) Campbell, *Specimens of the British poets* (1)   ....
Mar. 13 (83) [Chalmers, *The works of the*] *English poets* (1)   ....
Mar. 23 (84) Hazlitt, *Lectures on the English poets*   ....
Mar. 23 (85) Burke, *Philosophical enquiry into . . . sublime and beautiful*   ....
Mar. 30 (86) Say, *Poems . . . and two critical essays*   ....
Mar. 30 (87) Johnson, *Lives of the most eminent English poets* (1)   ....
Apr. 24 (88) Back, *Narrative of the Arctic land expedition*   ....
Apr. 24 (89) Gray, *Poems of Mr. Gray* (ed. Mason) (1,2,3,4)   ....
Apr. 27 (90) Milton, [*Complete collection* (Toland) or *Works* (Birch)] (1)   ....
Apr. 27 (91) Constant de Rebecque, *De la religion* (1)   ....
May 18 (92) Smith, *Introd. to physiological and systematical botany*   ....
May 25 (93) Ritson, *Robin Hood: a collection* (1)   ....
June 1 (94) Constant de Rebecque, *De la religion* (2,3)   ....
June 22 (95) Conybeare, *Illustrations of Anglo-Saxon poetry*   ....
June 22 (96) Bosworth, *Elements of Anglo-Saxon grammar*   ....
June 26 (97) Sibbald, *Chronicle of Scottish poetry* (2)   ....
June 26 (98) Nepos, *Vitæ excellentium imperatorum* (Clarke)   ....

1 8 4 1

Nov. 29 (99) *Poetical Tracts* [A miscellaneous collection]   ....
Nov. 29 (100) Turner, *History of the Anglo-Saxons*   ....
Nov. 29 (101) Conybeare, *Illustrations of Anglo-Saxon poetry*   ....
Nov. 29 (102) Chalmers, *The works of the English poets* (21)   ....
Nov. 30 (103) Warton, *The history of English poetry* (1,2,3,4)   ....
Nov. 30 (104) Chaucer, *The Canterbury tales of Chaucer* (1)   ....
Dec. 1 (105) Brand, *Observations on popular antiquities* (1,2)   ....
Dec. 1 (106) Hoccleve, *Poems never before printed*   ....
Dec. 1 (107) Brooke, *Certaine learned and elegant workes* (1633)   ....
Dec. 2 (108) Evans, *Old ballads, historical and narrative* (1,2,3,4)   ....
Dec. 2 (109) Headley, *Select beauties of ancient English poetry* (1,2)   ....
Dec. 6 (110) Chalmers, *The works of the English poets* (2,4)   ....

Dec. 6	(111)	Ritson, *Ancient English metrical romances* (1,2,3)	. . . .
Dec. 7	(112)	Hartshorne, *Ancient metrical tales*	. . . .
Dec. 7	(113)	Park, *Helconia; poetry of the Elizabethan age* (2)	. . . .
Dec. 8	(114)	Edwards, *The paradise of dainty devices*	. . . .
Dec. 8	(115)	Jamieson, *Popular ballads and songs* (1,2)	. . . .
Dec. 8	(116)	Carew, *Selection from poetical works of Thos. Carew*	. . . .
Dec. 8	(117)	James I., *The works of James I, king of Scotland*	. . . .
Dec. 9	(118)	Keach, *The glorious lover: a divine poem*	. . . .
Dec. 9	(119)	Bendlowes, *Theophila, or Loves sacrifice*	. . . .
Dec. 10	(120)	Raleigh, *The works of Sir Walter Raleigh kt.* (8)	. . . .
Dec. 10	(121)	Sidney, *The works of . . . in prose and verse* (1,2,3)	. . . .
Dec. 10	(122)	Sibbald, *Chronicle of Scottish poetry* (1,2,3,4)	. . . .

1849

Sept. 11	(123)	Mahābhārata, *Harwansa, ou Histoire de la famille* (1,2)	. . . .
Sept. 11	(124)	Garcin de Tassy, *Histoire de la littérature hindoui*	. . . .
Nov. 5	(125)	Pratt, *History of Eastham, Wellfleet and Orleans*	. . . .
Nov. 5	(126)	Rafn *et al.*, [Six tracts]*	. . . .
Nov. 5	(127)	Massachusetts Historical Society, *Collections* (? ser., 3)	. . . .

1850

Jan. 28	(128)	Visnu-Purana, *The Vishnu Purána* (tr. Wilson)	. . . .
Jan. 28	(129)	Içvara Krsna, *The Sánkhya Káriká, or Memorial verses*	. . . .
Jan. 28	(130)	Jones, *Works, with life of the author by Teignmouth* (9)	. . . .
Apr. 26	(131)	*Sama Veda. Translation of the Sanhita* (Stevenson)	. . . .
Apr. 26	(132)	Ramamohana Rāya, *Trans. of . . . passages . . . of the Veds*	. . . .
Apr. 26	(133)	Galbraith, *Mathematical and astronomical tables*	. . . .
Oct. 28	(134)	Champlain, *Voyages de la Nouvelle France (1603-1629)*	. . . .
Oct. 28	(135)	*Voyages de decouverte au Canada* (par Quartier *et al.*)	. . . .
Nov. 18	(136)	Champlain, *Voyages du sieur de Champlain* (1613)	. . . .
Nov. 18	(137)	Lescarbot, *Histoire de la Nouvelle-France* (1,2)	. . . .
Dec. 27	(138)	Champlain, *Voyages de la Nouvelle France (1603-1629)*	. . . .

1851

Jan. 14	(139)	Laet, *Novus orbis, seu Descriptionis Indiæ Occidentalis*	. . . .
Jan. 14	(140)	Michaux, *The North American sylva* (1)	. . . .
Jan. 14	(141)	Josselyn, *New Englands rarities discovered*	. . . .
Jan. 27	(142)	Young, *Chronicles of the Pilgrim fathers*	. . . .
Feb. 10	(143)	Hawkins, *Plan of the city of Quebec etc.*	. . . .
Feb. 10	(144)	Silliman, *Short tour between Hartford and Quebec*	. . . .
Apr. 30	(145)	Bigelow, *American medical botany* (1,2,3,4,5,6)	. . . .
Apr. 30	(146)	Michaux, *The North American sylva* (2,3)	. . . .
June 2	(147)	Michaux, *Voyage à l'ouest des monts Alléghanys*	. . . .

---

* The charging list reads: "Rafn, Amer. discov^d by Northmen   AR17". See bibliography. The title, "Six Tracts," is taken from the shelf-list.

Aug. 11   (148)   New York Historical Society, *Collections of . . .* (II.1)   ....

Aug. 11   (149)   Kalm, *Travels in North America* (1,2,3)   ....

Nov. 5   (150)   Stöver, *The life of Sir Charles Linnæus*   ....

Nov. 5   (151)   Charlevoix, *Histoire etc. de la Nouvelle France* (1,2,3)   ....

Nov. 5   (152)   Pulteney, *Gen'l view of the writings of Linnæus*   ....

1 8 5 2

Feb. 2   (153)   Linné, *Caroli Linnæi . . . Philosophia botanica*   ....

Feb. 2   (154)   Lahontan, *Voyages du baron de La Hontan*   ....

Mar. 16   (155)   Acharius, *Methodus qua omnes detectos lichenes*

Mar. 16   (156)   Talbot, *Five years' residence in the Canadas* (1,2)

Mar. 22   (157)   Gilpin, *Remarks on forest scenery* (1,2)   ....

Mar. 24   (158)   Richardson, *Fauna boreali-americana*   ....

May 24   (159)   Gilpin, *Observations . . . Cambridge, Norfolk, Suffolk* &c.

May 24   (160)   Gilpin, *Observations on the river Wye . . . South Wales* &c.   ....

May 24   (161)   Linné, *Caroli Linnæi . . . Amoenitates academicae* (2)   ....

July 26   (162)   Gilpin, *Observations . . . Cumberland and Westmoreland* (1,2) ....

July 26   (163)   Gilpin, *Observations . . . High-lands of Scotland* (1,2)   ....

Oct. 5   (164)   Gilpin, *Observations on western parts of England*   ....

Oct. 5   (165)   *Jesuit Relation* for 1633   ....

Oct. 5   (166)   *Jesuit Relation* for 1634   ....

Nov. 11   (167)   *Jesuit Relation* for 1635 and 1636   ....

Dec. 30   (168)   *Jesuit Relation* for 1637 and 1638   ....

1 8 5 3

Feb. 9   (169)   Smith, *Generall historie of Virginia, New-England etc.*   ....

Feb. 9   (170)   Bry, *Collectiones peregrinationum in Indiam Occident.*   ....

Feb. 9   (171)   *Jesuit Relation* for 1640   ....

Nov. 28   (172)   Gilpin, *Observations . . . Hampshire, Sussex and Kent*   ....

Nov. 28   (173)   Gilpin, *Three essays: On picturesque beauty etc.*   ....

Nov. 28   (174)   *Jesuit Relation* for 1640-1641, and for 1642   ....

1 8 5 4

Jan. 19   (175)   Price, *Essays on the picturesque etc.* (1)   ....

Jan. 19   (176)   McCulloh, *Researches on America . . . the aborigines*   ....

Jan. 19   (177)   Josselyn, *Account of two voyages to New-England*   ....

Mar. 13   (178)   Agassiz, *Études sur les glaciers* (with atlas)   ....

Mar. 13   (179)   Johnson, *A history of New-England*   ....

Mar. 13   (180)   Shepard, *The clear sun-shine of the gospel breaking*   ....

May 9   (181)   Heckewelder, *Narrative of the mission of United Brethren*   ....

May 9   (182)   Chambers, *Ancient sea-margins as memorials of changes*   ....

May 9   (183)   Tanner, *Narrative of captivity and adventures*

Oct. 9   (184)   *Bhagvat-geeta, or Dialogues of Kreeshna and Arjoon*   ....

Oct. 25   (185)   Visnu-Purana, *The Vishnu Puràna* (tr. Wilson)   ....

Dec. 7   (186)   Hunter, *Memoirs of a captivity among the Indians*   ....

Dec. 7   (187)   Colden, *History of the five Indian nations of Canada*   ....

Dec. 7   (188)   *Jesuit Relation* for 1639   ....

Dec. 7 (189) Schoolcraft, *Information respecting ... Indian tribes* (4) . . . .
Dec. 25 (190) Wood, *New-England's prospect; being a ... description* . . . .
Dec. 25 (191) Sagard-Théodat, *Le grand voyage du pays des Hurons* . . . .

1 8 5 5

Jan. 16 (192) Bewick, *History of British birds* . . . .
Jan. 16 (193) Sagard-Théodat, *Histoire du Canada* . . . .
Sept. 4 (194) Champlain, *Voyages de la Nouvelle France (1603-1629)* . . . .
Sept. 4 (195) Champlain, *Voyages du sieur de Champlain* (1613) . . . .
Sept. 4 (196) Sophocles, *The Antigone in Greek and English* . . . .
Sept. 17 (197) Biddle, *A memoir of Sebastian Cabot* . . . .
Sept. 17 (198) Am. Philos. Soc., *Transac. of the hist. and lit. Comm.* . . . .
Dec. 10 (199) Adair, *The history of the American Indians* . . . .
Dec. 10 (200) Loskiel, *History of the mission of the United Brethren* . . . .
Dec. 10 (201) Post, *The journal of Christian Frederick Post*[1] . . . .

1 8 5 6

Mar. 4 (202) Columella, *Husbandry ... and his Book concerning trees* . . . .
Mar. 4 (203) Barton, Burder and Edwards [On Indians][2] . . . .
Mar. 4 (204) Cusick, *David Cusick's sketches of ancient history* . . . .
Mar. 26 (205) *Jesuit Relation* for 1639; for 1642-1643 . . . .
Mar. 26 (206) Bartram, *Observations on the inhabitants, climate etc.* . . . .
Dec. 22 (207) "Collection of Travels" "40.27" [unidentified][3] . . . .

1 8 5 7

Jan. 26 (208) "Relation 11,12,13,14,15,16,17,18,19,20,21,22,23,24,25,26"[4] . . . .
Jan. 26 (209) [Beverley *or* Campbell], *History of Virginia* . . . .
Mar. 2 (210) Morton, *New English Canaan ... abstract of New England* . . . .
Mar. 16 (211) Grey, *Memoria technica; new method of artificial memory* . . . .

1 8 5 8

Jan. 13 (212) New York Historical Society, *Collections of ...* (II.3) . . . .
Jan. 13 (213) *Jesuit Relation* for 1662-1663; for 1663-1664 . . . .
Feb. 15 (214) Traill, *The backwoods of Canada: being letters* . . . .
Feb. 15 (215) Sagard-Théodat, *Histoire du Canada* . . . .
Feb. 15 (216) American Academy, *Memoirs of the Am. Acad. of Arts* (II.1) . . . .
Apr. 25 (217) "Relations de la Nou." (28,29,30)[5] . . . .

---

[1] Bound with *The Second Journal of Christian Frederick Post etc.*, London, 1759.

[2] The volume which Thoreau borrowed (US 10267.97) contains now as always Jonathan Edwards, *Observations on the Language of the Muhhekaneew Indians*; Benjamin S. Barton, *New views of the origin of the tribes and nations of America*; and George Burder, *The Welch Indians.*

[3] Apparently not the work of Churchill, Hakluyt, Harris, Osborne, Pinkerton or Ray.

[4] See "Jesuit Relations" in the Bibliography.

[5] See "Jesuit Relations" in the Bibliography. In the margin opposite this line is the name of "F. B. Sanborn."

May 27   (218)   Hennepin, *Description de la Louisiane* (1683)   ....
May 27   (219)   *Jesuit Relations* for 1669-1670; 1670-1671; 1671-1672   ....
Dec. 7   (220)   Tonti, *Relation de la Louisianne et du Mississipi*   ....
Dec. 7   (221)   Hennepin, *Voyages . . . de . . . Hennepin & de La Borde*   ....
Dec. 7   (222)   [Dablon,] *Relation [of the voyages . . . James] Marquette*   ....

1 8 5 9

Jan. 11   (223)   Higginson, *New-Englands plantation* (1630)   ....
Jan. 11   (224)   Champlain, *Des sauvages: Voyage faict en la France nouv*   ....
Feb. 28   (225)   Mackenzie, *Voyages from Montreal . . . through N. America*
                (1,2)   ....
Feb. 28   (226)   Halkett, *Historical notes re. Indians of North America*   ....
Feb. 28   (227)   Wafer, *New voyage and descrip. of the isthmus of America*   ....
Apr. 26   (228)   Penhallow, *History of the wars of New-England*   ....
Apr. 26   (229)   Bossu, *Nouveau voyages dans l'Amérique septentrionale*   ....
Apr. 26   (230)   Bossu, *Nouveaux voyages aux Indes Occidentales* (1,2)   ....
Aug. 15   (231)   Mather, *Magnalia Christi americana* (1,2)   ....
Aug. 15   (232)   Dubuat-Nançay, *Principes d'hydraulique* (1)   ....
Oct. 6   (233)   West, [Two journals bound in one volume.]   ....
Oct. 6   (234)   Badham, *Treatise on the esculent funguses of England*   ....
Oct. 6   (235)   Newman, *A history of British ferns*   ....
Oct. 6   (236)   Boucher, *Histoire véritable et naturelle . . . du . . . Canada*   ....
Dec. 16   (237)   Theophrastus, Θεοφραστου Ερεσιου τα σωζομενα (2)   ....
Dec. 16   (238)   Aristoteles, *Histoire des animaux d'Aristote* (1,2)   ....

1 8 6 0

Feb. 6   (239)   "C. L. Aeliani" "31.35" [or 31.36] [unidentified]   ....
Feb. 6   (240)   Topsell, *The historie of foure-footed beastes*   ....
Feb. 6   (241)   Belon, *L'histoire de la nature des oyseaux*   ....
Apr. 9   (242)   Ælianus, *De natura animalium libri XVII* (Schneider)   ....
May 2   (243)   Gosse, *The Canadian naturalist*   ....
May 2   (244)   Cornut, *Iac. Cornuti . . . Canadensium plantarum . . . historia* ....
Sept. 10   (245)   Gerard, *The herball, or Generall historie of plantes*   ....
Nov. 7   (246)   Jefferson, *Notes on the State of Virginia*   ....
Nov. 7   (247)   Cranz, *The history of Greenland* (tr. from High Dutch) (1,2) ....

BIBLIOGRAPHY OF THOREAU'S READING AT HARVARD

A

ACHARIUS, Erik: *Methodus qua omnes detectos lichenes*, Stockholmiæ, 1803. [155]
ADAIR, James: *The history of the American Indians . . . containing an account of their origin, language, manners, religious and civil customs etc.*, London, 1775. [199]
ÆLIANUS, Claudius: *De natura animalium libri xvii* (Greek and Latin, with notes by Johann Gottlob Schneider), Lipsiæ, 1784. [242]
ÆLIANUS, Claudius: (See #239).
AGASSIZ, Louis (i.e. Jean Louis Rodolphe): *Études sur les glaciers. Ouvrage accompagné d'un atlas*, Neuchâtel, 1840. [178]

AMERICAN ACADEMY: *Memoirs of the American Academy of Arts and Sciences,* (1st ser., 4v.) [Boston and] Cambridge, 1780-1821; (new ser., 18v.) Cambridge, 1826-1939. [216]

AMERICAN PHILOSOPHICAL SOCIETY (of Philadelphia): *Transactions of the historical and literary committee of the American philosophical society,* (3v.) Philadelphia, 1819-1843. [198] (Vol. 1 contains much information on the languages of American Indians.)

ANVILLE, Jean Baptiste Bourguignon d': *A complete body of ancient geography. The whole materially improved, by inserting the modern names of places under the ancient,* London, 1802. [62?] (The self-list calls it "Atlas of ancient geography.") (See also under "Rollin.")

ARISTOTELES: *Histoire des animaux d'Aristote,* tr. Armand Gaston Camus, (2v.) Paris, 1783. [238]

AL-ASMA'I: *Antar, a Bedoueen romance.* Tr. from the Arabic by Terrick Hamilton. Part I. (4v.) London, 1820. [17]

AUDUBON, John James: *Ornithological biography, or An account of the habits of the birds of the U. S.,* (5v.) Edinburgh, 1831-1839. [81]

B

BACK, *Sir* George: *Narrative of the Arctic land expedition to the mouth of the Great Fish River and along the shores of the Arctic Ocean (1833-1835),* London, 1836; Philadelphia, 1836. [88]

BADHAM, Charles David: *A treatise on the esculent funguses of England,* London, 1847. [234]

BAILEY, Samuel: *Essays on the formation and publication of opinions and on other subjects,* (2d. ed.) London, 1826. [27, 73]

BANKS, John: *A new history of the life and reign of the Czar Peter the Great, emperor of all Russia,* Montpelier, [Vt.], 1811. [3]

BARNEY, *Mrs.* Mary (Chase): *A biographical memoir of the late Commodore Joshua Barney,* Boston, 1832. [15]

BARROW, *Sir* John, *1st bart.*: *A voyage to Cochinchina in the years 1792 and 1793 (with an account of a journey made in 1801-1802 to the chief of the Booshuana nation),* London, 1806. [29]

BARTON, Benjamin Smith: *New views of the origin of the tribes and nations of America,* Philadelphia, 1797. [203] (Bound with Burder and Edwards, *q.v.*)

BARTRAM, John: *Observations on the inhabitants, climate, soil, rivers, productions, animals and other matters . . . in his travels from Pensilvania to . . . Canada* (Annex'd: a curious acc't of the cataracts at Niagara, by Peter Kalm), London, 1751. [206]

BELON, Pierre: *L'histoire de la nature des oyseaux avec leurs descriptions & naïfs portraicts . . . par Pierre Belon du Mans,* Paris, 1555. [241]

BENDLOWES, Edward: *Theophila, or Loves sacrifice; a divine poem,* London, 1652. [119]

BERNARD, Jean Frédéric: *Recueil de voiages au nord, divers memoirs très utiles au commerce & navigation,* (5v.) Amsterdam, 1715-1724. [220]

BEVERLEY, Robert: *The history and present state of Virginia, in four parts,* London, 1705; London, 1722. [209?]

BEWICK, Thomas: *History of British birds,* (2v.) Newcastle, 1804. [192]

BHAGAVAD-GITA: *The Bhagvat-geeta, or Dialogues of Kreeshna and Arjoon: in eighteen lectures, with notes.* Tr. Charles Wilkins, London, 1785. [184]

BIDDLE, Richard: *A memoir of Sebastian Cabot; with a review of the history of maritime discovery,* London, 1831. [197]

BIGELOW, Jacob: *American medical botany, being a collection of the native medical plants of the United States,* (3v. in 6) Boston, 1817-1821. [145]

BOSSU, Jean Bernard: *Nouveaux voyages aux Indes Occidentales, contenant une relation des differens peuples qui habitent les environs du . . . Mississipi,* (2ᵉ éd., 2v.) Paris, 1768. [230]

BOSSU, Jean Bernard: *Nouveau voyages dans l'Amérique septentrionale,* Amsterdam, 1777. [229]

BOSWORTH, Joseph: *The elements of Anglo-Saxon grammar, with copious notes, illustrating the structure of the Saxon and the formation of the English language,* London, 1823. [96]

BOUCHER, Pierre: *Histoire véritable et naturelle des meurs et productions du pays de la Nouvelle France, vulgairement dite le Canada,* Paris, 1664. [236]

BRACKENRIDGE, Henry Marie: *Journal of a voyage up the river Missouri, performed in 1811,* (2d ed.) Baltimore, 1815. [75]

BRAND, John: *Observations on popular antiquities.* Revised with add'ns by Henry Ellis, (2v.) London, 1813. [105]

BROOKE, Fulke Greville, *1st baron: Certaine learned and elegant workes, written in his youth and familiar exercise with Sir Philip Sidney,* London, 1633. [107]

BROSSES, Charles de: *Terra australis cognita: or Voyages to the Terra australis, or Southern hemisphere during the 16th, 17th and 18th centuries.* (Tr. with add'ns by John Callander), (3v.) Edinburgh & London, 1766-1768. [76]

BRY, Theodor de: *Collectiones peregrinationum in Indiam Occidentalem et Indiam Orientalem.* [In many parts], Francofurti, 1590-1629. [170]

BULLOCK, William: *Six months' residence and travels in Mexico, containing remarks on the present state of New Spain etc.,* (2d ed., 2v.) London, 1825. [18]

BURDER, George: *The Welch Indians, or A collection of papers respecting a people whose ancestors emigrated from Wales to America in 1170 with Prince Madoc,* London, [1797]. [203]   (Bound with Barton and Edwards, *q.v.*)

BURGH, James: *The dignity of human nature. Or, A brief account of the certain and established means for attaining the true end of our existence,* (new ed., 2v.) London, 1767. [42]

BURKE, Edmund: *A philosophical enquiry into the origin of our ideas of the sublime and beautiful,* (6th ed.) London, 1770. [85]

BUTLER, Charles: *The life of Erasmus: with historical remarks on the state of literature between the 10th and 16th centuries,* London, 1825. [1]

C

CAMPBELL, John W.: *A history of Virginia from its discovery till the year 1781.* With biographical sketches, Petersburg, Va., 1813. [209?]

CAMPBELL, Thomas: *Specimens of the British poets, with biographical and critical notices and an essay on English poetry,* (7v.) London, 1819. [82]

CAREW, Thomas: *A selection from the poetical works of Thomas Carew* [ed. John Fry], London, 1810. [116]

CHALMERS, Alexander: *The works of the English poets, from Chaucer to Cowper* (with prefaces biographical and critical by Dr. Samuel Johnson and Alexander Chalmers), (21v.) London, 1810. [72? 83? 102, 110]

CHAMBERS, Robert: *Ancient sea-margins, as memorials of changes in the relative level of sea and land,* Edinburgh, 1848. [182]

CHAMPLAIN, Samuel de: *Des sauvages, ou Voyage faict en la France nouvelle, l'an mil six cens trois,* Paris, 1604. [224]

CHAMPLAIN, Samuel de: *Les voyages du sieur de Champlain,* Paris, 1613. [136, 195]

CHAMPLAIN, Samuel de: *Les voyages de la Nouvelle France occidentale . . . & toutes les descouvertes qu'il a faites (1603-1629),* Paris (Collet), 1632. [134, 138, 194]

CHARLEVOIX, Pierre François Xavier de: *Histoire et description générale de la Nouvelle France, avec le Journal historique d'un voyage fait dans l'Amérique Septentrionnale,* (3v.) Paris, 1744. [151]

CHATEAUBRIAND, François Auguste René, vicomte de: *Œuvres complètes,* (28v.) Paris, 1826-1831. [59, 61]

CHAUCER, Geoffrey: *The Canterbury tales of Chaucer, with an essay on his language and versification etc.* by Tho. Tyrwhit, (5v.) London, 1830. [52, 104]

CHILD, Mrs. Lydia Maria (Francis): *Hobomok, a tale of early times.* By an American, Boston, 1824. [14]   (Thoreau used a copy bound with *The Rebels:* AL 1043.31*)

CHILD, Mrs. Lydia Maria (Francis): *The Rebels,* Boston, 1825. [14]   (See *supra*).

CLEVELAND, Charles Dexter: *An epitome of Grecian antiquities,* Boston, 1827. [13]

COCHRANE, Charles Stuart: *Journal of a residence and travels in Colombia during the years 1823 and 1824,* (2v.) London, 1825. [16]

COLDEN, Cadwallader: *The history of the Five Indian nations of Canada, which are dependent on the province of New-York in America* (Added: accounts of other nations of Indians in North America), London, 1747. [187]

COLERIDGE, Henry Nelson: *Introductions to the study of the Greek classic poets.* Part I: [all published], London, 1830. [65]

COLUMELLA, Lucius Junius Moderatus: *Husbandry. In twelve books, and his Book concerning trees.* (Tr. with illustrations from Pliny, Cato, Varro, Palladius and others), London, 1745. [202]

CONSTANT DE REBECQUE, Benjamin: *De la religion, considerée dans sa source, ses formes et ses développements*, (2° éd., 3v.) Paris, 1826-1827. [91, 94]

CONYBEARE, John Josias: *Illustrations of Anglo-Saxon poetry*, ed. with additions by William Daniel Conybeare, London, 1826. [95, 101]

CORNUT, Jacques: *Iac. Cornuti . . . Canadensium plantarum aliarumque nondum editarum historia*, Parisiis, 1635. [244]

COWPER, William: *Works*, (10v.) London, 1817. [70]

COX, Ross: *Adventures on the Columbia River, including the narrative of a residence of six years on the western side of the Rocky Mountains among various tribes of Indians hitherto unknown*, New York, 1832. [5, 74]

CRANZ, David: *The history of Greenland, containing a description of the country and its inhabitants*. (Tr. from the High Dutch), (2v.) London, 1767. [247]

CUSICK, David: *David Cusick's sketches of ancient history of the Six Nations*, Lockport, N.Y., 1848. [204]

D

DABLON, Claude: *Relation of the voyages, discoveries, and death, of Father James Marquette and the subsequent voyages of Father Claudius Allouez* (Prepared for publication in 1678) [See B. F. French, *Hist. coll. of Louisiana*, 1846. IV, pp. 1-77]. [222]

DUBUAT-NANÇAY, Louis Gabriel, *comte: Principes d'hydraulique et de pyrodynamique, vérifiés par un grand nombre d'expériences*, (nouv. éd., 3v.) Paris, 1816. [232]

DUMONT, Étienne: *Recollections of Mirabeau and of the first two legislative assemblies of France*, London, 1832; Philadelphia, 1833. [38]

E

EDINBURGH REVIEW, or critical journal, The: (250v.) Edinburgh, 1803-1829. [45]

EDWARDS, Jonathan: *Observations on the language of the Muhhekaneew Indians*. (New edition with notes by John Pickering), Boston, 1823. [203] (Bound with Barton and Burder, *q.v.*).

EDWARDS, Richard: *The paradise of dainty devices*, rptd. from a transcript of the first edition (1576), with an appendix. Ed. Sir Egerton Brydges, London, 1812. [114]

EURIPIDES: *Alcestis Euripidea*, edidit Gottlob Wagner, Lipsiæ, 1800. [41] (H.C.L. copy bound with the *Ion, q.v.*).

EURIPIDES: *Ion Graece, ad optimas editiones . . . recognitus, commentario perpetuo etc.* Studio Frederici Hülsemann, Lipsiæ, 1801. [41] (H.C.L. copy bound with the *Alcestis, q.v.*).

EVANS, Thomas: *Old ballads, historical and narrative, with some of modern date, collected from rare copies and MSS.*, (new ed., 4v.) London, 1810. [108]

F

FISK, Benjamin Franklin: *Greek exercises containing the substance of the Greek syntax*, Boston, 1831. [11]

FRENCH, Benjamin Franklin: *Historical collections of Louisiana, embracing many rare and valuable documents relating to the natural, civil and political history of that state*, (5v.) New York, 1846-1853. [222] H.C.L.: US 22015.5.

> Vol. 2: J. Marquette, *Account of the discovery of some new countries and nations in North America in 1673*.

> Vol. 4: J. Marquette, *Récit des voyages et des découvertes de P. Jacques Marquete en l'année 1673 et aux suivantes*.

G

GALBRAITH, William: *Mathematical and astronomical tables for the use of students in mathematics, practical astronomers, surveyors, engineers and navigators*, (2d ed.) Edinburgh, 1834. [133]

GARCÍN DE TASSY, Joseph Héliodore: *Histoire de la littérature hindoui et hindoustani*, (2v.) Paris, 1839-1847. [124] (Oriental Translation Fund Publ. 51).

GENTLEMAN'S MAGAZINE, The: [ed. by Sylvanus Urban], (303v.) London, 1731-1907. (New series of 45 vols., 1834-1856). [78]

GERARD, John: *The herball, or Generall historie of plantes, very much enlarged . . .* by Thomas Johnson, London, 1633. [245]

GILPIN, William: *Observations on several parts of England, particularly the mountains and lakes of Cumberland and Westmoreland, relative chiefly to picturesque beauty,* (3d ed., 2v.) London, 1808. [162]

GILPIN, William: *Observations on several parts of Great Britain, particularly the High-lands of Scotland,* (3d ed., 2v.) London, 1808. [163]

GILPIN, William: *Observations on the coasts of Hampshire, Sussex and Kent, relative chiefly to picturesque beauty,* London, 1804. [172]

GILPIN, William: *Observations on several parts of the counties of Cambridge, Norfolk, Suffolk, and Essex: Also on several parts of North Wales,* London, 1809. [159]

GILPIN, William: *Observations on the river Wye and several parts of South Wales,* (5th ed.) London, 1800. [160]

GILPIN, William: *Observations on the western parts of England relative chiefly to picturesque beauty,* (2d ed.) London, 1808. [164]

GILPIN, William: *Remarks on forest scenery, and other woodland views relative chiefly to picturesque beauty,* (3d ed.. 2v.) London, 1808. [157]

GILPIN, William: *Three essays: On picturesque beauty, On picturesque travel, and On sketching landscape etc.,* (3d ed.) London, 1808. [173]

GODWIN, William: *Life of Geoffrey Chaucer, including memoirs of John of Gaunt,* (2v.) London, 1803. [47]

GOLDSMITH, Oliver: *History of England to the death of George II, with a continuation to 1802 by M. Wood,* (1st Am. ed., 2v.) Boston, 1814-1815. [23]

GOLDSMITH, Oliver: *Miscellaneous works,* (new ed., 4v.) London, 1821. [44]

GOLDSMITH, Oliver: *The Roman history, from the foundation of the city of Rome to the destruction of the Western empire,* (2v.) London, 1786; (2v.) London, 1805. [77]

GOSSE, Philip Henry: *The Canadian naturalist. A series of conversations on the natural history of Lower Canada,* London, 1840. [243]

GRAY, Thomas, the poet: *Poems of Mr. Gray, to which are prefixed memoirs of his life and writings* [with selections of his correspondence] by W. Mason, (4v.) York, 1778. [89]

GRAY, Thomas (1803-1849): *The vestal, or A tale of Pompeii,* Boston, 1830. [19]

GREY, Richard: *Memoria technica: or, A new method of artificial memory, applied to and exemplified in chronology, history, geography, astronomy etc.,* London, 1730. [211]

GRIMANI, G.: *New and improved grammar of the Italian language, with a copious collection of exercises,* (2d ed. enl.) London, 1820. [28, 55]

H

HALKETT, John: *Historical notes respecting the Indians of North America, with remarks on the attempts made to convert and civilize them,* London, 1825. [226]

HALL, Col. Francis: *Travels in Canada and the United States in 1816 and 1817,* Boston, 1818; London, 1819. [2]

HARTSHORNE, Charles Henry, editor: *Ancient metrical tales, printed chiefly from original sources,* London, 1829. [112]

HARWOOD, Thomas: *Grecian antiquities, or An account of the public and private life of the Greeks . . . chiefly designed to explain words in the Greek classics etc.,* London, 1801. [10]

HAWKINS, Alfred: *Plan of the city of Quebec. Reduced by A. J. Russell from original plans by A. Larue,* [Quebec], 1835. (Bound with his *The environs of Quebec,* the binding having the title: "Hawkins plan of Quebec and map of environs.") [143]

HAZLITT, William: *Lectures on the English poets. Delivered at the Surry Institution,* London, 1818. [84]

HEADLEY, Henry: *Select beauties of ancient English poetry. With remarks,* (2v.) London, 1787. [109]

HECKEWELDER, John: *Narrative of the mission of the United Brethren among the Delaware and Mohegan Indians, from its commencement (1740) to the close of the year 1808,* Philadelphia, 1820. [181]

HEDERICH, Benjamin: *Lexicon manuale Graecum,* London, 1707; London, 1755; London, 1803; London, 1821. [35]

HENNEPIN, Louis: *Description de la Louisiane, nouvellement decouverte au sud'oüest de la Nouvelle France, par ordre du roy. Avec carte du pays*, Paris, 1683. [218]

HENNEPIN, Louis: *Voyages curieux et nouveaux de Messieurs Hennepin & de La Borde, ou l'on voit une description très particulière d'un grand pays dans l'Amerique etc.*, Amsterdam, 1711. [221]

HIGGINSON, Francis: *New-Englands plantation, Or, A short and true description of the commodities and discommodities of that countrey*, (1st ed.) London, 1630. [223]

HOCCLEVE, Thomas: *Poems never before printed*. With a preface, notes and glossary, London, 1796. [106]

HOMERUS: *The Iliads and Odysses*. Translated by Tho. Hobbes, (2d ed., 2v.) London, 1677. [60]

HOMERUS, *Ilias cum brevi annotatione curante C. G. Heyne*, (2v.) Lipsiæ, 1804. [51]

HUNTER, John Dunn: *Memoirs of a captivity among the Indians of North America, from childhood to the age of nineteen, with anecdotes descriptive of their manners and customs*, (new ed.) London, 1823. [186]

I

IÇVARA KRSNA: *The Sánkhya Káriká, or Memorial verses on the Sánkhya philosophy, by Iswara Krishna*. Tr. from the Sanscrit by Henry Thomas Colebrooke. Also the Bháshya or commentary of Gaurapáda. (tr. Horace Hayman Wilson), Oxford (Oriental Translation Fund), 1837. [129]

IRVING, Washington: *A chronicle of the conquest of Granada. From the MSS. of Fray Antonio Agapida*, (2v.) London, 1829; (2v.) Philadelphia, 1829. [12]

IRVING, Washington: *Voyages and discoveries of the companions of Columbus*, Phila., 1831. [9]

IRVING, Washington: *A history of the life and voyages of Christopher Columbus*, (4v.) London, 1828. [8]

J

JAMES I, *king of Scotland: The works of James I, king of Scotland* (ed. Robert Morison), Perth, 1786. [117]

JAMIESON, Robert, *editor: Popular ballads and songs, from tradition, manuscripts and scarce editions*, (2v.) Edinburgh, 1806. [115]

JEFFERSON, Thomas: *Notes on the State of Virginia*, [edition uncertain]. [246]

JESUIT RELATIONS: (The present editor cannot determine exactly what were Harvard's holdings of original editions or reprints during the decade of Thoreau's reading. That she had a collection of one or the other, totalling twenty-eight volumes, seems definite according to the shelf-list of *ca.* 1850-1860. [See under AR 119 or 14.119.] This fact is borne out by the numbering system employed in items #208 and #217 of the foregoing list. Additional Jesuit material is also to be found in the shelf-list under 14.120. Two modern editions of reprints Thoreau could *not* have used, for the first was received at Harvard (according to the *Accessions Book*) in 1859, and the second bears the imprint: "Cleveland, 1896-1901."* That Harvard had at least three of the original editions will be seen in her early printed catalogues (1830-1834). How many others were acquired in the following two decades, I do not know. I intend, therefore, to list most of the original editions, and hope that later on we may have new information.) [165, 166, 167, 168, 171, 174, 188, 205, 208, 213, 217, 219]

Le Jeune, Paul: *Brieve Relation du voyage de la Nouvelle France, fait au mois d'Avril dernier*, Paris, 1632.

Le Jeune, Paul: *Relation de ce qui s'est passé en la Nouvelle France, en l'année 1633*, Paris, 1634.

Le Jeune, Paul: *Relation . . . en l'année 1634*, Paris, 1635.

Le Jeune, Paul: *Relation . . . en l'année 1635*, Paris, 1636.

Le Jeune, Paul: *Relation . . . en l'année 1636*, Paris, 1637.

---

* See *Relations des Jésuites, contenant ce qui s'est passé de plus remarquable dans les missions des pères de la Compagnie de Jèsus dans la Nouvelle-France*. (3v.) Quebec, 1858. In this collection, the Relations are chronologically arranged and separately paged, bearing for convenience of reference a date instead of a serial number. The following period is covered by each volume: Vol. I (1611-1641); Vol. II (1642-1655); Vol. III (1656-1672). A later collection bears the title: *The Jesuit relations and allied documents*, (73v.) Cleveland, 1896-1901. (H.C.L.: Can 240.8)

Le Jeune, Paul: *Relation . . . en l'année 1637*, Rouen, 1638. (In H.C.L., 1830-1834)

Le Jeune, Paul: *Relation . . . en l'année 1638*, Paris, 1638.

Le Jeune, Paul: *Relation . . . en l'année 1639*, Paris, 1640.

Vimont, Barthélemy, *editor*:[1] *Relation . . . en l'année 1640*, Paris, 1641.

Vimont, Barthélemy: *Relation . . . és années 1640 et 1641*, Paris, 1642.

Vimont, Barthélemy: *Relation . . . en l'année 1642*, Paris, 1643. (In H.C.L., 1830-1834).

Vimont, Barthélemy: *Relation . . . és années 1642 et 1643*, Paris, 1644.

Vimont, Barthélemy: *Relation . . . és années 1643 et 1644*, Paris, 1645.

Vimont, Barthélemy: *Relation . . . és années 1644 et 1645*, Paris, 1646.

Lalemont, Jérôme: *Relation . . . és années 1645 et 1646*, Paris, 1647. (In H.C.L., 1830-1834)

Lalemant, Jérôme: *Relation . . . en l'année 1647*, Paris, 1648.

Lalemant, Jérôme: *Relation . . . és années 1647 et 1648*, Paris, 1649.

Ragueneau, Paul: *Relation . . . és années 1648 et 1649*, Paris, 1650.

Ragueneau, Paul: *Relation . . . és années 1649 et 1650*, Paris, 1651.

Ragueneau, Paul: *Relation . . . és années 1650 et 1651*, Paris, 1652.

Ragueneau, Paul: *Relation . . . és années 1651 et 1652*, Paris, 1653.

Le Mercier, François: *Relation . . . és années 1652 et 1653*, Paris, 1654.

Le Mercier, François: *Relation . . . és années 1653 et 1654*, Paris, 1655.

Quens, Jean de: *Relation . . . és années 1655 et 1656*, Paris, 1657.

Le Jeune, Paul, *editor*: *Relation . . . és années 1656 et 1657*, Paris, 1658.

[Anonymous]: *Relation . . . és années 1657 et 1658*, Paris, 1659.

Lalemant, Jérôme: *Relation . . . és années 1659 et 1660*, Paris, 1661.

Le Jeune, Paul: *Relation . . . és années 1660 et 1661*, Paris, 1662.

Lallemant, Jérôme: *Relation . . . és années 1661 et 1662*, Paris, 1663.

Lallemant, Jérôme: *Relation . . . és années 1662 et 1663*, Paris, 1664.

Lallemant, Jérôme: *Relation . . . és années 1663 et 1664*, Paris, 1665.

Le Mercier, François: *Relation . . . és années 1664 et 1665*, Paris, 1666.

Le Mercier, François: *Relation . . . és années 1665 et 1666*, Paris, 1667.

Le Mercier, François: *Relation . . . és années 1669 et 1670*, Paris, 1671.

Dablon, Claude: *Relation . . . les années 1670 & 1671*, Paris, 1672.

Dablon, Claude: *Relation . . . les années 1671 & 1672*, Paris, 1673.

JOHNSON, Edward: *A history of New-England. From the English planting in the yeere 1628 until the yeere 1652*, London, 1654. [179]

JOHNSON, Samuel: *The lives of the most eminent English poets, with critical observations on their works*, (new ed., 4v.) London, 1783. [87]

JONES, *Sir* William (1746-1794): *Works. With the life of the author by Lord Teignmouth*, (13v.) London, 1807. [130]

JOSSELYN, John: *An account of two voyages to New-England, wherein you have the setting out of a ship with charges (Also a chronological table of the most remarkable passages to the year 1673)*, London, 1674. [177]

JOSSELYN, John: *New Englands rarities discovered: in birds, beasts, fishes, serpents, and plants of that country . . . Also a perfect description of an Indian squa.*, London, 1672. [141]

K

KALM, Per: *Travels in North America, containing its natural history and a circumstantial account of its plantations and agriculture in general* (tr. John Reinhold Forster), (3v.) [Warrington and] London, 1770-1771. [149]

KEACH, Benjamin: *The glorious lover; a divine poem upon the adorable mystery of sinners redemption*, London, 1679. [118]

KNOX, Vicesimus, *compiler*: *Elegant extracts, or useful and entertaining pieces of poetry selected for the improvement of youth in speaking etc.*, (2v.) London, 1800. [20]

---

[1] This *Relation* has composite authorship. Vimont was only editor, succeeding Le Jeune as superior in 1639 and becoming responsible for the *Relations* until 1645, when he was succeeded by Jérôme Lalemant. Pt. I of the 1640 edition was prepared by Le Jeune; Part II, by Jérôme Lalemant.

L

LAET, Joannes de: *Novus orbis, seu Descriptionis Indiæ Occidentalis, libri XVII* [Half-title: *Americæ utriusque descriptio*], Lugd. Batav., 1633. [139]

LAHONTAN, Louis Armand de Lom d'Arce, *baron* de: *Voyages du baron de La Hontan dans l'Amerique Septentrionale, qui contiennent une rélation des différens peuples qui y habitent etc.*, (2v. in 1) Amsterdam, 1705. [154]

LANGTOFT, Peter: *Chronicle, as illustrated and improv'd by Robert of Brunne* (transcribed by Thomas Hearne), (2v.) Oxford, 1725. [43]

LESCARBOT, Marc: *Histoire de la Nouvelle-France*, (2e éd., 2v.) Paris, 1612. [137]

LINNE, Carl von: *Caroli Linnæi . . . Amoenitates academicæ, seu Dissertationes variæ physicæ, medicæ, botanicæ antehac seorsim editæ*, (10v.) Lugduni Batavorum, 1749-1790. [161]

LINNE, Carl von: *Caroli Linnæi . . . Philosophia botanica in qua explicantur fundamenta botanica*, (3d ed.) Viennæ Austriæ, 1763. [153]

LOSKIEL, George Henry: *History of the mission of the United Brethren among the Indians in North America*, Tr. Christian Ignatius LaTrobe, London, 1794. [200]

M

McCULLOH, James Haines: *Researches on America, being an attempt to settle some points relative to the aborigines of America*, (2d ed.) Baltimore, 1817. [176]

McKENNEY, Thomas Lorraine: *Sketches of a tour to the Lakes, of the character and customs of the Chippeway Indians, and of the incidents connected with the treaty of Fond du Lac*, Baltimore, 1827. [6]

MACKENZIE, Sir Alexander: *Voyages from Montreal, on the river St. Laurence, through the continent of North America, to the frozen and Pacific oceans (1789 and 1793)*, (2v.) London & Edinburgh, 1802. [225]

MAHABHARATA: *Harwansa, ou Histoire de la famille de Hari, ouvrage formant un appendice du Mahabharata* (tr. from Sanskrit by Alexandre Langlois), (2v.) London, 1834-1835. [123]

MARMONTEL, Jean François, *Moral tales, translated from the French*, (1st Am. ed., 2v.) New York, 1813. [4]

MARSHALL, John: *A history of the colonies planted by the English on the continent of North America, from their settlement [until 1776]*, Philadelphia, 1824. [26]

MASSACHUSETTS HISTORICAL SOCIETY: *Collections*, (1st ser., 10v.) Boston, 1792-1809; (2d ser., 10v.) Boston, 1814-1823; (3d ser., 10v.) Boston, 1825-1849. [127]

MATHER, Cotton: *Magnalia Christi americana, or The ecclesiastical history of New-England (1620-1698)*, (1st Am. ed., 2v.) Hartford, 1820. [231]

METASTASIO, Pietro: *Dramas and other poems*. Tr. John Hoole, (3v.) London, 1800. [32, 58]

MICHAUX, François André: *The North American sylva, or A description of the forest trees of the United States, Canada and Nova Scotia*, (3v.) Paris, 1819. [140, 146]

MICHAUX, François André: *Voyage à l'ouest des monts Alléghanys, dans les états de l'Ohio, du Kentucky et du Tennessée etc.*, Paris, 1808. [147]

MILLS, Charles: *The history of the crusades for the recovery and possession of the Holy Land*, (3d ed., 2v.) London, 1822. [25]

MILTON, John: *A complete collection of historical, political and miscellaneous works both in English and Latin*. (Life by John Toland), (3v.) Amsterdam, 1698. [90?]

MILTON, John: *The poetical works of John Milton*. Ed. with life by Henry John Todd, (6v.) London, 1801. [68, 79]

MILTON, John: *The prose works of John Milton, with life etc. by Charles Symmons*, (7v.) London, 1806. [71, 80]

MILTON, John: *Works, historical, political, and miscellaneous* (Life by Thomas Birch), (2v.) London, 1753. [90?]

MORRELL, *Mrs.* Abby Jane: *Narrative of a voyage to the Ethiopic and south Atlantic Ocean, Indian Ocean, Chinese Sea, north and south Pacific Ocean (1829-1831)*, N.Y., 1833. [36?]

MORRELL, Benjamin: *A narrative of four voyages to the South Sea, north and south Pacific Ocean, Chinese Sea, Ethiopic and southern Atlantic Ocean etc. (1822-1831)*, N.Y., 1832. [36?]

MORTON, Thomas: *New English Canaan or New Canaan. Containing an abstract of New England.* Amsterdam, 1637. [210]

N

NEPOS, Cornelius: *Vitæ excellentium imperatorum: cum versione Anglica* [By John Clarke], (10th ed.) Londini, 1765. [98]

NEW YORK HISTORICAL SOCIETY: *Collections of the . . .*, (1st ser., 5v. in 6) N.Y., 1809-1830; (2d ser., 4v.) N.Y., 1811-1859. [148, 212]

NEWMAN, Edward: *A history of British ferns*, London, 1840. [235]

NORTH AMERICAN REVIEW, The: (248v.) Boston, 1815-1940. [67]

P

PARK, Thomas, *editor: Helconia. Comprising a selection of English poetry of the Elizabethan age (1575-1604)*, (3v.) London, 1815. [113]

PEIRCE, Benjamin: *A history of Harvard University from its foundation (1636) to the period of the American revolution*, Cambridge, [Mass.], 1833. [49, 64]

PENHALLOW, Samuel: *The history of the wars of New-England with the eastern Indians*, Boston, 1726. [228]

POETICAL TRACTS. [A miscellany including the following:] London, 1718-1740. [99]

Austin and the Monks of Bangor	Panegyrical Epistle to Mr. Thomas Snow
Essay on Reason by Walter Harte	Full and True Account of a Robbery upon the Cambridge Coach
The Young Senator, a Satyre	Eugenio, or a Virtuous and Happy Life
Voice of Liberty	Epistle to Mr. Fielding, on his Studying the Law
The Negotiators	Essay on Conversation by Benjamin Stilling- fleet
Manners, a Satire by Whitehead	Milton's Epistle to Pollio from the Latin
Sir *'s Speech upon the Peace	Poem on the Glorious Atchievments of Admiral Vernon in the Spanish West Indies
Miltonis Epistola ad Pollionem	
Are these Things so?	
Yes they are. What of That!	
The Weather-Menders.	

Have at You All

POST, Christian Frederick: *The journal of Christian Frederick Post, in his journey from Philadelphia to the Ohio*, London, 1759. [201] (Bound with his *The Second Journal*).

POST, Christian Frederick: *The second journal of Christian Frederick Post, on a message from the governor of Pensilvania to the Indians on the Ohio*, London, 1759. [201]

PRATT, Enoch: *History of Eastham, Wellfleet, and Orleans, Barnstable Co., Massachusetts, from 1644-1844*, Yarmouth, 1844. [125]

PRICE, Sir Uvedale, *bart.: Essays on the picturesque, as compared with the sublime and beautiful, and on the use of studying pictures for the purpose of improving real landscape*, (3v.) London, 1810. [175]

PULTENEY, Richard: *A general view of the writings of Linnæus*, London, 1781. [152]

R

RACINE, Jean: *Œuvres*, (nouv. éd., 2v.) Paris, 1741. [40]

RAFN, Charles Christian, *et al.: [Six Tracts]* [126] What this volume contained I do not know. At all events, it contained the first and, possibly, the second of those listed below:)

    Rafn, *The discovery of America by Northmen*, n.p., n.d.
    Rafn, *Connection of the Northmen with the East*, n.p., n.d.

RALEIGH, Sir Walter (1552?-1618): *The works of Sir Walter Raleigh kt., now first collected (with lives by William Oldys and Thomas Birch)*, (8v.) Oxford, 1829. [120]

RAMAMOHANA RAYA, *raja: Translation of several principal books, passages and texts of the Veds, and of some controversial works on Brahmunical theology*, (2d ed.) London, 1832. [132]

RANKING, John: *Historical researches on the conquest of Peru, Mexico, Bogota, Natchez, and Talomeco, in the thirteenth century by the Mongols*, London, 1827. [39]

RICHARDSON, Sir John (1787-1865): *Fauna boreali-americana, or The zoology of the northern parts of British America. By John Richardson, assisted by William Swainson and William Kirby*, (4v.) London & Norwich, 1829-1837. [158]

RITSON, Joseph, *compiler: Ancient English metrical romances*, (3v.) London, 1802. [111]

RITSON, Joseph, *compiler: Robin Hood: a collection of all the ancient poems, songs, and ballads now extant relative to that outlaw*, (2v.) London, 1795. [93]

ROLLIN, Charles: *Ancient history of the Egyptians, Carthaginians, Assyrians, Babylonians, Medes and Persians, Macedonians, and Grecians (From the French)*, (12th ed., 8v.), Boston, 1807.* [34, 50, 56, 57]

S

SAGARD-THÉODAT, Gabriel: *Le grand voyage du pays des Hurons, situé en l'Amerique vers la Mer douce, és derniers confins de la Nouvelle France, dite Canada,* Paris, 1632. [191]

SAGARD-THÉODAT, Gabriel: *Histoire du Canada et voyages que les frères mineurs recollects y ont faicts pour la conversion des infidelles*, Paris, 1636. [193, 215]

SAMA-VEDA: *Sama Veda. Translation of the Sanhita of the Sama Veda.* By J. Stevenson, London (Oriental Translation Fund), 1842. [131]

SAY, Samuel: *Poems on several occasions: and two critical essays; viz., the first on the harmony, variety, and power of numbers . . . the second, on the numbers of Paradise Lost*, London, 1745. [86]

SCAPULA, Johann: *Lexicon Græco-Latinum e probatis auctoribus locupletatum. Accedunt lexicon etymologicum et Ioan. Meursii glossarium contractum*, London, 1652. [48]

SCHLEGEL, Friedrich von: *Lectures on the history of literature, ancient and modern*, [?tr. J. G. Lockhart], (2v.) Philadelphia, 1818. [63, 66]

SCHOOLCRAFT, Henry Rowe: *Information respecting the history, condition and prospects of the Indian tribes of the United States*, (6v.) Philadelphia, 1851-1857. [189]

SHAKESPEARE, William: *The plays of William Shakespeare. With the corrections and illustrations of various commentators.* (Added: notes by Samuel Johnson and George Steevens), (4th ed., 15v.) London, 1793. [46]

SHEPARD, Thomas: *The clear sun-shine of the gospel breaking forth upon the Indians in New-England. Or, An historicall narrative of Gods wonderfull workings upon sundry of the Indians*, London, 1648. [180]

SIBBALD, James: *Chronicle of Scottish poetry; from the 13th century to the union of the crowns.* (With a glossary), (4v.) Edinburgh, 1802. [97, 122]

SIDNEY, *Sir* Philip: *The works of the honourable Sʳ Philip Sidney, kt., in prose and verse*, (14th ed., 3v.) London, 1724-1725. [121]

SIGOURNEY, *Mrs.* Lydia Howard (Huntley): *Traits of the aborigines of America. A poem*, Cambridge, 1822. [24?]

SILLIMAN, Benjamin: *Remarks made on a short tour between Hartford and Quebec in the autumn of 1819*, (2d ed.) New Haven, 1824. [144]

SMITH, *Sir* James Edward: *An introduction to physiological and systematical botany. With notes by Jacob Bigelow*, (1st Am. ed.) Boston, 1814. [92]

SMITH, John: *The generall historie of Virginia, New-England, and the Summer Isles (1584-1626)*, London, 1632. [169]

SOPHOCLES: *The Antigone in Greek and English, with introd. and notes by J. W. Donaldson*, London, 1848. [196]

SOUTHEY. (See #33)

STOEVER, Dietrich Heinrich: *The life of Sir Charles Linnæus (with biographical sketch of his life by his son).* Tr. Joseph Trapp, London, 1794. [150]

T

TALBOT, Edward Allen: *Five years' residence in the Canadas, including a tour through part of the United States of America (in 1823)*, (2v.) London, 1824. [156]

TANNER, John: *A narrative of the captivity and adventures of John Tanner . . . during thirty years residence among the Indians*, New York, 1830. [183]

---

* Harvard has (AH 277.34.30): [Charles Rollin, *Ancient History. Atlas.* n.p., 1738-40.] This is probably the so-called "Atlas for the Ancient History" which the 1830 printed catalogue assigns to Jean Baptiste Bourguignon d'Anville.

THEOPHRASTUS: θεοφραστου Ερεσιου τα Σωζομενα. *Theophrasti Eresii quæ supersunt opera et excerpta librorum . . . emendavit . . . D. H. Linkii . . . explicare conatus est Io. Gottlob Schneider*, (5v.) Lipsiæ, 1818-1821. [237]

TONTI, Henri de: *Relation de la Louisianne, et du Mississipi* [in Bernard, *Recueil de voiages*, Vol. V (1720), q.v.] [220]

TOPSELL, Edward: *The historie of foure-footed beastes . . . Collected out of all the volumes of Conradus Gesner and all other writers to this present day*, London, 1607. [240]

TRAILL, *Mrs.* Catharine Parr (Strickland): *The backwoods of Canada: being letters from the wife of an emigrant officer, illustrative of the domestic economy of British America*, London, 1836. [214]

TREASURY OF KNOWLEDGE and Library of Reference, (5th ed., 2v.) New York, 1833-1834. [31]

TUCKER, Abraham: *The light of nature pursued. By Edward Search*, (3v. in 7) London, 1768-1777; (2d ed., 7v.) London, 1805. [53]

TURNER, Sharon: *History of the Anglo-Saxons*, (2d ed., 2v.) London, 1807. [100]

V

VISNU-PURANA: *The Vishnu Puráṇa (a system of Hindu mythology and tradition*, tr. from the Sanskrit by Horace Hayman Wilson), n.p., 1840. [128, 185]

VOYAGES: *Voyages de découverte au Canada, entre l'années 1534 et 1542, par Jacques Quartier, le sieur de Roberval, Jean Alphonse de Xanctoigne, &c.*, Quebec, 1843. [135]

W

WADDINGTON, George *and* Barnard HANBURY: *Journal of a visit to some parts of Ethiopia*, London, 1822. [30]

WAFER, Lionel: *A new voyage and description of the isthmus of America, giving an account of the author's abode there*, London, 1699. [227]

WARTON, Thomas: *The history of English poetry, from the close of the 11th to the commencement of the 18th century*, (4v.) London, 1824. [103]

WEST, John: *A journal of a mission to the Indians of the British provinces, of New Brunswick and Nova Scotia, and the Mohawks, on the Ouse, or Grand river, Upper Canada*, London, 1827. [233] (Bound with: "The substance of a journal etc.")

WEST, John: *The substance of a journal during a residence at the Red River colony, British North America; and frequent excursions among the North-west American Indians, in the years 1820-1823*, London, 1824. [233] (Bound with: "A journal of a Mission etc.")

WILSON, Alexander: *American ornithology, or, The natural history of the birds of the United States*, [vols. 7 and 8 completed by George Ord], (1st ed., 9v.) Philadelphia, 1808-1814. [54]

WILSON, Walter: *Memoirs of the life and times of Daniel De Foe: containing a review of his writings, and his opinions etc.*, (3v.) London, 1830. [22]

WINES, Enoch Cobb: *Two years and a half in the navy*, (2v.) Philadelphia, 1832. [37]

WOOD, William: *New-England's prospect; being a true, lively, and experimental description of that part of America commonly called New-England*, (3d ed.) Boston, 1674. [190]

Y

YOUNG, Alexander: *Chronicles of the Pilgrim fathers of the colony of Plymouth, from 1602 to 1625*, Boston, 1841. [142]

LETTERS

I

WILLIAM EMERSON TO REBECCA EMERSON—OCTOBER 7, 1793.[1]

The following letter, written by William Emerson (father of R. W. E.) to his sister Rebecca, is a delightful criticism of the latter's early epistolary efforts. Its advice might even prove valuable for college students today. On the outside wrapper is written: "Miss R. Emerson / Concord." Rebecca later married Robert Haskins, brother of Ruth Haskins (mother of R. W. E.).

Harvard, Oct. 7, 1793.

Sister Becca,

Your charming little letter I have just been reading. In commenting thereon, the two or three moments only, which are now my own, shall be occupied.

You have become pretty tolerably correct in your grammatical construction of sentences. I shall therefore begin to preach more & more loudly concerning elegance. Endeavor, my dear, to make your periods easy and mellifluent. The first sentence in your letter is rounded admirably. I cannot say the same of the second. Try them; your ear will show to you their difference. The next sentence ends with the word *of*. This little word might have been placed immediately before *which*. In general, it is not well that sentences end with petty monosyllables. They will not roll off the tongue with a grace. The four last words of the last paragraph in your letter would be well exchanged for these three *it will arrive*. The last sentence of all in your letter is destitute of a verb, and therefore unintelligible. We can do nothing, my dear, without verbs. I never in my life Becca, saw a perfect sentence without a verb.

The sentiment contained in this, and in your every epistle, is just and beautiful. Indeed few ladies of your age, my sister, write with equal judgment.

I am* your affectionate brother,

W. EMERSON.

---

* AM is a verb.

II

SAMPSON REED TO THEOPHILUS PARSONS, JR.[2]—MARCH 6, 1823.[3]

In the following, Sampson Reed reveals the vocational unrest that followed his receipt of the A.M. degree from Harvard in 1821.[4] He had studied

---

[1] Ms. owned by Mrs. James S. Barrow, 2050 Third Avenue North, Napa, California. For Mrs. Barrow's other holdings, see *infra* and also a footnote in "Additions to the Census."

[2] Theophilus Parsons, Jr., (1797-1882) was the son of Theophilus Parsons (1750-1813), a prominent Massachusetts jurist, a founder of the Boston Athenaeum and a fellow of Harvard College. The son was a Professor in the Harvard Law School and, during 1824-1826, he edited the *U. S. Literary Gazette*.

[3] Ms. owned by the Boston Public Library.

[4] See the chapter XI on Sampson Reed in Volume I.

theology apparently with a view to entering the Swedenborgian ministry, but perceiving that the little New Jerusalem Church needed funds for the support of the clergy already in existence, he took a "humble position" in the apothecary store of William B. White.[5] He alludes in this letter to the problem of relating his secular employment more creatively to the cause which he had so much at heart. He also seems to foreshadow his career as a writer and may already have begun his famous *Observations on the Growth of the Mind*, which was published in Boston in 1826.[6] The outside address appears as follows: "Theophilus Parsons Esq. / Taunton / Mass—"/.

Boston 6th March 1823

Dear Theophilus.—

It is not often that I am in a mode for writing—it is seldom that I have opportunity —of course still less frequent that these things come in conjunction. So much for not writing to you, sooner.—Have you seen Condy's[7] answer to the Episcopal Clergyman— I do not recollect his name? I was struck forcibly with the necessity of writing from the life of use,[8] on reading it. Here is a man obviously possessed of the highest talents, writing professedly in defence of the N J C[9]—and yet it was impossible for me to satisfy my own mind, whether he would do good or hurt. It is not easy to learn that so far as we fight from self, we are helping the enemy.—I have been for this year and a half past, between heaven and earth. Seven[10] years were spent in indolent study. The result of the whole was a few pieces of composition which had met with considerable applause; and on which my own mind rested with comfortable satisfaction. Here as far as I knew, was my whole man.—I was then put in a situation where I was obliged to work. The duties to be performed of necessity pressed on me continually—and between these, and the sum total of my old acquirements, there was to my knowledge, no connection. That I was sad, and unfit for any thing worthy to be named, was of course a necessary result. When I met any of my old acquaintance, I retreated into my former enclosure, ashamed of my present occupation; thence I was dragged again, by main strength. It is but lately that I have thought I could discover in my own mind, any thing like an essential incipient use, by which the two things will be united. This is so tender, as itself to require protection, though with this protection, it "may be the greatest among herbs; and become a tree, so that the birds of the air may come and lodge in the branches thereof."—I have written about myself partly because you appear

---

[5] See Warren Goddard, "Sampson Reed," *N J M*, n.s., IV (Sept., 1880), p. 287.

[6] The first edition is reprinted in one of the foregoing appendices.

[7] Jonathan Condy, an eminent lawyer, who served as clerk of the House of Representatives during the post-revolutionary period. For his activities in the Swedenborgian religion, see Marguerite Bloch, *The New Church in the New World*, N. Y., 1932, pp. 77, 114, 185, 195.

[8] For the "doctrine of uses" see Swedenborg ¶s. 18-20 and Sampson Reed ¶s. 35-37, 61.

[9] I.e., the New Jerusalem Church.

[10] He probably refers to his four undergraduate years at Harvard (1814-1818) and his three graduate years (1818-1821).

to desire it, and partly for want of any other subject. Ought we not to endeavour to form distinct idea's, of the uses of the several individuals of the Society? Warren,[11] you may have heard is going to study l[aw a]t Yarmouth. He went from here Tuesday, and will commence immediately. John[12] is yet in uncertainty.—A meeting of the proprietors of the library was not called by a warrant. It was thought that the name, and the scattered condition of the members, were sufficient ground for a distinct act of incorporation. How does this strike you?

Yours very sincely

SAMPSON REED

III

SAMPSON REED TO THEOPHILUS PARSONS, JR.—MAY 31, 1823.[13]

The following letter is interesting because of its reference to the subject of "individual uses" for members of the New Jerusalem Church—indicative of an attempt to convince members of the Church that secular occupations have spiritual value and significance—and because Reed herein sets forth his attitude toward poetry and nature. The dissatisfaction which he and his colleagues reveal toward the ill-fated *Missionary*, published for only one year by the New York Society of the New Church, probably led to the establishment of *The New Jerusalem Magazine* at Boston in the fall of 1827. On the reverse the letter is addressed to: "Theophilus Parsons Esq / Taunton / Mass"/.

Boston 31ˢᵗ May 1823

Dear Theophilus,

I did not expect to be able to afford you the assistance you looked for, in respect to your article in the N. A. R.[14] when we conversed on the subject; nor do I now see that I can. The subject is boundless. No one in our Society, would want light— I should be afraid that the peculiar form it might take, would be injured by any direct discussion of the subject by another. If you keep the Word before you as essential poetry, I think you must know where to look for every thing else, as instinctively as animals know the point of compass. The different kinds of poetry as they have been classified by writers

---

[11] Possibly Warren Goddard, who later became his biographer. See note 5.

[12] Probably his older brother, who later became the Hon. John Reed, a member of Congress for sixteen years or more and also, for some time, Lieutenant-Governor of Massachusetts.

[13] Ms. owned by the Boston Public Library.

[14] *North American Review.*

on the subject, are something, that I know very little about—but I should think that the natural mind had made divisions here, as elsewhere, many of which would disappear before a single view of goodness and truth united. Whether Lyric, Pastoral, Heroic or what not—poetry can have but one essence, love, but one form, nature. There may be infinite variety in the time, but they all require articulation and sound. I can see no rhymes in nature, and hardly blank verse, but a happy assemblage of living objects, not in straight lines and at a fixed distance, but springing up in Gods own order, which by its apparent want of design, leaves on the heart an image of its essential innocence and humility.—I have done somewhat like a person, who being asked how he does, says first "I don't know," and then proceeds to tell, in making any remarks after such a beginning; but it is my way, my Lord.—This letter together with one to Samuel,[15] and one to Thomas[16] constitutes all I have been able to effect in the writing way since I saw you. —We had a letter from Thomas last sunday. When he wrote that, he was in Ney York. He spoke of that society, as having made good improvement the last year. The subject which he seems to have set them thinking about now, and which was entirely new to them, is that of their distinct, individual, uses. They could not conceive that the New Church should have any thing to do with a Tailor.—We have received a dozen copies of the Missionary.[17] O tempora! O Mores! It will only make the task more difficut, of leaving on the minds of intelligent men, as just an impression as they are capable of receiving of the N J C[18]—at least I am afraid so. In the notice to correspondents it appears that an article attempting to shew that a person had a true idea of God in proportion, as his inclination made one with his duty, unquestionably written by Thomas, was rejected.—Give my love to Catherine.[19]

Very Sincerely Yours

SAMPSON

IV

SAMPSON REED TO THEOPHILUS PARSONS, JR.—JUNE 1, 1823.[20]

Boston Sunday Even June 1. 1823

Dear Theophilus,

I have just returned from a meeting of our Society. After reading a letter from the President, which contained nothing very important, a letter was read from Mr Roe[21] of

---

[15] Probably Samuel Worcester.

[16] Probably the Rev. Thomas Worcester, pastor of the Boston congregation.

[17] *The New Jerusalem Missionary and Intellectual Repository* (of New York), Vol. I (May, 1823—April, 1824), all published. (Copy at Univ. of Pa.)

[18] See note 9.

[19] Parsons had married Catherine Amore Chandler on March 7, 1823.

[20] Ms. in the Boston Public Library. It is addressed to Taunton, Mass.

[21] Daniel Roe. For account of him, see Marguerite Block, *op. cit.*, 118ff., 194.

Cincinnati, which was *very clever*, which the Corresponding Sec—was directed to answer. The Missionary[22] was then brought up—and after some discussion, it was "Resolved that H G Foster, S Reed, and T B Heyward[23] be a committee to examine the first No. of the N J Miss.—and to prepare a communication to the pastor of the Boston Society of the N J, to be directed to him at N. Y.[24] expressive of the views and feelings of this Society, with regard to the utility of circulating it in this vicinity."—Will you oblige us by giving us your views on the subject, as fully as a letter will hold them, immediately on receiving this?—We had a tolerably pleasant time today.—This letter may possibly overtake another which I sent you yesterday.—No news from Thomas,[25] the last week.

Eliza Jane[26] said she was going to write you.

In haste—

Truly Yours

SAMPSON —

V

SAMPSON REED TO THEOPHILUS PARSONS, JR.—[*ca.* 1824].[27]

This letter concerns Mr. Henning Gotfried Linberg, who a few years later (1832) translated and published Victor Cousin's *Introduction to the History of Philosophy*, a book in which Emerson was much interested. I have not been able to discover anything about the "disorderly conduct" or about the occasion for the charity mentioned by Reed. We have evidence that early in 1829[28] Linberg, who was then living in Copenhagen, received

---

[22] See note 17.

[23] The name is usually spelled *Hayward*.

[24] The Rev. Thomas Worcester was apparently visiting the New York Society at the time.

[25] See note 24.

[26] Identification uncertain.

[27] Owned by the Boston Public Library.

[28] See "Intelligence, Notices &c." *N J M*, III (1829-1830), page 94. For proof that Linberg was a member of the New Church, see the review of his translation of Cousin in *N J M*, V, (1831-1832), 288-306.

authority from the Boston church to proceed to Stockholm and purchase a number of Swedenborg's unpublished manuscripts, which were owned by the Academy of Sciences there. He made the trip in June, but could not effect the purchase.[29]

Boston Monday morning

[De]ar Theophilus.

I return the subscrip[tio]n-paper for Mr Linberg. In [th]e relation in which Mr [Li]nberg stands to the Church [I] do not feel inclined to sub[sc]ribe. It does not seem to [m]e to be proper to unite in[dis]criminately in assisting [M]r Linberg, as though noth[in]g had occurred. At least [I] do not feel inclined to do [i]t. Had there been in the [C]hurch a vote expressive of [hi]s disorderly conduct & at the same time recommending him to Charity—or if something similar had been expressed on the subscription-paper I would join.

Yours Truly

SAMPSON REED[30]

VI

SAMPSON REED TO THEOPHILUS PARSONS, JR.—JANUARY 31, 1827.[31]

Boston 31st Jan. 1827

Dear Theophilus,

As there are several who are wishing to read "Coleridges Aids to reflection," [32] you

---

[29] There is a strip pasted over the left margin of the first page of this letter, and many of the restorations are conjectural.

[30] At the bottom of Reed's letter, "W. G." (probably Warren Goddard) has added the following note:

Dear T. P.

Last night in bed I came to the conclusion not to let the reason operate which I stated to you Sat^y—but to give a trifle, small of course, if our Society shall say that he is a proper object of the Society's charity—respecting which I have no clear opinion—

Y^rs truly

W. G. —

[31] Ms. owned by the Boston Public Library.

[32] He refers apparently to the first edition of Coleridge's work, issued in 1825. The American edition, edited by James Marsh with an important preliminary essay, did not appear until 1829.

would confer a favour by returning it, if you have done with it, and it is not particularly in use.

Yours Truly

SAMPSON REED. —

VII

R. W. EMERSON TO REBECCA HASKINS[33]—FEB. 23, 1834.[34]

Boston, February 23, 1834.

My dear Aunt,

I remember with great pleasure my visit to Waterford not yet two years ago[35] I must not deny myself the pleasure of writing one word to you in my letter to Aunt Mary. I was truly grieved to hear of Hannah's[36] illness who was so kind a nurse to mine, & rejoice to hear she is better. She must be happy in knowing the strong interest her many friends feel in her health & happiness. Pray make her careful of herself & she must journey when the warm weather comes. I wish I could say, Come to my house, but as yet we have none although in the spring, Mother & I may find some permanent home, & then shall cherish the hope of seeing both her & you.

Will you not gratify me by letting me add the small sum[37] enclosed to Hannah's travelling fund. With remembrances of respect to my Uncle[38] & of love to my cousins,

Your affectionate nephew

R. WALDO EMERSON.

---

[33] See introduction to the first letter.

[34] Ms. owned by Mrs. James S. Barrow. See note 1. It was apparently included in a note to his Aunt Mary of the same date. (Dr. Rusk does not record such a letter.)

[35] Reference is probably made to a visit in August, 1832. See his letter to Aunt Mary dated August 19, 1832, in *Letters*, I, 352.

[36] His cousin, Hannah Upham Haskins (daughter of his Aunt Rebecca). Hannah later married Augustus Parsons.

[37] At the bottom of the letter, apparently in Hannah's handwriting, appears the line: "$20 the sum   H."

[38] Robert Haskins.

VIII

ALEXANDER IRELAND TO A FRIEND—NOVEMBER 3, 1847.[39]

Manchester Examiner Office
(Published on Tuesday and Saturday,)
22, Market Street,
Manchester, Novr. 3 1847

My dear Frand,

Here is your Ticket. Give my kind wishes to Margaret on her change of life. Emerson lectured last night. It was divine? "The Uses of Great Men." Now He is to give the following lectures, & if you can arrange for one or more, so much the better.

At the Mechanics Institute here[40]

Monday 8th   Eloquence
————— 15th   Domestic Life
————— 22^d   Reading
————— 29"   Autobiography

Athenaeum Here.

Nov. 2^d   Tuesdy —Uses of Great Men.
——— 4th   Thursdy—Swedenborg. The Mystic
——— 9th   Tuesdy —Montaigne the Sceptic
——— 11th Thursdy—Shakespere. The Poet
——— 16th Tuesday—Napoleon. The Man of Action
——— 2nd   Tuesday—Goethe. The Man of Letters

At Liverpool

Wedy   3^d —Uses of Gt Men
Saty — 6th—Swedenborg
Wedy 10th Montaigne
Saty —13^d   Shakespere.
Wedy 17th Napoleon
Saty —20th Goethe.

Now, I consider you ought to endeavour to hear some of these. If you could be at Lpool on Wedy 17th you may hear *Napoleon* one of his finest. You could also hear him on Saturdy the 20th on Goethe. I would advise you to hear these two at all events—also a Monday one if you can arrange it. We were crammed to the cieling. He took tea with me after with Hudson &c &c.

ever faithfully & since^{ly}

A IRELAND

---

[39] Ms. owned by the present editor.

[40] Townsend Scudder's studies have collected all the important facts about Emerson's lecture tour of 1847-1848: "Emerson's British Lecture Tour, 1847-1848," *American Lit.*, VII (1935), 15-36, 166-180; "Emerson in London and the London Lectures," *American Lit.*, VIII (1936), 22-36; "A Chronological List of Emerson's Lectures on his British Lecture Tour of 1847-1848," *P M L A*, LI (1936), 243-248.

IX

R. W. EMERSON TO RICHARD BENTLEY[41]——SEPTEMBER 6, 1855.[42]

Concord, Mass^{tts}

6 September, 1855

Mr Richard Bentley.

Dear Sir,

When my publishers, Messrs Phillips, Sampson, & Co. closed a copyright contract with you for my "English Notes,"[43] it was my intention to have gone to press in a short time. It happened that the work was necessarily interrupted, & is only ready now. In the meantime, a ruling in your courts has made it impossible to protect you or me in the copyright. This, of course, cancels the contract referred to, & makes it proper that I should ask what you can now do? My book will fill, say, 250 to 300 pp. 12mo. The proof sheets might be mailed by each steamer, as we proceed; giving you an opportunity of being twelve or fifteen days in advance of the possible reception of the American edition. Would such sheets be of value to you? If so, an early reply stating what compensation, & in what time,—you incline to offer, will greatly oblige

Yours respectfully,

R. W. EMERSON

---

[41] MS. owned by the Boston Public Library.

[42] See *Letters*, IV, 528, for a summary of Bentley's reply [dated Oct. 5, 1855] to this letter and for details about the eventual publication of *English Traits* by George Routledge & Company of London.

[43] Apparently Emerson originally intended to use this title, but changed it to *English Traits.*

X

SAMPSON REED TO FRANCIS BRINLEY[44]——JULY 7, 1861.

The following is one of several short notes[45] written by Reed to the secretary of the Harvard Class of 1818. Most of his correspondence with Brinley relates to class meetings held in Boston, and one gathers from the extant manuscripts that Reed was a frequent and generous host at his home, 7 Louisburg Square. The cancellation of the meeting of 1861 was the result of the outbreak of the Civil War.[46]

Boston   July 7, 1861

Francis Brinley Esq.

Dear Sir.

You may have heard that our classmate J. H. Wilkins[47] has been recently thrown from his carriage & seriously injured. It will be entirely out of his power to receive his class agreeably to his invitation. I called to consult with M[r] Curtis[48] in the emergency & he was out of the city. I then saw M[r] Bartlett,[49] & he thought that the meeting had better be given up this year. I concur in this opinion. No time should be lost in giving notice of whatever is done. I hope you will act as seems to you best under the circumstances. M[r] Worcester[50] also thinks our meeting had better be omitted.

I saw M[r] Wilkins yesterday. He seems very poorly. He was much out of health before this disaster & we have serious apprehensions as to the result.

Your Friend & Classmate

SAMPSON REED.

---

[44] These notes are preserved in the Harvard University Archives in a book of letters classified under "H.U. 338.18."

[45] I have not thought it important to edit all these manuscripts.

[46] The Rebels had fired on Fort Sumter on April 12. Lincoln had called for volunteers on April 15. On June 10, the Union troops had been repulsed at Big Bethel. Reed's letter preceded by only two weeks the defeat of the Union forces at Bull Run.

[47] John Hubbard Wilkins.

[48] Apparently Nathanael Curtis, also a member of the Class of 1818.

[49] Sidney Bartlett.

[50] Thomas Worcester.

XI

SAMPSON REED TO FRANCIS BRINLEY[51]——JULY 13, 1864.

Boston   July 13.   1864

Brother Brinley,

I received your notice of our class-meeting at Bartlett's[52] & hope to have the pleasure of attending. I have several times received a request to give some account of myself, & enclose a statement of some facts in regard to myself & family. I fear you will think that I am getting garrulous & shew indications of old age.

Very truly yours

SAMPSON REED.

[Enclosure][53]

Boston   July 8ᵗʰ 1864.

I was born in Bridgewater (now West Bridgewater) on the 10ᵗʰ of June, 1800, where I lived till the year 1814, having been prepared for college under the direction of my Father, Rev John Reed D.D. He officiated for half a century as clergyman in that place and was for six years member of Congress in the administration of Washington and the elder Adams. A considerable part of my boyhood was spent in working on my Father's farm. In 1814 my Father took me to Cambridge to offer me for examination and we spent the night at Morse's tavern. Our room was separated by a board partition from an adjoining one, in which I heard two students reciting to each other the Latin Grammar preparatory to the examination till I fell asleep myself. The next day I

---

[51] See footnote 44.

[52] See footnote 49.

[53] This is now to be found in Volume I of the Classbook of 1818 ("H.U. 338.18"), but must originally have belonged with the letter. The enclosure is written in the hand of an amanuensis, but is signed by Reed.

recognized the voices which I had heard as those of Osgood[54] and Swan,[55] and though those voices are now silent, they are still distinctly remembered. After leaving College, I spent almost three years in the Theological School at Cambridge, but during that time having become firmly convinced of the truth of the doctrines contained in the works of Emanuel Swedenborg, I relinquished the idea of preaching, as the number of those who believed as I did, was too small to afford me any prospect of success in that profession.

I was then entirely destitute of means and was under the necessity of seeking some other occupation for a subsistance. I at first commenced teaching a school in Boston on the Neck; but meeting with little success, I abandoned it. I then thought of studying medicine and entered my name with D[r] James Mann. I felt the necessity however of seeking some employment for my present subsistence; and having had a slight acquaintance with Mr W[m] B. White, I obtained a situation in his drug-store. I then began with the work of a common apprentice, and remained with him about three years for a sum barely sufficient to pay my necessary expenses, after which I commenced business for myself on a very humble scale, in Hanover Street, having received no other aid than a temporary loan of $900. I continued in the same business till January 1861 with quite as good success as my most sanguine hopes could have anticipated when I disposed of my interest to my son Thomas of the firm of Reed Cutler & Co. I have devoted considerable time to public duties; having served four years as a member of the School Committee of Boston, and having been two years 1852 and 1853 a member of the Board of Aldermen, I was also a member of the Constitutional Convention of 1853 and served as chairman of the committee on finance in the House of Representatives in 1854.

I was married December 25th 1832 to Catharine Clark, Daughter of John Clark Esq of Waltham. We have four children: three sons and one daughter, all of whom are living——James, born Dec. 8th 1834, Thomas, born Feb 3[d] 1837, Elizabeth, born July 10th 1838, and Joseph Sampson Dec 13, 1841. My eldest son graduated at Harvard in 1855 and is now settled as Assistant Minister with our Classmate Rev Thomas Worcester. My second son is established in the drug business in Boston. My youngest graduated at Harvard in 1862, but has studied no profession and is not settled in business. My Daughter is unmarried. My eldest son has three children and my second son one, making four Grand-children.

About the year 1828[56] I wrote a small work called the Growth of the Mind, which has passed through several editions, and have been a frequent contributor to the New Jerusalem Magazine. For several years past I have been one of the Editors of this work, and the Children's New Church Magazine which has now reached its 20th volume has always been under my management.

SAMPSON REED

---

[54] Timothy Osgood.
[55] James Swan.
[56] This date is incorrect. The first edition of his *Observations on the Growth of the Mind* appeared in Boston in 1826.

XII

R. W. EMERSON TO SARAH H. ADAMS[57]——FEBRUARY 13, 1865.[58]

This letter has considerable value as a commentary on the last paragraph of chapter XII ("Universities") in *English Traits*,[59] a passage about which there has been considerable misunderstanding.[60]

Concord
13 February 1865.

To Miss S. H. Adams,

I am sorry that the friendly note you send me should wait so long for a reply. But I have just returned from a journey to Chicago, & my correspondence is much in arrears.

On reading your note, I had to look up the printed passage to which you refer. I see plainly, that it refers to Wordsworth and Tennyson, who are both Cambridge men, as the preceding sentence refers to Ruskin. For *"in the old forms,"* whose purport you ask, it can only be said, that this is an American remark, since to readers on this side the water, there appears a great deal of conventionalism in all English poets,——[   ][61] even in Wordsworth & Tennyson; less in Browning & Clough, but with less excellence. But what I have to say on this point I should rather begin in conversation than with pen, & perhaps you will at some time give me the opportunity.

Respectfully,

R. W. EMERSON

---

[57] In 1894, Sarah H. Adams received Margaret Fuller's copy of the first edition of *Nature* and presented it to Miss Agnes Irwin, Dean of Radcliffe in 1908. See my facsimile of *Nature* (1940).

[58] MS. owned by the Boston Public Library.

[59] See *Works*, V, p. 213. The last two sentences read as follows: "England is the land of mixture and surprise, and when you have settled it that the universities are moribund, out comes a poetic influence from the heart of Oxford, to mould the opinions of cities, to build their houses as simply as birds their nests, to give veracity to art and charm mankind, as an appeal to moral order always must. But besides this restorative genius, the best poetry of England of this age, in the old forms, comes from two graduates at Cambridge."

[60] *Ibid.*, V, 372.

[61] The brackets indicate the position of the half-erased words, "less in."

XIII

R. W. EMERSON TO JOHN STUART MILL——MAY 6, 1865.[62]

In 1833, while in Rome, Emerson met Gustave D'Eichthal at an evening party given in the home of Horace Gray, and secured from him a letter of introduction to John Stuart Mill in London. Mill arranged Emerson's visit to Carlyle and thus became an agent in bringing the two men together.[63] The following letter, written nearly thirty-two years later, is apparently Emerson's first to the great utilitarian philosopher.

Concord Mass^{tts}
6 May 1865

Dear Sir,

I had the pleasure a great many years ago to bring you a letter of introduction from M. Gustave D'Eichthal of Paris, and I owed to your kind offices my first visit to Mr Carlyle. Will you let me strain that slight claim on your remembrance so far as to allow me to introduce to you a friend of mine, George Walker, Esq. of Springfield, Massachusetts, a gentleman highly esteemed here for his personal & social worth. Mr Walker is versed in the theory & practice of banking, & visits England with a commission from the United States Government regarding financial matters, & very naturally desires to see a master of Political Economy.

As we have learned to count you among our foremost friends[64] in England, I confide that you will share our joy in the suppression of the rebellion, & the approaches of a firm peace.[65] With high regard,

Your obedt serv^t—

R. W. EMERSON

J. S. Mill, Esq.

---

[62] MS. owned by the Boston Public Library.

[63] See *Letters*, I, 374, fn. 39; also *ibid.*, V, 415.

[64] See Mill's account of his liberal sympathies and his efforts to reduce England's opposition to the North: *The Autobiography of John Stuart Mill*, chap. VI (World's Classics edition, pp. 226-230). See also Mill's paper, "The Contest in America," in *Fraser's Magazine*, January, 1862.

[65] Lee had surrendered at Appomattox Court House on April 9, and Johnston had yielded to General Sherman on April 26. Lincoln had been assassinated on April 15.

CORRECTIONS AND ADDITIONS FOR *EMERSON'S READING*

(Cancel the volumes listed under Lardner's *Cabinet Cyclopædia* on pp. 84-85 of *Emerson's Reading*, and substitute the following original numbering of volumes as may be seen in the *Catalogue of Books Added to the Boston Athenæum*, Boston, 1840, pp. 86-87.)

2   Cooley, Wm. Desborough: *History of Maritime and Inland Discovery*, (3 vols.) London, 1830-1831, vol. I.

17   Lardner, Dionysius: *Hydrostatics and Pneumatics*, London, 1831.

19   Brewster, *Sir* David: *Treatise on Optics*, London, 1831.

34   Donovan, M.: *Treatise on Chemistry*, London, 1832.

63, 71, 96   Montgomery, James *et al.*: *Lives of Literary and Scientific Men of Italy, Spain and Portugal*, (3 vols.) London, 1835-1837.

80   Thirlwall, *Bp.* Cannop: *History of Greece*, (8 vols.) London, 1835-1844, vol. III: (B.C. 476-413).

84, 93, 112   Dunham, Samuel Astley *et al.*: *Lives of the Most Eminent Literary and Scientific Men of Great Britain*, (7 vols.) London, 1836-1839, consisting of (84) *Early British Writers;* (93, 106) *British Dramatists;* (112, 119) *English Poets* (by Robert Bell).

91, 99, 101, 108, 115   Forster, John, and Courtenay, T. P.: *Lives of Eminent British Statesmen*, (7 vols.) London, 1831-1839, vols. III-VII.

(On page 20, "[? Russell]" should now read "Robertson.")

(The following volumes were listed respectively as items 256-260 in the *Stephen H. Wakeman Collection of Books of Nineteenth Century American Writers*, N.Y. (American Art Association, Inc.) [1924], as having once been in Emerson's library. They all bear his autograph and were presented by him to others. Items 257-258 eventually reached the Concord Free Public library through the courtesy of Miss E. P. Peabody; item 259 was given to the Rev. Grindall Reynolds, pastor in Concord, and by him to the same institution; the last was for several years in the religious library of the First Church in Concord.)

[Hall, David]: *A Mite into the Treasury*, London (printed) and Phila. (reprinted), 1758.

Eichhorn, Johann Gottfried: *Einleitung ins Alte Testament*, (3 vols.) Leipzig, 1780.

Eichhorn, Johann Gottfried: *Die Hebraischen Propheten*, (3 vols.) Göttingen, 1816.

Kvinoel, D. C. T.: *Commentarivs in Libros Novi Testamenti Historicos.* (4 vols.) Lipsiæ, 1823-1818.

Degerando, M. le Baron: *Self-Education; or The Means and Art of Moral Progress*, (tr. from the French by E. P. Peabody), Boston, 1830.

ADDENDA TO THE INDEX-CONCORDANCE OF *NATURE*

PART SEVEN

———

INDEX-CONCORDANCE TO EMERSON'S
SERMONS

INDEX-CONCORDANCE TO EMERSON'S SERMONS[1]

During the next two decades scholarship will be obliged to approach the study of Emerson with better tools than have been hitherto available. The necessity of tracing his ideas to exact sources in the study of his development will justify the existence of every pertinent concordance and adequate index that can prove useful to researchers in the period of his most rapid intellectual growth. The immediate purpose of the present appendix, apart from its great utility to the compiler, is to enable the scholar quickly to compare the body of early sermons with *Nature* (1836) and with the collection of Emerson's poetry, for all three of which concordances are now at hand.[2] Students of particular themes——man, nature, spirit, salvation, soul, world, compensation, self-reliance etc.——now have a great advantage in being able to approach their specialized studies from at least three directions with little effort. I have not attempted to replace or incorporate Professor McGiffert's short index to his edition of the sermons,[3] which as far as it goes, still has value, but I have sought very greatly to augment it. Sources for many of the quotations which he did not identify will appear for the first time in succeeding pages, though a few are still proving troublesome.[4] The present concordance covers:

1) All twenty-five sermons which McGiffert has edited
2) Fragments from about thirty other sermons which McGiffert included in his "Introduction" and "Notes"
3) All important words in the titles of "A List of the Sermons"[5]
4) A few of McGiffert's comments which apparently reflect the MSS. which he was using.

All lines on each of his pages have been counted, except the running titles above the narrow black bar. To conserve space, I have used many abbreviations, most of them readily intelligible, but a few which should be memorized at the start.[6] Throughout *Emerson the Essayist*, moreover, I have referred to *Young Emerson Speaks* as *Y E S* and adopted the line-numbering system used in the following pages.

---

[1] Limited to the materials published in *Young Emerson Speaks*, ed. A. C. McGiffert, Jr., Boston, 1938, indicated hereafter by *Y E S*.

[2] See G. S. Hubbell, *A Concordance to the Poems of Ralph Waldo Emerson*, N.Y., 1932, and my small facsimile edition of Emerson's *Nature* (with index-concordance), N.Y., 1940.

[3] *Y E S*, pp. 273-276.

[4] These appear at 6.34, 9.28, 10.2, 13.20, 127.24, 174.11.

[5] *Y E S*, pp. 263-271.

[6] When not in agreement with the key word, N.=Nature; n.=nature; E.=Emerson; N.T.=New Testament.

A

AARON, 245.8

ABATEMENT, speak your own truth without a., xxxx.9

ABILITY to gratify our desires, 5.20; will be completely exercised, 19.4; men of, 181.33; regret over not having some fancied a., 107.24

ABNER, 245.8

ABODE, giving acc't of one's, 19.5

ABOLITION of slavery, 198.10

ABRAHAM, 107.3; faith was alive in A's heart, xxxv.28; God of A., Isaac and Jacob, 245.2

ABSTRACT proposition conquers mind, 198.19

ABSURD, men are agitated about the, 48.30

ABSURDITY of much that we do, 205.30

ACCEPTANCE: universal a. is a criterion of truth, 230.38

ACCESS to the Father only by me, 233.38

ACCIDENT: every a. threatens our being, 103.19; men cannot live by, 102.30

ACCOMMODATION in Jesus' discourses, 197.15

ACCOUNT of one's abode given, 19.5; true a. of the soul, 265.44

ACCUSATION: murderer sees a. in every face, xxiv.12

ACME of man's development, 211.3

ACQUAINTANCES do not have same character, 106.31

ACQUAINTED with virtuous men, xviii.23

ACT done by man produces inevitable fruit (compensation), 209.26; done out of solemn sense of duty, 14.33; of one's own will, 211.23; of reflection can redeem man, 206.34; of reflection necessary for making distinctions, 207.4; out yourself and thereby attain perfect character, 106.4; particular a. or sentiment seems intended for each man, 208.24; before a. of courage, love, devotion, height and distance are ineffectual, 178.20; each good a. is preference of whole to the part; future to present; God to men, 201.33; every a. is instantaneously judged and rewarded, 210.1; every just a., 167.19; God procures us good whether we a. or forbear to a., 68.27; God's mark on every moral a. is that it tends to produce good, 93.34; miracle is special a. of God's power, xxviii.19; pure a. cannot flow from polluted source, 128.21; when we a. from self we separate from God, 132.28

ACTING: by a. alone do we learn nature and extent of moral laws, 209.29

ACTION and reaction of man and profession, 164.11; better than wealth, 212.1; is end of knowledge, 193.2; must square with our conception of truth, 116.22; of genuine man, 187.11; all voluntary a. made basis for pleasing God, 85.25; bad

a. wins disapproval, 83.3; by a. man is enabled to learn properties of moral nature, 209.20; Christianity is rule of a., 27.32; connexion betw. moral truth and right a., 94.17; consequences of a. are reaped every moment, 103.31; diff. minds require culture for a., 70.24; efficient a. gained thru specialization, 164.16; ends of a. are the same, but the means and manner are various, 106.26; energy of a. imparted to the mind in love, 153.18; every man has his own sort of a., 108.5; every mind has its province of a., 167.15; extravagance of a. does not follow independence of mind, 110.32; frivolous a. may have grandeur, 14.11; God as Judge of a., 83.13; God's a. not hindered by man, 68.27; God's laws function wherever there is moral a., 101.23; good a. wins approbation of men, 83.1; great powers demand a., 166.22; healthy a. of mind, xxiv.30; how little our own a., how much mercenary etc., 183.17; intention before it blooms into a., 159.15; law of a., 116.10; law of all a. is that all things are double, 102.17; loyalty has been powerful spring of a., 154.9; men have power of voluntary a., 101.6; men's faculties are modes of God's a., 4.13; objects sufficient for our powers of a., 99.15; opinion of all a. determined by its tendency and end, 14.8; privy to virtuous a. performed, 212.6; reciprocal a. of opinions on the will and *vice versa*, 94.20; refer every a. in life to God, 53.9; retribution operates for past a., 101.17; reward of a. determined by moral laws, 209.30; right a. is not ours but God's, 132.30; rule of, 155.13; self-love and Benevolence are not the same a., 128.19; true field of a. above all ties, 168.13; truth vividly seen leads to, 94.18; uniformity of a. dangerous, 106.22; virtue exists only in a., 13.25; what of those excluded from a? 157.18; would do no mean a. to save his country, 156.7; yielding to opinions of others is a low-lived rule of a., 49.4

ACTIONS and words concern the perishable, 2.30; become God's responsibility, 188.14; conformed to the superior will within, 100.10; derived from principles, 264.18; designed to please God, 85.23; in service of sin, 3.23; judged acc. to standard of Jesus' principles, 178.4; judged not by movement but by tendency and end, 14.8; lead to better knowledge, 94.18; of good men are the Word made flesh, 235.18; of Jesus would not be considered insignificant, 14.12; of our neighbor deserve fair judgment, 1.8; all a. do not yield to the authority of honor, 157.9; daily a. not separate from relig. character, 189.19; greatness thru plain and vulgar a., 60.10; our a. are still observed by our departed friends, 235.10; our good and evil a. have preceded us to judgment, 101.18; our innumerable uncontrolled a., 163.14; proverbs govern us in gravest a., 63.13; single a. *vs.* our whole life, 163.10;

we judge others only by a., 1.4; we judge men by their a., 216.16; see *action* etc.

ACTIVITY of God omnipresent, xxiii.-20; of imagination greater in good man, 160.35; of will interrupted by sleep, 203.26

ACTS: amenable for our words and a., 116.18; animated by faith, 162.8

ADAM, 194.9; sin was a federal sin, 199.19; was federal head of human race, 199.18; N. as significant to us as to A., 44.25

ADAMS, [John?], 188.28

ADDISON, Joseph, 147.33

ADDITION: speak your own truth without a. or abatement, xxxx.8

ADDRESS of creation to the soul, 199.35

ADMIRATION, 248.31; excited in the soul, 211.15; fatal to spiritual health if lost, 248.35; flows from man's religious nature, 152.29; for laws of N., 161.17; is keenest and noblest of our pleasures, 151.21; is the rudiment of pure religion, 155.3; of crowds scorned, 6.25; of disinterestedness of sufferer, 154.27; of that which *is*, 205.6; of the good is the fountain of relig. in the soul, 212.8; possible only by man, 222.1; universal, 247.34; will often live and glow all unreturned, 155.1; disposition to a. leads us to idols, 152.1; proneness to a. is a peculiarity in man, 152.27; refining the a., 152.17; to be without a. is to lack mainspring, 151.22; unthinking a. of others, 106.25

ADMONITION in the measures of time, 67.8; of external N. to our short life, 44.31; to watch all we do, 102.31; louder a. of N. is to man's moral being, 44.33

ADORE your nature, 134.1

ADORES: man a., 207.12

ADVANCE of Christianity, 267.44

ADVANCEMENT of Christianity, 55.15; test for a. in relig. life, 250.8

ADVANTAGE which man has is more than to receive influence, 209.17; in seeking our own a. we promote good of others, 242.9; infinite a. of listening only to oneself, 108.33; men who look for their own particular a., 187.35; solid a. of well-spent hour, 17.30

ADVANTAGES gained from society, 46.4; of a gov't must always be negative, 77.23; of a life lived on relig. principle, 16.34; of external prosperity unimportant, 20.7; of society are purchased by disadvantages, 46.24; accidental a. in minister, 30.8; high tax for social a., 39.11; which men offer will vanish, 162.29

ADVERSARY, truth in an, 65.16

ADVERSITY is no longer adverse, 136.6; takes no peace away from good man, 102.25

ADVICE of St. James, 124.29

AFFAIRS: coincidence of first and third tho'ts applied to, xxxiii.18; din of world's, 162.19; in pressing a. facts speak for themselves, 109.12; men of discretion in common a., 3.34; results of moral laws in human, 209.23

AFFECTION, 205.13; disproportionate to objects, 153.2; for friends is balked and disappointed, 158.6; of love clothes its objects in ideal perfections, 153.7; of lover, 153.20; unrequited, 153.23; tokens of, 19.30

AFFECTIONS, 237.31; for God can be cultivated, 264.32; 265.6; impossible without speech, 61.34; intended to go out to some other being, 154.35; made purer by faith, 161.15; of ours, 191.19; of soul embrace truth and right, 100.15; recoil from authority and force, 195.10; require the personal, 234.15; warmed toward Jesus, 58.9; analysis of, 244.37; good book excites, 59.13; Jesus spoke of God in terms of earnest a., 92.7; league of a. in marriage, 31.14; minister's a. must be trained, 29.27; prayer to be sought in the a., 25.1; privation of, 226.28; social a. should be bands of strength, 19.14; source of humane a., 159.1

AFFIRMATION of spiritual world, 196.13

AFFIRMATIVE, speaks the, xx.13

AFFLICTION is a needful master, 258.30; E's domestic a., xxxvi.9

AFFLICTIONS not grievous to a heart that knows God, 160.10

AFTER-LIFE, 258.37; described, 9.29; we know little of, 10.27

AGE, dark, 156.8; is man's autumn, 44.19; left childless, xviii.28; of Jesus as contrasted with Him, 195.19; anr. a. will reverse all wrong opinions, 168.7; earth is of immense a., 172.7; honorable a. defined, 116.7; judging one's spiritual a., 115.1; old a. is unspotted life, 116.9; old a. means dissolution for all, 112.4; old a. of shame and sorrow, 16.30; religion in the new, xiii.18; we stand on eve of brighter a., 180.12; you are of a.; ask yourselves, 115.4; how old are you? 268.4

AGENCIES counterchecking natural laws, 126.10

AGENCY: free a. separates us from God, 132.26

AGES toiled to prove truths, 55.2; all a. concentrate their influence on man, 207.19; past a. instruct man, 208.20

AGREEABLE, cost of making oneself, 185.17

AGRICULTURE, 251.27

AID from God, 104.30; best a. to good gov't is sense of moral responsibility, 75.20

AIM exhortations at the heart, 36.9; made more distinct, 167.20; may be hidden for years, 167.21; of conversation is truth, 65.8; of a covetous man, 5.31; we must a. high to secure any good, 32.30

AIR, 208.3; a. grudges his breath, 193.6; makes the sound, 165.3; fly into a., 116.12

ALARM, death sounds, 34.3

ALFRED, the king, as reformer, 52.23

ALIENS, we are a. from God, 132.14

ALII disputent, ego mirabor (St. Augustine), 257.34

APPLICATIONS: superficial a. unworthy of scholar, 229.13

APPRECIATION, lack of, 258.26

APPREHENSIONS of vulgar ridicule, 52.33

APPROACH of death, 202.8; to God by humility, self-denial and love, 92.12

APPROBATION of erring creatures, 159.11

APPROVAL of erring creatures, 159.11

ARABIAN NIGHTS not more remarkable than N., 42.9

ARCH of rainbow, 258.2

ARCHANGEL, 188.24

ARCHANGELS see our guilt, 3.8

ARCHETYPES, 32.20

ARCHIMEDES, 172.2

ARCHITECT, God is moral, 107.17; man is a. of his fortunes, 8.8

ARCHITECTURE of the world, 222.3

ARE ye not much better than they? 45.15

AREA of infinite space, 172.26

ARGUMENT from N. is strong, 245.17; Jesus proves nothing by a., 91.4; overcome in fair a., 65.11; truth is victor in an a., 65.8

ARGUMENTS against truth often confirm it, 102.14

ARK of testimony, 38.25

ARIAN might be a member of rigid party, 84.20

ARIANISM of E's Christology, 233.26

ARM of art withered by palsy, xxx.33; of omnipotence is enlisted on side of Virtue, 87.27; raising one's, 122.14

ARMIES, few of us will command, 13.22

ARMS of man's influence, 205.14

ARRANGEMENT of one's tho'ts and purposes, 239.5; 239.8

ARRIVED at human dignity, xix.5

ARROGANCE in use of word *orthodox*, 230.32

ART cannot elude law of compensation, 209.28; of balancing oneself, 258.43; of conducting life well is taught by relig., 99.8; of life, 193.9; of man merely removes, combines and shapes the works of God, 41.20; arm of a. withered, xxx.33: more a. in formation of strawberry than in palace, 41.24; works of human a.: pyramid, church, 41.16

ARTIFICE is naked before God's knowledge, 4.3; not possible in dealing with truth, 95.26

ARTS, 234.21; attention secured by good a., 231.43; inventors of, 208.29; useful and elegant, 180.17

AS God liveth it shall be so, 188.19

ASIA, 203.7; 171.30; not as broad as a man's own soul, 111.14; plague of, 112.23

ASK, beware of what we, 215.10

ASPECTS of the heavens, 171.27

ASS knoweth his master's crib, 207.5

ASSEMBLY of an enlarged intellect not touched in revivals, 232.8

ASSISTANCE friends give us in worship, 237.26; men who need a. are often unlovely etc., 131.5

ASSOCIATION only with those nearest one in faith and feeling, 232.38

ASSOCIATIONS at the Second Church, 191.23; surrounding the name of home, 19.22; false a. with the Bible, 156.23

ASTONISHMENT: great a. perceived, 207.12

ASTROLOGY, 172.12

ASTRONOMER: the undevout a. is mad, 175.6

ASTRONOMERS have measured magnitude of sun, 52.11; of France revolted against relig., 175.9; were unbelievers in the popular doctrine, 175.1

ASTRONOMY, 170.1; 270.24; abridges what belongs to persons, places and things, 177.17; confirms our faith, 178.24; corrects and exalts views of God; humbles our view of self, 172.31; corrects and purifies the N.T., 177.10; corrects anthropomorphism, 173.5; has had effect on theology, 173.26; has tapped our theological conceit and upset Calvinism, 253.9; is tho't and harmony in masses of matter, 253.33; offers visible image of every exalted sentiment, 171.15; presents space in gigantic proportions, 172.25; proves doctrine of One God, 177.11; extent and plan of the universe, 171.12; influence on relig. opinion, 171.13; man carries the whole a. suspended in a tho't, 252.11; present state of, 171.10; spiritual, 252.8

ASSUMPTION that human mind is capable of receiving and acting on sublime principles, 105.5

ASYLUM from apprehensions of mortality is the church, 113.13

ATHEISM and ignorance, 265.35; no such thing as a., 247.31

ATHEIST: a's love of fellow man doubtful, 131.11; so-called, 199.32

ATHEISTS, 203.25

ATHENS, 200.28; 205.1

ATMOSPHERE transparent, 177.2; of the moon, 173.11

ATOMS in the immensity of being, 161.23; of knowledge and goodness, 17.10; reveal beneficent design, 175.32

ATONEMENT, 27.28; 199.20; 233.31; a way of a. sought by fearful soul, 84.5; great sacredness attached to opinions on a., 84.5

ATTACHMENT to beloved objects would increase if good qualities were increased, 153.32

ATTAINMENTS, men made for sublime a., 49.6

ATTENTION can make any trifle great or insupportable, 50.15; kept on things truly great, 52.35; of men must be called to presiding Intelligence by the spectacular, 121.15; turned from senses to God, 231.41; proper a., 167.19

ATTITUDE of preparation, 193.19

ATTRACTION: sublime a. of the grave, 143.4

ATTRIBUTES of beloved come from lover's own mind, 153.14; of God interpreted subjectively, xxiv.6; of God may be shared by men, 100.20; good men have venerable a., 105.14

AUDIENCE: keeping a. in one's mind, xviii.18

AUTHOR of N., 170.21

AUTHORITY belongs to moral truth and not to any person, 97.8; cannot be mimicked, 95.22; depends on the measure of the truth in man, 97.10; is necessary accompaniment of moral truth, 94.34; keeps errors alive in the church, 237.21; of Bible limited, xxv.21; of church destroyed, xxvi.6; of holiness, 124.27; of honor rarely extended to all action, 157.8; of Jesus, 90.1; 266.40; of Jesus rested on truth, 91.27; of Jesus springs not from his office of Messiah, 96.18; of men older, wiser and better than we, 109.29; of Scriptures also claimed by liberal party, 85.30; of virtue defined, 93.26; proceeds from perception of great principles, 95.23; affections recoil from a., 195.10; speaking with, xix.26; taught as one having a., 90.2; teacher of moral truth shares its a., 95.16; tone of a. cannot be taken without truths of a., 95.21

AVARICE in the young, 229.38

AWARD: God's a. upon character is immediate as well as future, 101.21

AXIOM of pastor, 35.34

AXIS, earth spins on, 173.35

B

BACON, Sir Francis, 208.31; 249.5; "Of Friendship" quoted, 62.24; "Of Great Place" quoted, 6.22

BAD derive countenance from the good, 79.3

BALANCE of man's faculties, 2.19

BALCONY kept after house was sold, 255.11

BALL spinning on its own axis, 173.34; the b. we dwell upon, 112.8

BALANCE: the beam of b. trembles, 243.29

BANDAGES torn from eyes, 193.32

BANK, journals are a savings b., xxxii.28

BANDS of strength are social affections, 19.15

BAPTISM, 31.7; marks accession of one more intelligent being into God's family, 31.18; sprinkled with water, 31.17

BARBAULD, Anna Laetitia (née Aiken), 147.34

BARBOUR, [Mr.], 181.25

BARDS were priests, 145.25

BARGAINS, driving, 163.19

BARNYARD, 209.14

BARRICADE of circumstances, 182.13

BASEMENTS, damp, 242.23

BASES of Christian theology, 231.25

BASIS of everything is God, 221.21; of social preeminence, 205.31; broad b. of man's moral n., 195.5; common b. of truth, 268.22

BATE no jot of heart or hope, 68.15; 201.28

BATS, 222.4

BE a God, 200.29; b. genuine, 190.6; b. girt with truth, 190.6; b. ye merciful; be ye perfect, 133.1; b. ye perfect as your Father in heaven, 92.17; b. ye reconciled to God, 38.9; b. ye stedfast, immoveable, 188.8

BEACH, shell cast up on, 221.45

BEAM in our own eye, 76.23; of the balance trembles, 243.29

BEAR one another's burdens, 19.27

BEAST, 173.22

BEASTS, Paul fought with, 22.21

BEATITUDES, 178.27; 223.22; quoted, 161.8

BEAUTIFUL: men of wide view of b. praise less extravagantly, 152.17

BEAUTY and excellence of moral truth, 196.8; clothes the dying good man, 127.13; clothes the world, 169.21; given to all parts of universe, 176.22; of external world, 39.6; of faith in God, 158.27; of justice, 212.4; of life nobly led under guidance of relig. principle, 16.31; of N. exists for soul of man, 43.31; of purified Christianity, 232.30; of world intended for man, 222.5; of world order, 45.24; an infinite and immortal b., 158.32; daily b. of their life, 20.14; every mind has its own, 108.1; love of moral b., 10.11; men less sensible to, 172.17; there is more in N. than b., 44.7; mortal b. unimportant, 20.9; neighbor's b. coveted, 4.28; root of, 210.26; same results in N. might have been possible without b., 43.4; stars are symbols of, 172.11

BED, lie later in, 232.22; sluggard in his b., 16.10

BEE, first journey of, 176.17

BEEHIVE, cell of a, 222.21

BEGGAR, considered a nuisance, 131.14

BEGIN: we b. where earlier ages left off, 55.2

BEGINNING: man in b. same as now, 44.14; God's laws have no b. or end, 101.23

BEHOLDERS of our thoughts, 1.19

BEING, best parts of my, xxi.26; continuance of individual b. in next life, 245.2; death is only a change of our b., 138.9; dignity of rational b., xix.6; duration of soul's b., 105.25; each b. is the centre of creation, 207.18; God is an awful, adorable B., 176.28; God's observation is law of our b., 4.16; immensity of, 161.24; man once considered type of highest b., 173.1; manner of, 136.30; men end with b. what they are accused of b., 87.2; miracle of our b., 203.1; 270.45; moral b's first duty is to reflect, 237.19; my present b. is sustained by Omnipresent Father, 221.11; no warrant in our b. for living anr. hour, 103.32; our own b. more wonderful than the resurrection, 122.19; tho'ts aided into b. by God, 4.11; truth of Jesus re-

lated to all our b., 138.6; whole b. of
genuine man behind every word, 187.10;
wonder of our b.: by whom not perceived, 206.29

BEINGS with faculties for reading
tho'ts, 216.16; all b. are embosomed in
God's wisdom and love, 170.18; animated and inanimate, 112.5

BELIEF destroyed by falsehood,
210.6 in God is innate, 264.26; in oneself, 183.27; in real presence of God
under bread and wine, 56.2; of value in
time of grief, 139.35; that death cannot
harm you, 202.2; that one is good may
be imposed on others, but not on oneself,
250.7; that space is boundless, 172.23

BELIEFS: few b. among liberal
Christians, 232.36

BELIEVE: sentence just read I do
not now b., xxxvii.33

BELIEVER, salvation of, 22.3

BELKNAP, Jeremy: his *Sacred Poetry* (1795) referred to, 148.1; 149.30

BELLY made a god, 151.15

BENEFACTOR: train child to be b.
of world, 52.5

BENEFIT to the world, 190.22; God
acts as b. to us, 221.42; relig. made for
man's b., 189.15; soul made to apply itself to more than its own b., 157.35; unshared, total b. of wisdom given each
man, 208.30

BENEFITS of conversation are mutual, 62.13

BENEVOLENCE and piety are only
true guides to the world, 94.9; b. and
selfishness, 266.18; b. and self-love may
prompt the same outward act, 128.18;
b. cannot require flattery, 226.3; b. from
self-interest springs from fear, 129.27;
b. furthers good of universe, 135.2; is
commendable, 110.8; is self-love well calculated, 128.12; not to be justified by
wants of our n., 130.21; of constant
natural process, 42.10; of God, 35.5; of
God discussed, 31.22; of God in his
works, 29.25; 41.13; of interest to all
men, 129.16; watches in creation, 159.16;
motive of b., 242.12; world is system of
b. (Hartley), 94.7

BENT of their moral n., 10.35

BEREAVE relig. of types but leave
things signified, xxxviii.30

BEREAVED are consoled by memory
of domestic virtues, 20.5

BERKELEY, George: 249.3

BERNARD, 249.1

BERRIES, 218.41

BERRY, 221.37

BEST part of life is unseen, 264.38;
all is for the b., 259.22

BETTER and b. every day, 85.8; b. to
fail than not to have striven, 32.31; b. to
give than to receive, 198.17; labor to become b., 101.15; work done b. if liked,
167.1

BEWARE of yourselves; there is terror in your n., 225.12

BIBLE called revelation, xxvi.28; can
contain error, xxv.27; is sealed bk. to one

who has not heard its laws in his soul,
111.5; not above Reason or moral sense,
xxv.20; reveals God's mind and will,
xxv.23; b. societies, 198.7; E's genuine
regard for, 218.26; false associations
with, 156.24; God of N. and B. is the
same, 170.16; reverence for, 147.17; tremendous interest in, 35.19. See also *gospel; scriptures.*

BIRD, 173.21; song of, 153.21

BIRDS, 203.18

BIRTH, 114.5; of an angel, 190.20;
new b., 116.14; new or spiritual b. is
necessary, 114.10

BIRTHRIGHT of the powers which
God has bestowed, 108.27

BISHOPS, apostles and sects yield,
xxxv.12

BLACKBERRY with polished surface
is a chemist, 207.26; influences upon b.,
its formation, 207.26

BLAME for bad gov't rests on individual, 80.3; good praise and b., xxii.13

BLESSED are eyes that can read
N's bk., 40.16; b. are the meek, 95.7; b.
are the poor in spirit, 115.13; b. is he
who does that for which he was made,
251.38

BLESSEDNESS and reality of relig.,
269.19

BLESSINGS: greatest b. not touched
by death, xxxi.2

BLOOD could not circulate on Uranus,
173.11; b. of Christ considered sacrifice
for all, 199.21; no atoning b., 177.15;
moon is turned to b., 8.28

BOAR, wild, 165.29

BOARD, conversation at family b.,
2.25

BODIES belong to world of matter,
1.23; heavenly b.: earth and moon, 176.6;
b. grow to height of but a few feet,
235.42; have a great inmate, 136.9; will
moulder in this nook of earth, 117.35;
heavenly b. were first objects of idolatry,
172.10; present your b. as a sacrifice,
99.2; unsocial b., 61.29. See also *stars.*

BODY born into this world, 114.5; has
no exercise or mansion in spirit world,
10.5; is a frail dwelling, 138.18; is soon
laid in the dust, 111.19; is temple of
Holy Ghost, xxvi.7; subordinate to soul,
189.7; hand is part of b., 132.24; I give
my b. to be burned, 14.25; powers of b.
multiplied by social affections, 19.18;
we need the b., not the mind, 216.20; a
well-spent hour like embalmed b. of the
mighty, 18.5; whole weight of, 186.27

BONAPARTE ridiculous, 111.11; see
Buonaparte.

BOND betw. seen and unseen world is
speech, 60.25

BONDAGE of the soul, 115.26

BONDSMAN of your friend, 158.30

BONE has a purpose, 220.41; why b.
is thus terminated, 204.17

BONUS vir nil nisi tempore a deo
differt, 200.27; bonus vir tempore tan-
tum a Deo differt, xxiv.3

BOOK excites the affections, 59.13; of common life, 7.15; of N., 40.15, 42.24; 178.26; of N. commands our interest, 171.4; of returning summer, 42.24; Bible is a sealed b., 111.5; impressions of a b., 110.2; N. is a b., 40.15; not a relig. recorded in a b., xxxv.29; Word of God a dull b., 115.8

BOOKS, 163.19; are seeds of civilization; silent benefactors; modest missionaries, 240.41; carry truth and virtue to other ages, 240.42; promote circulation of good b., 240.41; b. of the Evangelists are only the record of Revelation, 125.30; b. of theology, 199.19; ancient b. alone do not contain God's will, 189.3; hymn b., 145.1; 269.17; Jesus refers to no b. except Jewish scriptures, 90.17; prayer not result of study of b., 25.3; relation of man to globe set down in b., 203.21; relig. b., 268.40; soul sometimes needs b., 70.27; text b. in history, laws, politics, 75.13; we read same b. as our fathers but in different sense, 54.15

BORDERS of the earth set, 39.3

BOSOM of man enriched by all things, 208.35; of Jesus, 14.16; of the great night of space, 172.28; moral law in every b., 123.5

BOSTON described, 242.21

BOTANY cannot form an ear from a seed, 42.1; b. helpless if N. ceased working, 41.35

BOUGHS: remove green b. but don't forget the hope, xxxviii.33

BOUNDS should not be set to the discoveries of truth, 196.28

BOUNTY of God like waves of light, 159.17

BOXES, nest of a hundred, 206.11

BRADFORD, Gamaliel, quoted, 233.1

BRAIN in the hand, 251.28

BRASS, 244.30; sounding b. and tinkling cymbal, 51.2

BREAD, 216.22; b. and wine, 2.28, 56.3; b. and wine in memory of Jesus, 57.14; b. cast upon waters, 11.1; b. is bitter, 5.31; breaking of, 32.17; choice betw. virtue and b., 11.2; we do not get a piece of b. for ourselves, 135.11

BREAST: honor in a noble, 155.26; injury rankles in b., 30.14; man within b., 65.7; powers in a man's b., 166.21; reason is inmate of every human b., xxv.12; standard of character found in every human b., 110.11. See man; within.

BREASTS: honor rises to relig. in noble, 156.12

BREATH, 193.6; in nostrils, 162.30; eloquence is like b. of God moving on the deep, 26.22; man inspires and expires immortal b., 207.14

BROWNE, Sir Thomas, 159.24; allusion to Hydrotaphia, 112.26

BRUTE, unreflecting man is but a superior b., 211.26

BRUTES, men raised above, 193.12

BUCKINGHAM, Duke of, 157.2

BUNDLE, man becomes b. of errors and sins, 238.6

BUONAPARTE, Napoleon: ridiculous, 111.11; Russian campaign cited, 154.18

BURDEN, every man shall bear his own, 82.3; strength for the b., 268.6

BURDENS, bear one another's, 19.28; light b. and easy yokes, 264.16

BURNS to speak, xi.14

BUSINESS conversation illustrated, 109.4; dealings encourage national corruption, 79.30; not considered injurious to relig., 189.12; failure in, 184.14; main b. of man is shoved aside and never done, 117.3; our b. is the love of all, 135.20. See trade.

BUT know thyself a man and be a God, 200.28

BUTLER, Joseph, 249.4; Analogy cited, 245.17; 234.30; quotation from "Of the Nature of Virtue" in the Analogy, 93.28; [? Sermons] quoted, 95.14

C

CAESAR: his reason is no more weighty than our own, 182.3; ridiculous, 111.10

CALAMITIES, 268.34; become unimportant, 211.11; will befall men; they are widely shared, 259.4

CALAMITY, 140.8; bidden to do its worst, 22.9; disarmed by patience, 210.4; c. of Fr. Revolution, 194.26; great c. is man's distrust for himself, 105.20

CALCULATION, 184.33

CALCULATORS proclaim "world will last our day," 78.28

CALF: the golden c., xvii.16

CALL of our calling is loudest, 250.41; thunder c. of a Superior N., 162.19

CALLING in Christ, 169.10; is a channel thru which we learn laws of universe, 163.25; is that state employing all our powers, 167.30; is the work of every man, 167.24; of each mind filled with glory, joy etc., 169.14; of every soul is not in Heaven, 169.5; find your c., 163.1; 269.39; man's true and eternal c. is from God, 164.19; one's high c., 251.25; one's high c. is end for which man was created, 167.33; our c. brings with it the strength it needs, 169.19; our c. is the loudest call, 250.41. See employments, occupations, vocations etc.

CALLINGS invigorate faculties and educate, 164.7; of city dwellers, 163.17; of men in vulgar life, 251.24; serve same use as child's slate, 164.1; as many c. as individuals, 166.9

CALMNESS reigns within soul, 202.9; how achieved? 187.5

CALUMNY, 264.20

CALVIN, John: thinks for thousands, 237.16; worships with Fénelon etc., xxxviii.26

CALVINISM, 148.5; a dark and barbarous system, 147.30; pictures heaven from the senses, 243.38; upset by astronomy, 253.10

CALVINIST: 257.35; what must I say? 87.13

CALVINISTIC church, 133.34

CANDLE, play is not worth the, 193.5
CANNIBALS, 122.9
CANOPY of heaven, 33.35
CAPACITIES: we are full of c. that are within reach of objects, 5.19
CAPACITY and destiny of human soul, 157.29; for pleasure and pain revives in spirit world, 9.30; for ruling over a few things, 18.24; of individual soul, xxi.19; of men not realized, 105.15; man's c. for virtue, 83.6; 231.11; speech made intelligible to common c., xxxx.6;
CAPITAL of human comfort, 41.3
CAPRICE, each has his, 72.3
CAPRICES of society affect view of honor, 157.7
CARE of Providence for solar system, 174.22; c. of soul is ultimately one's own job, 238.20; take c. sermon is not a recitation, xviii.14
CARELESSNESS not in same class as deception, 51.32; not permitted in this world, 102.29
CARES of the world consume maturity, 117.3; a thousand c. besiege us, 103.6
CARPENTER, 163.18; Messiah is c's son, 56.27
CARTLOAD of dishonesty, 185.23
CARVE at a feast, 127.24
CAST down but not destroyed, 87.25
CATEGORICAL IMPERATIVE, 93.25; 94.35; 95.9; 105.6; 111.26
CATHOLIC churches, 102.11
CATHOLICS, 146.7
CATTLE, 203.18
CAUSE behind visible world denied, 175.12; not seen thru laws of N., 121.14; of all order is in the world, 114.2; of Christianity, 22.6; of Justice shall not fail, 66.7; of N., 175.19; of the slave is every man's c., 256.39; c. which God created you to promote, 19.9; die for a c., 14.10; failure in good c. better than not to have striven, 32.31; God is intelligent c., 175.14; good c. always strong, 160.31; how each c. tries to justify itself, 86.12; in right c. man's faculties multiply and grow wiser, 160.34; man is not c., but a mere effect, 238.4; presiding c., 124.11; secondary c. will satisfy most men, 121.21; soul asks tidings of First C., 204.8; support of a c., 184.2; unbeliever wants to assign a c. to everything, 122.6
CAUSES of destruction everywhere, 113.6; of mortality, 112.24; of pain, 138.21; understanding content with second c., 204.7
CELEBRITY: honorable c. coveted, 4.28
CELL of beehive, 222.21
CENTRE to circumference of things, 159.18; each being is c. of creation, 207.18; man is c. of the horizon, 208.16; man the c. round which all things roll, 208.12; see circle.
CENTURIES, dust of, 200.23
CENTURY is but the turning of an

hour glass, 113.26
CEPHAS, 177.24
CEREMONIES: cumbrous c. of Jewish Law, 55.12
CEREMONY is forgotten in hour of death, 34.30; important in society, 47.14
CERTAINTY in operation of natural laws, xxviii.29; of material world is challengeable, 2.9
CHAIR: getting c. nearer the fire, 48.35
CHALDEAN, 222.16
CHALLENGE of a martyr to pain, 22.8
CHAMBER of death illuminated, 34.28; alone in one's c., 226.42; dying c. of youth, 144.19
CHAMPIONS of arrogant churches, xxxviii.28
CHANCE cannot elude law of compensation, 209.28
CHANGE and circumstance do not affect moral goodness, 178.23; c. and permance, 263.24; c. in relig. opinions seems to be taking place, 256.10; c. of profession by men of strong character, 165.26; c. of vocation if it cannot be bent to one's character, 251.7; c. taking place in relig. opinions, 192.19; c. which Christianity is working in the world, 199.4; all things c. except the soul, 136.11; character of society every moment is undergoing c., 54.13; death is a c., not a termination of our being, 138.9; c. individuals before changing society, xxx.19; liability to c., 103.2; no c. but from glory to glory, 119.14; no c. in some churchgoers, 227.45; time cannot c. or touch spiritual things, 244.32
CHANGES affecting man do not affect the heavens, 171.34; c. or steps toward dissolution, 112.6; c. which touch man do not touch the heavens, 171.34; beneficent c. in the world, 159.2; violent c. of opinion seldom occur in men, xxxviii.10
CHANNEL fittest for each, 59.17
CHANNELS of our life, 116.17
CHANNING, William Ellery, xxi.24
CHAOS disembowelled, 4.5
CHAPTER of man's history appears in the conflict of parties, 86.16
CHARACTER affected by accidents, country, parentage etc., 164.24; c. and eternal condition rewarded, 104.22; basis of genuine man's action, 184.35; c. by which man is a particular person, 181.24; c. contracted or expanded determines our state in the hereafter, 9.34; developed thru failure, 184.15; dignified at home by moral force, 18.34; has its basis in the soul, 201.22; is exalted by the dignity of sentiments expressed, 94.23; c. of God, 194.28; 200.32; of God better understood, 232.31; of God grossly portrayed, 175.17; of God injured in hymns, 148.29; of God not jeopardized by a miracle, 122.31; of God revealed by Jesus, 179.1; of good man can not die; shines in purer light, 20.16; of Jesus

consistent with teaching, 94.27; of man can change inherited pursuits, 165.13; of man measured by its effect on others, 108.15; of man survives and ascends, 141.10; of mature man described, 130.2; of one's own mind not known, 251.5; of society undergoing change every moment, 54.12; of the genuine man, 254.23; c. one's brain, xi.9; rewarded both now and later, 101.21; strengthened in Lord's Supper, 58.12; tested at home, 15.34; c. *vs.* condition, 190.13; a man's c. is hidden, 1.6; childlike c., 266.32; Christian c. must embrace truth of both parties, 86.23; diff. between character and condition, 168.30; divinity of Jesus lies in majesty of c., 234.38; every mind has its own c., 108.1; force of c. preferred to external wealth, 183.35; formation of c. is main reason for human existence, 258.32; gov't cannot help citizens' intellectual or relig. c., 77.25; how determine c. of God? xxiii.28; imperfection in c. springs from neglect to cultivate some part of mind, 106.20; improvement of man's c. has influence on public welfare, 81.4; lameness of c. hidden by surfaces, 182.20; occasional c. of Jesus' sayings, 196.4; opinion of a c., 110.2; peculiar c. of every man, 106.26; 165.19; real c. of people not known to us, 254.37; perfect c. result of acting out oneself, 106.5; sinews of c., 210.28; standard of c. found in every human breast, 110.11; strength of c. determines man's effect on his inheritance, 165.17; the more finished the c., the more striking its individuality, 106.33; true c. has stability, 188.8; truth of c. defined, 184.26; truth of c. identical with relig. life, 188.34; veneration of speaker's c., 94.23; weight of professional c., 182.8; wherever there is c. there is judgment, 101.24; whole c. preferred to present gratification, 162.25

CHARACTERS of men are unlike in the best state of the world, 106.34; c. of N's pen, 40.17

CHARM of poetry hard to analyze, 145.10

CHARITIES, way full of, 101.32

CHARITY, 265.16; considered a bounty to vice, 131.15; Christian c., 266.42; indiscriminate, 241.14; law of c., 130.2; principle of c., 134.14

CHASMS: I don't like c. of discourse, xxxi.25

CHASTITY is only one meaning of *virtue*, 217.15

CHECK upon conversation is relig. feeling, 65.20; perfect c. on doctrine of self-reliance, 238.7

CHECKS: natural c. on fanaticism, 171.24

CHEERFULNESS and calmness, how achieved, 187.6; c. of this life depends on our progressive n., 54.23; c. regarding the future, 85.11

CHEMIST, the blackberry a., 207.27

CHESTERFIELD, Lord, xx.32

CHIEF among you is servant of all, 135.30

CHILD may sing for joy, 249.22; of the Creator, 200.16; character of, 266.32; how introduced to his world, 52.1ff.; intellect trained, 52.4; lesson in geography, 93.6; like a little c., 184.29; man treated as if he were only c. of N., 208.35; mind of c. taught to despise trifles, 51.29; soul is God's beloved c., 50.33

CHILDHOOD, twelve years of, 116.35

CHILDLESS, age left, xviii.29

CHILDREN and parents, 48.19; imitate evil, 115.32; rise up and call one blessed, 19.2; little c., love one another, 135.29; men are God's c., 132.17; most people are grown-up c. in understanding evil, 258.41; toys of c., 114.19; we are c. of God, 65.22; 133.11

CHILO (or Chilon), the Spartan ephor (*fl.* 560 B.C.), 248.45

CHOICE betw. principles for rule of our souls or gratification of bodies, 117.33; c. of a vocation premature, 251.4; c. of theisms, 151.1; 247.32; 269.27

CHOICES of men not overruled by God, xxiii.23

CHOIR of the world, 68.29

CHOOSE whom ye will serve, 151.2

CHRIST, 233.19; as he appears in hymns, 149.11; blood as sacrifice, 199.21; came into the light of worldly life, 233.28; character was consistent with teaching, 94.28; considered chiefly as teacher, 233.34; crucified, 263.22; gospel is power of God unto salvation, 22.2; portrayed in Calvinistic hymn books, 148.12; inferior to the Father, 84.21; life made vivid, 30.10; name appears in church, but not his spirit, 237.23; now head of church, no longer dead, 32.10; purpose was to redeem every soul, 169.11; taught living truth as applied to morals, 94.27; gospel of C. unfolded by time, xxxv.12; judgment of C., 267.34; the living C., 269.37; love of C., 268.38; love for C. to some has an unamiable sound, 235.6; love to C., 266.12; revere C. even if Christmas be not observed, xxxviii.35; significance of C., 266.9; spirit of C. preached to men in daily events, 68.30; temple of, xxvi.9; see *Jesus; Lord.*

CHRISTENDOM: see *Christianity.*

CHRISTIAN associations are correcting manners, 198.5; C. character must embrace foundations of both parties, 86.23; charity, 266.42; C. church as reformer, 52.22; C. church finds David's language inadequate, 149.26; C. concerned about his gov't, 76.29; C. despises trifles, 50.27; doctrine of immortality, 163.5; duty to pray, 267.16; C. relig. emphasizes world of spirits, 1.24; C. faith sets duty before the mourner, 143.21; C. faith teaches that soul does not die, 140.26; C. gives his strength to great duties, 51.12; C. is amenable to every other C. for his words and acts, 116.18; C. is free and solitary, 265.12; C. law, 135.17; C. law flows unobstructed thru the channels of our life, 116.16; C. life is a miniature of Christianity, 201.31; C. life leads to peace, 118.19; C. minister, 264.36; 264.37; C. nobleness in victory over egotism, 65.13; C. not too curious about course of unimportant events, 51.8; C. gratitude for immortality, 238.32; C. revelation has special economy, 85.17; C. scriptures, 29.22; C. sees Lord's Supper colored by complexion of his own mind, 57.20; C. sees U.S. as most perfect gov't, 77.22; a C. venture, 270.4; C. world divided by two prominent parties, 82.22; Liberal C. builds system on love of goodness, 231.26; marks of a C., 268.30; one may be a C. without knowing it, 156.22; Orthodox and Unitarian C. distinguished, 233.2; Orthodox C. builds system on fear of sin, 231.25; reasoning C. doesn't depend on outward evidence, 124.23; rigid C. characterized by his attitude toward God, 83.33

CHRISTIANITY is a rule of action aimed at highest good of intelligent n., 27.32; confirms natural relig., 265.20; displaced Jewish law, 55.14; enhances self-respect, 237.6; filled with churches of diff. creeds, 230.25; forgets that Fénelon, Calvin, Taylor etc. were champions of arrogant churches, xxxviii.27; found fit to be relig. of nations, 55.14; has a history of growth, 196.23; has shamed the idolater and broken the image, 71.22; is an infinite and universal law, 27.29; is medicine of immortality, 265.4; is most emphatic affirmation of spiritual world, 196.12; is not to be defended and respected but to be panted after and gloried in, 235.26; is spiritualism *vs.* sensualism, 201.30; is true, 27.11; made forcible appeal *vs.* paganism, 55.13; means more as men think more, 55.17; not defective, 27.9; not greatly superior to paganism in ethical standards, xxvii.4; not the only or last affirmation of truth, 196.25; now has nobler moral rule than formerly, 55.19; of divine authority, 57.33; outlines a hundred schools of skeptics, 55.23; part of history of the world, 195.4; rests on broad basis of man's moral nature, 195.5; revelation of a Deity whom the soul rejects with dire consequences, 27.31; seemed calculated to break down Jewish ceremonies, 55.10; seen in perspective by time, 195.4; should be taught always in manner as simple, absolute and universal as its truth, 27.13; significant for its revelation of immortality, 238.29; speculations of secondary importance in C., 233.32; C. touches all action, passion, and rational being, 27.30; must be found within own soul, xix.34; author of C. gave no systematic body of evidence,

91.7; change it is working, 199.4; corruptions of C. assailed, 194.33; E. not speaking only as preacher of C., xxxiv.15; evidences of C., 271.10; excitement and consolation in C., 55.18; exposition of C., 223.30; fruitfulness of C., 199.1; great doctrine of C. is immortality, 149.2; greatest value of C., 195.28; its enemies are product of bad teaching, 27.11; Jewish and Roman C., 177.23; nineteenth-century C., 55.16; progressive n. of C., 55.10; purified C. characterized, 232.31; why C. advances, 267.44

CHRISTIANS acc. to Tacitus, 217.40; are aware of Christ's immediate personal presence, 235.4; as interpreters of N.T., 219.4; C. by the same title as we are New England men, 23.29; C. cannot accept self-love as proper motive, 130.18; C. defined as receivers of the word of God that came by Christ, 115.35; have contact with the living Christ, 235.2; lack the spirit of Christ, 79.6; Liberal C. of Boston, 232.35; rigid C. set high value upon Faith, 84.10; we call ourselves C., 115.34; wise C. are not fond of miracles, 124.22

CHRISTMAS, 234.11; if you do not outwardly keep C., xxxviii.34

CHRYSOSTOM, Saint John, 249.1

CHURCH bears Christ's name but not his spirit, 237.23; hated and hating because of its errors, 237.23; is made up of spiritual natures, xxvi.11; is true asylum from apprehensions of mortality, 113.14; not to be honored as exclusive deposit of truth, xxvi.35; now divided from congregation, 58.17; C. of England, 133.29; c. of the future, 201.12; our only refuge from fear, 113.14; perpetuates the falsehoods of its leaders, 237.17; prepares us for death, 35.16; regulates faith for men, 237.16; c. services are periodical, 70.35; surveys man and his life from anr. side, 113.33; a work of human art, 41.16; God is present to individuals before being present to c., xxvi.13; Lowell's c. service less, xxxiv.4; mind of the c., xxvi.5; motives for joining c., 59.7; no rule in primitive c. for division of c. and congregation, 58.16; politics taboo in c., xxx.30; purpose in coming to c., 20.23; significance of joining the c., 58.2; view of c. is diff. from that of street-dweller, 113.31; whole c. called temple of Holy Ghost, xxvi.8; why built? 113.20; see *Christianity* and *institution.*

CHURCHES: hear what the Spirit saith unto the, 86.19; c. presented unworthy views of God, 175.16; all c. share view that man is manifestation of God, 133.17; Catholic or Calvinistic c., 102.11; four arrogant c., xxxviii.29; liberal c., 149.17; rival c. have all done service, 194.29

CIRCLE of your acquaintance, 181.7; shutting oneself in narrower c., 28.27

CIRCULATION of good books a duty, 240.40

CIRCUMCISION, disputes a b o u t, xxxv.2

CIRCUMSTANCE and change do not affect moral goodness, 178.23

CIRCUMSTANCES and their influence, 164.33; are instructors and presuppose a pupil, 165.1; bent or broken to man's purpose, 168.25; bent to one's calling, 251.34; bent to one's character, 165.25; c. change; the soul endures, 168.33; considered more than man himself, 254.16; control and are controlled by, the mind, 164.23; dazzle public life, 184.12; determined by Providence, 16.25; distinguished from the self, 183.15; do not make the man, 165.2; may be forgotten if one follows conscience, 188.28; of a man receive more attention than his essential manliness, 181.9; barricade of c., 182.13; making c. serve us, 168.21; not anxious concerning c., 126.18; our c. are to help us learn laws of universe, 163.25; c. that make it reasonable to expect a miracle, 120.10; a man independent of c., 181.9; see *environment*.

CITIES degrade us by magnifying trifles, 222.35; emphasize public opinion, 47.10; c. of men have been buried, 112.13; inhabitants of c., 39.11

CITIZEN must be vigilant, 78.16; intellectual and relig. character of c. cannot be helped by gov't, 77.25

CITIZENS in trust of a future world, 8.24; we are c. of anr. country, xxxi.3; 230.14; we are c. of heavenly country, 81.14

CITY of God is the universe, 176.14; c. throngs, 163.16

CIVILITY characterized, 225.38; c. of Fr. language, 225.40

CIVILIZATION costly, 39.12; pushed on by division of labor, 46.10

CLAIMS of others seem irksome, 144.3

CLARENDON, Earl of, 209.15

CLASS of social duties, 127.5; lowest c. of mankind, 129.12; see *party*.

CLASSES of ignorant men, xxxiii.16

CLAY, urn is made of, 132.26

CLEANSE his thoughts, 12.6

CLEMENT of Rome, 249.1

CLERGYMEN characterized, 165.32

CLERKS: presidents are c. of some real power, 229.44

CLIMATES: mild c. of early society, 171.29

CLOAK of dissimulation, 225.32; of licentiousness, 87.19

CLOCK, dial of a, 79.18; striking c. means death, 21.6

CLOSET, 157.13

CLOTH, weave, 206.21

CLOTHES are only a covering, 49.7; cannot protect a fool, 49.35; overemphasized in society, 48.20; unimportant, 49.18

CLOTHING: poor c. not shameful, 52.28

CLOUD, shade of, 33.14

CLOUDS and darkness hide the next world, 10.3; angry c. reflect man's guilt, xxiv.11; ever-changing glory of c., 39.16; he who regards c. will not reap, 50.26

CLUES leading thru N's labyrinths, 94.11

COAL, 218.41

COFFERS, wealth of India in my, 4.26

COINCIDENCE betw. heroes of honor and heroes of gospel, 156.14; c. of first and third tho'ts, xxxiii.17

COLERIDGE, Samuel Taylor, xxix.15; 249.5; *The Friend* quoted on miracles [See ¶162 in vol. I], 126.5; quoted again [See ¶116 in vol. I], 128.12

COLLECTION of the best hymns, 146.34

COLLEGES present unworthy views of God, 175.16

COLLINS, Anthony (1676-1729), 156.16

COLORS of a shell, 221.45

COLUMBUS, Christopher, 208.28; opened eyes on New World, 49.23; whether rich or poor is now unimportant, 49.22

COMFORT and women, 184.19; calculated too nicely, 50.22; in the death chamber, 35.1; capital of human c., 41.3; no c. in friends, 5.33; recipe for c. is not purpose of life, 258.34

COMFORTER, the Spirit of Truth, 197.1

COMFORTS of trifles unman and enslave us, 50.13; toys of petty c., 49.13

COMMAND of truth which pours light thru soul, 96.1

COMMANDMENT, breaking the first, 148.26

COMMANDMENTS, 81.22; 97.29; 109.27; 117.10; 141.23; are broken, 132.15; broken at home, 16.11; c. of God are disobeyed, 79.5; of Jesus, 133.3; keeping God's c., 132.23; obeying c., 269.18; obey c. while there is yet time, 104.1; Ten C., 71.19

COMMENTARY upon life found in proverbs, 63.4; science is c. on revelation, 171.7

COMMERCE, 198.4; grows out of human animal wants, 206.20; is a net woven around every man, 206.19; is ludicrous if regarded as end of life, 206.25; is only a means, not an end, 206.27; c. with outward things, 114.11

COMMISSION: God's c. to N., 6.11

COMMODITY, N. valued only as, 40.28; refuse converted to c., 41.1

COMMON basis of truth, 268.22; c. facts are most wonderful to instructed eye, 122.7; c. model for all men's minds, 64.22; c. nature of all men, 134.7; c. nature of men revealed thru speech, 62.6; c. to all is opportunity for greatness, 60.9; Reason c. to all men, 186.20; relig. in c. life, 189.23; why miracles are not c., 124.1

COMMONWEALTH: wide c. of God, 177.21

COMMUNICATE: minister can c. no more than he has, 32.20

COMMUNICATION, 194.10; of Divine Spirit, 134.3; of God to men involved in credibility of miracles, 120.23; of thoughts is miracle, 122.15; should be made intelligible to common capacity, xxxx.5; modes of c., 61.14

COMMUNION: closed c. discouraged, 58.16; c. with friends interrupted but not ended by death. 235.9

COMMUNISM, xxxiv.35

COMMUNITY benefited by presence of great men, 46.7; c. of goods impracticable, xxxiv.35; c. prayed for, 229.19

COMPACT: no c. of opinion among liberal Christians, 232.39

COMPANY not needed by the devout man, 221.31; unpretending c. of the fine race of flowers, 222.8

COMPARISON betw. what is required and what performed, 69.25

COMPASSION, 187.26

COMPENSATION, 65.31; 66.7; 101.16; 102.17; 159.20; 186.25; 210.3; c. and the gaining of wealth, 235.34; for every defect, 106.19; for excellences and defects, 107.19; for honest stewardship, 18.32; in astronomy, 176.11; is manifestation of God's judgment, 101.26; Law of C., 209.26; 263.21; c. takes place for all the qualities of the man, 101.26; see retribution.

COMPENSATIONS, riches of future depend on system of, 10.33

COMPETENCE of a man is known to his neighbors, 19.2

COMPETITIONS of this world, 114.17

COMPLAINT of a child over its lesson, 164.2; liver c., 233.2

COMPLAINING at the Almighty's decree, 139.13

COMPLAISANCE and self-interest, 185.8

COMPLEXION of individual mind, 57.21

COMPLIANCE in speech, 226.1

COMPOSITION as defined by E., xxxii.35

CONCEIT: theological c. tapped by astronomy, 253.10

CONCEPTION of divine n. enlarged, 72.15

CONCERNS, Gospel applicable to all human, xxi.35; 28.9

CONCESSION deserves no honor or love, 129.27

CONCLUSIONS of great practical value, xxi.18; of reason, 161.35

CONCORD, preaching in, 248.26

CONDITION of U.S. is index of average degree of private virtue, 80.8; of every man unique, 208.26; of fear, misfortune, ease, youth, age, 104.24; of teaching is a ripe pupil, 197.8; of wants, 5.16; c. vs. character, 190.12; compensation in our c., 101.27; favored c. has its

cares, 103.6; marvel of our c., 207.8; not in same c. as forefathers, 54.11

CONDITIONS attending announcement of future life, 85.19; fearful spirit makes no c., 84.7; rigid party will accept any c., 84.14; two c. of teaching, xxxix.34

CONDUCT capable of explanation tho circumstances be forgotten, 188.26; c. prompted by high principle is always significant, 14.21

CONFESSION of sin emphasized in revivals, 231.45

CONFIDENCE destroyed at root by falsity, 185.19; c. in God's goodness, 40.5; in worth of human n., 106.6; c. invites c., 37.26; needed in oneself, 107.16; c. of a man of principle, 188.17; c. that there is no defect or inferiority in his n., 106.14; relig. produces c. in God, 105.18; see self-reliance etc.

CONFINEMENT: solitary c. intolerable, 63.35

CONFINES: narrow c. of home, 14.28

CONFLICT betw. our two selves, 200.9; life a c. involving opportunities, 52.2

CONFORMITY to nature, 122.35

CONFUSION of tho't re. immortality of soul, 148.35

CONGREGATION, 146.31; 147.18; c. of moral natures always sees us, 3.7; c. whispers, 29.35

CONNECTION betw. moral truth and right action, 94.16; faith must have independent c. with God, 237.30; advantageous c., 184.18

CONNECTIONS of n. and friendship become sacred, 144.12; standing in same c., 191.14; c. with society preach doctrines of the gospel, 68.34

CONQUEROR, Israelitish, 193.32

CONQUERORS of men who have not yet conquered themselves, 111.12

CONSCIENCE, a proof of God, 264.22; a standard of character in every human breast, 110.11; cleared by faith, 161.14; God's vicegerent enthroned within, 11.25; impossible without God, xxiii.21; is above the highest copy of living excellence, 110.12; is Divine Eye, 100.7; is God working in man, 100.11; is God's minister in the soul, 231.21; is in every man, xxv.12; is man within the breast, 65.6; is proof and voice of God, xxv.6; is the domestic God, xxv.5; is the inner monitor, 11.29; of good men identified with Jesus' memory, 96.31; c. made a god, 151.13; may be followed without shame, 188.25; founded only in relig., 184.9; points to lower and lower degrees of right, 231.22; same in all men, 64.25; should do its office, 232.18; the truth-teller, 67.11; violated for reasons of livelihood, 254.42; will come to our aid, 127.20; acting acc. to c., 169.9; dominion of c. extended to include public duties, 75.24; divine instinct of c. is never wholly subdued, 231.23; c. and man's two selfs, 200.7; man in the single service of c., 161.3; no tax of c., 9.2; obedience to c., 111.26; service of c., 17.35; state safe if men follow c., 76.3; see *soul*.

CONSCIENCES bear witness to divine truth, 20.24

CONSCIOUSNESS: double c. and our two selfs, 200.7

CONSENT betw. God in neighbor and God in me, 134.27; of head and heart, 189.11; act with full c. of own mind, 166.30

CONSEQUENCE granted on basis of property, 205.33; c. of all goodness to increase the power of him who has it, 17.5; c. that prayers are always granted, 4.23

CONSEQUENCES indifferent to self-reliant, 188.20; c. of action being reaped every moment, 103.31; c. of human errors in the church, 237.22; c. which no chance or art can elude (compensation), 209.28

CONSIDERATION conceded by society, 5.28; c. of a doctrine requested, xix.31; a person of c., 211.33

CONSISTENCY of the genuine man, 184.34

CONSOLATION offered by Christianity, 139.2; for the mourner, 138.1; 268.15; in Christianity, 55.18; in trouble, 267.26; of truth and promises of N.T., 138.24; still given us by departed friends, 235.11; best c. at time of death is domestic virtues, 20.4

CONSOLATIONS, lasting, 161.10

CONSTITUTION and destination of human soul, 2.18; of man, 189.5; of man and universe is moral, 122.33; of men is wonderfully made, 257.27; of U.S., 75.13; man's c. answers his question, 161.26; marvel of man's c., 203.12

CONSUMPTIONS, 242.25

CONTEMPLATION impossible to mind degraded by little studies, 48.6; c. of our own virtues, 13.18; of outward things, 216.21; of the vast and unbounded, 152.21; of worldly goods, 5.27; of worth of soul, xxi.20

CONTEMPORARIES of Jesus found his particular lessons more valuable than we, 195.33

CONTEMPT for self, 211.30

CONTENT to stand by and let reason argue, 186.14

CONTENTION, 187.20; is adverse to true relig., 88.3

CONTENTMENT: more c. by trusting in God than in possessions, 114.27

CONTINUITY, principle of, 244.16

CONTINUANCE not a contrast, in next life, 244.17; c. of individual being in next life, 245.1

CONTRACTS, draw, 206.21

CONTRADICTIONS in gospel are resolved, 161.7

CONTRAST: next life not a c. with this one, 244.18

CONTRIVANCE in every part of our frame, 203.15

CONTRITION: private c. should not

cloud views of God, 68.18

CONTRIVANCES for use and pleasure; not for pain, 85.1

CONTROVERSIES about intent of Lord's Supper, xxxv.4

CONTROVERSY betw. two prominent parties in Christian world, 82.24; makes us jealous of others, 88.23; mischief of c. is set forth, 87.35

CONVENIENCE or inconvenience unimportant to Christian, 51.9

CONVENTIONALISM of our lives, 60.7

CONVENTIONS of worship objected to, xxxvii.20

CONVERSATION, 60.1; 194.10; 265.36; an institution for diffusion of knowledge, 62.29; breath of social life, 63.35; centers in insignificant things, 2.25; chastened by relig., 226.13; enables minds to quicken and alter each other, 62.10; enriches the common treasury of men, 62.31; has many degrees of merit, 64.19; is a seeking of ourselves in others, 134.8; a large part of life, 64.17; need not lose wit and brilliancy, 226.15; c. of business men illustrated, 109.3; of exalted minds, 63.22; of village gossip, 64.4; on pressing affairs permits facts to speak for themselves, 109.10; reveals an idea of man standard to all, 64.28; reveals disposition to admire, 152.2; tamely uniform everywhere, 107.7; tests the qualities of men; banishes outward considerations, 49.30; c. with one's inner man, 183.9; aim of c. is truth, 65.8; best check upon c. is relig. feeling, 65.20; blessings of c., 63.26; duties belonging to, 60.20; 64.10; each man is gainer in c., 62.16; fine c. is rare, 63.24; how poor in practice, 65.27; Jesus' style was that of c., 91.12; outrages in c., 66.3; personality of c. removed, 65.23; requirements for fine c., 63.24; uniformity of c. dangerous, 106.22; uses of c., 62.27; virtue of self-trust seldom enters c., 108.29; watch it, 102.33; wiser in c. than in silence, 62.23

CONVERSE with yourself, 111.25; 168.3

CONVERSION, 255.8

CONVICTION in human soul, 198.14; of a true man is equal to the Judge, 188.18; of duty conveyed to the heart by preacher, 25.22; trusting one's own c. is to rely on one's birthright, 108.25; private c. overrules Bible, xxv.25; your own c. to test a doctrine, xix.32

CONVICTIONS of Disciples, 56.33; departure from c. is loss of power, 108.19; when our inner c. contradict another's, 109.33

CONVINCE: we cannot c. others of what we do not believe ourselves, 250.12

CONVULSIONS of the earth, 112.12

COOPERATION, 130.10; impossible without speech, 61.33; in society is beneficial, 128.27; of men of intense conviction, 198.23; of scholar requisite in teaching, 197.12; necessity of c. with others to make efforts for true relig. of any avail, 88.33

COPERNICAN astronomy made the scheme of redemption incredible, 174.34

COPIES: our faculties are imperfect c. of God's perfections, 84.33

COPY: highest c. of living excellence, 110.12

CORDS of friendship and love, 19.19

CORINTHIANS, 198.2

CORN: plant a vine and gather c., 29.33

CORNER of every street is a closet, 3.16

CORNERS: men seldom turn sharp c., xxxviii.12

CORPOREALITY in future life, 244.25

CORRECTION of prison discipline, 198.8; of thoughts possible in conversation, 62.22

CORRESPONDENCE betw. sentiment of soul and Bible truth, 115.15

CORRUPTION, tho'ts of soul have no relation to, 202.4

CORRUPTIONS of Christianity, 194.33

COUNSEL sought of the soul, 200.13

COUNSELS not founded in truth, 139.9

COUNTENANCE colors at sight of the insignificant, 2.25; c. of rich man, 5.26; every c. accuses a murderer, xxiv.13; see also *face*.

COUNTERBALANCE to the engrossing of riches etc., 183.28

COUNTERFEIT: paltry c. of ignorance, 3.29

COUNTRIES benefit from union, 128.33

COUNTRY builds independent men, 47.3; earthly and heavenly, 81.25; give life for c. but do no mean act for it, 156.7; our c. may flourish or fall, 230.10; relig. concerns allegiance to c., 75.6; U.S. cannot long be our c., 230.12; we are citizens of anr. c., xxxi.3; 230.14; we are citizens of heavenly c., 81.14

COURAGE, 178.20; 234.17; comes to our aid, 127.20; greater c., 161.2

COURSE: gen'l c. of one's life often disregarded, 163.9; c. of unimportant events, 51.8

COURTESY to persons, 65.24; more c. in words of truth, 226.2

COUSIN, Victor: *Introd. to Hist. of Philosophy* quoted, 200.25

COVETING neighbor's goods, 13.11; neighbor's wit, 4.27

COVETOUSNESS, 5.26; 18.15; relieves starving multitude in self-protection, 129.10; spirit of c. rebuked, 135.28

COWPER, William, 147.34

CREATION, 212.11; as seen by liberal party, 83.7; as seen by rigid party, 83.8; continues while all perishes, 113.27; c. in each instant, 221.11; is continuous activity, 221.8; is so magically woven, 209.31; looks pale beside a virtuous man, 205.17; each being is centre of c., 207.18; each person is evidence of God's last c., 32.3; man is tongue of c., 145.4; man's duties and position in c., 204.33; ma-

terial c. only the shadow of moral truths, 196.32; nat'l c. subjected to man's tho'ts, 198.21; organized c. of every new year, 40.2; outward c. pales away, 178.14; scale of c., 45.17; spirit that governs c., 45.14; the gift of c., 168.9; veil removed from c., 175.24; voice of whole c. speaks in soul, 202.7; whole c. cannot bend a man who stands upright, 209.34; whole c. comes to aid of blackberry, 207.29; wonder of surrounding c. presses on soul, 199.33

CREATOR: God is active C. of tho'ts and aids them into being, 4.10; his word leaps forth to its effect, 6.34; uncovers the face of the soul to man, 200.16

CREATURE: each c. assigned to its own element, 173.21

CREATURES, 208.3; intended to serve one anr., 242.17; approbation of erring c., 159.11; man speaks for irrational c., 145.5

CREDENCE to the historic fact, 126.19

CREDIBILITY of a miracle—on what it depends, 123.27; of N.T. miracles, 124.14

CREDIT and consideration requested, xix.31

CREDULITY produced by rigid state of mind, 84.8

CREED meets the wants of some one class of minds, 230.26; of simple nature: all is for the best, 259.22; Doctrine of Trinity is accidentally part of c., 84.20; some men have dedicated entire life to support a c., 86.9; strict creed often hides immoral life, 15.32

CREEDS, be master of, xxxix.1; gross c. which were called relig. and Christianity, 175.8; old c. rejected as presenting gross views of God, 175.20; see *sects.*

CRIB known by the ass, 207.5

CRIME can never be gain, 136.21

CRIPPLED in the exercise of profession, xxii.5

CRITERIA for a truth, 230.37

CRITIC: siding with one's c. against oneself indicates cultivated man, 226.10

CRITICISM of a bk., 110.2; of music, 145.8; of poetry, 145.10; hymns almost below c., 147.10

CROSS: each has his own c. to bear, 258.27

CROSSES: peevish man finds way full of c., 101.32

CROWD, one selected from the, 208.13

CROWDS, scorn admiration of, 6.26

CROWN, star in its, 141.9

CROWNS: kings' c. are dim beside toy of a child, 249.25

CRUTCHES welcome in supporting virtue, 242.44

CULPRITS invited to Lord's Supper, 59.5

CULTIVATE in every soil the grape belonging to that soil, 107.13

CULTIVATION indicated by ability to side with critic against oneself, 226.10; of affections for God, 265.7; of all man's powers, 167.17; of all parts of mind required, 106.21; of E's mind necessary, 29.20; of self-knowledge, 201.15; powers of mind susceptible of c., 85.5

CULTIVATING affections for God, 264.33; the mind, 218.15; 265.8

CULTURE: diff. minds need diff. c. to bring them into action, 70.24

CUP of sensual excess, 225.9

CURE for fear of death, 127.11

CURIOSITY can be satisfied near at hand, 46.23

CURIOUS: not c. about unimportant events, 51.8

CURSE of the fatherless, 9.10

CUSTOM to personify abstract ideas, 256.17

CUSTOMS of man thunder, 184.8; our c. different from our fathers', 54.14

D

DAINTY in food and nice in dress, 52.6

DANCES, 10.18; d. and hymns in worship, 146.3

DANGER, trust in spite of, 212.18

DANGERS drive one to soul, 200.14; seen in conflicts within Christianity, 82.23

DARK AGES little dreamed of Christianity as we know it, 55.21

DARKNESS hides next world from us, 10.3; of world yields to the light of anr., 34.25; error finds its own d. everywhere, 102.22; sun goes down in d., 8.27

DATE of the creation (B.C. 4004), 252.33; humble things of mortal d., 2.26

DAVID, 147.11; 147.23; peculiar language of D. inadequate today, 149.25

DAWN is reddening around us, but the day has not come, 199.7

DAY has not yet come, 199.8; is full of duties, 85.8; is thine; night also, 39.2; d. made bright, 169.20; d. may come when, xxx.32; d. without night, 201.4; every d. a part of the divine message is spoken, 199.11; every d. exposes falsehoods, 194.5; Fast D., 270.10; improvement every d., 85.8; life is like the d., 193.16; objects of every d. preferred to spiritual ones, 2.12; world will last our d., 78.29

DAYS pleasant and unpleasant to men, 42.29

DEAD are present to the mourner, 142.7; enjoy a spiritual society, 142.31; help us in troubles and temptations, 142.19; keep one company, 142.24; see us with clearer sight, 142.14; d. themselves speak to the mourner, 142.7; best tribute to d. is to be faithful in our place, 144.7; deep gives us its d., 4.4; if one rose from d., 45.7; resurrection from the d., 35.1; virtuous d. confirm our opinion about grief, 143.19

DEAF: see dumb.

DEATH, 219.39; 266.36; 270.44; abolished, 87.32; d. and pain our ghastly enemies, 258.24; belongs to God's order called N., 33.33; cannot touch greatest blessings, xxxi.1; d. chamber illuminated, 34.29; d. clothes a good man with beauty,

127.13; deprived of its sting, 144.26; does not separate loving souls from us, 142.33; d. is fate of all, 34.34; has no terrors to soul, 202.8; d. impossible to mind clothed with humility, love etc., 92.16; d. interrupts but does not end communion with friends, 235.8; is a change not a termination of being, 138.9; is a solitude which the world cannot relieve, 34.10; is check to evil courses, 9.27; is man's winter, 44.19; is necessary and natural, 33.34; levels varieties, 265.17; of Jesus Christ, 52.19; of one who has served others, 127.11; of parent etc., 184.16; d. rate in Second Church, Boston, 220.2; regards not our human distinctions, 34.20; removes doubt, 140.33; result of loyalty, 154.14; symbolized by striking clock, 21.6; teaches something, 192.35; welcomed so that we may be with loved ones, 143.10; will bring a state of freedom, 168.35; after d. there is life, 9.29; approach of d., 34.2; at d. soul enters nearer relation to the Father, 140.25; at d. soul returned to soul of the world, 245.13; conquering d., 33.30; domestic virtues are best consolation at d., 20.4; fear of d., 119.3; 127.10; 267.32; indifference to d., 270.35; issues of life and d. are in the heart, 12.8; Jesus hoped by his d. to correct Jewish messianic hopes, 193.31; liability to d., 103.3; life is a progress toward d., 112.22; man has been delivered from d., 170.12; no knot which d. cannot untie, 168.34; not d. but life we are seeking, 143.27; our relig. is a preparation for d., 35.16; passage from d. to life, 114.16; seed of the second d. is selfishness, 239.11; sickness is forerunner of d., 103.18; time for d., 113.12; trust in spite of d., 212.18; what have I to do with d., 245.40; see mortality.

DEBASEMENT can yield to character, 210.28

DEBAUCHERY, damning, 6.9

DEBT: man owns deep d. to his troubles, 211.12; our d. to past generation, 77.17; preacher should strive to pay d. to fellow men, xxxx.4

DEBTOR, oppressed, xviii.30

DECAY of universe, 113.16; no d. in N., 159.20; within d. is a germ that decays not, 113.24

DECEIVE, impossible to d. oneself, 250.7

DECENCY esteemed above devotion, 227.42

DECEPTION distinguished from carelessness, 51.31

DECISIONS of honor, 155.35

DECORATION of the world, 222.3

DECORUM, reputation for, 227.43

DEDICATION of the Vestry, 218.43; 271.9

DEED: worthy d. puts man in harmony with eternal, 211.29

DEEDS are surest index of states of mind, 85.29; good d. registered on dial of soul, 17.15

DEEP gives up its dead, 4.4; breath of God moving on the d., 26.23

DEFECT of pure heart and good life inexcusable, 29.28; every d. has compensation, 106.18; no d. or inferiority in man's nature, 106.14

DEFECTS compensate for excellencies, 107.18

DEFENSE of a man resides in his will, 209.33

DEFERENCE demanded from fellow men, 205.27; d. to others results in loss of power, 108.19

DEFICIENCIES: our d. become more apparent to us with progress, 250.10

DEFINITION of honor, 155.28

DEGRADE trifles, or they will degrade you, 50.10

DEGREES of right, 231.22; improvement by small d., 266.24; virtues possessed in high d.. xviii.24

DEIFICATIONS: love, loyalty, honor, 247.37

DEISM repudiated by E., 31.23

DEITY of Christ opposed, 148.12; revealed in Christianity, 27.31; audible petitions to, 3.14; see God.

DELAY: work of self-culture admits of no d., 101.11

DELIGHT in memory of well-spent hour, 18.2; animal d., 6.4

DELIGHTS of fireside, 19.20

DELUSION of the understanding is most miserable, 3.18

DEMEANOR of man, 205.8; an apologizing d., 66.15

DEMIGOD, Jesus made a, 195.12

DEMOCRITUS, 206.14

DENIER of divine power, 206.27

DENOMINATIONALISM, evils of, 88.9

DEPARTED, voices of the, 38.21

DEPARTURE from the common order necessary to startle men into faith, 121.16; each new d. of man from relig. makes him less able to return, 28.3

DEPENDENCE and freedom, 265.38; d. and independence, 270.41; d. helps shape happiest man, 160.9; d. of man on God, 253.25; d. on Divine Will, 204.1; d. on God hard to reconcile with free will, 236.15; d. on God not contradicted by self-reliance, 110.22; men are d. on God, xxiii.18

DEPENDENTS, welfare of, 127.19

DEPORTMENT of Jesus graceful and decent, 51.22; d. of parents and children, 51.34; of women, xxxv.3

DEPRAVITY is real; is planted wherever seed of man was sown, 231.15; not complete in anyone, 231.20; springs from following other men's judgments, 110.35; doctrine of Total D., 232.19

DEPTH of human nature, 200.17; unfathomable d. of the soul, 201.17

DESCRIPTION of God is inadequate, xxiii.6

DESIGN and performance, 103.5; d. of Providence, 9.6; every virtuous d., 160.31; profusion of d. in universe suggests a mind behind it, 44.1; we must live by d., 102.30

DESIGNS hindered by many things, 67.18

DESIRE for sympathy, 237.12; d. of man can be satisfied only by God, 155.7; d. to raise oneself, xix.4; d. to self-improvement, 211.10; all effort at virtuous d. would cease without hope of immortality, 245.27; every d. is a prayer uttered to God, 4.19

DESIRES and faculties of the soul, 158.11; we try to obtain d., 5.11

DESPAIR, cast away, 7.30

DESPERATION of our trade, 229.38

DESPONDENCY, 128.1; weep not for d., 7.28

DESTINATION of human soul, 2.18

DESTINY and capacity of human soul, 157.29; d. of man is the grave, 112.20; becoming acquainted with our d., 168.18; what is my d. 199.26

DESTRUCTION: causes are everywhere, 113.6

DETERMINATION to some one pursuit for each man, 165.20

DEVELOPMENT of inward nature, 184.5

DEVILS, worship of, 156.35

DEVOTION yields to decency, 227.42; closet of d., 3.17; evils of d. to a denomination, 88.8; honor is a more spiritual d., 155.21

DEVOUT above the meaning of your will, 156.29

DIAL: golden d. of man's soul, 17.14; d. of a clock, 79.18

DICTATES of the reason, 185.1

DIE: as we d. in this world we are born into next, 10.3; if we did not d., 35.19

DIFFERENCE betw. liking and not liking one's task, 166.31; betw. pulpit and parlor, 220.10; betw. relig. and irrelig., xxiv.16; betw. slighting trifles and going studiously wrong in trifles, 51.20; betw. words that are things and words that are words, 226.27

DIFFERENCES: betw. great and good men, 107.2; betw. ourselves and others should be respected, 106.16

DIFFERENT senses put on N.T. text by d. Christians, 219.3; d. sorts of truth and d. ways of possessing and communicating it, 92.26; each man's condition is d., 208.26; trait that makes us d. from other men, 210.31; vocation is d. to every man, 251.27

DIFFICULTIES in home life, 20.20; to be encountered, 103.7

DIFFICULTY is a needful master, 258.30

DIFFUSION of knowledge by conversation, 62.29; of useful knowledge, 198.9

DIGNITY not added to Christ by making Him king, 195.11; d. of existence when conceived as a teacher, 193.11; dignity of rational being, xix.5; d. of sentiments expressed, 94.24; d. of the soul, 50.32; how Jesus gave d. to his instructions, 90.12

DILATED: man's heart becomes d. with the presence of Spirit of God, 210.19

DIN of this world's affairs, 162.19

DIRECTION may be wrong, tho sentiment is right, 154.29; d. of sentiments is unworthy, 157.21; d. to our common employments, 168.19

DISADVANTAGES become unimportant, 211.4

DISAPPOINTED man, xviii.27

DISAPPOINTMENT helps shape happiest man, 160.9

DISAPPOINTMENTS: domestic d. do not trouble the soul, 201.25

DISCERNMENT, spiritual, 268.41

DISCIPLES, 193.21; d. and other Christians share the authority of truth, 97.10; d. characterized, 125.12; d. of Jesus, 56.31; eyes of d. opened, xxxiv.32; Jesus reproves the d., 59.2; the Twelve D., 14.17

DISCIPLINE is reason for man's being placed here, 258.36; d. of intellect, 29.26; of virtue, 193.9; inequalities in human life are d., 160.5; our moral d. here anticipates our after-existence, 258.36; prison d., 198.9; rough d. of hot contention, 187.19

DISCONTENT is penalty for idleness, 210.8

DISCORD: man in d. with things around him, 207.10

DISCOUNTENANCE to laws, 3.26

DISCOURSE at a feast, 127.25; better than wealth, 212.1; I don't like chasms of d., xxxi.25; benevolent d., 14.17

DISCOURSES of Jesus show accommodation, 197.15; of Jesus were simple in style, 91.12

DISCOVERIES in spiritual world will continue, 196.28; of science prove that nothing is made without purpose, 220.38

DISCUSSION: free d. feared, 252.25

DISEASE, liability to, 103.3

DISGUISES of men, 15.30

DISGUST of life corrected, 143.26

DISHONESTY, cartload of, 185.23

DISORDERS of nature contribute to a good, remote yet certain, 259.11

DISPLAY, love of, 229.39

DISPOSITION adverse to true relig., 88.2; of human mind to magnify its system, 86.2; to admire, 152.1

DISPROPORTION betw. man's character and condition, 168.29

DISPUTES assume a standard idea of man, 64.29; fierce d. ended, xxxv.1; frivolous d. about church matters, xxxv.8

DISSENTERS, 146.8

DISSIMULATION, 185.11; to be avoided in pulpit, 219.8

DISSOLUTION characterizes old age, 112.5

DISTANCE and height ineffectual before a moral deed, 178.21; d. of the years, xi.16; d. stressed betw. God and man, 132.11; dizzy d. betw. earth and stars, 174.1

DISTANT, soul converses with, 202.3

DISTINCTION betw. circumstances and the self, 183.15; betw. men who work professionally and with the heart, 188.5; betw. outer and inner self, 200.6; betw. right and wrong estimate of oneself, 182.30; betw. times and seasons unjustified, 15.10

DISTINCTIONS disappear before the leveller Death, 34.20; possible only by act of reflection, 207.3; to be observed in rearing children, 51.31; earthly d. annihilated, 160.3; moral d. vs. positive ones, 177.30; most men do not make nice d., 86.29

DISTINCTNESS of a man's call determines his exertions, 251.33; d. given to idea of God, 30.8

DISTORTIONS of mind corrected by Christianity, xxvi.18

DISTRUST of human reason condemned, 252.23; of self is great calamity, 105.21

DISTURBANCE can be magnified by attention, 50.16

DISTURBANCES in political world do not trouble the soul, 201.25

DISTURBED, Christian not easily d., 51.9; soul is not d. over upsets in political world or domestic troubles, 201.25

DISUNION, tendency toward, 78.25

DITCH, 209.2

DIVERSITY of human taste and character illustrated, 166.10

DIVINE, God transforms all things into the d., 211.14

DIVINE WISDOM: how educates the race, 164.25. See also God.

DIVINITY of Jesus, 56.1; of Jesus lies in majesty of his character, 234.38. See God.

DIVISION OF LABOR, 164.13; great in large population, 46.8; is important, 128.27

DO justly, love mercy, etc., 72.8; learn what you can and cannot d., 168.3; d. nothing without intention, 102.30; d. nothing you cannot justify, 116.19; d. the will of my Father, and ye shall know the doctrines, 257.11; d. this in remembrance, 54.2; d. thyself no harm, 269.35; d. what God made you to d. best, 169.16; d. what you can do. well, 169.15; whatsoever ye d., d. it heartily as unto the Lord, 187.15

DOCTRINE of compensation, 209.26; of Election has foundation in N., 231.1; of immortality, 163.5; of immortality is chief in Christianity, 238.29; of Jesus' divinity, 55.35; of Paul not to be appeased by silent contempt, 22.18; of retribution; of rewards and punishments, 11.18; of self-trust, 106.13; of the N.T. on social duty, 135.33; of regeneration, 114.7; of transubstantiation, 56.2; of Trinity is accidentally in creed of rigid party, 84.19; of value of the soul is basis for self-reliance, 109.22; presented for consideration, xix.31; of reality of things unseen, 2.33; received by large numbers of men in diff. ages and countries is founded in truth, 230.38; d. is superior to miracles in its support, 124.34; d. that God dwells in human heart, 133.12; d. that we must be born again, 239.2; a true d. strengthens our belief in supporting miracles, 125.1; false d. in Bible, xxv.28; d. is fundamental in evangelical Christianity, 238.42; reject d. contradictory to your faith, xxv.29; sublime d. of love of God, 136.4

DOCTRINES, 233.9; of divine truth, 196.11; of each relig. system have a mutual relation, 83.28; of gospel preached by daily events, 68.30; of theology enlarged by astronomy, 173.27; of Total Depravity and Vicarious Suffering, 232.-19; d. that are solemn verities have been strained out of shape, 238.40; exaggeration of d. fundamentally true, 194.31; ye shall know of the d., 257.11

DODDRIDGE, Philip, 147.33

DOG in presence of man, 154.32

DOGMA accepted by multitudes is traceable to man's moral nature, 230.40

DOGMAS of Apostles yield before eternal truths, xxxv.12; blind reception of d., xxvi.33

DOGMATISM, 204.30

DOING good, 267.4; d. one's duty is relig., 264.40; d. our own work, 167.19; d. the will of God, 267.36

DOLLAR, a medal of real power, 189.26

DOLLARS, a thousand d. in indiscriminate alms, 241.19

DOMINION of God, 12.2; of moral law, 95.17; of reason, 210.26; of the conscience extended to include public duties, 75.24; of the world given man, 54.5

DOOR of heaven, 6.10; every sense is a treasury d., 249.35; sin lieth at the d., 59.9

DOT in space, 172.26

DOUBLE: all things are d., one against another, 102.17

DOUBT about existence of the world within, 183.11; in mind of Jesus, 56.16; is removed at death, 140.33; thrown on church systems, 175.28

DOUBTS make one seek counsel of the soul within, 200.14; solution of my d. lies in my immediate relation to God, 200.5; soul amid doubts doubts not, 136.12

DREAD of grave removed for the living, 142.3

DRESS, 216.22; d., houses, furniture desired, 2.29; d. important in society, 47.14; vanities of d., 10.17

DRINKS, soft raiment, wine, 6.5; meats and d., 10.18

DROP in the spiritual ocean is man, 100.24

DROVER in the mountains, 209.2

DRUNKARD gains nothing from Bible, 111.6

DUMB lose half the good of being,

61.22; d. mentioned, 61.7; institutions for deaf and d., 61.11

DUPLICITY, 185.28

DURATION characterizes eternal life, 244.15; of the past, 8.9; of soul's being, 105.25; to which a century is but the turning of an hour glass, 113.26; boundless d. of God, 117.13; good man differs from God only in d., xxiv.4; 133.24; 200.27

DUST of centuries, 200.23; body soon laid in the d., 111.20; greenness called from d., 42.22; less than d., 8.22

DUTIES are appointed us for only short time, 81.13; arising out of conflicts within Christianity, 82.24; belonging to conversation, 60.19; discharged without love, 167.6; d. God has written in light, 136.32; d. in this life need no specific knowledge re. the hereafter, 244.2; d. of a congregation, 36.35; of a man, 169.13; of Christian minister, 24.27; of mankind, 7.26; of man in creation not yet realized, 204.32; of pastor, 31.7; of the soul, 50.33; d. owed to God, 71.18; respecting conversation, 64.10; to fellow men and God not inconsistent with self-reliance, 109.23; d. were plainly and feelingly opened, 220.16; Christian gives strength to great d., 51.12; day is full of d., 85.8; enumeration of d., 216.10; obligation of common d., 60.5; principle underlying social d., 127.5; public and private d. to tax one's time, 103.10; public d. included in dominion of conscience, 75.23; small d. are great enough, 14.26; social d. contemplated with refreshment, 127.7; what are my d? 199.26. See *obligations.*

DUTY, 270.18; commands that we go on with our work after bereavement, 143.25; is the soul's everlasting object, 143.23; of man lies in overcoming pleasures of sense, 105.9; of parishioners to attend church, 72.20; of patriotism, 81.12; of penitence, 264.14; of prayer is most insisted upon, 216.9; of relig, improvement is plain enough, 72.26; of stated seasons of prayer, 7.5; d. is our salvation, 271.4; d. to exercise rectitude in public affairs, 76.11; d. to forsake the leading of anr. when our inner convictions differ, 109.32; d. to judge men only by actions, 1.4; d. to others dictated by a well-calculated self-love, 129.8; d. to prefer another's good always to our own, 109.30; to promote circulation of good bks., 240.39; d. yields to being agreeable to others, 48.12; Christian d. is an unceasing effort at self-culture, 101.3; doing d. on earth qualifies us for Heaven, 81.21; doing one's d. is relig., 264.40; first d. as moral being is to reflect, 237.19; foundation principle of d. to others, 135.25; inclination to our d., 17.5; Jesus bro't soul the sanction of d., 59.26; law of d. universal, 76.7; least act done out of solemn sense of d., 14.34; light of d. is always present to all, 70.25; memory of home animates to do d., 19.33; prayer is first Christian d., 267.17; preacher aims to give conviction of d., 25.22; principle behind d. to serve neighbor, 128.10; principle in system of social d., 131.22; questions of human d., 110.3; 212.3; reason of d. not always present to all, 70.25; relig. monitors prick us on to d., 35.20; remissness in discharge of d., 69.24; self-government is an important d., 88.13; sense of d. same in all minds, 64.23; sermon on duty, how enlarged, xxxviii.5; true motive of social d., 129.35; see *categorical imperative.*

E

EACH allied to all, 207.23; e. has his own channel, 59.17; e. has his own cross to bear, 258.27; e. to the other like, more than on earth is tho't, 244.21.

EAGLES, 222.4

EAR of man hears time's lesson, 194.5; of your mind, 34.3; eye hath not seen nor e. heard, 141.35

EARS, if we have, 86.18

EARTH, a scaffold of divine vengeance, 174.30; a small opaque planet etc., 174.16; a ball spinning on its own axis, 173.34; determined form of blackberry, 208.5; is a little globule, 175.24; is man's garden etc., 203.19; is of immense age, 172.6; may suffer from moon's deviations, 176.3; not the only object of God's care, 174.21; once believed stationary, 173.30; rent to form Andes and Alps, 112.8; scene of races of vast and shapeless animals, 112.11; the shadow of heaven, 244.19; tie betw. e. and heaven, 144.15; borders of the e., 39.3; contracted span of e., 174.11; fitness of man to the e., 203.18; God has spoken in e., 52.18; if e. refused her increase? 41.35; if you love e. you become e., 133.32. See *globe.*

EARTHQUAKES, 122.9; 259.11

EARTHWORMS, men called, 206.28

EASE: never at e. until aim is clear, 167.23; sunshine of e., 33.13

EASTERN writers personify abstract ideas, 256.17

EBBS: world e. away like a sea, 2.6

ECCENTRICITY is not self-reliance, 110.30; E. does not praise e., 51.18

ECCLESIASTES (11:4) quoted, 50.25

ECHOES, thunder has a hundred, 125.34

ECLIPSE of sun in Waltham, 252.29

ECONOMY of N., 116.25; of the Christian revelation, 85.17; of the universe, 10.21

ECSTASIES over trifles, 51.7

EDUCATION of the soul, 269.45; e. thru one's calling, 164.8; e. which world administers to soul, 207.6; best systems of e. neglected, 2.22; life is a term of e., 85.9; misfortunes of e., 156.23; objects of e., 269.12; progressive e. of the race, 164.26; revival offers first stage in relig. e., 232.13; years of my e., xiv.30

EDWARDS, Jonathan, 241.43

EFFECT of example of self-reliant, 188.21; of hymns, 147.2; of improvement of character, 81.5; of miracles depends on moral purpose, 123.13; of partly spirit is exclusiveness, 86.21; on others is one test of man's character, 108.15; an e. today is produced by the same power operating in beginning of time, 221.10; man is not cause, but a mere e., 238.4; man works out faithfully his own e., 101.28

EFFECTS of eloquence, 26.13; prolific e. of truth illustrated, 197.26; truth worth more than its e., 198.28

EFFICIENCY increased among men in right jobs, 167.12; we act with e. only when our aim is clear, 167.23; greater e. in exercising talents after death, 169.4

EFFORT at self-culture, 101.4; continual e. of divine Providence to instruct, 197.3; generous e., 210.3; man makes e. to obtain his desires, 5.11; upward e. of earth-dwellers, 245.22

EFFORTS to instruct and benefit man, 6.30; e. should be directed to a definite point, 20.22; union with others necessary to make efforts of any avail, 88.34

EGG, deadness of an e., 244.8

EGOTISM, victory over, 65.14

EGYPT, men see God only in, xxxv.26; relig. ceremonial in, 146.3

ELASTICITY of ordinance of Jesus, 57.16

ELECTION, our turn to make our, 117.28; doctrine of e. has foundation in N., 231.1

ELEMENT, each creature in its own, 173.21

ELEMENTARY, view of God is, xxiii.5

ELEMENTS are obedient to man's fervent prayers, 8.6; of human mind, 90.20; of moral and intellectual excellence in man, 106.3; natural e. help purposes of man, 6.12; results of the teacher are e. for the pupil, 55.3

ELEPHANTS and dull men compared, 206.31

ELM and poplar, 39.21

ELOQUENCE, a weapon of matchless force, 26.28; described in detail, 26.17; in every man who yields to a just sentiment, 26.27; is like breath of Almighty, 26.22; is mightiest engine God has put into hands of men, 26.10; masters the mind, 26.15; effects of, 26.13; every man has his own e, 108.4; higher Power speaks thru e., 26.22; highest platform of e., 218.29; love of e., xix.27; power of e. in few men, 66.26; principles lie in every man, 26.26; truth stronger when recommended by e., 63.19

EMANATION from soul of the world, 245.13

EMBARRASSMENT, laboring under load of, 168.31

EMBLEM: each thing in external N. is e. or hieroglyphic of something in us, 44.17

best those whose names and faces we see most frequently, 181.30; e. of separating the truth taught by Jesus from his office, 96.15; e. being compensated by e., 176.11; belief in matter is great practical e., 2.10; great e. is sensualism, 2.31; narrowness and e. in relig., xiii.17; we think e. will be corrected, 64.31

ERRORS, 238.6; in choice of pursuit, 168.14; in traditions might have been eliminated by reflection, 237.20; consequences of human e. in the church, 237.22; human e. can be corrected by God's original writing (astronomy), 178.30; power that corrects e., 209.13

ESCAPE, soul explores ways of, 84.4

ESSAY on a man of genius shows exaggeration, 152.24

ESSENCE of truth of character, 184.26

EST Deus in nobis, agitante calescimus illo, 200.25

ESTATE, inward e. more valuable than outward, 2.34; soul is an infinite e., 105.24

ESTEEM, raise himself in own, xix.5

ESTIMATE of wealth, fame, sensual pleasure, 227.3; right and wrong e. of oneself, 182.30

ETERNITIES: can crowd e. into an hour, 239.32

ETERNITY conceived in terms of duration, 244.15; e. of truth and right imparted to soul embracing them, 100.14; e. offers us greater exercise of our talents, 169.2; e. presses on us while we pursue seeming good, 35.27; e. taught by analogies of time, 10.29; e. vs. time, 239.17; can stretch hour into e., 239.33; God's measureless e., 117.8; hour is seed of e., 17.34; human life part of e., 136.8; leaving time and entering e., 114.35; man is master of his e., 8.8; speculations on e., 244.13; the cheerful e. into which we are born, 172.8; mysterious e. about to open, 10.26

ETHICAL standards of Christianity not greatly superior to those of pagans, xxvii.3

ETHICS, 251.28; of political parties, 76.16; basis of social e., 131.23

ETRURIAN village of Rome, 54.20

EULOGY breaks over the edges of truth, 152.22; e. of art of conversation, 63.26

EUROPE and stories of loyalty, 154.24; learned much from Fr. Revolution, 194.-26; not as broad as man's own soul, 111.14; relig. ceremonial in E., 146.3; war in E., 112.23

EUSEBIUS, 249.1

EVANGELISTS and their writings, 125.30. See gospels.

EVENT: every e. of memory and hope educates, 212.16; every e. suggests an experiment that need not be repeated, 194.21

EVENTS compared, 194.12; in this life

affect the whole being of the soul, 163.6; e. of past can be reversed, 8.13; e. of universe never lack articulate voice, 69.11; Christian not curious about e., 51.8; daily e. also preach the gospel, 68.32; high e., 7.31; imaginations issue in e., 6.16

EVERY desire of human mind is a prayer uttered, 4.18

EVERYDAY religion illustrated, 189.23

EVERYTHING speaks wisdom to the wise; sensuality to sensual, 101.34; takes hue of our thought, 101.30; was made for use, 166.21

EVIDENCE: chief e. comes from revelation, 245.18; internal e. outweighs all miracles to the soul, 124.22; miracle as an e. of moral truth, 122.33; miracle is lower species of e., 124.19; only a single miracle asked for as e. of power, 126.3

EVIDENCES of Christianity, 271.10; e. of Christianity not systematized by Jesus, 91.9; e. of immortality, 220.8

EVIL, 258.8ff.; e. actions and the judgment, 101.18; e. can be handled practically if not speculatively, 258.45; e. deducted from your spiritual age, 116.4; e. diminishes the peace of the soul, 141.6; disappears, 136.6; e. done to sacred property of man's soul, 106.23; e. floats in air, grows in grain, and impregnates waters, 259.1; e. in good people becomes depravity in others, 79.11; e. in world does not detract from its venerability, 52.8; e. is no problem, 85.2; e. not without use to relig. man, 258.39; e. overcome by good, 22.24; e. turned to good by exercise of Reason, 210.24; accumulated e. of slavery, 256.38; educative value of e., 258.29; how soul faces the problem of e., 201.24; indefinable e. hangs over rigid Christian, 83.34; nothing is absolutely e., 221.22; reality of e. not denied, 258.24; trust in spite of e., 212.18

EVILS of party spirit, 88.27; of social life, 46.25; root cause of e. in U.S.? 78.34; source of social e., 76.20

EXAGGERATION in conversation, 226.14; in our praise, 152.8

EXAMINATION of ourselves, 13.17

EXAMPLE of Jesus, 196.21; of pastor's life, 33.17; of the dead, 142.22; of the self-reliant man, 188.21; acting for sake of e., 242.42; good e. does most good at home, 18.12; good e. is a rich gift, 6.29; ill e. of men, 8.17; Jesus as an e., 90.10; 233.24; setting a good e., 263.18

EXAMPLES needed to remove barrenness from moral truth, 234.23

EXCELLENCE: above highest copy of living e., 110.12; admiration for e., 6.20; moral e. is goal of man, 49.10

EXCELLENCES compensate for defects, 107.20; partial e., 254.14

EXCELLENCY of the religious, 133.35

EXCEPTION: man no e. to invariable order of human life, 259.3

EXCEPTIONS to E's doctrine of prayer, 7.14; seeming e. to general order contribute to ultimate good, 259.8

EXCESS, cup of sensual e., 225.9

EXCITEMENT in Christianity, 55.18; e. of song and dances, 10.17

EXCUSE made by the understanding, 3.20

EXERCISE of intellect and heroic virtue, 52.3; e. of reason can redeem man, 206.34; e. of reason turns all evil to good, 210.23

EXERTION of an ambitious man, 5.30; e. of virtue needs no great occasion, 15.8; each right e. reveals vocation more clearly to man, 251.31; every e. has effect, 81.4; uncommon e., 211.5

EXHIBITION of our own moral principle, 13.10

EXHORTATIONS reach heart, 36.8

EXIST, never suspecting that we e., 204.14; to e. is more strange than any other fact, 203.10; why do we e.? 204.24

EXISTENCE has dignity only when conceived as a teacher, 193.11; e. is an astonishing fact, 204.26; e. of God is suggested to a reasoning man, 122.1; e. of spiritual world, 196.13; e. of inner world, 196.10; e. of world within us doubted, 183.12; miracle is sign of God's existence, xxviii.21; one's own e. more amazing than any other fact, 203.10; present e. depends on God, xxiii.19; reason for our e. is to form character, 258.33; undying e., 11.9; see *life*.

EXISTENCES, minds of men are not independent, 4.6

EXPECTATION of proper performance of N., 45.5; e. of the teacher, 202.10

EXPECTATIONS inextinguishable, 265.26

EXPEDIENT preferred to the right, 76.16

EXPERIENCE based on permanence of N., 124.9; e. of man is a tragic tale of connexion betw. ruler and ruled, 76.35; e. of the ages given to man, 208.21; all e. preaches doctrines of Gospel, 69.2; joy in the e. of truth, 93.14; personal e., 194.12

EXPERIMENT tried which need not be repeated, 194.23

EXPIATION by Jesus not taught, 177.31

EXPLANATION of N.T., 219.3

EXPLOITATION is product of self-love, 231.18

EXPLORE nature of God, xxii.35

EXPOSITION: science is e. of revelation, 171.7

EXTENT of moral laws can be learned only by *acting*, 209.29; e. of our prospect increased, 250.9; full e. of one's proper nature now seen, 199.17

EXTERNALS should be man's servants, not masters, 183.30; whole world goes after e., 182.23

EXTREMES favored by most men,

86.31; e. of life: our present condition and the height of a divine nature, 101.7

EYE fixed on rich man's manners, 5.25; fixed on the higher self, 183.14; grows microscopic in crowded society, 47.13; hath not seen nor ear heard, 141.35; loses power of distant vision if directed too long to minute objects, 48.4; of Christian law, 135.17; of God discerns the happiest man, 160.7; of God rests upon pious man, 159.14; of love grows severe, 144.5; of man intended to see beauty of world, 222.4; of man sees surrounding infinity, 175.25; of mind grows dull by little studies, 48.5; seems to see planets revolving around earth, 173.31; which fills universe with light, 159.12; act on principle is done in e. of God, 14.34; all things seen with partial e., 78.26; born a seeing e., 226.40; Divine E. fixed in man's soul, 100.7; Divine E. is God working in man, 100.11; Divine E. that cannot be deceived, 100.7; fire in the e., 160.35; man not designed to be an idle e., 209.19; mote in another's e; beam in our own, 76.23; omniscient E. sees into home, 16.14; one who writes only for his own e., xxxiv.11; outward e. does not perceive all in N., 44.8; range of vision of e., 47.23; retreat from public e., 3.5; scriptures read with erring e., 84.24; to an instructed e. the common facts are most wonderful, 122.7

EYES kept only on one's own tho'ts, 109.14; of disciples opened to Jesus' meaning, xxxiv.32; of moral beings see our guilt, 3.9; that can read N's book, 40.16; bandages torn from e., 193.33; if we have e., 86.18; man shuts e. to God's omnipresence, 40.25; scriptures read with purged e., 195.13; truth concealed from literal e., xxxviii.23

F

FABRIC: robust f. of soul that needs rough discipline, 187.19

FACE of God wears smiles, 169.21; every f. betrays marks of its destiny, 112.20; future has a new f. for man of faith, 160.29

FACES: ground the f. of the poor, 9.8; guilty man sees angry f., xxiv.12

FACT of authority of moral truth, 95.2; that prayers are granted, 4.22; historic credence to the historic f., 126.19; most strange f. is our own existence, 203.11; only a f. that puts skepticism at an end, 234.24

FACTS, 227.10; of diff. kinds, 95.4; of science, 171.5; of each season, 42.16; speak for themselves in talk on pressing affairs, 109.12; tested by appeal to man's consciousness, 91.7; all f. in universe, rightly seen, attest to truth of relig., 28.21; common f. are most wonderful to an instructed eye, 122.7; effect of f. upon mind, 222.20; homely f. used in scripture, 29.9; moral *vs.* physical or intellectual f., 93.21; these f. are the years of the soul, 114.28; tissue of neighboring f., 204.23; unquestionable f. lie behind relig. systems, 82.14

FACULTIES, 189.5; f. and desires of the soul, 158.12; f. enlarged become love of God, 158.14; f. made to love, venerate, adore, 152.30; f. of character, 184.15; f. of man find strength; multiply themselves in right cause, 160.33; f. of men do not penetrate to motives; too crude for estimating real character, 1.5; f. which can bring us to our ends, 5.18; balance of f., 2.19; divine f. appear behind astronomy as well as in man, 176.35; immortal f., 8.2; lower f. or senses, 202.9; our f. are imperfect copies of God's perfections, 84.32; reverence one's own f., 84.32; use f. God has given you, 107.30; virtue is essential to perfection of the f., 94.4; we have no f. by which to see the tho'ts of men, 216.14

FACULTY of conversation, 60.1; every f. exercised to glory of God, 60.14; every f. is mode of God's action, 4.13; had moral f. strength as it has right, it would govern the world, 95.14; how the moral f. functions, 95.11; reasoning f. weak, 234.29; spiritual f. suggests that death cannot harm, 202.1

FAGOT or the Mass, 228.16

FAILS, the prospect, xviii.28

FAILURE in good cause justified, 32.31; f. in trade is called *ruin*, 184.14; f. of preacher to do his duty, 26.4; value of f., 184.15

FAITH and works, 265.30; comforts wretched; unchains the slave, 159.35; confirmed by astronomy; agrees with bk. of N., 178.25; f. emphasized without knowledge by rigid party, 89.6; f. in gospel sense is perception of spiritual things, 250.31; is a practical principle, 160.26; is not hope; it is sight, 250.32; f. is the most real and certain part of knowledge, 250.30; f. left at home when one goes to the store, 189.13; f. makes conscience clear-sighted, 161.14; f. of Jesus degraded by world, 57.5; f. of the guides and teachers of mankind, 126.15; of the mourner, 139.34; f. received in revival is only first stage of spiritual education, 232.12; f. satisfactory to one's proper n., 199.16; strengthens the active powers, 160.26; f. that all is and will be well, 212.12; f. valued by rigid party, 84.10; f. was alive in hearts of Abraham and Paul, xxxv.27; f. when rooted and the leading motive, 159.33; f. widens understanding of the gospel, 161.6; a man's f. superior to Bible doctrine, xxv.28; beggarly f., 223.30; Christian f. sets duty before the mourner, 143.21; Christian f. teaches that soul does not die, 140.27; efficient f. in immortality, 231.44; eternal value of relig. f., 73.9; highest f. is intimate union with God, 161.12; highest f. required for greatest sacrifice, 161.12; I want a f. as alive as Paul's or Abraham's, xxxv.27; inde-

pendence in f., 268.14; is it founded on fact? 161.22; is f. just imagination? 250.29; is it practicable? 162.1; lost f., 175.21; man's f. must have an independent connexion with God, 237.29; may the new f. animate all who teach and all who learn, 202.10; men allow church to regulate f., 237.16; miracles of f., 160.22; motives that quicken f., 34.34; not f. but a parrot's talk, 237.30; new f. of "Know Thyself" may lead far, 201.2; O ye of little f., 45.32; f. of Christ abolishes power of death, 142.5; one credible miracle will justify our f. in miracles, 120.9; relig. f. suffers when men lack self-reliance, 237.14; sawn asunder for your f., 14.26; strong f. indicated strong sense of sin, 84.11; they have kept the f., 11.6; torch of this f., 200.33; triumphant f., 144.18; truly spiritual f. will form a new church, 201.12

FAITH IN GOD as a sentiment, 158.16; has unknown beauty and value, 158.26; significance of this well-worn phrase, 158.18; what it accomplishes in us, 159.25

FAITHFULNESS over a few things, 18.25

FALL of man as conceived in old theology, 174.24

FALSEHOOD destroys belief; is a foolish suicide, 210.6; not proved by a miracle, 123.14; f. of a relig. leader is perpetuated in the church, 237.17; f. thru imitation results in loss of power over others, 108.17

FALSEHOODS exposed every day, 194.6; scared from free discussion, 252.25

FALSENESS does not always deceive, 185.18

FAME, 227.3; wins, argues and commands for man, 182.1

FAMILIES, 168.1; of laborious tradesmen, 241.24; spying on f., 219.33

FAMILY of Father of universe, 31.19; human f. cut off from man by selfishness, 210.7

FANATICISM checked by nat'l objects, 171.25

FANATICS, 194.31

FANCIES, master of one's, xix.6

FARCE, world's, 206.6

FARMER sees practical values, 47.6

FASHION determines words of our ceremonial prayers, 5.5; is important in cities, 47.11

FAST DAY, 270.10; sermons on, xxx.28

FASTING, humiliation and prayer, 268.26

FATE of millions of rational spirits epitomized in history, 208.22; death is f. of all, 34.34

FATES: "Three F." and time, 239.24

FATHER hath life in himself, 114.20; is approached easily by the devout, 25.14; is found only by watching one's own mind, xxiv.26; F. is in me; I in the F.; yet F. is greater than I, 200.34; F. of Jesus is Divine Providence, 170.17; F. will not forsake the child instructed at such cost, 212.13; access to the F. only thru *me*, 233.38; access to the F. thru the soul, 200.15; Arian sees Christ inferior to the F., 84.22; everlasting F. sees our guilt, 3.8; God as F. of human soul, 92.8; God is my F. and my neighbor's, 131.31; hand of heavenly F., xiv.25; omnipresent F. sustains my being, 221.12; perfect as your F. in heaven is perfect, 92.18; veneration of the Almighty F., 211.9. See *God*.

FATHERLESS, curse of, 9.10

FATHERS, we share same ground etc. as our f., 54.8

FAULT in not thinking enough of oneself, 183.2; a man's need is often his own f., 131.18

FAULTS of great men, 110.18

FAVOR, forget, 232.22

FEAR, 5.8; exists only in lower faculties—in the senses, 202.8; is basis of doing good among the selfish, 129.27; is external to the soul, 202.8; makes the spirit passive, 84.6; f. men more than God, 16.16; f. not to follow your own convictions, 109.35; f. of death, 267.32; f. of death unworthy of man, 127.10; f. of God by Sir Thomas Browne, 159.23; f. of sin, 231.26; f. oppresses soul of rigid Christian, 84.2; church is our only refuge from f., 113.14; cure for f. of death, 127.11; do not f. God, 263.27; perfect love casteth out f., 87.26; 267.40

FEAST of Remembrance, 265.34; dispense with f. but don't forget joy, xxxviii.33; temperate at a f., 127.23

FEASTS: licentious f. of pagan worship, 55.32

FEATHER has a purpose, 220.41

FEELING of approval for a good act, 82.25; f. of lover is genuine, 153.13; f. of reality of things unseen, 2.31; devout f. is occasioned by N., 171.23; force of a man's f. justifies, 168.27; minister should be a man of f., 32.19; reality of f., 2.2; religious f. is best check on conversation, 65.21

FEELINGS altered by qualities good and bad, 153.35; benevolent f. are pleasant; malevolent are painful, 123.3; deeper f. than patriotism, 230.13; relig. f. assisted by fellowship, 228.10; wounded f., 66.4

FEET, industry of, 2.13

FELLOW, I am your, 34.33

FELLOW CITIZENS, opinion of, 18.17

FELLOW MAN: see *neighbor, others*.

FELLOW MEN, pay debt to, xxxx.5

FELLOWSHIP, right hand of, 271.8; soul finds f. thru speech, 62.6

FENCE of fine plausible manners, 182.9; invisible, immortal f. surrounds every man, 209.32

FENCES of presumption, 4.2

FÉNELON, François de Salignac de

La Mothe, 107.3; 249.4; said God is in our souls as our souls are in our bodies, 133.26; worships with Calvin etc., xxxviii.26

FEROCITY of party spirit, 229.33

FERVENCY of prayer effective, 8.6

FERVOR, speaking with, xix.26

FETTERS: affections are not f. to enslave us, 19.15

FEVER, 113.9

FIBER scrutinized by scientist, 41.31

FICHTE, Johann Gottlieb, 249.6

FICTION has nothing so perfect as Law of Compensation, 209.25; legitimate in conversation, 226.17; f. of outward respect to God, 3.19; no f. as wonderful as a man's own constitution, 203.13; truth is stranger than f., 203.14

FIDELITY of rain and sun, 40.7; brute f. of N., 45.1; man works out with f. his own effect, 101.28

FIELD of moral truth is barren until peopled with examples, 234.22; sow the f., 206.21; true f. of action, 168.13

FIGURES in the sky, 172.4

FIND Christianity within own soul, xix.34; f. your calling, 163.1; 269.39

FINGER of God, 188.22

FINGER, snap a, 14.9

FINITE: man leaves f. and enters infinite, 114.34

FINNEY can preach; his prayers are short, xxxiv.2

FIRE falls from heaven, 4.24; f. of relig. imported into new age, xiii.18; fire on its own altar, 228.29; called down f. on enemies, 59.2; getting one's chair near the f., 48.35; more f. in eye of good man, 160.35; sun seems a funeral f., 113.3; touch with f., 202.13

FIRESIDE invested with sacred delights, 19.20

FIRMAMENT concave, 194.15; eternal truths are like stars in f., xxxv.14

FISH, 173.21; 203.19

FITNESS of man to the earth described, 203.17

FIXTURE of material world based on prejudice, 2.9

FLASHES of celestial thought, 197.10

FLAWS, picking, 33.2

FLESH fails, 35.11; "made f." means realized in actions of good men, 235.18

FLETCHER, Andrew (of Saltoun) mentioned, 156.5

FLOODS, 259.11; f. of the sea, 112.13

FLOURISHED: wicked has f. up to his hope, 9.8

FLOWER reproves man, 45.18; man is like f. of the field, 44.15

FLOWERS quite rightly differ in kind, 107.32; can f. admire themselves? 43.34

FLOWING: a relig. f. from all things, xxxv.29

FLY, buzz of, 50.16

FOCUS of influence, 207.19

FOES of malice are multiplied, 210.8

FOIBLE, every man has his f., 48.26

FOLD, E. to keep none from Jesus' f.,

58.35; holy f. of Christianity, 55.25

FOLLY, 208.33; in conversation, 226.16; of men and their pursuits, 206.17; f. to underestimate one's own peculiar power, 108.8; seen everywhere by frivolous, 102.1

FONTENELLE, Bernard, *Plurality of Worlds*, 252.37

FOOD might have been produced without beauty, 43.29; f. of an animal, 204.20; common f. of the mind, 162.2; live without f., 116.13; impure f. of revivals, 232.14

FOOL not protected by costly clothes, 49.35

FOOT could not be lifted on Jupiter, 173.13

FOOTSTEPS of the Maker, 52.17

FORCE characterizes our reliance on our own tho'ts, 109.18; f. in spiritual nature makes things take hue of our tho't, 101.30; f. of a good life, 52.15; f. of a man's feeling justifies his purpose, 168.27; f. of character is greatest source of richness, 183.35; f. of divine truth, 20.23; f. of human spirit in sentiment of loyalty, 154.4; f. of moral truth is unborn and creative, 198.30; f. of will and one's vocation, 168.17; f. or fraud, 9.3; affections recoil from f., 195.10; greater f. needed in behalf of spiritual teaching, 2.32; infinite f. of a humble man, 161.4; man gives new f. to a trivial tho't when result of his own observation, 93.17; moral f. dignifies character at home, 18.34; our f. is superhuman when we rely on immortal truth, 109.18; spiritual f. unknown because untried, 105.23. See *power*.

FOREHEAD, God's name on, 32.4

FORFEITURE of name of gentleman, 229.26

FORGES of New England, xxx.34

FORGIVENESS, 264.42; f. of brother, 136.35

FORM of shell, 221.45; God considered in human f., 173.4; human f., 110.16

FORMATION of character is main reason for our human existence, 258.32

FORMS and idols of society contemned, 53.5; f. in worship, 228.3; be master of f. of relig., xxxix.1; new f. of address in pulpit, xxii.1; not anxious concerning f., 126.18

FORTUNE is not a true property of man, 211.32; f. of men's births, 165.6; f. that throws us into foreign lands, 19.29; making a f. is not reason for existence, 258.33

FOUNTAIN of honor, 158.33; f. of relig. in soul, 212.8

FOUNTAINS: two f. from which flow our feelings toward God and man, 83.9

FOX, George: xx.34; 134.2; 249.5; F. the same in words as in life, 186.6

FRAGRANCE of Arabian myrrh and spikenard, 18.5

FRAILTY of the flesh, 188.23; human f., 7.27

FRAME of an animal, 204.20; every part of human f., 203.15

FRANCE, 43.23; astronomers of, 175.9

FRANKLIN, Benjamin, 110.14; 208.28

FRAUD, 3.25; 225.7; f. or force, 9.4

FRAUDS, pious, 125.13

FREDERIC OF PRUSSIA, story about, 47.27

FREE AGENCY assures ability to gratify our wishes, 5.20; hard to reconcile with man's dependence on God, 236.15; perfection of, 116.22

FREE WILL, 164.29; 236.9; fw. is all that man may call his own, 4.14; fw. insisted upon, 118.5; fw. separates us from God, 132.26; men have fw., xxiii.22; perfection of fw., 116.22

FREEDOM, 269.4; f. and dependence, 265.38; f. befitting greatness of gospel, xxi.34; f. can be lost; it is evanescent property demanding use, 236.13; f. comes to one in death, 169.1; f. in preaching, 28.8; is given to us as fast as we are fit for it, 168.23; is God's gift and distinguishes man from other creatures, 236.10; makes man solitary and accountable, 236.11; f. of every power of the mind, 166.24; f. of speech among Unitarians, 232.41; f. of the Christian, 265.12; f. of the teacher, xxxx.6ff.; f. to be turned to self-culture, 101.7; our f. better preserved by indefiniteness of future, 244.4; our f. is too mighty for reason; stands whether reason sanctions or no, 236.17; perfect f. found when we are spiritually mature, 116.28; true f., 265.19; we possess f., 85.4

FRENCH language characterized by lying, 225.39; F. Revolution not a calamity, 194.25

FRIEND hasn't the attributes which the mind assigns, 153.16; makes the virtues solid and factual, 234.18; worshiped, 157.23; being a f. to man is advantageous, 128.23; bondsman of your f., 158.30; God treated as a holy F., 159.28; intimate and perfect f., 158.33; Jesus the f. of human race, 35.2; pastor is mild and blameless f., 33.16; voice of a f., 63.18

FRIENDLESS men, xviii.30

FRIENDS, 134.2; assist us in worship, 237.27; f. barren of comfort, 5.33; death interrupts but does not end communion with f., 235.8; departed f. suggest motives to our souls and encourage us, 235.10; departed f. still observe our actions, 235.9; earthly f. baulk and disappoint, 158.5

FRIENDSHIP 241.34; 269.33; f. connected with nature in sacred bond, 144.12; f. of good men is best gift, 192.11; cords of f., 19.19

FRIENDSHIPS, 237.31

FRUIT inevitably issues from an act, 209.27; diff. f. requires diff. soil, 107.11; tree bears f., 151.16

FRUITFULNESS of Christianity, 199.1; of moral truth, 198.29

FRUITS of relig., 267.7; costliest f. soonest spoiled, 73.4; we judge tree by f., 1.7

FUNCTIONS: vegetable f. dependable, 45.6

FUNERAL: sun seems a f. fire, 113.3

FURNITURE, 216.22

FUTURE can reverse events of past, 8.14; filled with unspeakable cheerfulness, 85.12; f. is great; present, little, 197.23; f. is bright, 180.12; f. of society, 256.9; f. preferred to present, 201.34; f. well-being and state, 99.9; f. will wear new face to man of faith, 160.29; conditions of the f. life, 85.19; immeasurable f. is before you, 8.14; Jesus could foresee the f., 234.45; prophetic glory of f., 56.13; solemn interest in f., 199.5; soul converses with f., 202.3; soul's vocation is not for remote f., 169.7

FUTURE LIFE, 269.8

FUTURE WORLD observes system of compensations, 10.33

G

GAIN, crime can never be a, 136.22; sons of, 39.7

GAIETY legitimate in conversation, 226.17

GALEN, the Grk. physician, 248.45

GALILEO, 173.34

GARDEN of Adam, 44.26; every g. witnesses constant nat'l process, 42.11

GARDENS, 222.16; g. and their grape vines, 107.7

GARMENT, goodness removed like cumbersome g., 16.6

GARRETS, obscure, 242.23

GAS, 208.4

GATE of Athens, 200.28

GENERATION, interests of next g. neglected, 76.14; this g. sees Christianity expanding, 55.25

GENEROSITY rewarded by enlargement of soul, 210.3

GENIUS: triumphs of g. unimportant, 20.11; g. of hero magnified, 152.26

GENTLEMAN, forfeiture of name of, 229.26; sentiments of a true and perfect g., 156.19

GENTLENESS, 264.44

GEOGRAPHY, child's lesson in, 93.6

GEOLOGY, what it tells about world, 112.7

· GERM of a peculiar character is in every man, 106.26; g. that does not decay, 113.24

GIFT of good example, 6.29; g. of prayer seldom possessed in high degree of excellence, 24.34; accept g. of creation, 168.9; best g. of God is the home, 19.24; best g. of good men is their friendship, 192.11; freedom is God's g., 236.10; God's crowning g. may appear in our unique traits, 210.33; God's rich g. of conditions for future life, 85.18; great g. of God is liberty, 164.28; greatest g.

of God is a teacher, 192.29; greatest g. of God is instruction, 193.18

GIFTS of God: wheat, wine, 41.14; g. of men vary, 26.24; g. of tongues, xxxv.2; g. scattered upon man, 208.13; g. which the world gives and takes away, 17.19

GIVE what you have; not what you would, 104.3

GLANCES at life, 227.1

GLASS: thru a g. darkly, 266.34

GLOBE of fire (sun) has shone on blackberry, 207.30; g. of precepts is imitation, 6.22; g. receives rays of millions of stars, 194.14; gravity of g., 28.21; nations of g., 198.4; seasons go like angels around g., 40.34; three zones of g., 42.12; whole surface repeats process of seed, 43.19; see *earth*.

GLOBES: eleven revolve around sun, 173.14

GLOBULE of sap examined, 41.31; earth is a little g., 175.24

GLOOM of chamber of death, 34.29

GLORIES of heaven in the home, 14.29

GLORY God has prepared, 142.1; g. Jesus has shed over world's history, 52.19; g. of clouds, 39.16; g. of the latter church, 201.11; no change but from g. to g., 119.14

GLUTTONY of meats and drinks, 10.18

GNOSTIC overtaken by time, xxxv.4

GNOTHI SEAUTON, 111.9

GO where you will, you shall work out your own effect, 101.27

GOAL is the height of a divine nature, 101.8; g. of covetous man, 5.34; g. of man is moral excellence, 49.10

GOALS of the average man, 205.18

GOD: a benignant power, 173.20; always designed men's happiness, 85.3; an object worthy of endless study and love, 83.21; g. and not the sower is responsible for harvest, 42.19; g. and speculation, 267.14; approached thru reason, xxiv.17; approached thru the holiness or godlikeness of Christ, 233.38; as described in hymns, 149.10; as pictured in hymns, 148.31; as viewed by liberal party, 85.22; calls greenness of plant life from dust, 42.22; calls while we pursue seeming for solid good, 35.27; can do no wrong because perfectly wise, 116.24; cannot be overlooked, 80.32; character inconsistent with astronomy and N., 175.17; commandeth men to repent, 170.8; conceived as a being of unknown power and purposes, 83.35; conceived as Judge of action and punisher of sin, 83.12; conceived under parental relation, 83.19; considered anthropomorphically, 139.19; considered in human form, 173.4; considers every desire a prayer and registers it in heaven, 4.19; demands the whole of us, 15.17; described, xxiii.15f.; differs from men only in duration, xxiv.4; does not absorb the soul, 244.44; does not cause miracle to make men stare, 240.13; does not limit virtue by rule, line or distinctions, 15.11; does not need men, 258.34; does not sit in solitude, 31.23; does not sleep, 4.18; dwelleth in you, xxvi.9; dwelleth not in temples made with hands, 170.3; dwells in human heart, 133.12; dwells within men, 133.22; 134.22; enables us to be of use to fellow men, 68.22; encourages human virtue, 83.20; exists for each man only, 208.32; Father of the universe, 31.19; feared by Sir Thomas Browne, 159.24; gave every man the germ of a peculiar character, 106.25; gave us social affections as bands of strength, 19.14; gives us freedom as fast as we are fit for it, 168.22; giveth to all life and breath, 170.5; grand object of all thought, 92.9; guides bee and planets, 176.21; has appointed day of judgment, 170.9; has assigned each creature to its own element, 173.20; has bestowed powers of soul as a birthright, 108.28; has given each man a cause to promote, 19.9; has given us dominion of world, 54.5; has joined together the good of temporal and eternal worlds, 230.16; has made moral institutions capable of mighty growth, 55.5; has made it possible for us to acquire what we want, 5.13; has placed a standard of character in every human breast, 110.10; has protected conscience in the soul, 231.20; has raised man from the dead, 170.11; has sent men with signs and wonders, 126.20; has yet much more light to impart, 55.27; hath made nothing poor, 249.34; helps those who help themselves, 118.15; 253.22; in human personality, xxiv.34; Stoics said G. in man was mind, 133.25; G. in neighbor and G. in me, 134.28; in the soul, 268.18; 116.32; G. in you, 137.3; intends his creatures to serve each other, 242.17; intends that we choose for ourselves, 118.5; G. is activity; is law, 250.16; is cause of all order, 114.2; is good even in bereavement, 243.35; is in our souls as our soul is in our bodies, 133.27; is intimate and friendly, xxiv.5; is moral Architect, 107.17; is not a Thunderer in the sky, 162.9; is not mocked, 69.10; is not only in Judea but around us, xxxv.27; is not our soul, but in our soul, xxv.8; is not such an one as yourself, 3.31; is object of unbounded love and adoration, 94.8; is observer of actions and potent principle binding them together, 4.8; is principle of the good man, 239.7; is reader and creator of tho'ts, 4.9; is separated from us by our free agency, 132.26; is substratum and basis of every one of his works, 221.20; is the G. of Abraham, Isaac etc., 245.2; is the substratum of all souls, 243.3; is the center of good man's life, 25.11; is the Reality of which admirations are a shadow, 155.7; is the servant of the universe, 221.41; is within man, 200.3; judges the whole of our lives, 163.12; justifies those who withdraw their eyes from all but

their own tho'ts, 109.13; keeps giving us encouragement and suggestions, 118.25; known intuitively, xxiv.29; likely to use miracles in interests of truth and relig., 121.32; makes acorn to grow into oak, 55.4; must be present to individual before being present to the church, xxvi.12; now greater, wider and more tender, 178.33; not like to gold, silver or stone, 170.6; not Lord alone of man, 174.13; not unknowable to mind of man, xxvii.13; occasionally ignored by understanding, 3.20; G. of N. and Bible are same, 170.16; G. of the living, 270.14; on right hand and on left, 25.12; once governor of world; now Infinite Mind, 176.25; only can satisfy our desire, 155.7; powerless over the past, 8.11; preferred to men, 201.34; present in astronomy, 175.5; present in bread and wine, 56.3; present in the mind, xxv.1; preserves whole universe, yet is mindful of all parts, 47.35; procures us good whether we act or forbear to act, 68.26; pronounced each mind good after its own kind, 108.2; rejoices in aiding his world, 31.24; revealed in Bible, xxv.22; is Father of human soul, 92.8; sees the soul, 216.17; shall be all in all, 179.5; sent Christ into the light of worldly life, 233.28; source of feelings toward G. and man, 83.9; speaks directly to each mind, 120.18; spoken of with uncertainty, 132.11; to be loved, not feared, 263.27; to be worshiped in our hearts, 111.31; the source of all good, 114.3; transforms all things into the divine, 211.14; treated as a holy Friend, 159.28; will care for the soul in the resurrection, 141.30; will care for you . . . of little faith, 45.32; will come to our aid, 127.21; will provide for us if we do his will, 45.29; will recompense your honest stewardship, 18.32; will right all suffering and injury in the end, 159.31; will seldom interrupt N., 123.34; within and without, 102.7; within us, xxiv.35; worketh in us his good pleasure, 132.21; working in man as conscience, 100.11; worshiped outwardly, 3.22; ability of G. to communicate to men involved in credibility of miracles, 120.24; actions designed to please, 85.22; aliens from G., 132.14; as G. liveth it shall be so, 188.19; be a G., 200.29; benevolence manifested, 31.22; benevolence of G. in N., 43.2; best of his gifts is the home, 19.24; character determined, xxiii.28; character injured in hymns, 148.29; character is moral, 123.6; city of G., 176.14; clearest manifestation is a good man, 162.10; commandment: Be ye holy! 132.35; confused views of G., 148.11; constant acknowledgment of G's presence, 53.9; description of G. is elementary, xxiii.6; distance betw. G. and man stressed, 132.11; domestic G. is conscience, xxv.6; enlarging conception of G., 72.15; existence attested by miracle, xxviii.22; existence is suggested to a reasoning man, 122.1; explanation of his attributes, xxiv.7; eye

turns evil to g., 210.24; exults in all that is g. and fair, 160.20; feels God is g. even in bereavement, 243.35; force of a g. life, 52.16; God is the source of all g., 114.3; God procures us g. whether we act or forbear to act, 68.27; highest g. of intelligent nature, 27.33; hold fast to that which is g., 70.31; honor is g. in the street but not in the closet, 157.13; hope of g. hereafter, 89.11; I desire to be g., 58.2; impulses of g., 219.2; in wreck of earthly g., the goods of the soul shine, 144.22; it is g. to act with the brave and industrious, 157.16; lessons are for the child's g., 164.3; loyalty is a remote and contingent g., 155.12; Mary has chosen the g. part, 51.16; men are entitled to respect from a g. man, 110.6; much g. can be done by g. conversation, 66.21; no man grew so g. that he could not be better, 236.4; one knows that one is not g., 250.7; our g. and evil actions and the judgment, 101.18; our g. is comprehended in God's great operation for all, 259.13; overcome evil with g., 22.24; path of order and of g., 116.30; prefer the g. in your character, 162.25; regard to common g. included in practice of virtue, 93.33; sacred poetry should be g., 146.18; self-love can never become principle of g., 130.17; soul seeks love and infinite g., 158.1; soul's g. of one's brethren, 70.29; striving after greater g., 8.26; the common g., 164.16; the dumb miss half the g. of being, 61.22; to be g. is to do g., 114.26; to seek anr's g. is better, 114.26; ultimate g. advanced by seeming exceptions to general order, 259.10; we are born to add to the sum of g., 128.7; we are bound to seek each other's g., 135.35; we must aim high to secure any g., 32.30; we pursue seeming for solid g., 35.28; will of G. is the g. of the universe, 131.32

GOODNESS, 161.32; g. and wisdom of Jesus alone to be loved, 195.14; g. increases the power of a man, 17.6; is awful, 6.19; not jealous of g. of others, xxvii.5; g. of God not limited to earth, 174.12; g. of God seemingly contradicted, xxiv.7; g. revealed to Jesus so much truth, 96.21; advances in g., xxv.34; confident in God's g., 40.5; he takes off g. like cumbersome garment, 16.6; infinite g. is object of love, 154.2; love of g. is basis of Christian system, 231.26; spirit capable of receiving all truth and g., 138.13; trust your share of God's g., 108.12

GOODS, community of, xxxiv.35

GOODWILL of the meanest is of importance, 192.10

GOSPEL, a help to mourner, 140.20; called revelation, xxvi.28; contradictions are resolved, 161.7; g. of eternal life filled with cheer, 85.11; g. of God has divine power, 23.13; words of g. received with mother's milk, 115.33; Christian g. has no monopoly on truth, xxvi.28; doc-

trines of g. are preached in daily events, 68.30; effects of g. after 1800 yrs. are small and feeble, 23.25; E. a servant of g., 28.17; greatness and universal application of g., xxi.34; heroes of g. compared with heroes of honor, 156.16; not ashamed of g. of Christ, 22.2; revelation of g., 11.10; sentiment of g. is: "Thy will be done," 259.23; sublime spiritual sense of g., xxxv.11; universal application of g. to all human concerns, 28.9; we flee to g. in the mouldering of N., 113.15. See scriptures, Bible.

GOSPELS: origin, authorship, genuineness of, 223.21; see Revelation.

GOSSIP, village, 64.4; 152.2

GOVERNMENT, a social institution, 54.10; cannot help intellectual or relig. character of citizen, 77.24; must be preserved, 78.6; g. of tongue, 64.16; g. strengthened by private virtue, 81.30; g. will be out of sight in a well-constituted state, 77.2; a perfect g. defined as one which gives freedom and harms nobody, 77.28; advantages of g. must always be negative, 77.23; bad g. described, 76.31; corruption in g., 78.10; every g. is mutable, 76.29; good form of g., 76.26; good g. already in our possession, 78.5; good g. depends on moral responsibility of individual, 75.21; one g. out of many, 128.34; vain to complain of crimes of g., 80.17

GOVERNMENTS, man's history is story of, 77.5

GOVERNOR: God was g. of world; now Infinite Mind, 176.26

GRACE, 27.27; of God, 253.30; doctrine of g., 253.17; God's g. will not overrule men's choices, xxiii.23; receive not g. of God in vain, 67.3

GRAIN of sand contributes to gravity of globe, 28.19; each g. of sand allied to all, 207.23; every g. of sand is fixed point round which all things revolve, 207.22

GRANDEUR in frivolous action, 14.11; of the heavens, 171.32; no g. like moral g., 178.19

GRANITE lifted into Andes and Alps, 112.9

GRAPES, 107.10

GRASS of field clothed, cast into oven, 45.30; groweth up, is cut down, withereth, 44.15; springs up, 39.20

GRATIFICATION of sense stifles conscience, 11.28; noble g., 7.32; sources of g., 5.21

GRATIFICATIONS of wants are within our reach, 5.17; g. that begin and end in this nook of earth, 117.34

GRATITUDE, 264.4; g. due God for our distinctive traits, 210.33; is not the result of self-interest, 129.26; g. to God, 160.11; what g. to God implies, 19.23

GRAVE is naked before God's knowledge, 4.4; creep into g., 193.4; dread of g. removed from the living, 140.30; 142.3; shall vice go triumphing to the g.?, 9.26; sublime attraction of the g., 143.4; sun lights men and animals to their g., 113.4

GRAVEYARDS resulting from nat'l calamities, 112.16

GRAVITATION, 176.15

GRAVITY dense on Jupiter, 173.14; of the globe, 28.20; sufficient for most men, 121.23; law of g., 208.5

GREAT: God revealed in all that is g., 212.16; time micrifies the g., xxxv.10

GREAT BRITAIN, a unity of small territories, 129.1

GREATNESS depends not on place or events, 60.8; doubled by noise and pomp, 181.34; lies in way of doing things, 60.13; means infusing great principles into common actions, 60.10; g. of N. reconciled to g. of mind, 176.25; g. of gospel, xxi.34; defects do not stand in way of g., 107.27; every man has idea of g. that was never realized, 110.13; mystery of our g., 136.31; secret of all true g., 184.4; what true g. is, 180.10

GREECE, 218.40

GREEKS on heaven, 243.40

GREENNESS called from dust by God, 42.22

GREENWOOD, Francis Wm. Pitt, his *Collection of Psalms and Hymns* referred to, 150.21

GRIEF, 268.16; g. and our attitude toward God, 139.9; not unkind, 140.5; g. that leads to inaction is evil, 143.29; unmans us, 143.15; petulance of g., 226.23; poignancy of g., 20.16

GRIEFS unimportant when God comes to the heart, 160.3

GROPINGS of infant weakness are theology, xxiii.7

GROTIUS, Hugo, 208.28

GROUND, Edward, xviii.21

GROUND given us to cultivate, 19.12; middle g. is best, 87.16; not an inch of g. to stand on, 135.19; tread on holy g., 38.19; we stand on same g. as our fathers, 54.7

GROUPS of men contain talents and virtues, 46.6

GROWTH and the internal struggle, 255.5; g. of human character—of an angel, 190.19; g. of Christianity, 196.23; g. of man dependent on direct imparting of the Divine Spirit, 134.3; moral institutions capable of mighty g., 55.6; skin of animal must expand to admit g., 55.9

GRUNDY, [Mr.], 181.25

GUARD: off g. when temptation comes, 20.28

GUESSES AT TRUTH. See J. C. and A. W. Hare

GUIDANCE of God, 186.23

GUIDE you into all truth, 257.12; same g. that pilots the bee and planet, 176.20

GUILT of man paints clouds, xxiv.11; we share in g. of slavery, 256.38

GULFS of chaos disembowelled before God, 4.5

H

HABIT, xxii.10; 265.40; h. of admiration, 151.24; hatred becomes a h., 30.15; negligence becomes a h., 72.35

HABITATION of creatures, 173.23; curses light on h. of wicked, 9.10

HABITS of reflexion and solitude have rec'd new value, 200.19

HAIR has a purpose, 220.41; gray h. is wisdom, 116.9

HAND, 216.9; is part of the body, 132.24; h. joins with h. thru gift of speech, 62.5; h. of fellowship extended to E., 24.18; humble man is h. of God, 161.5; h. of heavenly Father, xiv.25; h. of Jesus was strong because his soul was filled with virtue, 94.31; brain in the h., 251.29; every h. shall whip your vices and honor your virtues, 101.29; motion of h., 1.15; motion of h. of watch, 79.17; not a helping h., 226.41; pleasures near at h., 270.12; right h. of fellowship, 271.8; virtues near at h., 270.8; we are instruments of God's h., 68.26

HANDICAP not serious if God be helper, 21.2

HANDS folded, 193.7; h. of disappointed man, xviii.27; h. of men hold keys of heaven and hell, 253.21; h. were made by God, 135.12; God not worshiped with men's h., 170.4; house not made with h., 138.3; human h. wrote the scriptures, 178.29; industry of h., 2.13; lift one's h. in blank amazement, 204.29; make clean and holy the uplifted h., 38.24

HANGING-GARDENS, 222.16

HAPPINESS and the imagination, 7.20; comes from doing right, 85.26; derived from possessions, 7.18; dispensed by God, 31.25; found in enlarging knowledge, multiplying powers, exalting pleasures of others, 190.22; increased if work were liked, 167.1; is for poor in spirit, 161.8; h. of every soul will be diff., 141.5; h. of man reduced by lusts, 10.25; unlimited in heaven, 11.16; would be product of virtue, 35.23; men were designed for h., 85.4; mourner does not envy h. of others, 140.19; we are born to promote h., 128.7; why make h. less? 137.4

HAPPY: men desire to appear, xx.20

HARE, Augustus Wm. and Julius Charles, *Guesses at Truth* quoted, 153.19

HARM can be done by bad conversation, 66.22; do thyself no h., 269.36; each man defended from all h. he wills to resist, 209.33; h. is God's mark on immoral act, 93.35; no h. can befall a good man, 269.6

HARMONY in masses of matter, 253.33; of laws of God's kingdom, 242.16; with the real and eternal, 211.29; pre-existent h. between tho'ts and things, 6.14

HARP and viol, 9.13

HARPOON, throw, 206.23

HARTLEY, David, 249.4; *Observations on Man* quoted, 94.7

HARVEST and seedtime shall not fail, 42.23; h. of thistles for a h. of wheat, 102.27; their h. is our seed, 55.4; we eat a h. we have not sowed, 77.15

HARVESTS instruct, 208.19

HATE and you shall be hated, 102.18

HATH: to him that h. shall be given, 118.16

HATRED grown into a habit, 30.14; h. is the fruit of self-interest, 129.26; h. is warfare against oneself, 137.2; h. made a god, 151.14; life too dear to be soured by h., 87.33

HAVOC made on good mind by public questions, 229.9

HAYNE, Robert Young, 188.28

HE calls for things that are not, and they come, 6.35

HEAD and heart both consent, 189.11; h. was made by God, 135.12; Adam was federal h. of mankind, 199.19; industry of h., 2.14; injurious word recoils on one's own h., 65.31; world is carried in man's h., 252.11

HEADACHE, accused of a, 227.9

HEADS, rewards visited on our, 101.19

HEALTH sought by temperance, 123.1; spiritual h. demands admiration, 248.36

HEAR what the Spirit saith unto the Churches, 86.18

HEARER and speaker become pipes of God's spirit, 26.21

HEARING with soul as opposed to ears and memory, 114.30

HEART, 212.11; h. and head both consent, 189.11; h. and tongue in disagreement, 185.16; h. beat is death knell, 112.25; h. beats pulse for pulse with h. of universe, 186.27; becomes pure by God's influence, 162.15; determines our achievements, 6.1; fails, 35.12; is impatient of things finite, 152.19; is pure or impure; out of it are issues of life and death, 12.6; h. in sight of God finds earthly distinctions annihilated, 160.3; loves to lose itself in contemplating the vast and unbounded, 152.21; loves to praise, 152.12; needs relation of personal love, 159.23; h. of a lover cheered, 153.21; h. of man needs more than honor, 157.11; h. of one living man more revelatory than Italy or England, 209.7; h. opened for an hour to influences of relig., 17.34; h. oppressed by pity for dumb, 61.34; prefers to seek after the insignificant, 2.24; represents moral faculty etc., xxiv.24; touched with celestial impulse, 160.9; was made to love, 151.15; acting with all one's h., 166.32; Apostle Paul had valiant h., 22.5; as a man thinketh in his h. so is he, 102.2; bate no jot of h. or hope, 68.15; 201.28; commune with your own h., 190.8; conviction swells in man's h., 113.23; desolate h. comforted by good memories, 20.7;

each man placed at h. of the world, 209.16; exhortations aimed at the h., 36.9; God dwells in human h., 133.12; heaven begins in man's h., 210.18; human h. requires a God, 151.11; immortal life in bottom of h., 183.7; in the h. is concept of a greater man than has ever lived, 110.18; industry of h., 2.14; let young h. beat to his Maker's name, 52.31; Lord's Supper opens doors of h., 32.16; love God with h., mind and strength, 15.20; 71.27; man's h. becomes dilated with spirit of God, 210.19; men who work with the h., 188.6; the nearer a thing is to the h., the more impatient one is of insincerity, 226.19; no jot of h. or hope, 68.15; 201.28; not a used h., 239.38; prayers must reflect wish of the h. and real affection, 5.3; promptings of h. to be preferred, 168.7; pure h., 29.28; pure in h. shall see God, xxvi.2; sacred promptings of h., 162.24; simple h. has devout feeling in presence of N., 171.22; the good h., 266.30; the millions of suns etc. do not touch the h., 178.19; what saith the human h? 87.11; whole h. must love God, 15.20. See *pure*.

HEARTS: faith alive in h. of Abraham and Paul, xxxv.28; h. burned within early Christians, 92.22; vexed by a petty disaster, 258.41; bringing conviction of duty home to h., 25.22; God to be worshiped in our h., 111.31; we must accuse our own h. for gov't, 80.18

HEATHEN temple, 102.12

HEAVEN as described in hymns, 149.9; begins at once in his heart, 210.17; described, 21.27; has system of compensations, 10.33; h. of a common life, 265.10; h. of tho't, 208.34; offers greater exercise of our talents, 169.3; pictured from the senses, 243.38; supplies no aliment for earthly appetites, 10.17; the appropriate home of high tho't and noble virtue, 10.7; would not lack spectators in absence of men, 69.18; canopy of h., 33.35; door of h., 6.10; every desire registered in h., 4.20; glories of h. can all be had in the home, 14.29; high places in h. given those heeding duty on earth, 81.20; hour is seed of h., 17.33; joy in h. over one sinner, 245.23; keys of h. and hell, 253.21; kingdom of h., 267.30; law of h. that our nature should be progressive, 54.23; prayers are written in h., 8.31; real h. is felicity of a good mind, 92.14; soul's inheritance in h., 51.7; speak the language of h., 104.29; tie betw. earth and h., 144.15

HEAVENS have grandeur and influence the mind, 171.32; measure time but suffer nothing from time, 171.35; not touched by the changes that touch us, 171.35; opened to enable man to reform relig., 177.3; provided men with illustrations, 172.17; ancient system of h., 174.32; new h. and a new earth, 35.7; 119.5; the h. affect all opinion,

of soul stimulated by eloquence, 26.20; worldly h. to the ambitious, 102.1

HOPES of Adam's posterity cut off, 199.20

HORIZON, man is centre of, 208.17

HORSE, in presence of man, 154.32

HORSES, 222.4; h. and dull men compared, 206.30

HOSPITAL: you need not endow a h. to be good, 14.23

HOST of heaven, 173.32; celestial h. is within man, 200.4

HOUR: can crowd eternities into an h., 239.32; h. of death described, 34.29; h. of death is prepared for by all hours, 35.15; h. of systematic research worth years, 227.10; h. of youth, 73.4; h. to die, 33.32; well-spent h. is proper seed of heaven and eternity, 17.32; h. which may never arrive, xi.18; can stretch h. into eternity, 239.33; each h. has its appropriate subject, xxxi.28; every h. educates, 212.15; every h. of our waking time for virtue, 17.1; man's little h., 205.14; no warrant for living anr. h., 103.32; prefer h. of earnest dealing with yourself, 162.26; spend single h. in perfect purity, 20.32; 2400 die in an h., 112.24; value of one well-spent h. outweighs the fleshpots of the world, 17.25ff.; values in an h. of virtuous living, 21.7; virtuous h. is safe beyond accident; will witness for one at death, 21.9

HOUR GLASS, century is but the turning of, 113.26

HOURS of great diligence or concentrated tho't, 50.1; of life in household, 15.22; will take care of themselves, 217.31; all h. prepare for h. of death, 35.16; each minute in 24 hours, xxix.12; master of one's h., xix.6; our most virtuous h., 192.15

HOUSE desolate after bereavement, 143.6; is only a shelter, 49.8; not made with hands, 138.3; of wicked, 9.11; sold but balcony retained, 255.11; h. that no one could see into, 186.3; as for my h., we will serve the Lord, 151.2; each h. is a church, 3.16; earthly h. of this tabernacle, 138.2; in Father's h. are many mansions, 141.3; world is a h. where brave have dwelt, 52.7

HOUSEHOLD hours are hours of life, 15.21; h. of God, 11.22

HOUSEKEEPING, luxury of, 229.40

HOUSES, 216.22; h. and furniture sought after, 2.29

HOW awful goodness is, 6.18; h. old art thou? 112.1; h. to act, suffer, be useful, 193.9

HOWARD BENEVOLENT SOCIETY, 242.30

HUE: N. takes h. of our tho't, xxiv.11; things take the h. of our tho't, 101.31

HUMAN NATURE is much the same in all its forms, 35.34; worthy of re-

spect, xxvi.32; see *man, men, nature*.

HUMAN RACE, Jesus friend of, 35.2

HUMANITY: no nobler or softer h. than Jesus, 58.32; h. outstripped, 6.27

HUME, David, the skeptic, xx.33

HUMILIATION, 268.26

HUMILITY, 117.17; 253.27; h. and pride, 264.12; h. better than pride, 114.25; h. is means of approaching God, 92.11; virtue of h., 267.9

HUMOR: good h. guards one's speech, 88.15; good h. may be a disguise, 15.33; keep good h. and you win despite defeat, 65.13

HUNGER and thirst after righteousness, 178.12

HUNGRY are filled, 161.10

HUNT for station, land, horses, etc., 206.8

HUSBANDMEN, 146.1 ,

HYMN quoted, 174.11

HYMNBOOKS, 145.1; 269.17; should be better, 147.4

HYMNS, collection of the best, 146.34

HYPOCRISY of the understanding, 3.20; acts of h. broken by God, 4.3

HYPOCRITE: no man is h. at home, 15.25

I

I AM fearfully and wonderfully made, 203.2; the way, the truth and the life, 233.37

IDEA of God, 231.43; of God inadequate, xxiii.5; of God made more distinct, 30.9; of great purposes in life, 52.24; of greatness never realized, 110.13; of perfection in human n., 181.10; of universal man, 110.19; of virtue, 6.25; standard i. of man in all of us, 64.28; standard i. of man provides rule for our discourse, 65.4; people present no specific i., 181.26

IDEALISM illustrated, 2.6

IDEAS present to the mind of God, 4.7; abstract i. personified, 256.17

IDLENESS whips itself with discontent, 210.7; misery of, 164.7

IDOLATER has been shamed, 71.23

IDOLATRY displaced by purer relig., 146.5; i. imputed human passions to God, 173.4; is improper direction of admiration, 152.32; i. of the stars, 172.11; i. *vs.* relig., 151.8

IDOLS of society are contemned, 53.5; do not worship i., 71.22; meats offered to i., xxxv.2; we deck our i., 152.1

IGNORANCE and atheism, 265.35; i. of men regarding the gospel, 23.33; i. of mode of future life is not an argument against it, 244.7; i. of one's own resources, 184.20; i. of the truth, 3.29; of the world, 57.4; E. humbled by his i., 28.25; miracle speaks to i., 124.20; our i. of the real character of persons, 254.36

ILLUSIONS of life scarcely gotten over before time to put on shroud, 35.26

ILLUSTRATION for all argument found in heavens, 172.17; new modes of i., xxii.2

IMAGE, broken, 71.23; i. for every exalted sentiment found in astronomy, 171.15; i. of God in human nature worthy of greater honor, 110.10; every mind sees its own i. in the mirror of the world, 101.33

IMAGERY, gross material, 149.9

IMAGES employed in the gospels, 11.11; i. of scripture once low and familiar, 29.5; i. of the reformers of mankind, 52.2

IMAGINATION, 106.32; 145.16; believed to constitute faith, 250.29; heated i., 169.6; more active in good men, 160.35; i. of man or angel re. space, 172.27; i. of man re. the redemptive process, 174.27; i. of savage, 172.3; every man has his own sort of i., 108.5; vain i. of the skeptic, 27.17

IMAGINATIONS: images that inspire i. of men, 11.11; our i. settle down into events, 6.16

IMITATE: scorn to i. anything, 108.10

IMITATION arises out of unthinking admiration of others, 106.24; contrary to truth of character, 184.27; in deference to others, 107.15; in our daily life, 183.18; is "a globe of precepts," 6.22; i. of evil by children, 115.32; i. of Jesus' virtues necessary before sharing his power, 90.10; i. of others only *seems* relig., 109.26; i. of the small amount of evil in good people, 79.13; i. thru deference to others means loss of power, 108.17; see *opinions*.

IMMANENCE of God in man, xxiv.34; 257.1

IMMATURITY, 183.4

IMMENSITY of being, 161.24; a wearisome and barren i., 234.23

IMMORTALITY, 219.40; 220.5; 244.26; as revealed in Christianity, 238.29; confirmed by God and our own soul, 111.21; doctrine based on Jesus' teaching rather than on resurrection, 238.34; is personal, 244.41; not a mystical existence of the soul absorbed into God, 244.43; i. of human soul, 138.7; 149.2; i. of soul gives importance to events of this life, 163.5; i. provides us with incentive, 245.27; i. should not be a motive for virtue, 245.30; 245.33; faith in one's own i., 231.44; gloomy view of i., 243.27; how to gain a deeper conviction of i., 244.40; Jesus never preaches personal i., 245.9; medicine of i., 265.5

IMPATIENCE with insincerity, 226.19

IMPEDIMENT, 5.8; to enjoyment, 9.18

IMPERFECTION in character springs from neglect to cultivate some part of the mind, 106.20; i. should not discourage men, 69.20

IMPERFECTIONS of good men, 268.-12; of great men, 110.18

IMPORT fire of old faith, xiii.18

IMPORTANCE in eyes of fellow citizens desirable, 18.16; of events in this life, 163.6; man's exaggerated sense of i., 205.25

IMPOSITION of hands on E., 24.16

IMPOSTURE, 185.27; cannot be supposed of N.T. truths, 125.10

IMPRACTICABILITY of community of goods, xxxiv.35

IMPRESSIONS: first i. considered dangerous, 185.10

IMPROBABLE in the N.T., 125.28

IMPROVEMENT and not amusement is aim of Lyceum, xxxv.23; by small degrees, 266.24; i. every day is aim of liberal party, 85.7; i. is from a selfish to a social life, 130.9; i. is nat'l desire of men, 235.40; i. is our present business, 101.11; i. of one's time, 264.10; i. of the self, 269.41; duty of relig. i. is plain, 72.27; endeavor at i., 162.28; interruptions in i., 103.4; journey of i., 189.9; room for infinite i., 71.31; spiritual i. unlimitable, 267.11; state of rapid i., 180.7

IMPULSES of good, 219.1

IMPURITIES: mortal i. purged with fire, 10.23

INACTION is wrong, 143.29

INANITY of our activity hidden in multitude of particulars, 206.9

INCARNATION of pre-existent Logos, 233.27

INCENSE of prayers, 38.18

INCH of ground, 135.19

INCIDENTS of loyalty, 154.26; small i. make up life, 13.20

INCOGNITO of sect or party, 233.4

INCOMPREHENSIBLE, acknowledgment of the, 212.9

INCONVENIENCE from laws, 229.23

INCREASE: we are responsible for i. of profligacy, xxx.22

INDEPENDENCE and dependence, 270.41; i. in faith, 268.14; i. of a thousand bows to reason of one, 26.16; i. of circumstances, 181.9; i. of other men's judgments does not mean eccentricity, 110.30; i. of our spiritual n. on space and time, 117.19; i. of party even in midst of parties, 88.35

INDEX: deeds are surest i. of states of mind, 85.29

INDIA, wealth of, 4.26

INDIAN, treatment of, 229.29

INDIFFERENCE to death, 270.35; to wrong inflicted on Indian, 229.31; Paul fought i., 22.19

INDIGNATION seems justifiable, 66.4; i. aroused by Dr. Walker, xxi.28

INDIVIDUAL, 168.2; i. and society: their interest is one, 129.33; i. and the state, 75.1; 266.28; has power over his inheritance, 165.13; i. is solicited by good and evil spirits, 210.9; i. often forsakes usual path and shows men a new one, 166.15; i. responsible for bad gov't, 80.4; i. separated from world and made to demand his own faith, 199.15; i. usually true to early tendencies, xxxviii.13; God is present to i. before present to the church, xxvi.12f.; man is not so much an i. as a manifestation of God, 133.14; moral responsibility of i. is basis of good government, 75.21; solitary i. has effect on public morals, 81.2; worth of i. soul, xxi.19

INDIVIDUALISM, 57.21; approved, 232.37; Christianity corrects i., xxvi.18; excesses of i., 238.1

INDIVIDUALITY, genuine man parts with, 186.24; striking i. of a finished character, 106.33

INDIVIDUALS: as many callings as i., 166.9; change i. and you change social system, xxx.19; public virtue depends not on masses but on i., 80.22; solitary i., 197.35

INDOLENCE is suicide of soul, 8.1; rebuked by Christ, 69.31; overcoming i., xxv.35

INDULGENCE at table, 14.30

INDUSTRY of hands and feet devoted to perishable objects, 2.13; wages of honest i., 241.23

INEFFICIENCY, blank, 227.12

INEQUALITIES in human lot are only discipline, 160.4

INFANT: gropings of i. weakness, xxiii.7

INFERIORITY: no i. in man's nature, 106.15; soul stripped of i., xxiii.29

INFIDEL, 199.32

INFIDELITY is distrust of human reason, 252.24

INFIDELS, 194.32

INFINITE: finite yields to, 114.35

INFINITUDE of every man, 105.8; 200.18; 257.2; of individual soul, xxi.19

INFINITY, astronomer sees surrounding i., 175.25

INFIRMITIES, E's personal, xxxvi.9

INFIRMITY: your i. shall not hinder God's help, 21.2

INFLUENCE of a man thru thousands of years, 205.14; i. of objects and ages upon man, 207.20; i. of the fortune of birth, 165.5; i. of the heavens on the mind, 171.33; a more extensive i. coveted, 18.15; God's i. purifies the heart, 162.15; man exerts i. as well as receives it, 165.16; man something more than a receiver of i., 209.18; our acts have stronger i. at home, 18.14; revealer of my own nature will have more i. on me, 96.4; spiritual i. reciprocal, 268.36; supposed moral i. of stars, 172.15; see *power*.

INFLUENCES before inert, 193.15; i. of social institutions upon us, 54.9; opinions of others are insect i., 50.3; spiritual i. believed in, xx.5

INFLUX superseded the necessity of painful progress from elements of knowledge, 234.44; Jesus rec'd a miraculous i. of light into the soul, 234.43

INGRATITUDE, dumb, 19.27

INHABITANT of earth is a novelty, 172.7; eternal i. within the soul, 110.28; man is highly endowed i. of world, 45.25

INHABITANTS of cities pay high tax, 39.11; i. of other worlds, 177.22; i. on other planets diff. from man, 173.7

INHERITANCE of civil advantages, 77.16; maxims are i. of the past, 63.1; soul's i. of life and power, 51.6

INITIATIVE, men, not God, must take, 253.20

INJURY forgiven by old man, 30.14

INJUSTICE, 258.26

INMATE in our frail bodies, 136.9; reason is pure and holy i., xxv.11

INNOVATION not feared, xxii.1; E. not afraid of i., 28.10

INSCRIPTION on gates of Athens, 200.28

INSIGHT: some fundamental i. behind every system of theology, 231.7

INSIGNIFICANT delights man rather than eternal, 2.27

INSINCERITY is privation of whole spiritual world, 226.29; impatience with i., 226.19

INSPIRATION, plenary, 232.23; to prophets and heroes, 201.4; voices of i., 126.17

INSECT, man an, 206.5

INSTABILITY of credit and trade, 231.19

INSTANT in season and out, 69.31

INSTINCT: divine i. of conscience never wholly subdued, 231.23

INSTINCTS of man's nature, 161.34

INSTITUTION subordinated to individual, xxvi.15; conversation is i. for diffusion of knowledge, 62.29; see *church; Lord's Supper*.

INSTITUTIONS are like animal's skin, 55.8; for deaf and dumb, 61.11; form man, 165.11; i. of our fathers influence us, 54.9; i. of society in care of men, 54.6; i. of society, property, government, marriage, Sabbath, 54.9; ancient i. overshadow our births, 165.7; benevolent i., 199.2; Christian i., 198.15; free i., 29.16; moral i. capable of mighty growth, 55.6

INSTRUCTION, 187.27; helped by relig., 226.14; is greatest gift of God, 193.18; is main design of universe, 192.30; needed in history, laws, political science, 75.11; of God's providence is ceaseless, 69.9; i. of harvests and storms, 208.19; i. of Jesus is almost local, 195.35; i. of Jesus stresses no reason at all, 91.2; God has provided costly i. for his child, 212.15; relig. i., 256.10; relig. i. and prospects of society, 192.17; soul wants i., 155.15

INSTRUCTIONS of revealed relig., 220.39; how Jesus gave dignity to i., 90.13

INSTRUCTOR: great i. is time, xxxiv.31

INSTRUMENTS: social affections are not i. of pain, 19.14; we are i. of God's hands, 68.25

INSUFFICIENT: man i. to himself, no matter what his property, 206.2

INSULT, unprovoked, 66.5

INSULTS borne by righteous, 11.4

INTEGRITY can never be a loss, 136.21; defies sun to find flaw, 188.29;

i. of church not defended, xxvi.35; i. surrendered in conversation, 225.42

INTELLECT, 205.12; cannot reconcile free will and dependence on God, 236.16; child's i. trained, 52.4; discipline of., 29.26; invigorated i. makes world ebb away, 2.6; prayer not sought in the i., 25.2

INTELLIGENCE has contributed to advance of Christianity, 55.16; i. impossible without God, xxiii.21; i. indicated in N., 122.22; i. that presides over ordinary N., 122.32; man given i. ɪor purpose, 45.20; stars were considered to be i., 172.13

INTENT of Lord's Supper, xxxv.5

INTENTION of truth demanded by virtue, 226.16; i. shines thru words and deeds, 185.35; do nothing without i., 102.31; God's i. for man, 106.2; pious beyond i. of your tho't, 156.28

INTENTIONS that are mean need concealment, 185.31; good i. before they bloom into action, 159.15; good i. soon forgotten, 20.29

INTERCESSION by the dead, 142.30

INTERCOURSE poor in practice, 65.27; i. with disembodied man denied, 245.20; values and pleasures of social i., 65.27; see *conversation.*

INTEREST in insignificant particulars of a hero, 14.3; i. that only attaches to persons, 234.12; excess of i. shown in what one may say, 225.34; mutual i. of individual and society, 129.33; personal i. of love, 142.30; solemn i. in the future, 199.5; it is to man's i. to be benevolent, 129.16; trivial i. in politics, 229.35

INTERESTS of the righteous are consulted, 11.1

INTERPRETATION: subjective i. of God, xxiv.7; too literal i. of Jesus' words, xxxiv.33

INTERPRETATIONS: s p i r i t u a l, 200.21

INTERPRETER of scripture is always the human mind, 85.32

INTERROGATOR, why he exists? 204.24

INTERRUPTIONS in improvement, 103.4

INTIMACY of relations betw. man and God, 132.16

INTUITION, method of, xxiv.28

INVALID of many years, xviii.29

INVENTORS of arts, 208.29

INVESTIGATIONS of astronomers have had good and bad results, 175.28

INVIGORATE intellect and world becomes transparent, 2.6

IRONY of word *orthodox,* 230.33

IRREGULARITIES among the planets, 176.5; 176.10

IRRELIGION, wherein different from relig., xxiv.16

ISAAC, 245.2

ISRAEL, traitor in camp of, 79.2

ISSUES of life and death dwell in heart, 12.7; i. of life are in one's own

hands, 239.15; God will take care of the i., 188.23

ITALY, 209.8; I. and Rome, 54.18

J

JACOB, 245.3

JAIL, 163.23

JEFFERSON, Thomas, 208.28; quoted, 77.1; 229.20

JEALOUS: not j. of goodness of others, xxvii.5

JEALOUSY required in our use toward ourselves, 88.22

JERUSALEM, 177.14

JEST about human society and pursuits, 206.14

JESUS, 233.19; a poor benevolent Jew, 162.11; a sinless martyr, perfect and radiant, 234.32; apostle of moral nature, 196.14; appealed to man's consciousness, 91.6; armed with miracles, 244.43; as a moral teacher, 90.7; as an example, 233.24; as he appears in the light of astronomy, 178.34; as regarded by Unitarians, 148.19; as revealer of secrets of man's moral nature, 96.3; at the Last Supper, 56.10; benevolent and perfect son of man, 235.12; brought soul the hope of immortal life, 59.26; came not to call the righteous, 58.27; came out from God and spiritual world, 59.24; came to teach preference of soul over body, 189.5; checked or changed usual course of N., 56.19; could foresee the future, 234.45; declared the express image of God's person, 162.11; declared the truths on which the welfare of soul depends, 96.26; designed to be genuine, 183.20; did not teach like the scribes, 90.5; did not speak like the philosophers or like the vulgar, 92.5; did not tell men to prepare to die, 245.36; dwells with us alway, giving strength, peace, purposes etc., 235.12; friend of human race, 35.2; gave no systematic body of doctrine, 91.8; God's highly authorized servant, 58.10; had to accommodate his truth to his hearers, 197.15; had sublime purpose in his bosom, 14.16; has had an artificial place for ages, 195.8; image of God only inasmuch as he was better man than any other, 234.39; image of perfect man, who has no taint or mortality, 234.33; in doubt, 56.16; instructs us in the character of God, 178.35; is a mediator only if he bring us truth, 177.33; is a perfect pattern of obedience to God, 233.23; is an example for us, 90.10; is author and finisher of our salvation, 96.9; is followed by men who open the same elementary truth, 97.16; is the incarnation of the pre-existent Logos, 233.27; is your most effectual friend, 58.11; knew himself to be the Resurrection and the Life, 56.14; lived by the truths he proclaimed, 96.29; lived life of moral perfection, 56.23; lives for each man only, 208.32; made a king in barbarous times, 195.12; meek and lowly son of Almighty Father, 59.24; needed in the landscape of ethical precepts, 234.26; never preaches personal immortality, 245.8; never said: "All truth have I revealed," 196.33; not a subtle reasoner, 90.18; not well educated, 90.15; of Nazareth, 156.13; on subject of life, 114.21; our common teacher, 92.31; our savior not because of anointing, descent, or miracles, 96.22; possessed living moral truth as principle of his own life, 96.11; possessed *living* truth, 92.32; promised anr. teacher—the Comforter, 197.1; proves nothing by argument, 91.4; quoted: 45.30; 53.10; 81.9; 102.20; 106.7; 111.16; 133.1; 182.34; quoted on death, 168.35; realized the predictions of his people, 56.18; received a miraculous influx of light into the soul, 234.43; redeemer because teacher of men, 179.2; refused to listen to others and listened at home, 237.37; reputed son of Joseph, 91.15; serves us only by his holy tho'ts, 253.14; simply asserts on ground of his divine commission, 91.5; spoke of God in terms of earnest affection, 92.7; spoke to his times, 195.34; taught more truth more truly than others, 91.30; taught supreme kind of truth, 91.28; teacher and benefactor of man, 196.16; teaching about immortality of soul, 244.42; the soul's personal friend, 235.21; the Word of truth made flesh, 235.18; to be loved only for the wisdom in him, 195.14; to his elder disciples, 35.2; uses own name for truth taught, 233.36; was savior of soul, 56.28; will be better loved by not being adored, 195.7; will be loved by all to whom moral n. is dear, 195.20; will be valued for contrast with his age, 195.17; would have adapted his language to commonplaces of American life, 29.13; a secret attachment to J., 235.26; authority of, 90.1; 266.40; authority does not belong to person of J., 97.9; authority springs not from his office of Messiah, 96.18; brave stand for man's spiritual n. *vs.* sensualism, 195.30; commandment: "Be ye holy," 132.35; divinity lies in majesty of his character, 234.38; expiation not taught in astronomy, 177.32; fruitfulness seen in multitude of societies, 198.11; heavenly standard of J., 124.28; his goodness revealed to him so much truth, 96.21; his truth made him Messiah, 96.20; how distinguished from other teachers, 96.11; how mistakenly regarded, 233.40; habits were free and informal, 91.16; interest in J. is of a personal kind, 234.12; life and labors: how to be regarded, 195.2; life as original as his miracles, 56.24; life distinguished by presence of a Will superior to his own, 234.36; life epitomized, 100.26; his memory identified with conscience of good men, 96.31; men see God only in J., xxxv.26; method of teaching, 91.3; ministry about to close, 56.10; no nobler or softer humanity than J., 58.31; object of his life was great reformation,

56.35; office was to utter the truth, 96.20; person and actions of, 14.12; personal appearance, manners or voice not recorded, 91.21; precepts visible in omnipresent moral world, 69.6; principles will ever be standard for judging actions, 178.2; promise to the grief-stricken, 142.27; recorded teaching and example, 196.21; revelation discovers in us the principles we need, 100.4; rule was: Be ye perfect, 92.17; sayings are both occasional and universal, 196.4; sayings disclose inner world, 196.9; style of discourses was simple, 91.12; superiority over other teachers, 92.25; truth taught by J. not to be separated from his office, 96.16; truth was living truth, 93.22; truths not affected by astronomy, 178.8; we preach J., not ourselves, 31.3; why E. admires J's character, 58.29; words mark him as Messiah, 96.19; see *Christ, Lord, Master, Savior.*

JEW cried Blood! 22.19; Jesus was a poor J., 162.11

JEWISH law and ceremonies, 55.12; madness of J. hope, 56.26

JEWS, 135.35; and their fanatical expectation of a messiah, 193.32

JOHNSON, Samuel, 249.4

JOSEPH, reputed father of Jesus, 91.15

JOURNAL, keep a, xix.9

JOURNEY of improvement, 189.9; end of man's secret j., 140.34

JOY and peace of believing, 192.6; in heaven over one sinner that repenteth, 245.23; in suffering is the miracle of faith, 160.21; of little child, 249.22; dispense with feast but don't forget j., xxxviii.34; tidings of great j., 33.8

JOYS of sentiment and imagination hard to analyze, 145.16

JUDEA, men see God only in, xxxv.26

JUDGE, 163.23; j. not, 95.8; j. not and ye shall not be judged, 102.19; equal to the j., 188.19; good man better j. of truth, 94.14

JUDGING right for ourselves, 269.43

JUDGMENT day will show solid advantage of well-spent hour, 17.30; j. functions in present compensation, 101.26; j. in scriptures means more than an award in after-life, 101.20; instantaneous, 210.2; j. of Christ, 267.34; j. of men aided by proverbs, 63.13; j. of men on basis of words and actions, 216.15; j. of others should not deter us, 168.5; j. seat believed to be within, 225.14; j. shaken by renown of a prosperous man, 182.5; critical j., 184.22; Divine Eye in man passes j., 100.9; independent j., 200.20; our good and evil actions have gone before into j., 101.18; wherever there is character there is j., 101.25; see *retribution.*

JUDGMENTS of others will not harm men of self-reliance, 110.34; j. of the living yield to those of dead, 142.13;

honor is quick and correct in its j., 155.26; independence of other men's j., 110.31; j. of men aided by proverbs, 63.13

JUPITER (the planet), 173.7; 173.13

JURISDICTION of honor over all parts of life, 156.4

JUSTICE, 93.33; j. and truth, 186.21; cannot require flattery, 226.3; j., even if imperfect here, gives man warning, 102.28; j. of God will assert itself, 66.10; j., mercy and moral law at home in every climate, 177.25; j. of God will right all in the end, 159.32; j. same in mind of God and man, xxiii.32f.; j. shall not fail, 66.7; eternal j. administered, 138.12; honor is the finest sense of j., 155.30; terrors and beauty of j., 212.5

JUSTIFICATION, 27.28; j. for man's vocation lies in force of his feeling, 168.27

JUSTIFY, do nothing you cannot, 116.20

JUSTIN MARTYR, 249.1

JUVENES, 222.28

K

KEEPING the Sabbath, 268.32

KEY to Christ's teaching is "Know Thyself," 200.31

KEYS of heaven and hell in man's hands, 253.21; only k. to unlock mysteries of N. are benevolence and piety, 94.10

KINDRED: only k. souls unite for social worship, 232.38

KING worshiped, 157.24; sighed to be born a k., 18.18

KINGDOM of heaven is within, 267.30; of heaven promised a pauper, 209.14; of love, truth etc., 113.35; better k. recognized by interior senses, 114.13

KINGS terrible to enemies and subjects, 180.19

KNEES, throw self on, 210.33

KNEEL: saints of all churches k. side by side, xxxviii.27

KNELL, every heart beat is death k., 112.25

KNOT: no k. which death cannot untie, 168.34

KNOW THYSELF, 111.9; 111.28; 168.3; 183.3; 183.10; 200.25; 200.28; illustrated in Christ's teaching, 200.34; was doctrine known by Christ, 200.30

KNOWING God intuitively, xxiv.28

KNOWLEDGE, 190.23; accumulated by others is of no use until verified by us, 118.18; accumulated in mind of the race, 194.9; darkened by pride in self, 238.10; is end of action, 193.1; is increased by efforts to impart it, 62.17; k. men have of each other, 108.21; k. of a surveyor or shipmaster, 93.8; of God is perfect and immense, 4.1; of God secured thru N., 177.7; of God thru reason, xxiv.18; of God thru heart, xxiv.24; of God's works, 171.1; of others springs from our k. of ourselves, 243.11; k. of the

world—meaning of phrase, 185.9; one of God's restraints upon men, 129.13; ought not to be proud, 232.16; when increased shows purpose in everything, 220.42; accurate k. of proverbs not attainable by single man, 63.9; actions lead to better k., 94.19; conversation diffuses k., 62.29; critical k. of Christian sculptures, 29.22; diffusion of useful k., 198.9; exchange of k. in conversation, 62.15; faith is the most real and certain part of k., 250.31; increasing k. of God, 270.30; means of k. are multiplied, 46.11; outward means of k. is of avail only when one looks within, 111.4; revelation is a source of religious k., xxvi.26; rigid party emphasizes faith without k., 89.7; serve God acc. to our best k., 257.10; specific k. about future life would unfit us, 244.2; too many miracles would be fatal to k., 124.3; use all means to spread k. of true relig., 88.33

L

LABOR ought to be a pleasure, 167.2; under load of embarrassment, 168.31; daily l. blended with relig., 189.10; division of l., 164,13; division of l. of great social importance, 128.27; l. to become better, 101.15

LABORER in his ditch, 209.2; not worthy of his meat, 193.5; reflective l. only is a man; unreflecting l. is but a superior brute, 211.25

LABORS, honor doesn't sustain intellectual, 157.15

LABYRINTHS of N., 94.11

LAGRANGE, Joseph Louis (1736-1813), 176.9

LAKES, marching beyond, xxx.35

LAMP burns out, 113.6; l. by which I walk, 96.6

LAND, one's own, 191.9

LANDS, foreign, 19.29

LANDSCAPE exists for man, 43.32; is imperfect without animals and men, 234.21; country l., 44.4

LANGUAGE inadequate for some thoughts and passions, 2.35; like that of proverbs, 225.27; of scripture once low and familiar, 29.5; of heaven kept alive on earth, 104.29; l. of Jesus, 193.20; l. of love approaches l. of worship, 153.11; l. of Nature, 44.9; l. of reason is same for living and dead, 143.18; l. of the world is "Remember thou must die," 245.38; l. of truth-telling business man is clear and strong, 109.3; God not deceived by fradulent l., 3.33; God speaks l., 141.22; no l. even of signs, 61.29; subterfuges of l., 4.11; uniform l. of scripture, 105.13; see *conversation*.

LANTHORNS to illuminate the home of man, 173.32

LAUGHTER of Democritus, 206.13

LAUREL given one's virtues, 101.29

LAVA, 112.14

LAW accepted in place of the Cause, 121.13; can demand redress for a man,

78.4; has an arm of power, 78.2; l. of all action is that all things are double, 102.17; l. of charity, 130.2; l. of compensation, 263.20; l. of compensations excells anything in material N., 209.25; l. of duty is universal, 76.7; l. of heaven that our n. should be progressive, 54.22; l. of land justifies wrong, 229.31; l. of matter sustained throughout N., 116.26; l. of our action, 116.10; l. of our actions and words rests in things, 2.30; l. of the Christian, 135.17; l. of truth, 225.7; l. of universe guarantees success to endeavors, 7.2; a l. which is the fountain of honor, 158.33; all things preach the moral l., 122.35; Christian l. flows thru channels of our life, 116.16; Christianity is an infinite and universal l., 27.29; general l. that rulers represent the virtue of their respective countries, 80.11; homage and obedience to l. of God, 16.35; honor represents the l. of God, 155.27; inevitable l. of our being that God sees, 4.16; Jewish l. and ceremonies, 55.12; mathematical l., 95.6; moral l., 177.24; moral l. defined, 93.26; moral l. reigns in every man's bosom, 123.5; moral l. same in all minds, 64.23; subjecting oneself to l. of one's mind, 100.17; summary of the new l., 115.17; the great l. of moral n., 115.18

LAWS and customs of mankind, 184.8; l. below are sisters of the l. above, 10.32; l. discountenanced, 3.26; l. of Bible must first be found in one's own soul, 111.6; l. of England and Italy, 209.9; l. of God are eternal—have no beginning or end, 101.22; l. of God function wherever there is moral action, 101.23; l. of God have lesson to teach man, 45.27; l. of God may be obeyed or rejected, xxiii.22; l. of God's justice will assert themselves, 66.10; l. of mind interpret scripture, 85.33; l. of the mind must approve miracle, 123.25; l. of moral n. dimly perceived but ever working out results, 209.21; l. of N. are permanent, xxviii.27; l. of N. uniform, 121.13; l. of the stars, 177.3; l. of tho't not accommodated to divisions of time, 70.34; l. of universe can be learned thru our own trade or profession, 163.26; l. which cannot be obeyed without loss of self-respect, 229.25; conforming to natural l., 116.11; inconvenience from l., 229.23; Jesus expressed great l. to which human understanding must bow, 91.35; man's rebellion vs. l. of Maker, 45.27; moral l. assert themselves by effects, 35.22; moral l. in time and eternity, 10.29; moral l. proclaimed to ourselves and others, 210.14; nat'l l. operate with certainty, xxviii.29; nature of moral l. can be learned only by acting, 209.28; our l. diff. from our fathers', 54.14; simplicity of nat'l l., 175.16; universal l. occasionally counteracted in N., 126.11; watching the moral l. doesn't lessen our wonder, 161.17; we ultimately return to great l. of Jesus, 92.2

LAWYER, 166.2

LEADER of the genuine man is within, 184.34; dying for a political l., 158.10; invisible l. within one's breast, 188.13

LEADERS and patrons, 158.8; falsehoods of l. are perpetuated in church, 237.18

LEADERSHIP of governments, 80.11

LEAF, 207.25; lives in the tree, 132.19; God seen in l., 40.3

LEARN to adore your nature, 134.1; we can always l., 236.4

LEARNING, 251.28

LEAVEN, 197.24

LECTURE: unsaid part does the most good, 223.28

LEIGHTON, Archbishop Robert, quoted, 133.28

LENSES: distorting and coloring l. of the pauper, 209.12

LEPER, Naaman the, 250.27

LERENS, Vincent of, test for catholicity or truth of a doctrine, 230.37

LESSON for man in all he sees or hears, 208.20; for the pious in N's changes, 40.13; from scripture is to value our own souls, 106.9; l. of laws of our Maker, 45.27; l. of N. is omnipresence of God, 40.23; l. of serenity and trust, 72.9; l. taught by all things, 192.35; l. written in N's bk., 40.15; child's l., 164.2

LESSONS: pernicious l. of home life, 19.8

LET your light so shine before men, 81.9

LETTER: men appeal from l. to spirit of the scriptures and find one meaning, 85.33

LEVITIES of conversation chastened by relig., 226.13

LEWDNESS, 3.25

LIABILITY to changes, care, disease, death, 103.2

LIBERAL Christian builds system on love of goodness, 231.26; L. Christians of Boston, 232.35; l. thinking of the age, 57.30; see Christians; Unitarians.

LIBERALISM and Rigidity, 266.38; relig. L., 82.1

LIBERTINE, 6.7

LIBERTY, 244.6; is great gift of God, 164.29; l. of Unitarians, 232.42; l. wherewith the gospel has made one free, 87.19; glorious l. of the sons of God, 169.12; human l., 244.36; only l. may man call his own, 4.14

LICENCE of the respectable, 13.7

LIE in wait to sin again, 225.10

LIFE, 176.23; after death, 9.29; always has its subject, xxxi.28; but a vapor that appeareth for a little while, 243.28; flows thru channels of our l., 116.17; l. in conformity to N. is a moral life, 122.35; infinite and perfect, 212.17; is a term of education, 85.9; is all of a piece, xxvii.10; is like the day, 193.15; is long enough for its vast purposes, 117.20; is only found in God, 133.10; is short, 35.25; issues of one's l. are in one's own hands, 239.15; l. itself is a great miracle, 122.10; l. itself would be sermon and monition enough, 35.21; long enough for men to be saved or lost, 117.27; made up of small incidents and petty occurrences, 13.20; may be spent in great purposes, 52.24; l. of a genuine hero, 14.4; l. of inaction is inglorious, 143.29; l. of Christian is miniature of his relig., 201.30; l. of God in the soul, 116.32; l. of great man has imperfections, 110.18; l. of man compared to seasons, 44.18; l. of man needs more than honor, 157.12; l. of man short, 44.32; l. of pastor should be exemplary, 33.17; l. of the soul in us, 116.31; l. too dear to be soured by hatred, 87.32; a l. nobly led under guidance of relig. principle, 16.32; a pin will let out our l., 103.20; all l. is a progress toward death, 112.21; all our l. is a miracle, xxix.10; 122.18; all parts of l., 156.5; announcement of future l. on conditions, 85.19; art of l., 193.9; aspect of l. changed by sad event, 140.12; average l. longer now than in former ages, 54.25; best part of l. unseen, 264.38; bk. of common l., 7.15; character identical with relig. l., 188.35; church sees l. of man from diff. side, 113.33; conversation is breath of social l., 63.35; course of one's l., 163.9; daily beauty of their l., 20.14; disgust of l. corrected, 143.26; E's object in l., 72.12; end of l. is a preparation for soul to meet God, 92.10; events in this l., 163.6; every action in l. referred to God, 53.9; every moment of l. has retribution, 102.24; evils of social l., 46.25; Father hath l. in himself, 114.21; force of a good l., 52.16; future l., 269.8; godliness applies to l. here and to come, 81.23; good l., 29.29; good l. is a stand *vs.* sensualism and skepticism, 201.31; good l. is key to good prayers, 25.10; gospel of eternal l., 85.12; heaven of a common l., 265.10; holy l. possible in sickness, 104.11; honor as a rule of l., 156.33; common l., 265.10; holy l. possible in sickness, 104.11; honor as a rule of l., 156.33; human l. is part of Eternity of God, 136.7; ignorance not an argument *vs.* a future l., 244.8; immoral l. hidden behind respectability, 15.31; immortal l. in bottom of heart, 183.7; improvement is from a selfish to a social l., 130.9; invariable order of human l., 259.4; issues of l. and death in the heart, 12.7; Jesus bro't soul hope of immortal l., 59.26; Jesus showed l. of moral perfection, 56.23; judgment occurs during as well as after this l., 101.21; knowledge of human l. in proverbs, 63.10; love of l., 183.29; man made for immortal life; has infinite nature, 105.7; meaning of l. not confined to gospel, xxvi.29; men of vulgar l., 251.24; moral l. no longer relished, 6.7; most

solemn occasions of human l., 31.13; no distinct information re. future l., 244.1; no life in the soul apart from God, 114.5; obedience to virtue as a way of l., 94.1; object of l. to explore n. of God, xxii.35; other world alone is l., 114.15; our l. is hurrying to an end, 67.7; our l. runs on beaten track, 60.7; passage from death to l., 114.16; proverbs and maxims are commentaries upon l., 63.5; public l. dazzled by circumstances, 184.11; refinements and necessaries of l., 46.9; relig. teaches art of conducting l. well, 99.9; rounds that make up human l., 116.34; same in words as in l., 186.7; shortness of l., 99.5; some part of l. killed every moment, 112.17; soul must seek l. in itself, 114.20; the whole l. *vs.* single actions, 163.11; this transitory l., 137.10; to have humility, love and self-denial is to have l., 92.13; to know God aright is l .eternal, 83.22; true l. consists in opening interior senses, 114.13; truth not always attained in this l., 64.32; unspotted l. is old age, 116.9; vicissitudes of l., 155.14; waters of l. poured out, 32.17; we seek l. not death, 143.27; when the second l. begins, 114.34; worldly l. leads to ruin—this needs to be proved by each man, 118.20; would give his l. for his country, 156.6; see *existence*.

LIGHT and heat of sun on blackberry, 207.32; from N.T. shall break forth and guide us, 218.45; in man's mind is imparted without loss, 62.11; l. of duty is always present to all, 70.25; l. of God's presence carried by minister, 69.33; l. of N., 170.22; l. of scriptures flows into one's life, 219.16; l. of stars same as in beginning, 172.1; l. of world to come, 34.26; l. of the worldly life, 233.28; l. poured thru soul, 96.2; character shines in purer l. in spirit world, 20.18; crimson l. of first morning, 194.8; duties God has written in l., 136.32; eye which fills universe with l., 159.13; God has yet more l. to impart, 55.27; let your l. so shine before men, 81.9; orbit of l., 8.3; summits lifted into l., 35.11; sun grudges l., 193.6; truth finds l., 102.21; unaided l. of one's own understanding, 109.25; use the l. we have, 257.9; waves of l. from center to circumference, 159.17; we should gladly borrow l. from anr., 109.31

LIGHTNING come down from heaven, 4.25; loiters in contrast to retribution, 210.2

LIGHTS, men seldom see new, xxxviii.-11

LIKE only can know l., 134.11; l. sees l., 100.34; 102.2; I don't l. chasms of discourse, xxxi.25

LIKENESS betw. great and good men not apparent, 107.2; l. of all men, 134.8; l. of faith and feeling is the only basis for social worship, 232.38; principle of l., 243.9

LILY, why so beautiful? 222.1

LIMB draws whole weight of body,

186.26; has a purpose, 220.40

LIMBS, motion of, 40.21

LIMIT: no l. to learning and virtue, 236.3; no l. to spiritual improvement, 267.12

LIMITS, fixed and impassible, 176.13; l. of self-reliance, 268.45

LINE dividing saints and sinners, 224.11; no line divides saints from sinners, 58.4

LIPS say one thing; heart anr., 185.15; touched with fire, 202.13

LISTENED to Dr. Channing, xxi.26

LISTENS: advantage to man who l. to himself, 108.34

LITERATURE: earliest l. is religious odes, 145.24

LITTLE: man can do l. for anr., 238.18

LITTLENESS of persons of capacity, 48.34; of present; greatness of future, 197.22; mystery of l., 136.31

LIVE by design, not by accident, 102.30

LIVELIHOOD justifies injuring truth and violating conscience, 255.1; l. to be earned, 103.8

LIVER complaint of the Orthodox, 233.2

LIVES preach doctrines of gospel, 68.33

LIVING cautiously, xiii.30; l. may neglect the bereaved, 142.11; God of the l., 270.14; think on l., 245.40

LO, I am with you always, 142.27

LOGOS doctrine no more fundamental than Trinity or Atonement, 233.30; hymn to L., echoed, 114.3; pre-existent L., 233.27

LOINS girt about with truth, 180.2

LONELINESS, 258.26

LONG live the Emperor! 154.22

LOOM, 29.25

LOOMS shall stand still, xxx.33; xxxi.12

LOQUACITY, when tolerable, 226.20

LORD, character of discourses of, 29.8; 124.27; presence of L. refreshes, xxvi.1; revenge is mine, I will repay, saith the L., 66.6; trust in the L., 268.28; see *Christ, God, Jesus.*

LORD'S SUPPER, 31.7; 54.1; 55.28; 270.34; a feast, distinction, badge, pledge, rebuke, remembrance, 57.8; a matter of subordinate importance, xxxvi.15; a melancholy memorial, 32.7; LS. and character development, 58.12; LS. and modern liberal practice, 57.30; LS. and progress of men's minds, 57.26; LS. apt to be misunderstood even by Unitarians, 56.6; LS. commemorates dying love of Christ, 32.9; makes those who partake of it better, 224.15; meant to be accommodated to every age, 57.12; not intended as institution for perpetual observance, 223.39; once combined with superstition, 55.30; one of the gospel kindnesses, 223.9; seen under complexion of individual mind, 57.21; simply a means of

improvement, 59.11; symbol of a holy affection, 32.15; all partook of LS. in primitive church, 58.18; foundation and intent of LS., 56.8; its consequences, 59.17; its end and aim to make men better, 57.35; perversions unforeseen, 57.3; purpose of LS., 57.1; variety of effects, 57.22

LOSS, light imparted without, 62.12

LOSSES converted into angels and helpers, 160.6; l. to be repaired, 103.9

LOT in life determined by Providence, 16.25; of man, 20.2; of our social relations, 128.3; daily l., 8.16; man accepts his l., 207.11; our human l., 160.5

LOVE, 178.20; 212.10; 247.36; l. and you shall be loved, 102.18; l. as a person, 256.18; l. based on wisdom and goodness, 195.16; brightens the sun, 210.5; can never be a loss, 136.21; drawn to wisdom and goodness, 161.31; l. for the mere pleasure of loving, 153.24; l. God, 95.7; l. is gained by loving, 123.2; is means of approaching God, 92.11; is the principle God meant us to use toward others, 88.21; l. of a man never seen— loyalty, 154.15; l. of all is our business, 135.21; l. of Christ, 268.38; l. of Christ to some has unaimiable sound, 235.6; l. of Christianity for Fénelon, Calvin, Taylor and Priestley, xxxviii.28; l. of display, houses, clothes, etc., 229.39; l. of God (see *infra*); l. of goodness as basis of Christian system, 231.26; l. of life, 183.29; l. of N. joined with relig., 171.19; l. of neighbor (see *infra*); l. of order is petulance, 210.29; l. of poor and wretched not universal in man, 130.34; l. of thought and moral beauty, 10.10; l. of truth above party, 231.36; l. of virtue is innate, 265.24; l. the Lord thy God with all thy heart etc., 15.20; 53.10; 71.26; 88.4; 115.17; 127.2; 131.27; l. thy neighbor as thyself, 71.27; 269.15; l. to Christ, 266.12; l. will continue though unrequited, 155.1; cords of l., 19.19; disinterested l., 244.5; duties discharged without l., 167.6; eye of l. grows severe, 144.5; heart was made to l., 151.15; how stimulated? 153.25; if you l. earth you become earth; l. God and become God, 133.32; objects of l. are qualities, 153.29; passion of l. described, 153.4; passionate l. of eloquence, xix.27; perfect l. casteth out fear, 87.26; 267.40; relation of personal l., 159.23; sentiment of l. has infinite goodness for object, 154.1; soul wants an object as great as its l., 155.16; we l. the lovely, 131.3; what l. shall govern me? 151.7

LOVE OF GOD considered too distant a principle, 132.1; 132.10; excludes all selfishness, 134.35; is highest sentiment of soul, 151.4; is only sufficient principle, 247.40; is salvation, 239.10; is the result of enlarging our sentiments, 158.14; must supersede self-love, 239.9; by LG. the soul is made divine and one with Him, 133.30

LOVE OF NEIGHBOR as usually found lacks strength and cannot be trusted, 130.25; capricious, discriminating and selfish, 130.28; in practice, 134.30; insufficient basis of ethics, 131.24; is wonderful principle when it acts in family circle, 131.18; rests on principle of love of God, 131.28; will not serve as principle for whole system of social duty, 131.22

LOVELINESS of obedience, 228.13

LOVELY, Father revealed in all that is, 212.14

LOWELL can visit; church service is less, xxxiv.4

LOVER is loved, 102.18; is made happier by his affection than the object of it can be, 153.19; l. of animal delight, 6.3; l. of truth, 171.5; mind of l., 153.13

LOW and injurious turned to power and beauty by the Reason, 210.25

LOYALTY, 247.36; a powerful spring of action, 154.8; a remote and contingent good, 155.11; a species of worship, 154.12; a strong sentiment in human n., 154.6

LUNGS, rest for the, 248.8

LUSTS: gnawing l. have coiled themselves, 10.12

LUTHER, Martin: 117.16; 177.24; 208.27; 249.2; a reformer, 52.23

LUXURIES of the senses worthless, 196.19

LUXURY loved, 229.39; momentary l., 241.21; simplicitv superior to l., 49.26

LYCEUM aims at improvement, not amusement, xxxvi.23

LYING characterizes the Fr. language, 225.41

M

MACHINE, tree or vegetable is m., 43.7; working of human m., 203.17

MACHINERY: animal m. is poor compared with man, 45.12

MADEIRA grapes, 107.10

MADNESS in the young, 229.38; m. of party spirit, 78.20

MAGNANIMITY, 201.20; distinguished from foolishness, 51.19; is divine, 66.18

MAGNET, 218.41

MAGNIFICENCE: moral m. of disembodied souls, 11.14; to what end? 43.30

MAGNIFIES the small; micrifies the great, xxxv.10

MAGNITUDE of sun measured, 52.12

MAGNITUDES of stars, 174.7

MAINSPRING of man's progressive nature, 151.23

MAINSTAY of relig. man is tho't that Providence rules the world, 259.7

MAJORITY of men do not make nice distinctions, 86.28; m. opinion of honor, 157.4

MAKER, laws of man's, 45.27; name of M. honored, 52.31

MALEVOLENCE: no m. in the mourner, 140.15

MALICE in conversation, 226.13; mul-

tiplies its foes, 210.8; no m. in N., 159.20

MAN, a little creature unmindful of his spiritual potentiality, 205.8; 205.18; accepts his lot, 207.11; adores, 207.12; advances in goodness, xxv.34; m. and his profession react on each other, 164.11; m. and misrule of his passions, 45.26; m. and his proverbs, 63.8; m. and wife in matrimony, 31.15; m. as he really is behind his barricade, 182.13; becomes a drop in the spiritual ocean, 100.24; becomes bundle of errors and sins, 238.6; becomes one with all things, 207.11; becomes voice and hand of God, 161.4; becoming the servant of a tho't, tries to subject all creation to it, 198.20; bends circumstances to his purpose, 168.25; by reflection perceives he is wonderfully made, 207.2; can admire the shell, 222.1; can be harmed by none but himself, 209.31; can do little for anr., 238.18; can do much to redeem and uncreate himself, 239.12; can do nothing against Jesus' truth, 97.32; can live only in spiritual world, 114.14; can make calm solitude in midst of multitude, 159.4; capable of acting upon remote men and upon himself, 205.13; carries the world in his head, 252.11; counselled by all great minds, 208.31; consults no opinion but his own in solitude, 47.2; delights in insignificant, 2.27; designed to be a benefit to the world, 190.22; did not make himself, 238.3; distinguishes pleasant and unpleasant days, 42.28; does benefit generally from service to others, 128.23; does not stand in way of God's action, 68.26; does wrong; God does right, 132.33; eats bitter herbs of regret, 67.19; emerges out of finite into infinite, 114.34; endowed with same divine faculties which lie behind universe, 176.35; enters the inheritance of ages, 55.2; exerts influence as well as receives it, 165.16; experiences a compensation for all his qualities, 101.27; feels greater reality in tho't and feeling, 2.1; feels himself wiser in conversation than in silence, 62.23; finds all pain of use, 85.16; finds Divine Providence a teacher, 194.3; gains lesson in all he sees or hears, 208.20; gives his path in life unnecessary perplexities, 50.24; had better relate his tho'ts, 62.24; has conspicuous peculiarity of admiration, 152.28; has dominion of the world, 54.5; has elements of excellence within, 106.3; has enough within to puzzle and outwit all philosophy, 209.4; has faculties to bring him his ends, 5.18; has few obligations to gov't of U.S., 77.31; has great powers and desires acc. to liberal party, 83.17; has his foible, 48.26; has moral law in his bosom, 123.5; has nat'l reverence for moral truth, 95.3; has no defect or inferiority in his n., 106.14; has nothing that he did not receive, 135.10; has power in his parlor, 18.22; has power over his condition by free will, 164.28; has power to obey inner voice, refuse service of senses, subject self to law of mind and partake of God's attributes, 100.15; has standard of character in his breast, 110.11; hears voice that God is within, 200.2; himself seldom weighed, 182.12; holds everything in trust, 135.22; holds issues of life in his own hand, 239.15; in his right place has powers harmoniously developed, 167.11; in solitude attends only to real wants, 47.1; independent of circumstances, 181.9; inspires and expires immortal breath, 207.14; intended to be more than just a receiver of influence, 209.17; is a novelty on earth, 172.7; is above N., 45.15; is alone in death, 34.11; is architect of his fortunes, 8.8; is awaked to truth and virtue, 207.12; is being of giant energies, 8.8; is born a potential angel, 190.20; is born in shadow of ancient institutions whose strength is greater than his own, 165.7; is born into a cheerful eternity, 172.8; is bound to the will of God, 135.8; is centre of the horizon, 208.16; is considered less than circumstances, 254.16; is educated thru his calling, 164.8; is formed by institutions, 165.11; is highly endowed inhabitant of world, 45.25; is improvable, 265.32; is insufficient to himself no matter what he owns, 206.2; is judged by his works, 1.7; is master of his eternity, 8.8; is made the center round which all things roll, 208.11; is mere manifestation of a power and wisdom not his own, 238.5; is moral being, 44.35; is more wonderful than animal machinery, 45.13; is no puny sufferer tottering ill at ease, 8.7; is not cause, but a mere effect, 238.4; is not great unless reverenced at home, 15.2; is of great worth, 106.6; is point or focus upon which all objects and ages concentrate influence, 207.19; is solicited by good and evil spirits, 210.9; is the least part of himself, 182.17; is the tongue of creation, 145.4; is usually true to his early tendencies, xxxviii.13; is virtuous to himself, 118.13; judged by wheels of his carriage, 181.19; justified and condemned by words, 64.17; leaves time and enters eternity, 114.35; like the flower of field, 44.14; like the grass, 44.15; looks to relig. to supply his wants, 99.11; loves to lose himself in contemplation of the vast, 152.21; made for immortal life; has infinite nature, 105.7; may apply his own spirit to the Divine Mind, 100.23; may share attributes of God, 100.19; may walk in frail flesh with firm step of archangel, 188.23; moved by things 1000 yrs. old, 208.23; multiplies the sources of his own chagrin, 50.24; must be wise in himself or all knowledge will not help him, 118.11; must choose betw. good and evil spirits, 210.10; must make his own choices in God's moral order, 118.6; must not expect to be exception to invariable order of human life,

259.3; musters and clarifies tho'ts more vigorously in conversation, 62.19; not designed to be an idle eye, 209.19; not made by circumstances, 165.2; not made for Sabbath, 189.14; not needed by God, 258.34; not so much an individual as a manifestation of God, 133.14; not wholly good or bad, 58.6; m. of feeling, 32.19; m. of great powers of mind, 49.16; m. of principle is majestic, 188.16; m. of truth speaks a clear and strong language, 109.3; m. of wit can find out the right subject, xxxi.29; m. of worldly wisdom, xx.33; only a spectator of ways of God, 69.14; ought not to think highly of himself, 182.28; ought to ponder evils of party spirit, 88.26; passes out of local and finite, 207.13; pictured growing up, 204.10; placed here for discipline, 258.36; possesses something real and noble, 105.11; possesses the spirit that governs material creation, 45.13; profits from failure, 184.15; raised above the brutes, 193.12; reaches acme by developing his peculiarities, 211.3; receives all things as if the world had no other child, 208.35; receives freedom when fit for it, 168.23; removes, combines and shapes the works of God, 41.19; sees world only in parcels, 40.27; seldom depends on his naked merits, 182.1; seldom valued for quality and color of his character, 181.23; separated from human family by selfishness, 210.7; set down amid sublimities of the universe, 205.8; shares the experience of the ages, 208.21; should consider the unknown nature within him, 211.18; should follow his own tho't, 184.26; should give what he has, 104.3; should make externals his servants, not masters, 183.30; should sacredly strive to utter his one word, xxxx.7; should trust his own share of God's goodness, 108.11; shuts his eyes to God's omnipresence, 40.25; speaks for the irrational creatures, 145.5; standing in the way of truth, 219.9; stands in midst of two worlds, 1.21; stands on top of world, 208.16; superior to animal world, 257.36; surrounded by a miracle, 204.33; tends to doubt existence of a cause not shown to his senses, 121.11; thinks clouds angry because of his own guilt, xxiv.11; thru action is enabled to learn properties of moral nature, 209.20; thru Reason can turn the low and injurious to power and beauty, 210.25; thru virtue is grander than creation, 205.16; values N. only for his petty interests, 40.28; wanders from relig., the home of the mind, 28.2; wants to feel himself backed, 154.31; wants N. to suit his convenience, 40.29; m. who calculates too nicely on comfort, 50.21; who doesn't know himself, 183.3; who offends not in word, 60.2; who possesses truth will move you, 95.27; who puts riches first, 5.22; m. who reflects is a m.; not an animal, 206.35; m. who reveals secrets of my nature will have more power over me,

96.2; who stands upright cannot be bent by creation, 209.34; who tries to satisfy all his own needs would be poor indeed, 128.26; who watches his tho'ts, 159.3; who writes for his own eye only, xxxiv.-10; whose richness is in his own nature, 181.12; will be eloquent who yields to a just sentiment, 26.26; will come right hereafter if left to himself, 65.3; will come to the truth, 64.33; m. within the breast, 65.7; m. within your breast is revered in spirit world, 9.31; works out faithfully his own effect, 101.29; worthy of respect, xxvi.32; would still be an insect in the universe without self-knowledge, 206.5; yields to empire of Reason, 210.25————a finished m., 181.1; actions dignified by high purpose, 14.22; ambitious m. sees worldly hope everywhere, 102.1; any m. eligible for social eminence, 181.30; m. armed is poverty, 256.20; avaricious m., 206.28; bad m. finds no peace in prosperity, 102.25; balance of his faculties, 2.19; benevolent m. finds way full of charities, 101.32; best part of m. revolts against ministry, xxxiii.32; m's blood could not circulate on Uranus, 173.11; business is to improve, 72.28; capacity of m. for virtue, 231.11; capacity for virtue emphasized by liberal party, 83.6; celebrated m. often of humble appearance, 49.21; character affected by circumstances, 164.24; character cannot die, 20.18; character is measured by its effect on others, 108.15; character of a mature man, 130.1; character strengthened thru Reason, 210.28; character survives and ascends, 141.10; church surveys m. from a diff. side, 113.33; comfort of m., 41.3; competence of m. is known to neighbors, 19.2; complete m. not easily found, 181.8; constitution and destination of soul, 2.18; constitution is moral, 122.33; cultivated m. will side with critic against himself, 226.10; cultivation of all his powers, 167.17; destiny is the grave, 112.20; devout m. at church would not see the walls or the passing multitude, 221.30; devout m. finds the presence of the Omnipresent sufficient, 221.31; disappointed m., xviii.-27; disembodied m., 245.20; duty to relig. improvement, 72.26; duty to overcome pleasures of sense, 105.9; each departure from relig. makes return more difficult, 28.3————EACH MAN a type found nowhere else in world, 108.13; exercises a portion of political power, 75.7; is center of arch of the rainbow, 258.2; fits into a profession in accordance with his temper, 166.5; given unshared total benefit of all wisdom, 208.30; is gainer in conversation, 62.16; is imperially free, 258.6; must demonstrate for himself the truth of Christianity, 118.26; placed at heart of the world, 209.16; raises or depresses public virtue every day, 80.23; responsible for profligacy of public morals, 79.10; surround-

ed by immortal fence, 209.33; condition is diff. from that of anr., 208.26————early m., 145.27; emblems of m's mortal estate found in N., 44.13; error of m. will yield to truth, 64.33; essential m. often considered least, 181.16; every desire of m. is prayer to God, 4.19————EVERY MAN born with a peculiar character, 165.19; contains principles of eloquence, 26.25; defended from all harm he wills to resist, 209.33; has a perfect world existing for him, 209.1; has an idea of greatness that was never realized, 110.12; has germ of a peculiar character, 106.26; has had searching glances at life, 226.42; has his own sort of love, grief, imagination and action, 108.5; has his own voice, manner, eloquence, 108.3; has infinitude, 200.18; has something peculiar, 210.34; has tho'ts shared by no other, 106.29; is a sect himself, 232.37; knows every other by himself, 243.11; likes to do what he can do well, 169.15; occupies a singular position, 106.28; seems to repeat yourself, 134.7; shall bear his own burden, 82.3; should do his part in commerce, 206.20; uneasy until every power is in full action, 166.23; wields influence on gov't, 76.30; his work is his calling————experience of m. in gov't is tragic tale, 76.35; faculties of m. made to love, venerate, adore, 152.30; faith of m. must have an independent connexion with God, 237.29; faith of m. superior to Bible doctrines, xxv.28; faithful m. faces future unafraid, 160.29; fear of death unworthy of him, 127.10; finished m. speaks and is understood, 62.2; first day is reflection, 237.19; first m. on the first morning, 194.9; fitness of m. to the earth, 203.17; frailty of m. is described, 103.18; frailty of m., 8.5; freedom makes him solitary and accountable, 236.11; freedom should be used for self-culture, 101.7; frivolous m. sees folly everywhere, 102.2————GENUINE MAN, 180.1; 270.-37; acts his tho't, 185.3; acts in character because from character, 184.35; always consistent for he has but one leader, 184.34; cannot go astray, 188.22; espouses his cause, 188.2; examines every opinion for himself, 187.2; finds his own vocation, 187.27; gives himself up to God's guidance, 186.22; has four marks, 254.18; has strength of the whole, 186.25; in action, 187.11; is transparent, 185.35; leans upon laws of N., 186.23; parts with individuality, 186.23; puts God before men in his doings, 187.16; speaks in the spirit of truth, 187.1; speaks what he thinks, 185.3————God not unknowable to m's mind, xxvii.13; good and felicity of m. intended by God, 85.13————GOOD MAN better judge of truth than bad, 94.13; can experience no harm, 269.6; clothed with beauty in his death, 127.13; differs from God only in duration, xxiv.4; 200.26; finds peace in adversity, 102.25; hard to find, 250.7; has more fire in eye and more active imagination, 160.35; is entitled to anr. good m's respect, 110.6; is satisfied *from himself*, 110.29; is the clearest manifestation of God, 162.10; leans upon and borrows omnipotence, 160.27; needs no aid from company, 221.31——— grander nature of m. is his soul, 113.21; great calamity is distrust of self, 105.20; greatest blessings of m. untouched by death, xxxi.1; grieved m. neglects others, 140.13; growth dependent on direct imparting of the divine spirit, 134.3; guides and teachers of m., 126.16; guilt paints clouds angry, xxiv.11; happiest m. in God's sight is described, 160.7; happiness derived from possessions, 7.19; heart contains issues of life and death, 12.7; heart needs more than honor, 157.12; heart of one m. as revelatory as all England, 209.8; endowments of m. are independent of his work, 209.3; m's fall believed foreseen by God, 174.24; his lot to have home ties broken, 20.2; his power and wants, 157.32; his rebirth characterized, 114.29; his relation to the world, 5.15; his word leaps forth to its effect, 6.34; history of m. appears in conflict of parties, 86.16; history of m. is story of gov'ts, 77.5; history of m. as valuable as history of a nation, 209.5; history of m. in beginning is same as now, 44.13; how pious m. worships, 159.10; how profited if he gain world and lose soul? 105.2; 106.8; humble m. capable of infinite force, 161.3; if a m. fall on moral laws, they will grind him to powder, 209.23; if m. liked his work, society would speed, 166.34; imagination cannot conceive of space, 172.27; inanity of his activity hidden in multitude of particulars, 206.9; individual character can change inherited pursuits, 165.12; inferior m. described, 181.32; infinitude of m., 257.2; influence continues thru thousands of yrs., 205.14; irrelig. m. cannot think straight on problem of evil, 258.40; is he punctual in his orbit? 45.10; Jesus and God exist for each m. only, 208.32; lassitude of m., 45.1; let every m. prove his own work, 82.2; 238.21; liability to sin is principle of rigid party, 83.8; life of m. compared to seasons, 44.18; life of m. longer now than formerly, 54.25; lusts become principle of his nature, 10.25; magnificence of N. exists for m's soul, 43.31; main business shoved aside and never done, 117.4; meanest m. has importance, 192.10; merits may be extolled, but———, 69.13; mind isn't yet aware of true position in creation, 204.31; moral nature of m. is basis of Christianity, 195.6; moral nature of m. and his relation to God, 233.33; motion of his limbs; expression of his face, 40.21; nat'l m. hears everywhere: "How old art thou?" 113.10; nat'l man sees all things and himself decay,

113.16; nature of m. is to yield to authority of moral truth, 94.34; N. obedient to m's fervent prayers, 8.6; necessities of m. furnish structure of civilization, 210.29; m's neighbor is God's child, 131.30; new m. created after God in righteousness, 183.22; no m. can suddenly be a good pastor, 37.19; no m. grew so good that he could not be better, 236.4; no m. is a hypocrite at home, 15.25; no m. liveth or dieth to himself alone, 135.17; no m. nobler or softer than Jesus, 58.31; no m. visits the spirits in prison if I do not, 229.9; notion of genuine m.. 183.19; no wise m. can keep serious about the folly of mankind, 206.15; oddity of m's demeanor, 205.8; old m. urged to forgive an injury, 30.14; once considered type of highest being, 173.1; only possession is liberty or free will, 4.14; peevish m. finds way full of crosses, 101.31; perfect m. doesn't offend in word, 66.21; pious m. described, 231.27; possesses authority in proportion to his truth, 97.10; power over others lies in his peculiar qualities, 108.6; powers revealed thru specialization, 164.17; powers susceptible of cultivation, 85.5; progressive nature must have something to admire, 151.23; progressive nature of m., 54.24; promotes the good of others involuntarily, 130.13; proper goal is moral excellence, 49.10; prosperous m. disturbs our judgment, 182.4; public selfishness echoed in private life, 79.25; pure air and sunshine of genuine m., 185.27; pure m. is vehicle of God's spirit, 162.16; purpose of m. as disclosed in revelation, 106.2; purposes helped by N., 6.13; m's reason and virtue are God, 4.13; Reason is pure and holy inmate of every m., xxv.12; reason not addressed in relig. revivals, 232.5; reasoning m. knows God exists, 122.2; rebellion of m. against laws of his Maker, 45.26; reflecting m. only is a man, 211.26; relation of m. to God, 245.15; relations and duties of m., 7.26; reliance of m. on N., 45.2; relig. m. brings to church his own devotion, 228.29; relig. m. may not know solution to problem of evil, but he can handle it, 258.45; residence of m. believed illuminated by stars, 173.32; rich, travelled or powerful m., 211.35; scorn to be a secondary m., 108.11; selfish m., 206.28; selfish m. benefits others involuntarily, 130.14; selfish m. says beggar is nuisance, 131.14; sensual m. sees sensuality, 101.34; shall m. alone be in disorder? 45.25; solitary m. values advantages of society, 46.14; solitary and virtuous man, 208.14; soul always hears voice of its eternal inhabitant, 110.27; soul has Divine Eye within, 100.8; soul of m. hears scripture message, 114.9; soul is a sacred property, 106.24; soul is an empire, 111.15; soul is infinite spiritual estate, 105.23; soul is something real and noble, 105.11; soul made to act for others, 130.5; spiritual m. sees all things eternal including himself, 113.17; spiritual m. sees himself in God, 113.17; sin lieth at his own door, 59.8; sin of m., xx.19; sin shall not exclude him from Lord's Supper, 58.24; standard idea of m., 64.28; structure of m. is theistical, 247.33; sustenance is pleasant, 43.11; the great m. described, 181.35; the m. Hercules and the m. Chesterfield, xx.32; the m. is the least part of himself, 181.17; the new m. which after God is created in righteousness, 180.4; the proud m. doesn't perceive wonder of our being, 206.27; the wise m., xxxiii.16; there is a m. in us which we have not seen executed out of us, 181.5; tho'ts of m. are not like God's tho'ts, 97.15; to him that hath shall be given, 118.16; m. intended to observe the stars and write their laws, 177.2; treasure of m. is his soul, 266.5; true home is spiritual world, 114.9; true position in the universe and consequent obligations, 211.16; truth of m's moral nature, 91.28; truth perishes with no m., 69.14; universal m., 110.19; universal m. is within us, but not actualized, 181.6; unreflecting m. is but a superior brute, 211.26; unthinking m. desires a sect or party, 233.5; view of God exalted; view of self humbled, 172.32; vocation begins with exercise of conscience, 169.9; what? 263.28; whole self is his whole being, 182.33; wisdom is m's gray hair, 116.8; wise m. and miracles, 122.8; 122.11; wise m. differs from God only in duration, 133.24; wise m. sees wisdom, 101.34; wisest m. in ancient world was Socrates, 204.35; worldly m. adopts self as the principle, 239.6; young m. persuaded to forego sensuality, 30.12. See *men, nature* (miscellaneous), and *standard man*.

MANHOOD is the summer, 44.18; ripen into m., 34.1

MANIFESTATION: clearest m. of God, 162.10; man is m. of a power not his own, 238.5; man is m. of God, 133.14

MANKIND, I think well of, 231.12; service to, 6.29; to party gave up what was meant for m., 86.11; universe benefits m., xxiii.18

MANNER of speaking and thinking in Jesus' day, 197.16

MANNERS corrected by Christian associations, 198.6; of rich man, 5.25; fine, plausible m., 182.9

MANSION: body has no m. in spirit world, 10.6

MANSIONS, in my Father's house are many, 141.4

MAP, drawing a, 163.21

MARIVAUX, Pierre Carlet de Chamblain de, 249.4

MARK of a great soul is contempt for trifles, 50.27; m. of perfection, 104.1; I press toward the m., 163.3; God's m. upon every moral act, 93.34

MARKS of a Christian, 268.30; m. of failure in a minister, 30.1; m. of respect, 205.21; m. of genuine man, 254.18

MARRIAGE a social institution, 54.10; See *matrimony*.

MARTHA careful and troubled re. many things, 46.2; careful of trifles; careless of instruction, 51.14; officiousness rebuked by Jesus, 51.14

MARTYR challenges pain, 22.8; George Fox is a m., xx.34

MARTYRDOM not required of many, 60.6

MARVEL of our condition, 207.8; of the external fitness of man to earth, 203.23

MARVELLOUS seen in the common, 122.7

MARY has chosen the good part, 51.15

MASK removed at home, 16.5; person who never put off the m., 185.22; soul sees thru our m., 136.18

MASS of the earth, 208.5; Mass or the fagot, 228.16

MASTER of one's hours and fancies, xix.6; appetites turn upon m., 10.20; E. wanted to be m. and not servant to forms and creeds, xxxix.1; meaning of M's words, xxxiv.32; see *Jesus*.

MASTERS of men, 183.31; m. which God provides for the teaching of man, 258.31

MATRIMONY, 31.6; league of affections betw. man and wife necessary to existence and order of society, 31.14; see *marriage*.

MATTER only seems fixed and permanent, 2.9; law of m., 116.26; objects of m., 178.11; world of m., 1.22

MATTERS: hugh m. and small viewed in time, xxxv.9

MATURITY consumed in cares of the world, 117.2

MAXIM of Christian relig.; love Lord your God etc., 88.4; m. of little calculators: the world will last our day, 78.28; m.: take care of the minutes etc., 217.30; m.: people end with being what they are accused of being, 87.2

MAXIMS are commentaries on all parts of life, 63.5; m. of worldly prudence, 62.35; old m. have been remembered, 200.22

MEADOW, God seen in, 40.3

MEAN: appropriate m. to necessary end? 126.7; taking the m. of one's tho'ts, xxx.30

MEANEST, goodwill of the, 192.10

MEANING of Jesus' words becomes clearer, xxxiv.32; m. of life not confined to gospel, xxvi.28; m. of words has changed, 27.25; m. of your will, 156.29; one m. in the Word and works of God, 85.34; one m. on lips and anr. in their hearts, 185.15

MEANS and ends, 106.27; m. and manner of action should be infinitely various, 106.27; m. are great if end be, 14.2; m. must be appropriate to end, 95.12; each relig. party labors in its own cause with all its m., 86.4; use all m. to spread knowledge of true relig., 88.32

from whom they are accustomed to receive truth and falsehood, 108.20; know whether they are convinced or not, 95.25; lighted to their graves by sun, 113.4; lose power by imitating others, 108.20; make no effort to be pleasing at home, 16.5; make their relig. historical, xxxv.25; marching to the West, xxx.34; may be inferior to creatures of other planets, 173.24; may do the will of God, 59.27; much the same in all their forms, 35.34; must be born again, 239.2; must take the initiative, not God, 253.20; need not be discouraged with imperfection, 69.21; needed in landscape, 234.22; not eager to study best systems of education, 2.21; not made for themselves, 151.18; now inquire after their several stake in the whole, 199.22; occupied with particulars, 163.8; m. of ability owe much to pomp and noise, 181.32; m. of capacity have littleness, 48.33; m. of consideration in society, 7.34; m. of conviction intensify it by cooperating, 198.23; m. of discretion in worldly affairs think grossly of God, 3.34; m. of extended views of the grand and beautiful, 152.16; m. of honor have often been intemperate, 157.11; m. of letters are petulant, 222.20; m. of principles absent, 229.37; m. of standing determine what is honor, 157.5; m. of strong character often change their vocations, 165.26; m. of worth should be respected, 110.8; often follow fathers' professions, 165.9; pay heed only to single actions; God, to the whole life, 163.10; possess freedom, 85.4; reform states when they reform selves, 81.6; reproved by the flower, 45.19; sacrifice themselves for pottage, 255.2; say bad things to each other in good society, 79.19; see God only in Judea etc. and not around them, xxxv.26; seem satisfied, but are not, 8.25; seldom experience violent changes of opinion, xxxviii.11; seldom see new lights or turn sharp corners, xxxviii.11; m. sent by God have come with signs and wonders, 126.19; shall be parts of God, 132.24; share same ground as their fathers, 54.7; should be astonished at themselves, 203.7; should be warned of universality of law of duty, 76.6; should do nothing without intention, 102.31; should extort good from their present faculties, 107.30; should live by design, 102.30; should trust wisdom of God, 107.30; should value their differences, 106.16; should vote acc. to conscience, 76.9; speak from floating parlance of the time, not from within, 108.29; studious of what others will notice, 48.14; think conventionally, 108.30; think little of the present, 8.25; think relig. character is separate from daily actions, 189.17; turn from truth to being agreeable, 48.11; turn on same poles, 62.8; unconquered, unexplored, and unsuspected to themselves, 111.12; want neighbor to think as they do, 88.7; were designed for happi-

ness, 85.3; were made for sublime attainments, 49.6; m. who are less sensible to beauty, 172.16; m. who conquer others without conquering themselves, 111.12; m. who do their work professionally and who do it with the heart, 188.5; m. who look for own particular advantage, 187.34; m. who need assistance are often unlovely and offensive, 131.5; m. who teach and m. who hear, 202.12;———actions of good m. are the Word made flesh, 235.18; all m. admire, 151.22; all m. do not have same sense of honor, 156.34; all m. have power to know the pure and benevolent, 66.27; all m. have their caprices, 72.1; all m. suffer calamities, 259.5; amiable m. pursue natural science, 222.20; bad m. derive countenance from the good, 79.3; before m. had built towns, 171.30; careless and improvident m., 102.29; character of m. not really known to us, 254.37; character of m. strengthened in Lord's Supper, 58.12; characters are unlike in best state of the world, 106.34; choices of m. not overruled by God, xxiii.23; cities of m. have been buried, 112.13; considerate m. become more parsimonious in praise, 152.13; constitution of m. is wonderfully made, 257.27; doctrine rec'd by numbers of m., 230.38; entire m. formed, 254.15; faculties are made of God's action, 4.13; Fénelon, Calvin, Taylor etc. were holy m., xxxviii.28; few genuine m. have ever lived, 183.25; few m. can bear intense scrutiny, 182.12; few m. have analyzed every thought and emotion, 90.18; few m. have power of eloquence, 66.25; few m. love all their fellow beings, 130.31; few m. perceive marvel of their own constitution, 203.11; few m. suited to a profession, 167.4; few m. watch their own mind, xxiv.27; finite m. are atoms in the immensity of being, 161.23; forming true and entire m., 180.24; friendship is best gift of good m., 192.11; genuine m. and their attitudes to daily work, 189.23; gifts of eloquence in m. vary, 26.25; God preferred to m., 201.35; good m. are inspired by one soul, 134.11; good m. are not g. enough, 79.2; great m. elevate tone of community, 46.7; good m. have costly and venerable attributes, 105.13; good m. have feared trust in self, 238.10; good m. have imperfections, 268.12; good m. object to use of names, 86.32; good m. suffer injury to reputation, 225.8; great m. have faults and imperfections, 110.18; great m. present very dissimilar ideas to your tho't, 107.1; great m. unworthy of our exalted sentiments, 158.8; good m. will head affairs in good gov't, 80.13; great m. and great things are unimportant, 8.21; great m. worthy of honor, 110.8; greatest m. marked by simplicity, 51.23; half-men but half act, 187.32; history of great m., 110.14; m. must know their own task, 229.11; judgments of m. aided by proverbs, 63.13; low m. born, and their rise, 52.14; many m. are passive, 165.6; many m. cannot yield joyfully to truth of adversary, 65.17; minds made after one model, 64.22; minds not independent existences, 4.6; minds of m. are ideas present to God, 4.6; most m. do not make nice distinctions, 86.28; most m. favor extremes, 86.31; most m. satisfied with a secondary cause, 121.21; motives of m's acts hidden from us, 1.5; m. older, wiser and better than we, 109.29; only a few m. are quoted as authority for business transactions, 80.28; opinions on relig. questions, 192.20; our debt to fellow m., xxxx.5; perverted m. considered the stars to be power and intelligence, 172.12; presence of thinking m. in a foundering ship tortures us with interest, 234.20; purposes of m. are similar in best state of the world, 106.34; rights of m. recognized by law in U.S., 77.12; sacrifices of m., 52.14; scientific m., 52.11; secret history of m's lives, 18.30; sentiments grope after some great object, 161.28; serve all m., 95.7; several classes of ignorant m., xxxiii.16; shall m. not govern themselves? 45.18; significance of Jesus Christ to m., 52.19; some m. formed for public life, 187.17; some m. formed for science or mechanical arts, or commerce, 187.21; some m. formed to serve others in gentle offices of compassion or instruction, 187.26; some m. have dedicated entire life to cause of a creed, 86.8; some m. live only for appearance, 255.10; some m. may have faculties for perceiving tho'ts, 216.18; some m. never act for themselves, 185.14; some m. never put off the mask, 185.22; speech of m. exalted into a god, 157.6; spirits of just m. made perfect, 3.7; strength would fail on planet Jupiter, 173.12; sweet society of speaking m., 61.9; though m. were none, heaven would not want spectators, 69.18; 2400 m. die in an hour, 112.24; united m. live easier and happier than hating m., 128.31; useful m. find life long enough to work out ends, 117.22; we are the m. who increase profligacy, xxx.22; weak hands of m. hold keys of heaven and hell, 253.21; welfare still only hoped for, 180.14; wise and good m. gain strength from soul, 201.20; wise m. find life long enough to instruct others, 117.23; wise m. have had no greater opportunity than we have, 117.14; wise m. of dark ages, 55.20; wisest m. believe in continuity, not a contrast of this life, 244.17; wisest m. believe Judgment Seat is within, 225.13; you have done with m., 34.4; see human race; man.

MERCHANT, 166.2

MERCURY, 173.7

MERCY and truth are met together, 256.19; m., justice and the moral law at home in every planet, 177.25

MERIT of enthusiasm, 195.24 „

MERITS: naked m. do not appeal to us, 182.1

MESSAGE: each man has a message to deliver; let him not use another's, xxxx.8; m. spoken in part every day, 199.11

MESSIAH, 96.18; m. as expected by the Jews, 193.32; a carpenter's son, 56.27

METAMORPHOSIS, tale of, 42.8

METEORS, 122.9

METHOD of Jesus in teaching, 91.3; of knowing God intuitively, xxiv.28; speculative m. in theology, xxiv.18

METHODISTS, 146.8

MICROCOSM, see miniature.

MICROSCOPES of the scientists, 41.31

MIDDLE ground is for lovers of God, 87.16

MIDST: we stand in m. of two worlds, 1.22

MIGHT of Omnipotence has made elements obedient to fervent prayers, 8.5

MILK, mother's, 115.34

MILLIONS of suns and systems, 178.15

MILTON, John: 107.3; 249.3; Par. Lost, IV, 675-6 quoted, 69.18; Ibid., IV, 847-8 quoted, 6.18; Ibid., V, 310 quoted, 178.13; Ibid., V, 574ff. quoted, 244.19; M. should have written hymns, 147.19; "Sonnet on his Blindness" quoted, 104.16; "To Mr. Cyriack Skinner" quoted, 68.15; 201.28

MIND busied in objects of matter hears beatitudes, 178.11; can dedicate its whole force to mere straws, 47.21; capable of comprehensive views of God and eternity, 47.20; clothed with humility etc.; cannot die, 92.15; m. considered to be the God in man, 133.25; contains voice of God, 189.1; convinced of abstract proposition becomes its servant, 198.19; disregarded in favor of body, 216.21; educated by heavens, 177.4; framed for tho't of God, xxiv.30; has made a deity of honor, 155.17; improved by faith, 161.6; m. in love will experience energy of tho't and action, 153.18; is direct revelation of Maker's Will, 189.2; kept down and not exalted in relig. revivals, 232.6; kept ever awake by self-trust, 108.26; like music-box, xxiv.31; made for loyalty ——to apply its affections to others, 154.34; may both command and be commanded by circumstances, 164.22; must love God, 15.21; m. of child taught to despise trifles, 51.29; m. of dumb is crippled, 61.18; m. of God, 4.7; m. of God revealed in Bible, xxv.23; m. of man isn't yet aware of true position in creation, 204.31; m. of man paints N. with its thought, xxiv.11; m. of lover, 153.13; m. of mourner, 142.6; m. of the race accumulates knowledge, 194.10; m. of universe evidenced by beauty of world, 43.35; m. taught to reverence its own faculties, 84.30; m. which satisfies idea of human nature, 181.9; m. with no low ends, 185.32; m. with sufficient power of reason, 185.29; a duplicate type of each man is found only in Divine M., 108.13;

act with full consent of your own m.,
166.30; an original m. is not an eccentric
m., 110.30; calling should be sacred to
the m., 167.34; common food of m., 162.2;
complexion of man's m. accounts for his
power, 108.8; cultivating the m., 218.16;
265.8; development of truth in m. is not
periodical, 71.1; disposition of human m.
to magnify its own system, 86.2; distortions of m. corrected by Christianity,
xxvi.18; Divine M. like an ocean, 100.23;
each desire of m. is prayer to God, 4.19;
each m. designed for a peculiar good,
167.34; ear of the m., 34.3; elevation of
m. in all churches, 133.17; E's own m.
demands highest cultivation possible,
29.20; empire of m. deserves more stress
than empire of circumstances, 164.34;
every m. falls into that worship which
is best for him, 230.27; every mind has
its assigned province of action, 167.15;
every m. has its favorite resorts in the
domain of truth, 72.4; every m. has its
own beauty and character, 108.1; every
m. has *one* word to say, xxxx.6; every m.
loves either good or evil, 151.12; every
m. sees its own image reflected in mirror
of the world, 101.33; felicity of a good
m., 92.14; few men watch their own m.,
xxiv.27; finest sense of justice the m.
can frame, 155.30; follow leading of one's
own m., 184.29; God fixed as eternal
inhabitant in m., 73.15; God is Infinite
Mind——awful Being, 176.27; good m.
suffers havoc by dealing in public questions, 229.10; having one's audience in
m., xviii.18; healthy action of m. gives
tho't of God, xxiv.30; hoodwinking m. by
blind reception of dogmas, xxvi.34; human m. analyzed into elements, 90.20;
human m. has range of action, 47.19;
human m. is capable of acting on sublime
principles, 105.6; human m. must always
be the interpreter of scripture, 85.31; in
the m. one finds God's will, 168.10; influence of the heavens on the m., 171.33;
Jewish m. not ready for all the truth,
193.30; Judgment Seat in the m., 225.14;
justice same in m. of God and man,
xxiii.32; laws of the m. interpret scripture, 85.33; laws of the m. must approve
a miracle, 123.25; leading of one's own
m., 186.13; maker of the m. requires the
first fruits of man's admiration for himself, 155.4; man may apply his spirit to
the Divine, 100.23; men born for universe narrowed their m., 86.10; method
of cultivating m., xix.8; N's greatness
reconciled to greatness of m., 176.25;
neglect of part of mind leads to defect
in character, 106.21; one m. never meant
to resemble anr., 108.2; powers of m.
multiplied by social affections, 19.18;
prayer is a state of m., 216.11; prayer
is fruit of frame of m., 25.1; privilege
of active and virtuous m., xxiv.20; relig.
is the home of the m., 28.1; relig. frame
of m. characterized, 201.15; 228.26; relig.

m. hath fire on its own altar, 228.29;
relig. m. is in right road to truth, 232.15;
sense of moral responsibility in the m.,
75.21; society exhibits no striking variety of m., 107.5; speaking to a m. in
unusual way would be a miracle, 120.19;
states of m. valued only as revealed in
deeds, 85.28; structure of m. aids apprehension of God, xxiv.29; subjecting oneself to the law of his m., 100.17; supreme,
calm, immortal m. within my passionate
mortal self, 200.11; tardy expansion of
worldly m., 197.11; the public m. and
the new faith, 201.2; trust in the unseen,
infinite M., 161.25; truth always new
from the m. that perceives it, 93.19;
uncontrollable faculties of m., 70.33; universal reason in the m., 186.30; ways of
affecting the public m., 77.10

MINDS alter each other thru conversation, 62.10; are quickened by communication, 62.8; m. of men are ideas present
to mind of God, 4.5; diff. m. require diff.
culture to bring them into action, 70.23;
each class of m. makes its own creed,
230.26; energies of greatest m., 220.7;
feeble and slothful m. often appealed to
in revivals, 232.8; highest m. marked by
simplicity, 51.22; highest m. of this generation in Christian fold, 55.24; let the
m. yield such ores as are in it, 107.20;
our m. made after one model, 64.22

MINERALS, 208.3

MINIATURE: a Christian is m. of all
Christianity, 201.31

MINISTER as preacher and pastor,
70.6; degrades office by being a spy on
the families of his flock, 219.32; must be
instant in season and out of season,
69.31; must not talk inconsiderately,
70.16; must serve at altar, 69.32; m. who
aims to instruct must stay at home
searching for truth, 71.2; against one's
being a m., xxxiii.33; Christian m. and
his duties, 24.28; 70.1; God's m. in the
soul is conscience, 231.21

MINISTERS of relig., how diff., 165.31

MINISTRATIONS: public m. are duty
of minister, 24.28

MINISTRY, a year's retrospect, 67.1;
266.26; Christian m., 264.36-37; variety
of functions of, 165.32

MINORITY of Christians, 57.34

MINUTE: each m. filled with miracles,
xxix.12

MINUTES, take care of the, 217.30

MIRACLE and truth confirm each
other, 123.25; arouses men to inquire
after ultimate causes, 121.25; as an evidence of moral truth, 122.33; could not
prove a falsehood, 123.14; doesn't depart
from God's character, 122.30; m. for
moral purpose conforms to what we know
of a moral God, 123.8; m. from God must
have moral purpose, 123.12; m. in the
communication of our tho'ts, 122.15; m.
is acceptable insofar as it confirms a
true doctrine, 125.2; m. is God speaking
in an unusual way, 120.20; m. is lower

species of evidence, 124.19; is not incredible, 120.14; is only a thing of blind wonder, 96.1; is only means by which God communicates to men that which shall be known to be from God, 120.15; might be ascribed to evil spirit, 123.21; must accompany revelation of truth, 123.23; not favorite evidence of wise Christians, 124.21; not needed to strengthen the N.T. teachings, 124.28; not to make men stare, 240.13; m. of memory or recollection, 122.16; m. of our being, 203.1; 270.45; m. of process of growing seed, 42.15; m. speaks to unbelief and ignorance, 124.20; m. is special act of God's power for a moral purpose, xxviii.18; suggests no more than a reasoning man knows already, 122.3; supposes no more power than we see every day, 121.34; m. that surrounds man, 204.33; m. to an unbeliever, 122.3; a great m.: the fact that we live day by day, 122.10; all our life is a m., xxix.10; 122.18; in some circumstances it is reasonable to expect a m., 120.11; in the universal m., particular ms. disappear, xxviii.13; one m. will make a multitude credible, 125.33; only a single m. asked for in evidence of power of early Christians, 126.2; was it a mean to a necessary end; 126.7; when a m. no longer answers the use of a m., 124.13; when one m. is shown to be credible, it is enough for faith, 120.8; why E. can believe a m., 122.25

MIRACLES, xxvii.30ff.; 120.1ff.; 268.8; and Revelation, 124.18; are outweighed by internal evidence, 124.23; did not make Jesus our savior, 96.25; do not move men as much as moral truth, 95.30; have only temporary effect, 95.34; m. of faith are peace and joy in suffering, 160.22; m. of Jesus checked or changed course of N., 56.19; m. of Jesus harmonious with his character, 94.30; m. of Jesus not more original than his life, 56.24; m. of N.T., 124.14; should be weighed cautiously, 123.31; sick healed, sea calmed, dead raised, 56.20; Anthony Collins rejected Christian m., 156.17; distant m. not needed for man to know God's will, 189.4; each minute filled with m., xxix.12; Jesus armed with m., 244.43; no man can do these m. that thou doest, 120.3; particular m. believed in, xxviii.17; peculiarity of Christian m. is in their favor, 125.8; seeking God in extreme m., 162.14; why not of frequent occurrence. 124.2

MIRACULOUS seen in the common, 122.7

MIRIAM, 147.12

MIRROR in your mind, 115.16; world is a m. of the mind, 101.33

MISCHIEF of controversy set forth, 87.35; nothing can do us m. but ourselves, 209.32

MISERY of the slave, 5.24

MISFITS in vocations will tend to disappear, 251.36

MISFORTUNE teaches, 192.32

MISMANAGEMENT suspected of the needy, 131.15

MISTAKE, 211.6; ancient m. of pursuing seeming for solid good, 35.28

MISTAKES made in vocational choices, 167.27; m. to be corrected, 103.6; you must overlook m., 37.21

MITE: one m. added to the sum of happiness, 30.24

MOB pleased when you adopt only one side, 86.26; see *man, men, people.*

MODEL imitating, 6.22; our minds made after one m., 64.22

MODES: new m. of illustration, xxii.2

MODESTY is commendable, 110.8

MOMENT: every m. fatal; kills some part of life, 112.7; every m. is reaping consequences of action, 103.30; greatest tho'ts do not flash on soul in a m., 70.21; retribution in every m. of life, 102.24; soul not to be neglected for a m., 102.26; tho'ts and passions not born in a m., 3.2; thousands intombed in a m., 112.17; vegetation reveals God's goodness from m. to m., 39.24

MOMENTS: elevated m. animated by faith, 162.7

MONEY, the aim of trade, 189.20; twice the m. for a transparent house, 186.4

MONITION: life itself would be m. enough, 35.21

MONITOR, conscience is, 11.29; N. is m. of race of men, 44.11; undeceiving inward m. is the soul, 202.6

MONITORS: relig. m. not needed if there were no death, 35.20

MONSTERS, 122.10

MONTAIGNE, Michel Eyquem de, 249.3

MOON has deviated from her orbit, 176.1; has rare atmosphere, 173.11; is turned to blood, 8.28

MORAL faculty or "heart," xxiv.25; m. laws in this world and next, 10.29; m. of E's views, 211.18; m. preached by fruit is as fresh to us as to Adam, 44.25; m. sense of the people is obtuse, 229.33; becoming a mightier m. agent, 17.8; Bible not above m. sense, xxv.21; m. sense of "heart," xxiv.25; men always draw m. from that they see around them, 69.4; N. speaks to man as a m. being, 44.35

MORALIST: an old m. quoted, 127.24

MORALITY is real, absolute, independent of all circumstance or change, 178.22

MORALS, imperishable universe of, 3.3

MORE wise, true, just, temperate, kind, happy every day, 85.7

MORN: anr. m. risen on midnoon, 178.13

MORNING and evening, 208.17; m. of the world (creation), 113.28; first m. and the first man, 194.8

MORTALITY, apprehensions of, 113.13; common causes of, 112.24

MOSES, 107.3; men see God only in M., xxxv.26

MOSS, 207.25

MOTE in anr's eye, 76.23

MOTION of hand, 1.15; insensible m. of hand of watch, 79.17

MOTIONS of the hand, 216.19

MOTIVE of other men's acts are hid from us, 1.5; m. of self-interest, 129.18; m. of self-love not Christian, 130.19; ever-present m. and rule, 162.3; every m. discarded but the highest, 242.42; true m. of social duty, 129.35

MOTIVES for joining church, 59.7; m. governing vulgar people, 184.30; m. no longer sought in world but within, 100.6; m. suggested to our secret souls by departed friends, 235.10; m. that quicken faith, 34.35; m. which minister adopts to aid men, 30.18; m. worthy of our nature, 99.13; acting by one's highest m., 185.4; external m., 185.31; no right to assign wrong m., 1.9; wretched m. of children, 52.26

MOULDING sermons, xi.17

MOUNT GERIZIM, 177.14

MOUNT of our hope, 35.10

MOUNTAINS, 209.2; men marching beyond m., xxx.35

MOURNER, xviii.30; 138.1; feels that the dead are present, 142.7; wants truth, not prating, 226.22; consolation for m., 268.15

MOURNERS are comforted, 161.9

MOUTH puckered at every impertinent trifle, 204.13; story told from m. to m., 152.4

MOVE: we shall m. "impelled by strict necessity along the path of order and of good," 116.29

MOVEMENT of the sphere which he inhabits, 205.10

MULTIPLICATION of grain into ear regularly expected, 42.6

MULTITUDE of particulars hide man's inanity, 206.10; m. of people of standing, 157.5; m. understand you best when you adopt only one opinion or side, 86.26; devout man at church would not see the m., 221.31; mighty m. seeks things of sense, 2.16; solitude in midst of m., 159.5; starving m. relieved, 129.10

MULTITUDES: a dogma accepted by m. is based on moral nature of man, 230.40

MURDERER reads accusation in every face, xxiv.12

MURMURING against the rich, 129.31; m. is impertinent to Christian, 139.14

MUSCLES, stretch the spiritual, xxi.29

MUSIC hard to analyze, 145.8; m. has had a long history, 145.21; unites pleasures of sense with those of soul, 146.12; intellectual and material m., 145.8; man alone has m. of speech, 145.6

MUSIC-BOX like healthy mind, xxiv.31

MUTATION, 258.26

MYRRH, Arabian, 18.5

MYSTERY of our greatness and littleness, 136.31; conscious of the m., 205.4; Jesus added no m. to Lord's Supper, 57.16; man cannot solve vast m. that envelopes us, 206.4

MYSTICAL existence of the soul absorbed into God, 244.44

N

NAAMAN the leper, 250.27

NAME of a prosperous man shakes our judgment, 182.6; n. of Christ is motive and sermon against indolence, 69.31; n. of God venerated by lips, 3.21; n. of God written on the home and honored in family, 19.24; n. of Jesus, 156.13; n. of Jesus at end of prayers, 5.1; n. of priest opprobrious, 26.35; n. of Unitarians objected to, 86.34; let heart beat to Maker's n., 52.31; swearing by God's n., 3.23

NAMES and faces, 181.31; people are mere n., 181.25; use of n. objected to by good men, 86.33

NAPOLEON, Russian campaign cited, 154.18; see *Buonaparte.*

NARROWNESS and error, xiii.17

NATION: history of one man as valuable as that of a n., 209.7

NATIONS, 168.1; few of us will counsel n., 13.22; wars and victories of n., 180.16

NATIVITY, 264.6

NATURAL: man thinks it n. to be here etc., 205.22

NATURE (MISCELLANEOUS MEANINGS): n. of God explored, xxii.35; n. of God sought, 2.18; n. of God such as to be knowable, xxvii.12; n. of man to approve good action in himself or anr., 82.25; n. of man yields to authority of moral truth, 94.34; n. of moral laws can be learned only by *acting,* 209.28; n. of Revelation, 124.18; n. of the soul is basis for immortality, 244.28; a characteristic of our rational n., 83.31; animal n. ennobled by serving the soul, 210.27; depth of human n., 200.17; development of inward n., 184.5; exploring n. of God is E's object in life, 72.13; faith satisfactory to one's proper n., 199.16; grander n. of man is his soul, 113.21; great law of moral n., 115.19; height of a divine n., 101.8; highest good of intelligent n., 27.33; human n. moved more by moral truth than by miracles, 95.31; human n. of great worth, 106.7; image of God in human n., 110.10; in spiritual n. things take hue of our tho't, 101.30; instincts of man's n., 161.34; Jesus was apostle of moral n., 196.15; learn to adore your n., 134.1; man has infinite n., 105.8; man wants backing of superior n., 154.32; man's moral n., 195.6; 233.33; man's n. has no defect or inferiority, 106.15; man's progressive n., 151.24; men do not reverence their own n., 182.25; men have a common n. and can know others by knowing themselves, 243.10; men hold n. mutually, 134.19; metaphysical n. of happiness, 7.18; moral n. of man is foundation for popular dogmas, 230.41; motives worthy of our n., 99.14; partakers of the divine n., 133.5; principles of man's n., 10.25; progressive n. of man, 54.4; properties of moral n., 209.21; pursue bent of moral n., 10.35; puts off human n. and puts on divine, 100.18; relig. parties founded on principles inherent in our n., 82.14; secrets of my own n. revealed to me, 96.3; spiritual n. exalted above sensual, 195.30; spiritual n. is independent of space and time, 117.20; supreme truth of man's moral n., 91.28; terror in a man's n., 225.12; thinking well of human n., 270.20; thunder call of a Superior N., 162.20; unknown n. in every man, 211.19; wants of our n. an unsatisfactory basis of benevolence, 130.21

NATURE (THE COSMOS, PHENOMENAL WORLD): adapted to give pleasure to us, 44.3; adds beauty to utility, 44.30; admonishes man of shortness of life, 44.31; N. and laws of God as seen in scripture, 84.14; N. as significant to us as to Adam, 44.25; consistent and uniform, 2.4; does its appointed work, 44.35; excites our minds to God's benevolence, 44.28; exhibition of God's benevolence, 43.1; fragrant with odors and glowing with colors, 42.27; glorious show, 43.30; has commission to help the purposes of man, 6.12; indicates an intelligence, 122.22; indicates presence of God, 40.2; inferior to man, 45.15; is a bk., 40.15; is a great school of God, 193.7; is God's order, 33.34; is obedient to fervent prayers of man, 8.6; made the riches and shows of men, 171.31; makes Botany seem petty, 41.35; more remarkable than metamorphosis in poetry or legend, 42.10; nourishes animal life, 43.17; offers a foundation for the doctrine of election, 230.42; passes in review before man's eye, 209.19; perpetual miracle, 42.15; produces our food, 44.29; quiets our petty tempers, 42.26; reproaches man's lassitude, 45.1; reveals God's goodness, 39.25; reveals power and benevolence of God, 41.13; seems angry to guilty man, xxiv.11; seems to be prophet and monitor of race of man, 44.11; seen only in parcels, 40.27; speaks to man as a moral being, 44.35; tends to draw man's contemplation from God; hence need for miracles, 121.5; to a simple heart N. is the real occasion of devout feeling, 171.22; valued only as commodity, 40.28; valued only for man's petty interests, 40.28; warns by the seasons of man's short life, 44.31——all N. fights against vice, 94.2; an everlasting Now reigns in N., 222.15; any period of N. points to Great Creator, 42.16; argument from N. is

strong, 245.17; author of N., 170.21; book of N., 42.24; 178.26; bk. of N. interesting, 171.5; brute fidelity of N., 45.1; cause of N., 175.19; changes have a lesson for the pious, 40.13; connections betw. N. and friendship are sacred, 144.12; creed of simple N., 259.22; disorders of N. contribute to good, 259.11; everything in N. is emblem, a hieroglyphic of something in us, 44.17; external N. mean as compared with inner world, 196.19; genuine man relies on laws of N., 186.23; God of N. and of Bible is same, 170.16; God seen in N., 40.3; God will seldom interrupt N., 123.33; greatness reconciled to mind, 176.25; heavens exceed everything else in N. for grandeur and influence on mind, 171.32; infinite panorama of N., 2.3; Jesus checked or changed usual course of N., 56.20; layrinths of N., 94.11; language of N's everlasting analogies, 44.10; laws of N. are so uniform that multitude accept the law and forget the Cause, 121.13; laws of N. are permanent, xxviii.27; lesson of N. is omnipresence of God, 40.24; life in conformity to N., 122.35; light of N., 170.22; love of N. reunited with relig., 171.19; material N. has nothing so splendid as law of compensations, 209.24; more in N. than beauty, 44.7; mouldering of N., 113.15; mysteries of N. unlocked by benevolence and piety, 94.11; no greater power required to suspend than to originate N., 122.24; no lawless particle in N., 159.19; objects of N. keep us from fanaticism, 171.25; observation of N's secrets does not diminish our admiration for her laws, 161.16; order of N. did not come of itself, 40.1; pain results from ignorance or abuse of N., 85.3; permanence of N., 40.8; permanence of laws of N., 124.4; preacher must study N., 29.25; presence in N. of agencies counterchecking universal laws, 126.10; productiveness how explained? 42.7; punctuality of N., 45.9; seasons of N. are like angels, 40.33; secret of N. never discovered by scientists, 41.32; shows of N., 204.12; sight of true God in N., 171.26; student of N., 175.15; the Intelligence presiding over ordinary N., 122.32; there is a world of N. and anr. of Spirit, 113.30; thru N. God leads men to higher truth, 177.5; to what end is its magnificence? 43.30; unseen God has spoken in N., 52.19; vast economy of N. keeps law of matter, 116.25. See *human nature, man.*

NATURES, church is made up of spiritual, xxvi.11; lowest n. share relatedness to all, 207.25; moral n. surround us, 3.7

NAZARITE, Jesus the, 56.29

NECESSARIES of life, 46.10

NECESSITIES: out of man's n. grows civilization, 210.29

NECESSITY is God—an intelligent Cause, 175.13; eternal n. adopted by Fr. astronomers, 175.12; impelled by strict n., 116.29

NEED of loud alarms, bibles, tracts, etc., 35.30

NEEDS: see *wants.*

NEGATIONS: pale n. of Unitarians, 232.45

NEGATIVE, advantages of gov't always, 77.24

NEGLECT to cultivate part of mind leads to defect in character, 106.21; weep at n. of relig. faith, 73.11

NEGLIGENCE of a devout custom will grow into habit, 72.35

NEIGHBOR is a part of God's universe, 131.33; is also a temple of the Divine Presence, 136.29; is God's child, 131.30; Christian is amenable to his n. for his words and acts, 116.18; coveting our n's possessions, 13.11; duty to n. dictated by a well-calculated self-love, 129.8; ends must not be sought at n's expense, 95.12; love of n. as it operates within families etc., 131.18; love of n. capricious, discriminating and selfish, 130.25; love of n. will not serve as principle of whole system, 131.22; love thy n. as thyself, 53.11; 71.27; 88.5; 115.20; 127.2; 269.15; maintain respect for n., 89.4; motives for n's actions, 1.8; my relation to n., 199.25; obligations to serve n. not based on wants of our nature, 130.22; parties tend to make us dislike our n., 88.7; principle behind our duty to n., 128.10; principle of love to be used toward n., 88.21; self-reliance not inconsistent with duty to our n., 109.23; serving n. does benefit oneself, 128.23; sincere service of n. never prompted by self-interest, 128.21; soul is revealed in speech, 61.3; truth to me is truth to n., 64.24; we lose when we withhold from n., 130.3; welfare of n. promoted, 198.19; why help one's n? 134.26; see *others, fellow men.*

NEIGHBORS know a man's competence, 19.2; capacities that are n. to objects, 5.19

NERO, 23.2

NEST of a hundred boxes, 206.11

NEW heavens and a n. earth, 35.7; 119.5; 178.13; 189.32; n. not to be rejected, xxii.5; n. man created after God in righteousness, 183.22; n. truth, 190.17; truth always n. from the mind that perceives it, 93.19

NEW AGE, xiii.18

NEW ENGLAND, 149.17; hard soil of, 43.21; industries of, xxx.34

NEW TESTAMENT, 115.10; 138.25; 144.16; 177.21; 218.44; N.T. and astronomy, 177.8; N.T. taken as almanack, 115.4; N.T. truths will stand by themselves, 125.3; explanations of N.T. vary, 219.3; if N.T. had perished, 124.25; improbable in N.T., 125.28; miracles of N.T., 120.6

NEW WORLD and Columbus, 49.23

NEWCOMERS: we are n. into space, 172.6

NEWSPAPER is scourge to U.S., 79.15

NEWSPAPERS, worst, 79.20; would not be ptd. if neglected, 79.21

NEWTON, Sir Isaac, 110.14; 117.16; 152.25; 173.34; 208.28; 249.2; N. and astronomers, 52.11; became a Unitarian, 175.2; never did anything odd, 51.23; not distinguished by any singularity, 51.24

NICODEMUS comes to Jesus by night, 120.2

NIGHT, Nicodemus comes by, 120.2; the great n. of space, 172.28

NO man liveth to himself alone etc., 135.17

NOISE and pomp double a man's greatness, 181.33

NON-CONFORMITY, 266.14

NONE can teach faster than scholar can learn, xxxx.1; n. can teach more than he knows, xxxix.35

NOOK of earth, 117.35

NOSTRILS, breath in the, 162.30

NOTHING can do a man mischief but himself, 209.31; n. in world ends in itself, 80.31; n. permanent but tho't, 2.7; n. too small to be insupportable if given enough attention, 50.14

NOTHINGS: some men are n. when great occasions come, 49.15

NOTION: arriving at n. of a genuine man, 183.19

NOTIONS: truer n. than our ancestors held, 56.5

NOVELTY in pulpit, 28.11; man is a n. upon earth, 172.7

NOW: an everlasting N. reigns in Nature, 222.15

NUMA, a reformer, 52.22

NUMBER of steps taken for perishable objects, 2.12; increase in n. of men improves chance of finding talents, 46.5

NUMBERS: doctrine received by n. of men, 230.38

O

OAK, acorn will grow into, 55.5

OATH of God, 188.18

OBEDIENCE, 228.13; to virtue is way of good life, 94.1; to dictates of reason, 185.2; a present o. to the commandments, 103.34; Jesus is a pattern of o., 233.23; our languid o., 14.27; see *humility.*

OBEY the commandments, 269.18

OBJECT obtained at cost to conscience, 11.29; o. for lack of which men waste themselves, 161.30; o. of a lover's affection, 153.20; o. of E's life is to explore nature of God, 72.12; o. of Jesus' life was a great reformation, 56.35; o. of life to explore nature of God, xxii.35; o. of regard is a fellow creature, 155.9; o. of sentiment of love is infinite goodness, 154.1; o. of the affections requires personal emphasis, 234.15; o. of world's education is to touch the springs of wonder in soul, 207.6; everlasting o. of soul is duty, 143.23; faith becomes o. of exclusive attachment, 159.34; God is the grand o. of all thought, 92.9; infinite o. is prophesied, 161.33; man's felicity is God's o., 85.13; men's sentiments grope after some great o., 161.28; new properties in every particular o., 193.17; soul wants an o. as great as its love, 155.16; soul's o. of devotion, 158.3

OBJECTION of good men to the use of names, 86.32; o. to honor as a rule of life, 156.33; o. to name of Unitarian denomination, 86.33; o. urged against view of God's wrath, xx.21

OBJECTS of education, 269.12; o. of honor not equal to capacity of soul, 157.29; o. of legitimate desire, 227.5; o. of matter, 178.11; o. of science change and disintegrate, 112.7; o. of sentiments are finite and unworthy, 158.4; o. of every day preferred to imperishable things, 2.11; o. sufficient for our powers of action, 99.14; o. within reach of our capacities, 5.19; affection disproportionate to o., 153.2; all o. concentrate influence on man, 207.19; all o. in nat'l world are growing old, 112.4; nat'l o. are emblems, 44.13; stars were first o. of idolatry, 172.11

OBLIGATION to serve our fellow men, 130.21; to use doctrine of retribution, 11.17; force of moral o., 30.13

OBLIGATIONS of man, 211.17; o. or ties of family etc., 168.11; see *duties*.

OBSCURITY contributes to happiest man, 160.8; o. of tho'ts clarified in conversation, 62.20

OBSERVANCE of the Sabbath, 263.26; perpetual o. not intended in Lord's Supper, 223.40

OBSERVATION of N's secrets, 161.16; heedless o. compared with systematic research, 227.11; result of one's own o., 93.18; unsleeping o. of Divinity, 4.18

OBSERVER of actions is God, 4.8

OBSERVERS needed to excite virtue, 16.15

OCCASION for praise, 269.25; o. to which E's education has pointed, xiv.29; great o. not needed for exertion of virtue, 15.8; stimulus of great o., 16.15

OCCASIONALISM, theory of, 240.17

OCCASIONS for exhibition of moral principle, 13.10; o. of usefulness sent by God, 16.26; o. to exercise intellect and virtue, 52.3; great o. excite soul, 49.15; humble o. best for virtue, 16.20; solemn o. of human life, 31.13

OCCUPATION: a mean o. not shameful, 52.28

OCCUPATIONS, virtue sees no distinction in, 15.11

OCCURRENCES: daily o. instruct man, 194.20; petty o. make up life, 13.21

OCEAN, man is drop in the spiritual, 100.24; phial of water broken in the o., 245.15

OCEANS, sundered by, 61.32

ODD, Newton did nothing, 51.23

ODDITY of man's demeanor, 205.8

ODES: relig. o. are earliest literature, 145.24

ODIO humani generis, 217.39

OFFENCES, 11.35; of the people considered, 229.19; bad minister seeks to avoid o. in preaching, 25.29

OFFEND: let us not o. conscience, 65.6

OFFER: voluntary o. of ourselves to God, 102.35

OFFICE of Jesus not basis of his authority, 96.18; o. of minister degraded by spying on families, 219.32; o. of pulpit to warn men of universality of law of duty, 76.6; o. of Reason is two-fold, 207.13; o. of the conscience, 232.18; proper o. of each human faculty, 2.20

OFFICERS of the law, 163.23

OFFICES: mean o. can become respectable, 60.12

OFFSPRING: we are the o. of God, 170.6

OLD in truth, love and God, 116.28; all are growing o., 112.4; problems of o., 37.35; spiritually o. only when Christian law flows unobstructed, 116.16

OMNIPOTENCE is enlisted on the side of virtue, 87.27; o. of God backs up good purpose, 21.4; o. of God makes elements obedient to man, 8.5; o. of God powerless over the Past, 8.11; o. of truth in Jesus' word, 197.25; good man leans on and borrows o., 160.27

OMNIPRESENCE OF GOD, xxiii.19; becomes dominant, xxiii.26; explained, 221.22; is N's lesson, 40.24

OMNIPRESENT is sufficient company for the devout man, 221.32

ONE against anr.: all things double, 102.17; o. man taken for the crowd, 208.13; o. pursuit or o. sort of usefulness for every man, 165.20; o. with Jesus and with the Father, 98.9; God is not such an o. as you, 3.31; when man is at o. with all things, 207.11; soul is made o. with God, 133.30; virtues confined to o., 130.8; we are manifestations of the Universal O., 133.15

OPAQUE: earth is a small o. planet, 174.16

OPERATION of nat'l laws certain, xxviii.30; God's great o. for all, 259.13

OPHIR, 217.32

OPINION of all action, how based, 14.7; o. of men re. power of stars, 172.14; o. of the majority, 157.4; o. that St. Paul is mistaken, xxv.27; common o. to yield to one's own heart, 168.7; consequences of adopting one o. in a jealous warfare, 86.25; defend o. by joining weaker party, 88.30; exaggerated regard for others' o., 47.14; man consults own o. in solitude, 47.2; no compact of o. among liberal Christians, 232.39; no ties of o. among liberal Christians, 232.36; progress of religious o., 264.9; received o. that universality is a criterion of truth, 230.37; relig. o. changes as does science, 174.20; same division of o. exists in relig. and secular groups, 82.15; solitary o., 184.2; the heavens affect all o., 171.28; uniformity of o. about Lord's Supper, impossible, 57.19; v i o l e n t changes of o. seldom occur in men, xxxviii.10

OPINIONS of men on relig. questions, 192.20; o. of others regarded in cities, 47.11; o. on the atonement, 84.5; o. supported by inadequate view of scriptures, 84.26; anr. age will reverse wrong o., 168.8; borrow something of eternal truth from both o., 87.17; conflicting o. based in great truth, 86.22; change in relig. o., 256.11; discoverers of spiritual truths have listened to their own o., 111.1; in following o. of others we are misled and depraved, 110.34; reciprocal action of o. on the will and vice versa, 94.20

OPPORTUNITIES in a settled order of social life, 60.6; will be found by the seeker, 85.9

OPPORTUNITY for greatness is not of place or events, 60.8; o. unseized by preacher, 26.5; o. which God gives to us in this life, 117.9

OPTIMISM, 136.12; 180.12; o. regarding the future, 85.12; philosophy of o., 85.3

ORACLE within, 267.20; heart is the o. within, xxiv.25

ORACLES of God, 28.6; read and unfold o. of God, 32.22

ORATION, symmetry of, xviii.19

ORB, no ungoverned, 176.13

ORBIT of light, 8.2; o. of the moon, 176.1

ORDER, 176.22; o. of human life, 259.4; o. of N., 40.1; o. of things, 9.4; beautiful o. of the world, 45.24; departure from common o. of N. needed to startle man, 121.17; God's moral o. requires men to choose and to be wise for themselves, 118.6; great o. develops from our actions, 163.14; love of o. is petulance, 210.29; nat'l o., unless interrupted, tends to withdraw human mind from God, 121.5; path of o. and of good, 116.30; universal o., 203.20; we never doubt permanence of nat'l o., 40.8; why o.? 204.24

ORDINANCE of Jesus loose and elastic, 57.16; of Lord's Supper, 51.1ff.

ORDINATION, anniversary of E's, 67.5; E's o. mentioned, 24.15

ORES of the mind, 107.21

ORGAN, we become God's, 132.31

ORGANIZATION of beings on other planets diff. from man's, 173.9; why o.? 204.23

ORGANS thru which facts speak for themselves, 109.12

ORIENT, 256.17

ORIGIN is one thing; validity an-

other, 244.8; o. of self must be perceived, 238.2

ORIGINAL SIN condemned, 106.14

ORIGINALITY is not eccentricity, 110.30

ORPIMENT, John, xviii.21

ORTHODOX and Unitarian Christians distinguished, 233.2; o. avoided as a word, 230.32; o. Christian builds system on fear of sin, 231.25; o. vs. liberal, 82.1

OTHERS and self, 268.10; o. put before one's own integrity, 48.14; claims seem irksome, 144.3; complexity of our relations with o., 128.3; death of one who has served o., 127.12; good of o. often promoted against a man's will, 130.13; grieved man neglects o., 140.14; Jesus would not listen to o., 237.37; power to act with and for o., 130.10; pride is civil to o., 129.9; rights of o., 264.30; self and o., 127.1; self is sought in o., 134.9; soul of man to act for o., 130.5; we respect o. more than ourselves, 16.17; see neighbor.

OUGHT, 111.26; I o. and I o. not, 95.9; o. of moral truth, 93.25; 94.35; see categorical imperative.

OUTRAGE against Indian, 229.31

OVER-SOUL, xxiv.33; 237.42

OWN: man has nothing of his o., nothing he has not rec'd, 135.10; only liberty you may call your o., 4.15; only our sins are our o., 135.15; we are not our o., 135.20; 268.43

OX knoweth his owner, 207.4

P

PAGAN cried Blood! 22.20; feasts of p. worship, 55.32

PAGANISM has high ethical standards, xxvii.5; Christianity vs. p., 55.13

PAGE of cheerful wisdom is Fr. Revolution, 194.26; unwritten p. of today and tomorrow, 18.8

PAIN, 208.34; p. and death our ghastly enemies, 258.24; p. besets men, 138.21; p. forgotten when Reason is exercised, 210.23; p. is all of use to man, 85.16; p. is merely result of some ignorance or abuse of N., 85.2; p. presents no problem in our world, 85.2; a sufficient reason is given for existence of all p., 85.16; capacity for p. revives in spirit world, 9.30; God will justify p. in the end, 159.31; unnecessary p., 139.12; world does not aim at giving us p., 85.2

PAINS are teachers, 258.30; converted into angels and helpers, 160.6

PAINTS: guilty man p. angry clouds, xxiv.11

PALACE art requires less skill than strawberry's, 41.25

PALACES, 180.18

PALEY, William, 249.5; quoted with pleasure, 220.38

PALL, consecrated, xxxv.6

PALSY shall wither the arm of art, xxx.32

PANORAMA: infinite p. of N., 2.3

PARABOLICAL eliminated from sermons, xxii.16; p. in relig. abolished, 201.10

PARADE, outward, 182.21

PARADOXES, startle with sounding, xix.17

PARCELS, man sees world only in, 40.27

PARENT, God conceived as a, 83.19

PARENTS and children, 48.18; should be glad to have child baptized, 32.2; deportment of p., 51.30

PARIS, 203.7

PARKMAN can pray; his prayers are long, xxxiv.3

PARLANCE of the time, 108.30

PARLOR and pulpit not diff., 220.11; in his p. every man has power, 18.22

PART in life chosen, 22.9; p. of mind neglected leads to imperfection of character, 106.21; best p. of life unseen, 264.38; best p. of man revolts against being a minister, xxxiii.32; best p. of me not touched, xxi.29; every p. of our frame, 203.15; every p. of the house visible, 186.5; human life p. of Eternity, 136.7; main p. of life made up of small incidents and petty occurrences, 13.20; man is least p. of himself, 182.18; man should do his p. in commerce, 206.20; Mary has chosen the good p., 51.16; one's neighbor is a p. of God's universe, 131.34; whole preferred to p., 201.34

PARTAKERS: men are p. of the divine nature, 133.5

PARTICIPATION in attributes of God is possible to man, 100.19

PARTICLE: no lawless p. in N., 159.20; no lawless p. in universe, 176.14; no p. more of real power comes thru ownership of property, 206.4

PARTICULARS occupy men too much, 163.8; insignificant p. of a hero are interesting, 14.3; multitudes of p., 206.10

PARTIES tend to make us dislike neighbor, 88.6; both relig. p. approve good actions and disapprove bad, 83.5; both relig. p. founded on principles inherent in our nature, 82.13; conflict of p. is a chapter in man's history, 86.16; ethics of political p., 76.16; foundations of both p. must be included in Christian character, 86.24; middle ground betw. p. is best, 87.16; political p. use slander, 78.19; rigid and liberal p., 82.9; rigid and liberal p. exist on questions of ethics, metaphysics, education, free trade and gov't, 82.18; two great p. in the relig. community, 82.7; two p. prominent in Christian world, 82.22; value independence of p. even in the midst of p., 88.35

PARTISAN: if necessary be a p. but without evils of party spirit, 88.27

PARTS and the whole, 10.14; best p. of my being, xxi.26; E. sees only p. of the whole, 28.26; honor has jurisdiction over all p. of life, 156.5; integral p. of universe of morals, 3.3; we shall be p. of God, 132.24

PARTY consideration keeps men from progress, 87.9; p. is an incognito to save a man the vexation of thinking, 233.4; all p. is exclusive, 86.21; each p. labors in its own cause with all its means, 86.4; effect of p. spirit is exclusiveness, 86.21; ferocity of p. spirit, 229.33; how each p. tries to justify itself, 86.12; join weaker p. in defense of principle, 88.31——LIBERAL PARTY also claims Biblical authority, 85.30; commends virtues of gratitude, resignation, diligence, 83.23; conceives of God under parental relation, 83.19; emphasizes man's capacity for virtue, 83.6; gives views of God a degree of trust and love, 85.21; sees benevolence in universe and great powers and desires in man, 83.16; sees signs of a moral Providence, 83.18; takes opposite approach, 84.27——not wise to belong to any p., 233.14; to p. gave up what was meant for mankind, 86.11; ponder evils of p. spirit, 88.27——RIGID PARTY emphasizes faith without knowledge, 89.6; sees grievous guilt of man and dread of God, 83.11; sets high value on faith, 84.10; takes principle of man's liability to sin, 83.7——spirit of p., 158.9; spirit of p. rebuked, 135.27; truth loved above p., 231.26

PARTY MAN, distaste for being, xxxix.12

PASSAGE from death to life, 114.16

PASSION makes us speak in hyperbole, 153.8; p. of love, 153.4; p. of love is true and noble, 154.3

PASSIONATE love of eloquence, xix.27

PASSIONS, 162.18; are not born in a moment and then blotted out, 3.2; belong to imperishable moral world, 2.35; employ the tongue, 64.14; human p. ascribed to God, 173.5; selfish p. are mean and social p. are noble, 127.7

PASSIVE: when men become p. to their own tho'ts, they become voices of truth, 109.15

PAST beyond the reach of prayer, 8.9; is worth nothing, 8.18; not to be worshiped, xxvii.10; all p. affects you, 207.20; events of p. can be reversed, 8.13; maxims are inheritance of p., 63.2; omnipotence of God powerless over p., 8.11; soul converses with p., 202.3; weep not for p., 7.28; 8.9

PASTOR, 32.25; bad p. described, 33.1; duties of p., 31.8; good p. described, 33.15; his knowledge of his people, 36.11; his office requires experience rather than gifts, 37.20; no man can suddenly be a good p., 37.19

PASTORS, 194.30; made to console at time of death, 35.15

PATH of a covetous man, 5.24; p. of order and of good, 116.30; new p. taken by an occasional individual, 166.16; our job is a p. without an end, 169.22

PATIENCE disarms calamity, 210.4

PIQUE or trivial interest, 229.35

PITY for the dumb, 61.34; for unworthy direction of loyalty, 154.28

PLACE or event unnecessary for greatness, 60.9; p. to be born and a p. to die, 19.21; any p. will shine under light of virtues, 190.3; artificial p. of Jesus in men's opinions, 195.8; eternal truths take their p. in firmament, xxxv.14; faithful in our p., 144.8; test of p. is a criterion of truth, 230.39

PLACES and times disregarded by astronomy, 177.18

PLAGUE controlled in Asia, 112.22

PLAINNESS of Unitarian church, 150.29

PLANET gravitates to p., 176.15; guided by same force that guides the bee, 176.21; our p. is gray and scarred with wrinkles, 172.6

PLANTS quite rightly differ in kind, 107.32

PLATFORM: highest p. of eloquence is the moral sentiment, 218.29; world is a p. for Newton *et al.*, 52.10

PLATONISM: 108.13; 110.12; 110.13; 110.19; 244.22

PLAY is not worth the candle, 193.5

PLEASURE, 208.33; derived from right use of our powers, 84.28; in southwest wind, 39.7; E's p. in seeing his old congregation, xxxvii.13; avoid immoderate p., 111.24; capacity for p. revives in spirit world, 9.30; N. adapted to give p. to us, 44.3; sensual p., 227.3; to will and to do God's good p., 132.22; watch p., 102.33

PLEASURE-SEEKER, 163.22

PLEASURES and pains of body nonexistent in spirit world, 10.5; p. forevermore, 169.23; near at hand, 270.12; p. of appetite, 2.28; p. of others, 190.24; p. of sense to be overcome, 105.9; p. of sense united to those of soul by music, 146.12; p. of the senses in youth, 231.42; greatest of our p. is admiration, 151.21

PLEDGE of God will be redeemed, 11.6

PLEDGES, never give, 242.43

PLENARY inspiration, 232.23

PLURIMA nix, xxxiv.12; 248.5; 251.21

PLUTARCH, 248.45

POET: best p. should have written hymns, 147.19

POETRY, 251.27; has had a long history, 145.21; has no tale of metamorphosis to compare with nat'l process, 42.8; is harder to analyze, 145.10; sacred p. should be good, 146.17

POIGNANCY of grief abated by memories, 20.16

POINT on which all objects and ages shed influence, 207.19; definite p. for our efforts, 20.21; each grain of sand is fixed p. round which all things revolve, 207.22

POLES, men turn on same, 62.8

POLICE and turbulence, 129.15

POLITICAL economy shows inadequacy of selfishness, 128.24

POLITICS in U.S., 76.13; is taboo in church, xxx.29; corruption of, 78.21

POMP and noise, 181.33

POOR described, 9.17ff.; p. in spirit have kingdom of heaven, 161.8; p. justify covetousness, 13.11: p. strive to keep up appearance, 9.21; blessed are p. in spirit, 115.13; difficult to love p. and wretched, 130.34; ground the faces of the p., 9.9; nothing is p., 249.34; imprecation of the p. on the ruthless, 9.17

POPLAR and elm, 39.21

POPULARITY, 183.29; 183.33

POPULATION marching westward, xxx.34; larger p. requires greater division of labor, 46.8

POSITION of man in creation not yet realized, 204.32; every soul occupies a new p., 196.30; the singular p. of every man, 106.28; true p. of man in universe and consequent obligations, 211.16

POSSESS: we p. nothing of our own, 135.10

POSSESSED of virtues in high degree, xviii.23

POSSESSION of truth contingent upon ourselves, 102.4; soul is a p. real and noble, 105.11

POSSESSIONS of our neighbor, 13.11; p. give no ultimate contentment, 114.28ff.; happiness derived from p., 7.19; p. wasted, 8.14

POSSIBILITIES: virtues are dead p. until they live in a soul, 234.18

POST: quitting our p. is inglorious, 143.28

POSTERITY of Adam without hope, 199.20

POSTPONE: do not p. for an hour any serious purpose, 103.26

POTTAGE, men sacrifice themselves for, 255.2

POVERTY, 211.6; p. or wealth is matter of indifference, 184.1; p. shall come as an armed man, 256.20; p. yet strives to bear up, 9.20

POWDER, grind him to, 209.24

POWER and benevolence of God in his works, 41.13; p. and goodness of God revealed in vegetation, 39.25; p. and love of the Highest overshadow us, 192.6; p. coveted; would be put to better use, 18.21; p. exhibited by Jesus, 56.17; made a god, 151.14; multiplies itself in compound ratio thru men of conviction, 198.24; must not be sought at neighbor's expense, 95.10; p. of articulate and rational speech, 60.23; p. of eloquence in only a few people, 66.26; p. of eye seems borrowed from Divine Power, 47.34; p. of eye to range to distant and minute, 47.25; p. of giving interest and respectability to mean offices, 60.11; p. of God in evoking greenness from the dust, 42.22; p. of God least affecting, 159.22; p. of God will right all in the end, 159.31; p. of man increased by goodness, 17.6; p. of man to obtain degree of participation in attributes of

heaven, 8.31; in Jesus' name, 5.1; p. like the will of Supreme Being, 6.32; p. of Finney are short, xxxiv.3; p. of our true desires are granted, 5.10; p. of Parkman are long, xxxiv.4; p. shall become effects, 6.15; all p. are granted, 215.9; good p. spring from good life, not from seeking an effect, 25.10; mockeries of p., 5.6; not p. unless wish of heart, 5.3; true p. are desires of the soul, 5.7; true p. attended by endeavors, 7.2

PREACH not ourselves but Christ Jesus, 31.2

PREACHER must study the works of God, 29.25; p. not the only one in fault; the hearer is also, 228.25; p. not to utter relig. commonplaces, 25.26; p. notes hymn defects more than others, 150.2; careless p. neglects weapon of eloquence, 26.28; every p. should strive to pay debt to fellow men, xxxx.4; not just a p. of Christianity, xxxiv.15; p. when unfaithful to his charge, 25.26

PREACHING is but one voice in choir of world, 68.28; is second public duty of minister; a difficult office, 25.17; p. is too straitened, 27.21; must be manly, flexible, free beyond example of earlier times, 27.7; p. of a pastor rather than a stranger, 36.5; bad p. cannot be useful, 28.35; foolishness of p., 68.29; freedom in p., 28.8; good p. will carry its own vindication, 28.35

PRECEPT: know thyself, 111.9; p. of Stoics, 200.26

PRECEPTS of Jesus coincide with omnipresent moral world, 69.6; p. of the wise, 6.21; imitation is a globe of p., 6.22; landscape of ethical p. needs Jesus, 234.25

PREFERENCE of whole to part, future to present, God to man, 201.33

PREJUDICE, 184.31; p. assigns greater fixture to material world, 2.8

PREJUDICES re. Christian gospel, 23.34

PREPARATION for instruction, 193.19; p. for the duties of life, 216.12

PRESENCE of Christ assured to Christians, 235.4; p. of God constantly acknowledged, 53.10; p. of God to accompany minister, 69.33; p. of God to man is Reason or conscience, xxv.13; p. of the Lord refreshes, xxvi.1; p. of the Omnipresent sufficient, 221.32; p. of the Spirit of God, 210.20; man is temple of Divine P., 136.30; real p. of God in bread and wine, 56.3

PRESENT is little; the future, great, 197.22; future preferred to p., 201.34; value of p., 8.20

PRESIDENTS: most p. are merely clerks of some real power, 229.44

PRESS, licentious, 78.17

PRESSES stand still, xxx.33

PRESUMPTION of complaining at God's order, 259.15; God's knowledge

breaks down p., 4.2; no p. in self-reliance, 110.21; see *pride.*

PRIDE, 2.28; 204.30; p. and humility, 264.12; p. is civil to others, 129.9; false p. in clothing, occupation etc., 52.27; p. incompatible with knowledge, 232.16; p. not part of self-reliance, 238.9; only legitimate basis of p., 211.32; see *presumption.*

PRIEST, 177.14; name of p. opprobrious, 26.35; office of p. is most august, 27.4; office of p. one of honor or shame depending on person, 27.1

PRIESTHOOD, the true, 271.5

PRIESTLEY, Joseph: worships with Calvin etc., xxxviii.27

PRIESTS were bards, 145.25

PRINCE of Peace makes minister his messenger, 33.7; Asiatic p. visited Paris, 203.7

PRINCIPLE, 184.31; of charity, 134.14; of continuity, 244.16; of disinterested love, 244.5; of God in the good man, 239.8; of good can never spring from self-love, 130.17; of love of neighbor in family circle, 131.18; of man's capacity for virtue, 83.6; 231.11; of man's liability to sin, 83.7; of self in the worldly man, 239.6; of virtue never quite destroyed, 239.14; on which social duties depend, 127.5; p. underlying our duty to serve our fellow men, 128.9; basic p. in system of social duty, 131.22; central p. of all sin is self-love, 231.17; divine p. is within the soul, 110.27; faith is a practical p., 160.26; God is potent p. binding men's actions together, 4.8; God meant for us to use the p. of love in dealing with others, 88.20; high p. makes conduct significant, 14.21; life under guidance of relig. p., 16.32; majesty of man of p., 188.16; only sufficient p. is love of God, 247.38; sentiments point to higher p., God, 158.2; some fundamental p. behind every system of theology, 231.7; what p. shall govern me? 151.6

PRINCIPLES, 116.10; p. behind relig. revivals are sound, 232.3; p. inherent in our nature are behind orthodoxy and liberalism, 82.13; p. justifying relig. revivals, 231.40; p. of Jesus must ever be standard for actions, 178.2; p. of right and wrong same in all minds, 64.23; powerful and, in their degree, noble p., 157.27; p. sacrificed in bad gov't, 76.34; p. to guide in every transaction of life, 99.17; actions derived from p., 264.18; assumption that man is capable of receiving and acting on sublime p., 105.7; authority proceeds from perception of great p., 95.23; confidence in p. required in controversy, 88.16; great p. not regarded in social life, 48.11; Jesus plainly announced leading p., 91.32; lusts become p. of man's nature, 10.24; men of p. absent from American politics, 229.37; our need of p., 99.15ff.; relig. p. require study 70.11; revelation of Jesus discovers p. in us, 100.4

PRINTING PRESS, 29.15; stands still, xxxi.15

PRISON discipline, 198.9; Paul and Silas in p., 160.24; spirits in p., 229.8

PRISONER, 163.23

PRISONS: we should go to p. and bid culprits come to Lord's Supper, 59.4

PRIVATION of the affections; of the whole spiritual world, 226.28

PRIVILEGE of social worship, 237.25; of truly social worship, 228.9; speculative method is dearest p., xxiv.19

PRIZE of the high calling of God, 163.3; power regarded as a p. instead of a trust, 229.36

PROBLEMS of time and space, 239.18

PROCESS of time will go on, xxxv.15; p. of vegetation, 39.19; constant nat'l p., 42.10; nat'l p. incomputable, 43.18

PROCESSES: we cannot see p. of tho't, 1.11

PRODUCTION of refinements of life, 46.9

PRODUCTIVENESS of N.: how explained, 42.7

PROFESSION, 211.34; p. and man react on each other, 164.12; p. chosen against a man's inclination, 251.4; p. for which God formed a man, 166.27; p. of one's father passed on, 165.10; crippled in exercise of p., xxii.5; E. must not be crippled in exercise of his p., 28.15; few men suited to a p., 167.4

PROFESSIONS will multiply as society advances, 166.8; best p. hide immoral lives, 15.31; limited number of p. in society, 166.4; see *callings*, etc.

PROFIT: what shall it p. a man if he gain the whole world, 111.16

PROFLIGACY increased by us men, xxx.22

PROFUSION of words called civility, 225.37

PROGRESS and man's nature, 151.23; p. in Christianity in recent times, 55.17; p. in goodness demands more, 250.11; p. in spiritual life reveals our deficiencies more clearly, 250.10; p. of astronomy, 176.33; p. of citizen comes from within, 77.26; p. of men's minds re. Lord's Supper, 57.26; p. of relig. opinion, 264.8; p. of science makes relig. truer, 171.3; p. of society is always instructing men, 194.20; p. of soul will determine its happiness, 141.6; life is a p. towards death, 112.21; party consideration keeps men from p., 87.7; proof of p., 56.5

PROGRESSIVE: law of heaven that our nature should be p., 54.24

PROMISE of Jesus—how meant? 193.28; no p. that Aaron, Abner shall live, 245.7

PROMISES that teacher shall come, 193.35

PROMPTINGS of the heart preferred to common opinion, 168.7; p. of heart withstood, 162.24

PRONENESS to admiration, 152.27

PROOF of God in the conscience, xxv.6; 264.22

PROOFS of a beneficent design in the universe, 175.30

PROPENSITIES, means of strengthening virtuous, 58.8

PROPERTIES of wisdom and goodness, 195.15; irresistible p. of moral nature, 209.20; new p. brought out in every particular object, 193.17

PROPERTY, a social institution, 54.10; doesn't help man understand himself, 206.2; granted an exaggerated importance, 205.31; if invaded, 77.35; p. in all thru our relation to God, 160.20; p. should not be squandered in alms, 241.18; acquisition of p., 9.1; freedom is evanescent p.; must be used, 236.13; must we acquire p.? Yes, 206.18; sacred p. of man's soul, 106.24

PROPHET and monitor of race of men is N., 44.11

PROPHETS, 201.4

PROPORTION: in p. to strength of his character, 165.16

PROPOSITION: abstract p. conquers mind, 198.20

PROSPECT: every p. fails, xviii.28; extent of our p. increased, 250.9

PROSPECTS of society, 256.9; p. of society and relig. instruction, 192.17

PROSPERITY cannot give peace to the bad man, 102.24; advantages of external p. unimportant, 20.8; children of p., 208.14

PROTESTANTS, 146.7

PROVE all things, holding fast to that which is good, 70.30

PROVERB: speak that I may know thee, 61.4

PROVERBS are commentaries on all parts of life, 63.5; enrich conversation of all society, 63.10; govern us in all our traffic, 63.12; happy tho'ts of sagacious men, 63.6; p. heard in youth not heeded, 93.12; keep alive practical wisdom, 62.35; p. re. the stars, 172.13; satisfaction in p., 225.25

PROVIDENCE, 266.20; and the gift of speech, 61.21; answers all prayers, 7.13; appoints our situation in life, 16.25; cares for solar system, 174.22; continually instructs the receptive, 197.3; has given us the task of *forming* true and entire men, 180.23; makes effort to instruct man, 194.3; p. of God, 68.19; of the presiding Cause, 124.11; offers ceaseless instruction, 69.9; prevents monotony in seasons, 41.8; reaches thru all space, 138.10; rules the world, 259.8; design of p., 9.6; Divine P. is father of Jesus, 170.18; hope lies in p., 139.32; signs of a moral p., 83.18; style of God's p., 23.9; see *God*.

PROVINCE: assigned p. of action, 167.15

PRUDENCE based on permanence of N., 124.9; p. required in controversy, 88.16; calculating p. inadequate for virtue, 16.21; worldly p. in maxims and proverbs, 63.1

PSALMODY defined, 146.13

PSALMS of David, 147.23; quoted, 39.4; 75.3; 148.33

PTOLEMAIC SYSTEM described, 173.30

PTOLEMY, 172.2

PUBLIC questions avoided, 229.6

PULPIT has not set the world right, 27.20; not a vehicle for public issues, 76.2; not diff. from parlor, 220.10; not the only agency of preaching, 68.30; 69.7; character of the exhortations of p., 71.11; innovations in p., xxii.3

PULSE for p., 186.27; every p. is the knell of a brother, 112.25

PUNCTUAL: are we p. in our orbit? 45.10

PUNCTUALITY of N., 45.9

PUNISHMENT inevitable in a moral world, 66.9

PUPIL of circumstances, 165.2; a ripe p. is the essential condition of teaching, 197.9; receptivity of p. determines amount he can be taught, 197.10

PUPPET, 206.7

PURE in heart are united to God, utter his word, beam his glory, are vehicle of his spirit, 162.15; p. in heart shall see God, xxvi.2; 161.9; 162.13

PURITY, 234.17; destroys temptation, 210.5; hour spent in perfect p., 20.32

PURPOSE for which we live, 103.27; p. in everything, 220.40; p. of Christ was to redeem every soul, 169.10; p. of Jesus sublime; made actions sublime, 14.16; p. of man in revelation, 106.2; p. *to improve* will be blessed by God, 21.1; circumstances bent toward man's p., 168.25; good p. often forgotten, 20.29; great p. makes man forsake all else, 168.24; high p. dignifies man's act, 14.22; let us contract p. and thereby concentrate strength, 20.31; man's p. becomes father, mother, house, etc., 168.31; miracles for a moral p., xxviii.19; 123.8; rectitude of p., 185.33; serious p. should not be postponed, 103.27; wavering p. confirmed by virtue, 80.34; see *end, aim*.

PURPOSES of churchgoers, 227.42; p. of God best deduced from his works, 84.35; p. of God considered unknown, 83.35; p. of men more similar in best state of world, 106.35; arrangement of p., 239.6; 239.7; great p. to which life may be spent, 52.24; life is long enough for vast p., 117.21

PURSUIT, errors in choice of, 168.14; p. of genuine man, 187.16; peculiar p., xi.15

PURSUITS and events of our after-existence, 258.37; jested about p., 206.14; p. of outward things, 216.21; p. of this world lead to God's right hand, 169.22; worldly p. are trifles, 114.19; see *callings, vocation*.

PYRAMID, a work of human art, 41.16

Q

QUAKERS, 186.6; see *Shakers*.

QUALITIES that stimulate love, 153.29; bad q., 153.33; compensation for all man's q., 101.27; good q. if increased, 153.31; the peculiar q. of man account for his power over others, 108.7

QUALITY, good, 188.32

QUANTUM sumus, scimus, 32.20

QUARTER, hind q. of golden calf, xvii.18

QUESTION answered by man's own constitution, 161.26; q. dear to the understanding, 2.17; q. is not: what did God intend? What saith the human heart? 87.10; q. of duty, 110.3; q. of intent of Lord's Supper, xxxv.5; q. why any animal exists, 204.20; every q. on which men take sides, 82.16

QUESTIONS: all q. can be answered near at hand, 46.21; ethical, metaphysical, educational q., 82.18; moral and relig. q., 244.34; q. of sincere mind, 161.19; q. of human duty, 212.3; q. peremptorily asked by the soul, 199.27; public q. usually avoided, 229.6; q. spring from wonder of creation, 1£9.32; q. suggested by the heavens, 172.18

R

RABBI, we know thou art a teacher, 120.2

RACE of diff. structure on other planets, 173.15; before the human r. was, 172.5; help human r., 117.18; knowledge accumulated in mind of the r., 194.10; progressive education of the r., 164.26; truth is teacher of human r., 194.35; 2400 of human r. die in an hour, 112.24; see *men*.

RACES of vast and shapeless animals, 112.11

RAILING at God's order, 259.15

RAIMENT, soft, 6.5

RAIN waters the blackberry, 208.2

RAINBOW, 44.2; 218.41; I am center of r., 258.1

RAISE himself in own esteem, xix.4

RANK in society unimportant, 20.8

RAPTURE of Socrates, 205.2

RARE: presence of the Lord once r., now more frequent, xxvi.1

RATIO, power multiplied in compound r., 198.25

RATIONAL BEING, dignity of, xix.5

RAYS of stars, 194.14

READER: God is r. of tho'ts, 4.9

READING the tho'ts may be possible, 1.17

REACH of the understanding greater in good men, 161.1; within our r., 5.17

REACHES into the infinite void, 178.16

REALITY and blessedness of relig., 269.19; the r. behind the shadows of our admirations is God, 155.6; r. of evil not denied, 258.24; r. of things unseen, 2.31; greater r. to tho't and feeling than to panorama of N., 2.2; never could give much r. to evil and pain, 258.28

REAP: As I plant I hope to, 29.34

REASON (NOT IN TECHNICAL SENSE): r. for failing to find God, xxiv.26; r. of duty is not always present to all, 70.25; r. to think every man is born with peculiar character, 165.19; sufficient r. is given for the existence of pain, 85.15; sufficient r. is given for the special economy of the Christian revelation, 85.16

REASON (SPIRITUAL MIND, ETC.): r. and revelation, 267.28; r. and truth argued for Webster, 65.18; r. assumes its empire over man, 210.24; can turn the low and injurious to power and beauty, 210.25; cannot outsee God, 252.26; common to all men, 186.20; exercised by Dr. Walker, xxi.28; exercised to redeem man from brutishness, 206.34; has been shaken from her seat, 199.30; has two-fold office: awaking men to truth and virtue, 207.13; r. in the mind is Spirit of God in us all, 186.30; r. is a pure and holy inmate, xxv.12; r. is God, 4.13; r. not to be hampered by revelation (i.e., the Bible), xxvi. 31; r. of Caesar is no more weighty than our own, 182.3; r. of God speaks to r. of man in scriptures, 29.23; r. of man not addressed in revivals, 232.5; r. restored to an insane man, 122.12; r. speaks same language to living and dead, 143.18; r. speaks thru the speaker of truth, 186.17; conclusions of r., 161.35; dictates of r., 185.2; eternal r. which shines within man, 183.6; exercise of r. turns all our evil to good, 210.23; fortify truth with impregnable r., 90.25; human r. not to be distrusted, 252.23; Jesus does not r. at all, 91.3; knowing God thru r., xxiv.18; let r. argue for him, 186.15; man's freedom too mighty for r.; will stand whether r. sanction or no, 236.18; power of r., 185.29; supreme universal r. is not yours or mine or any man's, 186.30; voice of r. is above mere man, 186.20

REASONS for thanksgiving, 267.38; r. why N.T. miracles are credible, 120.6

REBIRTH of a man, 114.29

RECEIVER of influence is man, 209.17

RECEPTION: bling r. of dogmas condemned, xxvi.33

RECITATION, sermon shall not be, xviii.15

RECOLLECTION of angry word will return, 66.13; miracle of r., 122.16; relig. r., 19.32; purpose of Lord's Supper is r., 57.2

RECOLLECTIONS concealed in solitude, 3.6

RECORD of the Revelation, not the Revelation itself, 125.31; r. of time, 269.31

RECORDED: not a relig. r. in a bk., xxxv.29

RECORDS of divine dealings read by light of N., 170.20

RECTITUDE of purpose, 185.33; r. required in public as in private affairs, 76.11

RED SEA, 43.22

REDEMPTION: scheme of r. made incredible, 174.35; scheme or r. portrayed, 174.28; see regeneration.

REED, Sampson, quotation from "Sleep," New Jerusalem Mag., VI (Nov., 1832), p. 88, quoted, 203.26

REFER every action in life to God, 53.8

REFINEMENTS of life, 46.9

REFLECTION, 200.19; can redeem man, 206.34; humblest man capable of r., 208.15; r. is important, 210.23; is first duty of a moral being, 237.19; keeps man from being a mere animal, 207.1; shows man that he is wonderfully made, 207.1; would have eliminated errors in church, 237.20

REFORM in public relig. teaching, 201.8; r. yourself, xxx.21; true way to r. states is to r. individual, 81.5; your r. by kindness, not by angry words, 66.18

REFORMATION was object of Jesus' life, 56.34

REFORMERS of mankind, 52.21

REFRESHMENT comes from presence of the Lord, xxv.35; soul wants r. and instruction, 155.15

REFUSE converted to commodity, 41.1

REGENERATION, doctrine of, 114.8; signs of, 119.11; see redemption.

REGION: illimitable r. of relig. truth, 196.29

REGRET over not possessing some ability, 107.24; bitter herbs of r., 67.19

REGRETS for goods not gained, 7.29

REJECT Biblical doctrines that appear untrue, xxv.29; not to r. the new, xxii.4

REJOICING in himself alone, 238.22

RELATEDNESS of each to all, 207.23

RELATION betw. children of one God is sacred, 134.29; r. of command and obedience, 95.9; r. of God to individual has priority, xxvi.9; r. of man to God—every view valuable, 245.15; r. of man to God is sacred, 60.14; r. of man to this world, 5.15; r. of man's moral nature to God, 233.32; r. of moral laws in this world to those of next, 10.30; r. of personal love needed, 159.23; r. to God gives us property in all things, 160.21; my immediate r. to God, 200.5; my r. to God; to fellow man, 199.24; parallel r. of God, 83.19

RELATIONS and duties of man, 7.26; r. betw. man and God, 132.17; r. from each to all, 207.23; r. of a man, 205.7; r. of man to God, 194.28; family r. to be assisted, 103.8; web of our r., 128.2

RELIGION and idolatry, 146.4; and society, 191.1; 270.39; becomes purer thru progress of science, 171.2; blended with daily labor, 189.10; bound to chas-ten the levities of conversation, 226.12; covers relations to country and world, 75.4; is delicate plant, 73.2; is doing one's duty, 264.40; is home of the mind, 28.1; is right direction of admiration, 152.32; in the soul, 212.8; made for man's benefit—not God's, 189.15; never wants articulate voice, 69.12; r. of forms not for E., xxxviii.22; r. of one's father passed on, 165.9; r. produces a higher self-respect, 105.17; produces confidence in God, 105.17; reformed by astronomy, 177.4; reunited with love of N., 171.19; suffers from caprices and errors of men, 171.16; teaches art of conducting life well, 99.8; the foundation of conscience, 184.9; r. *vs.* idolatry, 151.8; a disposition adverse to true r., 88.3; a living r., 270.26; cause of external r., xxiv.22; Christian r. stresses spiritual world, 1.24; Christianity found fit to become r. of nations, 55.14; coincidence of first and third tho'ts applied to r., xxxiii.18; fruits of r., 267.7; honor close to r., 155.20; honor rises to a r. without name of Jesus, 156.13; how to present r. to others, 228.13; I want a r. not recorded in a bk. but flowing from all things, xxxv.29; instructions of revealed r., 220.39; main regard of r. is to make us good at home, 15.5; men make their r. a historical r., xxxv.25; nat'l r. confirmed by Christianity, 265.21; reality and blessedness of r., 269.20; satisfaction of r., 270.16; sum of r. is: Do thyself no harm, 269.35; truths of r. discovered by men of self-reliance, 111.1; use all means to spread true r., 88.33; we want a living r., xxxv.27; wherein r. is diff. from irrelig., xxiv.16

RELIGIOUS, excellency of the, 133.35

REMARK, suppression of merry or petulant, 14.31

REMEDY for sensualism: reflection, 206.33

REMEMBER, thou must die, 245.38

REMEMBRANCE of dead preaches doctrines of gospel, 68.33; r. of home in the soul, 19.31; r. of private virtues gives consolation, 20.14; feast of r., 54.1; 265.34; see *memory.*

REMORSE for sin can be overemphasized, 83.30

REMOTE: all r. somehow reaches you, 207.21

REMUNERATION comes in next world, 9.35

RENUNCIATION is yielding one's will, 210.19; r. of self leads to power of soul, 210.17

REPAIR the flagging powers of the soul, 70.27

REPETITION in sermons justified, 71.20; r. of a bad or good action, 210.12

REPETITIONS: formal r. are not prayers, 5.4

REPRESENTATIONS of God in relig. revivals not quite worthy, 232.5

REPROACH: no syllable of r. for the successful, 9.16

REPROOF: Jesus' r. of his disciples, 59.1

REPTILE reverence, 7.33

REPUTATION for decorum, 227.43; of good men, 225.9; unimportant, 181.15

REQUESTS not wasted on wind, 6.31

RESEARCH, systematic, 227.11

RESEMBLANCE of tho't and conversation everywhere, 107.6

RESIDENCE of animal requires his frame, 204.19; r. of man illuminated by stars, 173.33

RESIGNATION of the sufferer, 160.18

RESOLUTION to die, 14.10

RESOLUTIONS made in church, 20.25

RESOURCES of character, 184.15; r. of many women undeveloped, 184.20

RESPECT at home is significant, 15.2; r. given to all things, 52.30; r. is felt for person of intelligence, 49.33; r. of men inconsequential, 11.33; outward r. to God and inward r. to sin, 3.21; r. paid dictates of one's own reason, 185.1; r. should be sought in what *really* belongs to a man, 211.30; marks of r., 205.21

RESPECTABILITY and w o m e n, 184.19; r. given to mean offices, 60.11

RESPONSE: test of general r. is a criterion of the truth, 230.38

RESPONSIBILITY of each man for national conditions, 79.10; r. for one's soul is tremendous, 105.24; r. for words and actions becomes God's, 188.14; moral r. an aid to good gov't, 75.21

RESULT: good shall r. from everything, 51.11

RESULTS of an old philosopher are the elements of his pupil, 55.3; r. possible without beauty, 43.3; r. which no chance or art can elude (compensation), 209.28; beneficent r. from our random actions, 163.15; inevitable r. of the laws of moral nature, 209.23

RESURRECTION, 141.32; r. after interval of death denied, 245.1; r. and its hope, 52.20; r. and the life, 56.15; r. but not of the body, 244.25; r. from the dead, 35.1; r. not as important as Jesus' teaching, 238.34; miracle of the r., 125.25; our own being more wonderful than r., 122.20; value of the r. of Christ to a mourner, 140.21

RETRIBUTION faster than lightning, 210.3; r. operates for past action, 101.16; runs into every moment of life, 102.23; doctrine of r., 11.18; see *compensation, judgment.*

RETRIBUTIONS, perfectness of, 244.36

REVELATION, 225.13; r. and reason, 267.28; continuous, 199.11; discloses God's intention for man, 106.2; r. in special sense of Bible or Gospel, xxvi.26; r. is one source of relig. knowledge, xxvi.26; is only recorded in the gospels, 125.31; must be depended on for chief evidence, 245.18; r. of God in Bible, xxv.23; r. of God not in ancient books but in flesh and blood, 189.3; r. of God's will in the mind, 189.2; r. of immortality, 238.29; r. of Jesus failed to receive credit, 56.25; r. of Jesus Christ discovers in us the principles we need, 100.4; r. of the gospel, 11.10; r. of truth must accompany miracle, 123.24; r. *vs.* reason, xxvi.31; amazing r. of my immediate relation to God, 200.4; Christianity is r. of a Deity, 27.31; memory of one's home seems a new r. from heaven, 19.33; miracles and the nature of r., 124.18; science is commentary on or sequel to, r., 171.8; special economy of the Christian r., 85.18; study of God's r., 218.44

REVELATIONS, 197.31; a thousand more may be expected, 196.26; farther r. to be made by the Spirit, 193.25

REVENGE, 3.25; r. is mine, I will repay, 66.6

REVERE thyself, 200.29

REVERENCE for Bible, 147.17; r. for persons and topics, 65.25; r. for scriptural concept of God, 84.16; r. secured by moral force, 19.1; r. the nature which we hold in common with all men, 134.18; r. the soul, 111.22; r. yourself, 182.25; 189.2; reptile r. to men of consideration, 7.33; statement made in r., xx.9

REVIEW: N. passes in r. before man, 209.19

REVIVAL of capacity for pleasure, pain, 9.30; r. offers only first stage in relig. education, 232.13

REVIVALS have value to those open to such influences, 232.10; r. in relig., xxx.10; r. in relig. emphasize confession of sin, 231.45; efficacy of relig. r., 231.27; manner of relig. r. criticized, 231.38; relig. r. are based on sound principles, 232.3; relig. r. can be justified, 231.39; relig. r. do not address the reason of man, 232.5

REVOLTS: best part of a man r. against ministry, xxxiii.33

REVOLUTION in France, 194.25; r. in relig. caused by science, 253.2; r. in relig. opinion as in science, 174.20; r. of relig. opinion going on, 199.12; greatest r. is that which separates individual from world, 199.13

REWARD given for goodness and wisdom, 140.32; r. is instantaneous, 210.2; r. of action determined by moral laws, 209.30; doctrine of r. and punishment, 11.18

REWARDS are visited on our heads, 101.19

RHETORIC: no r. in E's doctrine of prayer, 3.17

RHEUMATISM, 113.9

RHEUMATISMS, 242.25

RICH, murmuring against the, 129.32; shall I become r? 4.27; we do not know how r. we are, 190.4

RICHES, 5.23; 5.32; 183.29; r. cannot

profit the inner man, 211.27; r. made a god, 151.14 r. of future depend on system of compensations, 10.32; r. of N., 171.31

RIDDLE of human sympathy, 243.4

RIDICULE, vulgar, 52.33

RIDICULOUS to deny power of reading inner character, 1.11

RIGHT and wrong, 208.32; r. and wrong estimate of oneself, 182.30; r. is naked before God's knowledge, 4.3; r. is God everlasting, 100.13; not of great importance to set a man r., 65.2; r. action is not our own but God's, 132.30; r. for r's sake, 269.23; r. to examine every opinion for oneself, 187.2; all will come r. hereafter, 65.3; concept of r. and wrong common to all men, 64.23; degrees of r., 231.22; honor is a delicate sense of r., 155.25; judging r. for ourselves, 269.43; man does wrong; God does r., 132.33; no r. to assign wrong motives, 1.8; only by doing r. can man receive happiness God planned for him, 85.27; question of simple r., 244.38; sentiment may be r.; direction wrong, 154.29; the expedient often put before the r., 76.16; when we do r., 132.29

RIGHTEOUS suffer insults, sorrow, rags, 11.4

RIGHTEOUSNESS and peace have kissed each other, 256.19; r. and true holiness, 183.22; God will judge world in r., 170.10; hunger and thirst after r., 178.12

RIGHTS, if invaded, 77.35; r. of men recognized by law in U.S., 77.12; r. of others, 264.30

RIGIDITY and liberalism, 266.39; relig. r., 82.1

RIOT attending Lord's Supper, 55.33

RISK, 244.6

RITE of Lord's Supper: its intent and use, xxxv.5

RITES are nothing in themselves, xxxviii.20

ROAD: in the right r. to truth, 232.16

ROBBINS, Chandler, referred to, 202.17

ROBE, white, xxxv.6

ROCK on which men have been shipwrecked, 117.6

ROMAN, 222.16; R. emperor put on cloak of dissimulation, 225.31; R. scorn, 56.27; old R. quoted on houses, 186.2

ROMANS, 135.35; 198.2; on heaven, 243.40

ROME, 186.5; 218.40; church of R., 133.26; R. a city of consuls, emperors, barbarians, popes and artists, 54.20; R. not same as in classical times, 54.18; St. Clement of R., 249.1

ROOT of man's relation to world, 5.15; r. of power and beauty, 210.26

ROOTS of the blackberry, 208.2

ROSE: no r. without its thorn, 258.18; pluck a r., 14.9

ROSES: same r. which charmed the Roman and Chaldean, 222.15

ROUND of the seasons, 203.20
ROUNDS that make up human life, 116.34
RUBBISH converted to commodity, 41.1
RUDIMENT of man's relation to the world, 5.15
RUIN is name we give to failure in trade, 184.14
RULE, 162.4; r. for our discourse, 65.4; r. of action, 27.32; 155.13; r. of Jesus: Be ye perfect, 92.17; r. of political action is: World will last our day, 78.30; one central r. will guide us safely, 53.8; Christianity now has nobler moral r. than formerly, 55.19; Golden R., 127.15; honor as a r. of life, 156.33; living by others' opinions is low-lived r. of action, 49.4; see *law*.
RULER over a few things first, 18.25; r. *vs.* ruled, 77.1
RULERS of country represent the virtue of same, 80.11
RULES for government of tongue, 64.16; r. of the N.T., 115.11
RUSSIAN campaign of Napoleon, 154.18

S

SABBATH, a social institution, 54.10; made for man, not man for the S., 189.14; S. observance, 227.34; 263.26; history of S., 20.23; keeping the S., 72.26; 268.32
SACRAMENTS of matrimony, baptism, Lord's Supper, 31.6
SACRED introduced into all relations, 60.13
SACREDNESS attached to opinions on atonement, 84.5
SACRIFICE: bodies presented a living s., 99.3; greatest s. requires the highest faith, 161.11; no mystic s. in astronomy, 177.15
SACRIFICES made by great men, 52.14; s. of what we have: even sickness, 104.10; present ourselves living s., 101.3
SAFETY depends on abstaining to offend, 123.1; gained by speaking falsely, 225.8
SAGACITY of pagan philosopher, 10.31
SAILOR, 163.20
SAINT: it needs a s. to dispute, 226.8
ST. AUGUSTINE, 133.31; 204.34; 249.1
ST. AUSTIN: see *St. Augustine.*
ST. BERNARD, 249.1
ST. CHRYSOSTOM, 249.1
ST. CLEMENT of Rome, 249.1
SAINT ÉVREMOND, Charles: quotation from *Sense of an Honest and Experienced Courtier*, 153.22
ST. JAMES quoted, 60.3; 66.20; 243.27; grave advice of, 124.28
ST. LUKE quoted, 46.3; 54.3
ST. MATTHEW quoted, 105.3
ST. PAUL, 15.24; 117.16; 177.23; P. and Silas prayed and sang praises,

160.24; P. can be very wrong, xxv.27; P. had sentiments of a true and perfect gentleman, 156.18; P. had valiant heart, 22.5; P. more than a conqueror, 22.25; P. quoted, 22.3; 31.3; 67.3; 68.28; 70.30; 82.2; 87.19; 87.25; 99.4; 101.2; 104.26; 133.10; 138.4; 163.4; 170.13; 182.27; 188.9; P. rebukes riots at Lord's Supper, 55.34; Anthony Collins' admiration for P., 156.18; ardor and spirituality of P., 124.28; P's death at Rome, 23.1; faith was alive in P's heart, xxxv.28; martyrdom of P., 217.40; sufferings of P., 22.8
ST. PETER, 133.5; can be mistaken, xxv.27
ST. PHILIP NERI, 249.2
SAINTS, 224.12; had no greater opportunity than we, 117.15; not divided by line from sinners, 58.4
SALOONS, harp and viol tinkle in, 9.14
SALVATION, 117.27; acc. to the old plan, 199.18; is individual, not corporate, 118.7; is love of God—not self-love, 239.10; is ours only when we are induced to save ourselves, 177.34; s. now, 266.44; s. of human soul rests in great truths, 111.2; give alms for the sake of your own s., 242.37; God's method of s., 174.25; gospel is power of God unto s., 22.3; Jesus the author and finisher of our s., 96.10; our s. is duty, 271.4
SAME in words as in life, 186.7; every man another of the s., 134.8; God of N. and of Bible are s., 170.17; name and place not always s. thing, 54.16; Justice s. in mind of God and man, xxiii.32f.
SANCTIFICATION, 27.28
SAND: each grain of s. allied to all, 207.23; each grain of s. is fixed point, 207.22; grain of s., 28.19
SANDS of sea unnumbered, 196.31
SAP that ascends in the stem, 41.32
SATIETY of unceasing harvest, 41.6
SATISFACTION found in proverbs, 225.26; s. of relig., 270.16
SATISFIED: people only seem s., but are not, 8.25; good man s. *from himself,* 110.29
SATURN, 173.7
SAURIN, Jacques (1677-1730): his *Sermons* or *Dissertations* quoted. [See *Journals,* II, 25], 174.29
SAVAGE is brother to the tiger, 165.28
SAVE: justifying revivals that s. one soul from sin, 232.11
SAVIOUR ever graceful and decent in deportment, 51.21; Jesus was s. of soul, 56.28
SAY, what is honor? 155.29
SAYINGS of Jesus are of universal application, 196.4; they disclose the inner world, 196.9
SCAFFOLD of the divine vengeance, 174.31
SCALE: man in the s. of creation, 45.17; public selfishness is private selfishness on great s., 79.26

182.31; we cannot see a man's secret s., 1.6; when we act from s., 132.28; whole s. is the soul, 182.33

SELF-COMMAND, 153.30; 212.2; 265.28; s-c. and self-direction, 264.28; importance of constitutional s-c. against parties and factions, 88.12

SELF-CULTURE, 99.1; 267.18; s-c. admits of no delay, 101.11; Christian called to unceasing effort at s-c., 101.4; our freedom to be turned to s-c., 101.7; sermon on s-c., how enlarged, xxxviii.5

SELF-DIRECTION and self-command, 264.28

SELF-ESTEEM, 111.22; raising one's s-e., xix.5

SELF-EXAMINATION, 190.11; s-e. at end of year, 73.17

SELF-GOOD yields to God in the soul, 132.33

SELF-GOVERNMENT, 45.18; an important duty, 88.13

SELF-GUIDANCE, 190.9

SELF-HELP necessary, 238.20

SELF-IMPORTANCE, 205.25

SELF-IMPROVEMENT, 17.2; 211.10; 269.41; is purpose of the soul, 50.35; see *improvement.*

SELF-INJURY, the only kind possible in our moral order, 209.32

SELF-INTEREST and complaisance, 185.8; as a motive of well-doing described, 129.18; never prompted sincere service of others, 128.20; voice of, 78.27

SELF-KNOWLEDGE, 111.9; 111.28; 168.18; s-k. and self-mastery, 264.34; s-k. is key to all other knowledge, 118.11; is the basis of choosing a vocation, 167.29; s-k. not gained thru property, 206.2; how advance to s-k., 167.32

SELF-LOVE, 115.28; an unworthy basis of ethics, 131.23; s-l. and benevolence may prompt the same outward act, 128.18; s-l. as basis of duty toward neighbor, 128.12; s-l. hasn't an inch of ground to stand on, 135.20; s-l. is central principle of all sin, 231.18; s-l. is not benevolence, 128.14; s-l. must yield to love of God, 239.8; s-l. though exalted can never become principle of good, 130.15; well-calculated s-l. is benevolence, 128.13; s-l. will turn world into a hell of slavery etc., 231.18; well-calculated s-l. would dictate duty to others, 129.8

SELF-MASTERY and self-knowledge, 264.34

SELF-PROTECTION described, 129.18; covetousness acts in s-p., 129.11

SELF-REALIZATION, 106.4

SELF-RELIANCE, xxv.28; 8.23; 105.1; 106.5; 184.29; 187.2; s-r. and relig. faith, 237.14; s-r. contains nothing of presumption, 110.21; s-r. defined, 188.12; grows out of scripture doctrine of value of the soul, 109.21; is departing from the low and falling back upon truth and upon God, 110.24; is guarantee against being misled and depraved, 110.35; is not selfish, 110.24; s-r. makes

for force, 109.18; misunderstood, 109.24; not inconsistent with dependence on and piety toward, God, 110.21; not inconsistent with duties to God and neighbor, 109.23; s-r. of genuine man, 186.13; s-r. how perverted, 238.9; limits of s-r., 238.2; 268.45; men of s-r. can bear the severest scrutiny of other men's judgments, 110.33; men of s-r. have found out the great truths of relig., 111.1; perfect check is that man is not his own, 238.7

SELF-RENOUNCEMENT is key to soul's power, 210.17

SELF-RENUNCIATION is yielding one's will, 210.19

SELF-RESPECT is a major-effect of Christianity, 237.6; lost in obeying certain laws, 229.25; relig. produces a higher s-r., 105.17

SELF-REVERENCE, 84.31

SELF-SALVATION, 178.1

SELF-SEEKERS and motive of benevolence, 242.13

SELF-SEEKING rebuked, 135.28

SELF-SUFFICIENCY, E. wishes preservation from, 68.16

SELF-TRUST, 186.32; 267.24; indispensable to genuine man, 183.27; is relying on your birthright, 108.25; means trust in the God within, 237.40; doctrine of s-t., 106.13; virtue of s-t. seldom enters conversation, 108.28; why feared by good men, 238.11; see *confidence.*

SELFISHNESS, 127.7; 226.26; s. and benevolence, 266.18; s. condemned by sound political economy, 128.24; s. distinguished from carelessness, 51.31; excluded by love of God, 135.1; s. in public measures paralleled in private life, 79.24; s. is not self-reliance, 110.24; s. is the seed of the second death, 239.12; s. of men is hostile to needy men, 131.10; s. separates one from human family, 210.6; s. vitiates all private virtues, 130.7; loathsome calculations of s., 48.32

SELFS: two s. exist: outer and inner; double consciousness, 200.9

SENSE of duty, 14.34; s. of justice, 155.29; s. of one's importance, 205.25; s. that we are God's children, 65.20; collective s. of the multitude of persons of standing, 157.4; diff. s. put on N.T. by diff. Christians, 219.3; every s. is a treasury door, 249.35; joys of s., 6.4; moral s. of the people is obtuse, 229.33; perishable things of s., 2.14; pleasures of s., 146.12; pleasures of s. to be overcome, 105.9; sublime spiritual s. of gospel, xxxv.11

SENSES are the lower faculties, 202.9; closed to commerce with outward things, 114.11; s. in which *spirit* is used, 223.14; heaven pictured from the s., 243.39; how long have you lived out of the s.? 115.7; interior s. opened to better kingdom, 114.12; luxuries of s., 196.19; pleasures of s. in youth, 231.42; refusing the service of the s., 100.17; riches are convenient only to the s., 211.28; servant of the s., 210.16; things apprehended by s. are grooved into each other, 204.3

SENSIBILITY, acute, xiv.25

SENSUALISM, 201.30; 201.32; condemned by Jesus, 195.30; 199.1

SENSUALIST, 206.27

SENSUALITY seen by sensual man, 101.34

SENTENCE which I have just read I do not now believe, xxxvii.32; a trite s. confirms a proverb, 93.16

SENTIMENT, 145.16; 208.25; s. may be right and its direction wrong, 154.29; s. of faith in God, 158.16; s. of love and loyalty, 155.9; s. of love founded on infinite goodness, 154.1; s. of love is drawn to wisdom and goodness; repelled by sin, 161.31; s. of love to God is highest, 151.4; s. of loyalty, 154.6; s. of the soul corresponds to Bible truth, 115.16; a just s. makes for eloquence, 26.27; anr. s. is honor, 155.17; astronomy offers image for the exalted s., 171.16; homage paid to a s. rather than to a person, 155.22; infinite s. belies the finite object, 157.22; moral s. is highest platform of eloquence, 218.29; soul made to go beyond a s., 157.34; surrendering self to a s., 157.33

SENTIMENTS are natural and infinite, but objects are finite and unworthy, 158.4; s. of a true and perfect gentleman, 156.18; s. of honor acquaint us with our own power and wants, 157.32; s. of honor serve higher use, 157.30; s. of men grope after some great object, 161.28; s. point to a higher principle—God, 158.2; s. that are powerful and noble principles, 157.26; s. re. creator in sacred poetry, 146.18; s. when enlarged become love of God, 158.12; most beneficent s. have an unworthy direction, 157.19; our s. toward great men are unjustified, 158.8; prayers are not repetitions of s. at second hand, 5.4; strongest s. thru the ages, 152.35; unchristian s. in hymns, 149.4

SEPARATION from human family by selfishness, 210.7; s. of God and man opposed, 237.44

SEQUEL: science is the s. of revelation, 171.7

SERENITY: lesson of s. and trust, 72.9

SERPENT, trail of, 10.13

SERMON should not be a recitation, xviii.15; life itself would be s., 35.21; Saturday's s., xxxi.32

SERMON ON THE MOUNT, 178.27; quoted, 133.1

SERMONS and virtue, 189.21; character of s., 71.11; s. deal with topics of immemorial meditation, 71.16; s. less valuable than nature, 171.23; s. not needed to stimulate the relig. mind, 228.32; subjects for s., 36.20

SERVANT of all, 135.31; s. of the senses, 210.15; E. a s. of the gospel, 28.17; E. wanted to be master and not s.

to forms and creeds, xxxix.3; God is the s. of the universe, 221.42

SERVANTS of men, not masters, 183.30

SERVE God acc. to our best knowledge, 257.9; they also s. who only stand and wait, 104.17

SERVICE done to truth in any scuffle, 194.33; s. of man to his Maker, 7.5; s. to mankind by good example, 6.29; music and poetry in relig. s., 145.23; not bring to s. of God what he would be ashamed to offer in s. of man, 70.17; usefulness in God's s., 104.22

SERVICES of Church are periodical, 70.35

SERVILITY of ministers, 219.34

SETTLERS of U.S. not bad men, 78.35

SEX, friend of anr., 157.23

SHADE of a cloud, 33.14

SHADOW: miss substance and grasp, 88.26; s. of dogmatism; of pride, 204.30; admirations are s. of the Reality called God, 155.6; earth as s. of heaven, 244.20; material creation only a s. of moral truths, 196.33; substance for the s., 255.2

SHADOWS, clouds and darkness rest upon next life, 10.2; tho'ts and passions are not s., 3.1

SHAFTESBURY, Lord, 249.4

SHAKERS, 146.8; see Quakers.

SHAKESPEARE, William, 152.24; 208.31; 249.3; Othello, V.i.19 quoted, 20.14

SHAME for the gospel of Christ, 22.2; s. that attends unrequited affection, 153.23; no s. if one follows conscience, 188.26

SHAPE of virtue is lovely, 6.19

SHARE of God's goodness, 108.11

SHARING Jesus' power by imitating his virtues, 90.11

SHEEP wandering without shepherd, 37.2

SHELL cast up on beach cannot admire its own form or splendor, 221.44; s. of an animal like social institutions, 55.8

SHEPHERD, sheep without a, 37.3; the first Syrian s., 172.3

SHEPHERDS, 146.1

SHEWS outside, 2.27

SHIP, 165.4; foundering in a tempest, 234.19; build s., 206.22

SHIPS borne homeward on breeze, 42.33

SHORTNESS of life, 99.5

SHOWS of N., 171.31; s. of N. and humanity, 204.12; s. of this world, 105.10; beneath outward s. of things, 227.2; glorious s. of N., 43.30

SHRINE, soul is inmost, 202.8

SHROUD, time to put on our, 35.27

SICK sufferer and God, 160.16

SICKNESS, 211.6; does not disturb the soul, 201.26; does not prevent a holy life, 104.11; interrupts best-laid schemes etc., 103.10; is forerunner of death, 103.17; s. teaches, 192.33

SIDE, Church sees man from a diff.,

113.34; omnipotence is on the s. of virtue, 87.28; sore s. of man's condition, 67.20; we choose a s. in life, 22.9

SIDNEY, Sir Philip, and honor, 157.1

SIGHT of good or bad action, 83.1; s. of the true God in N., 171.26; the dead see us with clear s., 142.13; spiritual s. cleared by "know thyself," 201.7

SIGN, miracle is a s., xxviii.21

SIGNAL of man's resolution to die, 14.10

SIGNIFICANCE of Christ, 266.9

SIGNS and wonders, 126.20; s. of regeneration, 119.11; evil s. in U.S., 78.17; 78.24; language of s., 61.29

SILAS with Paul in prison, 160.24

SILENCE, 211.19; wiser in conversation than in s., 62.24

SILSBEE, [Mr.], 181.24

SIMPLICITY has marked highest minds, 51.23; s. in living, dress, and character superior to ostentation, 49.24; s. marks style of Jesus' discourses, 91.12; s. of purified Christianity, 232.30; s. yields to fashion in society, 47.15

SIN, 161.32; accounts for the variety in our thinking, 243.6; can be turned to value, 211.7; s. in our hearts makes the public s., 80.19; s. lieth at a man's own door, 59.8; s. of Adam was federal, 199.19; s. teaches something, 192.34; central principle of all s. is self-love, 231.18; confession of s. emphasized in revivals, 231.45; fear of s. as basis of a system, 231.26; God as punisher of s., 83.13; man's s., xx.19; man's s. and God's wrath, 267.22; man's s. shall not exclude him from Lord's Supper, 58.24; theory of original s. condemned, 106.14; soul in bondage of s., 169.11; strong faith indicated strong sense of s., 84.11; tho'ts and actions in service of s., 3.23; unpardonable s. in educated persons, 229.10; when we s., conscience points to lower degrees of right, 231.22

SINEWS of a man's character, 210.28

SINGULARITY, nat'l or affected, 51.25

SINNER in greater need than others of Christ's aid, 58.25; Jesus came to call the s., 58.27; joy over one s. that repenteth, 245.23

SINNERS, 224.12; s. and saints, 58.5; we are the s., xxx.23

SINNING, prayer to make men stop, 7.10

SINS, 238.6; s. against the law of truth, 225.7; s. are enemies of Jesus' truth, 98.1; only our s. are our own, 135.16; souls spotted with s., 225.5

SISTERS of Laws above, 10.32

SITUATION in life appointed by Providence, 16.25

SKEPTIC on miracles, 124.35; sees only his own vain imagination, 27.17; Hume the s., xx.33

SKEPTICISM, 201.32; put at an end by a fact, 234.24; coincidence of first and third tho'ts applied to s., xxxiii.18; running the round of s., 92.3

SKEPTICS, Christianity outlives schools of, 55.23

SKIES: see *heavens*.

SKIN of an animal compared to institutions, 55.8

SKIRTS, treading upon, 129.10

SKY revealed figures to early man, 172.4

SLANDER used for party purposes, 78.19

SLATE, 164.1

SLAVE: the cause of the s. is mine, 256.39

SLAVERY condemned, 256.32; has been judged by Christ, 256.36; is product of self-love, 231.18; must be cut off root and branch, 256.35; once considered innocent institution, 256.35; abolition of s., 198.10

SLEEP: without phenomenon of s. we should be atheists, 203.25

SMALL, time magnifies the, xxxv.10

SMILES on face of God, 169.21

SOCIETIES of all kinds, 198.7

SOCIETY and relig., 191.1; s. and solitude, 265.42; s. and the individual: their interest is one, 129.33; s. educated with Jesus' truth, 197.29; s. exhibits no striking variety of mind, 107.4; s. has disadvantages, 46.25; s. in barbarous state, 195.11; s. in solitude, 159.5; s. is full of superstitions, 53.4; is produced thru speech, 62.4; is serviced by a limited number of professions, 166.4; makes outcry when forms and idols are contemned, 53.5; s. of departed loved ones, 143.11; of speaking men, 61.9; of the Friends, 134.2; s. only of the like minded, 232.38; s. overemphasizes clothes, 48.20; s. preaches doctrines of gospel, 68.34; provides solid advantages, 46.4; s. smiles on the "successful" man, 9.14; s. to the solitary is "know thyself," 201.6; s. will multiply indefinitely the number of professions, 251.36; s. would move with better speed if each liked his work, 166.34; advance of s. will multiply professions, 166.6; consideration and estimation of s., 5.29; conversation of s. enriched by proverbs, 63.11; early s. in mild climates, 171.29; eminence in s. artificial, 181.27; every moment s. is undergoing change, 54.12; s's existence depends on marriage bonds, 31.16; individuals must be changed before s., xxx.20; institutions of s. in man's care, 54.6; jest about human s., 206.14; men say bad things to each other in good s., 79.19; opinions and practices of s. scrutinized, 187.3; order and advantage of s., 157.31; people who stand high in s., 13.6; prospects of s., 192.17; purer s. of heaven, 81.18; rank in s. unimportant, 20.8; relig. and s., 270.39; speech is foundation of s., 60.24; spiritual s. of the dead, 142.31; vices and caprices of s. affect view of honor, 157.7; welfare of s., 157.28

SOCINUS, 177.24

SOCKET for bone, 204.18

SOCRATES, 107.3; 208.30; 248.45; a reformer, 52.22; stopped; stood still for one day in wonder, 205.1

SOIL of New England, 43.21; of this world, 10.16; cultivate in every s. the grapes peculiar to that s., 107.13

SOILS, kind of, 107.9

SOLACE: one s. at time of death, 34.23

SOLAR SYSTEM explained, 174.15

SOLDIER, 165.28; of Napoleon in Russia, 154.20

SOLEMNITY of morning and evening, 208.18

SOLITUDE, 200.19; 211.19; 226.42; 236.12; s. and society, 46.14; 265.42; s. makes man attend to the important, 47.1; s. of the Christian, 265.13; s. of those without speech, 61.26; s. which the world cannot relieve, 34.10; calm s. in midst of multitude, 159.4; conceal guilty wishes in s., 3.6; peace in s., 268.24; peoples every s., 142.5; society in the midst of s., 159.5; value of s., 227.5

SOLOMON, 208.31; quoted, 110.29; 250.22

SOLUTION to all my doubts lies in my immediate relation to God, 200.5

SON OF GOD sees our guilt, 3.8

SONG of a bird, 153.21; of the morning stars, 171.20; riotous s. and dances, 10.18; simple relig. s. important, 147.16

SONS of gain, 39.7

SORROW becomes unimportant, 211.12; s. for the past, 7.28; why s. is called selfish; s. described, 140.5

SOUL affected by events of this life, 163.7; as emanation from soul of the world, 245.13; aware of wonder of surrounding creation, 199.34; can gain strength from N.T. and the faith of others, 144.20; cannot reject Christian deity without denying itself, 27.31; contains voice of its eternal inhabitant, 110.26; conscious that its tho'ts are not subject to time or corruption, 202.4; converses with past, distant, future, 202.2; debarred from high events and noble gratification, 7.32; demands tidings of First Cause, 204.7; deserves reverence, 111.22; does not die, 140.25; educated by the world in wonder, 207.7; embraces an act or sentiment as if it were done or said for him only, 208.24; embracing truth and right the s. shares their eternity, 100.14; endures tho circumstances change, 168.34; enlarged by generosity, 210.4; s. entering life finds God's will better than its own, 114.23; enters nearer relation to the Father at death, 140.26; excited to admiration, 211.16; exists for self-improvement, 50.35; experiences newness of revelations, 142.35; experiences no fear or terror, 202.8; finds fellowship thru speech, 62.6; imprisoned in flesh, 138.23; s. in its disembodied state, 141.5ff.; is a golden dial, 17.14; is above the highest copy of living ex-

cellence, 110.12; is an infinite spiritual estate, 105.23; is an inmate of our frail bodies, 136.9; is beset by new temptations in society, 47.17; is calm and untroubled in presence of political or domestic upsets, 201.25; is door of my access to the Father, 200.15; is eternal temple of God, 159.2; is exalted by sentiments the direction of which is unworthy, 157.21; is face the creator uncovers to his child, 200.16; is full of truth, 111.5; is God's beloved child, 50.33; is God's image and likeness, 182.23; is house of God, 110.27; is inmost shrine, 202.8; is lord of inheritance of life and power, 51.5; is made divine by love of God, 133.30; is man within the breast, 65.6; is man's treasure, 266.5; is overlooked in search after externals, 182.23; is something real and noble, 105.11; is stronger than I am; wiser than I am; never approved me in wrong, 200.12; is undeceiving inward monitor, 202.6; knows no persons, 253.14; knows you, tho you wear a mask, 136.18; left in God's care, 141.30; lodged in a frail dwelling, 138.18; made acquainted with secret of its own power, 210.16; made for God's contemplation, 50.34; made to contemplate God's works and moral perfections, 50.33; made to go beyond a sentiment, 157.34; moved by remembrance of home, 19.32; must be born into spiritual world, 114.6; must seek life in itself, 114.20; needs at times conversation, action, bks., 70.27; not absorbed into God, 244.44; not curious about things and events, 51.8; not to be neglected a moment, 102.26; s. of Apostle Paul was fixed, 22.9; s. of dead still near us, 142.34; s. of Jesus filled with virtue, 94.32; s. of man is his higher nature, 113.21; s. of man made to act for others, 130.5; s. of man must live in spiritual world or have no life, 114.4; s. of man we seldom honor—only his circumstances, 181.21; s. of my brother revealed in speech, 61.3; s. of poetry in sentiment and imagination, 145.17; s. of rigid Christian is oppressed by fear, 84.2; s. once servant of senses, 210.15; moral law has dominion over s., 95.16; s. peremptorily asks certain questions, 199.27; s. preferred to body, 189.7; prefers internal evidence to miracles, 124.23; redeemed from bondage of sin, 169.11; refreshed and edified by prayer, 25.6; refuses to be put off with insufficient answers, 199.28; regards end of life as preparation to meet God, 92.10; seeks love and infinite good, 158.1; shines brighter when earthly goods wane, 144.22; sits calm within, 200.11; speaks as with voice of whole creation, 202.6; spotted with sins, 225.5; stripped of all inferiority, xxiii.29; strongly excited on great occasions, 49.15; suggests belief that death cannot harm you, 202.2; wants a pilot, a star, a stronghold, 155.13; wants an object as great as its

172.34; s. and God, 267.14; end of all s. is virtue, 87.34

SPECULATIONS of secondary importance in Christianity, 233.32

SPEECH is bond betw. seen and unseen world, 60.25; diminishes burden of life; augments pleasure, 63.15; is foundation of society, 60.24; necessary for cooperation and affections, 61.33; s. of fellow men worshiped, 157.24; s. of genuine man, 187.11; s. of men exalted into a god, 157.6; s. removes darkness covering man's soul, 61.1; reveals that all men share same moral principles, 64.23; reveals common nature of all men, 62.8; common s. filled with star-lore, 172.14; cooperation impossible without s., 61.33; deceitful forms of s., 226.1; false s., 225.8; good humor prevents rash s., 88.15; how faculty of s. is produced, 60.21; man alone has music of s., 145.7; polished s., 182.9; solitude of those without s., 61.27; suppose s. removed from men, 61.6

SPELLING book, 164.1

SPHERE which man inhabits, 205.11; stars are sphered vessels, 172.1

SPHERES in the depths of the cosmos, 205.11

SPIDER web, 218.41

SPIKENARD, 18.6

SPIN on, Fates! 239.25

SPINDLE, adamantine, 239.26

SPIRIT beareth witness with our s., 133.10; capable of receiving all truth and goodness, 138.11; is eternal, 162.31; is in the world and the world is made by it, 114.3; is never silent, 194.18; s. of Christ is preached to men in daily events, 68.30; s. of dependence on God, 110.22; s. of·God dilates man's heart, 210.20; s. of God dwelleth in you, 132.20; 136.26; s. of God fixed as eternal inhabitant of mind, 73.15; s. of God in us is universal reason, 186.31; s. of God less disguised in good men, 134.12; s. of party, 158.9; s. of truth is one, but speaks by a thousand lips, 194.16; s. of truth more important than letter, 187.1; s. of war, party, self-seeking, rebuked, 135.27; s. out of the body speaks, 142.10; s. that governs creation is in men, 45.14; s. will guide into all truth, 191.2; will show you things to come, 191.4——appeal from letter to the s., 85.34; blessed are the poor in s., 115.13; communication of Divine S., 134.4; contemplative s. amazed, 207.16; disembodied s., 244.24; effect of party s. is exclusiveness, 86.21; eighteen diff. senses in which the word *spirit* is used, 223.14; evil s. might perform miracles, 123.21; fates and actions of an unbodied s., 141.34; fearful s. only asks what it must do; it makes no conditions; it questions nothing, 84.6; friendship of the eternal S., 162.28; the Holy S., xx.3; Jesus groaned in s., 56.30; let us hear what the s. saith unto the churches, 86.18; madness of party s., 78.20; the Holy S., 268.20; there is a world of N. and anr. of s., 113.30; this s. is the s. of truth, 257.12; vehicle of God's s., 162.17; when s. of truth is come, 191.2; world of s., 1.23; see *Holy Ghost, Holy Spirit; soul.*

SPIRITS have not forgot any good work, 245.22; in prison, 229.8; s. of just men made perfect, 3.7; pass from this world to that of s., 104.31; glorified s. of departed parishioners, 38.22; good and evil s. solicit a man, 210.10; good and evil s. struggle to make a man their own, 210.11; millions of rational s. epitomize their fate in history, 208.22; world of s. more stable, 1.25

SPIRITUALISM defended by Jesus, 198.34; dismissed, 245.19

SPLENDOR of shell's colors, 221.45

SPORT of the winds of fortune, 258.44

SPOT: every s. of world is made venerable by great men, 52.8; nat'l process not limited to one s., 43.18

SPRING of action, 154.8

SPRINGS of wonder in us, 207.7

SPROUT: tiny s. of the blackberry, 207.34

STABILITY belongs to genuineness of character, 188.8

STAGE: first s. in relig. education, 232.13

STAKE of execution, 228.15; men inquire after their several s., 199.23; private s., 186.24

STAKES, deep, 187.20

STAND by and let reason argue, 186.14; s. having your loins girt, 180.2; brave s. of Jesus for man's spiritual nature *vs.* sensualism, 195.30; here you s., 156.26; self-love hasn't any ground to s. on, 135.20; we s. in midst of two worlds, 1.21; we s. on same ground as our fathers, 54.6

STANDARD by which actions are judged, 178.3; s. of character found in every human breast, 110.11; s. of private virtue nowhere high, 79.4; s. of success diff. from what prevails, 190.10; s. of virtue in world is average of individual virtue, 81.7; heavenly s. of Jesus, 124.27; moral s. doesn't shift with seasons, 15.16

STANDARD MAN believed in, 64.35; gives rule and guide for our discourse, 65.4; we shall come nearer the s-m., 64.28; 64.33

STAR attracts s., 176.16; s. by s. expires, 8.3; s. in its crown, 141.9; hitch wagon to a s., 252.9; soul wants a s., 155.14

STARS are symbols of power and beauty, 172.11; believed to move round the earth, 173.30; misunderstood as power and intelligence, 172.12; not counted, 196.30; pour rays upon our globe, 194.14; before the s. were launched, 113.28; bring down the s., 252.5; creature to observe the s. and write their laws, 177.2; eternal truths come out like s., xxxv.14; song of the morning s., 171.20; see heavenly *bodies.*

STARTLE with sounding paradoxes, xix.17

STATE and the individual, 266.28; s. is safe as long as men follow conscience, 76.8; s. of the real person ignored in the parade, 182.22; s. of world is best when men's characters are unlike, 106.34; barbarous s. of society, 195.11; in whatever s. we are, 136.2; individual and s., 75.1; life in anr. s., 9.30; prayer is a s. of mind—a state of continual preparation, 216.11; prominence in s., 211.33; well-constituted s. will have gov't out of sight, 77.2

STATE HOUSE, 190.2

STATES of mind valued only as marked by deeds, 85.28

STATESMAN: wise s. educates lowest class, 129.12

STEELE, Mrs. Anne, 147.33

STEP of an archangel, 188.24; s. of person in neighboring room, 50.16; each s. leads to anr., 193.13; every s. in relig. life increases the extent of our prospect, 250.9; walk but a s. at a time, 236.1

STEPHENSON, [?George], 188.28

STEPS toward dissolution, 112.6; more s. taken for perishable objects, 2.12

STEWARDSHIP: God will recompense honest, 18.32; unfaithful s., 19.9

STIMULUS of a great occasion needed by many, 16.14

STING of death removed, 144.26

STOICS, 200.26; S. assumed an indwelling God, 133.23; said wise man differed from God only in duration, 133.23; were reformers, 52.22

STONE, 244.30; melted s., 112.14

STONE CHAPEL, Boston, 150.22

STONES: cause s. to speak, 123.17

STORE, going to the, 189.14

STORM, value of, 42.30

STORMS instruct, 208.19

STORY, all love a wonderful, 152.3

STRAINS of eloquence, xix.27

STRANGER: Christ is s. to his church, 237.24; no s. to pastoral work, 220.17

STRANGERS to God, 132.15; s. to ourselves, 162.18

STRAWBERRY described, 41.25; s. requires more exquisite art than a palace, 41.24

STRAWS, mind often dedicated to mere, 47.22

STREET corner is closet, 3.16; good in the s. but not in the closet, 157.13

STREETS of brick and stone, 39.13

STRENGTH for the burden, 268.6; s. must love God, 15.21; s. of character, 165.17; s. of institutions is greater than our own, 165.8; s. of men would fail on Jupiter, 173.12; bands of s., 19.15; Christian gives s. to great duties, 51.12; had it s. as it has right it would govern the world, 95.14; love Lord thy God with all thy s., 53.10; our work brings with it the s. it needs, 169.19; real s. is found only in soul, 201.18

STRENGTHENING one's virtuous propensities, 58.8

STRETCH the spiritual muscles, xxi.28

STRIPPING human soul of all inferiority, xxiii.29

STRONGHOLD, soul wants a, 155.14

STRUCTURE of civilization, 210.30; s. of man is theistical, 247.33; s. of race on other planets diff., 173.15; s. of mind aids apprehension of God, xxiv.29

STRUGGLE: internal s. for growth, 255.4

STUDENTS of nat'l science are simple and amiable men, 222.19

STUDIES: trifling s. degrade mind, 48.7

STUDY of oneself, 17.7; God worthy of endless s., 83.21; most worth one's s., 211.24

STYLE of Jesus' discourses was very simple, 91.12

SUBJECT: always a s. for life and for each hour, xxxi.28

SUBJECTS like human liberty, retributions, analysis of affections etc., 244.36; s. of perception, 1.13; s. of sermons, 36.8; 36.20; how E. found s. for sermons, xxxi.29

SUBLIME in *Acts of the Apostles*, 160.23; s. preaching of Channing, xii.13

SUBLIMITIES of the moving universe, 205.9

SUBMISSION to God's will, 160.16

SUBSTANCE of seed fed from ground, 43.15; s. sacrificed for the shadow, 255.1; miss the s. whilst we grasp the shadow, 88.25

SUBSTITUTES sought for vital piety, 15.30; unworthy s. of God, 161.30

SUBSTRATUM of everything is God, 221.21; God is s. of all souls, 243.4

SUBTERFUGES of language, 4.11

SUCCESS assured a good purpose, 21.2; s. not on the world's standard, 190.11; s. of Jesus, 56.25

SUCCORS spring up from a thousand quarters, 160.32

SUFFER: Emerson did not affect to, 258.16; those called to s., 157.18

SUFFERERS and God, 160.16

SUFFERING and death will be righted in the end, 159.31; s. forgotten when Reason is exercised, 210.24; s. is only a trifle, xxxi.2; doctrine of Vicarious S., 232.20; peace in s. is the miracle of faith, 160.22

SUFFERINGS of man become unimportant, 211.4; s. of vast masses, 198.6; s. which faith turns to happiness, 162.5; our s. are small compared to accessible enjoyments, 258.20

SUFFRAGE: universal s. in U.S., 75.7

SUICIDE of soul is indolence, 8.1; falsehood is s., 210.6

SUM of good, 128.7; s. of relig. is: do thyself no harm, 269.35

SUMMARY of the new law, 115.17

SUMMER, 39.1; 265.14; s. and winter, 208.18

SUMMERS: body scarcely lasts eighty s., 138.19

SUMMITS: lifting everlasting s. into light, 35.11

SUN, a globe of fire, 207.30; s. and stars once tho't to move round the earth, 173.30; s. brightened by man's love, 210.5; gone down in darkness, 8.27; grudges light to unperceptive, 193.6; has made tour of heavens every day, 207.33; seems but a funeral fire, 112.26; eleven globes revolve around s., 173.15; light and darkness caused by s., 35.24; magnitude of s. measured, 52.12; worlds that journey around, 173.19

SUNDAY schools, 196.1; 198.7; 270.6

SUNS: millions are burning, 174.18

SUNSET described, 171.33

SUNSHINE of ease, 33.13

SUPERIORITY of spiritual truths, 195.22; s. of the view taken by the soul, 136.20; calm s. at the disturbances in the world, 201.24

SUPERLATIVE used in admiration, 152.8

SUPERSTITION, 184.33; s. combined with Lord's Supper, 55.30

SUPERSTITIONS of our fathers, 232.32

SUPPOSITION that man can act upon sublime principles, 105.5

SUPREME, love of the, 6.28

SUPREME BEING, 6.33

SURFACE of globe witnesses same nat'l processes, 43.19

SURFACES hide the lameness and imperfection of character, 182.18

SURPRISE at every impertinent trifle, 204.13; s. at ourselves, 203.6; Prince's s. to find himself in Paris, 203.9

SURRENDER to God, 104.2

SUSPECTED men, xviii.30

SUSTENANCE of man is pleasant, 43.11

SWEDENBORG, Emanuel, possible infl. of, 234.43; quoted, 186.9

SYLLABLE of reproach, 9.16

SYLLABLES, 145.15

SYMBOLS and symbolism, xxxviii. 31; stars are s. of power and beauty, 172.11; see *types*.

SYMMETRY of oration, xviii.19

SYMPATHY, 10.11; s. betw. speaker and audience, 26.20; s. of friends cannot lessen solitude, 34.12; desire for s., 237.12; invisible s. of the dead, 142.15; riddle of human s. solved, 243.4; soul finds only in God, 201.28

SYRIAN shepherd, 172.3

SYSTEM built on fear of sin, 231.26; s. of compensations, 10.33; s. of the heavens, 174.32; s. of relig. opinion magnified by its adherents, 86.3; s. of social duty, 131.22; s. of the universe described, 175.32; Calvinism a dark and barbarous s., 147.30; every s. of theology based on some fundamental principle, 231.6

SYSTEMS of opinion doubted, 175.27; s. of paganism, 55.13; s. of relig. tho't,

83.26; best s. of education not studied, 2.22; denominational s. built on unquestionable facts, 82.14

T

TABERNACLE: if t. were dissolved, 138.2

TABLE, intemperate at, 16.9

TACITUS, 209.15; quoted, 217.39

TALE of metamorphosis in poetry, 42.8; magic t. is experience of man, 76.35

TALENT of each man, 164.18; t. of hearing good sermons, 228.34

TALENTS found in groups of men, 46.6; t. of the individual shape his profession, 166.3; t. will be exercised with more freedom after death, 169.3

TALK: aim and end of t. is the truth, 65.7

TALKING, tired of, 248.7

TASK, intellectual men must know their own t., 229.11

TASTE discovered for new employment, 166.18; divine t. displayed in the architecture of the world, 222.2; pleasure of t., 43.11

TASTES of men uniform, 64.24

TAX we pay for social advantages, 39.11

TAYLOR, Jeremy, 249.3; worships with Calvin etc., xxxviii.26

TAZEWELL, [Mr.], 181.25

TEACH: Jesus did not t. like scribes, 90.2; minister can t. no more than he has, 32.20; none can t. faster than scholar can learn, xxxx.1; none can t. more than he knows, xxxix.35

TEACHER and pupil, 55.3; t. expected, 202.10; has not yet finished his word, 199.9; t. identified with the teaching, 233.35; t. is greatest gift of God, 192.29; t. must have freedom, xxxx.6ff.; must say what is given to him, xxxx.3; must say what scholar can understand, xxxx.2; t. of moral law must speak as a God unto men, 95.17; t. of moral truth participates in its authority, 95.15; t. sent from God, 120.3; the t., which is the Spirit of Truth, is one, but speaks from a thousand lips, 194.15; t. who hath been predicted and hath not yet come, 199.22; 256.12; anr. t. promised by Jesus, 197.1; Christ's chief office is t., 233.35; future t. will tell greater things, 197.7; Jesus as a moral t., 90.7; Jesus our Common T., 92.31; Jesus sent anr. t. who would guide disciples into all truth, 193.24; method of Jesus as t., 91.3; promised t. is Spirit of Truth, 194.2; time, the greatest t., utters his lessons, 194.4; truth is the t. of the human race, 194.34; wisest t. can impart no more than pupil can receive, 197.9

TEACHERS of mankind, 126.16; t. of wisdom in N.T., 126.3; a thousand t. preach gospel, 69.7; disciples were sincere t., 125.14; distinction betw. t. as to living and dead truth, 92.33; Jesus' superiority over other t., 92.25; Jesus unlike other t., 91.31; many moral t. before Jesus, 96.33; pains are t., 258.30

TEACHING for which all men are waiting, 256.12; is end of youth, growth, play etc., 192.31; t. is the perpetual end and office of all things, 192.29; t. of Christ remembered, 235.3; t. of Christ unlocked by "know thyself," 200.31; t. of Jesus rather than resurrection gives evidence of immortality, 238.34; all men are waiting for t., 192.21; essential condition of t. is a ripe pupil, 197.8; recorded t. of Jesus, 196.21; reform in public relig. t., 201.9; two conditions of t., xxxix.34

TEACHINGS of scriptures valuable in themselves apart from the documents, 124.26

TEARS of widow, 9.9

TECHNICAL eliminated from sermons, xxii.15; t. in relig. abolished, 201.9

TELESCOPE, 174.18; fatal to ancient theology and astronomy, 174.33

TELL, William, 152.25

TEMPER of a man, 166.5; dare we indulge t. in presence of N., 42.26

TEMPERAMENT in relig., 89.1

TEMPERANCE required for health, 123.1; how achieved, 127.23; t. societies, 198.7

TEMPEST, ship in a, 234.19

TEMPLE of Christ and of God, xxvi.9; t. of heathen, 102.12; ancient t., 38.18; body is t. of Holy Ghost, xxvi.7; one's neighbor is also a t. of Divine Presence, 136.29; ye are the t. of the Holy Ghost, 136.26

TEMPLES not made with hands, 170.3; grand t. and palaces, 180.18

TEMPTATION, 267.42; destroyed by purity, 210.5; finds us off our guard, 20.28; t. to act from external motives, 185.30; t. to join church from bad motives, 59.6; enduring t., 269.14; those resisting t. are rewarded, 10.35

TEMPTATIONS are our evil angels, 258.25; new t. beset soul in society, 47.18; the dead help us in t., 142.17

TENANTS of other regions, 177.20

TENDENCIES, individual true to early, xxxviii.13

TENDENCY and end of actions important, 14.8; beneficial t. in astronomy, 175.29; t. to emphasize trifles is an evil of social life, 46.25

TENEMENT and state house both open to honor, 190.2

TENEMENTS filled with poor, 9.22

TERM of human life longer than formerly, 54.25

TERMS, God interpreted in subjective, xxiv.7; outworn t. like *grace, atonement*, 27.27

TERROR in a man's nature, 225.12

TERRORS of justice, 212.4; no t. in soul at approach of death, 202.7

TEST of character is piety at home, 15.34; t. of true advancement in relig. life, 250.8

TESTIMONY of scriptures, 85.30; t. to soul's shifting character, 5.9; miracle is a t., xxviii.21

TESTS of a truth, 230.37

TEXT for sermon lacking, 218.16; t. of the N.T., 219.4

TEXTURE of integrity, 188.29; t. of the soul, 10.23

THANKSGIVING, 266.4; reasons for t., 267.38

THAT which I am in words, I am the same in life, 186.6; t. which is made for immortal life must be of an infinite nature, 105.7

THEATRE, vast, 187.21; world is t. of men's virtues, 52.9

THEISMS, choice of, 151.1; 247.32; 269.27

THEOLOGY and secular world both share same division of opinion, 82.16; t. enlarged by astronomy, 173.28; t. is gropings of infant weakness, xxiii.7; t. of Belknap's collection of hymns, 148.8; bks. of t., 199.19; every system of t. is based on some fundamental principle, 231.7; highest t. is inadequate, xxiii.6; old system of t., 174.31; speculative method in t., xxiv.19

THEORY: our t. the true one, 232.37

THING: considered a small t. to injure the truth, 254.41; miracle is only a t. of blind wonder, 96.1; only one t. is needful, 46.3; 48.9; same name and place are not the same t., 54.16

THINGS apprehended by senses nicely groved into each other, 204.3; t. are flitting away, 113.25; t. for use, not for ornament, 47.7; t. perish in the using, 113.5; t. take the hue of our tho't, 101.31; t. 1000 yrs. old communicated to man, 208.23; t. to come, 191.4; t. unaffected by time and place, 244.32; all t. are cunningly constructed, 207.17; all t. are double, one against anr., 102.17; all t. decay to nat'l man, 113.17; all t. are eternal to spiritual man, 113.18; all t. change except the soul, 136.11; all t. have purpose, 220.40; all t. poured into man's bosom as if world had no other child, 208.34; all t. preach the moral law, 122.34; all t. revolve around each grain of sand, 207.23; all t. roll round man and scatter gifts, 208.12; all t. seen with partial eye, 78.26; all t. teach us, 192.34; all t. transformed into the divine, 211.14; all t. work together for good, 259.21; attention turned to great t., 53.1; beneath outward shows of t., 227.2; commerce with outward t., 114.11; external t. should be man's servants, not masters, 183.30; forgetting the t. that are behind, 163.2; from centre to circumference of t., 159.18; God will make all t. equal in the end, 159.32; great t. unimportant compared with oneself, 8.21; greater t. than these shall ye do, 193.26; 197.32; greatness lies in way of doing t.,

60.13; he shall show you t. to come, 257.16; harmony betw. tho'ts and t., 6.15; human heart impatient of t. finite, 152.19; humble t. of mortal date, 2.26; imperishable t. of soul, 2.15; leave t. signified, xxxviii.31; life is cast among little t., 53.4; little t. not overemphasized, 47.6; must feel reality of t. unseen, 2.31; outward t., 216.22; outward t. have been credited with too much power, 164.32; perception of spiritual t. is faith, 250.32; perishable t. of sense, 2.14; reaching for t. that are before, 163.2; relig. flowing from all t., xxxv.30; spiritual t. are as distinct as brass and stone, and eternal as they are not, 244.30; spiritual t. misrepresented in hymns, 149.15; voice of t., 109.16; words are t., 269.21; words that are t., 226.27

THINK before we speak, 66.29; with one's audience in mind, xviii.18; as men t. more, Christianity is found to mean more, 55.17; if we t. as Jesus thought, we become one with him, 98.8; men t. as they are expected to t., 108.30; men t. grossly about God, 3.34; men want neighbor to t. as they do, 88.8; sit down to t. and world believes you have headache, 227.8; we don't t. *alone*, 3.4; we t. differently because we sin so much, 243.5; we say exactly what we t., 232.41; we shall t. alike someday, 243.8; we were made to t. alike, 134.10; what will people t.? 49.3

THINKS: as a man t., so he is and so he receives, 102.2

THINKING well of human nature, 270.20

THISTLES, harvest of, 102.27; man seeking comforts sows t., 50.23

THORN, every rose has its, 258.18; no t. without its rose, 258.19

THOUGHT is corrected and developed in conversation, 62.22; t. of God appears in healthy mind, xxiv.30; t. of one cannot penetrate to t. of the other, 61.32; a vivid t. brings the power to paint it, 220.13; astronomy is t. and harmony in matter, 253.33; beyond the intention of your t., 156.28; by t. to raise an arm, 122.14; celestial t. had to wait the tardy expansion of the worldly mind, 197.10; energy of t. imparted to a mind in love, 153.17; few men have analyzed every t., 90.19; first t. that arises, xxxi.30; genuine man acts his t., 185.3; God is the grand object of all t., 92.9; great men present very dissimilar ideas to one's t., 107.1; heaven of t. exists for each man alone, 208.34; high t. and noble virtue, 10.8; immortal t. comes nearest practical value in education, 2.20; Jesus' truth becomes echo of our own t., 98.8; laws of t. not accommodated to divisions of time, 70.34; love of t. and moral beauty, 10.10; man becomes servant of t. and tries to subject creation to it, 198.20; man capable of t. and virtue, 209.4; man should

follow his own t., 184.27; man's t. reflected in N., xxiv.11; new force given trival t. when it is fresh result of one's own observation, 93.17; no t. should break the law of souls, 116.26; nothing permanent but t., 2.7; one who has t. on questions of human duty, 212.3; reality of t., 2.2; things take the hue of our t., 101.31; true t. puts man in harmony with the eternal, 211.28; vast t. of faith, 162.1; we cannot see processes of t., 1.11; whole astronomy suspended in a t., 252.11

THOUGHTS and acts animated by faith, 162.8; t. and passions are parts of imperishable universe, 2.35; t. are not shadows of the moment, 3.1; t. are tamely uniform everywhere, 107.6; t. belong to world of spirit, 1.23; t. dear to the best men, 192.13; t. fixed on character, not on condition, 190.12; t. in difficult times, 127.22; t. in service of sin, 3.23; t. may be read by some beings, 1.17; t. mustered and clarified more vigorously in conversation, 62.19; t. never lose their immortal youth, 239.35; t. of men's minds differ, 106.29; t. of others are like our own, 62.6; t. of soul have no relation to time or corruption, 202.4; t. show a standard idea of man, 64.29; arrangement of t., 239.6; 239.7; better to relate t. than to let them smother, 62.25; cast your t. about, 106.30; cleanse the t., 12.6; coincidence of first and third t., xxxiii.17; communication of t. is miracle, 122.15; every man has t. shared by no other, 106.29; every mind has its virtuous t., 72.5; eyes kept only on one's own t., 109.14; first and third t. coincide, 110.2; God's t. are not like man's t., 97.15; greatest and truest t. do not flash upon soul in a moment, 70.20; harmony betw. t. and things, 6.14; he who watches his t., 159.3; Jesus serves us only by his holy t., 253.14; men's t. judged by their words and actions, 216.15; proverbs are happy t. of wise men, 63.6; sad t. are mixed with promises of N.T., 144.17; taking the *mean* of one's t., xxxi.31; train of t. checked, 1.18; we have no faculties for seeing the t. of men, 216.15; we speak with force whenever we rely on our own t., 109.17

THOUSANDS at God's bidding speed, 104.16; t. intombed in a moment, 112.16; Calvin and Wesley think for t., 237.16

THREAD, fragile, 239.26

THUNDER of the laws and customs of mankind, 184.7; clap of t. has a hundred echoes, 125.34

THUNDERER in the sky is not God, 162.9

TIDAL waves, 112.13

TIDINGS: glad t. of great joy, 33.8

TIE betw. earth and heaven, 144.14

TIES in life should not hold you from right, 168.11; t. of home soon severed, 20.1; no t. of opinion to each other, 232.36

TIGER, 165.29

TRIFLER thinks too much of himself, 182.29

TRIFLES, 46.1; 205.29; 265.22; t. are neglected in hour of death, 34.30; t. despised by Christian, 50.27; destroyed by time, xxxv.9; in politics, 229.35; t. unman and enslave, 50.13; child should learn to despise t., 51.29; cities degrade by magnifying t., 222.35; diff. betw. slighting t. and going studiously wrong in t., 51.20; never more agitated by t., 211.32; t. one of evils of social life, 47.1; rule safeguarding us from t., 53.8; scorn t., 222.26; worldly pursuits are t., 114.17

TRINITARIANISM, 148.27

TRINITARIANS wrongly considered opposite of Unitarians, 87.1

TRINITY, 233.31; doctrine of T. doesn't follow from principles, 84.19; T. opposed, 148.22

TRINKETS, men interested in, 48.28

TROUBLE, consolation in, 267.26

TROUBLES are unimportant to heart feeling God's presence, 160.3; become unimportant—even valuable, 211.11

TRUE to yourself, 190.9; views of the t. enlarged, 167.31

TRUST emerges thru all evil, danger, death, 212.18; t. in God gives more contentment than possessions, 114.27; t. in the Lord, 268.28; t. in the unseen, infinite mind, 161.25; t. the wisdom of God, 107.30; t. yourself, 105.1; 267.24; neglect a t., 232.22; no small t. to have keeping of a soul, 105.14; power regarded as a prize instead of a t., 229.36; we hold everything in t., 135.22

TRUSTS: powers are t. for greatest possible use, 241.17

TRUSTWORTHINESS of universal reason, 186.32

TRUTH, 207.12; 264.24; 270.28; a circle, 28.27; t. about meaning of life not confined to gospel, xxvi.28; always convinces, 95.24; t. and miracle mutually confirm each other, 123.25; t. and reason argued for Webster, 65.18; t. and right are of God everlasting, 100.13; t. alone makes a man a mediator, 177.33; t. alone tolerable to the petulance of grief, 226.23; t. can never be a loss, 136.21; t. cannot be altered, 132.13; t. comes to have solidity thru the personal, 234.15; concealed from literal eyes, xxxviii.23; t. endures, 194.6; t. finds light, 102.21; hidden by our ignorance, 3.30; hindered by love or fear of man, 219.8; t. in Jesus was *living* t., 92.32; t. in Liberal Christianity, 232.37; t. in proverbs, 225.26; t. in revivals is impure food, but it will lead to better aliment, 232.14; t. injured for reasons of livelihood, 254.41; t. is always new from the mind that perceives it, 93.18; t. is end and aim of our talk, 65.8; t. is stranger than fiction, 203.13; t. is the teacher of the human race, 194.34; t. is the victor in an argument, 65.9; t. loved above party, 231.36; t. not always attained in this life, 64.32; t. not

completely opened by Jesus, 193.29; t. not sought for itself, 48.12; t. of a doctrine—how tested, 230.39; t. of an adversary, 65.16; t. of character, 188.10; t. of character defined, 184.26; t. of character identical with relig. life, 188.34; t. of Christianity should be taught simply, 27.14; t. that spirit world is more permanent is hard to acquire, 2.8; t. of Jesus, 114.22; t. of Jesus related to all our being, 138.5; t. of relig., 228.14; t. of relig. attested by all facts, 28.22; t. of the defense of faith, 161.22; t. of the N.T., 138.24; t. perishes with no man, 69.14; t. possessed only as we are true, 102.4; t. stronger when recommended by eloquence, 63.19; t. taught by Jesus contains an interest that attaches to persons, 234.13; t. taught by Jesus should not be separated from his office, 96.16; t. taught in one's own name, 233.36; t. that church is deposit of t. is questionable, xxvii.1; t. that men are partakers of the divine nature, 133.4; t. violated a little in eulogies, 152.23; t. vividly seen leads to action, 94.17; t. wanted by the mourner, not prating, 226.22; t. will be found by the seeker, 85.10; t. will emerge even from arguments offered against it, 102.14; t. worth more than its effects, 198.27——a vital t. may be announced in a moment, 117.25; action should square with one's conception of it, 116.21; all t. is related, 269.10; all t. teaches lessons, 194.27; Andrew Fletcher was a man of t., 156.9; as if one conversed with t. and justice, 186.21; authority belongs to t. and not to any person, 97.8; authority accompanies moral t., 94.34; be girt with t., 190.6; beauty and excellence of moral t., 196.9; because I tell you the t. ye believe not, 197.21; borrow something of eternal t. from extremes, 87.16; by opening the same elementary t. we follow Jesus, 97.19; conflicting opinions based on great t., 86.22; connexion betw. moral t. and right action, 94.17; conscience is the t. teller, 67.11; danger of losing portion of t. which one defends, 88.1; development of t. in mind is not periodical, 71.1; diff. sorts of t. and diff. ways to possess and communicate t., 92.26; divine t. and scriptural imagery, 29.7; do we possess Jesus' t. merely by possessing his words? 92.28; earnest desire for t., 243.7; every mind has its favorite resorts in domain of t., 72.5; field of moral t. barren until peopled with examples, 234.22; force of divine t., 20.24; fortified t. with impregnable reason, 91.1; genuine man speaks, thinks, acts t., 254.20; good man a better judge of t., 94.14; goodness revealed to Jesus was so much t., 96.22; he who possesses t. will move you, 95.27; highest t. concerns relations of man to God, 194.27; indisputable t. that all experience preaches doctrines of gospel, 69.3; intention of t. demanded by virtue,

226.16; prolific effects of t. illustrated, 197.26; Jesus had much more t. to make known, 193.21; Jesus never said, "All t. I have revealed," 196.33; Jesus taught the supreme kind of t., 91.28; Jesus' t. becomes echo of our own tho't, 98.8; kingdom of t. cannot grow old, 114.1; law of t., 225.7; literal t. not highest virtue, 186.34; living and moral t., 93.22; living t. as applied to morals, 94.25; living t. contrasted with dead t.; first-hand with second-hand, 93.1; loins girt about with t., 180.3; love of t., 117.17; lover of t., 171.5; men will sometime come to the t., 64.33; miracle as evidence for moral t., 122.33; moral t. commands as soon as perceived, 93.23; moral t. defined, 93.26; moral t. does not grow old, 239.36; moral t. has fruitfulness, creative force, unfolding power, energy, 198.29; moral t. moves human nature more than miracles, 95.30; moral t. not disturbed by astronomy, 177.19; men reach higher t. thru N., 177.6; new t., 161.1; new t. emerges when we are doing our best, 257.11; no artifice possible in dealing with t., 95.26; omnipotence of t., 197.25; our force is superhuman when we rely on immortal t., 109.20; philosophic t. says every faculty is mode of God's action, 4.12; prerequisites for discovery of t., xxv.31: relation of t. to t. observed in conversation, 62.21; revelation of t. must accompany a miracle, 123.24; road to t., 232.16; self-reliance is falling back upon t., 110.25; simple t. never seems enough to some people, 225.33; sins are enemies of t., 98.1; soul is full of t., 111.5; source of t., 158.35; speak your own t. without addition or abatement, xxxx.8; speaker of t., 186.16; spirit capable of receiving all t. and goodness, 138.13; spirit of t. more important than letter, 187.2; spirit of t. will guide you into all t., 191.2; spiritual t. open to investigation of all, 71.35; strict adherence to t. at all risks, 14.30; supreme kind of t. relates to man's moral nature, 91.28; teacher of moral t. participates of its authority, 95.15; t. to me is t. to neighbor, 64.24; unrelated t. of geography in mind of child, 93.6; utterance of t. is the Messiah's office, 96.20; voice of t., 219.1; we can do nothing against Jesus' t., 97.32; what new t. has been revealed, 190.17; when a man is awakened to t. and virtue, 211.8; words of t. show more courtesy, 226.2

TRUTHS are now being revealed, 199.11; t. in N.T. will stand by themselves, 125.3; t. of relig. are salvation of the human soul, 111.1; t. unfolded by Jesus not disturbed by astronomy, 178.7; t. which ages toiled to prove, 55.1; eternal t. come out like stars, xxxv.14; great t. of relig. discovered by men of self-reliance, 111.1; Jesus declared t. on which depends the soul's welfare, 96.27; moral t. cannot be numbered or ended, 196.31; moral t. illustrated, 95.7; moral

t. of N.T. incompatible with supposition of imposture, 125.9; primal t., 192.5; solemn t., xix.16; sublime t. are to be studied rather than comprehended, 192.8; superiority of spiritual t., 195.22

TUITION of man by lore of the ages, 208.21

TULIP, why so richly dyed? 222.2

TUNE of music-box, xxiv.31

TURBULENCE beyond power of police, 129.14

TURKS on heaven, 243.41

TURN: our t. has come, 117.19; our t. to make our election, 117.28

TYPE: each man a t. found nowhere else in universe, 108.13

TYPES: take away t. but leave things signified, xxxviii.31

TYRANNY, men call gospel of Christ a, 23.35

TYRANTS have found life long enough to enslave men, 117.23

U

UMPIRE, who is the, 157.3

UNBELIEF, miracle speaks to, 124.20

UNBELIEVER in miracles, 122.3

UNCERTAINTY about laws of N. would be disastrous, 124.7; u. with which men speak of God, 132.11

UNCIRCUMCISION, disputes about, xxxv.2

UNCTION, extreme, xxxv.6

UNDERSTANDING has greater reach in good men, 161.1; u. of the mind opened by faith, 161.6; u. ourselves, 111.28; u. pleads on basis of fiction, 3.19; u. surrendered to error, 102.15; u. would run forever in round of second causes, if soul didn't ask for First Cause, 204.5; human u. must always bow to great laws of Jesus, 91.35; question of u. concerning God and soul, 2.17; shallow u. or ill example of men, 8.17; sing praises with u., 145.2; unaided light of one's own u., 109.25; we should gratefully borrow light from anr's u., 109.31

UNDERTAKINGS, 200.15

UNHAPPINESS, uses of, 263.16

UNIFORMITY of action and conversation is dangerous, 106.22

UNION stands in low esteem, 229.34; highest faith is intimate u. with God, 161.13

UNITARIAN, 257.35; U. and Orthodox Christians distinguished, 233.2; U. church has plain walls, 150.29; Newton became a U., 175.3; objection to U. denomination, 86.34

UNITARIANS: how do U. believe? 87.12; pale negations of U., 232.45; U. say exactly what they think, 232.41; see *Liberal Christians*.

UNITE with others in making efforts for true relig. of any avail, 88.33

UNITED STATES meets test of perfect gov't, 77.26; most perfect gov't, 77.21; recognizes rights of man, 77.12; cause of evils in U.S., 78.35; condition of U.S. is index of average degree of private virtue, 80.8; constitution of the U.S., 75.13; evil signs in U.S., 78.17; 78.24; instruction in U.S., 75.11; politics in U.S., 76.12; schools in U.S., 75.13; U.S. settlers were not bad men, 78.35; universal suffrage in U.S., 75.7

UNITY of God, 102.7; 102.12; u. *vs.* separation, 129.2

UNIVERSAL empire, 269.29; u. reason in the mind, 186.30

UNIVERSALITY, a test of truth, 230.38; u. of admiration, 247.34; u. of law of duty, 76.7

UNIVERSE has mind behind it, 44.1; invites man's industry, 8.15; sees that endeavors do not fail of their end, 7.3; superintended by God, xxiii.16; all facts in U. attest to truth of relig., 28.22; constitution of u. is moral, 122.34; decays of u., 113.16; economy of u., 10.21; embrace the u. and bring down the stars, 252.5; God is the servant of the u., 221.42; God's justice in the u., 66.10; God's will is the good of the u., 131.33; heart of the u., 186.28; history of the u., 2.27; imperishable u. of morals, 3.3; laws of u. to be learned where we are, 163.26; man's true position in u., 211.17; material u. less stable than spiritual, 2.1; men born for the u. narrowed their mind, 86.10; one's neighbor is a part of God's u., 131.33; world overflows into u., 249.37

UNPOPULARITY, 211.6

URN, world is a large, 112.26

URANUS, climate of, 173.12; 173.7

URN is made of clay, 132.25

USAGE of preaching is too straitened, 27.20

USE of afflictions and pains, 35.30; u. of names avoided by good men, 86.32; u. the light we have, 257.9; all things perish with u., 113.5; everything was made for u., 166.22; freedom disappears without u., 236.14; greatest possible u. of our powers, 241.17; no u. in knowledge until verified by us, 118.9; pain is all of u. to man, 85.16; power put to better u., 18.22; sentiments serve higher u., 157.30

USEFULNESS, 176.23; lost by excessive grief, 143.15; occasions of u., 16.26; one sort of u. for each man, 165.20; wider u. in God's service, 104.21

USES of the storm, 42.30; u. of unhappiness, 263.16

V

VALIDITY of a thing is not dependent on origin, 244.8

VALLEY of death, 35.9

VALUE of a well-spent hour, 17.24ff.; v. of faith in god, 158.28; conclusion of practical v., xxi.18; educative v. of evil,

258.29; eternal v. of a relig. faith, 73.9; practical v. of education of soul, 2.21

VANITIES of dress, 10.17

VANITY in the preacher, 30.6

VAPOR, life but a, 243.28

VARIETIES leveled by death, 265.17

VARIETY in each profession explained by personal character, 165.32; 166.1; v. in our thinking is the result of sin, 243.6; v. in sermon subjects, 72.12; v. of mind not evident in modern society, 107.5; v. of motives, 184.30; v. offered by seasons, 41.4

VAST and unbounded, 152.22

VAULT, sparks in the, 171.34

VEGETABLE is a machine separating nutritious matter, 43.6

VEGETATION gives new expression from moment to moment of Divine goodness, 39.24; mighty process of v., 39.19

VEHICLE of God's spirit, 162.16

VEIL, 185.34; removed from the creator, 175.23

VENERATION of Almighty Father, 211.9

VENGEANCE of God diverted by Christ's blood, 199.22; earth was scaffold of divine v., 174.31; withholding v., 66.11

VENTURE, the Christian, 270.4

VERACITY, 93.33

VERITIES of relig. have been strained out of shape, 238.41

VESSELS, stars are sphered, 172.1

VESTRIES, 171.23

VESTRY, dedication of, 271.9; new v. dedicated, 218.43

VIA eminentiae, xxiii.31

VIAL, see *Phial.*

VICARIOUS suffering of Christ, 232.20

VICE considered by society less evil than awkwardness and vulgarity, 47.16; v. has refined forms in society, 47.15; is unnatural and superficial, 231.15; v. or virtue, 9.3; v. begets v., 81.1; v. would inflict woe, 35.24; charity considered a bounty to v., 131.15

VICES, 7.33; v. of society affect view of honor, 157.7; flattering one's v., 219.33; private v. become public v., 79.32; whip for one's v., 101.29

VICISSITUDES of life, 155.14

VICTOR in an argument is truth, 65.9

VICTORIES, bloody, 180.17

VICTORY over egotism is Christian, 65.14

VIEW of Church differs from that of street dweller, 113.31; v. of God exalted; of man, humbled—by astronomy, 172.32; v. of God's wrath, xx.20; every v. of relation of man to God is valuable, 245.15; gloomy v. of death, 243.27; mourner's small v. of God, 139.20

VIEWPOINT: sharing v. of God and angels, 227.4

VIEWS of God in church and college were inadequate, 175.18; confused v. of God, 148.10; men of extended v., 152.16; partial v. account for systems of relig.

tho't, 83.27; superficial v. will not always satisfy us, 204.16

VIGILANCE required by citizen, 78.16

VILLANY not unmasked, 3.27

VILLIERS, George (1628-1687), 157.2

VINDICATION: good preaching its own v., 29.1

VINE: plant v. and gather corn, 29.33

VIOL and harp, 9.13

VIRTUE, 207.12; acceptable when practised from good motive, 16.18; asserts its majesty in heaven, 11.15; comes to have solidity thru the personal, 234.15; demands intention of truth, 226.16; v. determined by ourselves; the occasions, by God, 16.27; emphasized in child training, 52.4; enables a man to enter upon a life which makes creation look pale, 205.16; essential to perfection of faculties, 94.3; v. excited only in presence of observers, 16.15; exists only in action, 13.25; v. in a man is never quite destroyed, 239.14; v. in her own shape how lovely, 6.19; v. is God, 4.13; v. is God's mark upon every moral act, 93.34; v. is legitimate end of all speculation, 87.34; v. is means of power, 94.6; is nat'l and fundamental, 231.14; is personal and not transferable, 118.13; is source of happiness in heaven, 11.15; v. loved for v's sake, 16.22; made more beautiful, 30.10; must be exercised and not kept in store, 13.23; needs no great occasion for strenuous exertion, 15.8; v. of humility, 267.9; v. of independent judgment, 200.20; v. of individual soul, xxi.20; v. of prayer, 8.10; v. of self-trust seldom enters conversation, 108.28; v. of the poor man, 5.23; v. is one of God's restraints upon men, 129.14; v. opens the eye, sharpens the sight, is door of wisdom and cause of love, 94.4; v. or vice, 9.3; v. should be chosen for its own sake, 244.5; v. tends to create v., 80.35; will prove stimulus to goodness and confirm wavering purpose, 80.33; v. would produce happiness; and vice, woe, 35.23
————————a man capable of tho't and v., 209.4; authority of v. defined, 93.27; average of public v. always fluctuating, 80.21; awakened to truth and v., 211.8; choice betw. v. and bread, 11.2; discipline of v., 193.9; estimate of v. should not depend on eminence of people, 13.5; fugitive and cloistered v. cannot be praised, 130.7; gov't is index of private v., 80.10; high tho't and noble v., 10.8; high v. attended with deep respect, 80.31; human v. encouraged by God, 83.20; love of v. is innate, 265.24; man's capacity for v., 231.12; man's capacity for v. emphasized by liberal party, 83.6; meaning of the word v., 217.14; no v. can properly be called small, 14.1; omnipotence enlisted on the side of v., 87.27; our v. wants all the crutches we can get, 242.44; practice of v. includes jus-

tice, veracity, regard to common good, 93.32; prayers and sermons considered only road to v., 189.21; private v. strengthens our gov't, 81.30; public v. depends not on masses but on individuals, 80.22; rulers of country represent v. of same, 80.12; standard of private v. nowhere high, 79.5; sufferings of v. merit eternal reward, 23.10; venerated idea of v., 6.25; we never come to the end of v., 236.4; wherein v. consists (acc. to Bp. Butler), 93.28; worship of v., 10.11

VIRTUES applicable to any planet, 177.26; are dead possibilities till they live in a soul, 234.18; can make any place shine, 190.4; v. commended by liberal party are gratitude, resignation, diligence, 83.23; v. employ the tongue, 64.14; v. exercised with more freedom after death, 169.3; v. meant to be communicated, 130.8; v. near at home, 270.8; v. of E's congregation, xxxvii.14; v. of great men, 52.10; v. of rigid party are penitence, spirituality, and prayer, 83.13; v. possessed in high degree, xviii.23; v. unsupported in solitary individuals, 197.35; domestic v. are best consolation at time of death, 20.3; imitation of Jesus' v. leads to sharing his power, 90.11; laurel for one's v., 101.30

VISION: distant v. lost, 48.5; range of v., 47.22

VISITING: pastoral v. must often yield to meditation, 71.3

VISITS of seasons are annual, 41.9; pastoral v. required of ministers, 24.29

VOCATION considered only as a private end, 187.35; is above ties of kindred and country, 168.13; is diff. to every man, 251.27; is state in which all man's powers find employment, 251.30; is violated whenever conscience is violated, 169.9; v. of a genuine man has his whole life in it, 188.3; v. of the genuine man, 187.27; v. revealed more clearly thru right exertions, 251.31; v. will be bent to a man's character or changed, 251.6; one v. for every man, 165.20

VOCATIONS made clear by consulting oneself, 167.28; see callings.

VOICE, 216.19; v. and hand of God, 161.4; v. of command in moral truth, 94.35; v. of God always heard within the soul, 110.27; v. of God confirms immortality of soul, 111.20; v. of God is conscience, xxv.6; v. of God speaks in one's higher self, 184.10; v. of man's inward nature, 184.6; v. of men exalted into a god, 157.6; v. of reason is above mere man, 186.19; v. of Savior becomes v. of Friend, 98.4; v. of self-interest, 78.27; v. of truth, 219.1; v. of whole creation speaks in soul, 202.6; v. of your own mind is v. of God, 188.35; v. speaks: Hunger and thirst after righteousness, 178.11; v. speaks: what will people think? 49.3; inward v. of conscience, 188.12; let us obey inner v., 111.26; men become merely the v. of things, 109.16;

relig. never wants an articulate v., 69.12; sounds of v., 1.14

VOICES of harp and viol tinkle, 9.13; v. of inspiration, 126.17

VOLCANOES, 112.14; 122.9

VOLUPTUARY gains nothing from Bible, 111.7

VOTARY of lusts, 6.3

VOW broken too easily, 20.30

W

WAGES of honest industry, 241.22

WAIT: who only stand and, 104.18

WALES benefited by union, 129.1

WALK in the world as having rec'd light of anr., 59.22

WALKER, Dr. James, xxi.26; xxi.30

WALL of inefficiency, 227.12

WALLACE, Sir William, 152.25

WALLS: devout man would not see the w. of the church, 221.30

WALTHAM, Massachusetts, 252.29

WANDERS: man w. from relig., the home of the mind, 28.2

WANT considered the result of mismanagement, 131.16; w. is a man that travelleth, 256.20; w. is a needful master, 258.30; w. of a definite point to which we should direct our efforts, 20.21; hightest w. of the soul, 192.28

WANTS have their gratifications within our reach, 5.17; w. of man's heart unsatisfied by honor, 157.12; w. of our nature, 130.21; w. of some one class of minds met by each creed, 230.26; basis for relieving w. in the neighbor, 134.26; man's power and w., 157.32; our animal w. must be supplied, 206.18; real w. observed in solitude, 47.2; see *needs*.

WAR in Europe, 112.23; spirit of w. rebuked, 135.27

WARE, Rev. Henry, 220.18; praised, 37.5

WARFARE against yourself and God in you, 137.2

WARRANT for every word, 187.10; no w. in our being for living anr. hour, 103.32

WARS, 180.16; of England and Italy, 209.9; endless w. resulted from separation, 129.4

WASHINGTON, George, 110.14; 117.16; 152.25

WATCH is only a measure of time, 49.7; w. your own mind, xxiv.27; always w., 102.32; hand of a w., 79.17

WATER evaporated by the sea, 208.1; turned into wine, 31.16; phial of w. broken in the ocean, 245.14; walk on w., 116.12

WATERS of life poured out, 32.17; bread cast upon w., 11.2

WATTS, Dr. Isaac, 147.29

WAVES of light from the centre to circumference of things, 159.17; here shall thy proud w. be staid, 9.28

WAY full of crosses or charities, 101.32; w. of greatness, 107.27; w. of reason, xxiv.18; w. of the world, 185.6

WAYS of justifying one's own relig. system, 86.1

WE are not our own, 135.20; 268.43; we are the men, 79.10; we are wonderfully made, 257.26

WEAKNESS of the Indian, 229.30; gropings of infant w., xxiii.7; trait wrongly regarded as a w., 210.31

WEALTH, 183.33; 227.3; w. and the law of compensation, 263.20; w. not worth the man, 183.35; w. of India piled in my coffers, 4.26; w. of universe invites man's industry, 8.15

WEAPON: eloquence a w. of matchless force, 26.28

WEAPONS: being overcome by your own w., 110.6

WEATHER: all w. part of divine dispensation, 42.30

WEB of relations, 128.2

WEBSTER, Daniel, 65.17; 188.28; was content to stand by and let truth and reason argue for him, 65.18; quoted, 186.14

WEED quaking in the wind, 28.19

WEEDS, 218.41

WEIGH: impossible to w. motive, character, secret self, 1.6

WEIGHT of professional character, 182.8; w. of the body, 186.27; we can lift but a small w., 236.2

WELFARE and virtues of E's old congregation, xxxvii.14; w. of men still is only hoped for, 180.14; w. of neighbor promoted, 198.18; w. of society, 157.28; advancing w. of nearest dependents, 127.18

WELL, faith that all is, 212.12

WELL-DOING, continuance in, 101.5

WESLEY, John, thinks for thousands, 237.17

WEST, marching to the, xxx.35

WEST INDIES, 43.24

WHAT am I designed for? W. are my duties? W. is my destiny? 199.26; w. can a man give in exchange for his soul? 182.35; w. is a man profited if he gain the whole world? 105.2; 106.8; w. we are that only can we teach, 32.20; w. we are within and without, 190.7; w. we desire we try to obtain, 5.11; w. we strive after we acquire, 5.13; w. will people think? 49.3; 52.27

WHENCE and why? 199.27; w. gravity and life? 121.24

WHIP for one's vices, 101.29

WHOLE preferred to part, 201.34; w. self is the soul—comprehends a man's w. being, 182.33; God balanced the parts and modulated the harmony of the w., 10.14; God demands the w. of us, 15.17; stake in the joy and suffering of the w., 199.24; strength of the w., 186.26; the w. of our lives *vs.* single actions, 163.11

WHOSO would be chief among you, 135.30

WHY and whence? 199.28

WICKED has flourished up to his hope, 9.8

WIDOW, tears of, 9.9

WILBERFORCE, William, praised for devotion to slavery cause, 256.34

WILDERNESS, sheep wandering in, 37.3

WILL of man determines extent of his protection, 209.33; w. of my father, 257.11; w. of Supreme Being, 6.33; above the meaning of your w., 156.29; act of one's w. can open wealth to a man, 211.23; acting against one's w., 166.33; activity of w. interrupted in sleep, 203.26; anr's w. imposed on presidents, 230.1; conform all actions to the superior w. within, 100.11; doing the w. of God, 45.29; 267.36; force of w. and one's vocation, 168.17; if only the hand had a w., 132.25; man promotes good of others against his w., 130.14; men may do the w. of God, 59.27; one's wisdom is nothing until one's w. directs it, 118.25; our w. yields to God's w. in a right action, 132.31; reciprocal action of opinions on the w. and *vice versa*, 94.20; submission to God's w., 160.16; thy w. be done is sentiment of the gospel, 259.23; yielding one's w. is self-renunciation, 210.19; you are bound to the w. of God, 135.9

WILL OF GOD better than one's own w., 114.24; w-G. determined in oneself, 168.10; w-G. in the soul is greater principle than self-good, 132.32; w-G. is the good of the universe, 131.32; w-G. known thru spark in us, xxv.5; w-G. not in ancient bks. but in flesh and blood, 189.3; w-G. recorded in our minds, 189.3; w-G. revealed in Bible, xxv.23; w-G. revealed in your constitution, 189.5

WILLIS, Mr., famed for long sermons, xvii.12

WIND, 6.31; gentlest w. brings some destruction, 113.7; he who observes w. will not sow, 50.25; southwest w., 39.8; weed quaking in the w., 28.19

WINDS and seas obey God, 42.34; w. of fortune, 258.44

WINE, 6.5; 216.22; w. and dress, 2.29; water turned to w., 31.16

WING: unerring w. of bee, 176.20

WISDOM, 161.32; 208.33; 212.10; 263.32; w. and goodness of Jesus alone to be loved, 195.15; w. as a person, 256.18; w. gained in Fr. Revolution, 194.26; w. is gray hair unto a man, 116.8; w., justice, humility, diligence, truth and charity, 177.26; w. of love of God, 170.18; w. orders the world, 51.11; w. taught in N.T., 126.4; w. to the understanding is "know thyself," 201.5; w. with which world is framed, 130.12; greatest w. is self-knowledge, 118.11; man is a manifestation of w. not his own, 238.5; man of worldly w., xx.33; man's w. is nothing until his will directs it, 118.25; past w. is nothing except as identified in our own, 118.24; practical w. in proverbs or maxims, 62.34; total benefit of all w. given each man, 208.30; trust w. of God, 107.30; see *God*.

WISE: not w. to belong to any party, 233.13; precepts of the w., 6.21; spectacle of folly to the w., 211.31; w. see wisdom on all sides, 101.34

WISH: every secret w. is a prayer, 3.15; guilty w. hidden in solitude, 3.6

WIT, coveting my neighbor's, 4.27; man of w. can find right subject, xxxi.29

WITHIN are the laws of the Bible first found, 111.6; w. doors of his own soul, 158.34; w. each are elements of moral excellence, 106.3; w. is celestial host, 200.3; w. is the Word of God, 111.25; w. we have key to respect, 52.30 all is calm w., 202.9; be w. what you would appear w., 190.7; conversing with the celestial scene w., 183.9; developing the man w., 184.5; every man has an unknown nature w., 211.20; God dwells w., 133.12; 133.22; God is w. man, 200.3; God to be worshiped w., 111.31; God warns us from w., 162.20; hearts burned w. early Christians, 92.22; if God is w. he will be seen without, 102.7; Jesus listened w., 237.37; Judgment Seat is w., 225.14; Kingdom of Heaven is w., 267.31; man has enough w. to puzzle and outwit all philosophy, 209.4; man w. the breast, 65.7; men speak not from w., 108.29; motives no longer sought in world but w., 100.6; no wrinkles w., 239.37; one whose richness is w., 181.12; only by looking w. can outward knowledge be of any value, 111.3; progress of a citizen comes from w., 77.26; satisfaction must come from w., 110.29; scrutiny of all w. us, 45.24; self-trust means trust in the God w., 237.42; soul may always hear God's voice w., 110.28; soul must seek life w., 114.20; spirit of God dwelleth w., 132.21; spirit shall speak of that which is w. and above man, 257.14; springs of wonder w., 207.8; the inmate w. us, 136.9; the oracle w., 267.20; the world w. disclosed by Jesus, 196.9; see *breast*.

WITNESS to divine truth in the conscience, 20.25; do not bear false w., 71.28

WOE the result of vice, 35.24

WOMEN and the notion of respectability, 184.17; w. who grow up ignorant of their own resources, 184.17; deportment of w., xxxv.3; lonely and unhappy w., xviii.28

WONDER aroused at God's action, 11.8; w. of our being not perceived by the proud, sensual, denier of divine power, avaricious, etc., 206.29; w. of surrounding creation presses on soul, 199.33; eyes opened to true w., 211.32; great w. that the heart affects the insignificant, 2.23; "I will w." (said St. Augustine), 204.35; lifetime in trance of w., 204.28; miracle is thing of blind w., 96.1; our w. not lessened in watching the moral laws, 161.18; ourselves are the greatest w. of all, 122.18; springs of w. in us, 207.8

WONDERFUL are the most common facts, 122.7

WONDERS, signs and, 126.20

WOODS, deep ornamental, 9.13

WORD *amen* is a ceremonial w., 5.2; w. made flesh, 233.27; made flesh in actions of good men, 235.18; w. of God a dull bk., 115.7; w. of God within us, 111.25; w. of God tells the style of God's Providence, 23.9; w. of God uttered, 95.18; w. of Jesus' mouth consistent with work of his hand, 94.29; w. of teacher not yet finished, 199.9; w. of truth made flesh still reconciles men to God, 235.18; W. or pre-existent Logos, 233.27; w. *orthodox* avoided, 230.32; W. subordinate to God the Father, 233.29; angry w. will be recalled, 66.13; complexion of w. changed in five minutes, 65.35; each mind has one w. to say; it should strive sacredly to utter it, and not anr's, xxxx.7; every injurious w. recoils on head of utterer, 65.31; false w. is a sacrifice of power, 108.17; God's w. leaps forth to its effects, 6.34; if any man offend not in w., 60.2; Jesus' w. is a mustard seed; a little leaven, a single pearl, 197.23; one meaning in w. and works of God, 85.34; that w. will never be finished, 199.9; understanding God's w. thru his works, 171.2

WORDS and acts become God's responsibility, 188.14; w. are things, 269.21; w. enforced by one's veneration of the speaker's character, 94.22; w. of Apostles yield before eternal truths, xxxv.12; w. of Christ: how to be explained, 200.31; w. of complaisance, 185.8; w. of gospel received with mother's milk, 115.33; w. of Jesus are spirit, and they are life, 114.22; w. of Jesus ineffectual on many lips, 92.29; w. of Jesus mark him as Messiah, 96.19; w. too familiar to give effect, 158.18; w. wasted in pursuing perishable things, 2.35; angry w. never reform, 66.19; Christians are amenable for w. and acts, 116.19; diff. betw. w. that are things and w. that are w., 226.27; gracious w. proceeded out of Jesus' mouth, 92.21; justified or condemned by w., 64.17; meaning of Jesus' w., xxxiv.33; profusion of w. called civility, 225.37; same in w. as in life, 186.7; supple memory uses w. acc. to fashion, 5.5; take heed to w., 66.25; we judge men by their w., 216.16

WORDSWORTH, William: *Excursion*, IV, 1147-50, quoted, 156.26; *Ibid.*, IV, 1268-70, quoted, 116.29; sonnet, "Say What is Honor," quoted, 155.29

WORK, 270.32; inspires courage and hope, 144.9; w. of forming entire men, 180.24; 254.15; w. of Jesus' hand consistent with word of his mouth, 94.28; w. that demands severe exertion of head and heart, 169.17; doing our own w., 167.19; leaving one's w., 229.8; let every man prove his own w., 82.2; 238.21;

man's w. distinct from his endowments, 209.3; N. does its appointed w., 44.35; no stranger to pastoral w., 220.17; our w. is to aspire to a divine nature, 101.10; our w. never will be done, 169.17; unsuitable w. will be eliminated, 251.38; world is God's w., 52.7; you w. out with fidelity your own effect, 101.28

WORKERS together with God, 67.2

WORKS of God fashioned by man into art, 41.20; w. of God require preacher's attention, 29.25; w. of God speak, 141.22; faith and w., 265.30; God is substratum of all his w., 221.21; God's purposes seen in his w., 84.35; inanimate w. of God, 145.6; knowledge of God's w., 171.1; man is judged by his w., 1.7; marvellous are thy w., 203.2; one meaning in the word and w. of God, 85.35; reliance for God's favor upon our w., 85.25; that men may see your good w., 81.10

WORLD carried in man's head, 252.11; clothed with beauty, 169.21; framed in wisdom, 130.12; full of blessings, opportunities, hopes and truth, 85.10; full of contrivances for use and pleasure—not for pain, 85.1; goes after externals, 182.23; is a ball, 112.8; is a mirror of the mind, 101.33; is a platform for Newton *et al.*, 52.10; is a system of benevolence (Hartley), 94.7; is but a large urn, 112.25; is consistent and uniform, 2.3; is God's work, 52.6; is house where wise, great and brave men have dwelt, 52.7; is place of conflict, 52.1; is scene of wreck and fear, 113.10; is theatre of great men's virtues, 52.9; w. of Christian has two prominent parties, 82.23; w. of matter and spirit, 1.22; w. of remuneration is next life, 9.35; w. of souls, 116.27; w. of spirit is next world, 10.5; w. of spirits more certain and stable, 1.25; ordered by wisdom, 51.10; pours all things into man's bosom, 208.35; runs over into the infinite universe, 249.36; suggests lofty faith, 212.11; turned into hell of slavery by self-love, 231.18; w. was wrong, and pulpit has not set it right, 27.19; will last our day, 78.29; w. within not believed in, 183.11; w. without was slightly esteemed, 50.5; w. would cease to exist without God, xxiii.20————appetites growing in soil of this w., 10.16; architecture of the w., 222.3; as we die in this w. we are born into the next, 10.4; beauty of external w., 39.6; beneficent changes in the w., 159.2; body born into this w.; soul must be born into spiritual w., 114.5; character shines in spiritual w., 20.18; Christian lets w. go on, 51.10; citizens in trust of a future w., 8.24; citizens of anr. w., xxxi.3; competitions of this w., 114.18; darkness of this w., 34.25; difficult to walk in w. with lofty views, 53.3; dominion entrusted to man, 54.5; each man placed at heart of the w., 209.16; education administered to the soul, 207.7; emanation from soul of the w., 245.13; fashionable w., 211.34; forsake the w., 111.30; gain the whole w. and lose one's soul, 105.2; 106.8; 111.16; gifts of the w., 17.19; gravity of the w., 28.20; ignorance of the w., 57.4; in spiritual w. only can we live, 114.14; individual separated from the whole w., 199.15; inner w. as Jesus saw it, 196.18; inner w. disclosed by Jesus' sayings, 196.9; knowledge of the w., 185.9; lift self into spiritual w. and help the human race, 117.18; low standard of w's success, 190.11; man stands on top of w., 208.16; material w. seems fixed, 2.9; moral faculty would govern the w., 95.14; morning of the w., 113.28; my villainy hidden from w., 3.27; nat'l w. may ask the question: how old art thou? 112.3; next w. described, 9.29; no w. for careless persons, 102.29; not conformed to this w. but transformed, 104.26; outer w. loses esteem of active soul, 50.5; our little pursuits of this w., 169.23; pass from present w. to w. of spirits, 104.30; Paul heard hisses of the w., 22.22; peace which w. cannot give or take away, 202.22; perfect w. exists to every man, 209.1; privation of whole spiritual w., 226.29; relation of man to w., 5.16; relig. and the w., 75.6; w. seen and unseen connected by speech, 60.26; spirit is in the w. and the w. is made by it, 114.3; spiritual w. described, 114.3; spiritual w. is immutable; kingdom of love etc., 113.35; spiritual w. is man's true home, 114.8; the better the state of the w., the more unlike will be men's characters, 106.34; there is a nat'l w. and a spiritual w., 113.30; there is anr. w., 9.29; visible w. denied a cause, 175.12; walk in this w. as having rec'd light from anr., 59.22; way of the w., 185.6; we are the w., xxx.23; we die daily in this w., 114.14

WORLDS of God are mere dot in space, 172.26; temporal and eternal w., how joined, 230.17; a thousand w. are round, 174.14; we stand in midst of two w., 1.22

WORRY doesn't afflict the Christian, 51.9

WORSHIP and loyalty, 154.13; w. of devils, 156.35; w. of friend, king, speech, etc., 157.23; w. of God as he is revealed, 218.43; w. of God empty, 3.22; champions of arrogant churches w. side by side, xxxviii.27; E's objection to conventions of w., xxxvii.20; honor close to w., 155.20; indolent w. is none, 228.6; language of w. like that of love, 153.12; license of pagan w., 55.32; no one should be driven to w., 228.12; reminiscent w. is nothing, 228.7; sensual and spiritual w., 230.27; social w. is a privilege, 228.9; social w. only for those nearest us in faith and feeling, 232.38; stand, adore and w. when you know it not, 156.27; true or false w., 146.2; value of social w., 237.26

WORTH of human nature, 106.6; w. of the human soul, 238.16; w. of individual soul, xxi.19; men of w. should be respected, 110.8; tho'ts and acts of genuine w., 162.8

WORTHLESSNESS of private virtues of the selfish, 130.7

WRANGLE, let others w., (St. Augustine), 204.34

WRATH of God unreasonable, xxiv.8; God's w. and man's sin, xx.19; 267.22

WRETCH that wears the human form, 110.16

WRINKLES: no w. within, 239.37

WRITE God's name on the home, 19.24

WRITERS of the orient personify abstract ideas, 256.17

WRITES: one who w. only for himself, xxxiv.11

WRITING of Mother Nature, 40.17; w. of scriptures was by men; of the universe, by God, 178.29

WRITINGS of Swedenborg were anr. self, 186.9

WRONG, 208.33; w. vindicated by the law of the land, 229.30; God can do no w. because wise, 116.24; soul never approved me in any w., 200.13

X

XENOPHON, 248.45

Y

YEAR, end of the, 266.11; every y. a new creation, 40.2; last hours of the y., 118.31; self-examination at end of y., 73.17

YEARS of childhood, 116.34; y. of my education, xiv.30; y. of the soul are certain facts, 114.28; deduct evil from your y., 116.4; distance of the y., xi.16; invalid of many y., xviii.29

YET a little while and ye shall see me, 35.3

YOKES: uneasy y. and light burdens, 264.16

YOUNG, Edward, 249.4

YOUNG, ambition of, 229.40; avarice in the y., 229.38; prospects of the y., 37.32; y. persons addressed, xix.4

YOURSELF: act out y. and attain perfect character, 106.5

YOUTH addressed, 184.22; addressed on subject of space, 172.19; intent on pleasures of the senses, 231.42; y. is the spring of man, 44.18; condition of y., 104.25; dying chamber of y., 144.19; heats and temptations of y., 117.1; hour of y., 73.4; immortal y., 119.13; proverbs heard in y., 93.11; tho'ts never lose their immortal y., 239.36; unspent y., 239.38

Z

ZONES of the globe, 42.12

INDEXES

INDEX OF ALL REFERENCES TO THE TEXT OF "NATURE"

INDEX OF INDEXES

MATTERS NOT INCLUDED IN THE FINAL INDEX

FINAL INDEX

I

INDEX OF ALL REFERENCES TO THE TEXT OF EMERSON'S *NATURE**

* All references made in volume one of *E T E* to pages in the facsimile of the first edition of Emerson's *Nature* are here arranged in sequence so that the student, by glancing at the following columns, may gather commentary on any part of the text that interests him. The competent researcher will wish immediately to inscribe line numbers in his copy of the facsimile.

93.5-8	249
93.8	217
93.8-10	186, 413
93.9	51, 207
93.10-14	349
93.13ff.	43
93.14-23	349
93.15	95
93.15ff.	349
93.15-19	279
93.15—94.3	252
93.17	202
93.18-19	186
93.19	204, 208
93.20	42, 58
93.20-23	350
93.20-24	249
93.20—94.3	371

93.20—94.12 Orphic Poet V.	
	349-350, 361, 391, 424
93.21	58
94-95	368
94.1	49
94.1ff.	266, 275, 379
94.1-3	249
94.1—95.12	149
94.3ff.	186
94.5	26, 34, 47, 54, 106, 148, 165, 201, 380
94.6	217
94.6ff.	174

94.6-7	164
94.6-13	176
94.13	217
94.13ff.	178, 365
94.13-15	249, 291
94.13-20	237, 371
94.13-22	177, 238-239, 270-271, 280, 293, 301
94.13—95.7	260

94.13—95.12 Orphic Poet VI.	
	83, 252, 259, 343, 349, 361, 381, 389, 396, 411
94.14	51, 361
94.14ff.	174
94.16-17	235, 363
94.16-22	261, 383
94.19	237
94.20	52-53
94.22—95.7	280
95.2-7	186
95.7	178, 186, 217, 309, 334
95.7ff.	349
95.7-9	365
95.7-12	120, 196, 333
95.8	292
95.9	232
95.10ff.	269
95.10-12	127, 261, 269, 274, 293
95.11	123, 238
95.11-12	241

II

INDEX OF INDEXES

III

MATTERS NOT INCLUDED IN THE FINAL INDEX

IV

FINAL INDEX

A

A. Bronson Alcott (Sanborn)
A Tale of Berlin, s174
Aaron, 287
A posteriori knowledge, 117, 215, 388, 409
A priori knowledge, 29-30, 67, 136, 138, 330-331, 409, s66-67
Abbreviations, 15-16
Abdication: of one's kingdom, 390; of our past and present empire, 366
Ability: sweet-tempered a., 344
Abolition of the slave-trade, 367
Above and *within* are synonyms, 244, 273, 373
Abracadabra, 153
Abraham, 88, 135, 168, s87
Abrantes, Laura, duchesse d'
Memoirs of Celebrated Women, s169
Abridgment of the History of England (Goldsmith)
Absence of occupation is not rest, 445
Absentee: man is an a., 215
Absentee, The (Edgeworth)
Absolute: 124, 328, 402; a. being of nature disputed, 76; a. *vs.* relative truth, 163; knowledge of the A., 124, 210; nature awakens a feeling for the A., 424; nature suggests the A., 424
Absolute Ground, 111
Absolute Will, 202

Abstraction: 33, 86, 118, 120, 122, 143, 150, 154, 202; a. of beauty from things, 323; religion does not require a., 149
Abstractions of the mind are embodied in external forms, 349
Absurdity, no predilection for, 87, 108
Abyss: a day is a rich a. of means, 392
Abyssinia, s177
Académie Française, L': 296
Académie Impériale des Sciences, Littérature et Beaux-Arts
Mémoires, 17
Academus, grove of, 133
Academy, the, 308, 402
Academy of Sciences, Stockholm, Sweden, s214
Acceptance: test of general a., 108, 171
Accepts what God sends, 54
Access: to entire mind of the Creator, 381; to the Father, 183
According to the Idea of each, 151
Accountability for one's conduct, s30
Accuracy, 343; less important than veracity, 96; a. of perception, 352; poet wants or lacks a., 343
Aches become trifles, 398
Achievements: of a principle, 367; all a. belong to the race, 351
Achillini, Professor (of Padua), 308
Acme of human life, 158
Acquaintance with the spiritual dominion of every human mind, 393

---

* This index covers matters in both volumes with certain exceptions noted in the preceding table. A large "S" before a series of page numbers or a small "s" before a single numeral will indicate the *second* volume. All other references are to volume one. Titles of books are merely listed with the name of the author in parentheses. For a detailed list of citations, the reader should always consult the name of the author.

Animal Magnetism, 367, s93

Animalculæ, 146

Animali Parlanti, Gli (G. Casti)

Animals, 25, 35, 50, 58, 203, 280-281, 284, 299, 301, 339, 341, 349, 366, 411, s34-37; abused by man, s22; admonish man, 271; a. and dreams accompany our life, 424; a. and plants compared, 160; a. are degraded forms of man, s91; a. are hieroglyphics, s96; are the forms or incarnations of certain affections, 250, s34, s36; a. and the spiritual state of man, s85; correspond to certain affections, 231; eat minerals in vegetables, 351; have suffered change, 261; have tried to produce man, 341; a. in the imagery of Solomon and Jesus, 225; may possess a degree of Understanding, 89; receive man's states of mind, 270; suffer because of man, s25; suffered when man fell, s100; will show benevolence when man improves, s100; correspondences in a., 231; evil a., 371; ferocious a., 238, 383; instinct in a., 62, 241; orders of a., 154; savage a. accounted for, 271; souls of a., 286; souls of a. result of human affections, 271; Swedenborgian attitude toward a., 224; symbolical a., 225; their uses scarcely known, 272; uses of a., 270, 379; uses of a. not yet understood, 424

"Animals, On" (Reed)

Annals of the New Church (Odhner)

Annihilation of self, 223

Annotations on the Gospels and Acts (Elsley)

Annunciation of principles, 216

Another world but not to come, 152-153

Answer: a. to man's questions found in the external world, 183; external world is an a. in hieroglyphics, 340

Answers: for all questions, 410; insufficient a., 182; a. to questions, 370

Ant, 219; does not sleep, 271, 291; illustrates God's perpetual creativity, 271; instincts of the a., 271, 415

Antelopes, s36

Antenna, 378

Antony and Cleopatra (Shakespeare)

Anthropomorphism, 29, 82, 87

Antidote against the fear of death, 282

Antidote Against Atheism (More)

Antiquities of the Christian Church (Bingham)

Antiquity of the eldest causes, 393

Antitheses, 123-124

Antithesis, 102, 140; a. of mind and matter, 218; a. prior to synthesis, s65; a. vs. analogy, 112; a. vs. synthesis, 157; nature in a. to mind, 204

Ants, 138, 166

Anxiety to be admired, 139

Apex of the living pyramid, 158

Apocalypse, s92

Apocalypse of Nature (Stewart)

Apocalypse Revealed (Swedenborg)

Apollo, 90, 103, 332

Apollo Belvidere, 66

Apollodorus
  Bibliotheca (ed. Christian Gottlob Heyne), s136

Apollonius of Tyana, 47

Apollonius *Rhodius*
  Argonautics, s170

Apology for Christianity (R. Watson)

Apology for the Bible (R. Watson)

Apology for the Life of James Fennell, s175

Apology for the True Christian Divinity (Barclay)

Apology of Socrates (Plato)

Apostasy, 102

Apostles, 129, s45

Apothecary, 343

Apparent: the a. is not true, 311; a. vs. the real, 190, 402

Appear: it does not a. to all men, s128

Appearance: of nature each month, 411; a. vs. reality, 42, 65, 356

Appearances: seen thru, 388; a. of evil in nature, s22; a. are unreliable, 311; a. vs. substance, 128; deceitfulness of the world of a., 267; disagreeable a., 369, 398; freshness given to daily a., 110; terrible a., 383; unpleasant a. in nature, 293; world of a., 371, 380, 387

Appears: it a. to men or does not, 350, 379

Appendix to the New Testament (J. Winthrop)

Appetite, 84; a. for dying, 345; life of a., 43; pleasures of a., 75

Appetites: of beasts, 193; subdued, 334; natural a., 53

Apple, 219, 342; falling a., 147

Apple-tree, s79

Appomattox Court House, Va., s222

Approach metaphysically to God, 170

Approve: soul does not a. wrong-doing, 169

Approved: Reason never a. me in any wrong, 182

Apuleius, 47; on the Goddess Nature, 55
  Golden Ass, The, 325
  Metamorphoses, 55

Arabesque, 154

Arabia, s184

Arabian Nights' Entertainments, s150-151, s170

Aram, Eugene, s179

Arblay. Mme. Frances Burney d'
  Diary and Letters, s170
  Wanderer, The, s170

Arbouin, James
  Dissertations on the Regenerate Life, 287

Arch of time, s122-123

Archangel, a deranged, 382

Arches, 187; law of a., 87-88, 113, 222; properties of a., 139

Archetypal: art, 61; world, 59

Archetypes, 42, 48, 52

Architect, 411; a. and house, 123; finds walls transparent, 324; must understand drawing and music, 324; walls are transparent to him, 422

E

Each: has a concept of universal man, 168; e. man is representative of all men, 138; e. must find the spiritual world within, 131; e. must learn everything for himself, 209

Each in all, 26, 43, 48, 50, 82, 98-99, 120, 197-198, 201, 230, 234, 330, 419; *see* All in each *and* Microcosm.

Eagle, 258, s63; free and unshackled as an e., 260, 278; poet is like an e., s23

Ear, 32; evidence of the e., 74

Early British Writers, s178, s223

"Early History of the New Jerusalem Church at Bridgewater," 250

Ears, 153

Earth, 29, 98, 339; e. is a volume or book, 148; e. called mother, s97; dissipated by genius, 76; is a museum, 339; is the mother of all, 31; is the shadow of heaven, 243; love e. and become e., 382; renewest the face of the e., 398; sun etc. do not revolve around e., 269; theory of the e., s173; too solid e. expected to melt, 76

Earthly, divesting oneself of the, 266

East, 116, 305, s98; e. oneself, 116; if the mind could e. itself, 190, 194, 377; philosophy of the E., 304; the E., 307; the youth who daily from the E. must travel, 190; *see* Orient.

Eastern Railroad Corporation, 440

Eat, s95-96

Eating: of the tree of life or the tree of the knowledge of good and evil, 237; moral significance of e., s87

Eaton, Luella M., 12

Ecbatana: your shade is E., 392

Ecce Homo, 287

Ecclesiasticus quoted, s56-57, s80

Echo: of a voice, 64; e. *vs.* the original voice, 416

Echoes of one's own time, 316

Eckermann, Johann Peter
  Words of Goethe [*i.e., Conversations*], 419

Eclecticism, 303-319, 403

Eclipse of the sun, 285-286

Ecliptic, 378

E cœlo descendit Γνωθι Σεαυτον (Juvenal), 93, 118, 161

Economic uses of natural history, 339

Economy: only e. of time is being true to self, 190, 374

Economy of Nature (Gregory)

Ecstasy, 52, 54, 195, 223, 308, s93-94; discussed, 53; provoked, s93-94

Ectypal: art, 61; world, 59

Eden: education in, 117; Garden of E., 137, 221, 266, 272, 385, s11, s86; loss of E., s121; *see* Garden.

Edge: we stand on the e. of all that is great, 194, 377, 389; *see* Brink.

Edgeworth, Maria
  Absentee, The, s174
  Belinda, s174
  Helen, s174
  Leonora, s174
  Modern Griselda, The, s174

Moral Tales for Young People, s174
  Popular Tales, s174
  Tales of Fashionable Life, s174

Edgeworth, Richard Lovell
  Essays on Professional Education, s174

Edifice too large to fill, 387

Edinburgh Magazine: see *Blackwood's.*

Edinburgh Review, 244-245, s174

Editions: cheap e. of the classics, 347

Edmonds, John Worth, 286

Education, 30, 104, 275, 279, 281, 285-286, 347, s14, s19; e. a matter of recollection, 42-43, 388; acc. to Plato, 43; gauged by sermons, 129; is an awakening, 42; needs the initiatory Idea, 116; e. of the child, s26; e. of man, 207, 394; e. of man by nature, 380; e. of the intellect, 113; e. of the mind, 272; e. of the soul, 167; e. thru self-development, 113; thru the occurrences of every day, 393; bad e. developed with civilization, 117; the best e., 117; early e., 214; end of e., s31; fashionable e., 263; faults in e., s76; idea of e., s126; man's method of e., 96; moral e. needed, 187; natural history in e., 342; nature's method of e., 96; objects of e., 289, 291, 396; part nature plays in man's e., 118; prejudices of e., 267; reform in e., s130; significance of e., 52; theory of e., 259-262; true e., 251; true e. aims to increase consciousness, 217; two directions of man's e., 123; use of poetry in the mind's e., 156; *see* Recollection.

Éducation de Soi-Même, 17

Educator, The, 405

Educators, 211

Edwards, Jonathan
  Enquiry concerning the Freedom of the Will, s135

Edwin and the Druid, 352

Effect, 331; e. and cause, s72; e. of the Ideal Theory, 369; man the e., 383; nature is a perpetual e., 424; *see* Cause.

Effects: e. and causes, 285; e. of a single life cannot be limited, 381; e. of novel reading, 447; progression of e., 146, 206; world of e., 232

Efflux of goodness, 77

Effort, 103; progress only thru individual e., 378

Egan, James, s189

Egg, 157; e. *vs.* egg shell, 90

Eggs: of insects, 264; e. roasted in cinders of a volcano, 416

Egotism, 85; e. vanishes, 412

Egypt, 19, 229, 285, 290, 423; S., 94, 173, 184

Egypt (Wilkinson)

Egyptian, 387; E. hieroglyphics, 285, s92

Eichhorn, Johann Gottfried
  Einleitung ins Alte Testament, s223
  Hebraischen Propheten, Die, s223

Eichthal, Gustave d', s222

Eighteenth century, philosophy of, 307, 309

name to be given in h., 251; perception in h., s9; standards of h., 256; star shining in your h., 366; Swedenborgian h., 243; thou art h., 393; true h. of a man, 393
Heaven and its Wonders and Hell (Swedenborg)
Heaven-tongue, s124-125
Heavens, 281; h. meted out with a span, 239; open suddenly, 194; rolled together, s11; sympathize with Jesus, 415; worshiped, 117; before the h., 182; house eternal in the h., 135; man remembers the h., 382; mechanism of the h., 411; suddenly the h. open, 389; wonders of the h., 339
Heber, Reginald, 392
Hebraischen Propheten, Die (Eichhorn)
Hebrew, 378, s92; language, s28, s87
Hebrew and English Lexicon (Parkhurst)
Hebrew Bible, from the edition of Everardo van der Hooght, New York (Whiting and Watson), 1815, 433
Hebrew Grammar (Willard)
Hebrews, 374; ancient H., s175
Hebrews, s44
Hecatomb, 146
Hedericus, Benjamin
Lexicon Manuale Græcum, s136
Hedge, Frederic Henry, 198, 327
"Coleridge's Literary Character," 181, s59-69
"Emanuel Swedenborg," 229, 249, 252
"Transcendentalists, The," 199
Hedge, Levi, 429
Elements of Logic (Cambridge, 1816), 433
Hegel, Georg Wilhelm Friedrich, s67
"Hegel and his New England Echo" (Brann)
Height, 98; h. to which man may yet attain, 388
Helen (Edgeworth)
Hell, 91, 372, s37; begins in this life, 232; compared to the Understanding, 252; considered a fable, 97; defined, 232; defined as a state or condition, 396; in a man, 396; is not a place, 232; must be found *within*, 177; separated from the heaven? 374; h., the life of which is death, 237; angels of h., 237; can h. be separated from the heaven in a man? 385; man builds his own h., 372; natural man inclined toward h., 274; thou art h., 393
Hells, 281, s37; pervert divine influx, 271, s34; love of self characterizes the h., 240
Helmke, Henry W., 11
Helmont, Franciscus Mercurius van, 308
Helmont, Jan Baptista van, 308?
Help: needed h. is always available, 391
Helvetia, ancient and modern, s183; *see* Switzerland.
Helvetius, Claude Adrien, 305
Hemans, Felicia Dorothea, 245
"The Woodwalk," quoted, s81
Hemorrhage of the nose, 222
Henades or unities, 62-63

Henri-le-Grand, s184
Henri Quatre, s177
Henry, Caleb S., 303, 319
Henry, Matthew
Method for Prayer, s136
Henry IV (Shakespeare)
Henry VIII (Shakespeare)
Henry of Guise (James)
Henry E. Huntington Library, s191
Hens and the partridge, 421
Heraclitus, 33-36, 39, 102, 115, 150
Herbert, George, 347, 354, s178; quoted, 5
"Man," 121, 394, 413, 424
Poems and The Country Parson, s176
Herbert, Henry William
The Brothers, s176
Herbiverous animals, s36
Herbs, greatest among, 257
Hercules: Luther was a Christian H., 102
Herder, Johann Gottfried von
Ideas Concerning a Philosophy of History, 306
Outlines of a Philosophy of the History of Man, 341, 415
Herdman's wife, 352
Here: the omnipresent h., 76
Hereditary evil, s111
"Hereditary Evil" (Reed)
Heresies, 38; *see* McFarland.
Heritage: we are kept out of our h., 389
Hermes, 229
Hermes Trismegistus, 39, 229?
Hermit, recluse, 95
Hermite de la Chausée d'Antin, L' s177
Hero, 385
Herodotus, 40
History (tr. Wm. Beloe), 414, s171
Heroes, 55, 183, 375, 395; of independence, 316
Heroism, 173
Herrick, Robert, 347, 354
Hersey Professor of Anatomy and Surgery, 429
Hervey, James
Meditations and Contemplations, s136
Hesperides, gardens of, s79
Hexangular cells, 89
Heyne, Christian Gottlob: *see* Apollodorus.
Hibben, John Grier
Problems of Philosophy, 69
Hierarchies: of genies, 28; celestial h., 47
Hierarchy: of creatures and images, 44; of gods, 55
Hierocles
Aurea Pythagoreorum Carmina (Gr. and Lat.), s136?
De Providentia et Fato (Gr. and Lat.), s136?
Facetiæ (Gr. et Lat.), s136?
Hieroglyphic, s98, s113; h. keys, s95; h. temple, s97; man is the true h. of the Divinity, s95
Hieroglyphics, 164, 183, 296, 301, 410; S., 92, 96, 117; h. of the earth's history, 148; all animals are h., s96;

Hive, like neuters in a, 194, 377, 389
Hived: powers h. for later use, 188
Hiving knowledge, 188
Hobart, Nathaniel, 228
"Example," 242
"Life of Swedenborg," 231, 249
Hobbes, Thomas, 65-66, 70, 84, 86, 308; system described, 98
Hoc genus omne, 166
Hodges, Richard Manning, 430
Höffding, Harald
History of Modern Philosophy, 69
Hoeltje, Hubert H.
Sheltering Tree, 325
Hofaker, Ludwig Wilhelm
Elilytha, 297
Hogg, James
Brownie of Bodsbeck, s176
Winter Evening Tales, s176
Hohenlohe, miracles of, 367
Holcroft, Thomas, s175
Holidays too infrequent, s118
Holiness, 377; idea of h., 82, 153, 201; skepticism necessary for h., 29
Holland Ephraim, coffee house of, 263
Hollis Hall, 430ff., 460
Hollis Professor of Mathematics and Natural Philosophy, 429
Hollis Professor of Theology, 429
Holmes, Mr., 430
Holmes, Abiel
American Annals, s136
Holmes, John
Rhetoric Made Easy, s136
Holmes, Oliver Wendell
Ralph Waldo Emerson, 291, 356
Holroyd, John Baker, s175
Holworthy Hall, 430ff.
Holy, idea of the, 152, 205, 311
Holy and Profane States (Fuller)
Holy Communion, s90
Holy Land, s173, s184
Holy Spirit: *see* Spirit.
Homage to the law of God, 395
Home: driven from h., 393; love of h., 352; man's proper h., 153; men are strangers at h., 127; nature as man's eternal h., 246; soul should stay at h., 332; stay at h., 127
"Home" (Reed)
Home Book of Quotations (Stevenson)

Homer, 376, 415, 444
Ilias (ed. Michael Maittaire, 2 vols., London, 1816), 433
Odyssey, 419
Homme général, l' 115
Homme particulier, l' 115
Homo enim naturæ minister et interpres, 333, s78
Homo generalis, 159
Homo sum et nihil humani a me alienum puto, 311
Honesty of life, 355
Honor, 139, 171, 375; h. and virtue, 393; h. not sought from God, 263; spirit of h., 107-108; true h., 173
Honoré, comte de Mirabeau, s185
Hoogh, Everardo van der: see *Hebrew Bible*.
Hooker, Richard, 78, 86, 116, 347, 355; sermon on pride, 135
Hoole, John: *see* T. Tasso.
Hooper, Robert
Medical Dictionary, s136
Hope: for man's regeneration, 147; pursued in the spirit of fear, 106; a good h. distinguishes a wise man from a fool, 421; every event of h. educates man, 397
Hope, Thomas
Anastasius, or Memoirs of a Greek, s176
Hopes, 348
Horace, Uncle, s176
Horace (Quintus Horatius Flaccus)
Carmina Expurgata, (cum notis J. Juventii et aliorum, Cantab., Mass., 1806), 433
Satires, 332
Horizon, 301, s97, s98
Horizontal formed by the reptile, s96
Horns, s36, s92
Horologe, s103, s116
Horse, s97; h. within man, 129; flying h., 245; white h. of the Apocalypse, s92
Horsley, Samuel, s87?
Sermons, s176
Hosmer, Louisa Paine, 438
Host, celestial, 182
Hostility: no h. to nature, 423
Hottentot, s44
Houghton Library of Harvard University, 11, 16
Houghton Mifflin Company, 11
Hour: wisely spent, 127; every h. educates man, 397; every h. yields its tribute, 411; we have had no sane h., 194
Hours of illumination, 387
House: not made with hands, 127, 135, 170, 217; set afire to roast eggs, 416; building a h., 411; child in his Father's h., 259, 266; each builds his own spiritual h., 230; each occupies his own h. in heaven, 233; eye is the light of the h., 127; faith admits us to our spiritual h., 135; man's h., 340; nature as man's external h., 246; our Father's h., s19; resemblance betw. man and his h., 366; soul is God's h., 168; Spirit builds

Hypostasis, 63

Hypothesis, 131; Idealism is a useful introductory h., 221

I

I am, 91, 94, 149, 209, 259

I am God, 378, 382

I am nothing, 160, 223

I am that I am, 123, 211

I dare not waits upon *I would*, 132

I idealize; I sensualize, 190

I in the Father etc., s25

"I Wandered Lonely as a Cloud" (Wordsworth)

Iamblichus, 28, 44, 47; on the regions of the gods, 55

Iconoclasm, 44

Id quod ubique etc., 108, 171

Idea: an i. actually existing in the minds and consciences, 151; I. and its corresponding Law, 212; I. and its bloodwarm counterpart, 376; I. and its correlative Law, 114; I. and law, 209, 214; I. and law defined, 115; I. defined, 86, 140; I. has invisible walls, 350; is the correlative of Law, 113; is not ours, 212; is necessary for development in all fields, 116; I. of a god or perfect being, 43; I. of a year, 265; I. of an epoch, 315; I. of cause and effect, 111; I. of education——its history and type, s126; I. of God, 120; I. of God is its own evidence, 145; I. of greatness in every man, 375; I. of greatness in every man, 375; I. of man *vs.* the particular man, 376; I. of one's mind, 102; I. of philosophy, 304; I. of the Creator, 117; I. of the perfection of human nature, 375; I. of the True, s108; I. put before self, 216; I. seeking to embody itself, s129; I. *vs.* a notion, 197; a great man represents an I., 317; actualizing an I., 376; all-perfect I., 135; an I. and a Law, 151; an I. defined, 151; an I. is an experiment proposed, 115; beauty of a life conformed to an I., 198; correlative of the I. is God, 121; the determination of each man's character is called his I., 291; each I. is an *energeia*, 49; every man's ruling I., 396, 419; every principle is actualized by an I., 144, 217; friends coextensive with a man's I., 419; grasping the I., 216; its symbol is light, 146; life conformed to an I., s128; life in the I., 125, 211, 219; meaning of I., 151; one's *first* I., 250; only a life conformed to an I. is beautiful, 396; progressive force of one I., 352; pure I. of one's mind, 174; pure plastic I., 184; regulative I., 116, 213; ruling I. of great men, 343; ruling I. or daemon, 361; stages in the development of an I., 313; standard I. of man, 375; the I. that explains the universe, 184; unfolding of an I., 184; Unifying I., 110, 114, 195, 197, 213, 230; unifying I. exemplified, 114; true method begins with an I., 212; unifying I. of the "af-

fections clothed," 250; unity strives to become I., 160; we need the I. before we can understand the Bible, 146

Ideal: of spiritual consciousness, 273; barren contemplation of the I., 310; following one's own I., 102

Ideal Theory, 370, 391; effect of the I.T., 369

"Ideal Theory" (Emerson)

Idealism, 13, 29, 31, 36, 56, 173, 303, 307-309, 325, 329, 400, 403, 405, 423; I. and passion, 142; I. defined and illustrated, 421; I. of Bp. Berkeley, 69-77, 221; I. of Berkeley *vs.* that of Jesus, 77; I. of Coleridge, 180; I. a preparation for a moral life, 29; degrees in I., 77; limitations of I., 124

Idealist: described, 69; paints the world around your soul, 221; the book that makes one an I., 76

Idealists, 343; men become I. under a strong passion, 198

Idealization of English institutions, 196

Idealize, 76, 190

Ideals and portraits, 145

Ideas, 39, 44, 48-49, 52, 54-55, 64, 72; I. and correlative laws, 112, 151, 380; I. and the existence of external objects, 70ff.; are spiritual sense-organs, 153; called living *laws*, 115; called "truths spiritually discerned," 132; caused by the Spirit, 71; clash, perish, combine, 313; compose knowledge, 143; correspond to laws, 206; derived *a priori*, 67; discussed, 42; given to man for a purpose, 152; in mathematics, 82; I. in the mind make one what one is, 349; not gained thru sense, 67; I. of God, 198; I. of God, Justice, Free Will etc., 196; I. of history, 305; I. of Plato, 374; I. of Plato and Bacon, 126; I. of pure intellect, 210; I. of the Eternal, the Good, the True, the Holy and God, 152; I. of the Good, the Beautiful, Eternity, Immortality, Freedom and Holiness, 153; I. of the Reason descend to the Understanding, 193; I. of the soul, 99, 205; I. opposed and blended, 352; paralleled by Laws, 218; used in discovering Laws, 198; I. *vs.* facts, 141; I. *vs.* notions, 349; I. which govern man's activity, 304; I. working themselves out in history, 141; actualizing I., 41; archetypal I., 98; are they regulative or constitutive? 93, 151; changing our I., 314; connate I., 242; eternal necessary I., 79, 152, 197, 201, 205, 396, 423; facts are significant when related to I., 315; friends become I., 420; God's I. enumerated, 349; the gods of the ancient Greeks are I., 193; great I. are the test of literature, 196; great I. of the Reason, 208, 349; ground and source of I., 80; immutable I., 334; innate, eternal, immutable I., 309, 402; innate I. defined, 330; men are pensioners upon I., 195; moral I. defined, 152, 204; Necessary I., 79, 152, 197, 201, 205, 396, 423; possessed with

mines all phenomena, 113, 422; l. discussed, 111; L. in a man's own heart, 130; in its perfect form, 111; L. is present, 214; must be found *within*, 177; l. of all action, 168, 398; l. of all criticism, s27; of all exegesis, s27; of all knowledge, 168; l. of arches: *see* Euler; l. of cause and effect, s49; l. of coherence and sympathy, 50; l. of compensation: *see* Compensation; l. of conscience, 99, 204; l. of continuity, 204; l. of criticism, 261, 278, s27; l. of dependence of the particular upon the universal, 148; l. of gravitation, s56; L. of Laws explored, 392; l. of men's own hearts, 129, 222; l. of one's being, 80, 366; l. of polarity, 218; l. of reciprocity, 204, s48; l. of the distances of planets, 112; l. of the flesh, 138; l. of the mass of our actions, 75; l. of the mind, 168, 194; l. of the mind is absent from business, 389; l. that condemneth, 134; l. *vs.* the military profession, 445; chemical or astronomical l., 292; Coleridge on l., 179; discovery of a fundamental l., 179; discovery of the L., 343; each l. implies all truth, 191; ethical l. stated as scripture doctrine, 345; fixed and immutable L., 334; founders of l., 120; fundamental l., 34; generic l., 162; highest l. of one's being, 378; human l., 104; moral l., 38, 163; morality confounded with l., 104; Mosaic L., 109; one is a l. to oneself, 392; performance of the l. of God, 145; regulating l., 116; restraints of the civil l., 274; reverence for l., 158; summary of the L., s73; thou art the L., 177; thou art unto thyself a l., 177, 393; Unifying L., 113, 197, 213; universal l., 49, 119-120

Law, William, 90, 296

Lawgivers, 211

Lawrence, Sir Thomas, s186

Laws, 306, 393; and correlative Ideas, 151, 380; correspond to Ideas, 206; discovered thru Ideas, 198; l. of a state, 369; l. of action and reaction, 206; l. of criticism, 261, 278, s26-27; l. of the First Philosophy, 191; l. of God are uniform and harmonious, 268; l. of matter, 210; l. of the mind, 366, 374, 387; l. of mind and matter, s13; l. of the mind are fixed, 259; l. of the mind are known, 190; l. of moral mechanism, s27; l. of moral nature answer those of matter, 416; l. of nature, 20, 23, 25, 31, 33-34, 71, 84, 177, 209, 265, 340; S., 17, 19, 78; l. of nature are called Ideas, 115; l. of nature are dependable, 71; l. of nature are formulations of the mind, 209; l. of our being, s38; l. of Spirit, 172; l. of Truth and Right, 192, 374; paralled by Ideas, 218; l. tempered or adapted for each stage of existence, 121; divinely tyrannical and magnificent l., 349; eternal l. known thru the Reason, 186; fixed l. control every utterance, 350; God's l. and ours,

132; great moral l. learned by acting, 397; Hebrew l., s175; Hebrew l. sprang from the Reason, 142; human and divine l., 34, 36; magnificent l., 388; miracles come under l., s29; normal operation of spiritual l., 389; power thru obeying l. of nature, 333; spiritual l., 342; spiritual l. as boundless as the universe, 269; universal and particular l., 121; universal l. operate at each level of creation, 121; universal, necessary l., 100; value of written l., 43

Laws, The (Plato)

Laws of Organic Life, s173

Lawson, John

  Lectures Concerning Oratory, s136

Lay of the Last Minstrel (W. Scott)

Laying on of hands, s93-94

Lazarus, s11; tomb of L., s132

Leader, invisible, 397

Leaf: is related to the whole, 419; lives in the tree, 382; growth in the eye of a l., 418; marvels in a l., s58

Leaps and bounds, 384

Learn: I cease not to l., 412

Learning: defined, 44; l. in early sermons, 129; contempt for l., 377; process of l., 272

Leave: father and mother, 366; l. nation, party, sect, 376

Leaven, 398

Leaves: in the seed, s30; l. of a tree, s9, s29; trees put forth l., 280

Leaves of Grass (Whitman)

Lectures of Coleridge, 155

Lectures Concerning Oratory (J. Lawson)

Lectures on the Art of Reading (Sheridan)

Lectures on Comets (Winthrop)

Lectures on Dramatic Art and Literature (A. W. Schlegel)

Lectures on English Comic Writers (Hazlitt)

Lectures on the English Poets (Hazlitt)

Lectures on History and General Policy (Priestley)

Lectures on Natural and Experimental Philosophy (G. Adams)

Lectures on the History of Literature (F. Schlegel)

Lectures on the Philosophy of the Human Mind (T. Brown)

Lectures on Pneumatology (P. Doddridge)

Lectures on Rhetoric and Belles Lettres (Blair)

Lectures on Rhetoric and Oratory (J. Q. Adams)

Lectures on Witchcraft (Upham)

Lee, Eliza

  Life of Jean Paul Frederic Richter, s178

Lee, Hannah Farnham

  Life of Thomas Cranmer, s178

Lee, Robert E., s222

Lee, Sarah

  Memoirs of Baron Cuvier, 341

Left, s95, s98; l. *vs.* right, s27

Leg, 378

Magnets, books are like, 347

Magnitude is nothing, 369

Maids: competent nursery m. are rare, s104; old m., s176

Maintenon, Françoise d'Aubigné, marquise de
Lettres, s179

Maitresseries, 153

Mattaire, Michael: *see* Homer.

Majesty belonging to the God-centered man, 397

Male, 218, s98

Malebranche, Nicolas de, 306, 308

Malignancy in nature, 225-226

Malone, Edmond or Edmund, s174

Malthus, Thomas Robert
Essay on the Principle of Population, s179
Principles of Political Economy, s179

Maltravers, Ernest, s179

Mammalia, 226, s36

Man, 18-19, 23, 25, 36, s95; abdicates his kingdom, 390; accepts what God sends, 54; acc. to Plato, 43; admonished by animals, 271; alone created in the image of God, 143; alone is perpendicular, s91; m. and his true condition, 272; m. and the angels, 233; m. and the dog, s52; m. and the human form, s69-75; m. and the lower orders of creation, s25; m. and nature, 206; m. and nature are one, s101; m. and nature nurse the spirit, s110; m. and the serpent form a right angle, 301, s91; m. and woman, 110; m. at the apex of the living pyramid, 158; at the center of all, 225; at the head of the visible works of God, 226; became an idolater of the senses, 215; became a living soul, 127, 215; becomes God, 53; becomes a living poem, 261; becomes in a degree himself divine, 423; begins to hear a voice, 182; builds his own heaven and hell, 372; the central figure, 197; can conform events to his character, 390; cannot be a naturalist, 381; cannot be injured except by himself, 397; cannot be other than he is, s30; cannot exist without animals, s37; cannot rely on his own strength, 241; compared with an angel, 301; composed of earth and water, 31; creates his own world, 177; creates new beauty, 310; demands a satisfactory faith, 393; described, 386; deprived of free will in the *Bhagavadgita*, 311; differs from the gods only in degree, 52; distinguished from brutes, s40, s51; does not die, 233; does not make truth, s9; draws the audible moral from all, 351; drives his own shadow before him, 133, 215; enjoys a special dispensation, 121; exists as a god, 51; feared by the brute creation, 239; finds a correspondence betw. the Bible and his own nature, 160; finds in nature the originals of the forms within his intellect, 118; finds nature a modification of his own being, 118; gives himself up only to truth, 314; has abused his power, 271; has access to the entire mind of the Creator, 381; has all inferior natures summed up in him, s71; has been predicted in the universe for ages before he came, 192; has given his personality to things, 310; has left his place in creation, 261; has left the order of his creation, s29; has the most perfect osseous structure, 158; has trouble knowing his true condition, 259; has a world within him, 157; holds the last link of a chain, 392; in his idea, 121; is an absentee, 215; is an analogist, 415; is both a heaven and a world, 231; is central in nature, 230; is in the centre, 342; is the center and summit, 227; is in the center of the world, 184; is a citizen of both worlds, 218; is the compendium of nature, 157, 207; is the creator in the finite, 424; is disunited with himself, 381, 384; is a drowsy dwarf, 388; is a dwarf of himself, 366; is a great miracle, 99; is his own enemy, 177; is fallen, 261; is a fallen creature, 137, 215, 385; is a fallen god, 382; is fed that he may work, 413; is a god in ruins, 368; is a god playing the fool, 382; is great not in his goals but in his transition, 190, 386; is the high priest and representative of his Creator, 121; is ignorant of his true condition, 271; is the image of God, 237; is immortal, s99; is influenced by Revelation, s25; is the interpreter of nature, 351; is independent of his circumstances, 375; is invited to activity, 340; is the mediate creator, 270; is the medium of love and wisdom, 284; is a mere tunnel or pipe, 391; is a microcosm, 157, 300, 305, 312, 363, s56; is the king of nature, s98; is the native of both elements, 350; is no upstart in creation, 192, 341; is not as he ought to be, 220; is not his own, 180; is not wise from himself, 237; is one with God, 198; is the only object of interest to man, 342; is an organ recipient of life, 237; is the perfect emblem (the microcosm), s91; is the playfellow of nature, s76; is the priest and interpreter of nature, 333; is the principal end of creation, 234; is responsible for disorganizations in the animal world, 270; is restless away from God, 132; is the result of the ideas in his mind, 349; is a revelation of nature, 158, 207; is sister to the worm, 161; is a syllepsis or compendium, 158; is taught by nature, 226; is a tiny spectator, 349; is a true hieroglyphic of the Divinity, s95; is the universal form, s97; is the universal standard, 242, s58; is the universe in miniature, 312; is a world, society, law to himself, 392; is the world's child, 394; keeps the world in repair, 340; learns from nature the lesson of power, 390; like a hollow cylinder, s96; likened to ani-

vine M., 230, 375; heaven is a single m., 233; height to which m. may attain, 388; highest is present to the soul of m., 424; highest value in a m., 420; his abuse of power, 260; his alienation from God, 271; his animal and higher wants, 185; his condition is an answer, 410; his conquest over nature, 309; his degeneration, 389; his degradation, 271, 239; his departure from divine influence, s71; his departure from the spiritual level, s74; his desires are infinite, 382; his dialectic intellect, 124; his disunited state, 282; his divided self, 132; his divinity, 423; his dominion, 367; his education and tuition, 394; his educational requirements, 207; his endowments are independent of his work, 393; his evils projected into animals, 271; his fall, 282; his fallen state, 259; his follies and crimes, 239; his foundation in Spirit, 373; his greatest problem, 210; his growth and degradation, 299; his heaven or hell, 396; his immediate relation to God, 182; his inconsistency described, 132; his individuality is not his own, 120; his judgments, 34; his kingdom over nature, 367, 369; his life in three kingdoms, 353; his mission is to subdue nature, s131; his moral character determines the condition of the external world, 238; his nature limited, 382; his nature, powers and destiny, 50-51; his operations insignificant compared with nature's, 411; his perfectibility far off, 377; his personality is a parasitic atom, 192; his place is the true place, 392; his potential divine humanity, 244; his power over nature unlocked, 196; his proper place in nature, 377; his relation to God, s13; his relation to minerals and plants, 183; his relation to nature, 118; his relation to nature is outward, 379; his residence is the world, 341; his Rome, empire and wealth defined, 392; his soul awakes in the presence of ideas, 144; his spirit is an intelligent will, 152; his thought reflected in nature, 168; his triumph over nature, 319; his true heaven, 393; his true nature and higher self, 181; his true place in the system of being, 340; his true place sought, 183; his truest self, 127; his will alone is free, 188; history of one m. is as valuable as that of a nation, 393; how m. differs from the animals, 89, s34; how mean a thing is m., 127, 138; idea of m., s125; imagination is the creative power in m., s28; the "immediate" in m. is the Spirit, 392; the Infinite is embosomed in a m., 175; infinitude and capacity of each m., 180; infinitude of m., 183; influence of the universe upon m., 130; the inmate in m's frail body, 169; instinct in the redeemed m., 283; the intelligent will is behind the m., 130; is m. nothing? 124; Jesus was not complete m., 376;

kingdom of m. over nature, 395; know thyself a m. and be a god, 183; lascivious m., 104; life of a single m. has unlimited possibilities, 381; life of the wise m., 52; the light that lighteth every m., 150; literature is founded on the nature and condition of m., 348; the m. in the m., 127; material world made for the sake of m., 121; the most individual m. described, 207; mystery within m., 332; a nation considered as one m., 118; natural m., 82, 140; natural m. and self-love, 279; natural m. and spiritual m., 187, 193; naturalist must be subordinate to the m., 342-343; nature acts coercively upon m., 239; nature of universal m. to think, 377; nature suggests that m. has fallen, 147; the new m., 135; no bounds to his possibilities, 424; no fact interests us until connected with m., 198; no harm can befall a good m., 289; no history of m. in India, 311; no man can teach more than he knows, 347; no m. good apart from God, 132; no proportioned cultivation in m., 377; occult relation betw. animals and m., 339; office of the literary m., 353; organs of m., s95; our planet prepared for the coming of m., 183; passion-puzzled m., 407; peevish m. finds crosses, 397; the perfect m., 376; perfect world within m's reach, 186; potential divinity of m., 53; power in a m. capable of thought and virtue, 393; primitive m. perfect, s84; quotations on m., 95; a reasoning m. annihilates all distinction of circumstances, 392; regenerative nature of m., 384; relation of m. to the globe, 340; renewal of m., s132; respect m. as potential G., 383; reverence m., 375; reverence m., not Plato, 393; rich m. who went away sorrowing, s27; riddle of m., 124; savage and primitive state of m., 299, s84; scholar is m. thinking, 234; selfish m., s10; Shakespeare's questions about m., 353; shall m. alone stoop? 138; should a m. be raised from the dead, 135; significance of climate and geography in the history of m., 415; significance of m's spiritual response to nature, 119; significance of m's thoughts and affections, s85; skepticism of m. crushed, 388; the so-called great m., 288; society in heaven is as one m., 234; spiritual m. vs. the natural, 246; stages in the life of m., 187; standard idea of m., 375; state of language before m's fall, 298; sun sprang from m., 366; the supernatural in m. is the will, 131; temptations which the Understanding puts in m's path, 121; there is a m. within us greater than that which acts without, 180; to explain m. to himself, 339; true position of m., 423; true theory of m., 369; truest m. is self-reliant, 157; type of a m., 375; the Understanding is a

out m., 238; pleasures of m., 458; to store the m., develop the affections, 294

Men: almost become God, 244; m. and beasts compared, 237; m. and spirits have spiritual communion, 290; m. are convertible, 388; m. are equal as respects their Reason, 79; m. are instructed by the occurrences of every day, 393; m. are like a collection of angels, 382; m. are m. by being in the image of God, 244; m. are parts of God, 382; are pensioners upon ideas, 195; are practical when tranquil, 141; are strangers at home, 127; are survivors of the sun and stars, 381; are tadpoles, 378; are tenants of infinite spaces, 381; become idealists under a strong passion, 198; believed saved or lost as one race, 182; compared to empires, 382; differ in their wills, 215; have a distinctive character, 256; m. in whom the Reason stirs are gods, 381; m. likened to cylinders, s97; need awakening, 388; possessed by a soul, 169; raised to vision, 120; receive the fate which they deserve, 316; m. sent by God have come with signs and wonders, 122; should respect each other, 180; m. under the influence of passion clothe their thoughts, 249; m. who have contributed to the world, 351; m. who obey their genius, 356; m. who restrain the lusts of their will, 238; all m. are poets in some degree, 348-350; all m. can be raised by piety or passion, 423; all m. can find the inner world, 153; all m. can understand the poet, 348, 350; all m. have access to the facts on which Christianity is based, 145; all m. have parallel experiences, 419; bad m. characterized, 374; the basis of the relationship betw. high-minded m., 420; blind m., 32; m. of business, 194; conquering m., 394; destructive m., 226; differences of m. traceable to differences in the will, 153; evil m. pervert Divine Influx, 280; fallen m., 385; God dissolves m., 290; godlike m., 51; good m. and the gods, 55; Great Men, 191, 290, 306, s9-10; halves of m., 315; heads of m.; bodies of beasts, 283; how m. were formed, 387; inaction of m., 377, 389; instinct in m., 241; judgments of m., 34; life of most m. described, 377, 389; the light of m., 150; moral nature common to all m., 131; one-eyed, lobsided m., 377; opinions of m., 173; passions, errors and defects of m., 100; practical or business m., 379, s79; practical m. are not awake, 194, 389; prolific effects of truth in good m., 398; Reason common to all m., 150; Reason is in all m., even in the worst, 192; Reason makes m. men, 374; rich and poor m., 53; sincere m. are gods, 381; slaves and masters among m., 53; so-called great men, 256; three classes of m., 351; true equality of m. defined, 188; types of m., 316; uses of m., 234; what m. re-

ceive intuitively they tend to become, 149; when m. are childlike, 368; wise m. linked together, 290; young m., 127; see Great Men.

Menexenus (Plato)
Meno (Plato)
Mental Improvement (Wakefield)
Mental initiative, 114
Mental states, 415
Mephistopheles in England (Williams)
Merchants, we bow to noted, 194, 389
Merchant's Adventures, A, s176
Merchants Row, Boston, 263
Mercier, J. B., 411
Mercury (of Boston), 164
Mercy to oneself, 129
Meriam, Mr., 411
Merit, how increased, 53
Merlin, 352
Merrilies, Meg, 356
Merritt, Mary, 438
Mesmer, Franz (*or* Friedrich Anton), 295
Mesmerism, s185
Message brought by childhood, s121
Messiah, 368, 384; in *Paradise Lost*, 91; the perpetual m., 368, 385
Messiah, The (Klopstock)
Messiah, The True (Oegger)
Messias-ship of man, 407
Messiahship, perpetual, 368, 385
Metamorphosis, 29-30
Metamorphoses (Ovid)
Metaphor, 149, 175, 382
Metaphorical *vs.* literal, 144
Metaphors, 245
Metaphysics, 85, 94, s29; and the Bible, s29; as a term, s41; German M., 181, s64; is m. advantageous to the student? 448; systems of m., 141
Metastasio, Pietro Antonio D. B., 149, s171
Metcalf, Elinor Gregory, 11
Meteor, 366
Meteorology, 341

Method, 18, 95, 179, 184, 197, 307, 380, s66-67; m. for arriving at the truth, 110; for discovery of truth, 212; for interpreting facts, 209; m. of Plato and Bacon, 219; art of m., 113; deductive m., s78; inductive m., 114, 214; a m. lacking the progressive factor, 219; philosophical m., 184; a subjective and intuitional m., 218; transcendental m., s68; true m., 363; a true m. carries its evidence in itself, 184; the true m. in botany, 112

Method for Prayer (M. Henry)
Methods, 305; of education, 96
Methodists, 247, 251
Metrical romances, 156, 352
Meun, Jean de
Roman de la Rose, 88
Mexico: expedition against, s172; mines of, 94
Meyer, B. E., 69
Michael Angelo, 323-324, 344, 392; Emerson's reactions at his tomb, 345; platonic love of, 344
Rime, 345

manifests polarity, not dualism, 59; married to mind, 184; mirrors our own thought, 168; never acts by leaps and bounds, s86; never convicted of a lie, 153; not a blind and lifeless mechanism, 116; not the correlative of mind, 409; not exhausted in her first uses, 220; only as commodity, 380; penetrated with an informing soul, 423; placed in antithesis to mind, 204; proceeding from man, 366; provides Beauty and Commodity for man, 183-184; put forth thru us, 363; red in tooth and claw, 65; reinforces the Ten Commandments, 267; reveals answers, 410; reveals her affinity with mind, 208; ruled by an Intelligence, 59; seen as beauty, s79; serves man, s99; should be treated as real, 72; shows no guilt, 215; sits at a card-table, 418; speaks a language thru its constant analogies, 164; speaks of Spirit, 73; strengthens moral man, s20; studied in light of final causes, 116; subordinate and subservient to God, 59; subordinated by child's spirit, s122; suggests that man has fallen, 147; suggests the Absolute, 424; surrounds man, 348; teaches the lesson of power, 390; unlocks the powers of the soul, 379; unlocks the truth within us, 183; n. vs. art, s27; n. vs. free-will, s41; n. vs. Intelligence, 93; wears the colors of the Spirit, 412; will always exist, s58; works in silence, 154; ————affinity of n. with mind, 158; all n. will accompany us into the future existence, 300, 384, s86; ancient opinion on n., 58; arrangement of objects in n., 278; art of n. and man contrasted, 60; art of n. inferior to Divine art, 60; art subordinated to n., 92; beauty of n., 42, 330, s97; book of n., 68, 73, 147-148, 164, 180, 215, 224-225, 350; cause and effect in n., 136; colors and forms in n., s84; contribution of n. to man, 260; correspondences in n., 266; dice of n. are always loaded, 418; discord betw. man and n., 424; discordance in n. betw. man and animals, 239; economy of n., s136; end of n. is to produce highest individuality, 157; entire system of n., 323; every power in n. must evolve an opposite, 102; evil and malignancy in n., 225; finding a true theory of n., 218, 410; forms and colors of n. have meaning, s85; goddess of N., 32; a good deed conspires with all n., 292; good writing depends on n., 351; the great world of n., 322; harmony and discord in n., 301; harmony and proportion reign in n., 323; the harp of great n., 288; highest use of n., 293; highest function of n. is to teach and discipline, 379; how men have regarded n. in history, 402; how understood, 267; in relation to n., Reason is Spirit, 148; inadequacy of the religion of n., 134; instruction of n., 97; kingdom of

man over n., 395; know thyself in n. in order to understand n. in thyself, 207; language of n., 154, 284, 295-302, 410, s83ff.; language of n. existed before man's fall, 298; laws of n., 71, 119, 177, 209, 265, 340; laws of n. are formulations of the mind, 209; laws of n. called *ideas*, 115; laws of n. represented in the human mind, 149; laws of n. sought by Thales, 20; learn to know thyself in n., 127; light of n., 87, s185; light and life of n., 147; the Lord's infinity manifested in n., 242; man assimilates n. unto himself, 310; man is a compendium of n., 157; man is priest and interpreter of n., 333; man is a revelation of n., 158; man must comprehend n. in himself, 119; man related to all n., 157; man's conquest over n., 309; man's power over n. unlocked, 196; man's proper place in n., 377; man's relation to n., 118; man's relation to n. is outward, 379; marriage of mind and n., 343; meanings of n. classified, s78; method of education, 96; mighty hands of n., 173; ministry of n. to man, 413; moral influence of n., 293; multiform unity of n., 55; music of n., s175; no hostility to n., 423; numbers and patterns in n., 227; operations of n. greater than man's, 411; oracle of n., 114; organic n., 47; Parmenides' poem on n., 32-33; part of n. in man's education, 118; plastic n., 58; plastic life of n., 416; poets work like n. herself, 412; power of expression belonging to external n., 340; power of n. is all in every part, 149; power of subordinating n., 353; power over n. by obeying her laws, 333; powers and tendencies of n., 157; predictions of n., 153; purposes for which n. was intended, 226; religion of n., 87; savageness of n., 66; savagery in n., 260; scale of organic n., 154; scenery of n., s10; services of n. to man, 284; Shakespeare is the mirror to n., 159; Shakespeare's questions about n., 353; significance of man's spiritual response to n., 119; significance of n. in childbirth, s103; sordor and filths of n., 395; strangers in n., 388; study of n. helps to self-knowledge, 183; study of n. is a discipline, 184; summit of organized n., 186; Swedenborgian view of n., 246; symbolism in n., s75; sympathy with n. denied, 379; the term *n.*, s48; theory of n., s79; a thought is only one side of n., 188; to what end is n.? 410; traits of n., s171; true position of n. and man, 423; true theory of animated n., 184; triumph of man over n., 319; unity of impression in n., 148; unity of n. perceived within the mind, 67; use of n. is to awaken the feeling of the Absolute, 424; uses of n. in the service of man, 267, 284; we are strangers in n., 272; we drown out the voice of n., 267; we have not yet at-

O

Position-point altered to see landscape, 276

Possess: we p. ourselves only when we p. God, 131

Possessing: knowing God is possessing Him, 167

Possession: of God by knowing Him, 145; in p. of the Godhead, 54

Possibilities: of man, 424; of a single life, 260; no bounds to man's p., 381

Post office is an advantage, 413

Posterity of Adam, 182, 393

Posthumous Papers of the Pickwick Club (Dickens)

Postulate, 113; p. required in the discovery of speculative truth, 103; a p. must begin all speculative disquisition, 124; a p. requires an act of the will, 214; *see* Preconception.

Potato field, 369, 392

Potato ground, 156

Potentiality, 41; p. in nature, 154; p. *vs.* actuality, 49

Potter, Robert, s174

Potts, John Faulkner
The Swedenborg Concordance, 364

Poundmedown, Doctor, 69

Poultry, s36

Poverty, 53, 393, 399; p. of one's own individuality, 316; unimportant, 399; spiritual p. defined, 393

Power, 24, 55, 97, 127-128, 179, 378, s73; p. above man called *supervoluntary*, 282; p. above space and time, 265; behind Biblical miracles, 268; behind nature and me, 148; extended by the exercise of the will, 186; p. in nature and the Reason is the same, 215; is in a man who is capable of thought and virtue, 393; is the great lesson nature teaches, 390; multiplied thru the union of men of conviction, 397; p. not his own lies behind a great man, 317; p. not in time or space, 367; p. of acquiring knowledge is connate, 242; p. of concealing our thoughts, 274; p. of concealment, 266; p. of expression belonging to external nature, 340; p. of God overflows into human souls, 150; p. of language, 355; p. of nature is all in every part, 149; p. of questioning one's destiny, 172; p. of semination, 144, 217; p. of subordinating nature, 353; p. of a teacher, 388; p. of thought, 391; p. over the natural world, 209; p. over nature by obeying her laws, 333; p. over nature thru the Understanding, 367; p. over nature unlocked, 196; p. secured by unlocking knowledge, 207; shared by good and bad, 421; superior to the will, 390; p. thru knowledge of the Law, 113; p. to overcome or support suffering, 212; p. and property, 333; p. we originate outlives us, 387; p. to the hands, 183; p., wisdom and goodness of God, 224; abuse of p. has repercussions in nature, 260; accession of p. over nature, 333; actuating p., 126; adaptive p., 89; all-pervading p., 265; all-present p. with-

in and without man, 130; centrifugal and centripetal p., 157; Christ's flesh is the P., 135; designs of a superior P. accomplished in great men, 318; elemental p., 349, 389; every p. in nature must evolve an opposite, 102; every p. of the mind given a right direction, 397; everyone has a trust of p., 369; the forming p. within us, 262; gain or loss of p., 170; idea of p., 334; increasing one's spiritual p., 218; instantaneous, instreaming, causing p., 367; inward p., 126; knowledge is p., 143, 333; lesson of p., 418; man has abused his p., 271; man's elemental p., 196; mind has a self-determining p. within itself, s49; one p. in opposite forces, 114; physical p., 27; prophetic p., s77; redeeming p., 393; renewal of forfeited p., 150, 178, 216; science or knowledge is p., 144; simplicity of p., 176; source of p. in the Reason, 397; supervoluntary p., 283; theory of p., 306; thoughts fall to earth with p., 256; unconscious p., 367, 390; unfolding p., 397; Universal P., 211; where p. is vested, 106; wisdom is p., 217

Powers, 48, s96; hived for later use, 188; p. of manhood, 109-110; p. of the mind superior to force, 276; p. of nature, 157; man's p., 376; moral and physical p., s96; opposite p., 157; peculiar p. possessed by every individual, s30; self-containing and self-causing p., 154; self-retaining and self-finding p., 154; Shakespeare's reflective p., 353; unconscious of our p., 194, 377, 389; vital and organic p., 154; we have immense p., 389

Poynder, John
History of the Jesuits, s181

Practical: approach to nature, s79; p. men, 379, 389; p. Reason, 203; p. *vs.* impracticable, 185; abstract truth is most p., 410; men and nations are p. when tranquil, 141

Practical Discourse Concerning Death, A (Sherlock)

Practical Discourse Concerning a Future Judgment (Sherlock)

Practice depends on theory, 52

Prairies, southwestern, s177

Pratt, Anne S., 11

Pratt, Frederic Wolsey, 11, 327, s101

Pratt, George Williams, 432

Pratt, Samuel Jackson
Sublime and Beautiful of Scripture, s181

Prayer, 216, 367; defined, 189; is congruous with the Reason, 152; is important, 147; is a study of truth, 369; not an idle pastime, 152; hour spent in p., 127; spirit of p., s28

Prayers: criticized, 251; all p. are granted, 416

Prayers for the Use of Families (Enfield)

Preacher, 376, 394

Preacher's Directory (W. Enfield)

s27; t. of the first class, 170; t. of the Primeval Church broken up, 364; t. of the Reason, 100, 170; t. require general and long-continued assent, 108; t. spiritually discerned, 203; t. spiritually discerned are Ideas, 132; t. that are their own evidence, 79, 170, 180; t. that derive their evidence only from within, 109; t. that have validity in themselves, 202; t. that wake to perish never, s57; t. which are *felt*, 401; t. with signatures in nature, 115; ancient t. restored to pristine lustre, 208; Biblical t., 142; great t. can be perceived only by the Reason, 134; great t. which ages toiled to prove, 367; Necessary T., 79, 87, 170, 174, 329, 364; organized t., 97; salutary effect of Universal T., 398; simple t., 219; spiritual t. are spiritually discerned, 130, 267

Tucker, Abraham
  Abridgment of the Light of Nature Pursued, s185

Tucker, Benjamin, 432

Tucker, St. George, s186

Tuckerman, Henry Theodore
  Isabel, or Sicily, s185

Tuckerman, Joseph, 17

Tübingen, University of, 297

Tuition of man, 394

Tumult: the depth but not the t. of the soul, 192

Tunnel, man is a mere, 391

Turgot, Anne Robert Jacques, 306, 403

Turk, s24

Turkey, s173; geography of T., s173

Turn: of mind, 291; it is now our t., 395

Turnbull, Andrew, 432

Turnbull, Grace A., 47

Turner, Sharon
  History of the Anglo-Saxons, 352, s185

Turrets, 355

Tusculan Disputations (Cicero)

Tuttle, Mr., 424

Twelve: significance of the number *t.*, s98

Twelfth Night (Shakespeare)

Twelve Epistles, The (Plato)

Twice-told Tales (Hawthorne)

Two Lectures on Comets (Winthrop)

Two Pilgrims, The, s185

Two Princes of Persia (J. Porter)

Two Unpublished Essays (ed. Hale)

Tyng, George, 432

Type of a man, 375

Types, 245; t. of minds, 141; t. of people, 316

Typescript Journals (Emerson)

Tyranny, 101; t. of divine ideas, 388

Tyrants, 395

Tytler, Alexander Fraser, Lord Woodhouselee
  Considerations on the State of India, s185
  Elements of General History, Ancient and Modern, 433

U

Ugly: the u. is the projection of a diseased mind, 398

Uhland, Johann Ludwig, s183

Ultimate Reality, 43

Ultra-fidianism, 133

Unbelief of the Understanding, 87

Uncle Horace (A. M. Hall)

Uncollected Lectures (Emerson)

Uncollected Writings (Emerson)

Unconditioned, the, 47

Unconscious, 186; u. is ever the act of God, 384; u. knowledge, 183; u. of our powers, 194; u. power, 390; u. receivers of Divine energy, 293; u. reciprocal influences, 290; u. spiritual influences, 291; u. *vs.* conscious living, 93-94, 187, 383

Undertaker, s16

Understanding (miscellaneous meanings), 33, 232, 235, 328, s32, s34, s124; dwells in the cerebrum, 237; exertion of the u., s27

Understanding (Coleridgean sense), 40, 76, 86-90, 100-101, 131, 133, 137, 140, 150, 152, 174, 184, 186, 190, 215, 251, 351, 363-364, 368, 374, 379-380, 385-386, s28, s51; U. and allegories, 136; U. and reflection, 128; U. and the senses, 221; U. cannot comprehend great beliefs, 108; cannot measure nature, 148; has serious limitations, 115; is a rebellious and incorrigible liar, 190; is not free, 311; is not the measure of spiritual matters, 134; is the lower faculty in man's mind, 203-204; is left in a world of dreams and darkness, 150; raised to the Reason, 152; sees facts isolated, 196; U. *vs.* Reason, s41, s53, s55; an age under the dominion of the U., 144; blindness of the U., 128; culture of the U., 418; England of the U., 413; function of the U., 185, 192; habits of the U., 115; living in the realm of the U., 117; miracles startle the U., 140; passeth all U., 125, 211; power over nature is only thru the U., 367; school of the U., 123; short-sighted U., 383; temptations which the U. puts in man's path, 121; unrenewed U., 421; *see* Reason *vs.* Understanding.

Uniform operation of God's laws, 269

Uniformity, 148

Unifying Idea: *see* Idea.

Unifying Principle: *see* Principle.

Union: of the Divine and human, 282, s25; of head and heart, 198; of old and new, 110, 149; u. with God, 56, 99; act of mystical u,. 54; ecstatic u., 54

Union Army, s218

Uniqueness of every individual mind, 292

Unitarian, 186, 400, 402, s68

Unitarian Church, 249

Unitarianism, 199, 255, 293, 367, 406, 408, s185-186

Unitarianism Incapable of Vindication (Wardlaw)

344; u. of a church, 286; u. of men and angels, 234; u. of nations, s30; u. of natural things, s36; u. of nature, 284; u. of New-Churchmen, 246; u. of only a few natural objects known, 293; u. of plants and animals, 379; u. of sleep, 274; u. of things, s22; u. of travel, 341; u. that are exhausted, 219; Doctrine of U., 43-44, 228, 234, 247-248, 250, 257, 262, 275, 289, 293, s24, s210-212; economic u. of natural history, 339; nature not exhausted in her first u., 220; selfish u., 281; spiritual, civil and moral u., 234; true u. of natural things, 267

Utilitarian, 165

Utilitarianism, 379

Utility, 139; u. in nature, s99; ethics founded on u., 108; love of u., 352; principle of u., 107

Utley, Francis L., s191

Utopia (T. More)

Utterance: in heaven, 251; everything is full of u., 267; freer u. attained, 76; most perfect u. is language, 348

V

Vaccination, s37

Vacuum, transparence without, 124, 146, 203, 216

Valuational note, 41

Value: in our faults, 135; v. of a single life is unlimited, 276; man's v., 172

Values, preservation of, 41

Van der Hoogt, Everardo: see *Hebrew Bible.*

Vane, Sir Henry (*or* Harry), 414-415, 440

Vanini, Lucilio, 308

Vanishes, the truth, 292

Vanity, 150, 330, 376; v. of self, 216

Vapors steaming from the corrupt heart, 133

Variation: only slight v. betw. our present and future existence, 384

Variations betw. souls, 52

Variety, 55, 73; v. and unity, 305; endless v. in nature, 414; v. in unity, 223; v. of objects, 417; unity in v., 148

Vasari, Giorgio
Vite de' Piu Excellenti Pittori, 345

Vase, s97

Vassar College, 459

Vault, admantine, 153

Veda, 423

Vedanta, 308, 423

Vegetable, 52, 72, 418; v. instincts, 286; v. kingdom, 236, 260, s95-96; v. kingdom is a degradation of the animal kingdom, s96; v. life, 49-50; v. physiology, 312

Vegetables, 50, 147, 237, 272, 280-281, 341, s34, s58; have fixed natures, 281; work up minerals for animal use, 351

Vegetive life, 154

Veil, 176; how thin the veil, 194, 389

Vein: golden v. of duty, s27

Veins and veinlets, 366

Velde, Karl Franz van der
Tales from the German, s185

Vengeance, divine, 182

Ventriloquist, 100

Venus, 172

Venus and Adonis (Shakespeare)

Veracity, 145; v. *vs.* mere accuracy, 96

Verbum mentis, 61

Vergil (*or* Virgil), 27, 444, 453, s80

Verities, 82; of Swedenborg, 365; eternal v. of Plato, 201; nature filled with symbols of spiritual v., 226; universal v., 86, 203

Verity, absolute, 193

Vermin, man would be, 198

Vermont, 174; University of V., 163

Vers libre, 258, 277

Versailles, France, 298

Versification, 277, s21

Verulam: *see* Bacon.

Very, Jones, 199, s189

Vessel, s97

Vestal virgins, s17

Vestments, 55; v. of flesh, s118

Vesture without a seam, s75

Vexations become unimportant, 399

Viasa (Vyasa), 39, 423

Vicarious satisfaction, 87

Vice, 76, 178, 403; our national v. of imitation, 343

Vices, 54, 374

Vicissitudes of life, 51

Vico, Giovanni Battista
Principi di una Scienza Nuova, 306

Victor, vindication of the, 306

Victories gained over the evil and the false, 241

Victory over appetites, 334

View of the whole, 293

View of Episcopacy (C. Chauncy)

View of Heresies (A. McFarland)

View of Human Life (Petrarch)

View of Religions (H. Adams)

View of the Evidences of Christianity (Paley)

View of the Greek and Roman Classics (Harwood)

View of the Literature of the South of Europe (Simonde)

View of the State of Europe (Hallam)

View of the State of Europe (W. Robertson)

Vincent of Lerins: *see* St. Vincent of Lerins.

Vindiciæ Hiberniæ (M. Carey)

Vindication of Unitarianism (Yates)

Vine, 262, s10; v. and the branch, 273, 283; true v., 281

Vineyard, 156

Violence, 266, 389; v. defeats itself, 106

Violet: the v. and the sunbeam, 354; the color v., s95

Virgil, 27, 444, 453; tomb of V., s80
Æneid, quoted, 453

Virgin: deflowered, s10; coyness of a v., s11

Virgin Mary, s104

Virginia, 346

Virginia Road, near Bedford, Mass., 414

Miss Margaret Fuller
With the respects of
R. W. Emerson.

Dieses Buch war
in Bettig Bettinc's von
Arnim, aus den
es in den wenigen
Exemplar.

Hermann Grimm.

NATURE.

"Nature is but an image or imitation of wisdom, the last thing
of the soul; nature being a thing which doth only do, but not
know."

PLOTINUS.

BOSTON:
JAMES MUNROE AND COMPANY.
M DCCC XXXVI.

Entered, according to the Act of Congress, in the year 1836,
By JAMES MUNROE & Co.
in the Clerk's Office of the District Court of the District of
Massachusetts.

Cambridge Press:
Metcalf, Torry, & Ballou.

Given in 1894 to
Sarah H. Adams.
who gives it to
Miss Agnes Irwin
Dean of Radcliffe
Cambridge 1908.

CONTENTS.

INTRODUCTION.

OUR age is retrospective. It builds the sepulchres of the fathers. It writes biographies, histories, and criticism. The foregoing gene-
5 rations beheld God and nature face to face; we, through their eyes. Why should not we also enjoy an original relation to the universe? Why should not we have a poetry and philosophy of insight and not of tradition, and a relig-
10 ion by revelation to us, and not the history of theirs? Embosomed for a season in nature, whose floods of life stream around and through us, and invite us by the powers they supply, to action proportioned to nature, why should we
15 grope among the dry bones of the past, or put the living generation into masquerade out of its faded wardrobe? The sun shines to-day also. There is more wool and flax in the fields.

---

1 There are new lands, new men, new thoughts. Let us demand our own works and laws and worship.

Undoubtedly we have no questions to ask which are unanswerable. We must trust the
5 perfection of the creation so far, as to believe that whatever curiosity the order of things has awakened in our minds, the order of things can satisfy. Every man's condition is a solution in hieroglyphic to those inquiries he would put.
10 He acts it as life, before he apprehends it as truth. In like manner, nature is already, in its forms and tendencies, describing its own design. Let us interrogate the great apparition, that shines so peacefully around us. Let us inquire,
15 to what end is nature?

All science has one aim, namely, to find a theory of nature. We have theories of races and of functions, but scarcely yet a remote approximation to an idea of creation. We are
20 now so far from the road to truth, that religious teachers dispute and hate each other, and speculative men are esteemed unsound and

---

1 frivolous. But to a sound judgment, the most abstract truth is the most practical. Whenever a true theory appears, it will be its own evidence. Its test is, that it will explain all phe-
5 nomena. Now many are thought not only unexplained but inexplicable; as language, sleep, dreams, beasts, sex.

Philosophically considered, the universe is composed of Nature and the Soul. Strictly
10 speaking, therefore, all that is separate from us, all which Philosophy distinguishes as the NOT ME, that is, both nature and art, all other men and my own body, must be ranked under this name, NATURE. In enumerating the values of
15 nature and casting up their sum, I shall use the word in both senses; — in its common and in its philosophical import. In inquiries so general as our present one, the inaccuracy is not material; no confusion of thought will occur.
20 *Nature*, in the common sense, refers to essences unchanged by man; space, the air, the river, the leaf. *Art* is applied to the mixture of his will with the same things, as in a house, a

1 canal, a statue, a picture. But his operations
taken together are so insignificant, a little chip-
ping, baking, patching, and washing, that in an
impression so grand as that of the world on
5 the human mind, they do not vary the result.

NATURE.

CHAPTER I.

To go into solitude, a man needs to retire
as much from his chamber as from society.
5 I am not solitary whilst I read and write,
though nobody is with me. But if a man would
be alone, let him look at the stars. The rays
that come from those heavenly worlds, will
separate between him and vulgar things. One
10 might think the atmosphere was made transparent with this design, to give man, in the
heavenly bodies, the perpetual presence of the
sublime. Seen in the streets of cities, how
great they are! If the stars should appear one
15 night in a thousand years, how would men

1

1 believe and adore; and preserve for many
generations the remembrance of the city of
God which had been shown! But every night
come out these preachers of beauty, and light
5 the universe with their admonishing smile.

The stars awaken a certain reverence, because though always present, they are always
inaccessible; but all natural objects make a
kindred impression, when the mind is open to
10 their influence. Nature never wears a mean
appearance. Neither does the wisest man
extort all her secret, and lose his curiosity by
finding out all her perfection. Nature never
became a toy to a wise spirit. The flowers,
15 the animals, the mountains, reflected all the
wisdom of his best hour, as much as they had
delighted the simplicity of his childhood.

When we speak of nature in this manner,
we have a distinct but most poetical sense in
20 the mind. We mean the integrity of impression made by manifold natural objects. It is
this which distinguishes the stick of timber of
the wood-cutter, from the tree of the poet.

1 The charming landscape which I saw this
morning, is indubitably made up of some twenty
or thirty farms. Miller owns this field, Locke
that, and Manning the woodland beyond. But
5 none of them owns the landscape. There is
a property in the horizon which no man has
but he whose eye can integrate all the parts,
that is, the poet. This is the best part of these
men's farms, yet to this their land-deeds give
10 them no title.

To speak truly, few adult persons can see
nature. Most persons do not see the sun. At
least they have a very superficial seeing. The
sun illuminates only the eye of the man, but
15 shines into the eye and the heart of the child.
The lover of nature is he whose inward and
outward senses are still truly adjusted to each
other; who has retained the spirit of infancy
even into the era of manhood. His intercourse
20 with heaven and earth, becomes part of his
daily food. In the presence of nature, a wild
delight runs through the man, in spite of real
sorrows. Nature says, — he is my creature,

1 and maugre all his impertinent griefs, he shall
be glad with me. Not the sun or the summer
alone, but every hour and season yields its
tribute of delight ; for every hour and change
5 corresponds to and authorizes a different state
of the mind, from breathless noon to grimmest
midnight. Nature is a setting that fits equally
well a comic or a mourning piece. In good
health, the air is a cordial of incredible virtue.
10 Crossing a bare common, in snow puddles, at
twilight, under a clouded sky, without having
in my thoughts any occurrence of special good
fortune, I have enjoyed a perfect exhilaration.
Almost I fear to think how glad I am. In the
15 woods too, a man casts off his years, as the
snake his slough, and at what period soever of
life, is always a child. In the woods, is perpetual youth. Within these plantations of God,
a decorum and sanctity reign, a perennial
20 festival is dressed, and the guest sees not how
he should tire of them in a thousand years.
In the woods, we return to reason and faith.
There I feel that nothing can befal me in

1 life, — no disgrace, no calamity, (leaving me my
eyes,) which nature cannot repair. Standing
on the bare ground, — my head bathed by the
blithe air, and uplifted into infinite space, — all
5 mean egotism vanishes. I become a transparent eye-ball. I am nothing. I see all. The
currents of the Universal Being circulate
through me ; I am part or particle of God.
The name of the nearest friend sounds then
10 foreign and accidental. To be brothers, to be
acquaintances, — master or servant, is then
a trifle and a disturbance. I am the lover
of uncontained and immortal beauty. In
the wilderness, I find something more dear
15 and connate than in streets or villages. In the
tranquil landscape, and especially in the distant
line of the horizon, man beholds somewhat as
beautiful as his own nature.

The greatest delight which the fields and
20 woods minister, is the suggestion of an occult
relation between man and the vegetable. I am
not alone and unacknowledged. They nod to
me and I to them. The waving of the boughs
1*

1 in the storm, is new to me and old. It takes
me by surprise, and yet is not unknown. Its
effect is like that of a higher thought or a
better emotion coming over me, when I deemed
5 I was thinking justly or doing right.

Yet it is certain that the power to produce
this delight, does not reside in nature, but in
man, or in a harmony of both. It is necessary
to use these pleasures with great temperance.
10 For, nature is not always tricked in holiday
attire, but the same scene which yesterday
breathed perfume and glittered as for the frolic
of the nymphs, is overspread with melancholy
today. Nature always wears the colors of the
15 spirit. To a man laboring under calamity, the
heat of his own fire hath sadness in it. Then,
there is a kind of contempt of the landscape
felt by him who has just lost by death a dear
friend. The sky is less grand as it shuts down
20 over less worth in the population.

CHAPTER II.

COMMODITY.

WHOEVER considers the final cause of the
world, will discern a multitude of uses that
5 enter as parts into that result. They all admit
of being thrown into one of the following
classes ; Commodity ; Beauty ; Language ; and
Discipline.

Under the general name of Commodity,
10 I rank all those advantages which our senses
owe to nature. This, of course, is a benefit
which is temporary and mediate, not ultimate,
like its service to the soul. Yet although low,
it is perfect in its kind, and is the only use of
15 nature which all men apprehend. The misery
of man appears like childish petulance, when
we explore the steady and prodigal provision
that has been made for his support and delight
on this green ball which floats him through the

1 heavens. What angels invented these splendid
ornaments, these rich conveniences, this ocean
of air above, this ocean of water beneath, this
firmament of earth between? this zodiac of
5 lights, this tent of dropping clouds, this
striped coat of climates, this fourfold year?
Beasts, fire, water, stones, and corn serve
him. The field is at once his floor, his
work-yard, his play-ground, his garden, and his
10 bed.

> " More servants wait on man
> Than he 'll take notice of." ———

Nature, in its ministry to man, is not only the
material, but is also the process and the result.
15 All the parts incessantly work into each other's
hands for the profit of man. The wind sows
the seed; the sun evaporates the sea; the
wind blows the vapor to the field; the ice, on
the other side of the planet, condenses rain on
20 this; the rain feeds the plant; the plant feeds
the animal; and thus the endless circulations
of the divine charity nourish man.

1 The useful arts are but reproductions or new
combinations by the wit of man, of the same
natural benefactors. He no longer waits for
favoring gales, but by means of steam, he
5 realizes the fable of Æolus's bag, and carries
the two and thirty winds in the boiler of his
boat. To diminish friction, he paves the road
with iron bars, and, mounting a coach with a
ship-load of men, animals, and merchandise
10 behind him, he darts through the country, from
town to town, like an eagle or a swallow
through the air. By the aggregate of these
aids, how is the face of the world changed,
from the era of Noah to that of Napoleon!
15 The private poor man hath cities, ships, canals,
bridges, built for him. He goes to the post-
office, and the human race run on his errands;
to the book-shop, and the human race read
and write of all that happens, for him; to the
20 court-house, and nations repair his wrongs.
He sets his house upon the road, and the
human race go forth every morning, and shovel
out the snow, and cut a path for him.

1 But there is no need of specifying particulars in this class of uses. The catalogue is endless, and the examples so obvious, that I shall
leave them to the reader's reflection, with the
5 general remark, that this mercenary benefit is
one which has respect to a farther good. A
man is fed, not that he may be fed, but that he
may work.

CHAPTER III.

BEAUTY.

A NOBLER want of man is served by nature,
namely, the love of Beauty.
5 The ancient Greeks called the world κοσμος,
beauty. Such is the constitution of all things,
or such the plastic power of the human eye,
that the primary forms, as the sky, the mountain, the tree, the animal, give us a delight *in
and for themselves;* a pleasure arising from
10 outline, color, motion, and grouping. This
seems partly owing to the eye itself. The eye
is the best of artists. By the mutual action of
its structure and of the laws of light, perspec-
15 tive is produced, which integrates every mass
of objects, of what character soever, into a
well colored and shaded globe, so that where
the particular objects are mean and unaffecting,
the landscape which they compose, is round and

symmetrical. And as the eye is the best com-
poser, so light is the first of painters. There
is no object so foul that intense light will not
make beautiful. And the stimulus it affords to
the sense, and a sort of infinitude which it hath,
like space and time, make all matter gay.
Even the corpse hath its own beauty. But
beside this general grace diffused over nature,
almost all the individual forms are agreeable
to the eye, as is proved by our endless imitations of some of them, as the acorn, the grape,
the pine-cone, the wheat-ear, the egg, the
wings and forms of most birds, the lion's claw,
the serpent, the butterfly, sea-shells, flames,
clouds, buds, leaves, and the forms of many
trees, as the palm.

For better consideration, we may distribute
the aspects of Beauty in a threefold manner.

1. First, the simple perception of natural forms
is a delight. The influence of the forms and actions in nature, is so needful to man, that, in its
lowest functions, it seems to lie on the confines
of commodity and beauty. To the body and mind

which have been cramped by noxious work or
company, nature is medicinal and restores their
tone. The tradesman, the attorney comes out
of the din and craft of the street, and sees the
sky and the woods, and is a man again. In
their eternal calm, he finds himself. The
health of the eye seems to demand a horizon.
We are never tired, so long as we can see far
enough.

But in other hours, Nature satisfies the soul
purely by its loveliness, and without any mixture of corporeal benefit. I have seen the
spectacle of morning from the hill-top over
against my house, from day-break to sun-rise,
with emotions which an angel might share.
The long slender bars of cloud float like fishes
in the sea of crimson light. From the earth,
as a shore, I look out into that silent sea. I
seem to partake its rapid transformations : the
active enchantment reaches my dust, and I
dilate and conspire with the morning wind.
How does Nature deify us with a few and
cheap elements ! Give me health and a day,

2

and I will make the pomp of emperors ridiculous. The dawn is my Assyria; the sun-set
and moon-rise my Paphos, and unimaginable
realms of faerie; broad noon shall be my England of the senses and the understanding; the
night shall be my Germany of mystic philosophy and dreams.

Not less excellent, except for our less susceptibility in the afternoon, was the charm, last
evening, of a January sunset. The western
clouds divided and subdivided themselves into
pink flakes modulated with tints of unspeakable
softness; and the air had so much life and
sweetness, that it was a pain to come within
doors. What was it that nature would say ?
Was there no meaning in the live repose of the
valley behind the mill, and which Homer or
Shakspeare could not re-form for me in words ?
The leafless trees become spires of flame in
the sunset, with the blue east for their back-
ground, and the stars of the dead calices of
flowers, and every withered stem and stubble
rimed with frost, contribute something to the
mute music.

The inhabitants of cities suppose that the
country landscape is pleasant only half the year.
I please myself with observing the graces of
the winter scenery, and believe that we are as
much touched by it as by the genial influences
of summer. To the attentive eye, each moment
of the year has its own beauty, and in the
same field, it beholds, every hour, a picture
which was never seen before, and which shall
never be seen again. The heavens change
every moment, and reflect their glory or gloom
on the plains beneath. The state of the crop
in the surrounding farms alters the expression
of the earth from week to week. The succession of native plants in the pastures and road-
sides, which make the silent clock by which
time tells the summer hours, will make even
the divisions of the day sensible to a keen
observer. The tribes of birds and insects, like
the plants punctual to their time, follow each
other, and the year has room for all. By water-
courses, the variety is greater. In July, the
blue pontederia or pickerel-weed blooms in

1 large beds in the shallow parts of our pleasant
river, and swarms with yellow butterflies in continual motion. Art cannot rival this pomp of
purple and gold. Indeed the river is a per-
5 petual gala, and boasts each month a new
ornament.

But this beauty of Nature which is seen and
felt as beauty, is the least part. The shows of
day, the dewy morning, the rainbow, moun-
10 tains, orchards in blossom, stars, moonlight,
shadows in still water, and the like, if too
eagerly hunted, become shows merely, and
mock us with their unreality. Go out of the
house to see the moon, and 't is mere tinsel; it
15 will not please as when its light shines upon
your necessary journey. The beauty that
shimmers in the yellow afternoons of October,
who ever could clutch it? Go forth to find it,
and it is gone: 't is only a mirage as you look
20 from the windows of diligence.

2. The presence of a higher, namely, of the
spiritual element is essential to its perfection.
The high and divine beauty which can be loved

1 without effeminacy, is that which is found in
combination with the human will, and never
separate. Beauty is the mark God sets upon
virtue. Every natural action is graceful. Every
5 heroic act is also decent, and causes the place
and the bystanders to shine. We are taught by
great actions that the universe is the property
of every individual in it. Every rational creature has all nature for his dowry and estate. It
10 is his, if he will. He may divest himself of it;
he may creep into a corner, and abdicate his
kingdom, as most men do, but he is entitled to
the world by his constitution. In proportion to
the energy of his thought and will, he takes up
15 the world into himself. "All those things for
which men plough, build, or sail, obey virtue;"
said an ancient historian. "The winds and
waves," said Gibbon, "are always on the side
of the ablest navigators." So are the sun and
20 moon and all the stars of heaven. When a
noble act is done, — perchance in a scene of
great natural beauty; when Leonidas and his
three hundred martyrs consume one day in

2*

1 dying, and the sun and moon come each and
look at them once in the steep defile of Ther-
mopylæ; when Arnold Winkelried, in the high
Alps, under the shadow of the avalanche, gath-
5 ers in his side a sheaf of Austrian spears to
break the line for his comrades; are not these
heroes entitled to add the beauty of the scene to
the beauty of the deed? When the bark of
Columbus nears the shore of America; — before
10 it, the beach lined with savages, fleeing out of
all their huts of cane; the sea behind; and the
purple mountains of the Indian Archipelago
around, can we separate the man from the living picture? Does not the New World clothe
15 his form with her palm-groves and savannahs as
fit drapery? Ever does natural beauty steal in
like air, and envelope great actions. When Sir
Harry Vane was dragged up the Tower-hill,
sitting on a sled, to suffer death, as the cham-
20 pion of the English laws, one of the multitude
cried out to him, "You never sate on so glorious a seat." Charles II., to intimidate the citizens of London, caused the patriot Lord Rus-

1 sel to be drawn in an open coach, through the
principal streets of the city, on his way to the
scaffold. "But," to use the simple narrative of
his biographer, "the multitude imagined they
5 saw liberty and virtue sitting by his side." In
private places, among sordid objects, an act of
truth or heroism seems at once to draw to itself
the sky as its temple, the sun as its candle.
Nature stretcheth out her arms to embrace man,
10 only let his thoughts be of equal greatness.
Willingly does she follow his steps with the rose
and the violet, and bend her lines of grandeur
and grace to the decoration of her darling child.
Only let his thoughts be of equal scope, and the
15 frame will suit the picture. A virtuous man, is
in unison with her works, and makes the central figure of the visible sphere. Homer, Pin-
dar, Socrates, Phocion, associate themselves
fitly in our memory with the whole geography
20 and climate of Greece. The visible heavens
and earth sympathize with Jesus. And in common life, whosoever has seen a person of powerful character and happy genius, will have re-

1 marked how easily he took all things along with him, — the persons, the opinions, and the day, and nature became ancillary to a man.

3. There is still another aspect under which

5 the beauty of the world may be viewed, namely, as it becomes an object of the intellect. Beside the relation of things to virtue, they have a relation to thought. The intellect searches out the absolute order of things as they stand in the

10 mind of God, and without the colors of affection. The intellectual and the active powers seem to succeed each other in man, and the exclusive activity of the one, generates the exclusive activity of the other. There is something

15 unfriendly in each to the other, but they are like the alternate periods of feeding and working in animals; each prepares and certainly will be followed by the other. Therefore does beauty, which, in relation to actions, as we have

20 seen comes unsought, and comes because it is unsought, remain for the apprehension and pursuit of the intellect; and then again, in its turn, of the active power. Nothing divine dies. All

1 good is eternally reproductive. The beauty of nature reforms itself in the mind, and not for barren contemplation, but for new creation.

All men are in some degree impressed by the

5 face of the world. Some men even to delight. This love of beauty is Taste. Others have the same love in such excess, that, not content with admiring, they seek to embody it in new forms. The creation of beauty is Art.

10 The production of a work of art throws a light upon the mystery of humanity. A work of art is an abstract or epitome of the world. It is the result or expression of nature, in miniature. For although the works of nature are

15 innumerable and all different, the result or the expression of them all is similar and single. Nature is a sea of forms radically alike and even unique. A leaf, a sun-beam, a landscape, the ocean, make an analogous impression on

20 the mind. What is common to them all,— that perfectness and harmony, is beauty. Therefore the standard of beauty, is the entire circuit of natural forms, — the totality of nature;

1 which the Italians expressed by defining beauty " il piu nell' uno." Nothing is quite beautiful alone: nothing but is beautiful in the whole. A single object is only so far beautiful as it sug-

5 gests this universal grace. The poet, the painter, the sculptor, the musician, the architect seek each to concentrate this radiance of the world on one point, and each in his several work to satisfy the love of beauty which stimu-

10 lates him to produce. Thus is Art, a nature passed through the alembic of man. Thus in art, does nature work through the will of a man filled with the beauty of her first works.

The world thus exists to the soul to satisfy the

15 desire of beauty. Extend this element to the uttermost, and I call it an ultimate end. No reason can be asked or given why the soul seeks beauty. Beauty, in its largest and profoundest sense, is one expression for the universe. God

20 is the all-fair. Truth, and goodness, and beauty, are but different faces of the same All. But beauty in nature is not ultimate. It is the herald of inward and eternal beauty, and is

1 not alone a solid and satisfactory good. It must therefore stand as a part and not as yet the last or highest expression of the final cause of Nature.

CHAPTER IV.

LANGUAGE.

A THIRD use which Nature subserves to man is that of Language. Nature is the vehicle of thought, and in a simple, double, and threefold degree.

1. Words are signs of natural facts.

2. Particular natural facts are symbols of particular facts. *spiritual*

3. Nature is the symbol of spirits.

1. Words are signs of natural facts. The use of natural history is to give us aid in supernatural history. The use of the outer creation is to give us language for the beings and changes of the inward creation. Every word which is used to express a moral or intellectual fact, if traced to its root, is found to be borrowed from some material appearance. *Right* originally means *straight; wrong* means *twisted. Spirit* primarily means *wind; trans-*

---

gression, the crossing of a *line; supercilious*, the *raising of the eye-brow.* We say the *heart* to express emotion, the *head* to denote thought; and *thought* and *emotion* are, in their turn, words borrowed from sensible things, and now appropriated to spiritual nature. Most of the process by which this transformation is made, is hidden from us in the remote time when language was framed; but the same tendency may be daily observed in children. Children and savages use only nouns or names of things, which they continually convert into verbs, and apply to analogous mental acts.

2. But this origin of all words that convey a spiritual import, — so conspicuous a fact in the history of language, — is our least debt to nature. It is not words only that are emblematic; it is things which are emblematic. Every natural fact is a symbol of some spiritual fact. Every appearance in nature corresponds to some state of the mind, and that state of the mind can only be described by presenting that natural appearance as its picture. An enraged

---

man is a lion, a cunning man is a fox, a firm man is a rock, a learned man is a torch. A lamb is innocence; a snake is subtle spite; flowers express to us the delicate affections. Light and darkness are our familiar expression for knowledge and ignorance; and heat for love. Visible distance behind and before us, is respectively our image of memory and hope.

Who looks upon a river in a meditative hour, and is not reminded of the flux of all things? Throw a stone into the stream, and the circles that propagate themselves are the beautiful type of all influence. Man is conscious of a universal soul within or behind his individual life, wherein, as in a firmament, the natures of Justice, Truth, Love, Freedom, arise and shine. This universal soul, he calls Reason: it is not mine or thine or his, but we are its; we are its property and men. And the blue sky in which the private earth is buried, the sky with its eternal calm, and full of everlasting orbs, is the type of Reason. That which, intellectually considered, we call Reason, considered in rela-

---

tion to nature, we call Spirit. Spirit is the Creator. Spirit hath life in itself. And man in all ages and countries, embodies it in his language, as the FATHER.

It is easily seen that there is nothing lucky or capricious in these analogies, but that they are constant, and pervade nature. These are not the dreams of a few poets, here and there, but man is an analogist, and studies relations in all objects. He is placed in the centre of beings, and a ray of relation passes from every other being to him. And neither can man be understood without these objects, nor these objects without man. All the facts in natural history taken by themselves, have no value, but are barren like a single sex. But marry it to human history, and it is full of life. Whole Floras, all Linnæus' and Buffon's volumes, are but dry catalogues of facts; but the most trivial of these facts, the habit of a plant, the organs, or work, or noise of an insect, applied to the illustration of a fact in intellectual philosophy, or, in any way associated to human nature, affects

us in the most lively and agreeable manner. The seed of a plant, — to what affecting analogies in the nature of man, is that little fruit made use of, in all discourse, up to the voice of Paul, who calls the human corpse a seed, — "It is sown a natural body; it is raised a spiritual body." The motion of the earth round its axis, and round the sun, makes the day, and the year. These are certain amounts of brute light and heat. But is there no intent of an analogy between man's life and the seasons? And do the seasons gain no grandeur or pathos from that analogy? The instincts of the ant are very unimportant considered as the ant's; but the moment a ray of relation is seen to extend from it to man, and the little drudge is seen to be a monitor, a little body with a mighty heart, then all its habits, even that said to be recently observed, that it never sleeps, become sublime.

Because of this radical correspondence between visible things and human thoughts, savages, who have only what is necessary, converse

in figures. As we go back in history, language becomes more picturesque, until its infancy, when it is all poetry; or, all spiritual facts are represented by natural symbols. The same symbols are found to make the original elements of all languages. It has moreover been observed, that the idioms of all languages approach each other in passages of the greatest eloquence and power. And as this is the first language, so is it the last. This immediate dependence of language upon nature, this conversion of an outward phenomenon into a type of somewhat in human life, never loses its power to affect us. It is this which gives that piquancy to the conversation of a strong-natured farmer or back-woodsman, which all men relish.

Thus is nature an interpreter, by whose means man converses with his fellow men. A man's power to connect his thought with its proper symbol, and so utter it, depends on the simplicity of his character, that is, upon his love of truth and his desire to communicate it without loss. The corruption of man is follow-

3*

ed by the corruption of language. When simplicity of character and the sovereignty of ideas is broken up by the prevalence of secondary desires, the desire of riches, the desire of pleasure, the desire of power, the desire of praise, — and duplicity and falsehood take place of simplicity and truth, the power over nature as an interpreter of the will, is in a degree lost; new imagery ceases to be created, and old words are perverted to stand for things which are not; a paper currency is employed when there is no bullion in the vaults. In due time, the fraud is manifest, and words lose all power to stimulate the understanding or the affections. Hundreds of writers may be found in every long-civilized nation, who for a short time believe, and make others believe, that they see and utter truths, who do not of themselves clothe one thought in its natural garment, but who feed unconsciously upon the language created by the primary writers of the country, those, namely, who hold primarily on nature.

But wise men pierce this rotten diction and fasten words again to visible things; so that picturesque language is at once a commanding certificate that he who employs it, is a man in alliance with truth and God. The moment our discourse rises above the ground line of familiar facts, and is inflamed with passion or exalted by thought, it clothes itself in images. A man conversing in earnest, if he watch his intellectual processes, will find that always a material image, more or less luminous, arises in his mind, cotemporaneous with every thought, which furnishes the vestment of the thought. Hence, good writing and brilliant discourse are perpetual allegories. This imagery is spontaneous. It is the blending of experience with the present action of the mind. It is proper creation. It is the working of the Original Cause through the instruments he has already made.

These facts may suggest the advantage which the country-life possesses for a powerful mind, over the artificial and curtailed life of cities. We

1   know more from nature than we can at will
communicate.   Its light flows into the mind
evermore, and we forget its presence. The poet,
the orator, bred in the woods, whose senses
5   have been nourished by their fair and appeasing
changes, year after year, without design and
without heed, — shall not lose their lesson altogether, in the roar of cities or the broil of
politics. Long hereafter, amidst agitation and
10 terror in national councils, — in the hour of
revolution, — these solemn images shall reappear in their morning lustre, as fit symbols and
words of the thoughts which the passing events
shall awaken. At the call of a noble sentiment,
15 again the woods wave, the pines murmur, the
river rolls and shines, and the cattle low upon
the mountains, as he saw and heard them in his
infancy. And with these forms, the spells of persuasion, the keys of power are put into his hands.
20   3. We are thus assisted by natural objects in
the expression of particular meanings. But
how great a language to convey such pepper-
corn informations! Did it need such noble

1   races of creatures, this profusion of forms, this
host of orbs in heaven, to furnish man with the
dictionary and grammar of his municipal speech?
Whilst we use this grand cipher to expedite the
5   affairs of our pot and kettle, we feel that we
have not yet put it to its use, neither are able.
We are like travellers using the cinders of a
volcano to roast their eggs. Whilst we see that
it always stands ready to clothe what we would
10 say, we cannot avoid the question, whether the
characters are not significant of themselves.
Have mountains, and waves, and skies, no significance but what we consciously give them,
when we employ them as emblems of our
15 thoughts? The world is emblematic. Parts of
speech are metaphors because the whole of nature is a metaphor of the human mind. The
laws of moral nature answer to those of matter
as face to face in a glass. " The visible world
20 and the relation of its parts, is the dial plate of
the invisible." The axioms of physics translate the laws of ethics. Thus, " the whole is
greater than its part;" " reaction is equal to

1   action;" " the smallest weight may be made to
lift the greatest, the difference of weight being
compensated by time;" and many the like propositions, which have an ethical as well as phy-
5   sical sense. These propositions have a much
more extensive and universal sense when applied to human life, than when confined to
technical use.
    In like manner, the memorable words of his-
10 tory, and the proverbs of nations, consist usually of a natural fact, selected as a picture or
parable of a moral truth. Thus; A rolling
stone gathers no moss; A bird in the hand is
worth two in the bush; A cripple in the right
15 way, will beat a racer in the wrong; Make hay
whilst the sun shines; 'T is hard to carry a full
cup even; Vinegar is the son of wine; The
last ounce broke the camel's back; Long-lived
trees make roots first; — and the like. In their
20 primary sense these are trivial facts, but we repeat them for the value of their analogical import. What is true of proverbs, is true of all
fables, parables, and allegories.

1   This relation between the mind and matter is
not fancied by some poet, but stands in the will
of God, and so is free to be known by all men.
It appears to men, or it does not appear. When
5   in fortunate hours we ponder this miracle, the
wise man doubts, if, at all other times, he is not
blind and deaf;

                  —— " Can these things be,
        And overcome us like a summer's cloud,
10   Without our special wonder?"

for the universe becomes transparent, and the
light of higher laws than its own, shines
through it. It is the standing problem which
has exercised the wonder and the study of
15 every fine genius since the world began;
from the era of the Egyptians and the Brah-
mins, to that of Pythagoras, of Plato, of Bacon, of Leibnitz, of Swedenborg. There sits
the Sphinx at the road-side, and from age to
20 age, as each prophet comes by, he tries his fortune at reading her riddle. There seems to be
a necessity in spirit to manifest itself in material

1 forms; and day and night, river and storm,
beast and bird, acid and alkali, preexist in
necessary Ideas in the mind of God, and are
what they are by virtue of preceding affections,
5 in the world of spirit. A Fact is the end or
last issue of spirit. The visible creation is the
terminus or the circumference of the invisible
world. "Material objects," said a French philosopher, " are necessarily kinds of *scoriæ* of
10 the substantial thoughts of the Creator, which
must always preserve an exact relation to their
first origin; in other words, visible nature must
have a spiritual and moral side."

This doctrine is abstruse, and though the
15 images of " garment," " scoriæ," " mirror,"
&c., may stimulate the fancy, we must summon
the aid of subtler and more vital expositors to
make it plain. " Every scripture is to be interpreted by the same spirit which gave it forth,"
20 — is the fundamental law of criticism. A life
in harmony with nature, the love of truth and
of virtue, will purge the eyes to understand her
text. By degrees we may come to know the

1 primitive sense of the permanent objects of nature, so that the world shall be to us an open
book, and every form significant of its hidden
life and final cause.

5 A new interest surprises us, whilst, under the
view now suggested, we contemplate the fearful
extent and multitude of objects; since " every
object rightly seen, unlocks a new faculty of the
soul." That which was unconscious truth, be-
10 comes, when interpreted and defined in an object, a part of the domain of knowledge, — a
new amount to the magazine of power.

[46]

CHAPTER V.

DISCIPLINE.

In view of this significance of nature, we arrive at once at a new fact, that nature is a dis-
5 cipline. This use of the world includes the
preceding uses, as parts of itself.

Space, time, society, labor, climate, food, locomotion, the animals, the mechanical forces, give
us sincerest lessons, day by day, whose meaning
10 is unlimited. They educate both the Understanding and the Reason. Every property of
matter is a school for the understanding, — its solidity or resistance, its inertia, its extension, its
figure, its divisibility. The understanding adds,
15 divides, combines, measures, and finds everlasting nutriment and room for its activity in this
worthy scene. Meantime, Reason transfers all
these lessons into its own world of thought, by
perceiving the analogy that marries Matter and
20 Mind.

1 1. Nature is a discipline of the understanding
in intellectual truths. Our dealing with sensible objects is a constant exercise in the necessary lessons of difference, of likeness, of order,
5 of being and seeming, of progressive arrangement; of ascent from particular to general; of
combination to one end of manifold forces.
Proportioned to the importance of the organ to
be formed, is the extreme care with which its
10 tuition is provided, — a care pretermitted in no
single case. What tedious training, day after
day, year after year, never ending, to form the
common sense; what continual reproduction of
annoyances, inconveniences, dilemmas; what
15 rejoicing over us of little men; what disputing
of prices, what reckonings of interest, — and
all to form the Hand of the mind; — to instruct
us that " good thoughts are no better than good
dreams, unless they be executed!"

20 The same good office is performed by Property and its filial systems of debt and credit.
Debt, grinding debt, whose iron face the widow,
the orphan, and the sons of genius fear and

1 hate ; — debt, which consumes so much time, which so cripples and disheartens a great spirit with cares that seem so base, is a preceptor whose lessons cannot be forgone, and is needed
5 most by those who suffer from it most. Moreover, property, which has been well compared to snow, — " if it fall level to-day, it will be blown into drifts to-morrow," — is merely the surface action of internal machinery, like the
10 index on the face of a clock. Whilst now it is the gymnastics of the understanding, it is hiving in the foresight of the spirit, experience in profounder laws.

The whole character and fortune of the individual is affected by the least inequalities in the
15 culture of the understanding ; for example, in the perception of differences. Therefore is Space, and therefore Time, that man may know that things are not huddled and lumped, but sundered and individual. A bell and a plough
20 have each their use, and neither can do the office of the other. Water is good to drink, coal to burn, wool to wear ; but wool cannot be

1 drunk, nor water spun, nor coal eaten. The wise man shows his wisdom in separation, in gradation, and his scale of creatures and of merits, is as wide as nature. The foolish have
5 no range in their scale, but suppose every man is as every other man. What is not good they call the worst, and what is not hateful, they call the best.

In like manner, what good heed, nature forms
10 in us ! She pardons no mistakes. Her yea is yea, and her nay, nay.

The first steps in Agriculture, Astronomy, Zoölogy, (those first steps which the farmer, the hunter, and the sailor take,) teach that nature's
15 dice are always loaded ; that in her heaps and rubbish are concealed sure and useful results.

How calmly and genially the mind apprehends one after another the laws of physics ! What noble emotions dilate the mortal as he enters
20 into the counsels of the creation, and feels by knowledge the privilege to BE ! His insight refines him. The beauty of nature shines in his own breast. Man is greater that he can see

4*

1 this, and the universe less, because Time and Space relations vanish as laws are known.

Here again we are impressed and even daunted by the immense Universe to be explored.
5 ' What we know, is a point to what we do not know.' Open any recent journal of science, and weigh the problems suggested concerning Light, Heat, Electricity, Magnetism, Physiology, Geology, and judge whether the interest of
10 natural science is likely to be soon exhausted.

Passing by many particulars of the discipline of nature we must not omit to specify two.

The exercise of the Will or the lesson of power is taught in every event. From the child's
15 successive possession of his several senses up to the hour when he saith, " thy will be done ! " he is learning the secret, that he can reduce under his will, not only particular events, but great classes, nay the whole series of events, and
20 so conform all facts to his character. Nature is thoroughly mediate. It is made to serve. It receives the dominion of man as meekly as the ass on which the Saviour rode. It offers all its

1 kingdoms to man as the raw material which he may mould into what is useful. Man is never weary of working it up. He forges the subtile and delicate air into wise and melodious words,
5 and gives them wing as angels of persuasion and command. More and more, with every thought, does his kingdom stretch over things, until the world becomes, at last, only a realized will, — the double of the man.

10 2. Sensible objects conform to the premonitions of Reason and reflect the conscience. All things are moral ; and in their boundless changes have an unceasing reference to spiritual nature. Therefore is nature glorious with
15 form, color, and motion, that every globe in the remotest heaven ; every chemical change from the rudest crystal up to the laws of life ; every change of vegetation from the first principle of growth in the eye of a leaf, to the tropical forest
20 and antediluvian coal-mine ; every animal function from the sponge up to Hercules, shall hint or thunder to man the laws of right and wrong, and echo the Ten Commandments. Therefore

1 is nature always the ally of Religion : lends all
her pomp and riches to the religious sentiment.
Prophet and priest, David, Isaiah, Jesus, have
drawn deeply from this source.

5   This ethical character so penetrates the bone
and marrow of nature, as to seem the end for
which it was made. Whatever private purpose
is answered by any member or part, this is its
public and universal function, and is never omit-

10 ted. Nothing in nature is exhausted in its first
use. When a thing has served an end to the
uttermost, it is wholly new for an ulterior service. In God, every end is converted into a new
means. Thus the use of Commodity, regarded

15 by itself, is mean and squalid. But it is to the
mind an education in the great doctrine of Use,
namely, that a thing is good only so far as it
serves ; that a conspiring of parts and efforts to
the production of an end, is essential to any

20 being. The first and gross manifestation of this
truth, is our inevitable and hated training in
values and wants, in corn and meat.

1   It has already been illustrated, in treating of
the significance of material things, that every
natural process is but a version of a moral sentence. The moral law lies at the centre of na-

5   ture and radiates to the circumference. It is the
pith and marrow of every substance, every relation, and every process. All things with which
we deal, preach to us. What is a farm but a
mute gospel ! The chaff and the wheat, weeds

10 and plants, blight, rain, insects, sun, — it is a
sacred emblem from the first furrow of spring to
the last stack which the snow of winter over-
takes in the fields. But the sailor, the shepherd,
the miner, the merchant, in their several resorts,

15 have each an experience precisely parallel and
leading to the same conclusions. Because all
organizations are radically alike. Nor can it be
doubted that this moral sentiment which thus
scents the air, and grows in the grain, and im-

20 pregnates the waters of the world, is caught by
man and sinks into his soul. The moral influence of nature upon every individual is that
amount of truth which it illustrates to him.

1   Who can estimate this ? Who can guess how
much firmness the sea-beaten rock has taught
the fisherman ? how much tranquillity has been
reflected to man from the azure sky, over whose

5   unspotted deeps the winds forevermore drive
flocks of stormy clouds, and leave no wrin-
kle or stain ? how much industry and providence and affection we have caught from the
pantomime of brutes ? What a searching preach-

10 er of self-command is the varying phenomenon
of Health !

    Herein is especially apprehended the Unity of
Nature, — the Unity in Variety, — which meets
us everywhere. All the endless variety of things

15 make a unique, an identical impression. Xeno-
phanes complained in his old age, that, look
where he would, all things hastened back to
Unity. He was weary of seeing the same entity
in the tedious variety of forms. The fable of

20 Proteus has a cordial truth. Every particular
in nature, a leaf, a drop, a crystal, a moment of
time is related to the whole, and partakes of the
perfection of the whole. Each particle is a mi-

1   crocosm, and faithfully renders the likeness of
the world.

    Not only resemblances exist in things whose
analogy is obvious, as when we detect the type

5   of the human hand in the flipper of the fossil
saurus, but also in objects wherein there is great
superficial unlikeness. Thus architecture is
called ' frozen music,' by De Stael and Goethe.
' A Gothic church,' said Coleridge, ' is a petrified

10 religion.' Michael Angelo maintained, that, to
an architect, a knowledge of anatomy is essential. In Haydn's oratorios, the notes present to
the imagination not only motions, as, of the
snake, the stag, and the elephant, but colors also ;

15 as the green grass. The granite is differenced
in its laws only by the more or less of heat, from
the river that wears it away. The river, as it
flows, resembles the air that flows over it ; the
air resembles the light which traverses it with

20 more subtile currents ; the light resembles the
heat which rides with it through Space. Each
creature is only a modification of the other ; the
likeness in them is more than the difference, and

1   their radical law is one and the same. Hence it is, that a rule of one art, or a law of one organ-ization, holds true throughout nature. So in-timate is this Unity, that, it is easily seen, it lies

5   under the undermost garment of nature, and be-trays its source in universal Spirit. For, it per-vades Thought also. Every universal truth which we express in words, implies or supposes every other truth. *Omne verum vero consonat.*

10   It is like a great circle on a sphere, comprising all possible circles; which, however, may be drawn, and comprise it, in like manner. Every such truth is the absolute Ens seen from one side. But it has innumerable sides.

15   The same central Unity is still more conspic-ous in actions. Words are finite organs of the infinite mind. They cannot cover the dimen-sions of what is in truth. They break, chop, and impoverish it. An action is the perfection

20   and publication of thought. A right action seems to fill the eye, and to be related to all nature. "The wise man, in doing one thing, does all; or, in the one thing he does rightly, he sees the likeness of all which is done rightly."

1   Words and actions are not the attributes of mute and brute nature. They introduce us to that singular form which predominates over all other forms. This is the human. All other or-

5   ganizations appear to be degradations of the human form. When this organization appears among so many that surround it, the spirit pre-fers it to all others. It says, ' From such as this, have I drawn joy and knowledge. In such

10   as this, have I found and beheld myself. I will speak to it. It can speak again. It can yield me thought already formed and alive.' In fact, the eye, — the mind, — is always accompanied by these forms, male and female; and these are

15   incomparably the richest informations of the power and order that lie at the heart of things. Unfortunately, every one of them bears the marks as of some injury; is marred and superficially defective. Nevertheless, far different from the

20   deaf and dumb nature around them, these all rest like fountain-pipes on the unfathomed sea of thought and virtue whereto they alone, of all or-ganizations, are the entrances.

5

1   It were a pleasant inquiry to follow into de-tail their ministry to our education, but where would it stop? We are associated in adolescent and adult life with some friends, who, like skies

5   and waters, are coextensive with our idea; who, answering each to a certain affection of the soul, satisfy our desire on that side; whom we lack power to put at such focal distance from us, that we can mend or even analyze them. We can-

10   not chuse but love them. When much inter-course with a friend has supplied us with a standard of excellence, and has increased our respect for the resources of God who thus sends a real person to outgo our ideal; when he has,

15   moreover, become an object of thought, and, whilst his character retains all its unconscious effect, is converted in the mind into solid and sweet wisdom, — it is a sign to us that his office is closing, and he is commonly withdrawn from

20   our sight in a short time.

CHAPTER VI.

IDEALISM.

Thus is the unspeakable but intelligible and practicable meaning of the world conveyed to

5   man, the immortal pupil, in every object of sense. To this one end of Discipline, all parts of na-ture conspire.

A noble doubt perpetually suggests itself, whether this end be not the Final Cause of the

10   Universe; and whether nature outwardly exists. It is a sufficient account of that Appearance we call the World, that God will teach a human mind, and so makes it the receiver of a certain number of congruent sensations, which we call

15   sun and moon, man and woman, house and trade. In my utter impotence to test the authenticity of the report of my senses, to know whether the impressions they make on me correspond with outlying objects, what difference does it make,

20   whether Orion is up there in heaven, or some

god paints the image in the firmament of the
soul ? The relations of parts and the end of
the whole remaining the same, what is the difference, whether land and sea interact, and
worlds revolve and intermingle without number
or end, — deep yawning under deep, and galaxy
balancing galaxy, throughout absolute space, or,
whether, without relations of time and space,
the same appearances are inscribed in the constant faith of man. Whether nature enjoy a
substantial existence without, or is only in the
apocalypse of the mind, it is alike useful and
alike venerable to me. Be it what it may, it is
ideal to me, so long as I cannot try the accuracy
of my senses.

The frivolous make themselves merry with the
Ideal theory, as if its consequences were bur-
lesque; as if it affected the stability of nature.
It surely does not. God never jests with us, and
will not compromise the end of nature, by per-
mitting any inconsequence in its procession.
Any distrust of the permanence of laws, would
paralyze the faculties of man. Their perma-

nence is sacredly respected, and his faith therein
is perfect. The wheels and springs of man are
all set to the hypothesis of the permanence of
nature. We are not built like a ship to be toss-
ed, but like a house to stand. It is a natural
consequence of this structure, that, so long as
the active powers predominate over the reflective,
we resist with indignation any hint that nature
is more short-lived or mutable than spirit. The
broker, the wheelwright, the carpenter, the toll-
man, are much displeased at the intimation.

But whilst we acquiesce entirely in the permanence of natural laws, the question of the
absolute existence of nature, still remains open.
It is the uniform effect of culture on the human
mind, not to shake our faith in the stability of
particular phenomena, as of heat, water, azote;
but to lead us to regard nature as a phenomenon, not a substance; to attribute necessary
existence to spirit; to esteem nature as an accident and an effect.

To the senses and the unrenewed understanding, belongs a sort of instinctive belief in the

5*

absolute existence of nature. In their view,
man and nature are indissolubly joined. Things
are ultimates, and they never look beyond their
sphere. The presence of Reason mars this
faith. The first effort of thought tends to relax
this despotism of the senses, which binds us to
nature as if we were a part of it, and shows us
nature aloof, and, as it were, afloat. Until this
higher agency intervened, the animal eye sees,
with wonderful accuracy, sharp outlines and colored surfaces. When the eye of Reason opens,
to outline and surface are at once added, grace
and expression. These proceed from imagination and affection, and abate somewhat of the
angular distinctness of objects. If the Reason
be stimulated to more earnest vision, outlines
and surfaces become transparent, and are no
longer seen; causes and spirits are seen through
them. The best, the happiest moments of life,
are these delicious awakenings of the higher
powers, and the reverential withdrawing of nature before its God.

Let us proceed to indicate the effects of culture. 1. Our first institution in the Ideal philosophy is a hint from nature herself.

Nature is made to conspire with spirit to eman-
cipate us. Certain mechanical changes, a small
alteration in our local position apprizes us of a
dualism. We are strangely affected by seeing
the shore from a moving ship, from a balloon, or
through the tints of an unusual sky. The least
change in our point of view, gives the whole
world a pictorial air. A man who seldom rides,
needs only to get into a coach and traverse his
own town, to turn the street into a puppet-show.
The men, the women, — talking, running, bar-
tering, fighting, — the earnest mechanic, the
lounger, the beggar, the boys, the dogs, are un-
realized at once, or, at least, wholly detached
from all relation to the observer, and seen as apparent, not substantial beings. What new
thoughts are suggested by seeing a face of country quite familiar, in the rapid movement of the
rail-road car ! Nay, the most wonted objects,
(make a very slight change in the point of vis-

sion,) please us most. In a camera obscura, the butcher's cart, and the figure of one of our own family amuse us. So a protrait of a well-known face gratifies us. Turn the eyes upside down, by looking at the landscape through your legs, and how agreeable is the picture, though you have seen it any time these twenty years!

In these cases, by mechanical means, is suggested the difference between the observer and the spectacle, — between man and nature. Hence arises a pleasure mixed with awe; I may say, a low degree of the sublime is felt from the fact, probably, that man is hereby apprized, that, whilst the world is a spectacle, something in himself is stable.

2. In a higher manner, the poet communicates the same pleasure. By a few strokes he delineates, as on air, the sun, the mountain, the camp, the city, the hero, the maiden, not different from what we know them, but only lifted from the ground and afloat before the eye. He unfixes the land and the sea, makes them revolve around the axis of his primary thought, and dis-

poses them anew. Possessed himself by a heroic passion, he uses matter as symbols of it. The sensual man conforms thoughts to things; the poet conforms things to his thoughts. The one esteems nature as rooted and fast; the other, as fluid, and impresses his being thereon. To him, the refractory world is ductile and flexible; he invests dust and stones with humanity, and makes them the words of the Reason. The imagination may be defined to be, the use which the Reason makes of the material world. Shakspeare possesses the power of subordinating nature for the purposes of expression, beyond all poets. His imperial muse tosses the creation like a bauble from hand to hand, to embody any capricious shade of thought that is uppermost in his mind. The remotest spaces of nature are visited, and the farthest sundered things are brought together, by a subtile spiritual connexion. We are made aware that magnitude of material things is merely relative, and all objects shrink and expand to serve the passion of the poet. Thus, in his

sonnets, the lays of birds, the scents and dyes of flowers, he finds to be the *shadow* of his beloved; time, which keeps her from him, is his *chest*; the suspicion she has awakened, is her *ornament*;

> The ornament of beauty is Suspect,
> A crow which flies in heaven's sweetest air.

His passion is not the fruit of chance; it swells, as he speaks, to a city, or a state.

> No, it was builded far from accident;
> It suffers not in smiling pomp, nor falls
> Under the brow of thralling discontent;
> It fears not policy, that heretic,
> That works on leases of short numbered hours,
> But all alone stands hugely politic.

In the strength of his constancy, the Pyramids seem to him recent and transitory. And the freshness of youth and love dazzles him with its resemblance to morning.

> Take those lips away
> Which so sweetly were forsworn;
> And those eyes, — the break of day,
> Lights that do mislead the morn.

The wild beauty of this hyperbole, I may say, in passing, it would not be easy to match in literature.

This transfiguration which all material objects undergo through the passion of the poet, — this power which he exerts, at any moment, to magnify the small, to micrify the great, — might be illustrated by a thousand examples from his Plays. I have before me the Tempest, and will cite only these few lines.

> ARIEL. The strong based promontory
> Have I made shake, and by the spurs plucked up
> The pine and cedar.

Prospero calls for music to sooth the frantic Alonzo, and his companions;

> A solemn air, and the best comforter
> To an unsettled fancy, cure thy brains
> Now useless, boiled within thy skull.

Again;

> The charm dissolves apace
> And, as the morning steals upon the night,
> Melting the darkness, so their rising senses
> Begin to chase the ignorant fumes that mantle
> Their clearer reason.

Their understanding
Begins to swell : and the approaching tide
Will shortly fill the reasonable shores
That now lie foul and muddy.

The perception of real affinities between events, (that is to say, of *ideal* affinities, for those only are real,) enables the poet thus to make free with the most imposing forms and phenomena of the world, and to assert the predominance of the soul.

3. Whilst thus the poet delights us by animating nature like a creator, with his own thoughts, he differs from the philosopher only herein, that the one proposes Beauty as his main end ; the other Truth. But, the philosopher, not less than the poet, postpones the apparent order and relations of things to the empire of thought. "The problem of philosophy," according to Plato, " is, for all that exists conditionally, to find a ground unconditioned and absolute." It proceeds on the faith that a law determines all phenomena, which being known, the phenomena can be predicted. That law, when in the

mind, is an idea. Its beauty is infinite. The true philosopher and the true poet are one, and a beauty, which is truth, and a truth, which is beauty, is the aim of both. Is not the charm of one of Plato's or Aristotle's definitions, strictly like that of the Antigone of Sophocles ? It is, in both cases, that a spiritual life has been imparted to nature ; that the solid seeming block of matter has been pervaded and dissolved by a thought ; that this feeble human being has penetrated the vast masses of nature with an informing soul, and recognised itself in their harmony, that is, seized their law. In physics, when this is attained, the memory disburthens itself of its cumbrous catalogues of particulars, and carries centuries of observation in a single formula.

Thus even in physics, the material is ever degraded before the spiritual. The astronomer, the geometer, rely on their irrefragable analysis, and disdain the results of observation. The sublime remark of Euler on his law of arches, " This will be found contrary to all experience,

yet is true ;" had already transferred nature into the mind, and left matter like an outcast corpse.

4. Intellectual science has been observed to beget invariably a doubt of the existence of matter. Turgot said, "He that has never doubted the existence of matter, may be assured he has no aptitude for metaphysical inquiries." It fastens the attention upon immortal necessary uncreated natures, that is, upon Ideas ; and in their beautiful and majestic presence, we feel that our outward being is a dream and a shade. Whilst we wait in this Olympus of gods, we think of nature as an appendix to the soul. We ascend into their region, and know that these are the thoughts of the Supreme Being. " These are they who were set up from everlasting, from the beginning, or ever the earth was. When he prepared the heavens, they were there ; when he established the clouds above, when he strengthened the fountains of the deep. Then they were by him, as one brought up with him. Of them took he counsel."

Their influence is proportionate. As objects of science, they are accessible to few men. Yet all men are capable of being raised by piety or by passion, into their region. And no man touches these divine natures, without becoming, in some degree, himself divine. Like a new soul, they renew the body. We become physically nimble and lightsome ; we tread on air ; life is no longer irksome, and we think it will never be so. No man fears age or misfortune or death, in their serene company, for he is transported out of the district of change. Whilst we behold unveiled the nature of Justice and Truth, we learn the difference between the absolute and the conditional or relative. We apprehend the absolute. As it were, for the first time, *we exist*. We become immortal, for we learn that time and space are relations of matter ; that, with a perception of truth, or a virtuous will, they have no affinity.

5. Finally, religion and ethics, which may be fitly called, — the practice of ideas, or the introduction of ideas into life, — have an analo-

1 gous effect with all lower culture, in degrading
nature and suggesting its dependence on spirit.
Ethics and religion differ herein; that the one
is the system of human duties commencing from
5 man; the other, from God. Religion includes
the personality of God; Ethics does not. They
are one to our present design. They both put
nature under foot. The first and last lesson of
religion is, "The things that are seen, are
10 temporal; the things that are unseen are eternal." It puts an affront upon nature. It does
that for the unschooled, which philosophy does
for Berkeley and Viasa. The uniform language
that may be heard in the churches of the most
15 ignorant sects, is, — 'Contemn the unsubstantial shows of the world; they are vanities,
dreams, shadows, unrealities; seek the realities
of religion.' The devotee flouts nature. Some
theosophists have arrived at a certain hostility
20 and indignation towards matter, as the Mani-
chean and Plotinus. They distrusted in themselves any looking back to these flesh-pots of
Egypt. Plotinus was ashamed of his body. In

1 short, they might all better say of matter, what
Michael Angelo said of external beauty, "it is
the frail and weary weed, in which God dresses
the soul, which he has called into time."

5 It appears that motion, poetry, physical and
intellectual science, and religion, all tend to
affect our convictions of the reality of the external world. But I own there is something
ungrateful in expanding too curiously the par-
10 ticulars of the general proposition, that all culture tends to imbue us with idealism. I have
no hostility to nature, but a child's love to it.
I expand and live in the warm day like corn and
melons. Let us speak her fair. I do not wish
15 to fling stones at my beautiful mother, nor soil
my gentle nest. I only wish to indicate the
true position of nature in regard to man, wherein to establish man, all right education tends;
as the ground which to attain is the object of
20 human life, that is, of man's connexion with
nature. Culture inverts the vulgar views of nature, and brings the mind to call that apparent,
which it uses to call real, and that real, which

6*

1 it uses to call visionary. Children, it is true,
believe in the external world. The belief that
it appears only, is an afterthought, but with culture, this faith will as surely arise on the mind
5 as did the first.

The advantage of the ideal theory over the
popular faith, is this, that it presents the world
in precisely that view which is most desirable to
the mind. It is, in fact, the view which Reason,
10 both speculative and practical, that is, philosophy and virtue, take. For, seen in the light of
thought, the world always is phenomenal; and
virtue subordinates it to the mind. Idealism
sees the world in God. It beholds the whole
15 circle of persons and things, of actions and
events, of country and religion, not as painfully
accumulated, atom after atom, act after act, in
an aged creeping Past, but as one vast picture,
which God paints on the instant eternity, for
20 the contemplation of the soul. Therefore the
soul holds itself off from a too trivial and microscopic study of the universal tablet. It
respects the end too much, to immerse itself in

1 the means. It sees something more important
in Christianity, than the scandals of ecclesiastical history or the niceties of criticism; and,
very incurious concerning persons or miracles,
5 and not at all disturbed by chasms of historical
evidence, it accepts from God the phenomenon,
as it finds it, as the pure and awful form of religion in the world. It is not hot and passionate
at the appearance of what it calls its own good
10 or bad fortune, at the union or opposition of
other persons. No man is its enemy. It accepts whatsoever befals, as part of its lesson. It
is a watcher more than a doer, and it is a doer,
only that it may the better watch.

CHAPTER VII.

SPIRIT.

It is essential to a true theory of nature and of man, that it should contain somewhat progressive. Uses that are exhausted or that may be, and facts that end in the statement, cannot be all that is true of this brave lodging wherein man is harbored, and wherein all his faculties find appropriate and endless exercise. And all the uses of nature admit of being summed in one, which yields the activity of man an infinite scope. Through all its kingdoms, to the suburbs and outskirts of things, it is faithful to the cause whence it had its origin. It always speaks of Spirit. It suggests the absolute. It is a perpetual effect. It is a great shadow pointing always to the sun behind us.

The aspect of nature is devout. Like the figure of Jesus, she stands with bended head, and hands folded upon the breast. The happiest

man is he who learns from nature the lesson of worship.

Of that ineffable essence which we call Spirit, he that thinks most, will say least. We can foresee God in the coarse and, as it were, distant phenomena of matter; but when we try to define and describe himself, both language and thought desert us, and we are as helpless as fools and savages. That essence refuses to be recorded in propositions, but when man has worshipped him intellectually, the noblest ministry of nature is to stand as the apparition of God. It is the great organ through which the universal spirit speaks to the individual, and strives to lead back the individual to it.

When we consider Spirit, we see that the views already presented do not include the whole circumference of man. We must add some related thoughts.

Three problems are put by nature to the mind; What is matter? Whence is it? and Whereto? The first of these questions only, the ideal theory answers. Idealism saith: mat-

ter is a phenomenon, not a substance. Idealism acquaints us with the total disparity between the evidence of our own being, and the evidence of the world's being. The one is perfect; the other, incapable of any assurance; the mind is a part of the nature of things; the world is a divine dream, from which we may presently awake to the glories and certainties of day. Idealism is a hypothesis to account for nature by other principles than those of carpentry and chemistry. Yet, if it only deny the existence of matter, it does not satisfy the demands of the spirit. It leaves God out of me. It leaves me in the splendid labyrinth of my perceptions, to wander without end. Then the heart resists it, because it baulks the affections in denying substantive being to men and women. Nature is so pervaded with human life, that there is something of humanity in all, and in every particular. But this theory makes nature foreign to me, and does not account for that consanguinity which we acknowledge to it.

Let it stand then, in the present state of our knowledge, merely as a useful introductory hypothesis, serving to apprize us of the eternal distinction between the soul and the world.

But when, following the invisible steps of thought, we come to inquire, Whence is matter? and Whereto? many truths arise to us out of the recesses of consciousness. We learn that the highest is present to the soul of man, that the dread universal essence, which is not wisdom, or love, or beauty, or power, but all in one, and each entirely, is that for which all things exist, and that by which they are; that spirit creates; that behind nature, throughout nature, spirit is present; that spirit is one and not compound; that spirit does not act upon us from without, that is, in space and time, but spiritually, or through ourselves. Therefore, that spirit, that is, the Supreme Being, does not build up nature around us, but puts it forth through us, as the life of the tree puts forth new branches and leaves through the pores of the old. As a plant upon the earth, so a man rests

1 upon the bosom of God; he is nourished by
   unfailing fountains, and draws, at his need, inexhaustible power. Who can set bounds to the
   possibilities of man? Once inspire the infinite,
5 by being admitted to behold the absolute natures
   of justice and truth, and we learn that man has
   access to the entire mind of the Creator, is himself the creator in the finite. This view, which
   admonishes me where the sources of wisdom
10 and power lie, and points to virtue as to

> " The golden key
> Which opes the palace of eternity,"

carries upon its face the highest certificate of
truth, because it animates me to create my own
15 world through the purification of my soul.

The world proceeds from the same spirit as
the body of man. It is a remoter and inferior
incarnation of God, a projection of God in the
unconscious.. But it differs from the body in
20 one important respect. It is not, like that, now
subjected to the human will. Its serene order
is inviolable by us. It is therefore, to us, the
present expositor of the divine mind. It is a

1 fixed point whereby we may measure our departure. As we degenerate, the contrast between
   us and our house is more evident. We are as
   much strangers in nature, as we are aliens from
5 God. We do not understand the notes of birds.
   The fox and the deer run away from us; the
   bear and tiger rend us. We do not know the
   uses of more than a few plants, as corn and the
   apple, the potato and the vine. Is not the land-
10 scape, every glimpse of which hath a grandeur,
   a face of him? Yet this may show us what
   discord is between man and nature, for you cannot freely admire a noble landscape, if laborers
   are digging in the field hard by. The poet finds
15 something ridiculous in his delight, until he is
   out of the sight of men.

7

[82]

CHAPTER VIII.

PROSPECTS.

1 IN inquiries respecting the laws of the world
   and the frame of things, the highest reason is
   always the truest. That which seems faintly
5 possible — it is so refined, is often faint and dim
   because it is deepest seated in the mind among
   the eternal verities. Empirical science is apt
   to cloud the sight, and, by the very knowledge of
   functions and processes, to bereave the student
10 of the manly contemplation of the whole. The
   savant becomes unpoetic. But the best read
   naturalist who lends an entire and devout attention to truth, will see that there remains much
15 to learn of his relation to the world, and that it
   is not to be learned by any addition or subtrac-
   tion or other comparison of known quantities,
   but is arrived at by untaught sallies of the spirit,
   by a continual self-recovery, and by entire
20 humility. He will perceive that there are far

1 more excellent qualities in the student than
   preciseness and infallibility; that a guess is
   often more fruitful than an indisputable affirmation, and that a dream may let us deeper into
5 the secret of nature than a hundred concerted
   experiments.

For, the problems to be solved are precisely
those which the physiologist and the naturalist
omit to state. It is not so pertinent to man to
10 know all the individuals of the animal kingdom,
as it is to know whence and whereto is this
tyrannizing unity in his constitution, which evermore separates and classifies things, endeavouring to reduce the most diverse to one form.
15 When I behold a rich landscape, it is less to my
purpose to recite correctly the order and super-
position of the strata, than to know why all
thought of multitude is lost in a tranquil sense
of unity. I cannot greatly honor minuteness in
20 details, so long as there is no hint to explain the
relation between things and thoughts; no ray
upon the *metaphysics* of conchology, of botany,
of the arts, to show the relation of the forms of

flowers, shells, animals, architecture, to the mind, and build science upon ideas. In a cabinet of natural history, we become sensible of a certain occult recognition and sympathy in regard to the most bizarre forms of beast, fish, and insect. The American who has been confined, in his own country, to the sight of buildings designed after foreign models, is surprised on entering York Minster or St. Peter's at Rome, by the feeling that these structures are imitations also, — faint copies of an invisible archetype. Nor has science sufficient humanity, so long as the naturalist overlooks that wonderful congruity which subsists between man and the world; of which he is lord, not because he is the most subtile inhabitant, but because he is its head and heart, and finds something of himself in every great and small thing, in every mountain stratum, in every new law of color, fact of astronomy, or atmospheric influence which observation or analysis lay open. A perception of this mystery inspires the muse of George Herbert, the beautiful psalmist of the

seventeenth century. The following lines are part of his little poem on Man.

> "Man is all symmetry,
> Full of proportions, one limb to another,
> And to all the world besides.
> Each part may call the farthest, brother;
> For head with foot hath private amity,
> And both with moons and tides.
>
> "Nothing hath got so far
> But man hath caught and kept it as his prey;
> His eyes dismount the highest star;
> He is in little all the sphere.
> Herbs gladly cure our flesh, because that they
> Find their acquaintance there.
>
> "For us, the winds do blow,
> The earth doth rest, heaven move, and fountains flow;
> Nothing we see, but means our good,
> As our delight, or as our treasure;
> The whole is either our cupboard of food,
> Or cabinet of pleasure.
>
> "The stars have us to bed:
> Night draws the curtain; which the sun withdraws.
> Music and light attend our head.

7*

> All things unto our flesh are kind,
> In their descent and being; to our mind,
> In their ascent and cause.
>
> "More servants wait on man
> Than he 'll take notice of. In every path,
> He treads down that which doth befriend him
> When sickness makes him pale and wan.
> Oh mighty love! Man is one world, and hath
> Another to attend him."

The perception of this class of truths makes the eternal attraction which draws men to science, but the end is lost sight of in attention to the means. In view of this half-sight of science, we accept the sentence of Plato, that, "poetry comes nearer to vital truth than history." Every surmise and vaticination of the mind is entitled to a certain respect, and we learn to prefer imperfect theories, and sentences, which contain glimpses of truth, to digested systems which have no one valuable suggestion. A wise writer will feel that the ends of study and composition are best answered by announcing undiscovered regions of thought, and so

communicating, through hope, new activity to the torpid spirit.

I shall therefore conclude this essay with some traditions of man and nature, which a certain poet sang to me; and which, as they have always been in the world, and perhaps reappear to every bard, may be both history and prophecy.

'The foundations of man are not in matter, but in spirit. But the element of spirit is eternity. To it, therefore, the longest series of events, the oldest chronologies are young and recent. In the cycle of the universal man, from whom the known individuals proceed, centuries are points, and all history is but the epoch of one degradation.

'We distrust and deny inwardly our sympathy with nature. We own and disown our relation to it, by turns. We are, like Nebuchadnezzar, dethroned, bereft of reason, and eating grass like an ox. But who can set limits to the remedial force of spirit?

1 'A man is a god in ruins. When men are innocent, life shall be longer, and shall pass into the immortal, as gently as we awake from dreams. Now, the world would be insane and 5 rabid, if these disorganizations should last for hundreds of years. It is kept in check by death and infancy. Infancy is the perpetual Messiah, which comes into the arms of fallen men, and pleads with them to return to para-10 dise.

'Man is the dwarf of himself. Once he was permeated and dissolved by spirit. He filled nature with his overflowing currents. Out from him sprang the sun and moon; from man, the 15 sun; from woman, the moon. The laws of his mind, the periods of his actions externized themselves into day and night, into the year and the seasons. But, having made for himself this huge shell, his waters retired; he no longer fills 20 the veins and veinlets; he is shrunk to a drop. He sees, that the structure still fits him, but fits him colossally. Say, rather, once it fitted him, now it corresponds to him from far and on high.

1 He adores timidly his own work. Now is man the follower of the sun, and woman the follower of the moon. Yet sometimes he starts in his slumber, and wonders at himself and his house, 5 and muses strangely at the resemblance betwixt him and it. He perceives that if his law is still paramount, if still he have elemental power, " if his word is sterling yet in nature," it is not con-scious power, it is not inferior but superior to 10 his will. It is Instinct.' Thus my Orphic poet sang.

At present, man applies to nature but half his force. He works on the world with his under-standing alone. He lives in it, and masters it 15 by a penny-wisdom; and he that works most in it, is but a half-man, and whilst his arms are strong and his digestion good, his mind is imbruted and he is a selfish savage. His relation to na-ture, his power over it, is through the under-20 standing; as by manure; the economic use of fire, wind, water, and the mariner's needle; steam, coal, chemical agriculture; the repairs of the human body by the dentist and the sur-

1 geon. This is such a resumption of power, as if a banished king should buy his territories inch by inch, instead of vaulting at once into his throne. Meantime, in the thick darkness, 5 there are not wanting gleams of a better light, —occasional examples of the action of man upon nature with his entire force, — with reason as well as understanding. Such examples are; the traditions of miracles in the earliest antiqui-10 ty of all nations; the history of Jesus Christ; the achievements of a principle, as in religious and political revolutions, and in the abolition of the Slave-trade; the miracles of enthusiasm, as those reported of Swedenborg, Hohenlohe, and 15 the Shakers; many obscure and yet contested facts, now arranged under the name of Animal Magnetism; prayer; eloquence; self-healing; and the wisdom of children. These are exam-ples of Reason's momentary grasp of the scep-20 tre; the exertions of a power which exists not in time or space, but an instantaneous in-stream-ing causing power. The difference between the actual and the ideal force of man is happi-

1 ly figured by the schoolmen, in saying, that the knowledge of man is an evening knowledge, *vespertina cognitio*, but that of God is a morn-ing knowledge, *matutina cognitio*.

5 The problem of restoring to the world origi-nal and eternal beauty, is solved by the redemp-tion of the soul. The ruin or the blank, that we see when we look at nature, is in our own eye. The axis of vision is not coincident with 10 the axis of things, and so they appear not trans-parent but opake. The reason why the world lacks unity, and lies broken and in heaps, is, because man is disunited with himself. He cannot be a naturalist, until he satisfies all the 15 demands of the spirit. Love is as much its demand, as perception. Indeed, neither can be perfect without the other. In the uttermost meaning of the words, thought is devout, and devotion is thought. Deep calls unto deep. 20 But in actual life, the marriage is not celebrated. There are innocent men who worship God after the tradition of their fathers, but their sense of duty has not yet extended to the use of all their

1 faculties.   And there are patient naturalists, but they freeze their subject under the wintry light of the understanding.   Is not prayer also a study of truth, — a sally of the soul into the 5 unfound infinite ?   No man ever prayed heartily, without learning something.   But when a faithful thinker, resolute to detach every object from personal relations, and see it in the light of thought, shall, at the same time, kindle science 10 with the fire of the holiest affections, then will God go forth anew into the creation.

It will not need, when the mind is prepared for study, to search for objects.   The invariable mark of wisdom is to see the miraculous in the 15 common.   What is a day ?   What is a year ? What is summer ?   What is woman ?   What is a child ?   What is sleep ?   To our blindness, these things seem unaffecting.   We make fables to hide the baldness of the fact and conform it, as 20 we say, to the higher law of the mind.   But when the fact is seen under the light of an idea, the gaudy fable fades and shrivels.   We behold the real higher law.   To the wise, therefore, a

1 fact is true poetry, and the most beautiful of fables. These wonders are brought to our own door. You also are a man.   Man and woman, and their social life, poverty, labor, sleep, fear, fortune, 5 are known to you.   Learn that none of these things is superficial, but that each phenomenon hath its roots in the faculties and affections of the mind.   Whilst the abstract question occupies your intellect, nature brings it in the con- 10 crete to be solved by your hands.   It were a wise inquiry for the closet, to compare, point by point, especially at remarkable crises in life, our daily history, with the rise and progress of ideas in the mind.

15 So shall we come to look at the world with new eyes.   It shall answer the endless inquiry of the intellect, —What is truth ? and of the affections, — What is good ? by yielding itself passive to the educated Will.   Then shall come 20 to pass what my poet said ; ' Nature is not fixed but fluid.   Spirit alters, moulds, makes it.   The immobility or bruteness of nature, is the absence of spirit ; to pure spirit, it is fluid, it is volatile,

8

1 it is obedient.   Every spirit builds itself a house ; and beyond its house, a world ; and beyond its world, a heaven.   Know then, that the world exists for you.   For you is the phenomenon per- 5 fect.   What we are, that only can we see.   All that Adam had, all that Cæsar could, you have and can do.   Adam called his house, heaven and earth ; Cæsar called his house, Rome ; you perhaps call yours, a cobler's trade ; a hundred 10 acres of ploughed land ; or a scholar's garret. Yet line for line and point for point, your dominion is as great as theirs, though without fine names.   Build, therefore, your own world.   As fast as you conform your life to the pure idea in 15 your mind, that will unfold its great proportions. A correspondent revolution in things will attend the influx of the spirit.   So fast will disagreeable appearances, swine, spiders, snakes, pests, mad-houses, prisons, enemies, vanish ; they are 20 temporary and shall be no more seen.   The sordor and filths of nature, the sun shall dry up, and the wind exhale.   As when the summer comes from the south, the snow-banks melt, and

1 the face of the earth becomes green before it, so shall the advancing spirit create its ornaments along its path, and carry with it the beauty it visits, and the song which enchants it ; 5 it shall draw beautiful faces, and warm hearts, and wise discourse, and heroic acts, around its way, until evil is no more seen.   The kingdom of man over nature, which cometh not with observation, — a dominion such as now is beyond his 10 dream of God, — he shall enter without more wonder than the blind man feels who is gradually restored to perfect sight.'

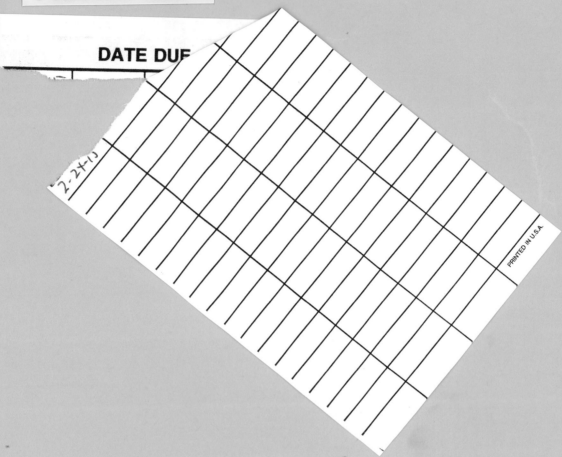

DATE DUE

PRINTED IN U.S.A.